Jeremy Beadle's
TODAY'S
! THE !
! DAY !

D1549721

Dedicated with Love

For Marji

who sacrificed so much to give her 'different drummer' the space to play . . . .

and Harry for making Marji so happy

Published September 1979 by
W. H. Allen & Co. Ltd,
44 Hill Street, London W1X 8LB

Printed and bound in Great Britain by
Hazell Watson & Viney Ltd, Aylesbury, Bucks

ISBN 0 491 02246 8

Cartoon on page 86 with apologies to Vicky of the London *Evening Standard*

Jeremy Beadle's

TODAY'S
! THE !
DAY !

A Chronicle of the Curious

W H Allen · London
A Howard & Wyndham Company
1979

Acknowledgements

Compiler: Jeremy Beadle
Writers: James Denley, Elisabeth Denley, Jeremy Beadle
Illustrator: Ken Taylor

Research: Marjorie Shaffer, Stephen Vandermere Fleming,
Joyce Mayes, Thérèse Birch, Vandra Butler, Bridgette Ennis,
Marion Taylor, Harry Shaffer. Editorial Help: Margaret Gartside,
Robin Thornber. Design: Nick Thirkell. Index: Derek Derbyshire.
Help, Inspiration and Kindness: That most amazing of agents Ed
Victor, Tony Elliott, Irving and Sylvia Wallace, Flora and Davvvvvy
Wallechinsky, Amy Wallybaby, Peter Jackson, Patrick Robertson,
Norris McWhirter, Pauline and Trevor Hatchett, Liz and Laurie
Hughes, Toni and Dave Arthur, Joan and Clive Doig, Rosemary Gill,
Denis Berson, Jackie and Bob Monkhouse, Grace Jean Denley,
Margaret and John Abbott, Alex Moose-Williams, Derek Dowsett,
Geoff Westley, Chris Godbeer, Esther Harrod, Caroline Daubeny,
Dasha Shenkman, Pamela George, Katrina Chalmers, The Buchanan
Company, Garrick, Squaw, Froggy, Sparrow, Wednesday Lobsang
Rampa and our glittering and unbelievably patient editor Amanda
Girling

Pssst . . . A Word in your Ear

Since *Today's the Day* is 'A Chronicle of the Curious', it's
not surprising that the tales it tells are a little strange – often
even incredible.

But nevertheless, with the possible exception of some
hearsay evidence and the occasional apocryphal anecdote
clearly indicated in the text, everything in this book of
anniversaries is true. Or at least, as true as can be ascertained
from the many hundreds of sources called upon during the
seven years it's been in research.

While it's packed with information, most of the material is
not of the kind you'll find in conventional text books.

But that too is hardly surprising.

Because it's to the odd, the entertaining and the unashamedly
bizarre that *Today's the Day* is dedicated.

Beadlebum, 24 May 1979

Today's the day...

Panting royal fiancé Henry VIII laden with love tokens arrived incognito at Rochester to meet his future fourth wife, Anne of Cleves. Henry's excitement was based on the flattering portraits painted by Holbein. But his first secret peek gave him quite a shock when he saw her looking out of a window at a bull-baiting. He was completely taken aback telling Cromwell, who had arranged the wedding, that she looked no better than a 'Flanders mare'. The marriage took place twelve days later and 'struck to the heart' by her ugliness he 'left her as good a maid as he found her'. Their seven-month unconsummated marriage ended in a swift amicable divorce and Anne, renouncing the title Queen, became known instead as 'the King's sister'. *1539*

Napoleon's greatest fan Marie Walewska at last had her dearest wish fulfilled when she met the Emperor at the village of Bronie, the last halt before Warsaw. Napoleon was smitten, but he forgot to ask her name. His spies soon located her, however, and he bombarded her with passionate notes, which the nineteen-year-old dutifully showed to her septuagenarian husband. A few evenings later, Napoleon arranged a cosy tryst, but in a sudden outburst he threw his fob-watch

6

to the floor and ground it with his heel, saying this is what he'd do to Poland if she didn't become his lover. Marie fainted and recovered only to find her underwear in disorder. The Emperor had raped her, but patriotic to the last, she sighed and said, 'I forgive you'.   *1807*

A piddling little incident upset the wedding plans of rich sophisticate James Gordon Bennett and his demure beloved, Caroline May. Bennett arrived, after imbibing a little too freely, to see his fiancée and her terribly proper Washington family. Stumbling into the sedate drawing room, he dimly perceived the fireplace, mistook it for a convenience and without so much as a by-your-leave, used it accordingly. In disgrace, the marriage was cancelled and he exiled himself to France – much to everyone's relief.   *1877*

Ecclesiastical hoarder the Reverend Mr Hagemore of Calthorn, Leicestershire, was knocked into his pond by a dog and drowned. Startled executors found he'd been collecting piles of odd items for years. They discovered thirty cassocks, 100 pairs of breeches and boots, 400 pairs of shoes and eight wigs. There were fifty-eight dogs, sixty horses, fifty saddles, eighty waggons and ploughs, thirty wheelbarrows, 200 shovels, 300 pick-axes, twenty-five ladders and no less than 250 razors!   *1746*

Big Daddy Field Marshal Idi Amin Dada was born. Sometime heavyweight boxing champion of Africa, his dizzy rise from the rank of sergeant to supremo in the 1971 military coup that took him to power is one of the true mysteries of the dark continent. In Amin's Uganda, anyone mentioning the superstition of the seditious talking tortoise was likely to be shot. Big Daddy really reached his apogee, however, in foreign policy. He asked Emperor Hirohito of Japan to send him a squad of kamikaze pilots and wished Nixon a speedy recovery from Watergate.   *1928*

Today's the day...

A quickie marriages ad appeared in the *Public Advertiser*. What it said was 'marriages performed with the utmost privacy, decency and regularity'. What it meant was secret or illegal marriages, and no questions asked. The venue was the Chapel Royal Savoy, in what was the smallest parish in London; the chaplain was Dr John Wilkinson, a gentlemanly Irishman, who was deeply in debt. He charged 'not more than one guinea' and in little over a year married 1,542 couples, and paid off most of his debts. He was worried that if he didn't stop it he'd be prosecuted, but he carried on regardless. One Sunday morning the constables arrived. He rushed into the vestry, threw off his surplice and made a run for it. He took refuge in Kent and gave surety to appear at the Old Bailey in July. In the meantime, he employed a curate called Grierson to continue the holy work. Both men were eventually sentenced to fourteen years' transportation, though Wilkinson was still on British soil when he died of a severe attack of gout. In their wake, 1,400 marriages were declared null and void.   *1754*

The world's first traffic lights exploded at the corner of Bridge Street and New Palace Yard near London's Parliament Square. The lights had been put up mainly for the benefit of MPs trying to get to the House of Commons and the red and green lights for 'Stop and Caution' were run on gas. The poor policeman responsible for pressing the lever which caused them to change sustained serious injuries to his eyes. This didn't deter the Metropolitan Commissioner of Police, however, and London's only traffic light continued functioning until 1872. When it went, there was to be no more stopping and going for over fifty years.   *1869*

Granada fell to Ferdinand and Isabella, monarchs of Aragon and Castile. The Moorish King Boabdil surrendered the keys of the city at a small mosque by the banks of the River Xenil. The Spanish King was merciful and the Moor appeared resigned. They exchanged courtesies, Ferdinand asking Boabdil to 'doubt not our promises', and then the vanquished Moslems set out for exile in the valley of Purchena. They paused on a rocky eminence to take a last look at the city, and the faint sound of artillery told them that it was finally, completely taken. The Moslem kingdom which had brought more than 700 years of culture and enlightenment to pre-Renaissance Europe was gone forever. It was all too much for Boabdil. '*Allah achbar*,' he said, – God is great – and then he burst into tears.   *1492*

One of Britain's greatest composers Sir Michael Tippett was born in London, the second son of a retired Cornish lawyer who owned a hotel in Cannes. An extremely self-critical man, he wasn't satisfied with anything he'd written until he composed his *String Quartet No. 1* in 1935, when he destroyed all his previous work. During the Great Depression he organised operatic performances for the unemployed, which was at least compassionate, even if they'd rather have had the money. He became first a Trotskyist and then a pacifist, and in 1943 he was imprisoned for three months in Wormwood Scrubs for refusing to comply with the conditions imposed upon him as a conscientious objector. He composes in the country, where he lives alone 'to find some kind of inner silence'. His music is notoriously difficult to play and when his *Symphony No. 2* was premièred at the Royal Festival Hall in 1958, the orchestra got in a terrible mess. The conductor Sir Adrian Boult stopped them, apologised to the audience, and went back to the beginning.   *1905*

A price list was agreed for 'women's complaints' by the New York County Medical Society. It was drawn up by the Associated Physicians and Surgeons of the City of New York and included $5 for inserting a catheter; $50 for removing a breast; $25 to $35 for normal births and $30 to $60 for 'tedious and difficult labours'.   *1816*

9

Today's the day...

Lord of the pen John Ronald Reuel Tolkien was born to English parents, with a name that comes from the German *tollkühn* for foolhardy, in Bloemfontein in the Orange Free State. He was brought up by his widowed mother in a cottage in Savehole, Warwickshire, which he later immortalised as Hobbiton. From an early age, words and languages fascinated him. His mother taught him Latin, Greek and French, and later he learnt Anglo-Saxon, Middle English, Old Norse and Welsh – and he invented languages of his own. The birth of the Hobbit occurred in peculiarly mundane circumstances. He was Professor of Anglo-Saxon at Oxford when he discovered that one of the students had 'mercifully' left a blank page. He wrote on it, 'In a hole in the ground there lived a hobbit.' He'd never thought of hobbits before, and thought he'd bother to find out what they were like. When he'd done so he said, 'I am in fact, a hobbit in all but size.'   *1892*

Hard-headed walker Simeon Ellerton died at Craike in County Durham. All his life he'd worked as a messenger and performed his long-distance duties 'with fidelity and diligence'. He lived in a neat stone cottage that he'd built himself, but what's more remarkable is the way he built it. On every journey he'd pick up a suitable stone, put it on his head and carry it home. Eventually he had enough perfect ones for the house, but by that time he was convinced the weight made him a better walker – so he kept up the habit ever after. If anybody asked him why he carried a stone on his head, he always answered, 'Why? 'Tis to keep my hat on.'   *1709*

Unassuming Prime Minister Clement Attlee was born. By a strange coincidence he succeeded Churchill as Prime Minister, and as a baby was looked after by 'the Governess who'd just finished looking after Winston'. No doubt peeved at his own displacement, Churchill variously described him as 'a sheep in sheep's clothing', and 'a modest little man with much to be modest about'.   *1883*

Tudor Mummy Queen Catherine de Valois died in the monastery of Bermondsey. She was buried with much pomp and circumstance in Westminster Abbey, where according to the custom of the time, her wooden effigy was carried before her coffin, dressed for the occasion in 'a satin mantle, surcote and tunic, all furred with ermine'. Henry VII redesigned the Abbey, pulled down the chapel and had Catherine's body placed in a wooden box, where its 'badly apparelled' state was left open to the curious gaze. She remained indecently exposed for 200 years and it was a favourite game for the boys of Westminster School to steal bits of her skin and bone. She was reburied in 1776, but it wasn't until Dean Stanley learned of her rough handling in 1878, that she got a more seemly and final resting place beneath the ancient altar slab in the Chantry Chapel of Henry V. One of her most famous visitors in her time in the outside world was the diarist Samuel Pepys, on his thirty-sixth birthday. With schoolboyish glee, he boasted in his diary that after bribing the keepers, 'I had the upper part of her body in my hands, and I did kiss her mouth, reflecting on it, that I did kiss a Queene.'   *1437*

Today's the day...

Strapping infant 'General Tom Thumb' was born. He weighed over 9 lbs at birth, grew normally until he was six months old, but at five years he was still exactly the same weight and only 2 ft 1 in tall. Not a dwarf, he was in fact a true midget – a perfect human being on a tiny scale. Phineas T. Barnum's half-brother Philo brought him to the showman's attention, and he hotfooted it down to Bridgeport, Connecticut, to see for himself. He signed up the five-year-old for $3 a week, as 'General Tom Thumb, a dwarf of eleven years of age, just arrived from England'. Barnum determined that his midget would be 'autocratic, impudent and regal' and set about schooling him night and day. Tom first appeared in public with a monologue of Barnum's terrible puns, followed by a variety of roles including Cupid, Yankee Doodle Dandy, a semi-nude gladiator and Napoleon. Overnight he was the talk of New York. A year later he was the toast of London and after three audiences with Queen Victoria was nicknamed the 'Pet of the Palace'. The Duke of Wellington came to see him perform several times. On the first occasion Tom was playing Napoleon, strutting about the stage wrapped in thought. The Duke asked him afterwards what he was thinking about. 'Sir,' replied the jaunty manikin, 'I was thinking of the loss of the Battle of Waterloo.'   *1838*

The first lynching of 'The Innocents' took place in Stinkingwater Valley, Montana. This was the largest of the gangs who'd been terrorising the area, committing robbery and murder in broad daylight. They'd finally overstepped the mark when they killed a popular young German, Nick Tbalt. One of the Sheriff's friends had been hanged for the murder, and shortly afterwards the Virginia City Vigilantes were formed. Masterminded by tubercular Englishman Thomas James Dimsdale, they captured two of the gang, G. W. Brown and Erastus 'Red' Yager. Brown begged for mercy but Yager admitted, 'I merited this years ago.' He went on to say he'd die happy, if he knew the rest of the gang would be hanged too – and promptly

January 4

gave Dimsdale a full confession. In it, he told the whole story of the 'Innocents' who'd killed 102 men in just over a year. The ringleader of this infamous band was none other than the Sheriff.   *1864*

Utah was admitted to the Union. Seventy-two per cent of the population are Mormon and the state capital, Salt Lake City, is the headquarters of the organisation. Perhaps this accounts for the thrift practised in 1919 by the citizens of Vernal. Building a new bank with bricks from Salt Lake City, they discovered that the cheapest way of transporting them was in packets of seven through the mail. So they had every single one delivered this way.   *1896*

Goya and Gauguin began painting seriously. Although over a century apart, they both decided on the same date that their only hope of happiness lay in painting. Goya was in the throes of his turbulent love affair with the Duchess of Alba and wrote to a friend, 'To occupy my mind which is mortified by consideration of my misfortunes . . . I have begun to paint.' Gauguin had been a model bank clerk up till now, supporting his wife and four children in comfort. He made his protest by staying in bed. His wife found him there at 10 am when he announced, to her horror, that he'd given in his notice and 'from now on I'm going to paint'.   *1794/1883*

The Russian Siamese twins Masha and Dasha were born. Joined at the pelvis, their spines are also linked but they have separate spinal cords and hence separate sense reactions, only feeling pain in their own half of the joined body. Surprisingly, they're very different in personality. Masha is 'a lightweight chatterbox who flirts with boys', while Dasha is serious and studious. They each have one leg which they control and a third vestigial one. Special exercises were necessary to teach them to walk, which they couldn't do until they were five. Now they can dance, ride a bicycle and even climb ladders.   *1950*

Today's the day...

Saint and King Edward the Confessor died after collapsing on Christmas Day. Edward had been a weak, self-absorbed, but extremely pious King. He was much revered for his holiness and his very touch was thought to cure the afflicted. The Normans liked him too, since they claimed he willed England to the Conqueror. So for religious and secular reasons, it was no surprise that he was canonised in 1161. What is surprising, is that in his tomb in Westminster Abbey – which he founded – he was not allowed to rest in peace. In 1098, Henry I wanted to know whether the body remained 'uncorrupt' and had the grave opened in the presence of Bishop Gundulf, who plucked out a hair from the beard. In 1163, Henry II had the coffin 'translated' to a new shrine and with the connivance of Thomas à Becket, removed Edward's robes. In 1269, Henry III had the Abbey re-built and Edward was moved yet again. During the Dissolution, he was disturbed by Henry VIII and as far as possible restored by Henry's daughter Mary. At last, after the coronation of James II in 1685, a rafter broke the coffin open; a crucifix and ring were given to the King, and hopefully, poor Edward was troubled no more. *1066*

January 5

Record-breaking pilot Amy Johnson was killed in a crash that has become one of the great mysteries of aviation. On a supposedly routine Air Transport Auxiliary solo flight from Blackpool to Oxford, this airwoman who had flown solo to Australia without a radio, crash-landed in Home Territory in the Thames Estuary, over 100 miles off course. Although visibility was poor, it was clear enough for sailors aboard HMS *Haslemere* to witness the fatal descent. They distinctly saw a man and a woman in the icy sea. By a cruel stroke of fate the boat ran aground and despite an heroic rescue attempt which cost the life of the *Haslemere*'s commander, they could not be saved and neither of the bodies were ever recovered. The Air Ministry denied the eye-witness reports, but never explained how such an expert navigator came to be so hopelessly lost and had also magically plucked a passenger out of mid-air. Miss Johnson hated flying on Sundays claiming all her crashes occurred on the Sabbath. Yet she willingly took off on a foggy Sunday. It is an interesting footnote that in 1940 she had personally requested 'some dangerous mission in the secret service'. They had said 'no' then – but did they change their minds ?   *1941*

Gilbert and Sullivan's *Princess Ida* was premièred at the Savoy Theatre. Sullivan, who thought he was wasting his genius on light opera, was suffering from his usual kidney trouble and was drugged with morphine. The piece was not a disaster, but it ran only nine months, and caused a rift between them. It seemed ill-omened from the start. The libretto was based on an early play of Gilbert's called *The Princess*, which was written in awkward blank verse. Gilbert's direction was 'as ruthless as a sergeant major's' and he didn't much help the struggling performers. 'Look here, sir!' said one of them, 'I will not be bullied! I know my lines.' 'That may be,' Gilbert replied, 'but you don't know mine.' 'I've rehearsed this confounded business until I feel a perfect fool,' said the leading man. 'Ah,' replied Gilbert, relieved, 'now we can talk on equal terms!'   *1884*

Today's the day...

Satirical prelate Seth Ward, Lord Bishop of Sarum, died. As a student at Cambridge he came close to being sent down after one particularly virulent speech. Elected a bishop when he was only forty, he suffered from inveterate diarrhoea which is said to have been cured by slow journeys on horseback. Perhaps this contributed to his 'black malice' which in the end quite disturbed his mind. For the month before his death he would hardly eat at all, drank only stock and died a virtual skeleton. *1689*

Incredibly lucky aviator Captain J. Hedley fell out of a plane at 1,500 ft. Hedley and his Canadian pilot, Lieutenant Makepeace, were trying to evade enemy German fighters when they put the plane into a steep vertical dive. It was so sudden that Hedley was plucked out of his seat and disappeared off into the wide blue yonder. Makepeace continued the descent but when he levelled off a few hundred feet down, he discovered he was not alone. The slipstream had pulled his companion down behind him and there he was sitting on the tail of the plane. *1918*

Generous Jewish banker Haym Salomon died. He'd helped finance the Revolutionary War, funding the rebel army and arranging for various loans. Jefferson, Madison and Monroe all acknowledged their debt to him as whenever the Treasury ran short of money he'd make an advance to tide them over. During the British occupation of New York he'd been arrested twice and the second time was condemned to death. Luckily he had a string of golden guineas concealed about his person and was able to bribe the jailer and escape to the American lines. When the war was over, he suffered heavy financial losses and on his death his family was left penniless. Despite repeated attempts by his heirs to obtain settlement from the government, his loans were never repaid and the only official gratitude expressed was when they printed his head on the ten-cent stamp. *1785*

January 6

Handsome, blond six-footer Richard II was born. Son of the Black Prince, he inherited none of his father's statesmanlike qualities but rather the beauty and pleasure-loving temperament of his mother. He succeeded to the throne aged only ten and was kept under the watchful eye of stern tutors until he was eighteen. Weak and indecisive by nature, this strict control only served to aggravate his faults and he became 'neurotic, introspective and revengeful'. He spent vast sums of money on clothes embroidered with gold and precious stones, and one Christmas entertained 10,000 house guests. When he had the body of his favourite Robert de Vere brought back from Holland, he opened up the coffin and lavished jewels and affection on the corpse before giving it a splendid burial. If he didn't accomplish much he at least left a lasting memento of his reign. He's said to have invented the handkerchief.   *1367*

Animal lover 'Humanity Martin' died in France, where he'd gone to escape creditors. The flamboyant MP was born in Dublin, owned a vast windswept estate near Galway and was so concerned about the cruelty of his tenants to their horses and cattle that he built a special stone tower there. Any offenders were unceremoniously thrown in and only released when they promised to be kinder to their animals in future. One of the founders of the RSPCA, he managed to get a bill passed through Parliament stating that anyone ill-treating an animal in their 'care or custody' could be prosecuted. Martin, who was also a barrister, brought a number of cases to court including one against a costermonger, Billy Burns, for flogging his donkey. The magistrates were reluctant to prosecute the man, feeling they were infringing on his liberty to do what he willed with his own property. With a characteristic flourish, Martin called his final witness – the donkey! When they saw for themselves the state of the wretched animal they relented and fined the owner. It was the only case in legal history where a donkey won the day.   *1834*

Today's the day...

The first aerial crossing of the English Channel was
accomplished in a hydrogen-filled balloon by a hot-tempered
Frenchman Pierre Blanchard and his wealthy American sponsor Dr
John Jeffries. At 1 pm they ascended from the White Cliffs of
Dover aboard their curious ornithopter. It was steered by a rudder
and propelled by a rotating fan and had four flapping wings. Loaded
down with such ridiculous equipment, maintaining a safe height was a
constant problem. By the time they were two-thirds of the way across,
they had already jettisoned all their ballast, but they were still
descending rapidly towards the sea. In a last ditch attempt to save
them from a disastrous ducking, they started to throw everything
overboard. After dumping the wings and the fan, there was nothing
left but their clothes. First went their heavy greatcoats and then their
trousers. Finally in a moment of farcical bravado they urinated into
the sea. Unbelievably, this brought the relief they sought. They rose
just high enough to clear the French coast. They had barely made it
and the historic first channel flight actually ended with two strangers
up a tree, wearing no trousers! *1785*

Portuguese paramour Ines Piras de Castro was brutally murdered on the orders of her father-in-law King Alfonso of Portugal. Against his father's wishes Don Pedro had secretly married Ines. When Alfonso discovered the truth he first tried to convince Ines to leave Pedro, when she refused his three henchmen cut her down. Don Pedro's revenge culminated in one of the most macabre ceremonies in the annals of history. He suppressed his grief until his father died two years later. Now as Pedro I of Portugal, he hunted down the murderers and had their hearts ripped out – from the back. The decomposed corpse of Ines was exhumed, clothed in fabulous raiment and enthroned next to him. He then staged a full coronation and all the courtiers were obliged to swear fealty kissing the withered hand of the Corpse Queen who reigned in death.   *1355*

Inter-galactic aliens are thought to have claimed their first victim. Kentucky Highway Patrol had been inundated with hundreds of anxious citizens making reports of a huge metallic saucer – 300ft in diameter – hovering above the woody lands of Maysville. Convinced they were dealing with authentic calls, the police notified Goodman Air Force Base who instructed World War II ace pilot Captain Thomas Mantell to investigate. Followed by two trainee pilots in Air National Guard F-51s, Mantell set off in pursuit. Because the jets were not fitted with the necessary oxygen equipment, they could fly no higher than 15,000ft. At this point, the two wingmen abandoned the chase but twenty-five-year-old Mantell continued upward attempting to close in. Excitedly, he radioed back that he had good visual contact but that it seemed capable of keeping a constant distance from him. His last message was, 'I'm going on up to 20,000ft. If I'm no closer, I'll abandon chase.' In the next moment his plane exploded. The official version claimed the experienced Mantell had passed out through oxygen starvation and his plane nose-dived and crashed. However the Air Force gave no satisfactory explanation of the run-away UFO.   *1948*

Today's the day...

The steady-handed painter Giotto died. When he was first recommended as an artist for the Vatican, Pope Benedict XI demanded proof of his ability. Simply but effectively the painter proved his worth, and with one sweep of his brush drew a perfect circle! *1337*

The last battle between England and America was fought at New Orleans and ended with the British being soundly thrashed. Over 5,000 Redcoats led by the blundering General Sir Edward Pakenham made a suicidal attack, through a narrow approach, on the American garrison held by 4,000 troops led by General Andrew Jackson. Along with 290 of his men Pakenham died – bleeding to death under an oak tree. The total American death toll was only thirteen. But the jubilation of the victorious Yankees turned sour when they learned it had all been in vain. Because of the vast distances and resulting slow communications, neither the British nor the Americans knew that the two countries had signed a peace treaty two weeks earlier. *1815*

Precocious parents Mr and Mrs Hsi of Amoy in China became the proud parents of a healthy baby boy. The father was nine and the mother was eight years old. *1910*

'The King' Elvis Aaron Presley was born to sharecropper parents in Tupelo, Mississippi, the surviving brother of twins. Inspired by local preachers 'jumpin' on the piano', he won a prize for singing at the age of ten – but the following year was disappointed to get his first guitar when he really wanted a bike. Hard times caused the family to pile their belongings into an old car and move to Memphis, where he cut his first record as a present for his mother. He grew sideburns, greased his hair and turned up at school in pink and black outfits. 'Acting kinda goofy' clearly paid off and from being the ultimate in rebellious youth, he became a thoroughly respectable multi-millionaire. His life must have been a strange and lonely one, nevertheless, and secluded in his palatial home of 'Graceland' he became terrified of assassination, amassed a huge collection of guns and a troop of bodyguards called 'the Memphis Mafia'. Perhaps his best friend was the one who wore scaled-down suits, got drunk and smashed up the telephones. He was called 'Scatter' and was Presley's pet chimpanzee.

1935

A munitions factory exploded in Stockholm, killing one person and injuring twelve others. The spark that caused the disaster was created by static – from a woman's nylon underwear.

1955

A suspected royal murderer Prince Albert Victor, Duke of Clarence, was born at Frogmore in Buckinghamshire – son of the Prince of Wales, grandson of Queen Victoria and heir to the throne. Despite his illustrious background, he's often accused of being 'Jack the Ripper', and his unexpected death at twenty-eight nothing more than a means of removing 'a deranged killer' from the Royal Family. In 1970, a retired surgeon, Dr Thomas Stowell, hinted he'd got secret files on the case but died shortly afterwards and his papers were destroyed. Recently a new biographer, American Frank Spiering, demanded that the Queen hold a press conference about him. She turned down his suggestion but offered the eager novelist complete access to the archives. Inexplicably the shy ex-private-eye refused.

1864

Chequers became an official residence when Lloyd George moved in. It was given to the country by Lord Lee of Fareham, and takes its name from a twelfth-century owner who was a clerk to the Exchequer. A party was held to celebrate the first Prime Minister's arrival and as Lord Lee drove into the night, he shouted back, 'Take good care of her!' According to the Chequers Trust he established, the house is available as the official country residence of the Prime Minister . . . even if his income should be limited to his salary!

1921

Today's the day...

Connecticut became the fifth state admitted to the Union. It actually granted rights for beavers to build dams and in 1975 debated what should become the official state animal. Candidates included the squirrel, the bald eagle and surprisingly, the sperm whale. A popular suggestion was the white-tailed deer, until red-faced senators were reminded that it is commonly called the Virginia deer. Finally a suggestion was accepted and although the decision still awaits final ratification, the official state animal of Connecticut is *Homo sapiens*.

1788

The first radio police appeal for a wanted murderer was broadcast in England. Six days earlier in a shed in Camden Town, London, a charred body was found seated on a stool. Beside it was a suicide note: 'Goodbye all. No work, no money.' It was signed by the appropriately named Sam Furnace. It wasn't long, however, before forensic experts established that the corpse had been shot in the back of the head, and shrewd detective work identified the victim as local rent collector, Walter Spatchett. The real Sam Furnace had murdered Spatchett to fake his own suicide. Police used the BBC to broadcast Furnace's description and he was quickly apprehended. He nevertheless escaped the long arm of the law by committing suicide in his cell – this time for real.

1933

January 9

Two calves were slaughtered in an oddly medieval ceremony at the opening of Egypt's most advanced technological achievement, the Aswan Dam. While the dam was being built by a team of Russian experts, a team of Swedish engineers worked against the clock to try and save the unique 3,200-year-old rock temples of Abu Simbel from the vast lake it would create. The operation involved cutting the two royal temples and the huge stone statues of the god-king Rameses II into 1,050 enormous pieces, and re-assembling them 690ft up a sheer rock face. With only three months to spare before the man-made Lake Nasser came flooding into existence, the fantastic monuments were saved when the world's most spectacular jigsaw puzzle was finally completed. *1960*

Mendacious, spaniel-loving US President Richard Nixon was born. His embittered father raised lemons, while his mother named Richard after the mean avaricious failure, Richard the Lionheart. At school he spent such long hours in the library he was nicknamed 'Iron Butt'. His perseverance paid off when he graduated from law school but his first case ended disastrously. The judge reprimanded him for unethical behaviour and his client successfully sued him for mishandling her case. During the vicious McCarthyite witch hunts Nixon impressed his political peers with his ruthless and often vindictive persecution of suspected communists and was rewarded by becoming, at the age of thirty-seven, the youngest Republican US senator. Surviving scandals and personal unpopularity, Nixon rose to become Vice-President. He lost his presidential fight with Kennedy by a whisker but eight years later his dream was fulfilled when he became the first Republican to take the Presidency on a second bid. Considering the subsequent disgrace, it is worth remembering Nixon's own words at the beginning of the 1968 campaign – 'Let us begin by committing ourselves to the truth – to see it like it is, and tell it like it is – to find the truth, and to live the truth . . .' *1913*

Today's the day...

The world's first underground railway was inaugurated by Mr Gladstone, with a maiden chug from Bishop's Road to Farringdon Street. It had taken three-and-a-half years to build and on its first day carried 30,000 passengers. The locomotives were powered by steam, and in the passenger compartments the oil lamp lighting was so weak, that people who wanted to read brought their own candles and stuck them on the carriage walls. After twelve months a total of nine-and-a-half million people had travelled by 'tube' and the rumbling vehicles were affectionately referred to as 'sewer trams'.   *1863*

The Penny Post was introduced, the brain-child of Rowland Hill. He'd worked out that the existing method of postage – which like modern telephone tariffs was charged according to distance – was both clumsy and uneconomic. Without any assistance from the General Post Office he calculated that preparing the letter for despatch, and delivering it at the other end, were the most costly parts of the service, while the actual transit was exceedingly cheap. So in 1837 he published *Post Office Reform*, which proposed a standard charge of one penny per

½oz weight, pre-paid regardless of distance. He pioneered the idea of 'little bags' called envelopes, and 'bits of paper' called stamps, and though all these revolutionary concepts were eventually adopted, he faced powerful opposition. Lord Litchfield, the Postmaster General, said in Parliament, 'Of all the wild and visionary schemes which I have ever heard, this is the most extraordinary.' He insisted that for the new scheme to pay as well as the old one, the number of letters carried would have to be multiplied six times over. He needn't have worried. Before Rowland Hill's death in 1879, twenty-four thousand million stamped letters had been sent.   *1840*

The artist without arms Cesar Ducornet was born in Lille, France. Apart from his two missing limbs, he was a digit short on his right foot, and had an abnormally large gap between his big toe and the rest. This enabled him to hold a piece of charcoal, with which he did drawings on the wall. His work was so good that he was financed to go to Paris where he became a famous painter and lived to be 100. One of his best known foot paintings showed Mary Magdalene and Christ. It was 11ft high.   *1806*

Unpunished outlaw Frank James was born. Neither as romantic, nor as vicious as Jesse, he also lacked his younger brother's good looks, quick intelligence, dry humour and commanding presence. These missing qualities he tried to make up for by quoting the Bible or Shakespeare at the drop of a hat, and writing self-righteous epistles to the press. The fact that he was a walking failure, however, didn't stop him from becoming a living legend. After Jesse had been murdered, Frank surrendered, and his trial attracted such enormous crowds that it was held in the Opera House at Gallatin, Missouri, instead of the County Court House. The posthumous reputation of the now defunct James Gang was still powerful enough to silence witnesses, and even after a second trial, Frank was acquitted of a double murder charge, and never broke the law again.   *1843*

Today's the day...

Hearty English writer Thomas Hardy died after expressing the wish that he should be buried in the churchyard at Stinsford, the original 'Mellstock' immortalised in his writings. The nation, however, wanted to honour him with a burial in Westminster Abbey. Finally a compromise was reached. Hardy should have his heart buried in Stinsford and his ashes kept at Westminster. The cremation took place in Dorchester and the ashes were duly placed with full pomp and ceremony in Poets' Corner. At the same time a casket containing the heart was buried in a quiet corner of Stinsford churchyard under an ancient yew tree. At least, that's what the world thought. Actually, the casket had been left on the kitchen table and Hardy's sister's cat got the heart and made off to the shrubbery with his prize. Although the cat came back, the heart was never recovered, and the casket so reverently placed in the humble grave was in fact empty. *1928*

The King of Shopping Mr Selfridge was born. He caused quite a furore when, with a great burst of advertising, he opened his American-style department store in Oxford Street. In 1909 London traders were still terribly genteel, catering for the 'carriage trade' with hardly a thought for the thousands of potential shoppers who poured into the city every day. Mr Selfridge put his transatlantic methods to work and in six days took a total of ninety-seven full page advertisements in the London newspapers announcing the opening of his store. The effect was staggering. The night before the event London bulged at the seams, and in the morning when the store opened the crowds were so vast that sixty policemen had to be called in to control them. A little less successful was Mr Selfridge's protracted wooing of one of the famous Dolly Sisters, Jenny Dolly. He'd fallen for the pair of identical twins when he saw them at the sleazy Kit-Kat Club in the Haymarket and lavished his fortune on them till the end of his days. With unlimited funds they had a gay old time mostly in the South of France where they became inveterate gamblers. In seven years he spent over two million pounds on these vivacious dollybirds – but their time was up. He owed £150,000 to the taxman and died with a mere £2,000 to his name.   *1864*

The racing 'Tinman' Fred Archer was born at Prestbury in Gloucestershire. He became Champion Jockey with 147 winners at the age of sixteen, and his skill was so consummate that it was said he could 'win on a donkey'. He held onto his Championship for thirteen successive years, despite the fact that he was the wrong build for a jockey. He was 5ft 9in tall, and in order to keep down to $8\frac{1}{2}$ stone he would eat next to nothing, breakfast on half an orange and a teaspoon of castor oil and purge himself with 'Archer's Mixture', a secret brew which somebody once tried, and was sick on for a week. Quite a competitor, he would furiously whip his horses, and tongue-lash other jockeys during races. Although his track record was an unmitigated success, his personal life was a complete disaster. His wife and son died, and he shot himself at the age of twenty-nine, by which time he'd ridden 2,748 winners.   *1857*

Today's the day...

A monstrous struggle occurred in Broadford Bay on the Isle of Skye. A local police constable named John Morrisey was strolling along the beach after a heavy storm when, half buried in the sand, he saw a gruesome slimy-looking mound. With complete disregard for his own safety, he gave it one almighty kick, but immediately wished he hadn't, for as he made contact an upset tentacle lashed out and lassoed his foot. The bizarre confrontation ended with the unfortunate policeman having to surrender his welly boot to the fierce hold of this mysterious but tenacious beast. PC Morrisey was outraged at this daylight robbery of one boot – size unknown. He hopped over to a nearby house, seconded a garden implement and returned to the scene of the crime. Then in a unique moment in criminal history, an armed British policeman killed a robber with a pair of garden shears. In the investigations that followed, it was established that the culprit was an unnamed 9ft squid. *1952*

Scarface Al Capone's closest shave came as he was getting out of his car to go into a Chicago restaurant. A sinister black limousine, carrying three gun-toting hoods, drew alongside the Capone car and raked it with a hail of bullets. Capone's bodyguards were quick enough to take cover, but his driver caught it in the back. A policeman who witnessed the shooting said that the hit men gave them 'everything but the kitchen stove'. Capone's answer was an immediate order to General Motors for a $30,000, four-wheeled fort. It weighed seven tons, had ½in thick bullet-proof windows, an armour-plated body, steel covered gas-tank, and an arsenal behind the back seat, which could be utilised through the removable back window to deter any over-zealous pursuers. From here on in, this incredible car would always be preceded by another, full of sharpshooters. His office was fitted with an armour-plated, high-backed swivel chair, and never again did Capone keep an appointment on time. The most infamous of all the hoodlums had effectively built himself his very own escape-proof prison. *1925*

January 12

Transvestite ex-bus conductress Margaret 'Bill' Allen was hanged for the murder of her sixty-three-year-old neighbour Nancy Chadwick. She was a big, butch lady who'd been a builder's labourer, and she seemed to know an awful lot about the movements of Mrs Chadwick. When confronted by bloodstains found in her house, she immediately confessed, claiming that in 'a funny mood' she'd beaten her gossipy old neighbour's head in with a hammer. Bill's peculiar lifestyle earned her little sympathy and only 152 out of 26,000 local inhabitants signed a petition for her reprieve. On the morning of her execution, she deliberately kicked over her breakfast tray, saying she didn't want it, and she didn't want anyone else to enjoy it. The actual hanging is odd in that men are traditionally allowed to wear their own clothes to the scaffold, but Bill wasn't. For the first time in many years, she was without her usual man's attire and plummeted to her death, wearing a striped prison frock.

1949

The fighting tank was first tested and given the official OK by the British military brass. The word 'tank' was originally thought to have been coined by Sir Ernest Swinton, who overheard two workmen describe the strange looking machine as 'that tank thing'. Another, perhaps less convincing suggestion, is that to fool German spies when the vehicles first went to France, they were sent over in enormous crates marked 'tanks'. The hard facts are that at this first test, the new device was so successful that the British Army immediately ordered forty-nine of them. It's interesting too, that in the early days, the only member of the War Office who was interested in Swinton's revolutionary machines was Winston Churchill, who was then First Lord of the Admiralty. Swinton never forgot Churchill's encouragement and that's why so many parts of a tank have nautical names like hull, deck and hatch. The Germans were so impressed with these fire-breathing monsters, that they invented a special long word for them. They called them *Schützengrabenvernitchtungsautomobiles*.

1916

Today's the day...

The amazing Thomas Crapper did it again. In a startling follow-up to his pioneering one-piece pedestal flushing toilet, he created for gentlemen everywhere the world's first self-raising seat. This splendid invention worked on an ingenious system of counterweights that left men free to concentrate on the job in hand. Like all novelties the seat was a great success at first, but its appeal has long since dwindled. Doubtless the ladies of the house didn't like the idea of mis-timing it – the result of which would be a soundly smacked bottom. *1863*

Jesus Christ was cremated in Wales, on a hill overlooking Llantrisant. This particular Jesus was the five-month-old son of sun-worshipper and nudist, Dr William Price, who was interrupted when smoke from the pathetic little body attracted the locals' attention. He took Jesus home again and kept what remained of him under the bed for a full week, after which time he was hauled before the magistrates. He was charged with obstructing the course of an inquest and otherwise disposing of a body which should have been buried in hallowed ground. Dressed in his Druidic robes, Price easily confounded the first charge by producing an authentic coroner's certificate, showing the death to be by natural causes. On the second charge, he simply challenged the judge to show him the law that expressly forbade the burning of the dead. There was none, and though the judge apprised the jury of the fact, they nevertheless found Price guilty of contravening a law which didn't exist. The exasperated judge insisted they discharge him, and when they did, Price immediately sued the police. He only got a farthing damages, but more importantly, he'd established the right of a person to be cremated if he so wished. By a curious coincidence, the Cremation Society of England, which sought that very end, had been created ten years to the day before young Jesus' conflagration.   *1884*

A cruel mockery of an article appeared in the *New York Times*. It heaped derision on the theories of Professor Robert Hutchings Goddard who had publicly announced that he believed a rocket could function in a vacuum. Though Goddard later became known as 'the Father of Space Exploration', the author suggested that he was the master of scientific follies and that he 'seems only to lack the knowledge ladled out daily in high schools'! Forty-nine years later, the bumptious writer got his come-uppance, when *Apollo II* headed for the moon. The paper was at least magnanimous, and published a gentle apology. It said, 'It is now definitely established that a rocket can function in a vacuum. *The Times* regrets the error.' The only problem was that the much wronged Goddard had been dead for twenty-four years.   *1920*

Home-loving English composer Richard Addinsell was born. His most famous work was the *Warsaw Concerto* which he wrote for the 1941 film *Dangerous Moonlight*. The music is remarkable since, despite its title, it is hardly a complete movement, let alone a complete concerto. In its first year, the eight-minute theme tune sold 300,000 records and half a million copies of the sheet music, and Poland was so proud she presented Addinsell with the country's Silver Cross of Merit. It was a marvellous achievement for a man who never set foot in Poland – and didn't even finish the work.   *1904*

Today's the day...

The saintly jungle doctor Albert Schweitzer was born, the son of a Lutheran pastor in Gunsbach, Germany. An infant musical prodigy, he became an organist and theologian of international repute. Yet at the tender age of thirty he gave up a brilliant career to found his mission-*cum*-clinic at Lambaréné, in the depths of equatorial Africa. 'I had had thoughts of becoming an intellectual,' he said, 'but I found it too difficult.' Instead, with only a disused chicken shack to work from and no previous experience in surgery, he treated 2,000 patients in his first nine months, and still found time to play his zinc-lined, damp and termite-proof piano. With money from books, lectures and organ recitals, he built Lambaréné into a complete hospital village, teeming not only with the ailing but all kinds of other inhabitants. There were 150 goats, a pelican who guarded the doctor's door, and a wild boar called Josephine who adopted him and followed him everywhere – even into church on Sundays.   *1875*

The first private phone call in the British Isles was made by Queen Victoria from her residence at Osborne House on the Isle of Wight. Its inventor Alexander Graham Bell demonstrated the machine, and though Her Majesty found it 'rather faint', she and her friends had great fun singing and saying poems into it with Sir Thomas Biddulph on the receiving end. In fact, they could just as well have shouted out the window – Sir Thomas lived in a cottage in the grounds.   *1878*

Westminster thrashed Bonn 2 – 1 in an international inter-parliamentary football match at Crystal Palace, using Hansards as shin-pads. There was a Tory on the left-wing, a Labour MP on the right and a star forty-three-year-old Dr Bernard Donoghue at the top of the age range. Just back from a tour of Asia, he'd had a hair-raising twenty-four hours. He'd breakfasted in Rawalpindi, lunched in Egypt, gone to bed in London at 2.45am, and arrived bright and breezy on the pitch at 10.30 next morning – the undoubted Man of the Match.   *1978*

January 14

The highest peak in the western hemisphere, Aconcagua, was climbed for the first time by Matthias Zurbriggen, the Swiss guide, in a party organised by the English mountaineer, Edward Fitzgerald. Battered by bitterly cold winds, gasping for breath and weak with sickness in the high altitude, the four-man party had struggled to within 1,000ft of the summit. There they rested and made the disastrous mistake of having a meal. Fitzgerald became violently ill and had to be helped back to camp, cheated from conquering the 22,834ft mountain himself – by a snack. *1897*

'Surly Bob' the swearing Lord Chancellor died after exclaiming in characteristic fashion, 'I'll be damned if I'm not dying.' Otherwise known as Lord Northington, Bob was also famed for his heavy drinking and cancelled evening sittings in the Court of Chancery so he could enjoy his after-dinner port. On his death-bed, he instructed his gardener to cut down a clump of his son's favourite trees. Knowing full well it was only ordered to spite the Northington heir, the man didn't do it and to his horror was summoned before Northington Snr. 'Sir, damn you, you have not done as I ordered you,' spluttered his lordship. 'You think I am going, so I am and be damned to you but you shall go first' – and he fired him on the spot. *1772*

An attempt to kill the Emperor of France Napoleon III seriously misfired, when three bombs hurled at him exploded and inflicted '500 wounds' on bystanders. The Italian revolutionary Count Felice Orsini had organised the plot and had his 'infernal machines' specially made in Birmingham and smuggled out to him in Paris. The explosions wreaked havoc. They killed a horse, seriously injured several soldiers and two footmen, wounded General Roquet who was sitting next to Napoleon and extinguished most of the nearby gas-lights. Orsini himself was hurt by flying shrapnel and yet Napoleon sustained only one small injury. His hat was perforated in the blast. *1858*

Today's the day...

Charles Dickens gave up his first and only diary. On New Year's Day, the twenty-six-year-old novelist who was just beginning to blossom, determined to commit to paper 'what rises to my lips – my mental lips at least – without reserve.' Although at this time he was starting to knock off the odd masterpiece, he kept up this steely resolve for a full fifteen days, before he could stand it no more. The last entry reads, 'Here ends this brief attempt – I grow sad over this checking off of days – and can't do it.'   *1838*

The passing wit of Henry Labouchere reached its apogee on his death-bed. The much loved English wit, journalist and MP had contracted what was at first a simple cold, but developed into bronchial catarrh that seriously weakened his heart. The day before he died, his dearest friend and future biographer Algar Thorold paid him a call. As the wilting Labouchere lay fitfully dozing, his visitor knocked a spirit lamp onto the floor, where with a soft crunch it ignited. The ailing Henry woke with a chuckle, 'Flames? Not yet I think!' They were his last words.   *1912*

The James-Younger Gang held up the Concord Stage just a few miles outside Malvern in Arkansas. The haul in cash and jewels was worth about $4,000 and would have been more had it not been for an uncharacteristically gallant gesture on the part of the droll and chubby Cole Younger. He was about to relieve a passenger of his expensive gold watch, when the man protested in a long Texan drawl. Younger looked at him with respect and asked if he was a Southerner. When he said he was, Cole asked if he'd been in the Confederate Army, and the poor man not knowing what to expect, bristled and bravely said indeed, he'd had that honour. The enthusiastic bandit gave him the third degree on regiments and place names, and when he was satisfied he was robbing an ex-Johnny Reb, he rectified the situation by giving the watch back. He gazed sardonically at the rest of the passengers,

said that he didn't go for detectives and damn Yankees, and completed
the raid. Perhaps Cole was feeling exceptionally generous that day
since it was, after all, his thirtieth birthday.   *1874*

Tight-fisted Welsh playwright and composer Ivor Novello
was born David Ivor Davies in the appropriately named house
'Llwyn yr Gos' – the Grove of the Nightingales. Money seems to have
dominated his life. His father was a tax inspector, and Ivor was always
careful. In his fabulous country house 'Red Roofs' he installed a
pay-phone, and wise party guests smuggled in extra bottles of drink,
since it never flowed freely. He once staggered actress Lilian
Braithwaite with the gift of a diamond brooch. She showed it to Noël
Coward, saying, 'Ivor gave me this tiny diamond. Can *you* see it?' *1893*

The mighty Pentagon was completed on the Virginia side of the
Potomac in Washington DC. Home to the US Defence Department,
its vital statistics are as amazing as the building itself. It covers 34 acres
and it has another 204 acres of lawns and terraces. Its total floor area
would fill a square whose sides were half a mile long, and it's all
condensed into a fairly compact series of five concentric pentagons
connected by ten spokes. The advantage of this ingenious design is
that, although there are $17\frac{1}{2}$ miles of corridor, no two offices are more
than 1,800ft – or a six-minute walk – apart. America sleeps safe in the
knowledge that all her most vital secrets are securely filed in this, the
largest office building in the world.   *1943*

London lost its head when James Heatherington appeared for the
first time in the very latest fashion. Such consternation was caused
that the unfortunate dandy was hauled before the Lord Mayor, who
bound him over and fined him £50 for appearing 'on the public
highway, wearing upon his head a tall structure having a shining lustre
and calculated to frighten timid people.' It was the first top hat. *1797*

Today's the day...

America went dry when the 18th Amendment to the Constitution went into effect. For over a century, temperance societies had been waging war against the ravages of alcohol and they finally had their way. All manufacture, sale and transportation of intoxicating liquor was declared illegal and even doctors' prescriptions and sacramental wine were checked for their alcoholic content! Prohibition revived the pioneer pastime of bootlegging, so named for the traditional way old-timers sold forbidden firewater to the Indians, often hiding the bottles in their boots.   1920

The Incredible Conjuror was supposed to astound the audience at London's Theatre Royal with devastating tricks. A newspaper ad in the *General Advertiser* promised that at 6.30pm the amazing magician would play the music of any instrument on a walking stick; identify any masked spectator; turn himself into any person alive or dead, and finally climb into a common wine bottle, and while inside, let any member of the audience handle it. By 7pm the theatre was packed, with more crowds outside clamouring to get in. When they were promised their money back if the performer didn't turn up, they realised they'd been had, and tore the place apart. One man gazed at the havoc with delight. He was the rascally Duke of Montague who'd laid a heavy wager with Lord Chesterfield that he could pack a playhouse, simply by advertising the impossible.   *1749*

The BBC caused panic and consternation with the most amazing newsflash. A straightforward speech was suddenly interrupted by an eye-witness report from London of violent clashes between police and rioters who were protesting about mass unemployment. The Houses of Parliament were being demolished by an angry mob armed with mortars, then in came the startling news that the Minister of Traffic had been hanged from a lamp post, and the loud noise of an explosion announced the destruction of the Savoy Hotel. Switchboards all over the country were jammed with people offering help, seeking information and demanding action from official sources. Bemused policemen were inundated with callers demanding to know what they were going to do about this disastrous situation. When they asked how people knew about it, and were told of the radio report, all was revealed. Few people had *really* listened to it, because if they had, they would have heard the announcer state that the following programme was a fiction.   *1926*

Gruesome American cannibal Albert Fish died in the electric chair at Sing Sing. The meek painter and decorator confessed to the murder of six children though it's thought he'd killed at least fifteen. One of his nastiest methods of disposing of the bodies was to chop them up, pop them in a pot with a carrot and an onion and serve them up as a stew. Although his defence pleaded insanity, the judge disagreed and sentenced him to death. Fish seemed quite tickled at the idea of roasting alive and even helped the executioner strap the electrodes to his legs.   *1936*

Today's the day...

American Renaissance man Benjamin Franklin was born in Boston,
the son of a chandler. He was the fifteenth of seventeen children, and
the youngest son of a youngest son for five generations. Starting life as a
printer's apprentice, he worked in England as a compositor and swam
the Thames from Chelsea to Blackfriars 'performing sundry feats in
the water as he went along'. Back in America, he contracted a bigamous
marriage with Deborah Read and launched himself on one of the
most amazing careers the world has ever seen. He became a writer,
publisher, scientist, philosopher and statesman; was Ambassador
to France and one of the five engineers of the Declaration of
Independence. Among other things, he invented bi-focals, lightning
conductors, the platform rocking-chair, and the water powered
harmonica. He created, organised or was involved in the founding of
Philadelphia's first fire department, the University of Pennsylvania,
the American Philosophical Society, and the country's first efficient
postal service, lending library, hospital and fire insurance company.
Though he was much loved, he made many enemies, both in his
lifetime and afterwards. William Carlos Williams described him as 'our

great prophet of chicanery'. D. H. Lawrence thought he was 'a snuff coloured little man with an unlovely snuff coloured ideal', and according to William Cobbett, he was a 'crafty and lecherous old hypocrite'. He certainly lusted after women and often made improper advances. He had an illegitimate son, frequent 'intrigues with low women' and claimed to believe that regular sex prevented gout.   *1706*

The original Siamese twins died aged sixty-three. The famous pair, Chang and Eng Bunker, had had a restless night, with Chang complaining of breathlessness and pains in his chest. In the early hours of the morning, Eng's son William found Chang dead and Eng in a deep sleep. When poor Eng was woken and told what had happened, he understandably panicked and went into nervous spasms. After an hour he appeared comatose, and an hour after that he was dead. An autopsy was performed and while the results were inconclusive, it was believed that Chang had died from the effects of a clot of blood, and Eng had died of fright.   *1874*

Richard Sheridan's great comedy *The Rivals* opened at the Covent Garden Theatre. Though it was later an enormous success and is now, of course, a classic of English theatre, the wordy first version was greeted with hisses on its opening night. When Sheridan told his wife, she said, 'My dear Dick, I am delighted. I always knew it was impossible you could make anything of writing plays.'   *1775*

A naval disaster occurred at a London pub and five people were killed. It happened when the captain of a ship lying off Rotherhithe made an agreement with the publican to secure the ship's cables to the premises. A small anchor was carried ashore and deposited in the cellar, while the cable was tied round a beam. In the night, which was a windy one, the ship veered about. It tugged at the cable, which pulled down the beam and the pub came tumbling down.   *1789*

Today's the day...

Word collector, physician and inventor Peter Mark Roget was born. His zest for work was staggering. Apart from a busy medical practice, in 1815 he invented the slide rule; then came the 'Economic Chessboard' – forerunner of the modern pocket chessboard; and finally his paper on *The Persistence of Vision with Regard to Moving Objects* which sowed the seeds for the invention of the movie camera. But his greatest invention was the mighty *Thesaurus of English Words and Phrases, classified and arranged so as to facilitate the Expression of Ideas and to assist in Literary Composition*. It began, when he was a young doctor, as a humble collection of 15,000 words in a penny notebook 'to supply my deficiencies' when giving lectures. He actually started the complete compilation at the age of seventy-one and it was published in 1852 after four years of incessant work. By the age of ninety he had edited twenty-eight new editions. It is remarkable that, although Roget was born in London, the compiler of the work second only to the English Dictionary did not have an ounce of English blood in his veins (that is blood vessels, arteries, aorta, veinlets, capillaries etc!). *1779*

Tanned smoothie Cary Grant was born – Alexander Archibald Leach – in Bristol, England. At the age of fourteen he joined a troupe of acrobats and travelled with them to New York. He made his way to Hollywood where he managed to get parts in several films. Strolling from the set of the disastrous *Madame Butterfly*, looking devastating in his white naval uniform, he was spotted by Mae West. On the spot she named him as her next leading man and he starred with her in *She Done Him No Wrong* and *I'm No Angel* in 1933. He freely admits that 'I learned everything from Mae West . . . well nearly everything', and his understated technique and innate sense of timing made him the superstar of sophisticated comedy. He retired from films in 1969, finally became a father in his fourth marriage and now spends his time running an international cosmetics firm – although he's never worn stage make-up in his life. His age has always been a source of wonder

January 18

and the subject of much gossip. One Hollywood columnist, determined to get to the bottom of the matter, sent him a brief telegram, 'How old Cary Grant?' With typical urbanity he replied, 'Old Cary Grant fine. How you?'

1904

A loser and a gentleman Captain Scott reached the South Pole under very different circumstances from those expected. Just one-and-a-half miles from where they had reckoned the Pole to be, Scott and his party found the tent and Norwegian flag of Roald Amundsen, who had beaten them there by more than a month. In the tent there was a note from Amundsen asking Scott to deliver a letter to King Haakon, and wishing him a safe return. There were also three reindeer bags containing an assortment of nuts and socks, and a number of pieces of navigational equipment. It is ironic that, among the items that helped Amundsen beat Scott to the Pole, were a hypsometer and a sextant of English make.

1912

Body-line bowling threatened the political peace between Australia and England in a strangely worded telegram sent to the MCC. During the Third Test at Adelaide demon bowler Harold Larwood had developed body-line bowling into such an art that Australian batsmen lived in fear of injury. After three were seriously clobbered and angry fans thirsted for revenge, the Australian Cricket Board of Control cabled the MCC in London, 'In our opinion it is unsportsmanlike. Unless it is stopped at once it is likely to upset the friendly relations existing between Australia and England.' The MCC calmly replied, 'In neither case was the bowler to blame.' The *London Mercury* was quite indignant at the complaint and commented, 'Where is that tough Australian grin?/When comrades did you learn to faint?/Can you not take without complaint/A dose of your own medicine?' Larwood settled Down Under and was treated as a folk hero even though one small child was heard to say, 'He doesn't look like a murderer.'

1933

Today's the day...

Voracious enquirer James Watt was born. Described by Wordsworth as 'perhaps the most extraordinary man that this country has ever produced', he didn't actually invent the steam engine but perfected its design by adding a separate steam condenser. Although a poor marksman, he enjoyed hunting on the Scottish moors but was irritated by the high cost of lead shot. He determined to find a cheap method of producing it but hours of work in his laboratory failed to come up with a solution. Fatigued and depressed, he was constantly visited by a curious dream in which raindrops falling on the ground were transformed into shot. With the help of the local squire, Watt tried to rationalise this idea and climbing to the top of a church steeple, poured a kettle of molten lead down into the moat. When the two men waded into the water they found handfuls of perfectly spherical lead shot and the principle of Watt's dream has been providing huntsmen with cheap ammunition ever since. *1736*

Dark brooding author Edgar Allan Poe was born of theatrical parents, who both died before he was two years old. He was adopted by wealthy tobacco merchant John Allan, and took his name. One of the richest men in Virginia, Allan was deliberately stingy with his adopted son and relations were somewhat strained. When he was sent to the University of Virginia, Poe was already in debt and took to gambling to try and resolve it. Instead his debts multiplied to some $2,500 which his foster father refused to pay. Poe had to withdraw from the college and after a violent argument left home to start a new life as a novelist, calling himself Henri le Rennet. His first work was published in 1827 obscurely under the *nom de plume* 'a Bostonian'. In the same year he enlisted in the army, adding four years to his age to get accepted. Army discipline rankled however and he was court-martialled for 'gross neglect of duty' and 'disobedience of orders'. He was drummed out with just twelve cents in his pocket. Secretly married to his thirteen-year-old cousin Virginia Clem, he began writing in earnest, with his black cat perched on his shoulder. Unfortunately, he was also drinking heavily and taking large amounts of opium. His weird and wonderful stories were acclaimed in France but not in England or America, and most of his life was spent in poverty. One of his short stories, *Berenice*, is a jolly little tale of a lover robbing his dead girlfriend's body of her teeth. Poe always claimed he'd written it to prove a wager that necrophilia and dentistry could be combined in a serious story. *1809*

Great Confederate General Robert E. Lee was born. His father was famous as the leader of Washington's cavalry and was nicknamed 'Light Horse Harry', though he ended his days a broken man in the West Indies, after two years in a debtors' prison. Son Robert nevertheless graduated from West Point with distinction and was promoted to colonel in the Mexican War. He rarely drank and a bottle of whisky, presented to him by a lady friend to sustain him in the Mexican War, was returned unopened when the war had ended. The Civil War presented him with the greatest distinction and gravest dilemma in military history when he was offered the leadership of both sides. His fair-mindedness and humanity inspired complete devotion in his men. When told that a junior officer he'd been wishing to promote had criticised his behaviour, Lee still insisted on the promotion saying, 'The question is not what he thinks of me, but what I think of him.' *1807*

The last 'Beetle' was made. The tough little VW runabout, originally designed by Ferdinand Porsche and encouraged by Hitler, enjoyed the distinction of being the first European car to sell over a million units of a single basic model. When its production run finally came to an end, over nineteen million cars had been produced since May 1938. It was originally sold as the 'KdF' which stood for *Kraft durch Freude* meaning 'Strength through Joy' – the motto of the National Socialist Labour Front in Germany. *1978*

Today's the day...

Edward the young Duke of Clarence was buried. At a festive gathering at Sandringham to celebrate his twenty-eighth birthday and make final plans for his wedding a month later, he'd caught a cold which developed into pneumonia and killed him after only a week's illness. The tragedy shocked the country but none was more bereft than his fiancée, the Princess May who sent her bridal bouquet of orange blossom to be placed on his coffin. She was to become Queen Mary, the wife of the future George V, and was widowed exactly forty-four years to the day after they buried 'young Eddy'. *1892*

That most conventional of monarchs George V died at Sandringham House in Norfolk, and though he was much loved, well cared for and well attended, his last words have always been a matter for conjecture. Some sources give us 'How is the Empire?' while others prefer 'Gentlemen, I'm sorry to keep you waiting. I am unable to concentrate'. But by far the most original is the popular version where a helpful courtier suggested a seaside convalescence at the monarch's favourite resort, to which the old King replied with admirable spirit 'Bugger Bognor'. At least there's no disputing the words in his diary – three days earlier he'd written with sorry accuracy 'feel rotten'. *1936*

Industrious Greek shipowner Aristotle Socrates Onassis was born not in Greece, but in Smyrna, Turkey. At the age of sixteen he took off for Argentina with about £60 in his pocket. Once he got there, he set himself a gruelling twenty-one-hour-day on the way to making his first million. Working as a telephone operator at night he spent the day, building up a tobacco business and by the time he was twenty-three was a dollar millionaire. In the slump that followed World War I, he bought up six ships, which were going cheap because of the lack of cargoes, and held on to them until trade picked up. From these modest beginnings he built up the most modern tanker fleet in the world and also the most efficient whaling fleet in history. It was this that got him into a private war with Peru – but needless to say, he won. He got into trouble with the USA too, and it took 375 of America's top lawyers to get him out of it. For a man whose wealth was reputed to increase at a rate of £2,000 an hour round-the-clock, he had a pretty poor opinion of his business. His great hero was J. Paul Getty whom he regarded as a 'real' rich man because he controlled oil from source to consumer. For himself he simply said, 'All I do is carry it, like a man in the station who carries your luggage. I am a porter.' This 'porter' however had a 350 acre island, a private eighty-four seater jet, a 1,700 ton yacht and a huge collection of priceless paintings by Picasso and El Greco.   *1906*

The first game of basketball was played at the YMCA gymnasium, Springfield, Massachusetts. Canadian doctor James Naismith was looking for an indoor game to keep his students fit during the long winter evenings. He decided to tie a cardboard box 10ft above the ground at either end of the gym and get his teams to throw the ball in. Unfortunately he couldn't find any boxes so he used peach baskets instead and 'boxball' became 'basketball'.   *1892*

Today's the day...

Hapless King Louis XVI was guillotined. He arose in the morning and heard mass at a makeshift altar which, with sad ineptitude, had been arranged on a commode. He was then taken to the Place de la Révolution, and on the way a feeble rescue attempt by Baron de Batz and friends was easily foiled. Though the thirty-eight-year-old King tried hard to maintain his dignity, there was a struggle with the executioner Sanson, before he'd have his hands tied, and when he made his famous little speech claiming his innocence of the charges laid against him, Santerre, the Commandant of the *Garde Nationale*, called on the drums to beat and shouted from his horse, 'I brought you here not to harangue the populace, but to die.' At 10.22am precisely Madame Guillotine severed his head, which was held up to the crowd and sprayed onlookers with royal blood. In the grisly aftermath, the crowd, chanting '*Vive la République*', clambered onto the scaffold. Marie Antoinette had said of the Revolution that she wanted to wash her hands in the blood of the French people, and now they washed their hands in her husband's blood. The awful irony of the scene was compounded by the fact that Louis himself had suggested an improvement to the design of the guillotine's blade, that it might cut more surely.   *1793*

The genie of Bolshevism V. I. Lenin died of a massive brain haemorrhage in the famous house at Gorki outside Moscow, two years after first complaining of bad headaches and prophesying, 'I will end in paralysis.' With remarkable tenacity, he had rallied from three previous strokes, even learning to write with his left hand, after he'd lost the use of his right. He devoted much of the time during his prolonged illness to composing his *Testament*, and wrote 'that the comrades should find some way to remove Stalin and find someone else who differs in all respects'. Lenin, who was only fifty-three, was lost to life. The post-mortem showed that his brain had atrophied to a quarter of normal size, and one of the doctors involved said, 'The

46

January 21

amazing thing was not that the thinking power remained intact in such a sclerotic brain, but that with such a brain, he could have lived so long.'   *1924*

Man struck a sexist blow for the environment, when in New York City the Sullivan Ordinance made it illegal for women to smoke in public.   *1908*

Hot shot golfer Jack William Nicklaus was born in Columbus, Ohio. He took a round of sixty-nine on a course of over 7,000yds when he was thirteen, and won the Ohio Amateur Open when he was sixteen. He often sings to himself as he plays, and once hit eighteen holes in sixty-six humming *Moon River* stroke by stroke. By July 1978, he'd earned himself a cool $3,336,342, the highest earnings of any golfer ever. His well-padded figure has earned him various nicknames like 'Blobbo' and 'Ohio Fats', and when in 1962 at the age of twenty-two he beat the great Arnold Palmer to become the youngest man to win the American Open since 1923, William Furlong wrote, 'He has short reddish fair hair, a face as innocent as milk, and a build like a chocolate eclair.'   *1940*

47

Today's the day...

The Black Widow Queen Victoria finally died in weary old age, at Osborne House in the Isle of Wight after years of mourning her beloved Albert. She was eighty-one, the longest reigning and the longest lived of all British monarchs. On the throne for sixty-three years, she outreigned George III by four years, and outlived him by four days. Her death marked the end of an era, and ironically she died in the arms of her grandson and great admirer, the not altogether sane Kaiser Wilhelm of Germany, who brought the era crashing to a war-torn close. The Prince of Wales was there too, though whether her last word 'Bertie' was addressed to him or her long-dead husband, we shall never know. She left minute instructions for her funeral and was, of course, interred next to Prince Albert, at Windsor. Her reign was among the most revolutionary of all times – though it was not so much due to her, as to the pioneering age in which she lived. She was the first British monarch to use a telephone; to travel on a train; to make a gramophone record; to be photographed; to use a lift; to appear in a film; to use a one-piece flushing pedestal toilet, and to live regularly in Buckingham Palace. James Pope-Hennessy called her 'an amiable fieldmouse', V. S. Pritchett described her as 'a mixture of national landlady and actress', while Henry James said, 'She's more of a man than I expected.' The nation grieved for its lost institution, however, and to one of her numerous sons-in-laws her death was like 'a great three decker ship sinking . . . she kept rallying and going down.' *1901*

Bright spark André Marie Ampère was born. He was, of course, the great French physicist after whom the 'amp' was named as a unit of electrical current, and the 'ammeter' for measuring it. Lucky in his choice of parents, the riches of his merchant father gave him plenty of facilities for learning. He mostly educated himself from a vast personal library; tackled Euclid without assistance and could recite large chunks of the *Great Encyclopaedia* wholesale. Though his career couldn't have been more successful, his personal life was a shocking disaster.

January 22

His father was guillotined in the Revolution; his first wife died after only four years of marriage; his second wife's father swindled him out of his inheritance; his son wassailed his life away on women and drink, and his daughter married a well-known army officer, drunkard and lunatic.

1775

Lame versifying womaniser Lord Byron was born, supposedly with a club foot. He was George Gordon, the sixth Lord; was educated at Harrow and Cambridge and took his seat in the House of Lords when he was twenty-one. In his short life, he managed to combine cricket, soldiering, swimming, dancing, boxing and fencing with his two major pursuits – poetry and the ladies. At twenty-three, he published his great epic *Childe Harold's Pilgrimage* and 'woke one morning to find himself famous'. He was the epitome of the romantic hero – classically handsome, with a look of pained nobility and very little sense of responsibility. He often kept his chestnut hair in rollers though, and his pale and interesting look may have had something to do with his lifelong devotion to purgatives. He practised hard to hide his limp and even some of his closest associates were not aware of his disability until after his death. When Trelawny, his great biographer, examined his body he first wrote that milord poet had 'the form and features of an Apollo, and the legs and feet of a Satyr.' Afterwards he replaced this fanciful description with a more scientific one, suggesting that Byron's trouble was merely a contraction of the Achilles tendon. Satyr he certainly was, however, for as well as an unhappy marriage, an affair with his sister, and another with the famous Lady Caroline Lamb, he was said to fall on chambermaids 'like a thunderbolt'. He had very little time for conventional morality or authority. It was typical of him that when he was forbidden by the University to keep dogs in his room, he kept a bear instead. He once said, 'Poetry is the lava of the imagination, whose eruption prevents an earthquake!'

1788

Today's the day...

Sickly genius William Pitt the Younger died in Putney. Though dogged by ill health, he'd become Britain's youngest Prime Minister before he was twenty-five. Now at forty-six, worn out by twenty years of government and a revolutionary and turbulent Europe, he finally succumbed. A grant of £40,000 was immediately voted by a grateful Parliament to cover his immense debts. He'd been a workaholic; he'd never been interested in money; had once refused a ministerial job worth £5,000 a year, and allowed servants and tradesmen to work their way through his considerable official income. Just a month before, Napoleon had won the Battle of Austerlitz and according to one account, the dying statesman's last words were a noble, 'Alas, my country.' According to another version, however, he had other things on his mind, and passed away saying, 'I could do with one of Bellamy's meat pies.'   *1806*

Naughty Pope Boniface VIII was confirmed in his holy calling in a bizarre ceremony which took place outside the Lateran Palace. He was ensconced in an ancient throne of red marble, which had originally come from the city's public baths. It had a seat with a hole in it, and looked suspiciously like a commode. Some said that's exactly what it was, and that the Pope's sitting in it was a gesture of self-abasement. Others believed it had a more scientific purpose, and was in fact used to facilitate a physical examination of the Pontiff, so there would never be a second pope-in-drag like the infamous 'Pope Joan'. They needn't have worried. Boniface was a healthy man, with a healthy sex life. He saw sexuality as no sin and added that going to bed with 'women and boys' was no more than rubbing one hand against the other.   *1294*

Bogie was born. His full name was Humphrey de Forest Bogart, and before he became a star he appeared in numerous gangster movies, playing in his own words 'the guy behind the guy behind the gun'. In *Casablanca* he never did say, 'Play it again Sam', but he did coin another famous expression in the last line of the film when he said, 'Louis, I think this is the beginning of a beautiful friendship.' Though Lauren Bacall claimed he wasn't a cynic, he was nevertheless renowned for his cynicism, and once gave Robert Mitchum a typical piece of Bogie advice. 'Whatever it is,' he said, 'be against it.'   *1899*

The first heart transplant was performed on a human patient at the University Hospital in Mississippi. The surgeon was James Hardy, who for eight years had performed similar operations on dogs and human corpses, and just seven months before had done the first human lung transplant. The recipient was a man in his late sixties, fatally ill with cardiovascular disease and arteriosclerosis, and the proposed donor a young man, still alive but only just, who had suffered irreparable brain damage. The older man was taken to the operating theatre; his heart was bypassed and failed completely. There was no going back now, but the younger man still clung to the tenuous threads of his life, and something had to be done quickly. As a failsafe, the patient had agreed to an alternative donor and so the operation went ahead. The replacement heart worked, but it was too small to cope with its new job and the patient died within hours. The heart's previous owner had weighed only 96lbs – a reasonable amount, in fact, since he was not a man, but a chimpanzee.   *1964*

Sam Taylor Coleridge's *Remorse* was first performed. Shortly afterwards the great poet was sitting in a hotel when he heard a man reading a newspaper mention his name in connection with an inquest. Curious, Sam asked to see the paper, and the man passed it to him, saying how odd it was that after the success of his play, this mad poet Coleridge should have hanged himself. As it turned out, Sam was in the habit of losing a shirt or two when he travelled and the anonymous dead man had appropriated one marked with a tab 'S. T. Coleridge'.   *1813*

Today's the day...

Nutty Emperor Caligula was finally assassinated as he left the Palatine games for a spot of lunch. Julia, the daughter of his incestuous relationship with his sister Drusilla, was also killed when her head was dashed against a wall. Caligula was twenty-nine; he had reigned for three years, ten months and eight days and committed more outrages than most of the Caesars committed in a lifetime. As he left the amphitheatre, the guard asked him for the password. Caligula replied, 'Jupiter, the bringer of death', and his chief assassin Chaerea yelled, 'So be it!' and split the Emperor's jaw with his sword. Caligula writhed on the ground, screaming, 'I'm still alive, I'm still alive.' He wasn't for long.   *AD 41*

Gold was discovered in 'them thar hills' near the south fork of California's America River, where it runs down from the Sierra Nevada mountains. James W. Marshall had been building a mill for cattle baron rancher John Sutter. Wanting to test the mill-race, he'd left the sluice open all night, and in the morning was amazed to find the glittering mineral lying there in considerable abundance. A workman wrote, 'This day some kind of mettle was found in the tail-race that looks like gauld – first discovered by James Martial.' It proved impossible to keep it a secret and before long the Forty-Niners were pouring in by the thousand and the Gold Rush had begun. They took over Sutter's land, wrecked his ranch, and built the shanty towns of Sacramento and San Francisco on property that was rightfully his. When the courts finally acknowledged Sutter's rights in the matter in 1855, the population went mad. They set light to the courts, dynamited Sutter's house, burnt his furniture, chopped down his fences and shot his cattle. One of his sons was murdered, one drowned trying to escape and the third committed suicide. Sutter had found a fortune, but not surprisingly in the circumstances, he lost his mind.   *1848*

Lovable, ugly Ernest Borgnine was born. His first big film *Marty* was meant to be a failure, so that its producers could write it off as a tax loss. The hero was an ugly-looking butcher and an all-time loser, so Borgnine seemed a natural for the part. He played it so movingly however, that he won an Oscar and the film was a huge hit.   *1918*

Two Churchills died. The first, Lord Randolph, of a crippling disease, which though it's never been proved showed many of the symptoms of syphilis, and killed him 'by inches'. The second, his son Winston, the great wartime leader, who finally suffered a stroke after a long decline into extreme old age. Both were buried in the country churchyard at Bladon, near Blenheim. Randolph at least had enjoyed a world tour before he went, but poor Winston was 'the chief mourner, at his own protracted funeral'.   *1895/1965*

Super soprano Farinelli was born. King Philip V of Spain was so enchanted with the silvery voiced singer that he employed Farinelli to sing the same four songs every night for ten years. Farinelli's christian name was Carlo, which wasn't all that surprising, since he was a man.   *1705*

Today's the day...

Wily writer Somerset Maugham was born in Paris. Fastidious and capricious, he was described by Gerhardie as looking 'exceedingly wicked'. Noël Coward once said of him, 'He hated people more easily than he loved them', while photographer Karsh saw him as 'the kind of man who has seen everything and doesn't think much of any of it'. Perhaps that's why he adopted a curious Moorish sign as his personal device – it's supposed to be a safeguard against the evil eye. *1874*

Jolly joker Empress Anne of Russia was born. She introduced gambling into Russia, was not above boxing the ears of her courtiers and had a thing about hens. Her jesters were made to sit in a row and cackle, then have fights and scratch each other until they drew blood, while one unfortunate prince was sentenced to sit on a nest of eggs and cackle – on pain of death. Perhaps her cruellest prank was on another prince, Michael Golitsyn. He displeased her by marrying an Italian Catholic during his travels and when his new wife died shortly after their return to Russia, the Empress decreed he should marry again to her choice of partner. She selected a particulary ugly Kalmuck girl and to complete the humiliation arranged an exotic marriage ceremony.

The bridal pair were mounted on an elephant followed by a train of carriages pulled by pigs, goats, dogs, reindeer and horses. They were then taken to a palace which the Empress, in her generous way, had specially built. In the worst winter for thirty years, the Classical style building was constructed entirely of blocks of ice. Inside, the couple were led to an elaborately carved four-poster bed with mattress, quilt, pillows and even nightcaps – all in ice. They were stripped naked and left to enjoy their wedding night. Amazingly they survived this chilly start to married life. Come the spring the ice melted, the Empress died and they lived happily ever after. *1693*

Millionaire mobster Al Capone died of neurosyphilis. Although he was the first syphilitic to be treated with antibiotics, they didn't help much and he finally collapsed with a massive brain haemorrhage. He had frittered away his huge fortune on gambling and extravagance, and when the King of Gangland died, he was virtually penniless. *1947*

Anne Boleyn secretly married Henry VIII at dawn. Egged on by her ambitious father, she'd captivated the King and helped convince him that only by marrying her and divorcing Catherine of Aragon, would he secure her lasting affection and an heir for his dynasty. For this he was prepared to open a deep rift in his kingdom and an historic and traumatic break with the Church. Vivacious, dark-haired Anne had arrived at court at the age of fifteen when her sister was Henry's mistress. Her high spirits in the gloomy household had entranced the King and he embarked on a passionate courtship, pleading with her to become his mistress in long and often lewd love letters. On the day of her wedding Anne was already pregnant and gave birth to a child in September. To the couple's dismay it was a girl – though as it turned out, their disappointment was unfounded. She was to be one of the most powerful rulers of England – the future Queen Elizabeth I. *1533*

Today's the day...

The first great woman photographer Julia Margaret Cameron
died. She was a typically British eccentric; didn't take up photography
until she was fifty; lived in chaos, and was the friend and confidante of
many famous artists and literary figures including Alfred Lord
Tennyson. In 1875 she made the sudden decision to go back to the
family's coffee plantations in Ceylon. She took with her two coffins,
filled for the journey with china and glass, just in case anything should
happen to her or her husband. Broke by the time she got to
Southampton, she gave the porters copies of her photographs instead
of tips. Once in Colombo she took up a collection to buy the ship's
captain a harmonium in thanks for an uneventful voyage. She never
did return, the coffins sadly both had to be used within a year of each
other, and the lovely lady's last word was 'beautiful'.   *1879*

'The diamond as big as the Ritz' was found by Captain M. E.
Wells as he strolled around the Premier Mine in South Africa. He saw
a flash of light, bent down and picked up the largest uncut diamond
ever discovered anywhere in the world. It weighed 1lb 4oz and was
called the 'Cullinan'. It was cleft by Jacob Asscher and gave birth to
the world's largest cut diamond the 530.2 carat 'Star of Africa', which
now adorns the British Royal Sceptre. Of the other six major stones
cut from it, three are set in royal crowns, two in royal necklaces and
one in a royal brooch. When it was originally sent from Africa, a
dummy came under escort, while the real thing – all 3000 carats of it –
was sent in the post.   *1905*

'Chinese' Gordon was slain in Khartoum. After a lifetime of
fighting, notably in the Crimea and against the Taiping rebels in China,
he'd been sent to the Sudan as Governor General, when the Mahdi –
the Chosen One – was leading his Moslem hordes in revolt. Besieged in
Khartoum for almost exactly a year, he was refused help by Gladstone
and the town was taken. Slaughtering everyone in their path, the

'whirling dervishes' cut a bloody swathe to the Palace where George Charles Gordon, London-born Scottish aristocrat, stood on the steps waiting for them, calm and unarmed. 'Where is your master, the Mahdi?' he asked – but the only reply he got was, 'Oh cursed one, your time has come!', as a man flung a huge spear at him, which struck him in the chest and tore through his back. The following day the belatedly-agreed-to British expeditionary force arrived, while the Mahdi, safely ensconced in Omdurman, studied the gory severed head of his most famous victim.   *1885*

Anti-superstar Paul Newman was born. Troubled by colour blindness in his baby blue eyes, he became a radio operator in wartime naval torpedo planes. Come the peace, he won an athletics scholarship, injured his knee and turned to acting. One of the 'method' generation, he's said to have lost lots of early parts because of his not very strong resemblance to Brando. Also famous as a racing driver, he seems happy to risk his life, while he takes great trouble to preserve his complexion by wearing a snorkel and dipping his head in cold water.   *1925*

Today's the day...

Mighty musical prodigy Wolfgang Amadeus Mozart was born, the son of a musician. At the age of four, he's supposed to have heard his first symphony and transcribed the complete score from memory. At five, he was composing the first of a lifetime total of over 600 works and the following year he was performing in the courts of Europe. He was a very frail and sensitive child, shaking and even fainting at the sound of a harsh discord. He'd once played at the Austrian court for Marie Antoinette, and his work-load had so wearied him that he slipped and fell to the ground. Princess Marie rushed over and picked him up, and as soon as he was on his feet again, he declared she was the most beautiful woman he'd ever seen and proposed to her on the spot. *1756*

The world's first public demonstration of TV was given by the Scottish inventor John Logie Baird in his attic workshop in Soho, London. Fifty eminent engineers and scientists were assembled for the occasion, but they nearly walked out when they saw the apparatus. The base of the motor was a tea chest, scanning discs were cut from cardboard and the whole projection lamp was housed in a biscuit tin.

January 27

Worse still was the sight of the complete machinery all being held together with darning needles, sealing-wax and string. Baird promised to transmit the face of an office boy seated in the workshop below, onto the screen in his attic. Despite the crude machinery he succeeded and television was born.   *1926*

Kaiser Bill was born, son of the German Emperor and grandson of Queen Victoria. He was a weak child and very nearly died at birth. When he was three days old, it was discovered that his left elbow was out of joint, causing the arm to be paralysed. Fearing that the shock of resetting it would kill the infant prince, his doctors decided not to operate. The arm remained stunted and withered for the rest of his life and he was exceedingly touchy about it – especially after he ascended the throne as Wilhelm II. He adopted cunning poses to hide the truth from his subjects, and few outside his immediate circle ever knew of his disability. He worked fanatically hard to make his right hand extra strong, and because of his massively powerful handshake, it became a crushing experience to meet him.   *1859*

The inventor of *Wonderland* Lewis Carroll was born Charles Lutwidge Dodgson. He went to Oxford, but because he was painfully shy, extremely sensitive and suffered from a stammer, he lived virtually like a recluse. The only company he really enjoyed was that of small children, especially the daughters of one of his few friends, Dean Liddell. Alice Liddell in fact, was the inspiration for the *Wonderland* and *Looking-Glass*, and she was very dear to him. Even his odd hobby of photographing little girls in the nude had a peculiar innocence about it, and even as a child, he'd befriended and cared for all the small creatures he could. He especially liked worms because no one else did, and he hated to think of them being eaten by ferocious snails and toads. He set to work and designed and built a little armoury of minute weapons, so his little friends could defend themselves.   *1832*

Today's the day...

The world's first chloroform fatality, fifteen-year-old Hannah Greener of Newcastle, succumbed under the knife. Two years earlier an historic operation in Boston had begun to make chloroform acceptable as an anaesthetic, but the public and many doctors were still sceptical and it wasn't realised for many years that it could have the rather unhealthy side-effect of stopping the heart. Sadly, this is exactly what happened to the pretty Miss Greener, who had only gone to the doctor to have an ingrown toenail removed.　　　*1848*

Speed freak Walter Arnold, a miller of East Peckham in Kent, was fined one shilling plus costs and became the first motorist ever convicted of speeding. Not using his loaf, he had whizzed past the policeman's house at a hair-raising 8mph – in a 2mph limit! Gallantly the officer interrupted his dinner and pursued him. The two hurtled breathlessly through five miles of twisting turning lanes and then, strangely, the world's first car chase ended with the felon being arrested by a bobby on a bicycle!　　　*1896*

Horace Walpole coined a word in a letter to a friend. He had just read a foreign fantasy entitled *The Travels and Adventures of Three Princess of Serendip* – the story of three heroes who repeatedly made marvellous discoveries by pure chance. Walpole was charmed by the idea and coined a word to describe that same faculty for making desirable discoveries by accident. He called it 'serendipity'.　　　*1754*

England's royal Bluebeard Henry VIII died in a room reeking of the fetid stench from his suppurating leg ulcers. At the end he couldn't speak, and when Archbishop Cranmer asked for a sign that he was prepared to commit himself to Christ's care Henry 'did wring his hand as hard as he could'. His huge 6ft 10in lead coffin was transported on the three-day journey from London to Windsor, making its first overnight stop at Syon in the same convent that had been Catherine

Howard's prison prior to her execution. There, a bizarre prophecy was
fulfilled. It had been said, 'The dogs will lick his bones as they did
Ahab's.' During the night his coffin burst open and when sentries
arrived with plumbers to repair it, they found dogs lapping up his
blood.   *1547*

The thriftiest King of England and the only one crowned on a field
of battle, Henry VII was born. Efficient and cold blooded, he managed
to drag England back from the verge of bankruptcy after the
disastrously expensive civil wars, which had almost ruined the country.
He was certainly ideally suited for the task. By nature mean and
calculating, he not only personally checked every national receipt
handled by the treasury, he also made his queen account for every
penny she spent. Though cynics suggested he preferred peace to
conflict only because it was cheaper, his reign was one of the most
peaceful and prosperous England had ever seen. Occasionally, though,
even Henry splashed out – like the time he paid the astonishing sum of
£38 1s 4d to John van Delf – for garnishing a salad!   *1457*

The world's first gas-lit street blazed into history. It was all the
bright idea of a German inventor named Winsor whose lack of English,
basic knowledge of chemistry and meagre mechanical ability made the
experiment both hazardous and open to ridicule. When he announced
he intended to light London's famous boulevard Pall Mall with coal
gas, Sir Walter Scott said he was a madman who proposed to illuminate
London with smoke, while Sir Humphrey Davy wondered whether he
was going to use the dome of St Paul's as a gasometer. On a bitterly
cold evening a huge crowd gathered to witness the downfall of the
shady foreigner. To their utter amazement Pall Mall suddenly burst
into light. Yet although the experiment was a dazzling success, it was
many months before the public accepted they would not be burnt if
they touched the lamp-posts!   *1807*

Today's the day...

'Farmer' George III King of England died, aged eighty-one years and eight months. He was the longest-lived and longest-reigning King of England and arguably the last British monarch to be a serious force in politics. A homely man, he was mad keen on agriculture, and in the last ten years of his life, when the poor man was afflicted by mental illness, this was almost literally true. When he wasn't wandering about the corridors of Windsor mumbling to himself, he was creating bizarre horticultural plans. At one point, he decided that beef grew like vegetables and to prove his point, planted 4lbs of it in the garden. On another occasion he was found shaking hands with an oak tree and talking very courteously to it because he thought it was the King of Prussia.

1820

Tragic lovers Crown Prince Rudolf and Maria Vetsera sealed their suicide pact in the hunting lodge at Mayerling. Both bodies had gun-shot wounds and it looked as if Rudolf had killed Maria before taking his own life. The whole affair was so efficiently hushed up, however, that nothing was ever proved. Thirty-one-year-old Rudolf, heir to the oldest established monarchy in Europe and direct descendant of the Holy Roman Emperors, suffered from venereal disease and morphine addiction. Emotionally unstable to start with, he'd been married off to a German princess who bored him silly, and launched himself into a life of dissipation. He became morbidly fascinated by death confessing to a friend, 'I'm trying to find an opportunity to see a dying man.' His lover Maria Vetsera on the other hand was a sprightly seventeen-year-old Baroness, whose only interests were clothes and horse racing. She'd adored the Prince from afar and finally managed to get her friend, Countess Larisch, to introduce her. Their affair only began on 13 January – just sixteen days before the tragedy. Rudolf's body was rushed back to Vienna, with the bullet holes carefully concealed, and he was given an elaborate funeral. Maria had expressed a wish in her suicide note to be buried alongside him but she was unceremoniously bundled off instead. Her body was hurriedly washed and dressed, and to avoid suspicion a carriage not a hearse was used to convey it to a monastery nearby. Her brothers carried her lurching body upright to the carriage and then propped her up on the seat. The foolish young romantic was then buried with indecent haste in a makeshift coffin, beside the monastery wall.   *1889*

The world's funniest misanthrope W. C. Fields was born. Unloved in childhood, he had an unhappy marriage with a dancer; a hugely successful film career and a bizarre friendship with King Edward VII. He had bank accounts all over the place, and during World War II kept $50,000 in Hitler's Germany 'in case the little bastard wins'. Children were not his favourite people and when asked if he liked them, he replied, 'Yes – if they're properly cooked.' One of his most famous quips 'anyone who hates small dogs and children can't be all bad' was in fact not his at all. It was coined by Leo Rosten when introducing the star at a dinner. Fields took a much more liberal view. He said, 'I am free of all prejudice, I hate everyone equally!'   *1879*

Today's the day...

The first assassination attempt on a US President was perpetrated on 'Old Hickory', the sixty-eight-year-old ex-soldier Andrew Jackson, who was in his second term of office and attending a funeral at the time. A man leapt out from behind a pillar and fired two pistols – both of which failed to go off. The usually violent and paranoic Jackson was in his element; he attacked the defenceless assassin screaming, 'Let me get at him.' The man was one Richard Lawrence, who was later confined to a lunatic asylum and actually outlived his intended victim by sixteen years. He sincerely believed his attempt was a righteous one, since he was convinced he was King Richard III of England and that the entire USA was rightfully his. *1835*

Reforming patrician President Franklin Delano Roosevelt was born. Once, when he was incarcerated with scarlet fever, his mother – to avoid going into quarantine herself – visited him by ladder outside his bedroom window. Although his political career was interrupted when he was stricken with polio, he nevertheless won the Democratic nomination for the 1932 election. He had six children; two official mistresses; and was the first President to appear on television. He was said to have 'started more creations than Genesis', and inevitably earned a lot of criticism. 'I wouldn't employ him,' said one observer, 'as a geek in a carnival!' *1882*

Pious English tyrant Charles I was beheaded outside the Banqueting House in London's Whitehall. He emerged through a window onto the scaffold wearing two shirts, lest the cold should make him appear to shake with fright. A ring of heavily armed soldiers between him and the uncannily silent crowd prevented his prepared speech from being adequately heard. A devout Christian, he said, 'I go from a corruptible to an incorruptible crown,' He then tucked his hair into a little silk cap, laid his neck on the block, mouthed a short prayer, and held out his hand as a signal for the executioner to strike. A 'dismal universal groan'

January 30

went up among the crowd and it was over. After some dispute, the body was interred in St George's Chapel, Windsor, alongside those of Henry VIII and his favourite wife Jane Seymour. In 1813, the vault in which they lay was disturbed by some workmen, and the Prince Regent gave his permission for it to be investigated. The long dead monarch's outer coffin of lead bore the plain inscription 'King Charles' and the wrong date – 1648. The tiny corpse – estimates of the King's height put him at between 4ft 11in and 5ft 2in – was well preserved, all but its nose, and the axe was found to have cleft the fourth cervical vertebra clean in two. The Royal Surgeon Sir Henry Halford, who carried out the examination, stole the bone and though it was later returned he kept it for years, and used to love to shock his friends by using it as a salt cellar. *1649*

The Mahatma Gandhi was assassinated in his own garden, four days after the celebration of Indian Independence Day. As he walked across the lawn, supported by his 'crutches' – his two grand-nieces – Narayan Godse, a fanatical Hindu, approached him, gave the traditional salute of the faithful to which Gandhi responded, and then shot the frail old man three times, hitting him in the chest, stomach and groin. Gandhi, vegetarian, creator of 'passive resistance' and architect of Independence was seventy-eight; he'd survived numerous attacks on his life, and that very morning had said that he must reply to all his important letters today 'for tomorrow may never be'. *1948*

Talkative beau Sir Everard Digby was executed. He was said to be among the most gallant, good looking and eligible knights in London, but was unwise enough to get involved in the Gunpowder Plot. He was sentenced to be hanged, drawn and quartered, a gruesome procedure involving ritual disembowelment. A contemporary report had it that when his heart was torn from his body and the executioner cried, 'Here is the heart of a traitor!' he replied, 'Thou liest.' *1606*

Today's the day...

Whistler's mother died in Hastings, England. The frail little woman had left America to join her son in London when it became clear the South was fighting a losing battle in the Civil War. Whistler loved her good old-fashioned American cooking but wasn't too happy about her good old-fashioned ideas on his free and easy life. When mother moved in, his mistress had to move out and there was such a violent row on one occasion, that it sent him scurrying off to Chile to fight in a minor war. They patched things up on his return however and that's when Whistler painted his famous portrait of her. An intensely religious woman, she'd travelled the world with her civil engineer husband. When they were living in St Petersburg she was so concerned about the creeds of the Orthodox Church, she imported religious tracts and distributed them to soldiers in the street. She was pleased to note they grabbed them eagerly. Little did she know that the illiterate soldiers were so keen because her tracts made excellent cigarette papers. *1881*

Husky-voiced actress Tallulah Bankhead was born. Remembered more for her exotic lifestyle and witty epithets than her acting, her sharp tongue made her quite a few enemies. Mrs Patrick Campbell summed it up when she said, 'Tallulah is always skating on thin ice.

January 31

Everyone wants to be around when it breaks.' Miss Bankhead described herself as being 'as pure as the driven slush', but said cheerfully, 'If I had to live my life again I'd make all the same mistakes – but sooner.'

1903

Poverty-stricken Austrian composer Franz Schubert was born. Despite his prodigious output, he had to rely on the charity of his friends and admirers and often sold his songs for only a shilling. From the age of thirteen until his untimely death at thirty-one, he wrote thirteen operas and over 600 songs, working at breakneck speed from dawn to dusk and rarely correcting anything. Shy and retiring, he lived alone, but one of his greatest enjoyments was to go to the tavern with his friends, and many of his works received their first airing in public in a jovial sing-song.

1797

Stalingrad won in the fight against Hitler. The crack German 6th Army had trapped the Russians in the city in November, but they'd held out and steadily gained ground in some of the fiercest hand-to-hand fighting of World War II. The German leader Field Marshal Paulus wanted to retreat but Hitler ordered him to stay and Goering promised 500 tons of airborne supplies a day to sustain his men in the cruel Russian winter. Actual supplies fell well below Goering's promises, sometimes as little as twenty or thirty tons and Russian guerrillas blew them up as soon as they arrived. While the Germans were reduced to eating dogs, cats and horses, the Russians brought up relief troops and completely surrounded them. Hitler ordered no surrender but Paulus, fearful for his starving men, capitulated and with twenty-five other generals surrendered the remains of his army. In the worst single defeat in German military history, thirty-two divisions and three brigades of the *Wehrmacht* had been destroyed completely – the remaining sixteen had been decimated by up to seventy-five per cent.

1943

Today's the day...

The King of Hollywood Clark Gable was born in Cadiz, Ohio. His father, a tough oil man, was disturbed by his teenage son's aspirations to be an actor and took him to work with him in the Oklahoma oil fields. At twenty-one he went back to acting and wound up in Hollywood. After playing as an extra in several films he was given a hilarious screen test. Dressed in a leopard skin loin cloth with a rose behind his ear, he was blacked up and sent out on the set to a chorus of jeers and cat-calls. It wasn't a success, largely because Gable's ears were too big and often caused comment. Howard Hughes said that 'his ears made him look like a taxi-cab with both doors open'. This slight drawback didn't seem to matter as he rose to fame opposite a selection of the world's leading ladies including Garbo, Joan Crawford, Jean Harlow and Norma Shearer. His rugged manliness had its effects outside Hollywood too. When he appeared outrageously bare beneath his shirt in *It Happened One Night*, sales of vests dropped dramatically and several underwear manufacturers went out of business.   *1907*

The wind-swept Bell Rock lighthouse was first lit. The 115ft edifice twenty-four miles east of Dundee had taken over four years to build and every single stone in its construction had been dragged from Arbroath by one horse. The valiant animal 'property of James Craw' was made a pensioner of the Lighthouse Commissioners, and ended his days grazing on the nearby island of Inchkeith.   *1811*

Penny Bjorkland's dream came true. The attractive eighteen-year-old blonde, a pleasant girl and a conscientious worker, harboured a blood-lust worthy of a thirties gangster. She dreamt obsessively about murdering someone and woke this morning deciding, 'This is the day I will kill someone. If I meet anyone that will be it.' After a hearty breakfast with her mother, she wandered off into the hills around San Francisco clutching the ·38 calibre pistol she used for target practice.

February 1

She came upon the unfortunate August Norry a landscape gardener who happened to be dumping some refuse by the side of the road. He offered her a lift and she shot him six times. Not content with that she reloaded and shot him again – and again. In all, eighteen bullets were found in the body. She was finally arrested a month later, confessed to the crime and said she did it, 'just to see if I could and not worry about it afterwards'. The judge sentenced her to life imprisonment for 'wanton murder' and Penny's only comment years later was, 'I consider myself a normal, average girl.'   *1959*

The first *Oxford English Dictionary* was published. It was a triumph for one man, James A. H. Murray who'd taken over the project five years earlier. Badly paid, overworked and badgered by the Oxford University Press, he'd finally achieved the mammoth task of sorting over two-and-a-half million handwritten slips into a definitive dictionary. The slips had been collected over the previous twenty years and left lying about in sacks, boxes and even a baby's pram. A dead rat was discovered in one bundle and a family of mice living happily in another. Murray had set to work to house the collection and built a corrugated-iron shed in his back garden. Which became known as the 'Scriptorium'. He'd had to build it 3ft below ground so he didn't spoil his neighbour's view and much of his time was spent working with his feet in a cardboard box.   *1884*

Tsar Alexei married Nadia Narishkina. He'd fallen madly in love with her when they met at boyar Matveev's house, and asked her to marry him after only a few days. But there were strict conventions for the choice of the Tsar's wife. A beauty competition had to be held and candidates rigorously checked by physicians and midwives. Matveev begged the Tsar not to flout this convention. The Tsar agreed and a line-up of sixty young girls was sent to the Kremlin – only this time the winner was fixed.   *1671*

Today's the day...

'Pretty witty Nell' Gwynn was born, the daughter of a fishwife. She sold her famous oranges outside the Theatre Royal until she was thirteen and then went into a brothel where, among other things, she learnt 'spelling, arithmetic and singing'. Her connections with actors eventually got her on to the stage, where she was a charismatic performer and often recited 'indelicate verses'. In 1668 the King took a keen interest in her; she later bore him a son and thereafter the poet and playwright Dryden 'gave her all his best parts'. Unlike a number of the tolerant King's ladies she was always faithful to him, and had a running feud with his concurrent mistress – the pretentious, unpopular and avowedly Catholic Duchess of Portsmouth, whose charms he often forsook for those of 'dear sweet Nellie'. When once she was travelling to Oxford, Nell's coach was attacked by a mob, who'd mistaken her for the popish Duchess. With her usual quick wit, she popped her head out of the window and brought a cheer from her attackers with a 'Pray good people be civil, I am the protestant whore!' *1650*

The very first public loo with flushing toilets was opened in London's Fleet Street by, of all people, the Society of Arts. Needless to say, it was a 'Gents' and the ladies had to wait another nine days to get a loo

70

February 2

of their very own in Bedford Street. Delicately dubbed 'Public Waiting Rooms' they were tastefully fitted out; the WC's themselves were boxed-in in polished wood and a staff of three made sure everything ran smoothly. The august Society published advertisements announcing the conveniences in *The Times* and handed out 50,000 explanatory leaflets. Unfortunately, the idea was abandoned, since by the end of the month only fifty-eight men and twenty-four women had used the loos. They failed to catch on probably because the Society of Arts charged tuppence for spending a penny.   *1852*

A literary high watermark was reached in Carson City, USA, when a journalist, who became one of America's best loved authors, appended his new *nom de plume* for the very first time to a report to the *Virginia City Enterprise*. He'd stolen the pseudonym from an old friend called Isiah Sellers who'd just died. It was a particularly suitable name for its new owner, however, since he'd been a Mississippi river pilot and the name was the sounding call the boatmen made for water two fathoms deep. The author was Sam Clemens; the name was Mark Twain.   *1863*

Master fiddler Fritz Kreisler was born. Early in his career he'd surprised the musical world by introducing a number of his own arrangements of previously unheard of works by significant, but mostly little-known composers like Louis Couperin, Padre Martini and Pugnani; there was even one by the great Vivaldi. They were everywhere rapturously received by musicians and critics alike, though in the early days at least, there was some reservation about Kreisler's playing. After one concert, a leading German reviewer wrote, 'He played beautifully, but naturally, his temperament lacks the strength and maturity to reach the heights of the Pugnani music.' The man would have undoubtedly been very red-faced, when finally, on his sixtieth birthday, Kreisler admitted he'd conceived and written all the pieces himself.   *1875*

Today's the day...

'The Petticoat of the Plains' Belle Star was ambushed and left for dead on the way back to her home at Younger's Bend. This angular hatchet-faced woman had first taken up with outlaws when she met the famous Cole Younger, believed to be the father of her daughter Pearl. After robbing an old prospector of $30,000, with another lover, Jim Reed, Belle took to queening it over the locals; wearing velvet gowns, plumed hats and a belt full of six-shooters, and riding her racehorse Venus at breakneck speeds through the streets. There followed a string of notorious outlaw lovers but it wasn't until Sam Starr, a Cherokee, came on the scene that she really got into her stride. Together they went on an orgy of cattle and horse stealing such as had never been seen in the history of Oklahoma. Just two days before her forty-first birthday, Belle was shot down and died in her daughter's arms. Over her grave topped by a statue of Venus, Pearl had a flowery epitaph inscribed, but perhaps Belle's own words are more fitting. With classic understatement she said, 'I regard myself as a woman who's seen much of life.'   *1889*

Tow-headed teetotal editor and statesman Horace Greeley was born. A harsh no-nonsense idealist, he believed that life was hard and earnest and there should be no 'trifling by the wayside'. Drink and infidelity were therefore the greatest of crimes because they wasted time, and there was no virtue more desirable than thrift. Convinced that the West offered unlimited opportunities, he popularised John B. Soule's phrase of 'Go West young man' by using it in an editorial adding 'and grow up with the country.' He'd sit and scribble away at his desk at the *New York Tribune*, frequently forgetting to eat. Despite all his industry his writing became a national joke – it was totally illegible. Compositors took bets on what certain words were on his corrected proof sheets; one bright young reporter used Greeley's handwritten letter of dismissal as a recommendation for several jobs, and another used his as a free pass on the railways.   *1811*

February 3

'Portrayer of Middle America' Norman Rockwell was born. Best
remembered for his *Saturday Evening Post* covers, he painted 317
of them and described himself as a 'hack illustrator'. His pictures are
regarded with affection by thousands, since they so accurately capture
the spirit of everyday life – especially the awkwardness of growing up.
Children and animals were his favourite subjects and he was aware of
his idealism saying that he always tried to paint life 'as I'd like it to be
without all the agonising crises and tangles'.   *1894*

John of Gaunt, the 'time-honoured' Duke of Lancaster, died. Thrice
married he left all his beds, including one of embroidered black velvet,
to his latest wife and long-time mistress Catherine Swynford. He also
left 100 marks to Newgate and Ludgate prisons, and eight children.
Henry, his son by his first wife, inherited Gaunt's title and later
usurped the crown of England from Richard II to become Henry IV.
Like many of his contemporaries, Gaunt had a terror of being buried
alive so he left strict instructions that he wasn't to be buried or
embalmed for at least forty days.   *1399*

Today's the day...

All American flyer Charles Lindbergh was born in Little Falls, Minnesota, His father, the famous C. A. Lindbergh, was not a man to be fooled with; he'd once undergone an abdominal operation by choice without anaesthetic, and instilled into his only male child the necessity of overcoming fear. The young Charles became obsessed with speed, motorcycles and eventually aeroplanes. He became the first pupil of a Nebraska flying school with one plane and one instructor, and as 'Daredevil Lindbergh' he went on to perform death-defying feats, flying with stunt pilot H. J. Lynch. He once clambered out onto the wing, was thrown off as Lynch looped the loop, only to save himself at the last minute by pulling the rip-cord on his parachute. He secured one of the first US mail contracts, flying between Chicago and St Louis but finally, of course, achieved international renown with his historic solo flight across the Atlantic in 1927. It's all that much more amazing when you consider that as a child he had an absolute horror of heights.

1902

A forty-nine-day ordeal in the ice began when a tiny monoplane, piloted by forty-two-year-old Mexican mechanic Ralph Flores, crashed miles from anywhere in a dark forest in the desolate Yukon Territory. Flores suffered a smashed jaw and broken ribs, while his twenty-one-year-old passenger Helen Klaben badly sprained her ankle and fractured her arm. They had no survival kit and no sleeping bags, and with temperatures plunging to −40°C, they were forced to use carpet as blankets and seat cushions as a bed. Flores managed to get a fire going and they survived the first night. Four tins of sardines, two of tuna, some fruit salad and a few biscuits were all the food they had and after nine days it was gone. They ate toothpaste and eventually subsisted on 'snowsoup'. Miraculously they survived the cold and hunger for a month, when in desperation Flores made snow-shoes from willow branches and set out to find a spot where they might more easily be sighted. He found one, and managed painfully to get Helen there too. Nearby, he discovered a clearing, and with an inventiveness born of despair, he spent three weary days working at an ingenious device that was soon to lead to a rescue. Their brilliant, but simple saviour was a huge SOS in the snow.   *1963*

Modest Roman Emperor Severus died at York in England where he'd suddenly been taken ill. While bed-ridden, he learned of a plot to depose him. He immediately summoned his officers and made them reaffirm their loyalty pointing out, 'It is not the feet but the head that discharges the duty of a general.' But the pledges were unnecessary, since it was obvious Severus was dying. Towards the end he recognised his own insignificance saying, 'I have been everything and everything is nothing. A little urn will contain all that remains of one for whom the whole world was too little.'   *AD 211*

Mr Spock's double visited Broadhaven Junior School at Dyfed in Wales. Pupils playing in the school grounds at lunchtime spotted a strange silvery green craft, shaped like a Chinaman's hat, landing in a nearby field. Stunned boys then saw a large silver-suited humanoid figure step out and observe the landing site. After a brief inspection the figure retraced his steps and the craft flew off. Although the boys later disagreed on several details, they all agreed on one thing – the strange alien had long pointed ears.   *1977*

Freaky rock singer Alice Cooper was born. Apart from making a name for himself with a string of hits like 'School's Out', he recently became an honorary 'Los Angeles Ambassador' in recognition of his contribution of nearly $30,000 for the renewal of the famous but sadly dilapidated Hollywood sign. When the star presented his cheque to the Mayor, he was careful to tell the man not to drop it, since it was actually written on a huge hunk of metal that was once a part of the sign. 'It won't bounce,' said Alice, 'but it might cut your foot off!' *1948*

Today's the day...

Courageous Roman leader Cato the Younger killed himself. Realising his army was hopelessly surrounded by Julius Caesar, he ordered his men to surrender but chose the honourable Roman way out for himself. After supper 'with a great deal of company', he withdrew to his room and read Plato's *Dialogue* concerning the soul. His sons knew what he had in mind and hid his sword, but Cato was outraged and demanded its return saying, 'To despatch myself I want no sword; I need but hold my breath awhile, or strike my head against the wall!' When they returned it, he was satisfied remarking, 'Now I am master of myself!' His servants left him but hastened back when they heard a noise. Cato had stabbed himself and in falling off his bed, had disembowelled himself – yet was still alive. The physician went to him to sew up the wound but Cato pushed him away, tore open the wound still further and died.   *46 BC*

Taciturn statesman Sir Robert Peel was born, son of a Lancashire cotton millionaire. Regarded as a member of the *nouveau riche* and one of the 'plebeian aristocracy of Mr Pitt', he was always painfully self-conscious. During an interview with King George IV he fiddled so much with the backs of chairs that the King implored him to sit down. His feet, too, were a great source of embarrassment and he would study them during conversation, turning his toes in and out 'as if practising the quadrille'. A humane man, as Home Secretary he worked towards the rationalisation of English laws and abolished the death penalty for over 250 petty crimes including impersonating a Chelsea pensioner and defacing Westminster Bridge. He founded the Metropolitan Police and thus they became known as 'Peelers' or 'Bobbies'. Renowned for his lack of humour, his smile was said to be 'like the silver plate on a coffin'. Nevertheless he was extremely generous in his patronage of the arts and regularly saved one artist from the debtors prison, who commented thankfully, 'and this Peel is the man who has no heart.' He once came upon a card-sharp in

February 5

Alexandra Park and was greatly interested in the three-card trick, remarking to his friends with great restraint that he wouldn't prosecute the man as he was 'but a sad bungler; he cannot do the trick at all'. Sir Robert seemed fascinated, spotting the right card every time and his companions left him to it. On their return some time later, they found the great man in a furious rage – he'd lost all his money. Strangely enough when he'd bet money on it, the right card had proved impossible to spot – the father of the police had been conned.   *1788*

***Peter Pan* was released.** J. M. Barrie left the play to the Children's Hospital in Great Ormond Street, London, and in 1939 Walt Disney negotiated the right to produce an animated film of the 'boy who never grew up'. Work didn't begin in earnest until ten years later and then the crew came upon a few problems – not least was how Tinker Bell should look. She'd only been shown as a beam of light before, even in the silent movie, and Disney's many artists were at a complete loss as to how to portray her. Finally they decided to model her on their ideal of womanhood, and they chose Marilyn Monroe.   *1953*

77

Today's the day...

Purged and plastered King Charles II finally died. He'd become violently ill five days before and doctors had worked frantically to try and save him. They'd purged him with enemas and emetics; bled him of nearly a quart of blood at a time; filled his nose with sneezing powder; swaddled him in hot plasters; daubed his feet with a pungent mixture of resin and pigeon droppings and even tried trepanning his shaved and blistered head. Not surprisingly, the King just became weaker and weaker, lapsed into a coma and finally died. His brother, James II, was anxious to carry out the King's last wishes 'not to let poor Nelly starve', but he couldn't openly give money to such a famous courtesan as Nell Gwynn. When her creditors threatened her with prison, however, he finally managed to extract a large sum from the Treasury. He told them it was for the Secret Service, though what the service was he didn't say!   *1685*

The phenomenal 'Babe' Ruth was born in Baltimore. Baseball was a great favourite of his at school, and George quickly became a star player. At nineteen, he was spotted by Jack Dunn, the owner of the Baltimore Club, and he was soon on the team. By 1927, 'Babe' was a national celebrity, greeted everywhere by adoring crowds, and by 1930 he was the most photographed American of the day. In the same year he was told that his $80,000 salary was more than President Hoover's. 'Babe' simply commented, 'Well, I had a better year!'   *1895*

King George VI died at Sandringham, his birthplace. He'd suffered from cancer for some time but had recovered well from an operation to remove one of his lungs. His doctors saw him on 29 January and pronounced themselves satisfied with his progress. On 31 January Princess Elizabeth and the Duke of Edinburgh left for an extensive tour of East Africa, Australia and New Zealand. The King went to London Airport to see them off and then returned to Sandringham for the rough-shooting. After a good day taking pot-shots at hare, the

February 6

King had dinner, then retired to his room. He died quietly during the night and was found by his valet next morning. There was no exact time of death, so all poor Princess Elizabeth knew, some 4,000 miles away in the Treetops Hotel, was that she'd been Queen of England since some time before dawn. Her accession set a great precedent, for at George VI's funeral, the sovereign's coffin was followed for the first time by a woman as chief mourner.

1952

Rolls Royce got a fitting mascot which was cast for the first time in bronze. The proprietors of the illustrious firm were somewhat disturbed by some of their less tasteful customers putting comic mascots on the front of their cars. So in 1910 they commissioned sculptor Charles Sykes, a member of the Royal Academy, to design something more refined. He came up with *The Spirit of Ecstasy*, a young lady who perched on the front of the car 'to travel in the freshness of air and the musical sound of her fluttering draperies'. The ethereal nymph was modelled on a rather more down-to-earth lady. She was Eleanor, secretary to Lord Montagu of Beaulieu, and in spirit form, she's been travelling the world ever since.

1911

Today's the day...

Non-conformist wordman James Murray was born. Son of a Teviotdale tailor, he taught himself Chinese by the age of seven; learnt French, Italian, German and Greek before leaving school at fourteen, and studied Latin on his first job as a cowherd. As editor of the first *Oxford English Dictionary*, he felt he enjoyed divine protection and delighted in telling how celestial visitors guided him whenever he was lost on country walks. He hated priests, Tories, drink and tobacco, and surprisingly, novels and plays. He had eleven children, named them such weird and wonderful names as Oswyn and Rosfrith because of his love of Anglo-Saxon, and enlisted the help of them all in working on the dictionary. With this in mind Murray, with his brood trailing behind him, soon became known as 'The Dic and the little Dics'.
1837

The Beatles arrived in America. They all felt sick and George was worried about his hair. 10,000 screaming fans greeted them at Kennedy Airport and the discreet Plaza Hotel where they were staying was besieged by thousands of hysterical teenagers. They appeared on the *Ed Sullivan Show* which had a record audience of seventy-three million and during transmission it's claimed that not one major crime was committed by a teenager in the whole of America.
1964

Dynamic man of letters Charles Dickens was born. From dismal beginnings in a blacking factory and a spell in a debtors' prison with his father, he eventually became a parliamentary reporter. In 1836 *Pickwick Papers* appeared in monthly parts and thereafter he produced a book every year. Amazingly, he also found time to start a magazine, edit a newspaper, manage a theatrical company, act in plays, found a campaign against capital punishment and a home for repentant prostitutes. He fathered ten children, toured America and understandably took long protracted holidays. He was very irritated by his poor wife Kate, however, who just couldn't keep up with him.

February 7

According to him, she walked too slowly, kept having babies and was
constantly ill. On the whole, he preferred her sister Mary Hogarth,
who lived with them and was 'the grace and life' of their home. When
she died at seventeen, he was distraught and insisted that on his death
he should be buried with her. She featured in his novels as Florence,
Agnes and Little Dorrit, and may well have been the inspiration for
another of his teenage heroines Little Nell, who also caused a furore
when she died. When the story was told, grown men wept, and at New
York Pier anxious crowds waited for incoming ships, calling out, 'Is
Little Nell dead?'   *1812*

Disney's *Pinocchio* had its world première. The story of the
metamorphosis of the little puppet had been a difficult one to produce
and at one point, five months' work had to be scrapped. Paulo
Lorenzini, nephew of Carlo Lorenzini – who wrote the original story –
wanted the Italian Government to sue Disney for making Pinocchio's
character too American, but nobody was very interested. The film
went on to become another children's classic, was dubbed into seven
languages and earned the dubious distinction of having some of the
most terrifying scenes in any of Disney's films.   *1940*

Compassionate realist Sir Thomas More was born. Erasmus
remarked that he had the eyes of a genius and 'the quickest sense of the
ridiculous of any man'. Kindly to a fault, he would have preferred to
marry his first wife's younger sister, but knew it would be a disgrace
if the elder girl were left on the shelf and so married her instead. When
it came to the time for his two daughters to marry, Will Roper was an
undecided suitor. To help him choose, More took him to their
bedroom, ripped off the bedclothes and exposed the pair of them
'their smocks up as high as their arme-pitts'. They promptly turned
over and Roper patted the bottom of the scholar Meg saying, 'I've seen
both sides and thou art mine!'   *1478*

T.D.—5   81

Today's the day...

Tragic Mary Queen of Scots was beheaded in the main hall of gloomy Fotheringay Castle, after a weary eighteen years of confinement. Having removed her funereal robe to reveal a scarlet undergown, she remarked that she 'had never put off her clothes in such a company', and almost cheerfully submitted herself, saying to her executioner, 'I forgive you with all my heart, for now I hope you shall make an end of all my troubles.' She laid her chin on the block, supporting it with both her hands, which would have been 'cut off had they not been espied'. As one executioner held her, a knot at the top of her undergown deflected the axe. At the second blow her head was still attached by 'one small gristle' and having been cut, her head was held up with a 'God Save the Queen'. In one final macabre scene, her little dog emerged from under her clothes and wouldn't leave her 'but came and lay between her head and her shoulders'. He'd been uncovered when, with 'unseemly haste', the executioner had removed the Queen's garters.   *1587*

Russian literary giant Alexander Pushkin was killed in an unfortunate and 'dishonourable' duel. Pushkin was a fierce fighter and at one time in his life, had fought duels practically every day. Today's event, caused by a slight on his wife's honour, was with his own brother-in-law, the less than fair-minded Baron Hecheren d'Anthes. The duel was kept as secret as possible, and though Pushkin's carriage passed that of his wife on the way to the killing ground, she was short-sighted, didn't see him and missed her opportunity to dissuade him. In knee-deep snow, the adversaries met and began to step out the twenty paces to their firing positions. Pushkin had already reached his when after only four paces, Hecheren turned and fired – felling and mortally wounding his foe. Pushkin insisted on taking his shot, but Hecheren stood sideways and covered himself with his arms so, though deadly accurate, Pushkin's shot merely pierced his wrist and bruised his ribs. Understandably, the great writer refused a reconciliation, and died two days later, gasping, 'Life is ended. It is difficult to breathe, I am choking.' As he had lain injured on the field of fire, he said, 'I thought it would give me pleasure to kill him, but I do not feel that now.'   *1837*

The Devil visited Devon in the dead of night and left a scarcely believable calling card. When startled residents awoke the following morning, they found a single line of hoof-prints, as if some demonic creature had hopped one-legged through the snow. More amazing still was that in one night, the creature appeared to have covered more than 100 miles of countryside, and when faced with walls, roofs and hayricks, had either clambered over them – or gone straight through. Eminent men studied the clues and concluded that no known quadruped or bird could have made the tracks individually – though barely conceivably a number of badgers, otters or rats might have done. The villagers' own conclusion that the tracks were 'manifest proof of the Great Enemy's immediate presence', seems scarcely less believable than one investigator's conviction that the culprit was of all things – a kangaroo.   *1855*

Conscientious hangman James Berry was born. He was a humane man; liked to meet his victims beforehand so they wouldn't be 'topped' by a stranger and perhaps misguidedly, gave them 'verses of comfort' to read. A pigeon-fancier and pet-rabbit breeder in his spare time, he was very secretive about his 'missions'. One landlady he stayed with clearly didn't know who he was and kept on and on about the hanging and what a fearsome man this Berry must be. Before he went to bed, her little scar-faced guest gave her his card which read '*James Berry – Executioner*', and he was most upset when she fainted. At the age of forty, he decided he'd had enough, and much to everyone's amazement took up lecturing, and became an outspoken opponent of capital punishment.   *1852*

Today's the day...

The world's worst actor 'Cockadoodle' Coates made his *début à débâcle* at the Bath Theatre. He was playing Romeo, the favourite role of his early days at home in Antigua, having first rewritten large chunks to 'improve it'. A crowd of 'abigails and butlers' had been hired to cheer him on, and the play struggled through to the fifth act amid catcalls and jeers from the rest of the audience. Finally, when he introduced the brilliant innovation of opening Juliet's coffin with a crow-bar, the playgoers dissolved into hysterical laughter and the curtain came down. Little did they know they'd missed the best part, which afterwards became famous. It was Coates' version of the bard's great death scene, where Romeo kills himself by the body of his love. Histrionically grief-stricken, he first dusted down the stage with a handkerchief, carefully removed his hat, and ultimately in his diamond studded costume lay down and gracefully died. On a rare occasion when this was greeted with tumultuous applause, he was so pleased, he got up and bowed to the audience, lay down and died again. The motto of this amazing man was, 'While I live, I'll crow!'   *1810*

A fowl story appeared in the magazine *Newsweek*. Originally written by journalist C. Louis Mortison, it told how Lester Green of Prospect, Connecticut, stopped his car freezing up on cold nights by putting two broody hens on the engine. He claimed that since each hen put out over 100 degrees of heat, the combined temperature was enough to make the car start on the button. There was, it appeared, no end to Lester's inventiveness and stories about him appeared in a number of respected publications. He hatched a clutch of furry chickens; made butter from milkweed and sprayed his apple trees with glue to stop the fruit dropping off in the autumn. He invented a new form of fox-hunting, where the fox chased the dogs, and made a concrete shell for a homeless tortoise, who in gratitude kept his house free of rats. Perhaps his greatest achievement, however, was to discover the fluid that put the curl in pigs' tails – a substance for which he was offered a

February 9

small fortune by a man who wanted to use it for making bed springs.
Unfortunately for the man there was no fluid, and unfortunately for
the editors Lester didn't live in Prospect, but only in Mr Mortison's
mind.   *1935*

Dashing George Custer married his beautiful sweetheart Elizabeth,
a linguist and reader of the classics. She called him 'Autie' and he called
her alternately 'Libby' and 'Old Lady'. On their honeymoon they
travelled in an army waggon piled high with hay, and at a posting soon
after, they 'romped' together so vigorously that the soldiers thought
their commanding officer was beating his wife. As the wife of a hero,
Mrs Custer had to tolerate the adoring females who clustered around
her handsome spouse. Vain in the extreme, he occasionally deigned to
cut his long yellow hair to give his admirers a lock, but he was deeply
fond of his wife and though he had plenty of opportunity, appears to
have had only one serious affair. That, if it happened at all, was with a
captive Indian Princess called Monahseetah, who is reported to have
had a child by him, and later became friends with Elizabeth. Custer
never openly admitted his involvement, but kept the girl by him for
four months as an interpreter – and she couldn't speak a word of
English.   *1864*

A peculiar double marriage took place at Sheffield. George Talbot
the Earl of Shrewsbury, 'the greatest subject in the realm', was
desperate to marry Bess of Hardwicke, the beautiful widow of Sir
William Cavendish. Bess, ambitious to a degree and a great dynast,
insisted on the intermingling of their families first. So she married her
son Henry to Shrewsbury's daughter Grace and married her daughter
Mary to Shrewsbury's son Gilbert. Thus she secured huge estates for
her descendants and when shortly afterwards she at last stooped to
marry her Earl, she became the stepmother of her son-and-daughter-
in-law, and the stepmother-in-law of her own son and daughter.   *1568*

Today's the day...

Long-serving Tory Prime Minister 'Super Mac' was born in Cadogan Place, London. Maurice Harold Macmillan by name and a publisher as well as politician by profession, he bought the rights to *Gone with the Wind*, and played an 'indispensable' role in laying the foundation for the Nuclear Test Ban Treaty of 1963. Perhaps most famous for his 'you've never had it so good' line which was afterwards borrowed by Lyndon Johnson, he was much admired by Churchill, Eisenhower, de Gaulle and Kennedy, and praised by, of all people, Labour Party Prime Minister Harold Wilson and Russian Premier Nikita Khrushchev. To Wilson's reminiscences of a penniless childhood, short on shoe leather, 'Super Mac' rejoined, 'If Harold ever went to school without any boots, it was merely because he was too big for them.' When Khrushchev started banging his shoe on the table during a Macmillan speech at the UN, the Prime Minister laconically responded, 'I'd like that translated, if I may.'   *1894*

Victoria married Albert. For her he was an 'Angel' and 'perfection'. For the populace, he was a fortune-hunting foreigner after England's 'fat Queen' and 'fatter purse', and Parliament was quick to dock his

February 10

proposed income from £50,000 to £30,000 a year. The two were
joined in the style of homely George III and Queen Charlotte in the
Chapel Royal of St James' Palace at 1 pm. Albert was 'awkward
with embarrassment'. It was freezing cold, the 300 guests were
crammed in and the Queen's dress, 'a tasteless muddle', had a train so
short that all the bridesmaids had to huddle together. The ecstatic
couple went off to begin their honeymoon at Windsor and the
following day they were up so early that they caused the diarist Charles
Greville to comment that it was 'not the way to provide us with a
Prince of Wales'.   *1840*

General Tom Thumb married Lavinia Warren, beating his rival
for her hand – the minute Commodore George Washington Nutt,
who stood 29ins tall, weighed 24lbs, and was best man at the wedding
which was solemnised in Grace Church, New York. The happy couple
towered over their best man by inches, but still had to stand on a piano
to greet the many and celebrated guests.   *1863*

Boy wonder aquanaut Mark Spitz was born. The idol of middle
American womanhood and an ad-man's dream, this handsome wind-
blown hero got off to a slow start at the Mexico Olympics, winning only
two golds, a silver and a bronze. By Munich, however, he'd overcome
mental and largely imagined physical problems and made a clean
sweep of seven golds – all in record-breaking time. Much encouraged in
his early days as a swimmer by his father Arnold, he stopped taking
Hebrew lessons when they got in the way of his training. As Arnold
explained to the Rabbi 'even God likes a winner'.   *1950*

Outraged East German Health Minister Herr Spiess complained
in a television broadcast that Western Europe had slandered the
USSR. They were calling the 'flu epidemic that was sweeping the
Continent 'Russian Flu' when, as every good Party member knew, it
was in fact, Chinese.   *1978*

Today's the day...

Scottish entrepreneurs Burke and Hare committed their first murder. They'd already discovered that dead bodies were worth money in Edinburgh when they'd sold that of Highlander 'old Donald' who died in their lodging house. A friendly unofficial anatomist Dr Knox had paid them well and they'd made a good profit, so when another lodger 'Joe the Mumper' fell ill they helped him on his way. Abigail Simpson was their first premeditated victim, however, and she was hale and hearty till she met them. They lured her to the house and plied her with whisky, then Hare suffocated her while Burke held onto her legs. Once again the body was disposed of to Dr Knox, the two men cheerfully counted their gold and in the six months before they were caught killed thirteen victims, including an Irish beggar woman, her dumb grandson, and a recalcitrant horse. *1828*

'The Wizard' inventor Thomas Alva Edison was born in Milan, Ohio. He only ever had three months of formal schooling and then his teacher rejected him as being 'addled'. By the age of nine, however, he'd read Porter's *Natural and Experimental Philosophy* and set up a laboratory in the cellar of his home. He only slept when he wasn't interested in anything and would work tirelessly night and day if something caught his imagination. Apart from his work on the telephone and electricity, he also invented the electric vote recorder, the dictating machine, the kinephone and kinetograph (which made the 'talkies' possible), the automatic railway signal and the first practical typewriter. At his death he held over 1,000 patents. His favourite was the phonograph. When he'd finished work on the prototype, he experimented by shouting 'Mary had a little lamb' into it and 'was never so taken about in my life' as when the machine mimicked him. He spent ten years working on the problem of incandescent light, experimenting with over 6,000 different materials for the filament including fishing line, human hair, grass and finally a singed piece of sewing thread. Not surprisingly he once remarked that, 'Genius is one per cent inspiration and ninety-nine per cent perspiration.'   *1847*

Asthmatic miller's daughter Bernadette Soubirous saw a vision of a 'lady in white' in the grotto at Massabielle on the banks of the River Gare in the Pyrenees. The 'lady' said she was the 'Immaculate Conception' and told Bernadette to drink and wash in a stream. The only trouble was, there wasn't a stream – until the visitant pointed to a spot nearby where a spring began to bubble and has flowed ever since. After four years of intense debate and strenuous cross-examination of Bernadette, it was decided that her story was true and that the Virgin Mary had in fact appeared to the young girl. Reports circulated of the miraculous cures of those who had bathed in the spring and the place which was Lourdes became the most famous shrine in the world. Bernadette herself retired to a convent at Nevers, and died there fifteen years later when she was only thirty-five.   *1858*

Red-frocked Cardinals gathered in Rome for the investiture of Pope John Paul II. Amongst their number was one whom commentators had fought shy of naming, simply referring to him as 'a Cardinal from the Philippines'. It wasn't surprising, his name was Cardinal Sin!   *1978*

Today's the day...

Poor incestuous Alice Burraway died aged seventy-six. Nearly fifty years before, her own father had fathered her son. The son was put in a home and the father died. Years passed, and Alice gave a job to an itinerant farm labourer. She became his paramour and eventually they wed. Shortly before her death, after twenty years of happy marriage, she discovered that she'd been his mother, his sister, his mistress and his wife.

1729

William the Conqueror invaded Britain again, though this particular one wasn't a Norman, but an Irish American mercenary, more familiarly known as General William Tate. He was meant to be attacking Bristol but in fact, along with a substantial force of French soldiers and impressed convicts, he ended up on the beach near the tiny village of Fishguard in Wales. The natives were distinctly unimpressed, and when the local guard turned out it was led by a crowd of women in traditional Welsh dress, whose stove-pipe hats and red shawls made them look at a distance like the official British army. Whether it was this optical illusion that made them quake in their boots, or the thought of tangling with a horde of mad Welsh fishwives, is something that will never satisfactorily be resolved. On any account, they gave up the ghost, and suitably enough the surrender was signed in a pub.

1797

The man who knew everyone – Lord Boothby Baron of Buchan and Rattray – was born to an aristocratic Scottish family of Norwegian extraction. Educated at Eton and Oxford, he became Tory MP for Aberdeen East, and Parliamentary Private Secretary to both Stanley Baldwin and Winston Churchill. He took an anti-appeasement stance in the thirties, was awarded the *Lègion d'Honneur* and when after the war his political career was blocked, first by Churchill and then by Eden, he shot to fame as a journalist, broadcaster, TV personality and 'character'. In 1978 he claimed to be the only man alive who had known intimately not only Baldwin and Churchill, but Sir Thomas Beecham, Somerset Maugham and Lloyd-George. Among his other friends and acquaintances can be numbered Asquith, Lawrence of Arabia, Mrs Wallace Simpson, King George VI and Harold Macmillan to name but a few. Perhaps his most famous meeting was with Hitler, who at first ignored him, then thrust his right arm in the air and shouted 'Hitler!'. Unabashed, m'lord also thrust his right arm in the air and shouted 'Boothby!'   *1900*

A snake committed suicide in the Philadelphia Zoo, or to be less anthropomorphic about it, the beast was found to have stabbed itself in the back with its own fangs. Since it was a Gaboon viper, a serpent that not only has a deadly and unusually quick acting venom, but has the largest fangs at nearly 2in of any snake extant, it was not surprisingly very dead.   *1963*

Abe Lincoln came into the world in a log cabin near Hodgeville, Kentucky. At a full grown height of 6ft 4in, with gangly limbs, huge hands and feet, and poor eyesight, he claimed he was 'the ugliest man in the world'. He was self-educated, had less than a year of schooling in total and suffered numerous electoral defeats before becoming the sixteenth President. He managed to combine great ambition with shyness; was incurably untidy, superstitious, uncomfortable with women, and sensitive to the weather. He was renowned for his wit, irony and generosity and once asked the Surgeon General where he could get smallpox, 'for then I shall have something I can give to everyone.'   *1809*

Gershwin's *Rhapsody in Blue* was first performed at the Aeolian Hall, New York. Conductor Paul Whiteman had asked him to compose it for a special concert, but Gershwin forgot until he read about it in a newspaper – and wrote it double quick!   *1924*

Today's the day...

The *Lady Luvibond* became a ghost ship when she sailed down the Thames on her way to Oporto. On board the three-master were Captain Simon Reed and his new wife, celebrating their marriage. It's said the mate John Rivers coveted the Captain's lady, and in a fit of jealousy decided to kill them all. He knocked out the bosun, took the helm and drove the ship onto the Goodwin Sands – the notorious sandbanks off Deal. Fifty years later to the day, Captain Westlake of the coaster *Edenbridge* narrowly avoided a collision with a three-master on the very same spot; the crew of a trawler saw the ship too and though they watched it break up on the sands, they could find neither wreckage nor survivors. Another fifty years passed and the phantom wreck was seen again by the Deal boatmen and fifty years after that, the Shore Watch saw it once more. In 1948, just weeks after an Italian ship had run aground on the sands, the *Lady* kept her bi-centenary, and sailors might beware that when she's next due in February 1998, the date will be Friday the 13th.   *1748*

The creator of *Maigret* Georges Simenon was born of Belgian stock, the son of a clerk. He became a boy-reporter in Paris, and to make ends meet wrote 'penny dreadful' romances and adventure stories, clocking up forty books and more than a dozen different pen names in four years. While he was writing *Maigret*, he would try to devote no more than ten days to a book, once turning out 90,000 words in three days. He has sold over 300 million copies of the *Maigrets* and written eleven books since his 'retirement' in 1973. Famous for his extravagant claims, he's boasted that he hates literature, has read nothing but medical reports for fifty years, and has made love to 10,000 women.   *1903*

Catherine Howard was beheaded on Tower Green. Wife number five for Henry VIII, she'd been condemned by Parliament for her manifold adultery. The King could hardly believe it, and debated the issue hotly with the Primate of England, the Lord Chancellor and her

February 13

uncle, the Duke of Norfolk. According to witnesses she died well, and this was clearly important to her, since before her execution she borrowed the block and rehearsed her own death.   *1542*

History's most famous turncoat was born. He was Charles Maurice de Talleyrand-Périgord – a lame, licentious, cunning and witty man. Under Louis XVI he became Bishop of Autun and was fortunate enough to be on a diplomatic mission to England when the Revolution began. He returned after a brief spell in America, and became Foreign Minister under the Directory. He played a double role in the plot which made Napoleon First Consul, and when the 'Little Corsican' made himself Emperor, Talleyrand became Grand Chamberlain. When Bonaparte began to totter in the wake of the Battle of Leipzig, the Grand Chamberlain saw the writing on the wall and helped smooth the way back for the Bourbons, serving under both Louis XVIII and Charles X. In 1830 revolution broke out again and Talleyrand watched the battle for Paris from his window. 'I see,' he said, 'we are winning.' 'Who is we?' asked a companion. 'Be quiet,' replied the statesman, 'I'll tell you tomorrow!'   *1754*

Today's the day...

Faithful lover Richard II died, imprisoned at Pontefract Castle. On the death of his beloved wife Anne of Bohemia he'd arranged for an elaborate tomb to be built in Westminster Abbey with his own effigy carved beside hers, each holding the other's hand. Legend has it, however, that the body which was conveyed to London and placed in the tomb with Anne, was not in fact that of Richard. Some say it was his chaplain who was a near double, and that Richard escaped his jailers and died an imbecile in Scotland. *1400*

The Importance of Being Earnest had its première at the St James' Theatre in London. Wilde had written it in three weeks when staying down in Worthing and had finally been persuaded to cut one act by George Alexander, the producer. Wilde protested vehemently against it for an hour, saying that the act had cost him 'terrible exhausting labour and heart-rending nerve-wracking strain' and apart from anything else 'it must have taken fully five minutes to write'. The opening night was a more than usually tense occasion. The Marquis of Queensberry was after Wilde's blood for his supposed homosexual relations with his son, and it was feared he might arrive and make a scene. Strict instructions were given not to let the Marquis in and Wilde stayed backstage in case he tried the stage door. The Marquis did turn up, complete with his heavyweight bodyguard, and obscurely clutching a bunch of carrots and turnips. He was refused admission at all the entrances. Disgruntled he waited about for three hours in the snow, then unceremoniously dumped his bouquet at the stage door and stomped off home. *1895*

The St Valentine's Day Massacre took place in a bleak garage in Chicago. It was a set-up. The night before, Bugs Moran – Capone's arch enemy – had received an anonymous phone call offering him a cheap consignment of bootleg whisky. He blithely told the man to deliver to his warehouse on North Clark Street at 10.30 next morning and agreed to meet some of his henchmen there to collect. Luckily for him, he was late. In the garage three empty trucks were waiting for their load and ex-safecracker Johnny May was repairing a fourth. The Gusenberg brothers, James Clark, Adam Heyer and Ali Weinshank were all hanging about waiting for the whisky, carrying about $5,000 between them to pay for the load and all heavily armed. Along with them was Reinhardt H. Schwimmer a thirty-year-old optician who got some sort of vicarious excitement out of being with criminals. A Cadillac drew up outside, five men got out, three dressed as policemen. Bugs, who saw it from the end of the street, assumed it was a raid and fled. The men walked into the garage, lined the gangsters up against the wall and systematically fired their machine-guns, first at the head, then the chest and finally at stomach level. Then they calmly walked out. Bugs Moran commented, 'Only Capone kills like that', while in his sumptuous Florida hideaway Capone remarked, 'The only man who kills like that is Bugs Moran.' *1929*

James I's daughter was married in a lavish display of extravagance. Her dress was made of 'Florence cloth of silver richly embroidered' and the train alone cost £130. Francis Bacon and Inigo Jones organised magnificent masques and there was a five-day spectacle on the Thames with Turkish galleys, floating castles and a reconstruction of the Battle of Lepanto. When the festivities were over and he'd paid his daughter's dowry, he found himself a staggering £72,794 out of pocket. *1613*

Debauched rake and gambler the Duke of Hamilton married eighteen-year-old Irish beauty Elizabeth Gunning at half past midnight in the Mayfair Chapel. He'd only met the lady two days earlier at a gambling party at Lord Chesterfield's. According to Horace Walpole, shortly after he met her he'd 'made violent love to her at one end of the room, while he was playing pharaoh at the other; that is, he saw neither the bank nor his own cards . . . and soon lost £1,000.' *1752*

Today's the day...

The battleship *Maine* blew up in Havana Harbour in what may well have been an accidental explosion. When a less than unbiased enquiry decided it was caused by a mine, the incident became the spark that ignited the Spanish-American War. Rebellion was already rife in Cuba. It had been providing reams of good copy for press baron Randolph Hearst's newspaper empire, and for him at least, the blasted battleship was a godsend. He drummed up an incredible jingoistic crusade, which added 300,000 to his circulation and piled the pressure on the politicians to engage directly in the fight. Eventually, in April, a reluctant President McKinley declared war. If it had done nothing else, the war had at least enabled Hearst to be a man of his word. He'd sent the artist Remington to Cuba to cover the rebellion. Remington had cabled back, 'There will be no war.' Hearst replied, 'You furnish the pictures. I'll furnish the war!'
1898

The assassination of Franklin Delano Roosevelt was muffed by the diminutive 5ft gunman Joseph Zangara. The thirty-one-year-old Italian immigrant and unemployed bricklayer of New Jersey knew that F.D.R., the then President-Elect, was going to speak at Miami's

Bayfront Park. He tried to get there early to get a ringside seat, but when he arrived at 8pm all the seats were taken, and he was prevented from getting a good vantage point by a citizen who gave him a lecture on good manners. Roosevelt duly arrived, gave his speech and called Miami Mayor Cermak to talk with him. As the crowd dispersed Zangara seized his opportunity, and fighting off a woman who hit him with her handbag, fired off five shots at the President-to-be. He missed, but injured four bystanders, and mortally wounded the Mayor. Before he was sent to the chair, thirty-three days later, this casual killer was exhaustively interviewed. It turned out he'd previously tried to assassinate King Victor Emmanuel; he'd considered Calvin Coolidge, Mussolini, the King of England and the incumbent but defeated President Herbert Hoover. When pressed at his trial he expressed no preference – 'any President, any King' would do!   *1933*

'A mummy's comfort' was registered as US Patent Number 516336. It was designed to save embarrassment for nursing mothers publicly compromised by the feverish hunger of their offspring. Worn under the blouse, it looked like a parachute harness. It had a cup for each breast and facilitated nourishment at waist level with artificial nipples that could be made 'to any desired length'.   *1910*

'The World's Greatest Actor' John Barrymore was born in Philadelphia. Despite fluffing his lines at his *début*, he established his reputation on the stage by attracting critical adulation in the 1915 production of Galsworthy's *Justice*. He went on to play *Hamlet* for a record 101 performances; became a star of the silent screen, and a winner in the talkies. He was married four times; pursued innumerable affairs and not surprisingly, had decided views on divorce. 'Alimony,' he said, 'is the most exorbitant of all stud fees!' 'A man . . . must pay the fiddler, but in my case . . . a whole symphony orchestra has to be subsidised!'   *1882*

Today's the day...

Travelling man of science Francis Galton was born in Birmingham, a Quaker and the cousin of Charles Darwin. Having studied medicine and inherited a fortune, he journeyed to Syria, Egypt and the Sudan, and won a gold medal from the National Geographical Society for his two-year expedition to South-West Africa through country 'hitherto unknown'. His book *Art of Travel or Shifts and Contrivances Available in Wild Countries* is full of handy hints like how to bait lice, fire a gun from a galloping horse and prevent 'the looseness of the teeth caused by scurvy'. When things got hot, he wore his 'patent ventilating hat', and if he got excited he'd 'manipulate its shutters . . . with remarkable rapidity'. With the use of statistics, he presented a paper on the posteriors of Hottentot women, and compiled a *Beauty Map of Britain* showing that all the most attractive girls lived in Aberdeen.   *1822*

The death sentence was passed on an entire country when the whole population of the Netherlands was condemned for heresy by the Inquisition brought in by their Spanish rulers. On this 'Day of Infamy' they proposed to stop the rot by executing three million people – and they managed to hang, burn or otherwise despatch 800 souls in the very first week.   *1568*

February 16

The tennis goddesses of the twenties fought it out on the clay court of the Carlton Hotel in Cannes. Twenty-seven-year-old Suzanne Lenglen, the French champion, was amazingly accurate, startlingly elegant and suffered from nerves, while her American opponent Helen Wills was seven years younger and relied more on power than accuracy. Shivering with nerves Suzanne won the first set, tired in the second and had to fight hard to reach match point. It looked as if she'd done it when a shot from Helen Wills went 'out'. But an indignant linesman insisted it was most definitely 'in' and Suzanne was so shaken, she lost six points in a row. When she finally won – eight games to six – she was so exhausted, she briefly shook her opponent's hand – then fled from the court in tears. *1926*

A haughty earl got his come-uppance in the House of Lords. He was Francis Norris, Earl of Berkshire, and when Lord Scrope had unavoidably jostled him in a narrow passage, he reacted in typically violent style by shoving Scrope out of the way. Unfortunately for Norris, Prince Charles was present. His action was taken as a mark of disrespect and he was flung into the Fleet Prison. There he brooded 'over these affronts' and on his release he committed suicide. He shot himself in the neck – with a crossbow. *1620*

Soviet surveyors surprised the world when they announced that they had overlooked something in Siberia. They'd just discovered a mountain they didn't know existed. It was 24,664ft high. *1955*

The famous inventor of oddities Arthur Pedrick patented his alternative to the lifeboat. To protect shipwreck survivors from the weather, he proposed to make survival capsules like man-sized vacuum flasks. At the order to abandon ship, men, women and children would hop into their own 'flask' and ask someone to throw them into the sea. What he didn't specify is what happens to the last man on board. *1968*

Today's the day...

Rapacious Mongol Tamerlane the Great died after a month of victorious feasting en route for China. A distant descendant of that other famous landwaster Genghis Khan, he'd conquered 'half the known world' before being laid to rest in an ebony coffin in the tomb of 'Gur Amir' in Samarkand. He emulated his antecedent by stacking the heads of murdered prisoners into pyramids – with the peculiar refinement that he arranged them facing outwards. He terrified his men as much as his enemies, killed people for telling jokes in his presence, and sacrificed twenty sheep a day for the souls of his dead father and son. Apocryphal stories about him abound, and in one he forbade his men to drink anything but boiled water, lest they die unnecessarily from poisoning. So tasteless did this prove to be that they added dried leaves, and invented the oddly refined drink of tea.

1405

The first female in space mystery got off the ground. Tracking stations around the world picked up the launch of a manned satellite from a base near the Aral Sea, deep in the USSR. To their amazement, they found the crew consisted of a man and the first ever woman astronaut. The stations followed their progress as the craft went into orbit. For seven days, the two voices were heard calling back to base. Then, on the 24 February, an unconfirmed report claimed the woman heard something outside the capsule. Then the man's voice said, 'Here, there is something. It's difficult . . . if we don't get out, the world will never hear about it . . .' That was the last that was heard. The Russians denounced the report as fabrication. They denied all knowledge of the unidentified flying female, and a little over two years after, Valentina Tereshkova officially became the first woman in space – but was she?

1961

Satirical French playwright and actor Molière died aged fifty-one. His real name was Jean Baptiste Poquelin, and he'd been suffering from tuberculosis for some seven years. Treated by incompetent and superstitious doctors, he decided to get his own back and wrote three inspired parodies, lampooning the noble profession. In the final one, *Le Malade Imaginaire*, the joke rebounded on him. He was playing a starring role as the hypochondriac when he suffered a for-real coughing fit, and burst a blood vessel. A true player to the last, he managed to finish the performance, and only then took his final bow.   1673

Medical eavesdropper René Théophile Hyacinthe Laënnec was born. He grew up to be a brilliant pathologist and teacher, and had a staggering inspiration while walking near the Louvre. There he saw some children playing with long sticks; tapping them at one end, and listening to the amplified sounds at the other. He rushed off to his laboratory at a nearby hospital, rolled up a piece of paper, went to the first patient he could find, and held the device against his chest. Much impressed, he made a more refined cylinder of wood, called it *stethos* – from the Greek for chest – *scope* – from the Greek to examine.   *1781*

A poet metaphorically lost his head for love of Mary Queen of Scots. He was the Frenchman Monsieur de Chatelard and until today had been one of Mary's favourites. As she was about to go to bed, however, she and her maids discovered him hiding in the closet. He was ejected from the room and the following day, more to save him from possibly worse consequences than to punish him, the Queen sent him into exile. Three days later, she was staying at Burntisland and again was about to go to bed when the poet popped out from behind the curtains. James Earl of Moray, the Queen's ruthless half-brother, was the next to arrive on the scene and for Chatelard there was no escape. The following day he was tried at St Andrews, and the day after that he lost his head once more – and this time for good.   *1563*

Today's the day...

A new world was discovered by self-taught astronomer Clyde
Tombaugh at the Lowell Observatory in Flagstaff, Arizona.
Continuing the work of its founder, Percival Lowell who died some
fourteen years before, he spent nearly twelve months searching the
heavens for proof of the theoretical body that made Uranus wander in
its orbit. By rapidly projecting pairs of photographic plates of the
same piece of sky, taken at different times, he'd found a movement
indicative of a 'new' planet. By 13 March, the seventy-fifth anniversary
of Lowell's birth, he was able to announce that the planet was indeed
a reality. It was the first new planet discovered for nearly a century,
and not surprisingly at over 3,500 million miles, it was the furthest
away from the Sun. It was called Pluto for Lowell's initials, and for
Pluto, the god of the dead and outer darkness.   *1930*

The great holy allegory *Pilgrim's Progress* was published only a few
months after its author John Bunyan had been released from his
second term of imprisonment. Bunyan, who in his youth had been
much noted for his colourful swearing, had married his first wife and
fought with the Parliamentary army in the English Civil War, before
he became a truly enthusiastic convert to the Baptist puritan faith.
In fact he was so enthusiastic that he was jailed for twelve years for
his preaching; pardoned by Charles II's *Declaration of Indulgence* and
locked up again for another nine months. As well as many pamphlets
and his spiritual autobiography *Grace Abounding*, he also wrote
Pilgrim's Progress during his incarceration, helped along by a friendly
jailer. The first three editions were immediate bestsellers; Part II was
published in 1685, and 100,000 copies had been sold by 1688 – and
this was when the vast majority of the population was illiterate. For
250 years, it outsold everything but the Bible, and though scorned by
the *literati* at first, it was soon accepted as a masterpiece. Its author
was described by no less a personage than George Bernard Shaw as
'better than Shakespeare!'   *1678*

February 18

The devilish 'Spring Heeled Jack' struck for the first time in the heart of London, having successfully terrorised much of the South Bank. Tall and abnormally thin, he generally wore a cloak, a white oilskin jumpsuit and a horned helmet; he had clammy skin, fiery eyes and long metal claws; and got his name from the huge and unearthly leaps he made escaping the scene of the crime. On this particular evening he attacked two teenage sisters, Mary and Lucy Scales, knocking Lucy to the ground and breathing blue fire in her face. He was chased off by her doughty brother Tom, a Limehouse butcher, but two days later, masquerading as a policeman, he struck again, badly mauling an eighteen-year-old girl in Bow. More attacks followed and all kinds of extravagant claims were made for Jack. He was the devil; he was a kangaroo; he was responsible for sundry rapes and murders; slapped policemen's faces and frightened the life out of the guards at the Aldershot barracks. Intermittent reports of his activities kept rolling in for more than half a century, by which time he must have been a very old horror indeed. The only certain thing about him is that the bounder was never caught. *1837*

Today's the day...

Revolutionary astronomer Nicolaus Copernicus was born in
Poland. When it first occurred to him that perhaps the sun, and not the
earth, was the centre of our universe, he set out to prove it. From his
own and other people's observations, he worked out the planets'
relationship to each other and to the sun, and embodied his findings
in a book called *De Revolutionibus Orbium Celestium*, which he
finished in 1530 but was just too frightened – or too cautious – to
publish. Disciples of his were later burnt at the stake for their belief
in his theories, so when he was finally prevailed upon to publish he was
sensible, if sycophantic, in dedicating the work to the Pope.   *1473*

The actor who changed the face of acting, David Garrick, was
born in a public house in Hereford. He was sent to Lisbon to learn the
wine trade and on his return joined his brother and the two became
vintners. David liked to sneak off from work to pursue his amateur
acting and writing career, and his earliest dated performance was in
1740 at 'Drury Lane' – the theatre he was to start managing seven
years later. Perhaps his most lasting contribution was to sweep away
the 'declamatory' style of acting for something altogether less formal –
a change that may have prompted Oliver Goldsmith to quip, 'On stage
he was natural, simple and affecting; 'twas only when he was off, he
was acting!'   *1717*

Homicidal Swiss miniature painter Theodore Gardelle committed
a life-size murder. A near neighbour of Sir Joshua Reynolds, he lived
with his landlady, Mrs Amelia King, at Leicester Fields in London.
This morning he sent the maid out to buy him some snuff, and when
she returned Mrs King had disappeared. He told the maid, as he told
all callers over the next few days, that the good woman had gone to
Bath. Then he made the fatal mistake of dismissing the maid, and
employing in her stead an inquisitive charwoman. When the plumbing
went wrong, the charwoman found an old water tub in the back

February 19

kitchen, and in it she discovered a pile of bloodstained bedclothes. The Bow Street Runners were summoned, hot-footed it to the scene of the crime, and found bits of Mrs King all over the house. Gardelle had apparently tried to burn her body piecemeal, but he didn't make a very good job of it. He was hauled off to Newgate prison where he twice tried to commit suicide, but failed on both occasions. He was sentenced to death anyway, and on the road to his execution the crowd, with somewhat superfluous enthusiasm, tried to lynch him.   *1761*

The worst crocodile attack in history took place on an island in the Bay of Bengal. In the battle for Burma, over 1,000 Japanese soldiers had been trapped in the mire, cut off from rescue and pounded with artillery and mortar fire by the assembled British forces. As darkness fell, another 'army' of huge and voracious crocodiles was attracted to the swamp by the smell of blood on the tide. All night long the British troops could hear the turmoil in the water as the huge reptiles snapped up the quick, the injured and the dead. By morning the battle was over and just twenty Japanese survivors could testify to the victory of the strangest allies the British have ever had.   *1945*

Today's the day...

King James I of Scotland was slain in a lavatory after his
sweeping liberal reforms inspired an assassination plot by a group of
powerful nobles. They followed him to the Black Monastery in Perth
where a fellow conspirator secretly removed the door bolts. About
midnight they stormed the King's quarters. Katherine Douglas, a lady-
in-waiting, put her arms through the bolt rings to hold the doors but
the assassins pushed so hard they snapped her arm in two.
The King ran and hid in a small private toilet but was quickly
discovered and, although he managed to kill two men, was fatally run
through with a sword. Within forty days all the murderers were
captured, horribly tortured and executed. Katherine recovered and
became known as 'Barlass' and as their family crest, all her descendants
have adopted a broken arm. *1437*

First American spaceman to enter earth's orbit was Lieutenant
Colonel John Glenn, aged forty, launched from Cape Canaveral
aboard *Friendship 7*. The flight was riddled with delays and faults and
the last orbit was flown entirely by manual control. The epic
mission lasted 4hrs 55mins at between 99 and 162 miles altitude
covering in three orbits a total of 81,000 miles. He dropped safely into
the sea and became a national hero. He received the largest ticker-tape
reception in the history of New York City – the Sanitation
Department estimated 3,474 tons of paper fell on the hero. He later
entered politics where again his rise to fame was hampered by a fall
which kept him out of campaigning for a year – he fell in his
bathtub. *1962*

The Englishman with the longest surname died of pneumonia in
the French trenches during World War I. His full name was Major
Leone Sextus Denys Oswolf Fraudati Tollemache-Tollemache de
Orellana Plantagenet Tollemache Tollemache. His men called him
'Sir'. *1917*

February 20

Old John Mealy-face, one of the stingiest men in Yorkshire, was
born in the Parish of Topcliffe near Thirsk. To make sure that his wife
didn't make sneaky loaves of bread in his absence, he would press his
face down in the flour and on his return would make sure that his
impression was still there.   *1784*

Master criminal Stephen Callaghan a twenty-two-year-old
Scotsman faced magistrates at Bedford for his part in an amazing
series of robberies. Unemployed and out of loot he spent his last £2
on a bottle of sherry and a toy gun. He then marched into a
newsagents in Luton and said, 'This is a stick up!' The young female
assistant, not understanding his broad accent, just looked at Callaghan
who pulled out his gun and said, 'Bang, bang.' She giggled and said,
'You're dead.' He ran down the street and tried the same caper in a
café where he told another girl cashier, 'I'm not joking,'; she just
laughed. Again he entered another store where the girl told him to
clear off. This time he proved he meant business by grabbing her, but
unfortunately he was immediately clobbered by two hefty male shop
assistants. He surrendered saying, 'This is the third store and all they
have done is laugh at me.' The court could hardly believe their ears.
Finally Judge Robert Lymbery QC put him on two years' probation
adding with judicial understatement, 'As a criminal you are thoroughly
incompetent, and not I think a potential danger.'   *1976*

Boy King Edward VI aged eight-and-a-half was crowned in
Westminster Abbey. To protect the new monarch the wet and frosty
streets were all freshly gravelled and new railings were installed to
hold back over-enthusiastic crowds. The short journey was made
tedious by endless speeches which Edward manfully endured. Light
relief came when he watched a tightrope-walker, balancing on a rope
tied between the summit of St Paul's and the Deanery Gate, glide down
to earth on his chest.   *1547*

Today's the day...

Mogul Emperor Aurungzebe died, murmuring happily that his soul was departing. For a devout Mohammedan – though not for a Mogul – his seizure of the throne was a little unorthodox. He imprisoned his father and murdered all his brothers. That done with, however, he dedicated himself to 'righteous government' and his reign is regarded as something of a golden age. He had a unique way of conquering kingdoms – he used a shoe. A golden slipper was enshrined in a magnificent howdah on the back of an equally magnificent elephant, and as the animal lumbered across the border, the king who was about to be conquered was supposed to meet it on foot, guide it to his palace and, with due reverence, place the slipper on his throne. If he knew what was good for him, that's exactly what he did. By playing this charming game of footsie, Aurungzebe brought a total of seventeen countries to heel. *1707*

The murderers of Sir Edmund Berry Godfrey were hanged on Primrose Hill, near where his body was found. Sir Edmund, who'd been knighted for bravery in the Great Plague of 1665, was the presiding magistrate in the case of a so-called Catholic conspiracy against King Charles II, 'revealed' by the devious and dubious Titus

Oates, and known as 'the Popish Plot'. The poor knight found himself tangled up in a wasps' nest of intrigue, and when he laid the matter before the Privy Council he was rebuked for 'meddling in so tender a matter'. He was very unhappy about it and believed he himself 'should be knocked on the head' for his involvement. In fact, he ended up in a ditch, with two sword wounds, a broken neck, bruises all over his chest and a rope burn around his throat. Strangely, there was no blood on his coat, no mud on his shoes, and no food in his stomach. His rings were still on his fingers, and a large sum of money in his pocket. The Catholics inevitably were blamed, and under torture Miles Prance, a silversmith in the Queen's Chapel, confessed only to be pardoned when he named his three accomplices, and later pilloried for perjury. The men went to their deaths protesting their innocence, and it's interesting to note that in those days Primrose Hill was known as Greenberry Hill. The men's names were Green, Berry and Hill. *1678*

Britain's most famous air ace Douglas Bader was born. Though at school he was better at games than studies, he earned himself a prize cadetship to the RAF College at Cranwell. He joined No. 23 Squadron at Kenley and in a bout of aerobatic hi-jinks at a nearby flying club he crashed his plane, and had to have both legs amputated. Despite the fact that with artificial limbs he could still fly – and proved it – he was invalided out until the war came, when the RAF no longer let his disability come between them and a good pilot. Within seven months he was Commanding 242 Squadron; won the DSO and the DFC; pioneered the tactically crucial mass fighter formation, and in August 1941 was shot down and captured. In the parachute landing one of his artificial limbs was badly damaged, and with a remarkably gentlemanly piece of behaviour, the Germans contacted the RAF and gave safe conduct for a British plane to fly in a replacement. With more spirit than gratitude, Bader made good use of the leg – and did his level best to escape. *1910*

Today's the day...

The world's first 'Woolworths' opened at Utica, New York – and closed three months later. Undeterred Frank Winfield Woolworth decided to open another store at Lancaster, Pennsylvania and extend his 'nothing over five cents' principle to include ten cent goods. It was a raging success and Frank was on his way to becoming a household name. As a boy his favourite game was 'playing store' and he'd worked unpaid for the village grocer just to gain experience. With a chain of stores across America, he decided to try his luck in Britain. The first store in Liverpool bemused shoppers with its well-stocked open counters; the second Liverpool store caused a riot, and crowd barriers had to be erected at the opening in Hull. Fred Woolworth and Bryon Miller were in charge of UK operations but Frank was still at the helm and ordered them to grow moustaches to look more commanding. So they did, every time they sailed to England – and every time they sailed back to America they shaved them off again! *1879*

The Austrian Ace racing driver Niki Lauda was born to a wealthy banking family in Vienna. Nicknamed 'the Clockwork Mouse', his singleminded determination helped him recover from his horrific crash at Nurburgring. Though his condition was so serious he was given the last rites, just thirteen months later he was driving in the Italian Grand Prix. *1949*

Gloomy old philosopher Arthur Schopenhauer was born in Danzig. His mother's apparent indifference to his father's suicide, and a severe bout of syphilis at university, hardened his views about women. He decided they were 'under-sized, short-legged creatures' created solely to tempt men's baser natures. Suspicious and full of passionate hatreds he believed that life was a curse and that the only way to get through it was to resign yourself to the fact. He survived by playing the flute, listening to the music of Beethoven and going for long walks with his poodle. *1788*

February 22

'The Father of America' George Washington was born at Bridges Creek, Virginia. His severe upbringing – he addressed his mother as 'Honourable Madam' – made him a dour man, who seldom smiled and rarely laughed. Spurned by the beautiful Sally Fairfax, he married plump and homely Martha Custis – who had the advantage of being the richest widow in the state. The $100,000 she brought him, combined with a 'lawyer's skill at drafting documents and a merchant's at keeping accounts', made him America's first millionaire. He was also the country's first mule breeder, and grew marijuana in his garden. A giant of a man, well over 6ft tall, strong framed and wearing size 13 boots, he always appeared deceptively calm and rational. However one of his many portrait painters Gilbert Stuart remarked that 'all his features were indicative of ungovernable passions'. These he kept on a tight rein – though it wasn't frustration that caused his characteristic clenched-jaw expression. It was badly-fitting false teeth!   *1732*

A dream of sunken treasure came true for William Phipps when he started to salvage a Spanish galleon. For years he'd dreamed of finding such a ship but in his native Maine, no one was willing to finance him. Phipps finally found a patron in England, the second Duke of Albemarle, and with his help he'd already led two unsuccessful expeditions. This time, with an extra ship and native divers, he'd discovered the *Almiranta*, which had plunged to the bottom forty-six years before. Using only strong knives and coral weights, the naked divers worked day after day for two months and raised over thirteen tons of silver ingots as well as silver plate, gold, pearls and emeralds. Ex-ship's carpenter Phipps sailed for England with his bounty and received not only his share of the loot but a knighthood and the Governorship of New England. Unfortunately the treasure-hunter wasn't exactly fitted for governmental duties. He quarrelled with the Governor of New York, got involved in brawls and was eventually recalled to answer for his behaviour.   *1687*

Today's the day...

The world's most remarkable diarist Samuel Pepys was born. For nine years of his life he kept his own unique and highly personal record of an age. In it, he tells of everything from his haircuts and the making of his famous periwig, to the movements of his bowels and his celebrated, unanaesthetised gallstone operation. Most noticeably of all, he tells of his sex life, of his many peccadilloes, the 'lewd' book he bought in a plain cover and the awful dénouement when his wife caught him with the maid, and by way of revenge, decided to pinch his nose with red hot tongs. *1633*

The awesome triple hanging of John Lee was enacted at Exeter jail. Convicted on largely circumstantial evidence of brutally murdering his employer, Miss Emma Ann Keyse, the nineteen-year-old Lee had protested his innocence. On the morning of the execution, he was uncannily calm, and laughed saying, 'You'll never hang me . . . You wait and see.' Executioner Berry arrived already unhappy with the new gallows, and led his victim to the scaffold. Lee stood on the trap door, pinioned and hooded. Berry threw the lever. The door creaked – but nothing happened. As the chaplain continued to intone the service, the frantic executioner stamped on the door, but still it wouldn't budge. Lee was led away. The door was tested and it worked. He was brought back, bound and hooded again, and this time Berry threw the lever with such force he bent it. Still nothing happened. Lee was taken to a nearby room. Again the door was tested and again it worked. Once more the victim was brought to the drop. But incredibly the door that was supposed to send him to his death still stayed firmly shut. The chaplain fainted and had to be held up by a warder. Berry was visibly shaken and the anguished Governor ordered a stay of execution. Lee's sentence was eventually commuted to life imprisonment, but the mystery of the door was never solved. Back in his cell, still cool as a cucumber, the condemned man ate a hearty breakfast. Ironically, the meal had been intended for his executioner, but unlike his victim, Berry couldn't face it!

1885

Lawn Tennis was patented by Major Walter Clopton Wingfield (retired) of Pimlico. Alternatively called 'sphairistike' or 'sticky', it borrowed most of its rules from similar outdoor sports that were being played in preference to the ancient enclosed-court game of 'Real Tennis'. Despite complaints of plagiarism, Wingfield marketed the equipment for 'sticky' in large wooden boxes at five guineas a throw. Two years later, down on its luck, the All England Croquet Club at Wimbledon sponsored the first lawn tennis championships. The winner, twenty-seven-year-old Spencer Gore, ran away with the match, but commented that the game was really too dull to be of any lasting interest.

1874

The Prince Regent was insulted in a way he'd no doubt have found hard to stomach. The Prince was an extremely rotund gentleman – not to say obese – and today his friend Lord Folkestone wrote of him: 'Prinney has let loose his belly', which as the awestruck peer then added 'now reaches his knees!'

1818

Today's the day...

Courageous Jacobite dandy James Radcliffe, 3rd Earl of
Derwentwater was executed on Tower Hill for his support of the
Stuart Rebellion of 1715. He appeared on the scaffold in a long wig of
flaxen curls, a beaver hat with a black plume, a black velvet suit and
high-heeled shoes with silver buckles, and while the executioners
argued over who should get his clothes, he inspected the block. Then
with a coolness that amazed spectators, he asked the executioners to
smooth it down a little – in case it bruised his neck.   *1716*

Toy-maker extraordinary Jacques de Vaucanson was born. He
created a tiny pianist that breathed, made an asp that attacked
Cleopatra's breast, and started on a man with a working heart, veins
and arteries. His masterpiece, however, was his duck – 'perhaps the
most wonderful piece of mechanism ever made'. Built life-size and
'bone-by-bone', it was complete to the last feather and walked,
quacked, drank and ate. Inside, its food was 'digested by clockwork
and dyed green', and much to the horror of the ladies, its droppings
were collected on a silver salver.   *1709*

February 24

Drury Lane Theatre suddenly burst into flames. The manager, playwright Richard Brinsley Sheridan, was in the House of Commons and when news was brought, the Speaker adjourned proceedings. Sheridan paused to complain about private interests being allowed to interrupt public business, and then returned to a coffee house near the Theatre, comforted by a bottle of port. A friend remarked that he was taking his disaster very calmly to which Sheridan replied, 'A man may surely be allowed to take a glass of wine by his own fireside.' *1809*

The King of French drag queens Henry III gave a spectacular ball. He appeared dressed as a woman, wearing a pearl necklace, three ruffs and an open blouse that exposed his hairy chest. *1576*

The ungallant King Matthias Corvinus of Hungary was born. He passed a law saying that all ladies-in waiting should sit in his presence, because they were so ugly that that way they'd be less of an eyesore. *1557*

Pious Imperial murderer the Emperor Charles V was born in Ghent, son of Philip and Joanna the Mad. From his father and grandfather he inherited the Netherlands, Spain and most of Germany and had to cope with a very aggressive France and Martin Luther's Reformation. He was betrothed ten times, married once, and found solace in making mechanical toys and clocks – which were always going wrong. 'Not even two watches can I bring to agree with each other, and yet fool that I was, I thought to govern so many nations.' In fact, it all got too much for him and he became the first Emperor to retire since Diocletian in 305. In his retirement, he continued to be an enthusiastic supporter of the Inquisition, and during his reign a total of 100,000 'protestant Netherlanders' were burned. It's likely that 'this one Holy Roman Emperor slew more Christians than all the pagan Roman Emperors put together'. *1500*

Today's the day...

The company that cleaned up was established by Hubert Cecil Booth, the inventor of the vacuum cleaner. A year earlier he'd seen a power-operated device that blew the dirt out of the way and since he'd been doused in dust, he became convinced the solution was to suck it up instead. He tried it out by sucking through a handkerchief and it worked, and soon his first machine was on the streets. It was huge and horse-drawn, and equipped with an 800ft hose for reaching into houses. It was called the 'noisy serpent' and Booth was frequently sued by cab-drivers because it made their horses bolt. The machine became distinctly trendy nevertheless. Hostesses asked for demonstrations at their *soirées* – and Booth supplied special transparent tubes so the fashionable guests could see the dirt sucked up!   *1902*

Ill-treated architect Sir Christopher Wren died. Probably his greatest single achievement had been to design and supervise the building of St Paul's, but it brought him nothing but trouble. There was a special penalty clause in his contract 'to suspend a moiety of the surveyor's salary until the said church be finished'; the commissioners never ceased to overrule his judgement and for all that, he was paid a measly £200 a year. He was buried in the crypt of his cathedral alongside his daughter who'd died twenty years earlier aged only twenty-six, and there's a lasting tribute to him in an inscription over the door. It says, 'If you seek his monument, look around you.'   *1723*

The condemned wit of Charley Peace stood him in good stead when he was hanged at Armley Jail in Leeds. Charley had been living respectably in a Victorian villa in Peckham, when it was discovered that this violin-playing churchgoer had tried to kill a policeman, was a confirmed housebreaker and had actually murdered a man in Sheffield. On his way to Leeds he made one last ditch attempt to escape by jumping off the train in his handcuffs, but when this was foiled, he cheerfully accepted his fate and admitted to another killing in

Manchester. He wrote his own funeral cards: 'Executed for that I done, but never intended', and sent many letters to his dubious relations exhorting them to live a religious life. On the morning of his execution he wondered if the executioner 'would cure this cough', complained about not having enough time in the toilet and 'the bloody rotten bacon', then delivered a pious little speech, before he was hanged by Marwood. He'd previously claimed to have met his executioner on a train and asked, 'If you ever have to do the job for me, be sure you grease the rope well to let me slip.' Marwood thought Charley was 'his best subject' and said, 'he passed off like a summer's eve!'   *1876*

'The greatest singer who ever lived' Enrico Caruso was born in the slums of Naples, one of twenty-one children, only three of whom survived infancy. Fastidious to a fault, he gargled frequently with warm salty water, took two baths a day and sung in them from music on a special rack, with an accompanist playing next door. He once had to work with a fellow singer who was not quite so particular, and was vociferous in his complaints. 'It is terrible to sing with one that doesn't bathe,' he said, 'but to be emotionated over by one who breathes garlic is impossible!'   *1873*

Eighty Indians were murdered for their scalps. They were members of the Raritan tribe who'd dared to attack Dutch settlers. Governor Kieft of the New Netherlands had offered a rival tribe 'ten fathoms of wampum' for every Raritan scalp they brought back and it set something of a precedent. Settlers started bounty hunting too and earned large amounts of money by virtually 'clearing' New Jersey and Southern New York of Indians before the Pilgrim Fathers even set sail. The awful irony of the situation was that while the Indians did bring back the odd head, arm or leg as a trophy, scalping was never an Indian custom. It was introduced by the white man and popularised by Kieft's bounty.   *1641*

Today's the day...

The faithful baboon soldier Private Jackie stayed with his wounded friend Albert Marr at the Battle of Agagia. Together they'd joined the Third South African Infantry, and Jackie in his special uniform smartly saluted his officers, lit cigarettes for his colleagues and made an outstanding guard. He saw front line action against both the Germans and Turks, and was wounded at Passchendaele while frantically piling up rocks to protect himself. His right leg was partly severed by shrapnel, but he licked up a saucer of chloroform and a field surgeon made a neat amputation. Jackie recovered, got a medal and a promotion to corporal, and at the Lord Mayor's procession he appeared astride a howitzer – captured by his own regiment.   *1916*

The self-made legend of Buffalo Bill began when William F. Cody was born on a farm in Iowa. When the family moved West and his father died, Bill became a cattle drover, Pony Express rider, friend to Wild Bill Hickok and thanks to some 'bad whisky', a medical orderly in the Kansas cavalry. Though he was later a buffalo hunter and army scout, Bill was never a war-hero; his rank of Colonel was an honorary one, and his reputation as an Indian fighter was based more or less on a single unfortunate incident when he killed and scalped Chief Yellow Hand. The truth is that Mr Cody drank a lot and told tall tales. The writer Ned Buntline published them, and overnight Bill was a star. He bought his 'dude-ranch', launched his Wild West Show and rode into myth dressed in white buckskin and doggedly believing his own image. When he was a Justice of the Peace, he used to marry people and say, 'What God and Buffalo Bill has joined together, let no man put asunder.'

1846

The smallest person who ever lived was born in Holland. One of a poor family of twelve normal sized children, Pauline Musters was exceptionally intelligent, spoke four languages fluently and grew only 7ins from birth to reach a strapping 23ins tall. Her parents cashed in on her diminutive stature, trained her as an acrobat and hired her out so often that she collapsed from overwork. To keep her going the family fed her whisky and at the age of twenty-two she died – the world's tiniest alcoholic.

1876

The miserly giant of literature Victor Hugo was born in Besançon, the son of a professional soldier. At seventeen, he was a 1,000-franc-a-year man, bathing his face in rosewater and wearing his hair long to accentuate 'his truly monumental forehead'. He was adored by the ladies, loved by King Louis XVIII and consequently hated by Emperor Napoleon III, who drove him into exile for eighteen years. Hugo was massively rich, but he kept not only his wife and daughters, but also his mistress on an extremely stingy allowance. He wrote one of the longest novels ever – *Les Misérables* – which runs to 1,995 pages and contains one sentence of no less than 823 words. But when it came to forking out for a cable to his publishers to find out how it was selling, he sent the shortest telegram ever. It said simply '?' and the publishers replied in kind with an affirmative '!'

1802

Today's the day...

Tough old 'Poker Alice' died aged seventy-nine. A genteel schoolteacher's daughter from Suffolk, she'd gone to America and was a widow and card sharp by the age of nineteen. Living from gambling, travelling from one frontier town to another, she dressed extravagantly, smoked long black cheroots and always carried a Colt ·45. In Deadwood, she married her arch rival William Tubbs and they became chicken farmers and adopted seven children. On William's death she was forced to go back to gambling to pay for his funeral, and when she was in her sixties she opened a gambling club in Fort Meade. One night after a tussle, she shot a man – though in fact she only intended to scare him off. She was found guilty, but the judge took pity on this silver-haired old lady and released her. Years later, she was rushed to hospital where a surgeon told her she desperately needed an operation, but it was a gamble. 'I've been taking gambles all my life,' she said, 'Go ahead and operate.' Sadly for Alice, she lost.   *1930*

The Reichstag went up in flames – exploding simultaneously from twenty different points. Hitler insisted it was either 'a sign from heaven' or the 'beginning of a communist rising', and used this very convenient disaster to help him take over Germany. A mentally sub-normal Dutchman, Martinus Van der Lubbe was accused of single-handedly setting fire to the building and was beheaded the following January. In 1967 a West Berlin court posthumously commuted his sentence to eight years in jail.   *1933*

A ghost's prediction came true when Borley Rectory burned to the ground. Known as 'the most haunted house in England', it had been the scene of a continuous and sophisticated ghost-hunt since 1929. It was claimed that at séances a French nun, Marie Lairre, had identified herself, saying she'd been strangled and her bones buried in the garden. Her spectre was seen both within the rectory and on the road to the nearby village, and strange writing appeared on the walls of the

February 27

rooms. Eleven months before the conflagration, another spirit calling itself 'Sunex Amures' prophesied how the rectory would go up in flames in a fire which would start 'over the hall'. It did, and as villagers watched the building crumble, they caught a glimpse of a cowled figure standing at one of the blazing windows – it bore the outline of a nun.

1939

Twice convicted murderer Walter Graham Rowland was hanged at Strangeways jail for the slaying of prostitute Olive Balchin whom he'd beaten to death with a hammer. Previously, he'd tried to strangle his wife and had succeeded in strangling his two-year-old daughter. In the very same death cell he left this morning, he'd been reprieved, and it looked as if the same thing might happen again when David Ware, a prisoner in Walton jail, Liverpool, confessed to Olive's murder. A month later, however, he recanted – said he did it 'out of swank' – and Rowland's execution went ahead. Four years later a woman was attacked with a hammer in Bristol and her assailant gave himself up at the nearest police station. His name was David Ware.

1947

Queen Victoria was libelled by the *Age* newspaper when she was an eleven-year-old princess. No action was taken, save an outraged letter to *The Times*, though what the scurrilous rag had suggested was that the heir to the throne had had to be wheeled in to her own birthday party because she was 'so weak in the ankles and legs'.

1831

Goldie the Eagle caused a sensation when he escaped from his cage at London Zoo. For over a fortnight the public were held spellbound by his exploits. He made front-page news every day; was cheered in the House of Commons, and caused traffic jams when 5,000 people turned up to watch him flit from tree to tree in Regents Park.

1965

Today's the day...

Classy killer and hoodlum Bugsy Siegel was born of poor Jewish parents in a slum in Brooklyn. He started a teenage protection racket by setting fire to market stalls, graduated to bootlegging and became New York's No. 1 hit man. Things got too hot for him, so he moved West to found nothing less than the gambling oasis of Las Vegas. 'Class – that's the only thing in life that counts,' he said, and as if to prove the point he had a passionate affair with a countess and began hobnobbing with stars like Cary Grant and Jean Harlow. It would have been interesting to know what they'd have thought if they'd known Bugsy had pioneered the 'stomach puncture routine' so corpses would sink in the river!   *1906*

'The Queen of the stage' French actress Rachel was born. She was exceedingly beautiful and a strange mixture of tragedienne, society lady and courtesan. Probably her most famous liaison was with the Prince Louis Philippe – sometime King of France. According to one less than delicate account of their first encounter, he sent her a card which read: *'Où? Quand? Combien?'* She was said to have written back instantly: *'Chez toi. Ce soir. Pour rien.'*   *1820*

February 28

The History of Tom Jones, a Foundling was published in six volumes, after its author Henry Fielding had spent nearly three years writing it. This rollicking romp of a book turned out to be one of the most influential of all English novels, though Fielding only got £700 for it and the critics disapproved of the naughty content. 'Everybody in it does what he or she ought to have done,' said one friendly reviewer, 'but I do not mean morally.' In 1896 Miss J. E. M. Fielding, a descendant of the author, expurgated the book – probably in answer to another critic Frederick Harrison, who ten years earlier had claimed that Tom Jones was 'so indecent that a Bowdlerised version would be scarcely intelligible'.

1749

Little John Dunlop tried out the first cycle tyres on his tricycle. The ten-year-old's daddy was John Boyd Dunlop, the Scottish veterinary surgeon. His prototype was prompted by the sight of little John's trike leaving great ruts in the lawn, and the originals were made of garden hose filled with water. The surprising thing was that Dunlop's pneumatic tyre was not the first. Robert Thompson had invented one in 1845 – but although he patented the idea, no one would use it. Dunlop didn't know of Thompson's patent when he came up with his tyre, but said that if he had, he wouldn't have bothered to get his registered, 'but would probably have kept it for my son's amusement only'.

1888

The first woman 'L' driver to sue her instructor did so in the High Court in London. She was the fifty-five-year-old Mrs Gladys Gibbons who, on her nineteenth driving lesson, had crashed into a tree. She claimed the instructor Howard Priestley should have taken steps to stop the crash, but the judge said it all happened so fast that unless Mr Priestley were an Olympic gymnast he couldn't possibly have done so. Three quarters of Mr Priestley's pupils are women. 'Most of them pass the test', he said, 'in the end.'

1978

Today's the day...

Speedy greedy composer Gioacchino Rossini was born to a trumpet player and touring soprano at Pesaro in Italy. His first opera was performed when he was only eighteen – but his second was closed by the police for being obscene. Incredibly he wrote the *Barber of Seville* in three weeks, panicking after the date of the performance had been brought forward, and frantically borrowing from his own – and everybody else's – work to get all the music together in time. In fact, it turned out so well that even dour old Beethoven praised it. At the height of his fame, Rossini sang duets with George IV, was given a snuff box by the Czar of Russia, settled down to a cosy sinecure in Paris – and didn't write a thing for nearly thirty years. In the meantime, he turned his attention to his second love – food. '*Tournedos rossoni* were named after him, and in fact he indulged his gourmet greed so much that a large portion of his dining table had to be cut out to accommodate his enormous paunch.   *1792*

The calendar usually hiccups and unless it's a leap year passes straight on to tomorrow. It doesn't happen every four years as everybody thinks it does, but only when the year can be exactly divided by four. That's except for centenary years, of course, which have to be divided exactly by 400. There was no today in 1900 but in the year 2000 there will be. W.S. Gilbert blamed it all on 'an ill-natured fairy'!
                                                  Every four years . . . occasionally

'The white man's farthest outpost' Deerfield, Massachusetts was attacked before dawn by a combined force of over 300 French and Indians from Canada. Though there was a sentry on watch, the marauders approached silently in the deep snow, massacred forty-seven inhabitants in their beds and carried off 120 more. Among the prisoners were the Reverend John Williams and his daughter Eunice. The Reverend eventually wrote a bestseller about his experiences, but Eunice never returned – for she married the Indian who caught her.

February 29

One of the main objects of the raid had been to take the bell which hung over the Deerfield meeting house. Shipped over from France, it had been captured by a privateer and innocently bought by the ill-fated citizens. What they didn't know was that the bell was originally destined for a tribe of Canadian Indians.   *1704*

The man with the longest name in the world was born in Bergedorf, near Hamburg. He was actually called Adolph Blaine Charles David Earl Frederick Gerald Hubert Irvin John Kenneth Lloyd Martin Nero Oliver Paul Quincy Randolph Sherman Thomas Uncas Victor William Xerxes Yancy Zeus – a Christian name for every letter of the alphabet – and his surname was Wolfeschlegelsteinhausenbergerdorft, Snr. Actually this was only an abbreviation of his full surname, which had a total of 590 letters. So tiresome did it all become that the gentleman, who moved to Pennsylvania, shortened it to Mr Wolfe + 585, Snr.   *1904*

'The woman clothed with sun' Mother Ann Lee, founder of the once thriving American Shakers, was born in Toad Lane, Manchester. Though illiterate, she was already a keen Shaking Quaker when she married Abraham Standerin, 'a man who loved his beef and beer', and when her four children died in infancy she became seriously ill. Celibacy, she decided, was the only holy state but few agreed with her – least of all her husband – and she was imprisoned for her preaching. With seven followers, including her recalcitrant spouse, she fled to America in 1774. Aboard ship, their ecstatic 'shaking' in prayer so annoyed the captain that he threatened to throw them overboard. But he soon changed his tune when the ship sprang a leak from a loosened plank. 'Not a hair of our heads shall perish,' said Mother Ann after a quick vision, 'and we shall arrive safely in America.' As she spoke a powerful wave struck the vessel and forced the loose plank miraculously back into place.   *1736*

Today's the day...

The perfect Englishman actor David Niven was born in Kirriemuir, Scotland. Sent to public school – a fate he described as 'cruelty to animals' – he failed his Royal Navy entrance exams, and ended up as an officer in the Highland Light Infantry, a bridge-builder and barman. In Hollywood, he was registered as Anglo-Saxon type 2008, though in fact in his first twenty-seven films, he played only Mexicans. His climb to fame was steady, rather than spectacular and was greatly assisted by his friendship with the likes of Bogart and Flynn – though when Bogey first met him he thought he was 'a really pissy Englishman'. Come World War II, Niven returned to the British Army. In one attack, he was said to have rallied his men with the cry: 'Come on you chaps. It's all very well for you – you'll only have to do it once. I'll have to go through it all again in five years' time with Errol Flynn!' Perhaps of all his adventures, the strangest occurred at Jersey Zoo, where he performed a marriage ceremony between two gorillas and was later godfather to their son.   *1910*

Cataleptics could rest easy when an Austrian patented a design for 'the saving of buried living persons'. His 'device' was connected by an air-line to the coffin, so that non-corpses could comfortably raise the alarm. In fact, the premature burial was a real danger in those days, and many people left instructions in their wills for test procedures to check they were dead. A favourite was the lopping off of fingers or toes! *1887*

The world's most infamous kidnapping occurred when baby Charles Lindbergh, son of the record-breaking aviator, was snatched from the upstairs nursery of the family's luxury New Jersey home by an intruder using a home-made ladder. On the window-sill was a ransom note demanding $50,000, along with the reassurance that 'the child is in gut care'. With stunning insight, a handwriting expert concluded that the writer was 'a German of meagre education'. The money was duly paid to 'a foreigner' in a Bronx cemetery who gave instructions that the child would be found in a boat in Massachusetts. It was a cruel lie and two months later the decomposing body was found only four miles from home. The ransom money was marked and traced to a thirty-six-year-old carpenter named Bruno Hauptman. He had a stash of marked bills and it was proved that the rungs of the ladder had come from his house. Though he protested his innocence, he was condemned to die – while ghouls outside the courtroom sold ten-cent kidnap ladder pendants as souvenirs. Strangely, when the nurse had first discovered the child was missing, she hadn't worried. By a gruesome coincidence, Lindbergh Snr had recently played a practical joke and had hidden the baby in a cupboard.   *1932*

An elephant went berserk in London at the Royal Menagerie in The Strand. For seventeen years, the twenty-two-year-old Chunee had been kept in cramped quarters, supposedly tranquillised with hundred-weight doses of salt. Finally, he could stand the frustration no more, and smashed the bars of his cage. Fearing terrible consequences, his keepers shot him repeatedly in the chest and he rushed round in agony 'with the speed of a racehorse'. He was shot several more times in the ear and eventually collapsed 'as if he'd lain down to rest'. Six days later, two large and rather high steaks were cut from his rump and eaten, and it was reported that the diners 'expressed no disrelish for this novel food'.   *1826*

Hundreds of ladies had a smashing time in two of London's most prestigious shopping centres, Oxford Street and Regent Street. At a pre-arranged moment, over 200 militant suffragettes produced hammers from their muffs and in one huge, synchronised attack smashed nearly every shop window in sight. Public outrage was accurately captured by an article in the *Standard* – which not only decried the militants' 'public degradation of woman-hood', but ended with the condemnation: 'It's worse than wicked, it's vulgar.'   *1912*

Today's the day...

Louis XVI improved the guillotine. Along with executioner Sanson, Dr Guillotin had come to the Tuileries to show his design to the king's physician. During their meeting Louis slipped into the room and took an interest in their discussion. A locksmith in his spare time, he'd some experience of mechanical instruments and pointed out that the crescent shaped blade wasn't practical: with all the varying sizes of neck 'it would be too wide for thin ones and too narrow for thick'. He suggested a blade with a slanting edge that could suit 'all sizes' and shear through them more quickly too. Little did he realise that barely nine months later his own neck would feel the sharpness of *Madame Guillotine*.   *1792*

***Pioneer 10* blasted off the earth** faster than anything else had ever done before. Its mission was to become the first space vehicle to break out of the solar system. Taking only eleven hours to reach the moon compared with *Apollo 17*'s eighty-nine, it survived the dangers of the asteroid belt and is now expected to continue travelling for at least another two million years.   *1972*

Faking fighter Kid McCoy became world welterweight champion when he beat Tommy Ryan in Long Island, USA. It's said that he approached Ryan, made up to look like a dying consumptive, and asked him for a fight. He was so convincing that Ryan didn't even bother to train and was amazed when his 'ailing' opponent sprang into life in the fifteenth round and knocked him out cold. After his great performance Kid was very careful to be billed as 'The Real' McCoy to show that his play-acting days were over.   *1896*

De Gaulle's premature death was hallowed with the *Légion d'Honneur* – fifty-four years before he actually died. He'd been in the thick of the fighting at the Battle of Verdun and was so badly wounded that he was left for dead. Unknown to General Pétain, who issued the honour, he'd been picked up by a German patrol and was now a convalescent prisoner. He made five bids to escape, but was caught every time – his lanky 6ft 4in frame gave him away. Officially he was allowed to keep the medal – dead or alive.

1916

The earliest cuckoo ever was heard and seen in Wantage, Oxfordshire. Over the years, hearing its call has provoked flurries of letters to *The Times* newspaper. Because it's so easy to imitate, letter writers have to be careful how they spot it too, or they may suffer the fate of R. Lydekker. Six days after reporting it in 1913, he had to send an apologetic note when he discovered 'the full double note' he'd heard was made by 'a bricklayer's labourer'.

1972

The first Concorde took off and zoomed across France. Flying at supersonic speeds in temperatures as low as minus 150°C, the windows of the flight deck are specially vulnerable. So, they're made up of thick glass panes with a coating of gold. You can't see the gold because it's two-millionths of an inch thick.

1969

Today's the day...

'The Blonde Bombshell' Jean Harlow was born Harlean Carpentier in Kansas City, USA. Her first major film role was in *Hell's Angels*, when her apparent sexuality caused a sensation and she coined the immortal line, 'Pardon me, while I slip into something more comfortable.' After a decade of flat-busted flappers her cleavage was riveting, and film-makers made the most of it by putting her into skin-tight sateen gowns or drenching her to the skin to make her clothes stick. Not surprisingly, when she was offered a new part, she'd ask, 'What kind of whore am I this time ?' Inevitably, she was stalked by scandal. Her second husband was found shot dead in the nude, and she divorced her third because 'he read in bed'. A fourth marriage to William Powell was in the offing, when she was making *Saratoga*, but she fell ill. Her mother refused her medical treatment on religious grounds, and within days she died of uremic poisoning. In her brief seven years of success, she'd had to put up with a lot. When she met Margot, Lady Asquith, she asked whether the 'T' was silent. 'Yes' replied Lady Asquith 'as in Harlow.'   *1911*

Forty-nine years in bed came to an end when William Sharp died where he lay at 'The World's Farm' in Keighley, Yorkshire. At thirty this thrifty farmer had been left at the altar by his true love after a disagreement over the marriage settlement. The trauma was too much for him and so he took to his bed. Over the years, his hair grew long and white, and his nails like claws. His legs gradually atrophied and one caller described him as a 'mass of inanimate matter'. So twisted were his limbs that when he was buried, his coffin had to be made 2ft 4in deep, and out of bed for the first time in ages, it took eight men to lower him into his grave.   *1856*

Bizet's *Carmen* was first performed at the Opéra Comique in Paris. The audience didn't think it was very funny, in fact they thought it was awful and jeered Bizet as he fled from the theatre. The critics

March 3

deemed it 'painful, noisy, blatant and eminently repulsive', and Bizet died broken-hearted three months later. Though *Carmen* is now one of the most popular of all operas, it has been given some pretty bizarre performances. It's been staged in a bull ring with real bulls; Beatrice Lillie played Carmen in a kilt, and one enterprising producer made the opera into a silent movie.   *1875*

The inventor of the telephone Alexander Graham Bell was born in Edinburgh. His mother was deaf and both his father and grandfather dedicated themselves to teaching the deaf to speak. Bell himself went to teach at the school for the deaf in Boston where he fell madly in love with Mabel Hubbard who, like his mother, was also deaf. Surprisingly, it was she who persuaded him to turn his attention from teaching to his pet idea, the telephone. Having made his fortune, Bell retired to devote his time to the problems of dynamic flight, and breeding twins from sheep. Ironically, he found telephone calls were a constant interruption, and so before he started work, he'd put his own invention out of action – by stuffing it with paper!   *1847*

Today's the day...

Over-enthusiastic vicar William Davy was born. Super-keen
on theology, his parishioners complained of his long-winded
abstract sermons and no one would support his scheme to write *A
Compendium of the Evidence of the Origin of the Christian Faith.*
Undeterred Davy completed his book, built his own printing press
and started to print it himself. Unfortunately he could only afford to
buy enough type for four pages at a time, so he had to set four, run
off the copies, then break up the type and set four more. With the
help of his servant, he laboured for fifty years and finally produced
the complete work in twenty-six volumes of 500 pages each.
Triumphantly he went to see his bishop and proudly presented him
with a copy. Lazily the bishop flicked through it and remarked, 'I
cannot be supposed to notice every trifle that appears in print.'   *1743*

Walt Disney's *Cinderella* was released. One of the moments in the
film which had the audience gasping was when the Prince drops the
glass slipper on the ground and it smashes to smithereens. But in the
original story Cinderella wasn't wearing dainty glass slippers at all.
Perrault who transcribed it from medieval French mistook the word
'*vair*' to mean glass. What it actually means is fur, so Cinderella
originally went off to the ball in fluffy fur slippers.   *1950*

A dubious honour for a star-gazer went to John Flamsteed when
he was appointed the first Astronomer Royal by Charles II. At the
time there was no observatory so Flamsteed had to work in the Tower
at Greenwich – formerly reserved for mistresses of royalty. £520 was
hurriedly raised from the sale of spoilt gunpowder, Sir Christopher
Wren designed a building and it was hastily built out of second-hand
materials. A year later Flamsteed entered this splendid new Royal
Observatory only to find there were no instruments. Not only that but
his only assistant was 'a surly labourer' and he had to teach two boys
from Christ's Hospital as well as 'rectify the tables of the motions of

March 4

the heavens' – all for £100 a year (£90 after tax). Flamsteed begged, borrowed, bought the minimum of instruments and took on 140 pupils to subsidise himself. Fourteen years later he'd catalogued 2,935 stars in his *Historia Coelestis* and it still wasn't complete. Against Flamsteed's wishes 400 copies were published, but he got his own back – he got hold of 300 and burnt them.   *1675*

The Queen joined the Army. Anxious to do her bit for the war effort, Princess Elizabeth finally persuaded George VI to let her join the ATS at Camberley. Every morning Second Subaltern Windsor No 230873 was driven to the camp and spent the day learning how to read maps, drive in convoy and strip and service an engine – often ended up covered in oil in greasy overalls. After taking her final test, the Princess was allowed to drive her company commander up from Aldershot to Buckingham Palace in the thick of London's traffic – and went round Piccadilly Circus twice on the way.   *1945*

The one-day President David Rice Atchison took the helm of the United States of America and he stayed with it – all day. President Polk's term of office had expired, but his successor Zachary Taylor refused to be sworn in on a Sunday. As President of the Senate, Mr Atchison automatically became President in the interim. He confessed afterwards that he slept all day – his entire term of office.   *1849*

Cool-headed racing driver Jim Clark was born. Quietly spoken, with a very calm approach to racing, he won twenty-five Formula One races to beat Juan Fangio's record of twenty-four. His equanimity wasn't even disturbed at Indianapolis in 1966 when he hit a patch of oil at 160mph. The car slithered out of control and started going backwards down the track. Clark calmly steered it into another spin until it was facing the right way. Then he put his foot down and carried on to take second place.   *1936*

Today's the day...

'Man of Steel' the Russian communist leader Joseph Stalin died aged seventy-three in circumstances that are never likely to be explained. Conflicting reports said he'd passed away both at a conference in the Kremlin and at his country *dacha* fifty miles from Moscow. Whatever really happened, he was laid in an open coffin in the Lenin Mausoleum. Moscow Radio announced that five million mourners filed past in seventy-two hours – and an American accountant worked out that if that were true, they'd have had to run past two abreast, three paces apart at a record breaking speed of 22 mph. *1953*

The first Plantagenet King Henry II was born to Geoffrey of Anjou and the English ex-princess and Empress, Mathilda. He grew to be a huge red-haired man with 'an enormous paunch' which he tried to get rid of by taking 'immoderate exercise', and apart from when he was riding, he hardly ever sat down. He married Eleanor of Aquitaine who'd been in the Holy Land where she was said to have been 'in carnal familiarity with a Turk'. She did the proposing and bore him four sons, all of whom hated him as she did. Henry's favourite lady was Rosamund Clifford, whom he hid in 'a labyrinth' near Woodstock. Unfortunately Queen Eleanor found her there and Rosamund died mysteriously shortly afterwards. Her body was taken to a nunnery but Hugh, Bishop of Lincoln, ordered her bones scattered 'as those of an harlot'. The nuns gathered them together again and kept them for Henry in a perfumed bag. *1133*

The fascist in drag 'Colonel Barker' was arrested for bankruptcy and found to be a woman. Her real name was Lillias Arkell-Smith and after an unsuccessful marriage, a long-standing love affair and two children, she decided she'd make a better life as a man. She disguised herself thoroughly, opened an antique shop, worked as a male actor, hunted and played cricket, joined Oswald Mosley's English Nazis, marched to the Cenotaph bedecked in phoney medals and actually married a woman! There was a great outcry in court when she was discovered; she was sentenced to nine months for making a false statement on a marriage register and was hurriedly transferred from Brixton Jail to the woman's prison at Holloway. She died years later in a quiet Suffolk village where she'd lived as 'Geoffrey Norton' – described by a local policeman as 'a big fattish man weighing about twenty stone, with a deep voice and his hair brushed back'.   *1929*

'The Dirty Duke' Charles Howard of Northumberland was born. 'Destitute of grace and dignity', he was a terrible rake and a drunkard, and was only ever clean when his servants dumped him in the bath in an alcoholic stupor. He sired lots of illegitimate children, all with 'blue eyes, Jewish noses, gipsy skins and woolly black hair grafted on to the unmistakable Howard features'. He did at least pay for their upkeep, but when their mothers came to collect, he'd spy on them from the back parlour and if any of them still took his fancy, he'd call them in and give them 'a generous lecture on morality', exhorting them to lead a more respectable life.   *1746*

Today's the day...

A robber turned confidence-trickster when Homer Van Meter joined the new Dillinger gang for its very first raid – the old one was mostly in prison. The victim was a bank in Sioux Falls, South Dakota, and in the middle of it all, there was some shooting and gang-member Tommy Carroll managed to round up the town's entire police force. A crowd of people stood by and watched, but they didn't try to do anything because the previous day a Hollywood producer had been rushing round telling everyone he was going to be shooting a gangster film there. The producer's name was Homer Van Meter.   *1934*

Jazz was first in the news when the word was used by Peter Tamony in an article in the *San Francisco Bulletin*. Though this was its *début* in print, the word had been heard in the lyrics of Southern black music years before and was presumed to mean 'dancing'. White authorities later spotted that it had an overtly sexual meaning, but on this occasion it was used rather obscurely in a sports report to describe a keen baseball player.   *1913*

A bird brained ornithologist released sixty pairs of starlings in New York's Central Park. His idea was to start a flying memorial to Shakespeare by importing every species of bird mentioned in the Bard's thirty-seven plays. Unfortunately in the case of *Sturnus vulgaris*, he was more successful than he could have hoped, for the starling is now America's worst avian pest and millions of them wreak millions of dollars' worth of damage every year.   *1890*

The first recorded gurning match in Australia took place on Batman's Hill, at the first ever horse races in Melbourne. Gurning is of course, crudely speaking, the noble old English art of pulling faces, but this particular antipodean variation was actually referred to as 'Grinning'. The five ugliest inhabitants stuck their heads through a horse collar and grimaced for all they were worth. The winner was

March 6

fifty-year-old Tom Curnew whose 'lips and palate were drawn in as if to be swallowed', and whose 'chin and forehead approached as if to meet'. Afterwards, everyone retired to the local hostelry where they consumed the entire 'limited stock of bad champagne'.   *1838*

The gross-featured genius Michelangelo di Lodovico Buonarroti-Simoni was born in Arezzo, where he claimed he 'sucked-in chisels and hammers' with his nurse's milk. He was not a pretty sight, for his temples stuck out beyond his ears, his ears beyond his cheeks and his massive forehead overhung his broken nose. Thus handicapped, his enormous talents were nevertheless brought on by Lorenzo de' Medici and indulged intermittently by successive popes. Michelangelo was aggressive, cantankerous, extroverted and homosexual, and he got more than his fair share of criticism. El Greco said he was 'an admirable man, but he knew nothing of painting'. A less friendly contemporary thought his work would be 'more at home in a brothel', while Pope Paul VI commissioned Volterra to go over 'The Judgement' and clothe the hosts of nudes. The poor man was referred to ever after as '*Il Braghettone*' – 'the Breeches Maker'.   *1475*

The first frozen foods appeared in grocery stores in Springfield, Massachusetts. They had been developed, believe it or not, by Brooklyn born Mr Clarence Birdseye who patented the process in the early twenties and had sold his company the year before for a cool twenty-two million dollars. Birdseye, who was fond of saying the credit should have gone to the Eskimos, first got the idea while he was doing a US Government fish and wildlife survey in Labrador. He saw 'the natives' catching fish in 50° F below and of course, the poor little creatures were frozen the minute they came out of the water. Vegetables were at a premium that far north, so inventive old Clarence tried freezing them too. In fact, later associates said he'd try anything – and on one occasion he produced the first frozen alligator meat.   *1930*

Today's the day...

The murdering maidservant Sarah Malcolm was hanged for the slaying of her mistress and two colleagues. She'd robbed them too, and when first taken to Newgate, £53 was found hidden in her hair. Sarah was a great one for publicity. Two days before her execution she dressed in red and posed for Hogarth, and on her way to the gallows she rouged her cheeks and chatted with her admirer, the Reverend Mr Paddington. Her dead body was exhibited for money by her undertakers; it was dissected and with an obscure turn of logic her skeleton was sent to the Cambridge Botanical Gardens. *1737*

England's pretend prophet Samuel Best died aged eighty-seven. He'd long since disowned his children and gone to live in the Shoreditch workhouse, calling himself 'Poor-help' and claiming he was a palmist. He told people's fortunes in rapid recitations of the scriptures, diagnosed their ailments by licking their hands and didn't sleep but 'conversed nocturnally' with the celestial powers. Such gobbledegook made him a tremendous hit with the upper classes and he died in commodious apartments, mollycoddled and convinced that single-handed, he'd rebuild Jerusalem. *1827*

March 7

American Superprude Antony Comstock was born. His mother died when he was ten, and over the years he channelled his vague feelings of guilt into a strange kind of censoriousness. He broke into a liquor store and poured all the booze away and then, intoxicated with his success, he formed the New York Society for the Suppression of Vice, was given virtually police powers and a percentage of all the fines he collected. In one year, he boasted he'd driven sixteen wicked people to their deaths; appropriated 194,000 naughty photos and 134,000lbs of books, which he said were 'the feeders of brothels'. He described George Bernard Shaw as 'an Irish smut dealer' and prosecuted one poor man for printing pictures of women in woolly underwear.

1844

'The Lonely Hearts Killers' Fernandez and Beck were executed. Hawaiian-born Raymond Fernandez had made a profession of seducing lonely women and swindling them out of their money. He met fat and thrice-married nurse Martha Beck and she said she'd like to join him, but suggested they murdered the women too. In two years, they killed twenty or more unfortunate ladies, including a young widow and her two-year-old daughter whose bodies were found in a cellar. Once arrested, the killers admitted everything and details of their sexual activities were 'so indecent' they were never published. In Sing Sing they waved to each other across the yard and were still declaring their undying love when they went to the electric chair.

1951

Kim the Korean genius was born, the son of parents who were both university professors born on the same day in the same year at exactly the same time. The brainy babe was soon writing poetry, spoke four languages and understood integral calculus by the time he was only 4yrs 8mnths old. Not surprisingly, Kim's IQ has been clocked up at 210 – the highest ever recorded.

1963

Today's the day...

A royal fit of the ague killed King William III. Doctors thought it
had been brought on by the shock of a riding accident that had
occurred a little over two weeks before. The King had been riding his
favourite horse 'Sorrel' in the park at Hampton Court, when the
animal had stepped into a mole-hole and fallen to its knees. William
went over the top and broke his collar bone and he was never well
again. Thereafter his enemies the Jacobites used to like to raise a toast
to the mole – 'the little gentleman in the velvet jacket'.   *1702*

A canine rescue took place when two little boys fell into the old
Grosvenor Canal near Pimlico. Both sank and 'their lives were greatly
imperilled' when Mr Ryan, an actor, happened by with his
Newfoundland dog. Guided by pebbles thrown by a bystander the
dog saved both boys, and was delighted to see them again at a special
dinner given in his honour. Since he was a puppy, the dog had been
called 'Hero'.   *1834*

A scorpion stung an Indian boy – only he was no ordinary boy,
but the thirteen-year-old Satyanarayana, which means 'true, all-
pervading God' – and something distinctly odd was about to happen.
The boy fell unconscious and when he awoke, he began to laugh and
cry, perform great feats of strength and recite poetry he could never
have heard before. Finally, he announced he had become the guru Sai
Baba – a reincarnation of another of that name – and soon after he
'materialised' some 'holy wood ash' to prove it. Since then, Sai Baba
has become for some 'the most impressive holy man for centuries',
while for others he's just another guru. He's said to be a great healer,
and has often been reported to cure people by taking their affliction
on himself and making a 'miraculous' recovery. He's been said to be
able to change rocks into sweets and flowers into diamonds – so when
he says, 'No one can understand my mystery,' it's not difficult to see
why.   *1940*

Mole's creator the author Kenneth Grahame was born. He was first a clerk and then the Secretary of the Bank of England, and though he gradually achieved acclaim as a writer he would never give up the security of the Bank to write full-time. He married his wife Elspeth late in 1899 and had an only son called Alistair, who sadly was killed by a train when he was twenty. For him Grahame created not only Mole, but Rat and Toad and Badger and the rest – and when it came to the summer holidays, Alistair refused to go off to Littlehampton unless his father promised to write him an instalment every day. He did – and of course the result was *The Wind in the Willows*.   *1859*

The Crimson Flash – the Australian sprinter with the unlikely name of Arthur Postle was born in Pittsworth, near a place with the even more unlikely name of Toowoomba. He became an immortal in antipodean athletics, clocking up a whole series of world records from 5.1 seconds for the 50yds to 19 seconds for the 200yds. He claimed that his secret was that he had trained his feet to do anything his hands could do. 'I could almost thread a needle,' he said, 'with my toes.' *1882*

A shaggy dog story was exposed in court and Christopher Mannion, the man who told it, was fined £150. When he'd been stopped by police for speeding he'd shown them a licence in Charles Mannion's name and when they checked up on it, it turned out that Christopher had actually taken a second driving test on Charles' behalf. He'd done it for a joke, and the reason that neither the police nor the magistrates were amused was not only the basic illegality, but the fact that Charles wasn't a man – he was a golden labrador.   *1978*

The cheekiest escape in Australian history took place when Moondyne Joe fooled guards into thinking he was asleep by draping his clothes over a sledge hammer used for breaking rocks. Then he just walked out of the forbidding Fremantle Prison in his underpants and boots.   *1867*

Today's the day...

Jumbo the elephant's fate was sealed when despite protests from Queen Victoria and *The Times*, the Court of Chancery declared his sale to P. T. Barnum legal and binding. All England had been horrified when they'd heard the great favourite of London Zoo was to be sold, and even Jumbo refused to co-operate. Taken out of his cage to be loaded, he just lay down and wouldn't budge. Similar antics went on for six weeks; the newspapers were delighted and told the heart-rending story of the poor lad not wanting to leave his home and his friends. Strangely enough it was true – or at least a part of it – for only after Jumbo's keeper had been given leave to accompany him to America did they manage to get him crated up, and down to the docks. Hoisted aboard the *Assyrian Monarch* Jumbo objected briefly, then settled down quietly to his transatlantic crossing. He'd been tranquillised rather unsubtly with vast amounts of beer.   *1882*

Napoleon took Josephine for his lawful wedded wife. Engrossed in plans for his Italian campaign, he'd forgotten his nuptials completely, turned up two hours late and had to wake the registrar who by now had fallen asleep. Both bride and groom gave their ages as twenty-eight, though in fact, Napoleon was only twenty-seven and Josephine was pushing thirty-three, a widow and a bit short of teeth. With only two days to go before he had to leave Paris for the fighting, Napoleon rushed his new wife off to her bedroom and launched into his love-making with characteristic brevity and enthusiasm.   *1796*

Monkish chess master Bobby Fischer was born in Chicago. He hates teachers, women and ready-made clothes; loves to see his opponent's 'ego crumble' and won't join a gym because they're 'too low-class with too much riff-raff'. An enthusiastic member of the 'Worldwide Church of God', he was last seen in Pasadena, sticking leaflets on cars telling people they were controlled by 'the Satanic secret world government'.   *1943*

The world's toughest army, the French Foreign Legion, was founded by King Louis Philippe. In true Beau Geste tradition, legionnaires still sign under a pseudonym, *'nom de guerre'*, but now the Legion checks their real identity to make sure they've never been involved in serious crime. There are three applicants for every place, despite the traditionally harsh discipline. One recent account stated that as a punishment, wrongdoers were made to clear leaves with their teeth and lick concrete clean with their tongues.   *1831*

The first man in space was born on a collective farm near Smolensk. He was, of course, the diminutive Yuri Gagarin and his surname means 'wild duck'. He was blasted skywards – all 5ft 2in of him – in 1961 and his epoch-making flight around the globe made him internationally famous. Tragically he died seven years later, but for a while at least he was a worldwide celebrity. He became a hero of the Soviet Union, went on a tour of foreign capitals and, no doubt much to his surprise, Comrade Gagarin ended up having lunch at Buckingham Palace with the Queen.   *1934*

Today's the day...

An ingenious hat-tipper was patented for 'automatically effecting polite salutations'. A cunning weighting system inside the gentleman's hat caused a block to swing which pushed a rod which released a stud which stressed a spring which tipped the hat to salute the ladies – even if the gentleman had his arms full.   *1869*

The first ever Cruft's Dog Show was held in London. It was a great success, and the first 'Top Dog' was a terrier – though that wasn't really surprising since the other 599 entrants were terriers too. Since then, just about every other dog has had its day, including 'Bossyboots' a twelve stone St Bernard, and a dainty toy poodle who answered to the name of Oakington Puckeshill Amber Sunblush.   *1886*

The Irish giant Cornelius MacGrath was born in Tipperary. 7ft 3in in his stocking-feet, he first attracted attention in Cork when he was sixteen and crowds followed him everywhere he went. He toured London and the European capitals, and back home in Dublin was a great favourite with students at Trinity College. When he died, aged only twenty-three, they were at great pains to obtain his body for the Anatomy School. Heavily disguised, four students went to his wake, dosed the liberal supply of whisky with laudanum and carried his body out over the unconscious bodies of the mourners. By the time they came to, Cornelius had already been dissected.   *1736*

'Bertie' got married. The rakish Edward, Prince of Wales, took Alexandra of Denmark for his wife in the first royal wedding held in St George's Chapel, Windsor, since 1361. The day before, Queen Victoria had taken her eldest and his bride to Prince Albert's mausoleum, where she'd morbidly assured them, 'He gives you his blessing.' At the wedding, she sat apart from the congregation wearing 'a hideous widow's cap' and surrounded by her ladies-in-waiting – all dressed in black. Alexandra arrived with her eyes and 'the tip of her nose . . . a tiny bit red' as if she'd been crying. She'd had to give up her beautiful gown of Brussels lace because it was 'unpatriotic' and was wed instead in a dress that was bedecked in orange blossom and myrtle and 'too much sunk in greenery'. After a magnificent 'standing lunch', the newlyweds drove off to Osborne for a week, and most of the guests were hurried off back to London by special train. It was terribly overcrowded and the Duchess of Westminster ended up in a third-class carriage – wearing half a million pounds' worth of diamonds.   *1863*

A phone call for help made history when Alexander Graham Bell summoned his assistant, Mr Watson, from the basement at 5 Exeter Place, Boston. Deserted by his patrons Bell had struggled on with his experiments and set up the mouthpiece of a telephone in his laboratory, with the receiver in Mr Watson's room. Today Bell spilt some acid on his clothes and shouted in alarm, 'Mr Watson, come here. I want you!' To his intense relief and utter amazement Watson came running up the stairs. In his panic-stricken state Bell had made the world's very first telephone call.   *1876*

The famous alcoholic gun-slinger Jack Slade was hanged by vigilantes. Renowned for the brutal killing of Jules Bene who'd been foolish enough to shoot at him, Slade had lashed the man to a post and in between swigs of whisky had shot him in the arms and legs, blown off the top of his head and sliced off his ear as a watch-fob. He wasn't hanged for that, however, but for getting drunk too often and shooting up the town. His distraught wife packed his body into a tin coffin, filled appropriately enough with raw alcohol, to take him to his native Illinois. Unfortunately the alcohol didn't work, the body started to decompose, and she hastily had to inter her drunken gun-toting husband in Salt Lake City – in, of all places, the Mormon Cemetery.   *1864*

Today's the day...

Outspoken jester Archie Armstrong met his downfall when he insulted Archbishop Laud once too often. The cheeky former sheep-stealer had enjoyed a privileged position at court for the last thirty years, been the cause of many a quarrel and treated everyone with 'the utmost freedom and familiarity'. Like his fellow Scotsmen, Archie was violently opposed to Laud's high-church policies and when he heard of the rebellion at Stirling, triumphantly taunted the Archbishop, 'Whae's feule now?' Laud promptly reported him to King Charles who ordered that Armstrong be banished from the court with 'his coat pulled over his head'.   *1637*

Mount Etna erupted at dawn when a twelve mile long fissure split it open down one side. By dusk a two mile wide river of lava was roaring down the mountain straight towards the town of Catania. Citizens there had built a 60ft high wall to try and stem the flow but the molten rock just built up and poured over the top. In all some 20,000 people were killed and the amount of rock and sand thrown up from fissures near Catania formed a hill 450ft high.   *1669*

The 'Intimate Revue' opened – and closed – at the Duchess Theatre, London. Incredibly complicated scene changes took up to twenty minutes a time and seven scenes were scrapped just to get it finished by midnight! The play did achieve fame, though. With just one performance, it had the shortest run on record.   *1930*

The profligate teenage Emperor Heliogabalus was murdered, aged only seventeen, after a reign so full of excess it had shocked even the Romans. He'd raped the Vestal Virgin, and 'married' his male favourite Zoticus. He wore make-up, bathed with the women at the public baths and removed all the hair from his body 'to arouse the lusts of the greatest number'! He served up jewels mixed with food (though sometimes he put in dung or spiders for a change), buried his

146

guests so deep in rose petals that several suffocated, and frightened them half to death with his pet lions and tigers – which unbeknown to them were both tame and toothless! He performed child sacrifices daily, fed human flesh to his conger eels and often arrived nude at State functions – in a wheelbarrow drawn by naked women. Finally his soldiers could stand it no longer. They murdered him, suitably enough, in a latrine, dragged his body through the streets, and had to throw it in the Tiber. They'd have preferred to have stuffed it down a sewer – but it wouldn't fit.

AD 222

Pipe-puffing ex-Prime Minister Harold Wilson was born in Huddersfield, Yorkshire. He first visited Downing Street when he was only eight and was photographed standing outside Number 10 in his short trousers. Forty years later he was back there as the youngest Premier this century. A vigorous speaker in Opposition to the Tory government of the late fifties and early sixties, he clashed frequently with Harold Macmillan, whom he nicknamed 'Mac the Knife'. When asked what the main differences between them were, he curtly replied, 'about twenty-two years!'

1916

Today's the day...

'The white-robed sybil of Mount Lebanon' Lady Hester
Stanhope, the great English eccentric, was born. While she was
housekeeper to her uncle William Pitt at 10 Downing Street, she
visited the mad fortune-teller Brothers, in Bedlam, and he predicted
she'd go to Jerusalem and become a Queen. After her uncle died and
she lost her favourite brother and her beloved, the General Sir John
Moore at the Battle of Corunna, she travelled eastwards and in a way
fulfilled the augury. She was a great believer in magic, alchemy,
phrenology and astrology, and the Bedouin, thinking her supernatural,
made her 'Queen of the Desert'. She lived among the half savage
tribes like some mystic potentate, surrounded by hordes of animals,
servants and supplicants, whom she'd occasionally beat in a friendly
fashion with a mace.   *1776*

Cure-all philosopher George Berkeley was born to a family of
English descent in Thomastown, Kilkenny, and ever afterwards
regarded the native Irish as foreigners. He became Dean of Derry and
Bishop of Cloyne, and developed his great philosophical thesis that
nothing exists except in the mind. Dr Johnson called this 'ingenious
sophistry' and Berkeley became much more famous for his treatise on
The Virtues of Tar Water, which he claimed held all the vital elements
of the universe. He believed that it could prevent or cure scurvy,
smallpox, hysteria, hypochondria, plague, erysipelas, gout, gangrene,
bloody flux and all disorders of the urinary passages. He had six
children – two of whom died and all of whom had delicate constitutions
– and every one of them had been fed on tar water.   *1685*

The Hebrides got 'Whisky Galore' around midnight, when in
their little boats, the islanders reached the abandoned wreck of the
8,000-ton cargo ship the *Politician*, which had run aground in a storm
on the rocks at the mouth of the Minch. In her holds were no less
than 22,000 cases of Scotch – over a quarter of a million bottles. The

March 12

islanders 'requisitioned' as much as they could carry. Just as in
Compton Mackenzie's novel, based on the story, the islands were
almost literally awash with whisky. It was buried in gardens, stacked
in sheds, hidden in barns and bathroom cisterns, and one old lady
poured hers into chamber-pots and kept it under the bed. The
customs got wind of it eventually, and a few men were locked up
briefly and a few more fired. It wasn't their fault, they claimed,
because 'it wasn't a normal shipwreck – it was the islands calling the
whisky'.   *1941*

A dreadful state of undress swept the stage at the Paris Opera at
the *première* of Filippo Taglioni's new ballet *Les Sylphides*. Maria
Taglioni danced the title role of '*La Sylphide*' and like the *corps de
ballet*, she was dressed in the first ever tutus, designed by Eugène
Lami. These elegant but outrageous white flouncy costumes exposed
the whole of the dancers' ankles and worse still – their bare arms up
to the shoulder!   *1832*

The dreaded Mohocks got a good lambasting in the *Spectator*. They
were the latest of a long line of gentlemen thugs who attacked people
at night in the ill-lit streets of London just for the fun of it. Under
their 'Emperor', they were classified into various drunken categories.
'The dancing masters' for instance, who specialised in making their
victims leap about by thrusting swords through their legs, and 'the
bumblers' who chose only women and upskittled them to 'commit
certain indecencies . . . on the limbs which they thus expose'.
Strangely these 'barbarians' were rather oddly concerned for the
people they bullied, albeit in a rather vicious sort of way. One 'Emperor'
decreed that their attacks should only take place in the early hours;
'pinking' should always be done to 'the fleshy parts' only and
whenever possible 'patients' should be taken in 'alleys, nooks and
corners' so that they 'may not be in danger of catching cold'.   *1712*

Today's the day...

An amateur astronomer discovered a planet. He was William Herschel, a German-born English-dwelling organist and music teacher who was obsessed by his heavenly hobby. Today he spotted a celestial body that was not a spot of light, but a disc. At first he thought it was a comet, but after consultations with other astronomers, he was amazed to realise it was his very own planet – the first discovered in recorded memory. It was called Uranus, and though it's a cold and inhospitable world that turns some 1,783 million miles from the sun, it earned Herschel a handsome pension from George III, and helped him to devote most of the rest of his life to astronomy. He lived to be eighty-four, which is exactly how many earth years Uranus takes to orbit the sun.

1781

An astronomical coincidence occurred when the famous American star-gazer Percival Lowell was born exactly seventy-four years to the day after the discovery of Uranus. Lowell made the most accurate predictions to date of the nature, size and orbit of yet another planet that was thought to exist only in astronomers' theories. That planet was Pluto; it was discovered in Lowell's observatory nearly fourteen years after his death, and it was announced to the world today in 1930. What had prompted the theory of its existence in the first place was an irregularity in the orbit of Uranus.

1855

The world's first motor cyclist Gottlieb Daimler was born in Schorndorf and started his career as an apprentice gunsmith. Of all the pioneers of the motor age, his contribution must be one of the very greatest, for it was fundamental to everything that followed. His original motorcycle was based on an ordinary pushbike and was developed with Nicholas Otto – a partnership which produced both the first four-stroke and the first two-stroke internal combustion engines. Later Daimler worked with Wilhelm Mayback and was the guiding genius behind the first high speed petrol engine, which was created in 1883 and was the direct ancestor of the modern car engine. Apart from the English motor car that carries his name, there is another lasting tribute to him. It's a car called the Mercedes; it was created in the Daimler factory, and named after his daughter.   *1834*

The first professional striptease was presented in a Paris music hall after amateur efforts had gained enough publicity to ensure this new art form would really take off. The act that was premièred consisted of variations on a theme of a girl removing clothes in order to go to bed, cool off from the heat or take a bath. Most imaginative of all, however, was the version called *La Puce* in which the lady stripped while she searched for a flea!   *1894*

The dreaded driving test was first introduced into Britain – one of the last countries in Europe to make it a legal requirement. As of today, the test was purely voluntary. It didn't actually become compulsory until June, and then you only had to take it if you'd got your first licence a year or less before the day it became official. Funnily enough that day happened to be April 1.   *1935*

Today's the day...

The child who died of old age Charles Charlesworth was born to perfectly normal parents in Staffordshire. He had slight imperfections in his shoulders and bottom jaw, but otherwise appeared to be an ordinary healthy infant. By the age of three, however, he was developing with frightening speed, and a year later he'd reached sexual maturity and had started to grow whiskers. Over the next three years, he aged rapidly. His hair turned white, his skin wrinkled, his veins stuck out, his shoulders drooped and he came to walk, talk and look like an old man. At the age of seven, he fainted and died – and as the coroner said, incredulous, it was old age that had carried him off. *1829*

A very fishy excuse was given to magistrates in Kendal, Cumbria, by a keen angler, twenty-two-year-old David Preston, before he was put on probation for a year for growing cannabis. A little hopefully, he claimed he'd grown it as fish-bait. *1978*

'Garbo talks!' appeared in ads, posters and newspaper headlines when this enigmatic silent film star's first sound movie *Anna Christie* was premièred. Thirty-four minutes into the plot, Greta/Anna made her virgin celluloid utterance: 'Gimme a visky with chincher aile on the saide – ant doan be stinchy baby!' *1930*

The Man who broke the bank at Monte Carlo, the tubby cockney con-man Charles Deville Wells, was sentenced to eight years penal servitude at the Old Bailey on numerous counts of obtaining around £50,000 by false pretences. In July 1891 he'd broken the bank on the roulette table at the famous Casino not once, but more than a dozen times, and scooped a million francs. In November he returned and broke the bank again and by his third visit the following year, he'd had a hit song written about him and was able to sail down to Monte Carlo in his 300ft yacht, the *Palais Royal*. Then inevitably, he started to lose. He was soon reduced to selling the coal from the yacht's bunkers to make ends meet, and finally he was arrested at Le Havre and sent back to London. It turned out that our hero was a demon inventor, who'd conned his stake money and thousands more out of investors who'd 'financed' his 'proved inventions' by post. Needless to say his envelope-openers, tunnel ventilators and barnacle removers came to nothing, and the only good idea he ever had he sold for £50. It was the original musical skipping rope.   *1893*

The father of the atomic age Albert Einstein was born in Ulm and grew up largely in Munich. He couldn't talk until he was three, was told by a teacher he'd 'never amount to anything' and worked out his earth-shattering *Theory of Relativity* in his spare time while he was employed in the Swiss patents office. With his scruffy clothes, white hair and spiky moustache, he was almost certainly the original for the archetypal 'absent-minded professor'. He didn't much like to wear socks, loved to wander about the house playing Mozart on his fiddle, and when he was a little confused about anything, he'd announce, 'I will go and do a little tink!'   *1879*

Today's the day...

Julius Caesar was assassinated as predicted by Spurinna the prophetess. His friends too, alerted by rumours, had warned him of what might happen and so had his wife Calpurnia who was alarmed by awful dreams and visions. He insisted on going to the Senate House anyway and went completely unprotected. Metellus Cimber grabbed hold of his toga and Servilius Casca struck the first blow. Then came the others; the 'lean and hungry' Cassius slashed his face, and Brutus – who may well have been not only Caesar's friend, but his illegitimate son – stabbed him in the groin. To put a stop to his 'overweening ambition' or to protect their own interests, the conspirators inflicted twenty-three separate wounds – probably only one of which was fatal. Caesar fell at the foot of the statue of his dead and defeated enemy Pompey the Great and before he fell, he modestly loosened his belt so his toga could fall and he could die with both legs decently covered.   *44 BC*

Burton married Taylor on the eighth floor of Montreal's Ritz-Carlton hotel, so ending their 'open and notorious association'. On their wedding night, according to Miss Taylor, they 'sat and talked and giggled and cried until seven in the morning'. Later in their connubial career, Burton was to say, 'I did not tame Elizabeth; she came, she saw and then I conquered.'   *1964*

'The world's most beautiful store' opened in London's Oxford Street. It was named after its forty-five-year-old American owner, H. Gordon Selfridge, who in his young days as a lace-salesman had been called 'Handsome Harry'. With the help of a massive and unprecedented advertising campaign, he promised his customers 'Integrity . . . Value . . . Courtesy . . . and Originality', as well as his own brand of cheerfully fake, mass-market exclusivity. 'We have issued 600,000 personal invitations to the opening,' ran one advertisement, 'but if you haven't received one yet, come along anyway.'   *1909*

March 15

A masochistic subaquanaut broke a record by spending the longest ever solitary, voluntary sojourn under water, in the pool of the Bermuda Palms Hotel, San Rafael, California. He was Robert Foster, a thirty-two-year-old technician, and very sensibly, he made sure he had both a doctor and a first aid man right there at the pool-side. Before he jumped in, he 'hyper-ventilated' – breathed oxygen direct from a tank – for half an hour. Then down he went, under 10ft of water and stayed there for a staggering 13mins 42·5secs.   *1959*

'Swifts Nicks' Gentleman of the road was hanged. He was called John Nevison, and as a child he'd stolen apples, poultry, a silver spoon and the school master's horse which he afterwards shot to avoid identification. He became alternately a soldier and a highwayman of high repute. Charles II was fascinated by him. It's highly likely that if anybody did, it was Nevison – and not Dick Turpin – who rode 190 miles to York in fifteen hours to establish an alibi for a robbery in London. Sadly, this 'valiant' man murdered 'one Fletcher' and 'threatened the death of Justices of the Peace whenever he met them'. He was caught near Wakefield, refused a pardon and swung at Tyburn – and that was 'the end of the remarkable Mr Nevison'.   *1685*

The fighting President of the United States 'Old Hickory' Andrew Jackson was born, the son of recent Irish immigrants. A boy-soldier in the Revolutionary War, he became the hero of the Battle of New Orleans in the War of 1812; a hard, but respected general, a tough lawyer and a harsh judge. He was accused of marrying an adulteress and legend has it that the poor woman died of shame. He took office in 1829, stayed there for eight years and kept racehorses in the White House stable. Jefferson said he was 'one of the most unfit men I know for such a place' – but another man said, 'He has slain the Indians and flogged the British and therefore is the wisest and greatest man in the nation.'   *1767*

Today's the day...

The Pilgrim Fathers met their first Indian and were amazed. He strode into their camp, bade them welcome and asked them for beer – all in English. He was naked except for a leather fringe about his waist and as they fed him 'bisket and butter and cheese and pudding and a piece of mallard', he told them his tale. His name was Samoset and he came from further up the coast where English ships frequently fished. One of his friends, a certain Squanto, had even visited England and been 'entertained by a merchant in London'. Samoset returned frequently to see the settlers and brought the famous Squanto who proved to be invaluable, and helped them fish and plant corn. On one occasion Samoset turned up with five more friends intent on a party. After drinking 'strong water' and eating 'liberally', they burst into song and danced 'like anticks'. The Pilgrims were horrified – after all it was a Sunday!   *1621*

Superstitious Londoners evacuated the city in the strange belief that it was going to be wrecked by an earthquake. It started with the Irish residents in St Giles and Seven Dials where 'frantic cries for deliverance' and 'heart-rending supplications for assistance' filled the air. The panic was infectious and as the rumour spread, crowds rushed to board boats to Gravesend, trains were packed out and other escapees took to the fields beyond Stepney, Hampstead and Primrose Hill. At a safe distance they expected to view 'the demolition of the leviathan city' but, as *The Times* reported with classic under-statement, 'The darkness of the day and the thickness of the atmosphere prevented it being seen.'   *1842*

Avenging wife Henriette Caillaux shot Gaston Calmette, editor of one of France's most influential newspapers, *Le Figaro*. In the past two months he'd written over 130 articles about her husband, the Minister of Finance, deriding his advocacy of income tax and his policy of friendship with Germany. The final blow came when he published one of the sexually and politically indiscreet letters Monsieur Caillaux had written to Henriette years before, when she was his mistress 'Ri-Ri' and he was still married to someone else. Frantic with worry, Henriette consulted a judge. He told her there was no legal action she could take so she took the law into her own hands. She drove to the newspaper offices in the official limousine, killed Calmette, drove to the police station and gave herself up. At her trial, she claimed the gun had gone off accidentally and she'd only meant to frighten him. Incredibly, she was acquitted and a disgusted *Le Figaro* claimed she'd covered 'the radical republic with mud and blood'.   *1914*

Slapstick clown Jerry Lewis was born Joseph Levitch in Newark, New Jersey. At school he was nicknamed 'Id' for idiot and discovered that by acting even more clumsily he could make people laugh. He's been doing it ever since and in 1963 signed the biggest ever TV contract for a five-year series worth twelve-and-a-half million pounds. The public had the last laugh, however. They didn't think it was very funny and it was taken off the air only thirteen weeks later.   *1926*

The worst Jewish massacre in English history took place at York. Richard the Lionheart was about to leave for his crusades in the Holy Land and at his coronation, fighting had broken out between Christians and Jews. It was followed by similar violence in Norwich, Stamford and Lincoln, and now the mob in York was on the warpath, harrying and murdering and driving most of the Jewish community of 150 into the castle. There they were besieged and rather than give themselves up to almost certain death, they buried their gold and silver and, in desperation, committed mass suicide. The few who surrendered were butchered as soon as they opened the gates. It was discovered afterwards that as well as the rampant Christian prejudice, there was another strong motive behind the attack. Many of the leaders of the mob were deeply in debt to the Jews.   *1190*

Today's the day...

A great leap in athletics history was made when the first ever recorded high jump of 6ft was made by the Hon. Marshall Jones Brooks at Marston near Oxford. Mr Brooks used to jump very decorously – wearing his top hat!

1876

The feast of the confusing saint St Patrick is celebrated. Though he's the Patron Saint of Ireland, the first thing to appreciate about him is that while he may have been English, Welsh, Scottish or French, he was definitely not Irish. He was carried off to Ireland as a slave and had no sooner escaped, after spending six years as a swineherd, than he had a dream that he should preach, became a priest and went back there. Of course, that is assuming that he ever existed in his traditional form at all, for a number of authorities believe 'he' may have been two people – Palladius and Patrick the Briton – who got all mixed up into one.

Feast Day

The gallant Captain Oates was born and died. A soldier and yachtsman, he was keen on fox-hunting and was appointed by Scott to look after the ponies on the 1910 Antarctic Expedition. He suffered terribly from the cold and on the march back from the Pole, his feet turned black from frostbite. On 16 March 'he slept through the night, hoping not to wake'. He did and it was his birthday. A terrible blizzard was blowing and he knew he was holding the others up. 'I am just going outside,' he said, 'and may be some time.' But both he and they knew he was never coming back.   *1880/1912*

'The Tartar Fury' Rudolph Nureyev was born on a train travelling to Vladivostock. By the age of six, he knew he wanted to be a dancer; at seven he saw his first ballet and was 'branded for life' and at seventeen he joined the Kirov Ballet School in Leningrad. He's been described as 'the Brigitte Bardot of Ballet' and as 'a great Muslim whore'. Age just doesn't seem to wither him. 'If I stopped dancing,' he says, 'then they'd have to take me to the hospital.'   *1938*

The last of the dare-devil Irish gentlemen Charles James Patrick Mahon – 'the O'Gormon Mahon' – was born in Ennis, County Clare. A Justice of the Peace at twenty-one, he helped fight an election campaign for O'Connell by swinging from a balcony wearing national costume and the self-styled medal of 'The Order of the Liberators'. He fought thirteen duels, and indulged much in foreign travel, accumulating more active army ranks than any other mortal. He served in the Irish Militia; the armies of Turkey, Russia, Austria, France, Brazil, Costa Rica, Uruguay, Peru and the United States, not to mention being the Governor of a province in Nicaragua and an Admiral in the Chilean Navy. He died aged ninety-one, still regarded as the handsomest man in Ireland.   *1800*

The guilty King of Scotland James IV was born. At fifteen, he was placed at the head of the rebellion that ended in his father's death, and thereafter he performed 'ostentatious penance' by wearing an iron chain belt, which he was said to increase in weight every year. *1473*

Today's the day...

Man walked in space for the first time when Lieutenant Colonel Aleksey Leonov clambered about attached to a 16ft 'umbilicus' outside the Russian satellite *Voskhod II* – which aptly enough means 'sunrise'. He was in space for a grand total of twenty minutes and during his 12min 9sec 'float' he travelled 3,000 miles at a speed of 17,500mph, rotating ten times a minute. Unfortunately, his space-suit 'ballooned' and so the last eight minutes of his cosmic promenade were spent trying frantically to get back in the hatch. *1965*

The lascivious Tsar Ivan the Terrible died probably of syphilis while lying down playing chess with his eventual successor Boris Godunov. He claimed to have deflowered 1,000 virgins and killed 1,000 offspring of his own begetting. He'd had eight wives, three of whom had died of poisoning along with most of their families, and he used to swap mistresses with his son Ivan, whom he later killed with a spear. In an early form of *Catch-22*, he was going to execute his soothsayer for predicting his death correctly, and was the more annoyed because with him the direct line effectively ended. Though he'd sired so many children, his only legitimate successor was Feodor – who not surprisingly was a complete imbecile. *1584*

The Tolpuddle Martyrs were sentenced to seven years' transportation. The 'six Dorchester labourers' led by George and James Lovelace had been worried by the continuing decline of agricultural wages, so they'd contacted the Grand National Consolidated Trade Union, and with their help set up a 'Friendly Society', which they were perfectly entitled to do. 'We were uniting,' they said, 'to preserve ourselves, our wives and our children.' Unaware that they'd done anything wrong, they were hauled before the bench for 'administering illegal oaths', and much to the satisfaction of local farmers, they were given the second severest sentence to hanging. They were sent to the prison hulks, and then on in chains to the penal colony of Tasmania, where they were to languish for two years before a public outcry brought about their release. The staggering thing about it all was that these pioneering trade unionists had never called a strike and hadn't even asked for an increase in wages. *1834*

The headless humorist Laurence Sterne died in poverty. The writer of *Tristram Shandy*, the first comic novel, he was nicknamed 'Yorick' after the exhumed jester in Hamlet. His body was interred in a pauper's grave and shortly afterwards, it was snatched and sold to Dr Charles Collignon in Cambridge who had no idea whose corpse it was. During dissection, one of the students recognised Sterne and the body was hurriedly returned. Collignon was said to have kept the skull and added it to Cambridge's collection, though in fact it's never been found there. In 1968, Sterne's grave was excavated and several skulls were found in the hole – one of them with the lid cut off as it might have been in dissection. It was the right size and shape for the writer and though there was no positive proof, it was given the benefit of the doubt. When it was reburied and a stone erected over it, the memorial began, 'Alas poor Yorick'. *1768*

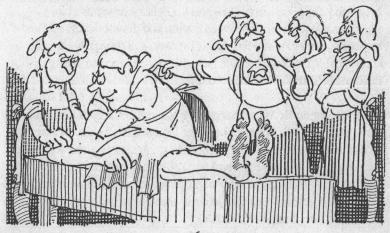

Today's the day...

An unsuspecting farmer was murdered without knowing it. On his way home after a game of dominoes at the local pub, John Dawson heard a click and felt a tap on his shoulder, but thought it was children throwing stones. Next day his back felt stiff and his sister discovered it was covered in blood from a gaping wound. He died two days later. Neither the murderer nor the murder weapon was ever found, but at the inquest the village constable admitted the locals liked 'a full-blooded joke'. *1934*

The manic missionary and explorer David Livingstone was born in Blantyre. An ex-cotton worker who joined the London Missionary Society, he nearly ruined his career at the start by going to preach in Essex. Paralysed by fear he said, 'Friends, I have forgotten all I had to say' – then picked up his hat and fled. Eventually he made it to Africa, married Mary Moffat, 'a little, thick black-haired girl', and was attacked by a lion that 'shook him as a terrier does a rat' and permanently disabled his arm. Plagued by illness, and unsuccessful as a missionary, he plodded on through the Dark Continent until he was 'a mere ruckle of bones'. It's now thought he suffered from 'cyclothymia' – a hereditary depressive insanity – and his behaviour seems quite symptomatic. He veered between elation and despondency, insulted his sisters, once brutally fought his brother, and though he was the archetypal Victorian Christian hero, he was often found sitting in the bush using 'filthy and abusive language'. *1813*

Wild West goodie Wyatt Earp was born in Kentucky. Though he came to fame as the honest lawman of Dodge City, he wasn't always so well behaved. He was imprisoned for stealing horses and worked as a card-sharp, debt-collector and legal pimp, taking licence fees from hookers. He deserted his wife, who became an alcoholic and committed suicide, and before he died he had the cheek to write, 'I am not ashamed of anything I ever did!' *1848*

March 19

Short-lived Welsh lightweight Hopkins Hopkins died, weighing just 13lbs. Son of the poet Lewis Hopkins, he was barely 31ins tall and had long suffered from appalling health. Three years earlier he was described as being 'weak and emaciated, his eyes dim, his hearing very bad and his countenance fallen'. Doctors pronounced that he died of old age – but in fact, he was only seventeen.   *1754*

Hard-drinking critic-hater, the German composer Max Reger, was born. 'A swollen myopic beetle, with thick lips and a sullen expression', he was excessively fond of marching songs, and after Wagner, was Hitler's favourite. He was offensive to everybody, but most particularly to reviewers. He wrote to one, 'I am sitting in the smallest room . . . I have your review in front of me. It will soon be behind me.'   *1873*

The most travelled man of his time Sir Richard Burton was born. He visited Africa, Arabia, America, Brazil, India and Fernando Po; discovered Lake Tanganyka and the source of the Nile; sailed up the Congo River and climbed the mountains of the Cameroons; studied polygamy in Salt Lake City and sexual perversion in Karachi. Disguised as an arab 'Al Haj Abdullah', he was the first Englishman to see Mecca and live, and was rumoured to have killed a man who spotted him 'performing an operation of nature in a non-oriental fashion'. He wrote extensively of his travels in fifty volumes, but his most successful work was *The Book of a Thousand Nights and a Night* in which 'certain subjects of curiosity are discussed with naked freedom'. Strangely enough his prudish Catholic wife published the book after his death as 'household reading'. She did take care, however, to burn his diaries and his other masterpiece, *A Scented Garden*. He'd warned her they contained some rather unsavoury facts about the Middle East, including 'fellahs copulatin' with crocodiles!'   *1821*

Today's the day...

A novel written by God was published. It was none other than *Uncle Tom's Cabin* penned by Harriet Beecher Stowe – she said at the dictation of the Almighty. Though it now tends to be seen as a paternalist and thus a racialist little story, it was in fact written to show what 'an accursed thing' slavery was. It caused an absolute storm of controversy, prompting books and speeches on both sides of the fence. When Abe Lincoln met Harriet ten years later, when the Civil War was in full cry, he said to her, 'So this is the little lady who made this big war.' *Uncle Tom* sold a million copies in a little over a year. When she'd finished writing it, the little lady had retired to bed for forty-eight hours and said, 'I hope it will make me enough to buy a new silk dress.'

1852

Derided dramatist Henrik Ibsen was born in Skien, Norway, the son of a bankrupt businessman. He became a pharmacist's assistant and started writing, finishing his first play *Cataline* when he was twenty-two. His work was greeted with massive indifference and even when plays like *A Doll's House* and *Ghosts* brought him international acclaim, the insults flew thick and fast. He was called 'a crazy fanatic',

March 20

'a Scandinavian Humbug' and 'a gloomy ghoul, groping for horrors by night'. His plays were accused of 'dramatic impotence', amateurishness, nastiness and vulgarity, and those who watched them were of course effeminate men, 'unwomanly women', 'unprepossessing cranks' and best of all, 'muck-ferreting dogs.!   *1828*

The unloved and unlovely Prince of Wales Frederick Louis died aged forty-four leaving the young George – later Farmer George III – as heir to the throne. His own father was, of course, George II and Frederick and he roundly disliked each other. Frederick was always pestering George for money and the Household was irritated with his 'powers of exasperation' and horrified by his excessive gambling and womanising. His death was brought about by an abscess, burst by a blow from a tennis ball, and the general feeling of the nation was well summed up in a rhyme of the time. It said: 'Here lies Fred/Who was alive and is dead/ . . . There's no more to be said.'   *1751*

A fishy pin-up was patented in America. It consisted of the figure – 'front, longitudinal and side elevation thereof' – of a small, naked mermaid, adorned with hooks.   *1928*

Part II came to an end for Henry IV when he died of a stroke, prematurely old at the age of forty-six. He'd had at least one stroke before and was thought to have been suffering from leprosy. To ease his conscience over his usurping of the throne from his cousin Richard I, he wanted to lead a crusade, and thus it was prophesied that he'd die in Jerusalem – a thought that gave him a sort of morbid pleasure. He never did make the crusade, but instead was visiting St Edward's shrine in Westminster Abbey when the fatal seizure took him and he was taken into a nearby room where he died. The room was called the Jerusalem Chapel.   *1413*

Today's the day...

The world's most determined composer Johann Sebastian Bach was born in Eisenach, Thuringia. His family had produced musicians for generations and four out of his ten brothers joined him in the profession. One of them was especially jealous of the ten-year-old Johann's talent and wouldn't let him look at the scores he'd composed. Undaunted, the young Johann crept downstairs every night and copied them out by moonlight – an activity which permanently impaired his eyesight. He would walk thirty miles to hear different organists play, travel over sixty to hear the Court Orchestra, and when he was first made church organist he confused the entire congregation by improvising on hymn tunes. He married twice, had twenty children and kept moving from job to job trying to earn the money to support them. He still managed to compose 300 cantatas, two oratorios, the 'St John' and 'St Matthew' Passions and the vast 'Mass in B Minor'. *1685*

Unhappy court poet Stephen Duck committed suicide. A humble farm labourer from Wiltshire, he'd had a skimpy education and improved on it by reading *Paradise Lost* with the aid of a dictionary. He took to writing verse, and Queen Caroline brought him to court and paid him a pension. In his fortunate position he incurred the wrath of many other poets and Swift wrote a particularly scathing epigram about him. Subject to depressions 'his mind gave way', and the unfortunately-named Mr Duck drowned himself 'behind the Black Lion Inn at Reading'. *1756*

The Duke of Wellington defended his honour in Battersea Fields. The Earl of Winchelsea, violently opposed to Wellington's policy of Catholic emancipation, had accused him publicly of giving generous donations to the Protestant King's College, London, simply as a pose. A 'voluminous correspondence' between the two gentlemen ensued but it seemed that honour would only be satisfied by a duel. Wellington had to borrow a set of duelling pistols and the two men faced each other in the misty morning 'among the cabbages', to the astonishment of about fifteen gardeners! Wellington shot wide, whereupon the Earl gallantly shot straight at the ground and then presented the Duke with a written apology. Afterwards one of the seconds, Lord Falmouth, explained that he'd only agreed to act for Winchelsea after he'd promised that under no circumstances would he shoot England's great hero.   *1829*

Schubert wrote a posthumous piece of music – 140 years after his death! Actually he sang it in 'not a very good voice' to London housewife Mrs Rosemary Brown. She wrote it all down for him just as she claims she's done for Liszt, Stravinsky, Beethoven, Bach, Rachmaninov and Chopin. Obscurely, the 'Moment Musical' Schubert dictated today is dedicated to 'Mrs Firth'.   *1968*

Creator of the fabulous 'Follies', Florenz Ziegfeld was born in Chicago. He disdained to work in his father's musical college, saying, 'Who needs peanuts?' and by the time he was twenty-two, he was already producing vaudeville shows. He found his first 'Follies' girl, Anna Held, in Paris and determined to make her a star. He put her in lavish productions; installed her in a luxury suite and told everyone he bathed her in mare's milk; and they went through a form of marriage. Starting with her success, Ziegfeld set out to 'glorify the American Girl' – a process which seemed to consist of placing her in extravagant surroundings and showing off as much of her anatomy as possible. His first Follies were in 1907 and he continued to be highly successful with them for over two decades. He was the original producer with a casting couch and in his later years was accused of 'satyriasis' – morbidly exaggerated sexual desire. He died in Hollywood, leaving behind a million dollars in debts. As he said himself, 'When you get as high up as I've been, there's only one way to go – and it's spelt d-o-w-n!'   *1869*

Today's the day...

Rags-to-riches showman Mike Todd was killed when his light aircraft iced up and crashed into the Zuni Mountains of New Mexico. His bride of thirteen months, Elizabeth Taylor, was ill at home with a fever, but had a feeling that something was wrong after Todd failed to phone her as promised. Todd's real name was Avrom Hirsch-Goldbogen, and he nicknamed Taylor Lizzie Schwartzkopf. She'd accepted the Jewish faith to marry him and they were wed in Mexico – in Spanish – by a rabbi. To cope with the demands of his jet-set existence, Todd had bought the aircraft that killed him. He'd called it *The Lucky Liz*.   *1958*

The highest-priced orchid of the time was bought by Baron Schroder of Egham for 1,150 guineas from Sanders Nurseries of St Albans. The exotic flower was one of the 'Odontoglossum' genus, found in the Andes and brought back by one of Sanders' scouts who travelled the world hunting for new species. Though incredibly expensive, this was the only way to acquire a new orchid before hybridisation took over and began to create the 40,000 hybrids which now exist. Orchids are incredibly fecund plants and Charles Darwin was much impressed by the vast numbers of seeds they produce. He worked out that if all the seeds produced by one European Spotted Orchid germinated successfully, in three generations it would cover the entire surface of the earth.   *1906*

An embarrassing diving record was claimed by Alex Wickham when he jumped off a cliff overlooking the River Yarra near Melbourne, Australia. Halfway down he lost consciousness and only regained it when he hit the water. He climbed out to claim a dive of 205ft but unfortunately it was later revealed that the actual measurement was only 95½ft. But what was more embarrassing still was the fact that the impact of the dive had ripped off his bathing suit!   *1919*

Sobersided comedian John Liston died and left a fortune. He'd started off as a straight actor, but when he came on stage the cast laughed so much they couldn't speak – so he took funny parts ever after. In London, 'the gravity of his face' kept them rolling in the aisles and he became the highest paid comic of his time. Like many other comedians, he suffered from depressions and would fortify himself with a bottle of brandy before every performance. He married the diminutive Irish singer Miss Tyrer, kept a tiny pug dog and bought a large house facing Hyde Park Corner. In his last years he could be seen crutch in hand, observing the times of the omnibuses passing his house and 'exhibiting signs of distress if any happened to be late'. *1846*

The incorrigible comic Chico Marx was born. He was an inveterate gambler and would disappear whenever his debts were due, leaving Groucho to soldier on with the act with only the silent Harpo to help. His other great pastime was women. He got his name from chasing 'the chicks'; was married three times and when one of his wives caught him kissing a chorus girl, he explained, 'I wasn't kissing her. I was whispering in her mouth.' *1891*

Today's the day...

The father of 'The Father of Clowns' died. Giuseppe Grimaldi, sometime dentist, ballet master and famed acrobat, was noted for his morbid disposition which earned him the nickname 'Old Grim'. So great was his fear of being buried alive that he insisted his head must be cut off first – and the family fulfilled his wishes. On a previous occasion, Giuseppe had once faked his death to see how everyone would react. The young Joseph, wary of his father's tricks, had shown every sign of sorrow, but his incautious elder brother had danced around the corpse in glee until it 'sat up and shouted at him'!   *1788*

The foppish playwright Sir Lumley 'Skiffey' Skeffington was born. A trend-setting dandy, he advised the Prince Regent about fashion, invented a new colour, 'Skeffington brown', and paraded round in 'white cord inexpressibles with large bunches of white ribbons at the knees'. He was caricatured by the cartoonist Gillray, and mocked by Byron for his 'skirtless coats and skeletons of plays'. His dark curly hair was one of his best features and he cut a strange figure one night when escaping from a fire. He appeared in the street 'in his nightgown without his hat and his hair in papers'!   *1771*

March 23

A key operation in medical history was performed in Edinburgh when surgeons removed a brass padlock from a woman's throat. She'd swallowed it over a month earlier 'while engaged in some pleasantry', but kept quiet about it – 'for fear of distressing her friends'.   *1837*

Master magician Chung Ling Soo was killed on stage at the Empire Theatre, Wood Green. For over twelve years, he'd toured the country with his beautiful handmaiden Suee Seen, and astounded audiences by catching marked bullets fired at him from a twelve-bore rifle. Tonight it all went wrong and when the shot rang out, the magician fell to the floor bleeding profusely from his chest. He died a few hours later. Wild rumours abounded: it was a quaint old Chinese way of committing suicide; he'd been killed by a secret society, a rival magician or a jealous lover of Suee Seen. At the inquest the plain truth emerged. Chung Ling Soo was none other than Bill Robinson, a fifty-seven-year-old New Yorker, his 'Chinese' handmaiden was his wife Dot and he'd died because his trick guns had gone wrong – and this time they'd got him for real.   *1918*

Steely superstar Joan Crawford was born Lucille LeSueur in San Antonio, Texas. She first appeared in films as a 'flapper' on the silent screen 'so long ago that Scott Fitzgerald wrote the script', yet she was still making movies in the seventies, with her cheeks taped-in to show off the Crawford cheekbones. She adopted four children and mistreated them cruelly; was married four times and had innumerable lovers picked at random from whatever men were available. She drank little until she was thirty-five, but then started hitting the bottle on 100 per cent proof vodka, which she carried round in her handbag or in a 'soft drinks' cooler. Obsessed with hygiene, she continually washed her hands, changed her clothes hourly, considered baths 'unsanitary' and would only shower in a hotel bathroom after she'd thoroughly scrubbed the floor.   *1904*

Today's the day...

Good Queen Bess died 'easily like a ripe apple from a tree' at 3am in Richmond Palace. It was New Year's Eve on the old calendar and she was sixty-nine. She'd ruled for forty-four years and for the last two she'd been mourning her rebellious and executed favourite the Earl of Essex. She'd lain in bed for fifteen days, 'sat on a stool for three' and stood for fifteen hours. 'I am not sick,' she insisted despite throat ulcers and 'flu, 'I feel no pain and yet I pine away.' Her coffin was installed in Westminster Abbey, on top of Bloody Mary's, and the two half-sisters, who were of different religions and at odds in life, lie there as the inscription says, 'in the hope of one resurrection'.   *1603*

Zealot and soldier Orde Charles Wingate was killed aged forty-one in a plane crash in the Naga jungle in Assam. Never one to conform or even be consistent, he was a crack-shot, a skilled horseman and thought most other soldiers were 'military apes'. Impressionable and enthusiastic, he was a keen Christian, thoroughly pro-Arab in the Sudan, and a rabid Zionist in Israel. He was nicknamed 'Gideon' and 'Lawrence of Judea', rode a pet ostrich, kept a baboon and would stride across the desert quoting the Old Testament and singing Psalms in Hebrew. In his way, however he was very successful. He helped sweep the Italians out of Ethiopia; created and led the famous 'Chindits' in Burma; became an acting major-general, DSO and two bars and almost made a career of disagreeing with top brass. Throughout the war, he kept a special grease-stained uniform to wear when greeting VIPs, and received one brigadier sitting on his bed, eating raw onions and scrubbing himself with a toothbrush!   *1944*

The only dead heat in the boat race caused a storm of controversy. At the very last minute an oar broke in the Oxford boat and Cambridge snatched the chance to draw level. The whole thing was 'so upsetting' that the very next year, they installed that rather ungentlemanly device – the winning post.   *1877*

March 24

The world's rarest stamp was sold for a staggering £116,666 to a syndicate of American businessmen. Issued in 1856, it revels in the name 'one-cent black-on-magenta British Guiana', and was kept a dark secret by its Australian owner Fred Small for thirty years – even his wife didn't know he owned it. The previous owner is said to have bought and burned the only other known example, and the one and only is now valued in excess of £350,000. So battered and poorly coloured is it, however, that it's often referred to as 'the Blob'.

1970

The Grand National's greatest drama stunned the Aintree crowd and shattered the dream of the first royal win since 1900. The Queen Mother's horse 'Devon Loch' had been in the first six all the way round. He cleared the last fence a length and a half in front of 'E.S.B.' and was going easily. It looked like nothing could stop him and then just a few yards from home the incredible happened – Devon Loch's hindlegs seemed to slip from under him, he skidded and belly-flopped. His jockey, Dick Francis, leapt off fearing his mount had broken a leg and E.S.B. swept past him to win. What caused the collapse is still a mystery. It's been suggested he had a heart attack or a convulsion, or that he tried to jump a shadow. Francis thought he may have got cramp or been frightened by the roar of the crowd. But whatever it was, the horse got up and walked away sound. Said the Queen Mother, 'That's racing I suppose.'

1956

Elvis Presley joined the army, his draft-board having postponed the momentous occasion so 'the King' could finish filming the movie *King Creole*. 'I'm kinda proud,' said apple-pie Elvis. 'It's a duty I've got to fill, and I'm gonna do it.' On day one they cut his hair and his sideburns, thousands of mourning girls wept and Private Presley made one of the worst gags of all time. 'Hair today,' he said without a blush, 'gone tomorrow!'

1958

Today's the day...

A shipwrecked racehorse ran in the Grand National. He was the antipodean thoroughbred Moifaa and he was on his way to England when his ship was wrecked in a storm off Cape Town and the horse, left to his own devices, swam and was swept a staggering 100 miles to land. His owners were found and notified, and Moifaa was brought to this country. It was decided to enter him anyway. Not surprisingly he started an outsider at 25-1, yet defying belief completely he not only finished, but romped home a winner.   *1904*

An unholy accident was narrowly avoided when Will Summers and his colleague Tipping were hanged for housebreaking. The hangman was drunk and thinking there were three to be despatched, was only 'with much difficulty' restrained from topping the parson!   *1738*

The maestro of abuse Arturo Toscanini was born in Parma, the son of a tailor. He became first a cellist, and having been asked to conduct when the regular conductor of a small orchestra fell ill, he went on to become the greatest baton-wielder of his day. He was, to say the least, temperamental and his musicians were lucky if it was only abuse he hurled at them. Ordinarily, he would break his baton or throw it into the pit, and one long-suffering violinist once had to throw it back to him six times, while another sued him for assault. 'After I die,' he screamed at some recalcitrant players, 'I shall return to earth as the gate-keeper of a brothel, and I shan't let any of you in!'   *1867*

A man fell 18,000ft without a parachute. He was rear gunner Sergeant Nicholas Alkemade, whose Lancaster bomber was badly shot up by a night fighter over Germany. In the blazing plane his parachute caught fire and he was faced with the choice 'burn or jump'. He rotated his turret, dived out and plummeted head first at 120mph. Incredibly, he survived. He woke up in thick snow and saw above him the trees that had broken his fall. 'Jesus Christ,' he said aloud, 'I'm alive.' Apart from burns to his hands, face and legs, a splinter wound and a twisted knee, he was all in one piece – though in fact, he lost his boots. The Germans, understandably, wouldn't believe his story. Finally, they found proof in the wreckage of the plane in which all but two of his fellows died. 'Gentlemen,' said the prison camp commandant when he heard the news, 'a miracle no less.' *1944*

'Fighting Mac' Macdonald shot himself at the Hotel Regina in Paris, having risen through the ranks to become Major General commanding his Majesty's forces in Ceylon. Along the way, he fought in just about every major battle from Kabul to Omdurman, became ADC to Queen Victoria and was dubbed Sir Hector, a Knight Commander of the Bath. Suddenly in 1902, an 'opprobrious accusation' was made against him, to wit that this famous war hero was a practising homosexual. He returned home to face his superiors, but was promptly sent back to face a court of enquiry. He then took what was supposedly the notorious womaniser, Edward VII's, advice to take 'the gentleman's way out'. No sooner had he done so, than the legend grew up that he hadn't died at all but had gone off to join the Kaiser. Strangely, in World War I, there was a German Field-Marshal Mackensen, who looked uncannily like him. *1903*

It wasn't New Year's Day any more. It always had been up to and including 1751, when England finally decided to ditch the old Julian Calendar and became one of the last countries in Europe to adopt the Gregorian alternative. It had taken us nearly two centuries to catch on to the fact that the old calendar was falling behind at the rate of three days every 400 years, and the result was absolute chaos. The New Year now began on January 1; eleven days were lost in September and in 1753 not only was today no longer New Year, it became April 5 – and that's why the income tax year starts then. It's obvious really. *1752*

Today's the day...

'A famous thief of England' the much loved highwayman Gamaliel Ratsey was hanged at Bedford. The hero of many ballads, poems and pamphlets, he was the son of a wealthy gentleman from Market Deeping, well educated and a distinguished soldier. After an expedition to Ireland, he fell in with two cut-throats called Snell and Shorthose and only then became a gentleman of the road. He always wore 'a hideous mask' to terrorise his victims and was called by some 'Gamaliel Hobgoblin'. He gave freely to the poor, but extracted payment in money, in jewels and in kind from just about everyone else. He once demanded a learned oration from a scholar and before robbing an actor, insisted on a speech from Hamlet. *1605*

Vienna shook as Beethoven died. It was in the grip of a tremendous storm of snow and lightning, and in the eerie light the great composer 'looked more like a skeleton than a living man'. He was now suffering not only from his cruel deafness but from cirrhosis of the liver, jaundice, dropsy and pneumonia. He asked for wine and when it arrived, he said with his last words and some accuracy, 'Too bad. Too bad. It's too late.' *1827*

A model prisoner killed his guards. He was the convicted mother-murderer Irving Latimer, an ex-dandy and pharmacist. In fact, so well behaved a convict was he that he was made the prison pharmacist's assistant – and that's where the authorities made their big mistake. Latimer very decently prepared his warders some supper, and served it up with a cocktail of lemonade, prussic acid and opium. One man died, the other went into a coma and Latimer escaped. When he was caught a few days later he said he hadn't meant to do it, it was an accident, he just put in a little too much acid. He was given forty-two years to reflect on his mistake.   *1893*

The architect of Blenheim Sir John Vanbrugh died of a quinsy at his house in Whitehall. He created many fine buildings, and what's not often remembered is that he was a comedy playwright too. He left a wife and a son behind and his famous epitaph, often wrongly attributed to Dean Swift, reads: 'Lie heavy on him, Earth! for he/Laid many heavy loads on thee!'   *1726*

The Bird Man of Alcatraz Robert Franklin Stroud committed his second murder. He'd previously killed his mistress's ex-lover in Juneau, Alaska, when he was eighteen and had been given a maximum sentence of twelve years. Today, for no apparent reason, he killed a prison guard in Leavenworth jail in front of 1,200 witnesses. He was sentenced to death, but after three trials and four years, his punishment was commuted to life imprisonment. He was to spend the rest of his existence – forty-two years – in solitary confinement. His birds helped him come to terms with it. He began by nurturing two adopted sparrows and eventually, given an extra cell and plenty of equipment, he became an acknowledged expert. He had an authoritative work published on bird diseases and ran a successful little business selling patent medicines and, aptly enough, caged birds. One of his customers was J. Edgar Hoover.   *1916*

Today's the day...

One of the worst earthquakes ever recorded struck Alaska. Emanating from the ineptly named Fairweather Fault, around 100 miles south-east of Anchorage, it registered a cataclysmic 8.9 on the Richter Scale. In the city itself, buildings toppled and cars flew across streets that 'rippled like waves'. On Kodiak Island an entire village disappeared, and further round the coast, a fishing boat ended up in a school yard five blocks inland. A 90ft tidal wave struck Chenga on Prince William Sound, drowning a third of the population, and similar if smaller waves wreaked havoc as far south as Crescent City, California. While the shock claimed 118 lives and wrought an estimated 300 million dollars' worth of damage, Alaska's top seismologists were safely elsewhere in Washington State at a conference – discussing earthquakes!   *1964*

Cranky English writer Arnold Bennett died of bravado. The sixty-three-year-old author of *Clayhanger* and *The Card* had been to Paris and insisted on drinking the local water to prove how pure it was. It wasn't, and a sick Arnold returned to London, where his illness was diagnosed as flu. A sympathetic Council allowed straw to be laid on Marylebone Road to deaden the noise of the traffic – probably the last time the pre-rubber tyre practice was ever used. It didn't do any good, for the flu turned out to be typhoid.   *1931*

The Vicar of Wakefield was published, having enabled its author Oliver Goldsmith to pay his rent. Dr Johnson had called one morning to find that Ollie's landlady was going to have him arrested for non-payment. The good doctor found that his friend had a novel ready for the press, and persuaded the landlady to let her tenant pop out to see his publisher Neweberry, to whom he sold the manuscript for £60. What naughty old Ollie didn't tell the poor man was that he had already sold a third share of it to Collins of Salisbury who eventually published the first edition.   *1766*

March 27

Engineer and perfectionist Henry Royce was born, the son of an insolvent miller. His childhood was grindingly poor, and it was only after a doting aunt financed him, that he was able to get an apprenticeship with the Great Northern Railway, and eventually set himself up with a small electrical business in Manchester. For nearly twenty years, he manufactured dynamos, motors and cranes, addicted to work and obsessed with improving everything he laid hands on. It was to this obsession that he owed everything – his partnership with the aristocratic Charles Rolls and all that followed – for in 1902, he bought a twin-cylinder *Deauville*, and was so appalled by its poor standard of workmanship, that he resolved to build a car of his own. He did exactly that, and though the company afterwards tried to hide the fact, the first prototype of 'the finest car in the world' was tested in 1904 – on April Fool's Day. *1863*

A bizarre punishment was given to a knight and MP. He was Sir Giles Mompesson, who'd misused his power as a Royal Commissioner to extort money from innkeepers and makers of gold and silver thread. He was fined £10,000; condemned first to life imprisonment and then to perpetual banishment, and finally made to walk along the Strand with his face to a horse's tail! *1621*

Archbishop Cornwallis of Canterbury was buried at Lambeth. In the vault where the pall-bearers were about to place him, they were amazed to find the remains of Bishop Thirlby, the one and only Bishop of Westminster and later Bishop of Norwich and Ely. More than 200 years before, this lucky prelate had served King Henry VIII and Edward VI as a Protestant, and Queen Mary as a Catholic. Elizabeth I had imprisoned him in the Tower, where he'd said he'd enjoyed himself more than when he was in high office, and where indeed he died in 1570. The noble Bishop's body was largely undecayed. He had a hat on his head and another hat under his arm! *1783*

Today's the day...

The distant film star Dirk Bogarde was born. After an idyllically happy childhood and a horrifying war, he ended up at an interview at the Rank Organisation only to be told his head was too small, he was too thin and his neck 'wasn't right'! Small wonder he says he lacked confidence, and to make up for it was rude, arrogant and often drunk. He became a great star anyway and at one point had to have his flies sewn up to protect him from his more enthusiastic female fans. He'll never act on television because, 'I don't want my audience making the tea while I'm hard at work on the screen!'   *1921*

A terrifying tornado hit Chicago killing twenty-eight people and wreaking three million dollars' worth of damage. It started with 'hailstones as big as pigeons' eggs' and a looming 'funnel-shaped' cloud. Cars flew up in the air and birds were thrown down to the ground. Houses collapsed and burst into flame, and one was found completely upside down standing on its chimney.   *1920*

Hero married Heroine when Douglas Fairbanks wed Mary Pickford on a special secret licence supplied by County Clerk 'Cupid' Sparks. The bride wore one stocking inside out for luck and to preserve the secrecy, she covered her wedding ring with adhesive tape. Within three days, the news had exploded, and serious doubts were expressed about the validity of Miss Pickford's 'quickie' Nevada divorce from Owen Moore. Asked a bitchy Hollywood press – if Mary was pregnant would the child be called Moore, Fairbanks or Pickford?   *1920*

The world was sold by auction. After the assassination of the Roman Emperor Pertinax by his own official bodyguards, the Praetorian Guard, nobody wanted the vacant throne. Pertinax had been much loved by the populace and being Caesar might soon be even more dangerous than usual. The Guards decided to sell the Empire and since somebody always wants to rule the world, they soon had two serious bidders. One was Sulpicianus, Pertinax's father-in-law, and the other was the sixty-one-year-old Didius Julianus, the richest Senator in Rome. Didius won with an unbeatable bid of 300 million sesterces and he became Emperor Julianus. It didn't do him much good though – for the General Septimius Severus wasn't happy about the deal and bribed his soldiers to march the 800 miles from his Pannonian camp to take Rome. They did and after only sixty-six days poor old Julianus was beheaded. Septimius Severus got Rome without an auction, and it didn't cost him a single sesterce. *AD 193*

'A modern-day Moby Dick' attacked two men in a small boat about half a mile off shore, thirty miles north of San Francisco. The creature was thought at the time to be a killer whale – though now it's considered more likely to have been a 'Jaws-style' great white shark. Whatever it was, the beastie circled the 14ft craft, passed underneath it then charged and took a large bite out of the hull. The two men aged fifty and seventy-two only escaped when one of them grabbed an oar and poked Leviathan 'right in the eye'. *1952*

Today's the day...

The first batch of 'Coca-Cola' was brewed up over a woodfire in his backyard by graduate chemist John S. Pemberton. Launched as an 'Esteemed Brain Tonic and Intellectual Beverage' it was recommended for headaches, hangovers and as a general pick-me-up. Not surprisingly one of its chief ingredients was the dried leaf of the 'Coca' plant – a principal source of cocaine – but of all the fifteen ingredients the most mysterious is the famous 7x, the secret of which is never known by more than three people at any time. To ensure the secret is safe, they never travel together. *1886*

Captain Scott made the last entry in his diary as he lay in a tent with his two surviving companions, Bowers and Wilson. Trapped by a howling blizzard he wrote, 'We can stick it out to the end but we are getting weaker and the end cannot be far.' Beaten by Amundsen to the South Pole, their 'wearisome return' had cost them two men: Evans, who was found aimlessly crawling around in the snow and died the same night, and Oates who with his frost-bitten feet had heroically walked off to his death to avoid holding up the others. Now the food had run out, the blizzard still raged and they were too weak to move. 'For God's sake look after our people', were the last words Scott wrote. Eight months later, they were found perfectly preserved by the ice – Bowers with his hands crossed on his chest and Scott with his arm thrown over his dearest friend, Wilson. Nearby was a bottle of opium pills, which though it would have given them a quick and easy death, lay untouched. Tragically, they were just eleven miles from safety. *1912*

England's bloodiest battle raged for ten hours around the village of Towton in Yorkshire, between the opposing armies of York and Lancaster. Enraged by the killing of his father and brother, the nineteen-year-old Edward Duke of York had swept north from London with 36,000 men and here, on the banks of the River Cock, near

March 29

Tadcaster, he confronted 40,000 Lancastrians. The appalling weather was on his side and when the Lancastrian bow-men launched a hail of arrows, the driving snowstorm made their shafts fall short. They charged forward anyway, but stumbled in droves over their own fallen arrows sticking up from the ground, and were slain where they lay. When the Duke of Norfolk arrived with Yorkist reinforcements, the Lancastrians finally broke and fled down the road – ironically towards York. Edward, who had ordered no prisoners be taken, personally helped hack them to pieces. It was said that over 28,000 died and that the York road literally ran red with blood. Henry VI was deposed and Edward became King Edward IV. Sadly this wicked slaughter took place on Palm Sunday – one of the holiest days of the Christian year.

1461

A greyhound marathon was run by a determined dog in the 8.15 race at Wimbledon Stadium. Though last in the race he kept on running and went round – and round – and round for a record 30mins 29secs before he finally stopped! Aptly enough his name was Mental's Only Hope.

1961

Today's the day...

The sorry tale of a double loss was recorded in the *Domestic Intelligencer*. A Miss Clark, recently in service, had set fire to her master's house in Southwark and had been sentenced to death. A man decided to marry her 'under the gallows', but she thought she'd get a reprieve and demurred. The man's friends talked him out of marrying the ungrateful wench – and since no pardon was forthcoming she lost, in the words of the *Intelligencer*, 'a husband and her life together'.

1680

The world's first anaesthetised operation was performed by Dr Crawford Williamson Long when he 'extirpated' an encysted tumour from the neck of James Venable, having first rendered him unconscious by administering sulphuric ether on a towel. The operation cost Mr Venable $2, and so painless was it that he wouldn't believe it had been done until he was shown the $\frac{1}{2}$in-round tumour. Dr Long had conceived the idea after attending 'a nitrous oxide frolic' – a laughing gas party – where people staggered and fell, but felt no pain from their bruises. He later performed the first anaesthetised amputation when he removed a boy's finger, but after a few more operations he had to desist. The citizens of Jefferson, Georgia, where he practised, thought it was magic. They accused him of witchcraft – and threatened to lynch him.

1842

The best deal in history was concluded by the American Secretary of State, William H. Seward. The previous evening, the Russian Minister in Washington, Baron de Stoeckl, had interrupted him during a game of whist to announce that the hard-up Tsar Alexander II was prepared to sell America 586,400 square miles of land for $7,200,000. That amounted to 375 million acres for less than two cents an acre, and the offer included rights to fur, fish, timber, minerals and gold. Seward, who was an enthusiastic believer in the United States 'Manifest Destiny' to expand, jumped at the chance, and a treaty securing the deal was signed at 4am. The land was called Alaska, and though the huge wilderness was almost immediately dubbed 'Seward's Folly', the purchase was to prove ultimately wise. Within 100 years of the signing, an oil company had bought a single acre of Alaskan soil for $28,233, while in total Alaska had yielded 757 million dollars' worth of gold.

1867

Gagsters robbed a bank. Butch Cassidy, Tom McCarty and another member of the notorious Hole-in-the-Wall gang, came up with an unusual opening gambit when they stole $20,000 from the First National Bank in Denver, Colorado. McCarty rushed up to the manager and told him he knew there was a plot afoot to rob the place. 'How do you know?' asked the manager. 'We planned it,' said McCarty, 'Hands up!'

1889

The short and unhappy life of Vincent Van Gogh began in the house of his father the pastor, in the village of Groot Zundert in Holland. He was twenty-seven years old before he decided he was an artist, and by then he'd been a depressed art dealer in The Hague, London and Paris, and a miserable self-appointed missionary in a Mons mining village. He had three disastrous platonic love affairs, and one equally disastrous, but less than platonic one with a prostitute. Painting didn't seem to help. He was kept alive, but only just, by his younger brother Theo, fought bitterly with Gauguin who was one of his few friends, and relied more and more on the bottle and 'the sisters of charity' in the local brothel near 'the little yellow house in Arles'. There his mental illness finally overtook him – he sliced off half his left ear with a razor, incarcerated himself in the asylum of Saint Remy and within twelve months he shot himself. In all, he was painting for only ten years, yet he managed to produce over 800 paintings and more than 700 drawings. Incredibly, and despite the frantic efforts of his brother, he only ever sold one of them.

1853

Today's the day...

A pampered golf ball was patented in Britain. Since golf balls travel further when they're warm, its inventor suggested a transparent sphere with a dark interior, which was supposed to absorb the heat of the sun. On cloudy or particularly cold days, there was a further refinement – inside the ball was a heating element.

1969

A better rat-trap was patented in America. It consisted of a complicated frame through which the unsuspecting rodent had to poke his head to get the cheese. When he did so, a collar fitted with bells sprung onto his neck. In theory, he would then hurtle back to his rat-hole making such a noise that his friends and relations would flee!

1908

Spiritualism was born in Hydesville, New York when it first became clear that the 'rappings' heard in the Fox family's home were no ordinary noises. Addressing the rapper as 'Mr Splitfoot' – presumably an epithet for the Devil – eleven-year-old Kate Fox engaged him in conversation. 'Talking in taps', he told her and her mother that he was the spirit of a pedlar murdered in the house some years before. The visitations continued and when the cellar was investigated, small pieces of bone were found. Medical tests couldn't positively identify them as human, however, and in 1850 the great showman P.T. Barnum whisked the girls away and presented them as the world's first professional mediums. Much accused of charlatanism, they eventually became alcoholics and died. Fifty-six years after the event, children playing in the 'Spook House' disturbed a crumbling wall – and there lay the skeleton of the pedlar.

1848

The Prince Regent's strangest friend George Hanger died of a convulsive fit, aged seventy-three. Soldier, socialite, gambler and Don Juan, he'd lost his virginity to a carpenter's wife at Eton, married a gipsy and once rode his horse into the attic of the royal mistress's house.

Refusing to use his title Baron Coleraine, he got heavily in debt and became a coal merchant and inventor, including among his brighter ideas a new kind of rat-trap, a cannon to deter poachers, a drum to keep the congregation awake in church and a tax on the urine of men who 'made water in the streets'. When he accompanied the Duchess of York for a trip on the Thames, the waterman said, 'Your Highness must wait for the tide.' Said George, 'Had I been the tide, I should have waited for Your Highness.'

1824

The first zip was patented by Whitcomb L. Judson of Chicago. It was designed for boots and shoes and was soon being manufactured by Colonel Walker's 'Automatic Hook and Eye Company' under the brand-name 'C-Curity'. Despite its name, it kept catching and bursting open. A Swede called Sundback refined the design, and it was successfully marketed in 1913 as the Talon Slide Fastener. It was first fitted to women's dresses in 1930 and finally made flies in 1935. Stories about it abounded. According to one, it was used on special shoes for sheep in a foot-and-mouth outbreak, and for ease of examination a surgeon sewed one into a patient's stomach.

1896

Today's the day...

It's April Fool's Day, a custom possibly dating back to the Roman celebration of the equinox or more likely to sixteenth-century France, where they changed New Year's Day from 1 April to 1 January, leaving fools to celebrate three months late. It's now the day when dupes are sent to find hen's teeth, rubber hammers, tartan paint and left-handed screwdrivers. Radio 4 reported the French were overfishing sea-borne frogs off Cornwall and television's *Panorama* ran a feature on spaghetti-tree farming in Italy. In 1868 the notorious Reno Brothers celebrated by escaping from jail, leaving a chalked message on the walls – it read 'April Fool'! *Annual Event*

Britain's other monarch the then thirty-nine-year-old Richard Booth declared himself King of Hay-on-Wye. Hay, population 1,500, nestles on the English-Welsh border. It's the second-hand book centre of the world, home of the badger-faced sheep and the Cusop Dingle snail and, according to His Majesty, it's been raped by creeping bureaucracy. At the time of the declaration, it could boast a cabinet, a field-marshal and its own currency, and there were plans afoot for a university and, rather more obscurely, a number of model pterodactyls. Passports cost £1, knighthoods £1.50, earldoms retailed at £5 with a free t-shirt and for £25 you could enjoy all the 'secret privileges' of a Hay Dukedom. *1977*

England's oddest guru Wednesday Lobsang Rampa first saw the light while walking in the hills above Oldham. Born in Beaconsfield of Anglo-Celtic descent and named after the great Irish Buddhist Tuesday Lobsang Rampa, he now lives in a tiny cottage called 'The Pimple', perched 700ft up in the Pennines. An advocate of free love by example, he lives with a eunuch called 'Sparrow', subsists almost entirely on rabbit meat and mealy biscuits, and devotes much of his days to the contemplative pursuit his disciples call 'seeking sticks in the grass'. Small, stocky, ginger-haired and handsome, he wears nothing but a fur coat and white socks whatever the weather, and is renowned for his gentleness, long thoughtful silences and strange periods of inspired trance-like moaning. Though considered by many to be an austere and humourless figure, he often shocks strangers by rolling on his back and appealing to them to tickle his tummy.   *1972*

The human book factory Edgar Wallace was born in Greenwich, the illegitimate son of an actor and actress, and brought up by a Billingsgate fish-porter. Once a newsboy, trawlerman and labourer, he became a £50,000-a-year writer, married twice, kept a special bank account to bail out friends in financial trouble, and died at fifty-six £134,000 in the red. Sitting at a desk surrounded by glass on three sides to keep out the draughts, this large expansive man wrote 10,000 words a day with his feet in a fur muff, fortified by thirty cups of tea, doughnuts and ginger beer. In his twenty-eight-year career, he wrote 173 books, twenty-two plays and literally hundreds of articles and stories. He wrote the screenplay for *King Kong* in nine weeks, and composed so fast, it was said he could turn out a novel in the back of a taxi in a traffic jam.   *1875*

The greatest race-horse that ever lived, 'Eclipse', was foaled during an eclipse, in the stables of 'Stinking Billy' the Duke of Cumberland. Sold to a Yorkshire meat trader for only eighty guineas, he was rising six before he started racing. 'Abominably bad-tempered', this big rangy chestnut panted like an old cart horse, yet even heavily handicapped could run four miles in eight minutes, and in his short seventeen-month career was unbeaten in twenty-six outings. He literally ran out of competition and was retired to stud, siring sons and daughters that won 344 races and a string of descendants that won over 100 Derbys. He was to say the least a big hearted horse, and this was admirably demonstrated after he died at twenty-five, and his heart was actually found to weigh nearly 14lbs.   *1764*

Today's the day...

A new play by Shakespeare – *Vortigern and Rowena* – was
performed at Drury Lane. Its discoverer William Henry Ireland had
been given a bundle of documents in a coffee house and found they
contained the Bard's originals of various bits of plays, a lock of his
hair and a love-letter to Anne Hathaway. They were all put on show
in Ireland's bookshop and among the people who flocked to see them
was Boswell, who reverently kissed the relics. Two months later
Ireland turned up with the play, and this unique masterpiece was
snapped up by Richard Brinsley Sheridan for £300. The leading
actor, John Kemble, had his doubts about the piece and when he
pronounced, with laborious grimacing, his line: 'And when this
solemn mockery is o'er', the audience saw his meaning and collapsed
laughing. A red-faced Ireland made a hasty exit and confessed that
he'd forged the lot.   *1796*

An ice meteor had a happy landing. It fell from the sky just
after a single flash of lightning and crashed to the ground in Burton
Road, Manchester. It was picked up by Richard Griffiths who rushed
home and put it in his freezer. It was given a thorough analysis, found
to contain fifty-one layers of ice and come from a larger meteor
weighing around 4lbs. All this was discovered because coincidentally
Dr Griffiths was a lightning observer for the Electrical Research
Association who'd happened to be walking down the street.   *1973*

The world's greatest lover, the incredible adventurer Giacomo
Casanova, was born. Though he was later a secret agent, gambler,
factory owner and writer, he started his nefarious career by taking
Minor Orders in the Church. On one of the few occasions when he
preached a sermon, however, the collection consisted largely of
propositions from ladies and thereafter he followed his true vocation.
Travelling around Europe from St Petersburg to Constantinople, he
waded through duels, scandals and swindles, chasing every female

that took his fancy. He never 'attacked' novices or 'those with strong prejudices' and he refused the famous courtesan Kitty Fisher on the grounds that he couldn't speak her language and, 'Without speech, the pleasure of love is diminished by at least two-thirds.' Surprisingly, with the licentious Empress Catherine of Russia, he only discussed the reform of the calendar and on one singular, and horrifying occasion, he was actually turned down by one he loved. She was the exquisite *demi-mondaine* La Charpillon who actually preferred a barber's apprentice. 'On that fatal day,' said Casanova, 'I began to die and ceased to live.'

1725

The original Ugly Duckling Hans Christian Andersen was born in Odense to a family that included a shoemaker and a brothel keeper. He was extremely gawky, had a high-pitched voice, 'long swinging arms', a big nose and colossal feet. For years he struggled with 'serious writing' and then finally developed his real talent for fairy stories. Andersen was agoraphobic, and a raving hypochondriac – he even got toothache in his dentures – and in all his life he never had a sexual relationship. Determined to deprive him of his virginity, his friends took him to a brothel in Paris. He found a nice young Turkish lady called Fernanda – and spent the entire evening talking to her about Constantinople!

1805

Nelson turned a blind eye at the Battle of Copenhagen. With the fleet 'dreadfully cut up', Admiral Hyde Parker signalled 'discontinue battle' to Nelson aboard the *Elephant*. With 'glorious disobedience' Nelson raised his 'glass' to his blind eye and remarked, 'I really do not see the signal.', continued to fight, and the English won the day. Although he admitted it was the most terrible of all the sea battles he'd ever seen, he was remarkably cool about the whole affair. When a cannon ball shot through the mainmast, he smiled and casually remarked, 'This is warm work!'

1801

Today's the day...

Caraboo the mystery princess appeared in the village of Almondsbury in Gloucestershire, clothed and turbaned all in black, and speaking a strange language which no one could understand. She was taken in by the local magistrate and a young Portuguese called Manuel offered to translate. She was, he said, a princess from Javasu in the East Indies who'd been captured by pirates, ransomed for a sack of gold and escaped off the English coast and swum ashore. She stayed in the big house, communicated her language to lexicologists, climbed on the roof every Tuesday, and terrified the villagers by occasionally going on the warpath – banging a tambourine and firing arrows. It was only when the *Bath Chronicle* reported her story that the truth came out, and it was revealed that the Princess was none other than Mary Baker, a runaway servant from Devon, who'd taken up with highwaymen and gipsies. The poor girl ended up in Bristol – selling leeches. *1817*

Jesse James was murdered, shot in the back at point blank range as he stretched up to adjust a picture on his cabin wall. The killer was his cousin Bob Ford and the two had been planning a robbery. Ford rushed back to Kansas City to claim the $10,000 reward and expected to find himself a great hero. To his dismay he was reviled and threatened, especially when it was discovered that Jesse had been unarmed. He ended up running a saloon in Colorado where he himself was killed eleven years later. It's often been claimed that Ford didn't in fact shoot Jesse James and that a lookalike Charlie Bigelow was killed instead. In 1948 a white-haired old gentleman from Oklahoma known as Frank J. Dalton said that he was the real Jesse. He was now 102 and had escaped to South America on the day of the shooting.   *1882*

Moody mumbler Marlon Brando was born in Omaha, Nebraska. Expelled from military academy, he dug ditches for a while then went to study at the famous Actors' Studio in New York. At twenty-two he was voted Broadway's Most Promising Actor and was finally tempted to Hollywood with an offer of $50,000. He arrived there aggressively 'anti-star' in blue jeans and t-shirt and became known variously as 'The Slob', 'The Male Garbo' and 'The Walking Hormone Factory'.   *1924*

Britain's rudest doctor John Abernethy was born in London. A brilliant surgeon who happily cared for the poor, he nevertheless found it hard to tolerate the whims of his private patients. He returned a shilling of his fee to one 'highly-strung' lady and told her to buy a skipping-rope, and when another over-indulged patient asked how he might live a healthy life, Abernethy replied sharply, 'Live on sixpence a day – and earn it!'   *1764*

Cradle-snatching Commander-in-Chief Frederick, Duke of York, issued his first official act. In it he ordered the recall to active service of 'every lieutenant-colonel under twenty, and every captain under the age of twelve'.   *1798*

Today's the day...

ACW/2 Horton accidentally took to the air, clinging on for dear life to the tail of a Spitfire – at one point with just three fingers! In rough weather flight mechanics had to lie across the tails of the aircraft when they were taxi-ing. The unfortunate Ms Horton hadn't managed to jump off before the plane took off and found herself hoisted up into the skies. The offending aircraft already had a reputation – it was nicknamed 'T' for trouble.

1945

Martin Luther King was killed by a single gunshot as he stood on the balcony of his motel in Memphis, Tennessee. The alleged assassin was James Earl Ray – a petty crook and an 'all-time loser' – who drove out of town minutes later in a white Ford Mustang, leaving behind his rifle, clothes and a single fingerprint. Dr King was always conscious his life was in danger – there had already been two attempts to kill him. Just the day before he'd said, 'Like anybody, I would like to live a long life . . . But I'm not concerned about that now. I just want to do God's will. And he's allowed me to go up to the mountain. And I've looked over, and I've seen the promised land.'

1968

Elizabeth I didn't knight Francis Drake aboard the *Golden Hind* at Deptford. She was supposed to, but as Drake had only recently returned from his Pacific voyage with a treasure trove plundered from the Spanish, for the Queen to knight him would be a direct insult to Spain. Instead the wily Elizabeth waved the ceremonial sword above the head of the nation's hero and laughingly commented that he really ought to be beheaded for piracy. Then with consummate grace she handed the sword to the French emissary at her side and ordered him to perform the ceremony. Naturally, at the order of the Queen, he had to comply. Thus with the Spanish Ambassador noting every action, Elizabeth neatly implicated France in the alliance against Spain – but so subtly that she could always plead innocent.   *1581*

The world's first woman mayor was elected by a two-thirds majority at Argonia, Kansas. This important milestone in feminine history came as a great surprise, especially to the victorious twenty-seven-year-old Susanna Salter. She didn't know she was a candidate until she arrived at the polling station.   *1887*

The Byzantine harlot empress Theodora was crowned alongside Emperor Justinian. The daughter of a bear-trainer who got hugged to death, she'd been on the streets since she was twelve, and married her first husband Emperor Justin after his wife had opportunely died. When he died too, she married his nephew Justinian and, on his behalf, quelled a riot by promising the people a grand circus at the Hippodrome. The wine flowed freely and everyone enjoyed the games. Then in came Theodora's guards and slaughtered the entire audience – all 30,000 of them. When her illegitimate son turned up years later, husband Justinian suspected he was her lover and slaughtered him. Horrified, Theodora turned to religion and spent the rest of her life commissioning churches. She did such a good job that when she died, this scheming ex-prostitute was promptly declared a saint.   *AD 527*

Today's the day...

The ill-matched royal lovers the Prince of Wales and Caroline of Brunswick met for the first time, three days before their arranged marriage. Under the influence of trendy Beau Brummel, the English court had recently adopted the novel custom of washing and changing their clothes regularly. Not so in Brunswick – so when the Prince came within range of his bride-to-be, she was a good deal less than wholesome. Risking her halitosis, he kissed her – carefully – and retired to a distant corner of the room and called for brandy. At the wedding, the Prince was again well fortified in spirit – so well in fact that he passed out and spent his wedding night in a drunken stupor on the floor.   *1795*

'The Witch Queen of Hollywood' Bette Davis was born of Pilgrim heritage in Lowell, Massachusetts, where the Davis clan had once been accused of sorcery. Never the standardised glamour-puss of thirties Hollywood, Miss Davis ran screaming from her first screen test and claimed that if she didn't make it in the movies, she was quite prepared to be 'the best secretary in the world'. Though now recognised as one of the greatest actresses the star system produced, she felt that she was treated like a factory worker, and put in so many outstanding performances in dreadful movies that one critic said, 'Only bad films are good enough for her.' When her film career was at its nadir, she wasn't too proud to put an advertisement in the trade press asking for work. She got *Whatever Happened to Baby Jane?* and though she only got a small fee, she also got a share of the profits. It made her a million.   *1908*

The original Peter Pan died – and would have been horrified to hear himself called that. All his life Peter Llewellyn Davies had suffered from his association with the perennially popular character that J. M. Barrie had created out of his strange and suffocating relationship with the boy and his three brothers. Peter came to refer

April 5

to the play as 'that terrible masterpiece' and said, 'If that boy so fatally committed to an arrestation of his development had only been dubbed George, or Jack, or Michael, or Nicholas, what miseries would have been spared me.' At the age of sixty-three, Mr Davies threw himself under a tube train. *1960*

Multi-millionaire recluse Howard Hughes died on board his private jet on its way to Houston, Texas. Since the early sixties the man who had so much money he could have bought literally anything he wanted, had lived in darkened rooms in hotels around the world and become so weak and emaciated he was like a 'frail long-legged child'. Not surprisingly, with an estimated £500 million at stake, there has been a flood of 'authentic' wills since his death – totalling some thirty-seven to date. One leaves everything to a former chief executive, another instructs that all his money should be stuffed into coffins and burnt, and a third leaves everything to his supposed illegitimate son – who says he used to communicate with Mr Hughes 'through a radio planted in his head'. *1976*

'The Scarlet Sodomite' English poet Algernon Charles Swinburne was born of aristocratic parents. He was small and fragile with 'the eye of a god and the smile of an elf', a mop of flaming red hair, a piping voice and 'a peculiar dancing step'. He was sent to Eton and the beatings he got there gave him a taste for flagellation. At Oxford he was dubbed 'Dear Carrots', joined the 'Pre-Raphaelites' and took to 'insanely and indecently' embracing his men friends. As he got older, and retreated more and more into sado-masochism and alcohol, he was rescued by his friend and legal adviser, Theo Watts-Dutton – who installed him in his peaceful home in Putney. The ageing poet spent the rest of his life there, earnestly writing and meticulously dusting his books. In fact, the high spot of his day in later years was nothing more wicked than to walk across the common for a pint of brown ale. *1837*

Today's the day...

Body-snatching shoemakers got little thanks when they brought home the cadaver of one of their colleagues to his widow after he'd been executed. She would have none of it so they tried to sell it 'to all the apothecaries from Horsley down to Rotherhithe at a very cheap rate'. There were no offers so they gave up and buried the unwanted body in St George's Fields.   *1739*

The painter Raphael was born and died on the same day thirty-seven years later. Named after one of the archangels, he came to Rome under the patronage of Pope Julius II. Both he and Michelangelo were at work beautifying the Vatican at the same time, but the two despised each other. Michelangelo jeered that the ever-popular Raphael went about the streets 'with a suite like a general', while Raphael retorted it was better than going about alone 'like the hangman'. Raphael didn't take kindly to criticism and when two cardinals complained that the cheeks of St Peter and St Paul were too pink he coolly replied, 'My Lords, they blush for shame that their church on earth should be governed by such men as you!'   *1483/1520*

April 6

Master escapologist Harry Houdini was born Ehrich Weiss in
Appleton, Wisconsin, the son of a Rabbi from Budapest. He spent
his childhood exercising in the family woodshed and became so supple
he could pick up pins with his eyelashes, thread needles with his toes
and flex every single muscle in his body. He adopted the name Houdini
in honour of the great French magician Robert-Houdin, and soon
became known as 'The Handcuff King' when with consummate
ease he would slip off a pair of locked handcuffs – even in the middle
of Scotland Yard. 'My chief task,' he once said, 'has been to
conquer fear. I have to keep absolutely calm. If I grow panicky I
am lost.'
                                                                    1874

An earthquake in London killed two people, the first such recorded
fatalities. It was Easter Wednesday, the churches were full and while
the faithful were at prayer, a violent earth tremor shook the city. All
the church bells rang out at once and two curious apprentices rushed
out of Christchurch to see what was happening – they were killed by
falling masonry.
                                                                    1580

The first Olympic gold medallist was James Connolly of America
who won the triple jump. His first prize medal was actually silver – but
he did get a diploma and a crown of olive branches too.
                                                                    1896

The first man at the North Pole Robert Peary arrived with his
negro servant Henson and four eskimos – Ootah, Egingwah, Seegloo
and Ookeah. He'd studied the Eskimos closely, adopted their clothing
and means of travelling, and with the help of 246 dogs finally achieved –
'The pole at last! My dream and goal of twenty years!' In celebration
he planted five flags including a silk 'Stars and Stripes' which he had to
confess looked 'somewhat worn and discoloured'. It was hardly
surprising, since on every expedition north for the last fifteen years
he'd been carrying it along – wrapped around his body.
                                                                    1909

Today's the day...

The lustful poet Sir William Davenant died in his lodgings at his theatre in Lincoln's Inn Fields. Many people thought he was Shakespeare's son, since Sir William's father had kept an inn on the road from London to Stratford and the Bard had often stayed there and been particularly friendly with the lady of the house. Sir William himself had never denied it and when he was 'pleasant' over a glass of wine, he often remarked that he wrote 'with the very spirit of Shakespeare'. His own love-life, however, was rather unfortunate. He got 'a terrible clap off a black handsome wench' that cost him his nose and he'd had to endure jokes about its loss ever after. One day a beggar woman accosted him and blessed his eyesight. Upon enquiring why she did so Sir William was told, 'Ah, good sir, should your sight ever fail you, you must borrow a nose of your neighbour to hang your spectacles on!'   *1688*

The first box of matches was sold by their inventor, chemist John Walker of Stockton-on-Tees. He'd been working to discover some combustible material for flintlocks, and the stick he'd been using to stir up his brew of potash and antimony had a blob on the end. Walker scraped it along the stone floor to remove it and it ignited! Eager to capitalise on his new invention he got the boys of the local grammar schools to cut up the tiny matchsticks and paid them just six pence a hundred. All went well until one bright spark used a jackplane to cut the sticks. They all came out curved, and wouldn't fit in the box, and the matchless Mr Walker put a damper on the whole business.   *1827*

The notorious highwayman Dick Turpin was hanged at York. Contrary to popular belief, he wasn't a romantic figure at all but a pock-marked cattle-thief, brutal house-breaker and rapist. Along with Tom King he committed so many robberies on the Cambridge Road that the inns would no longer shelter him and he had to live in a cave. He shot one man who came to arrest him and, in escaping from another, accidentally shot King – who died in Newgate prison. After such a close shave he took refuge in Yorkshire, changed his name to John Palmer and lived as a horse-dealer. He was arrested after deliberately shooting a neighbour's hen; his true identity was discovered and he was condemned to death. He bought a new coat and shoes, paid £3 10s for five men to be his mourners, and on arrival at the gallows, he stamped his leg impatiently when it began to tremble, then vigorously threw himself off the ladder.   *1739*

Farmer Thompson sold his wife. He led her through the streets of Carlisle, dressed in all her finery, and told the town crier to announce that he would be selling her at noon. As an introduction to the sale, Thompson advised the audience to avoid 'troublesome wives and frolicsome women' as they would 'a mad dog, a roaring lion, cholera morbus or Mount Etna'. Not surprisingly after such encouragement, there weren't any bids and a full hour passed by in silence. Finally one Henry Mears bid for Mrs Thompson and she was knocked down for him to twenty shillings – and a Newfoundland dog.   *1832*

Today's the day...

'The Beast of Germany' the multiple murderer Bruno Ludke died. A mentally defective sex-maniac, he started killing at eighteen and eleven years later when the war came, he had a field day. He was a laundryman by trade and when he wasn't stabbing, strangling, robbing and raping women, he liked to torture animals and once ran an old lady over with his horse-drawn cart just for fun. He was first convicted for sexual assault and sterilised by Himmler's SS. Then, in 1943, he was finally arrested for murder. In all, he confessed to a record eighty-five killings, but so many innocent men had already been executed for crimes Ludke admitted to, that the whole affair was hushed up. He was sent to a hospital in Vienna and used as a guinea pig for 'various experiments'. Today they tried a new injection on him. It didn't work.   *1944*

The Duke of Wellington's pigeon established a record that's never been reliably broken. The bird was released from a ship sailing along the coast of West Africa. If it travelled as the crow flies, it winged its way some 5,500 miles, but if as is more likely it made a detour to avoid the desert, it probably flew nearer 7,000. It was found about a mile from home in London – stone-dead from exhaustion.   *1845*

'The girl with the curls' champion hustler and superstar Mary Pickford was born in Toronto. She was really called Gladys Smith and before her New York *début* at thirteen, she'd quite happily toured the States – often unchaperoned – to earn the family's keep. For her first movie, she upped her price from $5 to $10 a day, and soon had a starring role in the less than immortal *Violin Maker of Cremona*. In 1910, with *The Little Teacher*, she was a smash hit and for the next twenty-three years she was never anything else. She once told a producer, 'I can't afford to work for less than $10,000 a week', and in 1919, to protect her interests, she formed 'United Artists' with Chaplin and husband No.2, Douglas Fairbanks. It was said that 'it took longer

to make one of Mary's contracts than it did to make one of Mary's
pictures', but until the advent of talkies she was 'the world's
sweetheart' and reigned supreme. Her films were mostly awful, but
nobody cared because 'it was Pickford'. When one was billed in
Scotland, they didn't even give the title. The sign just read 'What
happened to Mary – twice nightly'.   *1893*

Sorrowful monarch Philip IV of Spain was born in Valladolid. He
presided over the decline of his empire, was married twice, took advice
from a mystic nun, ruined horses with his riding, banned fictitious
plots in plays, forbade ruffs and starch, had hats trimmed to 'a decent
narrowness' and was refused point blank by the lady-in-waiting he
most desired as a mistress. Not surprisingly, it's recorded that he only
laughed three times in his life.   *1605*

A tragic attempt to assassinate Krushchev was made in the mining
town of Tatabanya in Hungary in the wake of the 1956 rising.
Krushchev was there to explain how the Russian invasion had been a
gesture of friendship and the assassins, twenty-five in number, were
out to stop him and avenge their dead. They unearthed a pile of arms
in the woods nearby and were testing them when a rifle went off and
killed its handler. In no time the woods were surrounded by secret
police, and all the would-be assassins were incarcerated in the
Virgin Mary prison in Budapest where many of them were tortured
and every one of them was executed. The eldest was hanged, the
youngest was shot. They were respectively aged seventeen and
twelve.   *1958*

It was warm for the time of year thought the great English
satirist Jonathan Swift, and he wrote as much in his *Journal to Stella*.
Well, what he actually wrote was that 'It was bloody hot out walking
today.'   *1711*

Today's the day...

The secret life of Edward 'Beau' Wilson came to an end as the result of a duel. Beau was the fifth son of a poor gentleman of Leicestershire, who lived so amazingly high off the hog in London that some thought he was a highwayman, while others said he'd found the philosopher's stone. He was challenged by the gambler and financier John Law for no apparent reason and killed in Bloomsbury Square. Fourteen years later, some letters were published which suggested that Beau was a kept man and that the 'unknown' lady who kept him was Lady Elizabeth Villiers, William III's mistress and Countess of Orkney. She'd arranged the affair, met Beau anonymously and always in the dark, and made him swear never to try and identify her on pain of death. He recognised her in society, however, by the 'feel' of 'a very particular ring' and as soon as she realised he'd discovered who she was, she arranged for his 'euthanasia'. Poor Beau left just a few pounds and never said a word.   *1694*

'Old Man River' Paul Robeson was born in Princeton, New Jersey, the son of an ex-slave and minister. He became an all-American footballer, lawyer, preacher, actor and singer, and was a good deal more popular in England – especially after his 1928 triumph in *Showboat* – then he ever was in America. He was a declared anti-fascist, labelled 'a commie' in the US, and was one of the few contemporary prominent blacks to be a vocal anti-racist. He was much criticised for slipping on a leopard skin as the African chief in *Sanders of the River*, and when he said to a real chief – 'What do you expect me to wear in Africa, tweeds ?' – the English educated Ashanti replied, 'Why not old boy – that's exactly what we do.'   *1898*

Britain's last beheading took place on Tower Hill with the very block and axe that now rests in the Bloody Tower. The victim was the incorrigible Lord Lovat who'd fought against the Jacobites in the 1715 Rebellion and mostly fought with them in the disastrous '45. The corpulent old scoundrel was said to have asked to be hanged because his neck was too short for beheading, and he told the executioner that if he hit him in the shoulders he might be able to rise again and 'should be very angry'.   *1747*

Bacon was killed by a chicken. The great philosopher and statesman Francis Bacon, Viscount St Albans, was 'taking the aire' near Highgate when the snow lay on the ground. He wondered 'why flesh might not be preserved in snow as in salt', stopped and got a woman to 'extenterate' a chicken, and helped stuff the snow inside it. He caught a chill in the process and thanks to a damp bed came down with 'such a cold' that he suffocated – and no one could save his bacon!   *1626*

Captain Jenkins lost an ear when his sloop *Rebecca* was boarded off Havana by the Spanish coastguard who suspected him of smuggling. The wicked Captain Fandino lopped off the lug supposedly claiming he'd do the same to the English King if he could but catch him. Jenkins kept the wrinkled piece 'wrapped in cotton' and not unreasonably complained bitterly about his treatment. He was largely ignored for seven years, until Britain wanted an excuse to throw its weight about in the West Indies, and belatedly 'outraged' by the removal of Jenkins' flap, declared war on Spain – the War of Jenkins' Ear.   *1731*

The Warrior King Henry V was crowned in his twenty-fifth year in Westminster. Supposedly, he'd given up his hard-drinking, womanising ways and 'appeared to be almost an angel', but more likely his 'bluff Prince Hal' image was a later invention and he was probably always the dour military zealot he afterwards seemed to be. At any rate, he was a bundle of fun at the coronation feast. He didn't eat anything then, and neither did he eat for the next three days.   *1413*

Today's the day...

The Chartists shook London when over 20,000 of them gathered on Kennington Common to march to Parliament with their petition for universal male suffrage and revolutionary electoral reforms. In a state of panic, London had adopted a 'warlike attitude'; cannon were planted along the Embankment, 8,000 troops were called in and the Duke of Wellington took command. To everybody's great relief, 'the intended tragedy' was avoided and the meeting dispersed quietly after the Chartist leader Feargus O'Connor was given leave to take the petition to Parliament himself. It was so bulky it filled up three cabs and was said to contain over five million signatures. However, some doubt was cast on its authenticity when it was discovered that not only had 'Cheeks the Marine' and 'Mr Punch' signed, but also 'seventeen Dukes of Wellington' and 'a baker's dozen of Queens'. *1848*

Father Mathew founded the Temperance Movement in Cork with his characteristic watchword, 'Here goes – in the name of the Lord!' He travelled the country spreading the word and converts flocked in droves to sign the pledge of total abstinence. Somehow he never managed to convert his servant, John, an old bachelor who sported an exceedingly red nose. One evening while John was serving supper there was a 'frightful smack of whisky'. When taken to task he innocently explained that it was purely by accident he'd drunk some of the spirit – he'd put it in the jug by mistake while he was 'cleaning his tins' with it! *1838*

'Vile versifier' John Wilmot, Third Earl of Rochester was born. Sent to Oxford at thirteen, he was put in the care of the licentious Dr Whitehall, and soon emulated his mentor by contracting venereal disease and becoming a heavy drinker. That year Charles II was restored to the throne, and Rochester soon found himself at Court with a fat income. He joined in the junketings led by the dissolute George Villiers, made a name for himself as a 'lewd and profane'

April 10

writer and excelled even his 'gross companions with his profligacy'. His poems were always at least indecent and often libellous, and it was he who dubbed Charles the 'pritty, witty King' who 'never said a foolish thing and never did a wise one'.   *1647*

The safety-pin was patented after the American inventor Walter Hunt had created the immortal concept in three hours flat. The ubiquitous safety-pin didn't do him much good, as he gave the idea, lock, stock and barrel, to a friend to pay off a $15 debt.   *1849*

'The Living Skeleton' Claude Seurat was born to robust peasant parents in Troyes, France. Normal to start with, he grew taller and thinner by the year, until when he was fully grown at 5ft 7½in he weighed only 5st 8lb. 'Pinched and poked in every direction' by inquisitive French doctors, he fled to England and made a fortune exhibiting himself at the 'Chinese Saloon' on Pall Mall. His wasted body was barely 3ins deep from chest to spine and his biceps were only 4ins round. What most tickled his audiences, however, was his outfit – 'a small piece of fringed purple silk' with holes cut in it for his huge protruding hip-bones.   *1797*

Today's the day...

William and Mary were crowned with disaster at one of the most unfortunate coronations in British history. The Archbishop of Canterbury refused to perform the service and a reluctant Bishop of London had to do it instead. Since they were to be joint monarchs, they had to go through everything in unison in a little duet of bowing, kneeling, kissing the Bible and swearing, and then after all that the Champion, Sir Charles Dymock, was late arriving to make the traditional challenge to the sovereigns' enemies. To crown it all, one of the speeches at the banquet was made by a gentleman who couldn't pronounce his aitches. 'Future ages', he said toasting William, 'regarding your majesty's exploits, will call you a Nero.'   *1689*

The brilliant and irritating Prime Minister, George Canning was born in 'narrow circumstances' and was financed at Eton and Oxford by his uncle. He started as a Whig, turned Tory and at thirty-seven became an outstanding but highly controversial Foreign Secretary. Sir Walter Scott said his tongue 'would have penetrated the hide of a rhinoceros'. He quarrelled with Wellington and pretty well all of the Tory hierarchy; fought his famous duel with fellow minister Castlereagh and drove Pitt insane because 'he was like a mistress – always affronted and always writing notes.'   *1770*

'The Princely Cheat' James Stuart de la Cloche was admitted as a Jesuit novice at St Andrea at Quirinale in Rome. He claimed to be the eldest natural son of Charles II of England and produced two letters from his Dad and one from the itinerant Queen Christina of Denmark to prove it. According to de la Cloche, it was all part of an elaborate plot to facilitate Charles's secret conversion to Catholicism; de la Cloche would become the King's clandestine confessor, and perhaps ultimately his successor. On this pretext, he twice extorted a small fortune from the Jesuits, then disappeared. Someone claiming to be him turned up in Jersey, where for a long time the story was that de la

Cloche was indeed Charles' son by a liaison with a local girl, and that he so much resembled his father that his half brothers had him locked in a French jail – the original of the Man in the Iron Mask. *1668*

A US President was arrested for speeding. It was Ulysses S. Grant's first offence – when he was still commander of the Army of the Potomac – and in July he was caught again and fined $5. As President, he took to hurtling around Washington in a carriage and was apprehended for the third time. A black policeman hurled himself at the horse and was dragged down the road. When he saw who the driver was the policeman apologised, but Grant said, 'Officer do your duty.' So he did and the President was taken to the station. *1866*

The tragedy of the elephant man came to an end when poor John Merrick died aged twenty-nine. He was hideously deformed with a massive bony head, a 'tusk' protruding from his mouth and 'bags' of wrinkled skin hanging down his back. Far from being brutalised by a life spent gawked at as 'an object of horror', he was a sensitive, intelligent soul. The Prince of Wales sent him gifts, and the actress Mrs Kendal arranged for secret trips to the theatre. Merrick, who always slept with his hugely heavy head on his knees, was found lying flat on his bed and it was assumed the weight of his head had dislocated his neck. He'd often wished he could lie down to sleep 'like other people' and it looked as if sadly, on this last night, he had tried. *1890*

A corker of an alarm clock was presented at the US Patent Office. Invented by a man called S.S. Applegate who had no time for ordinary alarms, it consisted of a frame hung directly over the sleeper, suspended by a cord with an automatic release mechanism attached to the clock. Fixed to the frame were sixty cork bricks and when the chosen hour came around, they fell on the sleeper's head. *1882*

Today's the day...

The first shots of the American Civil War were fired when
Confederate guns started shelling the fortified Federal outpost of Fort
Sunter in Charleston Harbour, South Carolina. They kept at it for a
wearing thirty-four hours, during which time not a soul was killed or
injured, but the Fort was thoroughly wrecked. Finally the Federal
Commander Major Anderson surrendered. He ordered a fifty-gun
salute and ironically, it was on the fiftieth discharge that a premature
explosion caused the first death. There were well over 600,000 more
to follow between then and the time, four years to the day later, when
the Confederate President Jefferson Davis was informed of the South's
surrender. Of this bloody and bitter struggle, sparked off by the
question of slavery, the British historian Thomas Carlyle was to say,
'They are cutting each other's throats because one half of them prefer
hiring their servants for life and the other half by the hour.'   *1861*

Death robbed Roosevelt of victory. F.D.R. was sitting for his
portrait in the 'Little White House' in Warm Springs, Georgia. As
President, he'd led America through World War II and now he
was resting with Lucy Mercer, the woman he'd loved for nearly

thirty years, by his side. He turned to the artist and said, 'We have just fifteen minutes.' Exactly fifteen minutes later he said, 'I have a terrible headache' – then he collapsed and three hours after he died. A fortnight later it was VE Day and the war with Germany was officially won.   *1945*

The classic British weather forecast was delivered to an expectant nation by BBC Radio. 'The weather will be cold,' their weatherman said. 'There will be two reasons for this. One is that temperatures will be lower.'   *1969*

Napoleon tried to commit suicide – a fact that was only confirmed in 1937. Faced with the near certainty of exile after the disaster of his Russian campaign, he took a large dose of poison. Forbidding General de Caulaincourt to fetch a doctor, he gave him a letter for the Empress and said, 'Soon I shall exist no more.' In fact, he only succeeded in making himself sick and in an attempt to prevent himself vomiting he developed violent hiccups. While he was thus prostrated, Caulaincourt disobeyed him and brought the physician. When the Emperor had recovered he said with his usual dramatic flair, 'It seems I shall live, since death cares as little for me in my bed as it does on the battle-field.'   *1814*

The Daddy of Rock'n'Roll, Bill Haley, recorded two songs that shook America and took Great Britain by storm. They were 'Shake, Rattle and Roll' and 'Rock Around the Clock'. They were both enormous sellers and 'Clock' became the first record ever to sell a million in Britain alone. It stayed at the top of the US charts for seven weeks, the British charts for five. It was featured in fourteen films; recorded in thirty-five different languages; made in 140 different versions, and to date its total sales amount to a staggering figure of more than twenty-two million copies.   *1954*

Today's the day...

The snoozing statesman Frederick Lord North was born, awkward, bulky, pop-eyed, and exceedingly careless. As Prime Minister he lost a file of secret papers which was found 'lying wide open in the water closet'. He also lost the American colonies. 'Even now,' said a sententious speaker for the Opposition, 'the noble Lord is slumbering over the ruin of his country'. 'I wish to God I was,' grunted North – who wasn't the only member of his family to be often insulted. At a high society gathering, a gentleman asked him who 'that frightful woman' was. 'That is my wife,' answered his lordship. To cover his embarrassment the gentleman said he didn't mean that one but 'the monster' next to her. 'That,' said Lord North, 'is my daughter.' At a dinner soon after a young wit was gaily regaling the lady next to him with the story. To his anguish she introduced herself as 'the very monster in question'. *1732*

The might of the British Empire cracked a very small nut, when General Sir Robert Napier, 17,000 troops, 19,000 horses and mules, 8,000 camels and forty-four elephants, captured Magdala, the mountain stronghold of Emperor Theodore of Abyssinia. Their object was to rescue one man, the British Ambassador Lord Cameron, who'd been seized by Theodore in a fit of pique. The cost to Britain for the nine-month expedition was a staggering £8,600,000. The cost to the Emperor was his life. He committed suicide with a gun given to him as a gift by Queen Victoria. *1868*

The most cunning of all Queen Mothers Catherine de Medici was born, the daughter of Florentine merchant princes. Orphaned, brought up by her uncle the Pope and married at thirteen to Henry of Orleans, she saw her husband become King of France and take over his father's mistress Diane de Poitiers. Reviled as 'the shopkeeper's daughter', she surrounded herself with a 'brigade of Amazons', popularised side-saddles and snuff, and bided her time. When the King died, she

gleefully kicked out Diane and for thirty years ruled France through
her three feeble sons. Ironically, for a woman who gained power
through her children, Catherine was childless for the first ten years
of her marriage and accused of being a lesbian. It was only with the
help of quacks and astrologers that she finally became pregnant and
then she produced ten children in quick succession – including a pair
of twins.   *1519*

'The moonshine philosopher' third President of the United States
and author of the Declaration of Independence, Long Tom Jefferson,
was born and for the rest of his life was 'as busy as a bee in a molasses
barrel'. Red-haired, freckle-faced and gangly, he rose before dawn,
strode around in carpet slippers, designed his magnificent house at
Monticello complete with self-opening doors and a refrigerator, and
among other things invented a pedometer, a perpetual clock and a
plough. He founded the University of Virginia, got through £5,000
worth of wine in the White House, and could often be seen clutching a
miniature violin, with his pet mocking-bird on his shoulder. When his
wife died he consoled himself with a young mulatto slave Sally Hemings
who's thought to have borne him five children. Though the press made
a great furore about it, having a slave-mistress was nothing new – Sally
was in fact his wife's half-sister.   *1743*

An explosion in space blew a faulty oxygen tank on moon mission
Apollo 13, leaving the crew of three short of air and fuel 205,000 miles
from home. Clambering into the cramped lunar module, they
—had just enough power to swing around the moon and get back to
the earth's atmosphere – fearful that the blast had damaged the heat-
shield. It hadn't and they returned in 'triumphant failure', having
achieved at least one remarkable first. On the way back they'd been
ordered to jettison their urine bags, and eleven little sacks were duly
cast adrift – destined to float in space forever.   *1970*

Today's the day...

The most famous decision ever made by the Jews was reached in the mighty fortress of Masada, perched high on a mountain top. For two years, 967 rebelling Jewish Zealots had held off the besieging Roman 10th Legion, and now it was clear they could hold them off no longer. On the prompting of their leader, Eleazar ben Jair, they chose to die free rather than face Roman retribution and slavery. Fathers put their families to the sword, then ten men chosen by ballot killed their comrades. When the slaughter was done, nine men bared their throats, and the last man despatched them before committing suicide himself. The following morning, the Romans poured over the wall and found a garrison of corpses. Just two women and five children had survived by hiding in a cistern, and in the face of such carnage, the Romans allowed them to live. *AD 73*

The last act of the dramatist Thomas Otway truncated his brief and unhappy life. His career in tatters, he was forced to go a-begging, and asked a gentleman for a shilling in a coffee house on Tower Hill. Touched by the fallen writer's sorry plight, the man gave him a guinea. The joyous Otway rushed off and bought a roll – and choked to death on the first mouthful. *1685*

The actor-assassin struck Lincoln down in very odd circumstances in Box 7 at Ford's Theatre in Washington – shooting him behind the left ear at point blank range. In the President's desk, eighty letters threatening his life were found, and that very morning he'd said, 'Do you know, I believe there are men who want to take my life. And I have no doubt they will do it.' So convinced was he that he went personally to Stanton, the Secretary of War, and asked him for a special bodyguard called Eckert – a man who could break five iron pokers over his arm. But the politically ambitious Stanton, who incredibly knew of the death-plot, refused – even though the guard had no other duties that night – and instead Lincoln was 'protected' by

April 14

Mayor Rathbone who was more interested in his fiancée and John F. Parker who had convictions for extortion, being drunk in a brothel and sleeping on duty. At the critical moment, the assassin John Wilkes Booth went unhindered, because Parker had gone for a drink!

1865

The world's most prestigious road race, the Monaco Grand Prix, first hurtled two miles through the narrow streets of the tiny principality. The tunnels, hills and hairpins, and the need for around 1,600 gear changes in seventy-eight laps, make this one of the most gruelling of all world championship motor races. The current lap record is 86.67mph, but the first race, won by Mr W. Williams in a Type 35B Bugatti, was driven at a breathless 49.83mph.

1929

A policeman's feet won £100 damages in a court action. An old press photograph showing P. C. Plumb all hot and bothered on point duty was used without his consent in an advertising campaign. The good constable was understandably insulted since the caption implied his feet were sweaty. 'Phew!' it read. 'I'm going to get my feet into a Jeyes' fluid bath.'

1937

Today's the day...

Dr Johnson's idiosyncratic dictionary was published. The good doctor had been working at it for eight years, sitting at an 'old crazy deal table' on an even older chair, which gradually disintegrated till he was left balancing on three of its legs and a single arm! Of his six assistants, five were Scottish, and with a typical stab of Scotophobic chauvinism, Johnson said they weren't much assistance at all. The complete lexicon contained 40,000 words and sold well despite its exorbitant price of £4 10s. Some of its more dubious definitions included: 'Net. Anything reticulated or decussated at equal distances, with interstices between the interections'; 'Oats. A grain which in England is generally given to horses, but in Scotland supports the people', and 'Excise. A hateful tax levied on commodities' – a jibe that had the Commissioners of Excise taking legal advice as to whether to sue or not.

1755

The unthinkable happened to the unsinkable in the middle of the North Atlantic, when the world's largest and most luxurious liner, the 46,328 ton *Titanic* struck a mountainous iceberg. The impact, which tore a 300ft gash through holds and boiler rooms, was hardly felt and some passengers actually went and played snowballs on deck. When the gravity of the situation became clear, all the passengers were assembled and it became horrifyingly apparent that to make way for luxuries, minor details like lifeboats had been neglected, and the great ship only carried enough to take a maximum of half the people to safety. Even then many refused to believe that the *Titanic* could sink and the first lifeboat left with only a dozen souls on board. Slowly, the terrible truth sank in and the panic grew. The General Director of the shipping company leapt aboard a boat, depriving a woman of a seat, while the millionaire Guggenheim and his valet courageously gave up their seats and calmly changed into evening dress so they could die in the style of gentlemen. All the while, the ship's band played a mixture of hymns and jolly ragtime tunes, and as the *Titanic* plunged to the depths 2hrs 30mins after the crash, the captain was last seen clutching the ship's flag, exhorting everyone to 'Be British!'   *1912*

The world's largest hamburger chain McDonald's was founded in De Plaines, Chicago, obscurely by Ray A. Kroe. Providing bumper burgers and using the curious motto 'QSC&V' – Quality, Service, Cleanliness and Value, by 1978 it had 4,671 restaurants to its name in twenty-three countries with a total aggregate of twenty-two billion all-beef burgers. Understandably, Mr Kroe takes his products very seriously. He's organised academic seminars on the subject and is himself a fully qualified BH – Bachelor of Hamburgerology.   *1955*

The one-eyed king of the slate table Joe Davis was born. He became the world billiard champion four times; world snooker champion fifteen times and in 1955 scored the world's first maximum snooker break of 147. Not recognising him, a cocky local in a small village once challenged him to a match. After a sound thrashing the man said, 'Blimey, you must know Joe Davis' – to which Joe replied, 'Not very well, but I sleep with his wife.'   *1901*

Today's the day...

Fastest portraitist of note Goya died. It was said he could complete a portrait in two hours. This amazing talent reputedly saved his life at the hands of an angry husband who learned his wife was posing nude. By the time he reached the studio Goya had painted a new portrait of her fully-clothed. Despite twice being rejected by the Madrid Academy of Art he rapidly earned the reputation of being the greatest painter in Spain. Although short, fat, bald and deaf, women found him irresistible; he charmed them by standing on his head. *1828*

Extraordinary matrimonial advertisement appeared in the London *Public Advertiser*. 'A Gentleman who hath filled two succeeding seats in Parliament, is near sixty years of age, lives in great Splendour and Hospitality, and from whom a considerable estate must pass if he dies without issue – hath no objection to marry any widow or single lady, provided the party be of genteel birth, polished manners and five, six, seven or eight months gone in her pregnancy.' The advertiser was the aged Edward Wortley Montague who wanted to prevent greedy relatives from inheriting his fortune. He received several replies and selected one but sadly died on his way to meet her. *1776*

The screen's greatest clown Charlie Chaplin was born in London. His parents were talented but unrecognised music hall artistes – Charlie claimed his mother was the most brilliant mimic he ever saw. His father died of alcoholism leaving the family so destitute they were forced to spend time in the workhouse. Charlie eked a meagre living as a boy actor, 'rouging' his face by pinching his skin rather than buy expensive cosmetics. His screen *début* is probably the strangest of any star – he recognised himself in a crowd scene from a newsreel. He has said, 'It's a desperate business being a clown' – a fact borne out by four marriages, two major scandals and losing a paternity case despite blood tests proving it was impossible for him to be the father.   *1889*

Darwin's 'missing link' died in New York at the age of forty-nine where she had been a famous show freak exhibited with Ringling Brothers and Barnum and Bailey Circus. Originally found in Siam her whole body was covered with smooth black hair, and she had the facial appearance of a gorilla. Because of this and her incredible prehensile feet and lips it was thought she was the first real proof of Darwin's theory that man is descended from ape-like creatures. For a gorilla she was also extraordinarily intelligent, loving literature and speaking several languages.   *1926*

Writer who named himself after his country Anatole France was born. His real name was Jacques Anatole Thibault which he changed to prove his patriotism. He never loaned books but claimed his library comprised of ones he had borrowed and never returned. In 1921 he was awarded the Nobel Prize for Literature snoring throughout the ceremony and wearing three overcoats to keep warm.   *1844*

Eccentric French publisher Aurelian Scholl died. His strangest venture was to publish *La Naïade* (The Water Nymph), a newspaper printed on rubber so it could be read while bathing!   *1902*

Today's the day...

Ebullient premier Nikita Khrushchev was born in the Ukraine. He joined the Red Guards and rose through the ranks to become one of Stalin's right hand men; he personally supervised the infamous purge of the Moscow Party, and twenty years later astounded the world by denouncing his now-dead mentor as a 'mass-murderer'. Fond of food and drink, he developed a passion for hot-dogs when visiting America, and denounced the Can-Can as pornographic. Despite the Cuban crisis and banging his shoe during Macmillan's speech in the United Nations, he was comparatively friendly with the West – a fact that upset Mao Tse-Tung, who called him a 'toady for the Imperialists'. Khruschev, however, never minded a joke at his own expense, and in fact once related to Kennedy the story of a man who ran through the Kremlin shouting, 'Khruschev is a fool.' 'He was sentenced to twenty-three years in prison,' said the premier, 'three for insulting the Party Secretary, and twenty for revealing a State secret!'   *1894*

Founding Father Benjamin Franklin died aged eighty-four. He'd long suffered from gout and believed it was caused by not enjoying 'more favours from sex'. Indeed his reputation for chasing the ladies prompted John Adams to remark, 'Franklin at the age of seventy-odd, has neither lost his love of beauty nor his taste for it.' Some time earlier he'd suggested his own epitaph. In it he likened himself to the cover of an old book, 'its contents worn out . . . yet . . . it will appear once more, in a new and more beautiful edition, corrected and amended by its author'.   *1790*

French-born Adelaide Bartlett was acquitted of the murder of her husband, Edwin. He'd believed a man should have two wives, one for 'use' and one for companionship. The nineteen-year-old Adelaide was to be his 'companion' so he packed her off to finishing school for three years! When her husband fell ill, Adelaide appeared to nurse him devotedly but on New Year's Day he was found dead with the entire

April 17

contents of a bottle of chloroform in his stomach. At the Old Bailey, Adelaide was eloquently defended, and the jury finally agreed that there wasn't enough evidence to convict her. But there still remained the question of how the chloroform had been given to Edwin without burning his mouth or rousing the neighbours with his screams of agony. Surgeon Sir James Pagett echoed many people's thoughts when he remarked, 'Now she's acquitted, she should tell us in the interests of science how she did it!'   *1886*

A public circumcision of the prophet John Wroe took place in the Quaker meeting house in Ashton-under-Lyne, Lancashire. Two months before this excruciating performance, he had been baptised in a freezing river, and had lived in a 'dark hole' for forty days, with nothing to eat but milk and honey. Four months after, he was baptised again in the River Medlock, and spent a fortnight wandering the fields subsisting on a diet that consisted largely of nuts!   *1823*

The first world title fight took place outside Farnborough in Hampshire when the little Englishman Tom Sayers took on the huge American John Heenan. Boxing was still officially regarded as a breach of the peace, but the fight had excited such 'wild patriotic enthusiasm' that the police turned a blind eye to it. The two men started slogging at 7.30am and battled on for a terrible thirty-seven rounds. By this time, Heenan had a broken hand and was nearly blinded by the swelling round his eyes, while Sayers was covered in blood and his right arm was useless. In a frenzy, the crowd cut the ropes and invaded the ring, urging the fighters on for another gruelling five rounds. The referee disappeared, the fight was declared a draw and the American had to run for it, hotly pursued by an angry mob. Apart from the novelists Dickens and Thackeray, the crowd included 'justices of the peace' and 'brethren of the cloth', and was said to have 'emptied' Parliament.   *1860*

Today's the day...

The San Francisco earthquake shattered the city just before dawn, killing between 500 and 700 people, destroying 28,000 buildings and causing an estimated 500 million dollars' worth of damage. Thanks to a corrupt and inefficient administration, chaos reigned as more than fifty fires blazed, firemen ran out of water and plague-carrying rats poured unheeded from the docks and sewers. Fifteen million gallons of wine were lost, thirty-four men were shot trying to loot the US Mint, and Enrico Caruso made for the streets, clutching a picture of Teddy Roosevelt and singing for all he was worth. Bizarre behaviour abounded, adding a touch of black humour to the terror and panic. William James, brother of novelist Henry, said to his wife, 'This is an earthquake, there is no cause for alarm'; an engineer called Saunders insisted on paying his bill as the hotel he'd been staying in crumbled around him; the landlady of a boarding house was arrested for indecent exposure as she escaped naked; and actor John Barrymore, who was wearing white tie and tails from a party the night before, was said to be 'the only man in the world who'd dress for an earthquake!' *1906*

The great scientist and thinker, Albert Einstein died in Princeton, New Jersey, still regretting the encouragement he'd given Roosevelt to instigate the development of the atomic bomb. The Catholic-educated, Jewish, German-Swiss-American genius had always claimed that less than a dozen people had really understood his Theory of Relativity though it had been written about in more than 900 books, and hailed as the greatest discovery since gravity. The great man's brain was preserved for study by Dr Thomas Harvey of Wichita, Kansas, and in 1978, with the project more or less complete, it was being kept in a cardboard box under a beer cooler.   *1955*

Callous murderer Frank Seddon was hanged at Pentonville Prison. An insurance agent by trade, he lived with his wife in a large house in Tollington Park, North London. The upstairs had been converted into a flat and there a dirty, ill-mannered old miser called Eliza Barrow came to stay. He swindled her out of money and shares worth between £2,000 and £3,000 in return for a lifetime tenancy of the flat and a small, but regular annuity. Secure in this arrangement, Eliza made a will making Seddon her executor. Shortly afterwards she died of 'epidemic diarrhoea' and was buried in a pauper's grave. Relatives became suspicious and informed the police. The body was exhumed and at the trial, Seddon was accused of having poisoned her with arsenic, coldly waited for her to die and then sat and counted her money. Before sentence was passed Seddon, who was a mason, swore his innocence by the 'Great Architect of the Universe', and the judge, who was also a mason, was so upset it was all he could do to finish. When he was first accused of murder, Seddon had said, 'It's scandalous. It's the first time anyone in our family has been accused of such a crime!'   *1912*

Australian skin-diver Henry Bource was shooting an underwater film about sharks in the sea off Melbourne. One of the stars got a little temperamental and bit off Henry's left leg. The diver was comparatively unpeturbed since it was an artificial leg – a shark had also bitten off the original!   *1968*

Today's the day...

Commander Lionel 'Buster' Crabb disappeared in Portsmouth
Harbour while investigating the hull of a Russian cruiser which had
brought the Soviet leaders Bulganin and Khrushchev to Britain.
Despite strict orders that there was to be no espionage, someone had
approached Crabb and offered him £5,000 to dive. Divorced,
penniless and a heavy drinker, he'd become increasingly depressed
since he retired from the Navy, and jumped at the chance of a new
'adventure'. Using special breathing apparatus that didn't make
tell-tale bubbles, he slipped into the water, surfaced briefly to say he
was having trouble with the equipment, dived once more and was
never seen again. Fourteen months later the headless, handless body
of a diver was found in Chichester Harbour and the coroner announced
it was Crabb's, even though there was no positive identification.
However in 1959 in a Russian forces magazine, there appeared a
picture of a group of Soviet naval officers. When Crabb's ex-wife saw
it she was convinced, as were many of her friends, that Lieutenant
Lvev Lvovich Korablov was in fact old 'Buster' himself. *1956*

Benjamin Disraeli died. In great pain during his final illness, he still
insisted on correcting the proofs of his last speech saying, 'I will not
go down to posterity talking bad grammar.' Asked if he wished to see
his friend the widowed Queen Victoria, he replied, 'Why should I see
her? She will only want to give a message to Albert!' *1881*

The regal Count Von Attems landed at the Circular Quay and took
Sydney society by storm. The genteel young man took the best suite
at the best hotel, charmed his way into the mansions of the rich and
discreetly hinted he was related to the Emperor of Austria. He
entertained lavishly and spent money freely, and his new-found friends
were only too happy to cash cheques for him, even though it would
take six months to clear them through his European bank. He gave a
grand farewell banquet before leaving Australia, regretting only that

he'd been unable to meet his old friend Major Samuel Wensley Blackall, the new Governor of Queensland. When Blackall arrived in town he was shown photos of his long-lost acquaintance. The Governor's verdict was short and to the point – 'That's not Von Attems. That's his valet.' The man was later arrested in Batavia and jailed for twenty-two years, but high society in Australia still winced when they remembered him – and the £60,000 he'd swindled out of them.   *1868*

Duryea's 'buggyant' made its first successful run in Springfield, Massachusetts. Built by the brothers Charles and Frank Duryea, it was powered by a gasoline engine and was to become the first automobile regularly made for sale. The Duryeas attracted great attention in 1895 when one of their cars won the fifty-four-mile 'Times-Herald' race – at an average speed of a staggering 6mph.   *1892*

The mysterious 'Major Martin' set sail aboard the submarine HMS *Seraph* – packed inside a 6ft metal canister surrounded by dry ice. The frozen British officer was in fact an anonymous body decked out to seem like a top-secret courier. He was to be set adrift off the coast of Spain in an elaborate plot to divert German attention from the site of the proposed Allied landing in Sicily. The false letters he carried, ostensibly addressed to General Alexander and Sir Andrew Cunningham, indicated that the Allies were looking to Greece and Sardinia instead. With careful attention to detail, the Intelligence Service prepared a personality for the dead man, and even provided him with a note from his bank about an overdraft. The body was discovered according to plan and when the letters were returned nearly a month later, tests confirmed they'd been opened. A whole Panzer division along with mine-layers and motor torpedo boats was diverted to Greece, the invasion of Sicily was successful and hundreds of lives were saved – thanks to a man who didn't exist.   *1943*

Today's the day...

The world's first motor race was run along the banks of the Seine from the centre of Paris to Neuilly. It was organised by the editor of *La Vélocipède* and won by Georges Bouton driving a steam quadricycle. He couldn't lose, not because his vehicle was particularly fast, but because he was the only competitor in the race! *1887*

The corporal who ruled Europe, Adolf Hitler was born in Branau, Austria. He hated his father, who had changed his name from Schicklgruber; was almost oedipal in his love for his mother and was later obsessed with the idea that his grandfather may have been Jewish. After winning two Iron Crosses in World War I and failing as an artist, he rose from being a dosser to Chancellor of Germany. He suffered from chronic flatulence and poor eyesight, and was quite possibly monorchid and died a virgin. He nevertheless had six mistresses, three of whom committed suicide including Eva Braun, who became his wife and died alongside him. He was passionately fond of wolves, ravens and decapitations, and is said to have been absolutely terrified of sexual intercourse and horses. He loved most other animals, hated hunting and was a keen vegetarian – a fact that prompted the American OSS to spike his carrots with female hormones in the hope of changing his sex. In looks if not in action, Hitler bore a marked resemblance to Charlie Chaplin, and this so worried the SS that they took the little clown's portrait from the 'Exhibition of Degenerate Art' and carefully removed his moustache.   *1889*

The second Bonaparte Emperor was born, the son of Napoleon's brother and Josephine's daughter. His mother Hortense was having an affair with an admiral at the time but though doubts were expressed, he was declared to be legitimate. He grew up in exile, avoiding imprisonment by fleeing to London. In the Chartist risings, the future French monarch became a volunteer constable, though as a London bobby his only achievement was to arrest an ancient female vagrant. Shortly afterwards he was made President of France and four years later made himself Emperor. He took the title Napoleon III in deference to Napoleon's dead son and married the beautiful Eugénie de Montijo. After the birth of an heir, his wife was forbidden to have any more children, and the enthusiastically unfaithful Emperor sought yet more adulterous conquests. Once sitting in a dimly lit room he perceived a shapely silken-clad leg right next to him. Delicately he caressed the thigh and was staggered to hear a deep bellow of rage. He'd been stroking the leg of a Bishop!   *1808*

Cromwell kicked out 'the Rump' – the sixty remaining members of the 'Long Parliament' who had been sitting since 1640, and were planning to continue to do so without re-election. 'I will put an end to your prating', he's reported to have said. 'You have sat too long . . . You shall now give way to honester men.' On cue, Colonel Harrison and his musketeers marched in and unceremoniously ejected the members. The following day a notice appeared on the door of the Commons. It read, 'This House to let – unfurnished.'   *1653*

Today's the day...

The 'Ace of Aces', scourge of World War I British fliers, Manfred von Richthofen, was shot down in his bright red Fokker tri-plane. Attacked in the air by Captain Roy Brown, he glided to the ground under heavy fire from Australian gunners – and both parties claimed the kill. Though mortally wounded by a single bullet in the chest, von Richthofen still made the perfect landing, then died. His day had started inauspiciously. Much to his annoyance, he'd been photographed before take-off – something he'd hated ever since his hero and mentor Boelke had crashed after a similar snapshot. To make matters worse, a mechanic then rushed up to ask for his autograph. 'What's the matter?' joked the Red Baron. 'Don't you think I'll come back?'   *1918*

Alfred the Great's thirty-sixth great grand-daughter, the weight watching Queen Elizabeth II, was born at 2.40am where there now stands an office building at 17 Bruton Street, London W1. She became heir-apparent when Uncle Edward abdicated in 1936; was helping Dad with dispatches at fourteen and fulfilled her first official function as a sixteen-year-old Colonel-in-Chief of the Grenadier Guards. These days, she likes to work with her shoes off, surrounded by numerous

228

dogs whose meat she cuts up herself and whose fleas she despatches personally. Her Majesty is a very busy lady. In the first twenty years of her reign alone, she held 5,600 official audiences, received half a million letters and travelled 275,000 miles around the world, visiting Canada five times. On a more recent visit there, she surprised a couple of intruders in the garden of the house where she was staying. At her regal glance they turned tail and fled. To a shame-faced security guard HRH quipped, 'Why do we need you? We seem to be able to frighten people away by ourselves!'

1926

The first public drinking fountain was turned on by the Archbishop of Canterbury's daughter, Mrs Willson, who celebrated by sipping some of 'the crystal stream' from a silver chalice. The Temperance Movement was especially pleased about it since, with touching optimism, they hoped the H_2O would tempt the 'thirsty mechanic' more than 'the chemical atrocities concocted for his ruin at the gin-palace'!

1859

Dr Cook beat Peary to the North Pole or so he claimed later in Copenhagen on his return from a fourteen-month sojourn in the Arctic. Along with two Eskimos, he said he'd spent two days there 'the only pulsating creatures in a dead world of ice'. Forty-eight hours later an incensed telegram from Peary said that he'd been first and Cook had never been anywhere near it. Claims and counter claims flew thick and fast, and though public victory went to Peary, neither story could ever be adequately substantiated. When the Royal Geographical Society gave Peary their gold medal, they made it clear that it was for his services in general and not for this particular achievement – and in 1915 his maps of Greenland proved to be so inaccurate they were withdrawn by the US Government. His 'Navy Cliff' was 100 miles from the sea, and a water-way he modestly named 'Peary Channel' was, in fact, an 'ice-free upland abounding with game'.

1908

Today's the day...

The Siren of the Salons – the brilliant, bossy, political vamp and writer Madame de Staël was born in Geneva. Pop-eyed and butch, with the 'thoracic development of a wet-nurse', 'she thought like a man, but felt like a woman'. No sooner had she married the Swedish Ambassador than she took three lovers – her 'kindergarten' or 'barnyard' – and had seven children, only three of which were legitimate. The first time she met Napoleon, she told him he was much too clever to be married to Josephine – 'that insignificant little Creole', and her attempts to seduce him included a raid at bathtime when she confronted the furious, naked Corsican with the defence that 'genius has no sex'. Napoleon threw her out of Paris and she spent a year in Dorking, confused the Prince Regent and bored Byron to distraction. In her forties, she married a man in his early twenties and conceived again at the age of forty-five. 'Love is the whole history of a woman's life,' she said, 'it's but an episode in a man's.'   *1766*

The legendary Wandering Jew last appeared in Brussels, gave his name as Isaac Laquedem, sat for his portrait and disappeared. Originally called Cartophilus, he was once Pontius Pilate's doorkeeper and had been doomed to wander till the Second Coming for striking Christ. Converted to Christianity, baptised and conveniently rejuvenated once every 100 years, he was first noted by the thirteenth century monks of St Albans and appeared all over Germany in the sixteenth century – ragged, hirsute and torn. In most accounts he's a pious beggar but perhaps typically, when he turned up in Italy, he became a successful gambler!   *1772*

The father of the English novel Henry Fielding was born, and from his youth was a great one for the ladies. He tried to abduct a fifteen-year-old girl when he was eighteen; eloped at twenty-seven with his beloved Charlotte, and when she died he outraged everyone by marrying her maid – who gave birth three months later! Faced with being 'a hackney writer or a hackney coachman', he scraped a living as a satirical playwright and travelling lawyer – which while it didn't make him any money, gave him a great insight into chambermaids and coaching-inns. He wrote late at night on tobacco papers after bouts at the tavern, and didn't finish *Tom Jones* till he was in his forties. Dr Johnson said, 'I scarcely know a more corrupt work' – which is rather ironic since Fielding ended his life as a magistrate.   *1707*

Another Rolls Royce legend was created when Henry Royce died and the red RR on the car's radiators was changed to black, supposedly as a sign of perpetual mourning. In fact, the decision to change had been made some time before and the timing was no more than a poetic and slightly morbid coincidence. Mr Royce had asked that his ashes be interred in the middle of the workshop in the Derby factory, and though this was done it proved to be a short-lived shrine. His remains were exhumed and buried in the church of Alwalton, the village where he was born, since staff felt the workshop was 'inappropriate'.   *1933*

The genie of Bolshevism Vladimir Ilyich Ulyanov – known as Lenin – was born in Simbirsk and was a chubby seventeen-year-old when his brother was executed for an attempt on the life of the Tsar. Revolution was his life and he allowed nothing to interfere with it. He loved music, but never listened to it because it made him 'say stupid, nice things', and though he was a masterful chess player who could handle several games at once, he gave it up as a waste of time. Lenin was 5ft 5½in, bald with a red beard, Mongol eyes and legs so short that when he sat in a chair they barely touched the ground. He liked bicycles and enjoyed gathering mushrooms, but was so austere that even at the height of his power, he allowed himself no luxuries, except for a humble Rolls Royce. For Ilyich, the Revolution was not a Russian phenomenon, but an international force. 'When we conquer the world,' he's reported to have said, 'we'll build lavatories of gold.'   *1870*

Today's the day...

St George the patron saint of England is believed to have been martyred by the Emperor Diocletian in Nicomedia in the early fourth century. His body was broken and he was sorely tortured, but before he died he called on God to destroy the pagan temple, and when this was done, he bled milk from his wounds. Nothing much was heard of him after this thoroughly nasty end, until he got mixed up with the ancient myths of Perseus the dragon slayer; was adopted as a knight-errant hero by the crusaders and became something of a cult figure. The irony is that though he's officially only a 'local saint' for the British Isles, he may never have existed at all, and if he did, he certainly never came to England.   *Circa AD 303/Saint's Day*

Literary enigma William Shakespeare was born in Stratford-upon-Avon. Though much has been written, little is really known about his private life. He was the third of the eight children of a successful tanner; married Anne Hathaway, probably when she was three months pregnant, and had three children of his own. He wrote thirty-seven plays as well as the sonnets and narrative poems, and while no playwright or poet has had such praise heaped upon him, few have been so disliked by so many eminent people. Tolstoy said, 'The works of Shakespeare have nothing in common with art or poetry', and Voltaire described him as 'an enormous dunghill'!   *1564*

Conductor extraordinaire, the great Jullien was born in Sisteron in alpine France. The son of a bandmaster, he was named after all his father's colleagues at the local Philharmonic Society and though he called himself Louis Antoine, he had a grand total of thirty-five Christian names! An outstanding self-publicist, he was fêted on both sides of the Atlantic and particularly endeared himself to audiences by using different batons for different composers. For his favourite, Beethoven, he would wear a new pair of white gloves and use a jewel-encrusted stick, which was presented to him on a silver salver.   *1812*

The saga of the incredible 'Rabbit Woman' of Godalming
began when pregnant mother of three, Mary Tofts, was frightened by
a coney while working in the fields. She later miscarried and began
'giving birth' to first a piece of rabbit, then a whole animal and finally
– according to legend – a litter of fifteen. Local apothecary and
man-midwife John Howard was called in, and insisted that he could
feel the beasts 'leaping in her belly'. He wanted a second opinion and
brought along the eminent Westminster surgeon Nathaniel St André,
who testified that he'd delivered two little bunnies himself. Mary had
been moved to Guildford, and since by this time George I and Queen
Caroline were spellbound by the story, her next visitor was the court
physician Cyriacus Ahler, who only got a portion of rabbit and was
ticked off by Howard for mistreating his patient. The King wasn't
satisfied and sent in the star obstetrician of the day, Sir Richard
Manningham, under whose sceptical gaze Mary could only produce a
piece of pig's bladder. Under threat of a 'painful experiment' she
finally confessed that the whole thing was a hoax. Interestingly
enough, she ended up in a prison for 'receiving stolen goods'.   *1726*

Today's the day...

Halley's Comet frightened a monk when it appeared over England. He was Aethelmaer, known as Oliver of Malmesbury, and almost immediately he made a telling prediction. 'Thou hast come,' he wailed, 'bringing sorrow and lamentation to many a mother . . . threatening the destruction of this country.' Five months later William the Conqueror invaded, thousands died and much land was laid waste. It has to be said, however, that this prophecy was Oliver's only success in life. As a youth he'd attempted to copy Daedalus, made himself a pair of wings and leapt from a tower. He's said to have flown a full furlong, but due to the lack of a tail he unbalanced, fell, broke his legs and was lame for the rest of his days. *1066*

The Royal Treasure was stolen from the Chamber of Pyx in Westminster Abbey, while its regal owner Edward I was away hammering the Scots. Grasping the opportunity Richard Podelicote, a priest turned merchant-adventurer, had hatched his plot – probably with the connivance of the Keeper of the Palace, the Abbot and forty-eight monks. When the heist was a rip-roaring success, they got a little carried away. Edward's spies smelt a rat when a fisherman netted a

April 24

silver goblet in the Thames, jewellery was found in St Margaret's churchyard, and golden plunder behind tombstones in Kentish Town. Caught and tortured, Podelicote spilled the beans, nobly if a little foolishly taking all the blame on himself. In the nineteenth century a hidden door to the treasury was discovered and nailed to it were several pieces of white leather that turned out to be human skin. For his sins, Richard Podelicote had been flayed alive.   *1303*

The postman's novelist Anthony Trollope was born in London and for most of his life worked for the Post Office, riding an average of forty-six miles a day for six pence a mile. He established the rural postal service; wrote 2,500 words before breakfast at the rate of 250 every fifteen minutes, and actually invented the post-box. 'A big red-faced, rather underbred Englishman of the bald-with-spectacles-type', he enjoyed foxhunting, and his works, said one critic, were 'like a leg of mutton, substantial but a little coarse'. He earned a lifetime total of £66,939 17s 6d, and claimed that all a writer needs is a pen, paper and 1lb of beeswax – the latter to stick the seat of his pants to the seat of the chair!   *1815*

The anthem of the French Revolution *La Marseillaise* was written and composed by Claude Rouget de Lisle, a captain of engineers stationed near Strasbourg, after he'd been asked by the mayor to provide a patriotic song in exchange for a bottle of wine. The song was originally called 'The War Song of the Army on the Rhine' and its defiance was aimed at advancing Austrian and German soldiers, not the French aristocracy. Some months after, a battalion of revolutionary volunteers picked the song up as they marched from Marseilles to storm the Tuileries in Paris, and that's how it got its familiar name. Three years later the revolutionaries officially adopted it as the French national anthem. The irony was that de Lisle had been a Royalist officer and only narrowly avoided the guillotine.   *1791*

Today's the day...

Britain's first and only dictator Oliver Cromwell was born in Huntingdon to a cadet branch of the family of Henry VIII's infamous lieutenant Thomas Cromwell. An unremarkable MP, he rose to prominence in the latter half of the Civil War; was largely responsible for creating the new Model Army; and was chief among the Regicides when 'that man of blood' Charles I was executed. He was a dour and dowdy man, 'his linen was plain and not very clean, his voice sharp and untuneable'. He was plagued by his conscience and religious scruples, and whatever the truth of the matter, his evil reputation was secured forever in his campaign to subdue the Irish. When the garrison of Drogheda refused to surrender he put more than 1,000 souls to fire and the sword 'in the heat of action'. Though he advised his men to have no fear, but 'to put your trust in God and keep your powder dry', he himself was terrified of assassination and was heavily guarded. When a Scottish soldier tried to shoot him, however, he was very cool about it. 'If a trooper of mine had missed such a mark,' he said, 'he should have had a hundred lashes.' *1599*

The first human being was executed by guillotine. He was the young highwayman Pelletier who had robbed, beaten and stabbed 'a private individual'. The machine had previously only been used on sheep, and though it was meant to be a 'humane' invention, its grim outline on the scaffold caused Pelletier to faint. He was dragged to the block and despatched by the executioner Sanson without ever regaining consciousness. The 'considerable crowd', used to more entertaining methods of execution, were understandably disappointed. *1792*

'The last great amateur sportsman' Charles Fry was born in Croydon, Surrey. Educated at Repton and Oxford, he gained a 'blue' for rugby and played soccer in the Southampton side in the 1902 Cup Final. He also played football for England, held the world long jump record for over twenty years, and captained his country's team at cricket, scoring a lifetime total of around 30,000 runs. Added to which he hunted, shot and fished; was a Liberal candidate for Parliament; and, for a short time, a diplomat. It was in this capacity that he received the most remarkable sporting offer of his life. He was approached to be King of Albania.   *1872*

'The Centre of the Universe' Reza Shah was crowned, including among his other titles 'King of Kings', 'Light of the Aryans' and 'Vice-Regent of God'. Surprisingly, this new incumbent of the 'Peacock Throne' of Persia, was the first of his dynasty and despite the splendour, he'd been born a peasant. From tending his father's sheep, he eventually became a cavalry man and after twenty years, an officer. Famed for his immense strength, he once broke a horse's neck with his bare hands, and in the chaos of World War I, he started his rise to power. Asked by English General Ironside if he could command a division, he replied, 'General, I am capable of commanding the entire British Army.' A year later, with Persia in disarray, he led an armed revolt, displaced Sultan Ahmed Shah who was holidaying in the South of France and made himself Prime Minister. From there, it was but a short if ruthless step to absolute power, which he exercised as if to the manner born. He would tour outlying provinces in his armour-plated Rolls Royce, and when he stopped over, all the dogs in the neighbourhood were killed lest they disturbed his royal sleep.   *1926*

The most famous of American broadcasters Ed Murrow was born. Described as 'the right man in the right place in the right era', he dominated US radio and TV news programmes for three decades, and in his *See It Now* series he was the first newsman to take on witch-hunting Senator Joe McCarthy. He once said, 'The ideal voice for radio should have no substance, no sex, no owner and a message of importance to every housewife.'   *1908*

Today's the day...

Emma, Lady Hamilton was born plain Amy Lyon. At seventeen she arrived in London and soon became an erotic dancer at the 'Temple of Aesculapius' – capering around the glass-pillared 'Celestial Bed' in the nude. Having been the mistress of various eminent men and adopted the fashionable name 'Emma', she was sent off to Naples by the artistic young aristocrat Charles Greville to stay with his uncle, Sir William Hamilton. Emma said, 'I will make him marry me', and although she was first Sir William's mistress for five years, that's exactly what she did. Famed for her beauty but considered 'uninteresting', her pronunciation was 'vulgar' and her manners had 'the ease of a barmaid'. Her passionate affair with Nelson offended many, including his friend Lord Minto who described her as 'cramming Nelson with trowelfuls of flattery, which he goes on taking as quietly as a child does pap.' It never upset Lord Hamilton, however, for to the end of his days he was convinced the relationship was 'pure' – even when Emma was pregnant with Nelson's child.   *Circa 1761*

Lincoln's assassin John Wilkes Booth was supposedly shot at Garrett's Barn, fifty miles south of Washington. When soldiers surrounded the barn his associate Herold was quick to surrender, but Booth stubbornly refused and asked for a chance to come out fighting. In reply they fired the barn and the figure of a man leaning on a crutch could be seen in the flames. A shot rang out, and the man fell dying, though whether it was his own gun or Sergeant Boston Corbett's which killed him, is not certain. Taken to the nearby house, he murmured, 'Tell Mother I died for my country', and passed away nearly five hours later. The body was returned to Washington and hurriedly buried at the old Arsenal. Reports circulated that Booth had escaped, was a theatre manager in San Francisco, had sailed for the Caroline Islands or left to live in India. His accomplices weren't asked for their opinion. Throughout the whole of their imprisonment and trial, they had to wear tight-fitting canvas bags over their heads, which made it impossible for them to hear, see or speak.   *1865*

Elizabeth Bowes-Lyon married the Duke of York at Westminster Abbey, the first royal wedding there since 1383. When the groom arrived with his two brothers, all splendid in their respective uniforms, the Dowager Queen Alexandra couldn't resist her three handsome grandsons and left her pew to give them all a quick hug. Elizabeth arrived in a landau with just four policemen as escort, since she was still a commoner. Her dress and those of her bridesmaids included Nottingham lace to give that depressed industry a much needed fillip, and at either side of her tulle veil she wore a white rose of York. Her bouquet, too, was of white York roses, and as she passed down the aisle she stopped and placed it on the Tomb of the Unknown Warrior in memory of her brother Fergus and the countless others who died in World War I. The couple emerged from the Abbey to the cheers of the crowd and, after a reception at Buckingham Palace, left for the first part of their honeymoon in Surrey. No doubt they were looking forward to a quiet life, little thinking that thirteen years later, Edward VIII would abdicate and they would become King and Queen of England.   *1923*

Today's the day...

The last touching for the King's Evil was performed by Queen Anne just three months before her death. She'd touched Dr Johnson when he was only a baby and he could always remember 'a lady in diamonds with a long black hood'. The touching, believed to cure the glandular tumours of scrofula, had been practised by English monarchs since the eleventh century and the apparent power to heal had been helped along by the gift of a gold 'touchpiece' with every cure. The most popular toucher of all time was Charles II, who in one four-year period touched 24,000 people. So great was the crowd's enthusiasm that when Charles was in exile, an enterprising businessman ran trips to the Low Countries, so the sores of the scrofulous could still be touched.   *1714*

An explorer's last trip proved fatal. Veteran of Africa and survivor of all the dangers and diseases of the 'Dark Continent', James Bruce hurried to the top of the stairs to hand a lady into her carriage. In the safety of his own home, he missed his footing, fell headlong and killed himself!   *1794*

The *Kon-Tiki* set out from Callao, Peru – its mission to prove that early man could have emigrated from South America to Polynesia. On board the 45ft rope and balsa raft, were the Norwegian explorer Thor Heyerdahl, five human companions, a parrot who got washed overboard and a crab called Johannes. Though the 4,300 mile trip was ultimately a success, *Kon-Tiki* frequently came near to disaster. They were visited – a little too closely – by a 50ft whale shark and a sinister sabre-toothed eel cuddled up on board for the night; two men were almost lost when the dinghy was swept away and another when he fell in the sea. Initially they'd been worried because they'd had to use green logs in building the raft. In fact it was a lucky accident, because it was only the sap in the wood that kept them out of the water and floating. Had they used dry logs, they'd probably have sunk.   *1947*

A kangaroo beat a racehorse in a specially staged race held in Sydney. As the horse, ridden by a leading jockey, got off to a flying start, the jumped-up roo swept by in a cloud of dust. It wasn't really surprising – in a single leap it could clear 33ft.   *1927*

The dots and dashes man Samuel Morse was born in Charlestown, Massachusetts. The inventor of the famous code, he in fact made his living as a portrait painter and when he decided to build an electrical telegraph he hadn't the foggiest idea about electricity. It was only with the unstinting help of physicist Joseph Henry that he managed to succeed and when he did, he promptly denied that Henry had helped him at all. Never a modest man, Morse wanted to rival 'the genius of a Raphael, a Michelangelo or a Titian'. He studied art in London, visited Paris and painted a huge picture of a gallery in the Louvre which he intended to exhibit. He painted the gallery complete with thirty-seven pictures, including the 'Mona Lisa' – all crammed onto a single wall!   *1791*

Twitchy philosopher Herbert Spencer was born in Derbyshire. An ex-railway engineer who became one of the greatest contributors to twentieth century philosophical thought, he was a nervous wreck. He had two breakdowns and suffered from 'cerebral congestion' – a peculiar feeling he got whenever he tried to think. If the poor man even so much as thought anyone was going to say anything to upset him, he blocked up his ears with earplugs.   *1820*

The toe-tapping 'La Cucaracha' was first published. The popular band classic is actually a Mexican revolutionary song celebrating the exploits of Pancho Villa in his fight against the rich. The title literally means the cockroach – a symbol of the oppressed poor – and a reference to the way Villa's men disappeared 'under the rocks of the mountains' like cockroaches in a crevice.   *1961*

Today's the day...

The mutiny on the *Bounty* began when Captain Bligh was dragged from his bed at 5.20am. So eager were the mutineers to tie up the captain's wrists that his nightshirt got tangled in the rope and he was bundled bare-bottomed on deck. Since they'd left Tahiti little more than three weeks earlier, Bligh had cut rations and grog, brutally flogged his crew on the slightest pretext and accused his first mate and old friend Fletcher Christian of being a coward. Cast adrift with his loyal sailors in an overloaded open boat in the middle of the Pacific Ocean, Bligh incredibly survived; he was made a vice-admiral and became Governor of New South Wales. Christian was not so lucky; his South Seas utopia on Pitcairn Island went sour and within four years he was dead. *1789*

Captain Cook's only female crew member died at his house in Mile End Road. She'd sailed twice round the world with him; Dr Johnson had written a verse in her honour which she wore engraved on a silver collar round her neck, and Greenwich Hospital had made her a pensioner with the Admiralty commendation, 'If ever a female deserved a pension, this is she.' She, oddly enough, was a goat. *1772*

A horse was the hero of the Cup Final when Bolton Wanderers
beat West Ham 2-0. It was the first final in the new Wembley stadium –
and just before it opened a full army battalion had marched around it
to test the strength of the terraces. Though its capacity was 123,000,
an estimated 250,000 were crammed in. In the crush they flooded onto
the pitch until 'not a blade of grass could be seen'. To save the day,
out rode PC Scorey on his white charger Billy and from a tiny gap in
the crowd he walked round in ever-widening circles with Billy gently
nudging the fans back to the sidelines. Though it was only due to them
that the game went ahead, neither Billy nor PC Scorey were football
fans. The doughty constable preferred cricket and despite being plied
with free tickets, he never went to a football match again.   *1923*

A prisoner with a dark secret, convicted perjurer Peter Lazaros
died suddenly in Pontiac Gaol, Michigan. When a post mortem was
carried out a four-carat diamond ring valued at £17,500 was discovered
in his stomach. It had disappeared over a year earlier when Mr
Lazaros, known as 'Peter the Greek', had had a selection of jewels sent
up to his room at Manhattan's Pierre Hotel. Duly cleaned up, the
recovered gem was returned to the firm who'd lost it – and presumably
put on sale again.   *1978*

Defeated dictator Benito Mussolini was shot with his mistress
Claretta Petacci. The couple had spent their last night in the huge
walnut bed of a farmhouse, usually occupied by the farmer's strapping
sons. At 4pm they were hustled to the gateway of the Villa Belmonte
and summarily shot by the partisan Audusio. The bodies were dumped
in a van and taken to Milan. In their haste, Claretta had had no time
to put her knickers on and when she was strung up by the heels, along
with her sixty-two-year-old lover in front of a jeering crowd, a
chivalrous partisan covered her nakedness by tying her skirt round her
legs with his belt.   *1945*

Today's the day...

The mischievious maestro Sir Thomas Beecham was born, son of
a mayor of St Helens who'd made a fortune from patent medicines.
He conducted the Hallé while still an amateur and wielded the baton
like 'a dancing Dervish'. 'What matters,' he told an orchestra, 'is that
you begin and end together. What you do in between doesn't matter
because the audience won't know anyway.' When he criticised a
soprano rehearsing the dying Mimi in *La Bohème* she complained
'One can't give of one's best when one is in a prone position.' 'I seem
to recollect,' Sir Thomas replied, 'that I've given some of my very best
performances in that position.' On his seventieth birthday, telegrams
pouring in from the great and the famous were read to him, 'What!' he
snorted, 'Nothing from Mozart!'   *1879*

The original Citizen Kane, press baron, multi-millionaire and
megalomaniac William Randolph Hearst was born very rich in San
Francisco. Creator of the 'yellow press', his newspaper empire was
devoted largely to crime, corruption, political manipulation and sex,
and he was said to have conjured up the Spanish-American War merely
to boost circulation. As a spendthrift he was without rival. He
imported a Spanish monastery and an entire Bavarian village; created
the fairytale castle of San Simeon on a 200,000 acre estate, and at one
time controlled a quarter of the world's art transactions, amassing a
collection of over 20,000 items – many of which were never unpacked.
Though he was visited by everyone from Chaplin to Churchill, he
remained essentially the lonely demagogue. 'The man has not a friend
in the world,' said writer Ambrose Bierce, 'nor does he merit one.' *1863*

The most immaculate Emperor, the son of Heaven, Hirohito was
born in Tokyo, the 124th direct descendant of Jimmu, the legendary
first Emperor of Japan. Shy to the point of extinction, Hirohito is a
poet and marine biologist of some academic distinction. He's the first
Japanese Emperor to travel abroad in 2,700 years; the first to eat

porridge for breakfast and the first to have never kept a concubine. He
ascended the Chrysanthemum Throne on Christmas Day 1926 and
twenty years later became the first Japanese Emperor to repudiate his
divinity. Ironically, in the light of Pearl Harbour, he'd been dubbed
'the Emperor of Shining Peace'. *1901*

Hannah Dustin took a terrible revenge on the Indians of the
Abnaki tribe who had attacked the settlement of Haverhill,
Massachusetts and killed her one-week-old baby by dashing its brains
out on a tree. Held captive by a handful of Indians in the forest, she
and a boy called Lenerson stole two tomahawks and in the dead of
night killed two men, two women and six children – Hannah
accounting for nine of the victims herself. When the deed was done,
she stayed behind, and so she could claim the Indian bounty, she
carefully scalped them all. *1697*

Aristocratic jazzman Edward Kennedy 'Duke' Ellington was born
in Washington DC the son of a White House butler. Called the 'Duke'
because he was 'prideful', he got the opportunity to go back there on
his seventieth birthday, after nearly forty years of stardom. President
Nixon had decided to honour him with a party and even played 'Happy
Birthday' for him on the piano. The Duke kissed the President four
times. 'One' he said, 'for each cheek.' *1899*

'Flash Harry' the great conductor Sir Malcolm Sargent was born in
Ashford, Kent. He 'inherited' the Promenade Concerts from Sir Henry
Wood and it was the promenaders who gave him his soubriquet. In
eighteen years, the elegant 'Flash' wore out twenty-five tail suits; he
always wore a red carnation during the day and a white one at night,
and occasionally, he conducted with his parakeet 'Hughie' on his lapel.
When Beecham heard that Sargent was conducting in Tokyo, he
quipped, 'Ah, Flash in Japan, eh?' *1895*

Today's the day...

Buffoon and astrologer William Lilly was born and spent a lifetime
upsetting everyone with his almanacks and predictions – numbering
among his early fiascos a confident search for buried treasure in
Westminster Abbey which only unearthed a corpse in a coffin. Come
the Civil War he managed to annoy both the Royalists and the Puritans
by loosely predicting the death of the King but adding a rosy future
for his son Prince Charles. The Roundheads, nevertheless, made him
official fortune-teller at the siege of Colchester where his job was to
encourage the troops by divining 'a speedy victory'. Somehow this
'imprudent and senseless fellon' managed to survive both the war and
the Restoration, and in 1666 he actually predicted the Great Fire.
When for once in his life he was right, it was so unusual that he was
accused of starting it himself.   *1602*

Princess Caroline got the big goodbye when at her own request,
her estranged husband the chubby Prince of Wales and future
George IV, sat down at Windsor and wrote her 'a disagreeable
correspondence'. The letter effectively, but unofficially, ended their
relationship and stated the terms on which they were to live in future.

246

Among other things, he couldn't stand her sluttish behaviour, and she could not stomach his obesity – or as he put it, rather more politely, 'nature has not made us suitable'. The terms were largely that they should no longer 'be answerable to each other', and when the letter arrived, she happened to be with the statesman George Canning, with whom she was 'unduly familiar'. He told her that it was a charter to do what she liked and, as he afterwards told the Duke of Wellington, they 'took advantage of it on the spot'. *1796*

The Nazi Messiah committed suicide. After a light lunch of spaghetti with a vegetarian sauce, the fifty-six-year-old Adolph Hitler took Eva Braun, his wife of one day, and shut the door of the sitting room in his underground bunker beneath the Chancellery in Berlin. There, so the official story goes, he shot himself in the mouth and she bit on a cyanide capsule. On Herr Hitler's instructions, their bodies were almost immediately taken outside and burnt so that no trace should be left. 180 litres of petrol were poured on the miserable corpses in a shell hole, but though the blaze lasted two-and-a-half hours, the bodies were apparently not entirely consumed and the Fuhrer's last order was bungled. *1945*

The United States doubled in size when the deal to buy Louisiana from the French was signed and sealed. This was not, of course, the present day Louisiana, but a vast tract of land stretching from the Mississippi to Canada. An overjoyed President Thomas Jefferson had only asked to buy New Orleans and the land around it but Napoleon, who needed the money and was disenchanted with the colonies after the slave revolt in the Caribbean, said take it all or nothing. After some haggling, a price of $27,267,622 was agreed for roughly 828,000 square miles at a little under three cents an acre. Napoleon was well pleased – he got fifteen million dollars for a wilderness he'd bullied Spain into giving him for nothing. *1803*

Today's the day...

The lone explorer, the thirty-seven-year-old Japanese Naomi Uemura, became the first man to reach the North Pole solo, having rushed his dog-team over 450 miles across the Arctic ice-cap. It was 4.45GMT; he'd left Cape Columbia in northern Canada over fifty days before, been attacked by a polar bear, trapped on an ice-floe, and one of his bitches had given birth to six puppies, which were flown out to safety. He took out his automatic bleeper, and via a satellite notified the Smithsonian Institute in Washington. The Japanese Prime Minister Mr Fukada happened to be at the White House and sent his congratulations back. Mr Uemura was only 5ft 3in and when he returned from his lonely trek he said plaintively, 'I don't like solitude.'   *1978*

A 'Come-As-You-Fancy-Ball' was given at the Haymarket by the Princess of Wales, and King George II was naughty. Elizabeth Chudleigh, the Duchess of Kingston, had turned up in a topless body stocking with only a bunch of flowers to protect her modesty. The lecherous old monarch sidled up to her and asked quietly if he could fondle her breasts. He could hardly believe his luck when the little coquette took his hand and said she would guide it to a much softer place. He wasn't so pleased when she put it on his own head.   *1749*

The Empire State Building was completed at a cost of over forty million dollars and seven million man hours. At a towering 1,472ft including a 222ft TV antenna, it was for nearly forty years the tallest inhabited structure in the world. It has 102 floors, 63 lifts, 1,860 steps, 6,500 windows and 60 miles of plumbing – and it can sway in a gale by nearly 3ins. The two-acre site was originally the small holding of one John Thompson, who sold it in 1799 for $7,000. In his 'For Sale' notice, he made a classic understatement when he advised that 'the rapid growth of the city . . . will cause the value of this property to be greatly enhanced'.   *1931*

May 1

The Great Exhibition was opened in Hyde Park by Queen Victoria. The first major international exhibition and the brainchild of Prince Albert, it was housed in a vast iron and glass edifice designed by Sir Thomas Paxton, exactly 1,851ft long to match the year. *The Times* called it 'a monstrous greenhouse', and it was *Punch* that dubbed it 'The Crystal Palace'. While more than a million people lined the streets for the opening, over 34,000 crammed inside and 'it was impossible for the invited guests of a lady's drawing room to have conducted themselves with more perfect propriety'. To save the Park's trees, the Palace had been built around and over them, and though Her Majesty was impressed with this act of conservation, she was worried that the sparrows it attracted might 'insult the illustrious guests'. She asked the Duke of Wellington to solve the problem, which he did on the spot. He said, 'Try Sparrowhawks Ma'am.'   *1851*

Hitler's death was announced to a less than grieving England. Asked if in the light of the tyrant's demise, he had anything to say about the state of the war effort, Churchill replied, 'Yes – it is definitely more satisfactory than it was this time five years ago.'   *1945*

The sex-mad sausage-maker of Chicago, Adolph Luetgert 'lost' his wife Louisa. Adolph, a strapping 6ft 3in and seventeen stone, was a prominent food manufacturer and a man of many mistresses. He even had a bed installed in his factory to accommodate them, and when Louisa got upset, he tried to strangle and shoot her. When she was found missing, her understandably worried brother called the police and they visited the Luetgert factory. There, in a vat, they found a strange brown fluid, pieces of human bone and two gold rings, one of which was inscribed L. L. At the trial Adolph was sentenced to life, a string of his mistresses having testified against him. What must have given his customers food for thought is that the vat used for Louisa was also used for preparing his sausage-meat.   *1897*

Today's the day...

An ignoble death at sea put an end to the powerful Duke of Suffolk after Parliament had condemned him for corruption and robbery. He'd been saved from an official execution by King Henry VI and sentenced instead to five years in exile, but on the way to Calais he'd been captured and taken on board another ship. 'Welcome traitor,' said the sailors, and after a mock trial they cast him adrift in a small boat with a few of the crew. A knave of Ireland – 'one of the lewdest men on board' – decided to kill him and sawed his head off with six strokes of a rusty sword.   *1450*

'The Bloody Red Baron' Manfred Freiherr von Richthofen was born to aristocratic parents in Prussia and groomed for a military career. He rode brilliantly but was blown off his horse in the élite Uhlan cavalry, and relegated to being supply officer. Incensed at having to look after 'cheese and eggs', he applied to join the new German Air Force. He crashed on his first solo flight, and only after intensive training from the flying ace Boelcke did he join the crack 'Jasta 2' squadron. He spurned drink and women and fought with single-minded ferocity. Disdaining the cowardly device of camouflage, he had his plane painted bright red – and earned his name. He loved the 'glory of the hunt', shot down a grand total of eighty aircraft and would have had a siver goblet made for each 'kill'. As it turned out, he was much too deadly and when he got to his sixtieth goblet, the German's wartime supply of silver ran out!   *1892*

The voracious Empress of Russia Catherine the Great was born, Sophia Augusta Frederica, in Stettin, Germany. At the age of fourteen she was carted off to Russia, re-christened Catherine Alexeyevna and married the heir to the throne – the teenage imbecile weakling Peter Ulrich. 'Child as I was,' she said, as her husband played with his toy soldiers, 'the title of Queen sounded sweet to my ears.' Her first affair with the handsome Sergei Soltykov was engineered by her own mother-in-law and later in her career she used a lover of her own choosing, Gregory Orlov, to dispose of her husband and make her Empress of Russia. Of all her lovers the longest lasting was the unkempt one-eyed Potemkin – her 'bow-wow' – who chewed garlic, walked round naked in his slippers and even supplied her with younger men. *1729*

'The Old Groaner' was born Harry Lillis Crosby in Tacoma, Washington. He was nicknamed 'Bingo' after a character in 'The Bingsville Bugle' cartoon strip, and was soon singing even though it was 'cissy'. He gave up lessons when his teacher wouldn't let him sing pop-songs, and untutored he made it as a radio star with 'The Rhythm Boys'. When he first arrived in Hollywood his big ears made him look like 'a taxi with its doors open', so the make-up men got to work with glue. For years the heat from the lights kept making them pop out again, until one day he couldn't stick it any more and said they'd have to stay that way. He claimed he had no glamour, no 'continental suavity', and fellow singer Dinah Shore probably came near to the secret of his success when she said, 'Bing sings like all people think they sing – in the shower!' *1901*

Today's the day...

The Momma of Israel Golda Meir was born in Kiev, the daughter of a cabinet maker. In 1906, Golda made it to America where she became a teacher and a committed Zionist. But Milwaukee was hardly the land of milk and honey, and so when she married Morris Myerson it was on condition they move to Palestine – which they did in 1921. Briefly they lived on a Kibbutz; then Golda took in washing in Tel Aviv, getting more politically involved all the time. After Israel achieved statehood in 1948 she became its first representative in Moscow, Minister of Labour and of Foreign Affairs, and had actually retired by 1969 when at the age of seventy she was made Prime Minister. Her defiant stance in the *mêlée* of the Middle East had once caused David Ben Gurion to say that she was 'the only man' in his cabinet. Now she was in his shoes as Premier she summed up her own attitude to her country. 'Israel has a secret weapon,' she said – 'no choice.'   *1898*

Dickens' dying friend the poet and satirist Thomas Hood finally popped off after a long illness during which he'd eked out a living by writing from his bed. 'I must remain a lively Hood,' he quipped, 'to earn a livelihood.' Previously he'd gotten by with advances made by his publishers to whom he'd temporarily 'mortgaged his brain' – and now he was determined to carry on working till the end. 'I must die in harness,' he said, 'like a hero – or a horse.'   *1845*

The passing of a great impostor occurred when Psalmanazar, whose real name was never known, died in London's Ironmonger Row aged about eighty-four. Though visibly European, he was introduced to the Bishop of London as 'a Formosan convert' by an unscrupulous Scottish chaplain, and since no one knew much about the Far East he was immediately lionised as 'a saved exotic'. Doted on by the wealthy, the learned and the pious, he was given chambers at Oxford and asked to translate the Bible into his 'native tongue' – which of course, he'd invented. Instead, he wrote a bestseller that was a totally fictitious and utterly believed survey of Formosa, where apparently eating flesh was considered 'unmannerly' but not a sin, and where 18,000 small boys were sacrificed every year. The public lapped it up – for a while – until Psalmanazar got a conscience, joined a Dragoon's regiment and really was converted. He lived his last years 'like a saint', saving only his 'sole indulgence' – he took ten to twelve spoonfuls of opium every night. Thinking it might be wicked, however, he sought to cut down by taking the same number of drops dissolved in a pint of punch!

1763

A premonition of Parliamentary murder came to John Williams, a Cornish mine manager, who dreamt that he stood in the lobby of the House of Commons and watched as a man wearing a coat with brass buttons shot and mortally wounded the Prime Minister Spencer Perceval, marking his spotless white waistcoat with blood. Williams' wife told him to go back to sleep, but he dreamt it again and this time was dissuaded from giving warning by his friends, who said he'd be exposed to 'contempt and vexation'. A week later, the identical dream was dreamt by Perceval himself, and the day after that, a lunatic called Bellingham mistook the Prime Minister for someone else and shot him. Bellingham wore a coat with brass buttons, and Perceval's white waistcoat was spattered with blood.

1812

An airborne duel took place over a field near Paris, fought between two crazy Frenchmen who'd argued over the love of an actress. Accompanied by their seconds, the men ascended in the baskets of two hydrogen balloons. At more than 2,000ft, floating less than 100yds apart, one man fired his blunderbuss and missed. The other returned fire and scored a direct hit in the canopy of the balloon, which burst and plummeted earthwards. The poor second plunged to his death along with the protagonist, whose 'honour' must have been seriously deflated.

1808

Today's the day...

The millionaire matador El Cordobes was born Manuel Benitez in Palma del Rio, in Andalusia, and was so poor and ill-educated he claimed he didn't even know the world was round until he saw film of a satellite on TV! He started fighting officially in 1959 and became a full blown matador four years later. By 1968 he was a millionaire, not once but three times over. He bears the scars of more than twenty gorings, and when the length of them all is added up, it comes to three times the measurement of his waist.   *1936*

The man who gave men back their faces, plastic surgeon Sir Archie McIndoe, was born in Dunedin, New Zealand. Introduced to cosmetic surgery by Harold Gillies, a distant cousin, he became fascinated with the idea of curing 'cringing introverts' of facial blemishes. When the war came he took over the Queen Victoria Hospital, East Grinstead, and worked marvels with terribly burnt young airmen of the Battle of Britain. His patients called themselves his 'guinea pigs', and with his new techniques he not only put their faces and hands, skin and bones back together, but bullied them into facing life again. He was by no means a modest or retiring gentleman, but in the circumstances his attitude is perhaps understandable. 'I am a renovator of men's faces,' he said, 'a restorer of confidence, and in a sense a spiritual healer. Thus I take to myself a God-like status.'   *1900*

The General Strike began in earnest having started officially at midnight the night before. This vast confrontation had grown from a dispute in the mines, and when the call came nearly three million people came out – almost a quarter of the nation's workforce. Lady Mountbatten buckled to and answered the switchboard at the *Daily Express*, while Lady Diana Cooper sat up all night folding copies of *The Times*. During the nine days it lasted, 3,149 prosecutions were made against strikers, and under the Emergency Powers Act many men

May 4

were convicted merely for possessing a copy of the strike bulletin. At the eleventh hour, Ernest Bevin had claimed that the Unions and the Government were within five minutes of a settlement, but the Cabinet determined to discontinue negotiations until the TUC repudiated an unofficial action by the *Daily Mail* printers. When they did so, and went to tell Prime Minister Baldwin at midnight, they weren't allowed to see him. A servant told them he'd gone to bed! *1926*

The first ever Derby was run at Epsom Downs, and to stimulate a little more interest it was followed by a cockfight. Inaugurated by the twenty-eight-year-old 12th Earl of Derby and his friend Sir Charles Bunbury, the race was designed for three-year-olds and made the gentlemanly distinction that colts should carry 9st, but fillies only 8st 9lb. Sir Charles' own horse 'Diomed' won this opening race, which as it turned out was a much needed consolation. There had been some disagreement over what the race should be called, and the name was only decided on when the two founders tossed a coin. Had milordship the Earl not won, this world famous race would now have been called the 'Bunbury'. *1780*

255

Today's the day...

The neglected Emperor Napoleon Bonaparte died at the age of fifty-one. Bonapartist doctors believed he'd been laid low by chronic hepatitis brought on by the climate of his 'sea girt dungeon of exile' on the Isle of St Helena. After-the-event opinion seems to concur that the little Corsican died of a combination of a gastric ulcer and stomach cancer, and his conviction that his doctors were 'worse killers than generals' was not far from the mark. The constant doses of calomel and arsenic they gave him seemed hardly conducive to saving his life, though since he was in perfect shape when his coffin was opened nineteen years later, they may have helped preserve him. *1821*

'The Sage of Highgate' and 'Father of Communism' Karl Heinrich Marx was born in Trier – the son of a Christian Jewish lawyer. He came to England after the revolutionary upheavals of 1848 and stayed in London for most of the rest of his life. For a long while he and his wife and children lived in two gruesome rooms in Soho, where the little daughter Franziska died and the manuscripts lay with the pipe-ash and dirty teaspoons on the table. Friend and disciple Engels gradually helped them to live a little better, but by that time the aristocratic Mrs Marx – Jenny von Westphalen – was already embittered by poverty. Karl, who had carbuncles and often couldn't sit down to write, only ever had one regular earned income – £1 a week – which came from his unlikely post as the European Economics correspondent of the *New York Tribune*. '*Das Kapital*,' he said of his masterwork, 'won't even pay for the cigars I smoked writing it.' *1818*

'The Lass with the Wings' Amy Johnson took off from Croydon on her historic flight to Australia. Nobody was particularly interested as they didn't think the twenty-six-year-old 'beginner' would get very far. It looked as if they were right when her little plane *Jason* sprang a fuel leak over the Channel and the fumes made Amy feel so sick she had to fly with her head out the window. She was forced down by a sandstorm near Baghdad and a monsoon in Burma, and narrowly missed a mountain in dense cloud on the Syrian border. When she arrived in Karachi the press began to sit up and take note, and publicity was so great she was greeted by a cheering crowd chanting 'Amy Wonderful Amy'. In the circumstances, it was odd that our international aviator heroine had only learnt to fly after a disastrously unhappy love affair. 'I wanted desperately to die,' she said, 'and flying seemed as good a way as any!' *1930*

The gift of a vulture was graciously accepted by London Zoo from the celebrated Doctor Joshua Brookes of Oxford Street. He kept quite a number of vultures, to gobble up the human remains left over after anatomy classes! *1826*

Virginia Woolf's baffling masterpiece *To the Lighthouse* was published. Virginia sent a copy to her friend Vita Sackville-West inscribed, 'In my opinion the best novel I have ever written.' A little taken aback by Miss Woolf's uncharacteristic immodesty, Vita opened the book – it was a dummy copy filled with blank pages! *1927*

Today's the day...

The Everest of athletics was conquered when Roger Bannister ran the first sub-four-minute-mile at the Iffley Road track in Oxford. The lanky 6ft 1½in medical student lined up with five other runners, including his friends, the Christophers Brasher and Chataway. The three of them had plotted and trained for the race together, and now they were ready to tear into history – but not straight away, for their first effort was a false start. Brasher paced them for the first two laps, then Chataway took the lead. With 300yds to go, Bannister accelerated past and cheered on by 1,500 spectators collapsed over the finishing line in 3mins 59.4secs. Suitably, the time-keeper of the race was the doyen of record-breaking, Norris McWhirter. It had taken nine years to lower the previous record and bring it down by two seconds, yet Bannister's new record was broken only forty-six days later. The Iffley Road track was a memorable one for Bannister, for here, seven years earlier, he had run his first major competitive mile – it took him over a minute longer. *1954*

'White Christmas' was published as the summer began. Composed by Irving Berlin against a tight deadline for the film *Holiday Inn*, it was destined to become the greatest selling record of all time, with a mind-boggling estimate of 140 million copies sold to date. While everyone on the set thought it was a nice little sentimental song, a confident Bing Crosby turned to Berlin and said prophetically, 'I don't think you need to worry about this one, Irving.' *1942*

The neurotic father of psychoanalysis Sigmund Freud was born in Freiberg, Moravia. As a young medical graduate, he pioneered the early use of cocaine as a cure for diabetes, but the experiments were 'conspicuous failures', and he turned his attention to curing hysteria by hypnosis. In the course of his work he came up with a novel technique of his own – and psychoanalysis was born. Freud was famous for his remarkable sympathy for his patients – which might be explained by

258

his own neuroses. He developed an Oedipus complex after seeing his mother naked, and though advocating sexual freedom, personally found intercourse degrading. He suffered from debilitating depressions, a fear of open spaces and railway trains, and lived in terror of dying at the age of fifty-one. Illness and depression, it seemed, were the source of his genius, and he claimed he could only really work when unwell. Bouts of furious creative activity were always heralded by stomach pains which increased as the work got better. His own mental health became an obsession, and religiously every day he spent half an hour practising self-analysis – convinced it made him calm and serene. In every analytical session, he had one dogged assistant – his favourite Chow, Jo-fi. She walked in with the patient, lay down beside the couch and at the end after precisely one hour, got up and trotted out again – so Freud knew the session was over.   *1856*

The male vamp Rudolph Valentino was born, the son of a vet, in Castellaneto, southern Italy. As a young man he emigrated to America arriving, he claimed, with $1 and two addresses. These he supplemented by becoming a gardener in New York's Central Park and later a ten cent-a-dance gigolo. He went to Hollywood where after a few false starts playing villains, he landed such a plum part in *The Four Horse Men of the Apocalypse* that after a sensational New York première, his name was lifted from the supporting roles to star billing. In a film career spanning just fourteen major films in five years, he made men laugh, critics cringe and women swoon. In his private life, however, he failed to live up to his screen image as The Great Lover. He married two butch ladies both noted for their lesbian tendencies. The first marriage ended on the wedding day after she locked him out of the bedroom and in the second, his wife made him wear a slave bracelet and call her 'Boss'. In fact Valentino was only a dream lover. He was vain, disinterested in heterosexual affairs and had only two real passions – food and men.   *1895*

Today's the day...

The real Sherlock Holmes was revealed when Sir Arthur Conan Doyle wrote a letter to Dr Joseph Bell freely admitting that it was on this eminent surgeon, who'd taught him at Edinburgh University, that he'd based the character of Holmes. Bell would mesmerise his students with his powers of observation. The way a man walked, the calluses on his hands, the shade of his tan and the state of his clothes could all add up, in the doctor's mind, to give a clear picture of his profession, where he'd been and what he'd done. Only on one occasion did he seem to come unstuck when he declared a man was obviously a piper in a Highland regiment. The man insisted he'd never been in the Army in his life, but when he was stripped all was explained by a small 'D' tattooed on his chest. It was true he wasn't a soldier – he was a deserter.

1892

'Britain's answer to the Red Baron' Captain Albert Ball was killed in action. The sensitive young man who loved playing the violin and hated 'this killing business' nevertheless became an air ace and a legend. With a record of twenty-nine downed German planes to his credit, he was eager to outdo the French ace Georges Guynemer's total of thirty-seven. On his last tour of duty, he flew so many missions that his speech became slurred, he was often incoherent and his eyes glazed over with fatigue. Intercepting the 'Richthofen Flying Circus' over Lens, he got his score up to forty-four but in the fierce fighting he disappeared into a bank of cloud. He never returned and when his body was found in the wreckage of his plane, his only injuries were those sustained on impact. He hadn't been shot down and why he crashed remains a mystery.   *1917*

'Mr Average Joe American' Gary Cooper was born in Helena, Montana. He was very much the 'guy next door' and was described as 'one of the most beloved illiterates America has ever known'. In 1939 he earned over $480,000 – which wasn't bad for an ex-cartoonist and baby photographer who'd started off as a cowboy extra at $5 a fall.   *1901*

The *Lusitania* was torpedoed by a German U-boat, and sank in eighteen minutes, just ten miles from safety off the coast of Ireland. The giant 762ft long passenger ship was carrying an illicit cargo, almost entirely ammunition. When the first torpedo hit, the contraband shells and cartridges exploded, the vast bunkers of coal ignited and she listed over at an impossible angle with one of her decks just 12ft from the sea. There were not enough crewmen to launch the lifeboats, which jammed on their frozen ropes and smashed against the side or plunged uselessly into the sea. 900 people were still on board as the liner went down and in all 1,198 perished. On the day the *Lusitania* sailed from New York an advertisement had appeared in the newspapers, placed by the 'Imperial German Embassy' warning travellers that 'the zone of war includes the water adjacent to the British Isles'; some passengers had received telegrams urging them not to embark and others had been stopped by strangers at the dockyard gates muttering the same warning. Everyone, of course, had dismissed it all as German propaganda.   *1915*

Today's the day...

Mount Pelée erupted on the island of Martinique. A 'boiling red river' of molten lava poured down the mountainside, obliterated the town of St Pierre, incinerated ten square miles of countryside and killed over 30,000 people in just three minutes. In an estimated temperature of 1000° C most of the victims were instantly burnt to death; others asphyxiated in the caustic sulphurous fumes and even after the initial blast, still more died when they were coated with red-hot mud and literally baked alive. In St Pierre there were only two survivors – a murderer who was incarcerated in a cell with only a tiny window and a cobbler who, despite being badly burned, managed to run to safety. Three months later the mountain erupted again. This time it claimed 2,000 lives, most of them rescuers trying to bring relief supplies to the stricken island.   *1902*

The royally deflated historian Edward Gibbon was born. He remained a bachelor all his life labouring away on *The Decline and Fall of the Roman Empire*, but was well looked after in his house in London by a housekeeper, butler, cook and four maids. When he delivered the second volume of his work to the Duke of Gloucester, the affable Duke received him and remarked, 'Another damned thick square book! Always scribble, scribble, scribble! Eh Mr Gibbon?'   *1737*

The secret of the treasure ship of Sutton Hoo began to be revealed when the owner of the land, Mrs Pretty, suggested they start to excavate the curiously-shaped burial mound in which it stood. With a little help, Mrs Pretty and Mr Basil Brown of the Ipswich Museum found an 89ft long Anglo-Saxon open ship with a burial chamber on deck full of the most magnificent treasure. The site was declared a national monument and leading archaeologists were called in to help. Throughout the long hot summer they hurried to finish excavations in the face of the approaching war with Germany. One by one the treasures emerged: jewelled shoulder-brooches, shields and scabbards, an intricately enamelled purse and a fearsome warrior's helmet. In materials alone the hoard was worth over half a million pounds; in historical terms it was priceless. An official Treasure Trove inquest decided that it all belonged to Mrs Pretty, but she handed it over to the nation. Hurriedly it was packed up and whisked off to a place of safe-keeping for the duration of the war – and the ancient ship ended up in a disused stretch of the London Underground. *1939*

Hitler's autopsy was performed – and anatomists discovered that the marching song of British soldiers was right! According to the report on what dental records proved were the remains of Hitler, 'the left testicle could not be found', and though it may have been destroyed when an attempt was made to burn the body, its absence was confirmed by his commander in World War I. Psychologically, it's supposed to have been extremely damaging and caused many of Hitler's obsessions – his belief in a special mission, mania for change, violent temper tantrums and insistence on his ruthless masculinity. It's also said to be the reason why he always crossed his hands in front of him when he was photographed. *1945*

Today's the day...

Colonel Blood stole the Crown Jewels from Charles II and the Tower of London. Dressed as a parson, this ex-puritan Irish adventurer had carefully cultivated the seventy-seven-year-old deputy-keeper, Talbot Edwards. He'd even suggested a match between Edwards' young daughter and his own nephew, and a meeting was arranged for today. With three accomplices, Blood turned up at the unearthly hour of 7am, and suggested they take a peep at the Jewels. Once in the chamber, they clubbed the old keeper and stabbed him. Blood flattened the crown and hid it under his cloak, while crony Parrott put the orb down his trousers. Just as they were about to file the sceptre in half, Edwards' son arrived home from Flanders with his friend Captain Beckman, and the thieves had to hot-foot it over the drawbridge. Blood was caught but far from being sentenced to death as everyone expected, he was not only pardoned, but given £500 a year and estates in Ireland! To the end of his days he was a favourite of the King and nobody ever knew why. *1671*

Twenty-five guineas reward was offered by the Henfield Prosecuting Society for information leading to the arrest of some barbarous villains who broke into Mr Thomas Page's stable on Furzefield Farm in Shermanbury. There, during the night, with bare-faced effrontery, these vandals stole valuable property from Mr Page in that they did 'maliciously cut-off and carry away' the hair from the tails of his horses. *1838*

The man who wouldn't grow up J. M. Barrie was born in Kirriemuir, one of the seven offspring of a weaver. His childhood was marred by the death of an elder brother and he became obsessed with the idea of eternal childhood – the 'arrested development' he was to immortalise in his masterpiece *Peter Pan*. Barrie never grew above 5ft, he didn't shave until he was twenty-four and never consummated his marriage. He was already a successful writer and an unsuccessful husband when he met Sylvia and Arthur Llewelyn-Davies and their sons – and started to take over their lives. Adults were puzzled by Barrie and he's been condemned for all shades of 'abnormal' conduct from being asexual to paedophilic. For children he was much simpler: he knew a lot about 'murders, hangings and desert islands' and besides, 'he could wiggle his ears'.   *1860*

A revolting animal nuisance was inspected by an Inspector of Nuisances at the request of the Newhaven Board of Guardians. Arriving at the home of one Mr Robert Dennis Chantreli in what turned out to be the aptly named village of Rottingdean, the poor inspector found the house and its inhabitants 'in a disgusting condition'. In the house, the garden, and an outbuilding, he discovered between 100 and 200 live cats, some loose and some in cages, as well as two dead ones, raw meat and gnawed bones, a fox, a goat, turkeys, geese, ducks and 'other fowls of every description'. In court, Mr Chantreli said he kept them all for a young lady who resided with him. She was an artist, he explained, and he kept his menagerie that she might never be short of animal models.   *1867*

Today's the day...

The Deputy Fuhrer took the plunge. In the early evening Hitler's right hand man, the notorious Rudolph Hess, parachuted onto the Duke of Hamilton's estate in Scotland from a *Messerschmidt 110* fighter he'd flown from Augsburg. Told by an astrologer that he was destined to bring peace between Germany and England, he must have cursed his faulty horoscope, because he was interrogated and eventually sent to prison for life. Churchill was so unimpressed by what he described as this 'devoted and frantic deed of lunatic benevolence' that, having been told of the solo peace mission, he returned to watching a Marx brothers' movie. Hitler was less impressed still. In fact he was furious. 'Lunacy is no excuse for what he has done,' he was reported to have said, and promptly arrested poor Willi Messerschmidt, the plane's designer.   *1941*

Mother's Day became official when the US Congress declared the second Sunday in May a national holiday dedicated to 'the best mother in the world – your mother!' Miss Anna M. Jarvis of Philadelphia had been campaigning for the idea ever since her own mother, a Methodist Sunday School teacher, had died on 9 May, 1905. In England, on the other hand, the fourth Sunday in Lent had been observed as Mothering Sunday for centuries, when apprentices and maids were allowed home for the day with a modest offering of a posy or a simnel cake. The American version arrived in Britain with the GIs in World War II – much to the delight of greeting card manufacturers and florists everywhere.   *1913*

Tap-happy dancer Fred Astaire was born in Omaha, Nebraska, to Austrian immigrant parents who battled through life with the name of Austerlitz. His sister Adele was something of a local dance star, and at four a bewildered Fred was bundled off to a New York dancing school as her partner – quite a shock really, since he'd never danced before. When Adele left the stage to marry an English peer, Fred

May 10

went to Hollywood on his own, teamed up with Ginger Rogers in 1933 and within a year was making so much money that the studio insured his legs for a million dollars. Quite a career for someone once categorised by a talent scout: 'Can't act. Can't sing. Slightly bald. Can dance a little.'   *1899*

The *Kraken* awoke in latitude 8.50 N, longitude 84.05 E, when one of the crew of the becalmed schooner *Pearl* fired a shot into a 'large brownish mass' which turned out to be a giant squid. Passengers on a passing steamer bound from Columbo to Madras described the overgrown cephalopod as being as wide as the schooner and about half as long, with a 100ft train of tentacles. The monster attacked the schooner and as the crew took to the boats, two of them were crushed beneath its tentacles, which were each as thick as a barrel. It squeezed onto the deck of the schooner and then, understandably upset, it simply pulled it over.   *1874*

The mutiny that shook the Empire erupted in Meerut after eighty-five sepoys had been sentenced to ten years' hard labour for refusing to bite off the greased end of the cartridges for new Lee Enfield rifles. The rumour had spread that the grease included the fat of pigs – unclean to Moslems – and the fat of cows – sacred to Hindus, and the native regiments rose while the Europeans were on church parade. They emptied the prison, fired British bungalows and massacred the women and children. The murder and mutilation spread to Cawnpore, Lucknow and Delhi, where the European officers guarding the magazine blew it and themselves up to stop the Indians getting it. The British inflicted a savage vengeance and the fighting continued sporadically for over a year. Ironically, though the animal fat led to the last flaring of the old India against British domination, it ended instead with the imposition of the direct and total rule of the crown and the founding of the Imperial Raj.   *1857*

Today's the day...

'Mr American Music' Irving Berlin was born Israel Baline in Ternun, Siberia. Harried by the Cossacks, the family emigrated to New York and young Israel became a singing waiter in the Bowery. He wrote songs on his shirt-cuffs as he was serving and his first hit earned him 37 cents in royalties! He's written over 3,000 songs but in fact he can't read music – and although his greatest success was of course 'White Christmas' he actually prefers to spend the Yuletide in sunny Florida!   *1888*

The biggest fibber of all time Baron Munchhausen was born in Bodenwerder. His tall-tales about his own incredible bravery as a soldier, hunter and sportsman were barely tolerated in his own time and when they were set down for posterity by his drinking companion Rudolph Raspe, they strained credulity to the limit. With little subtlety his hometown passed comment by erecting a statue of the Baron mounted on half a horse. The other half, he once said, had been severed by a falling portcullis!   *1720*

The original Siamese twins Chang and Eng were born of Chinese parents in Meklong, Siam, firmly joined together at the chest by a 6in arm-like band of flesh. The King of Siam thought they were an omen of disaster and wanted them killed, but he relented and allowed the Scottish merchant Robert Hunter to take them to America. They were an instant success touring both the United States and Europe, and when they'd earned enough money they bought a farm in North Carolina. They married the sisters Sarah Ann and Adelaide Yates and sharing a 'very large bed' between them sired twenty-one children. Chang drank excessively and though Eng didn't get drunk he liked to stay up playing poker. Chang often got violent and once caused the pair of them to be hauled before a court on an assault charge. The judge felt he should really sentence Chang to prison but he couldn't do it. It would just have been too unfair on Eng!   *1811*

May 11

Moustachioed Spanish surrealist Salvador Dali was born after nine months in what he described as 'divine paradise'. A nasty little boy, he took great pleasure in beating his sister, once took a bite from a dead bat and was so hated in his home town that the people stoned him in the streets.   *1904*

The First King of All England Edgar I was crowned at Bath, after fourteen licentious and war-like years on the throne. Having subdued all the other English kingdoms and given up his 'foreign vices' he was finally anointed by St Dunstan, Archbishop of Canterbury. He had two 'handfast unions' – one with a nun and one with a lady called 'White Duck' – before he married Elfrida, the beautiful widow of his best friend who was fortuitously found dead in a wood. She was crowned with him and the happy couple went to Chester where they accepted pledges of loyalty from the eight kings of Scotland, Wales and the Islands. Just to show he meant business, Edgar had them row him down the River Dee and back – with himself at the helm as coxswain.   *AD 973*

Today's the day...

'The Lady of the Lamp', and the woman who made nursing respectable, Florence Nightingale, was born in the city of Florence in Italy. Though Florence was considered a man's name, she was a good deal luckier than her sister who'd been born in Greece and called Parthenope! Florence was the child of a wealthy pleasure-loving family but she yearned 'for something worth doing'. To the family's horror she studied mathematics and reports on sanitation, trained as a nurse in Germany and Paris, and returned home to reorganise the Institute for Sick Gentlewomen in London. Concerned about the appalling conditions in the field hospitals in the Crimea, she went off to be a nurse-at-war, and after two years she came back a heroine, slipping into England unnoticed after having refused a passage on a battleship sent specially for her. She felt she'd been called to her mission by God and firmly believed that there was a heaven for animals – a fact that no doubt would have pleased the little owl that for years she carried around in her breast pocket.   *1820*

A mind-reader lost his head. He was Washington Irving Bishop and he went into a coma at a club in New York and was pronounced dead. Two doctors were present and so impressed were they with his psychic powers that they decided to take a peek at his brain and opened his skull in a post-mortem on the very same night. His brain was quite normal and they could find nothing to indicate the cause of death. Unfortunately, the man's mother then arrived, distraught, and announced that her son frequently went into cataleptic fits – often for as long as eighteen hours – and awoke perfectly healthy.   *1889*

'Dreamer of Decadence', the artist and poet Dante Gabriel Rossetti was born to exiled Italian parents in London and never set foot in Italy in his life. A precocious artist as a child, he became the leader of the Pre-Raphaelite set, married the beautiful ex-shop girl Elizabeth Siddal and was heartbroken when she committed suicide.

270

May 12

He put his only complete manuscript of poems in her coffin and it was buried with her, but seven years later he regretted his romantic gesture; the coffin was exhumed and the poems retrieved and published, with Rossetti in fear that the truth would 'ooze out'. He developed a mania for collecting things and filled his 'great barn of a house' in Cheyne Walk with bric-a-brac, peopling his spare bedroom with so many carved heads, gargoyles and buddhas that most of his guests found it impossible to sleep there. His other great collector's passion was for animals and he stacked his back garden with lizards and peacocks, wombats, deer, a raccoon and a zebra. His neighbours weren't very pleased – especially with his armadillos, who finding the garden a little crowded, burrowed under the fence and through their kitchen floor.   *1828*

Augustus the Strong was born in Dresden. He became the elector of Saxony and wangled his way on to the throne of Poland. He precipitated the Great Northern War, brought financial ruin on his country, was deposed and unfortunately restored. It was said by some that his soubriquet pointed not so much to his kingly qualities but to his virility, for legend had it that he sired near 1,000 children – though in fact 355 is thought to be nearer the truth. Amazingly, only one of that lot was legitimate and even more amazingly, Poland eventually allowed him to be King.   *1670*

Unhappy nonsense-man Edward Lear was born. He was actually an artist and gave drawing lessons to Queen Victoria, but is best remembered for his *Book of Nonsense* – which he sold outright for £125. He felt himself to be ugly and unattractive, suffered from epilepsy, bronchitis and asthma, and was intensely lonely. He sought refuge in the humour of his nonsense verse which may well have been *okulscratch abibblebongibo, viddle squibble tog-atog* – or at least you'd be hard put to prove it wasn't.   *1812*

Today's the day...

The illegal Empress, Queen of Hungary and Bohemia and
Archduchess of Austria, Maria Theresa was born. Since it was
unlawful for women to succeed, she came to the throne only by 'The
Pragmatic Sanction' of her father Charles VI, and was at war through
much of her reign because of it. She nevertheless managed to produce
sixteen children; she was 'insatiable' they said, and could be seen at
the opera before a birth and driving in the streets soon after. Of the ten
that survived, two became emperors, three became queens, and one
of them, Marie Antoinette, lost her head. Both personally and in power,
Maria Theresa was deeply religious and strongly intolerant, but was
not above a little political sleight of hand. She instituted a 'Chastity
Commission', officially for the protection of public morals. But in fact
it was little more than an intimate system of espionage, and the real
joke was that one of her best spies was none other than the world's
greatest lecher – Giacomo Casanova.   *1717*

The first fire insurance company started trading, run by financial
speculator Nicholas Barbon who suitably enough made his fortune
out of re-building London after the Great Fire. Fortunately for the
insurance industry, Barbon had changed his name; he was the son of
the famous Anabaptist Praise-God Barebones and had been christened
'If-Christ-had-not-died-thou-hadst-been-damned' Barebones.
To his father's horror, he was called 'Damned' for short.   *1680*

Painter-by-the-yard Sir James Thornhill died after a lifetime spent
decorating the walls and ceilings of the stately buildings of Britain with
'a liberal supply of gods and goddesses'. Queen Anne commissioned
him to work in Hampton Court and Kensington Palace, and it took him
twenty years to complete the great ceiling in Greenwich Hospital –
which left him with a permanent stoop. Though he constantly railed
against piece-work, he could never get out of it and was only paid
forty shillings a yard for one of his most famous works – the dome of

St Paul's. Working high in the dome on scaffolding, he stepped back to study a face he'd just painted, and his assistant was horrified to see he was teetering on the very edge of the platform. Frightened to say anything, he flung a pot of paint at the picture and Sir James rushed forward enraged. 'What have you done?' he exclaimed. 'Saved your life Sir,' came the reply.   *1734*

The longest reigning heavyweight champ, the 'Brown Bomber' Joe Louis Barrow was born in Alabama. Mother wanted him to be a fiddle-player, but instead he trained at the local gym with his friend Sugar Ray Robinson, and became a professional boxer at the age of twenty. On his way to the crown, his only serious defeat was at the hands of the German Max Schmeling – a victory much capitalised-on by Hitler. As soon as Joe was champ, he fought him again, and knocked him out in the first round with a punch so hard it snapped a vertebra in Schmeling's back. In his reign of eleven years, he successfully defended his title twenty-five times – but actually felt a pre-title fight to be his best one. It was with Max Baer in 1935, when he aimed 254 punches at his opponent – and only missed once.   *1914*

The poet Dryden was finally buried in Westminster Abbey, a full twelve days after he died. The funeral was originally supposed to have taken place the very day after, 'the Abbey had been lighted, the ground opened' and Bishop and choir were waiting. But as the eighteen mourning coaches set off, they were intercepted by a bunch of drunken 'aristocratic mohocks and disturbers of the peace', led by Lord Jeffreys, son of the infamous hanging Judge. On hearing it was the great poet's funeral, Jeffreys declaimed it was far too shabby an affair, insisted on providing something grander and ordered the body to be lodged at an undertakers in cheapside. His offensive generosity, however, proved to be an empty vessel. When he sobered up, milord swore he knew nothing about it.   *1700*

Today's the day...

Frank and earnest painter Thomas Gainsborough was baptised in the Meeting House in Sudbury in Suffolk, having been born nearly two years earlier in a house that was once a pub. He liked best to paint landscapes, but was 'encouraged out of his way' by the financial rewards of portraits and lured to the social high-spots, first of Bath and then of London. Always keen to get on, he painted eight portraits of George III, became a founder member of the Royal Academy and had something of a love-hate relationship with the portrait supremo of the time, Sir Joshua Reynolds. Both as painters and people, they were wildly different. When Reynolds painted the actress Sarah Siddons, he signed his name at the bottom of the picture and said, 'Madam, my name shall go down to posterity on the hem of your garment.' When Gainsborough painted her, the only thing he's supposed to have said is: 'Madam is there no end to your nose?' *1729*

'Vaseline' was made a registered trademark for petroleum jelly, it having been developed by a struggling London-born chemist Robert Augustus Chesebrough when he was working in the Pennsylvania oilfields. He'd noticed that a colourless residue that built up around the pump rods was used by the workers to soothe cuts and burns, so he analysed it and made a commercially acceptable version. To test it, this undoubted enthusiast cut and scratched himself and burned his hands with fire and acid, and so thoroughly satisfied was he with his product that he took a spoonful of it every day of his life. He lived to be ninety-six. *1878*

'The Christian Caligula' Pope John XII died, aged about twenty-seven, after a riotous reign of nine years. John was a sex-mad gambler who kept gangs of thugs to do his dirty work, violated female pilgrims and was said to have turned the Lateran Palace into a brothel. He plotted against the Emperor Otto, mutilated priests who upset him and once ordained a bishop in a stable. *AD 964*

Medicine got a shot in the arm when Edward Jenner, a country doctor from Gloucestershire, made his first 'vaccination' against smallpox. Previously, it had been the custom in the East and occasionally in Europe to inoculate by purposely infecting people – in which circumstances they usually, but not always, got a milder form of the disease. Twenty years earlier, Jenner had heard that milkmaids didn't get smallpox, because in the course of their work they got cow-pox – which made them immune. So took 'some matter' from the cow-pox infected hand of one Sarah Nelmes and inoculated eight-year-old James Phipps with it. Two months later, he infected him with a virulent strain of smallpox and yet the boy survived. This dangerous, not to say rather brutal, experiment validated a technique that was soon saving thousands of lives. Jenner called it vaccination from '*vacca*' – the Latin for cow.   *1796*

Another unfortunate Pope passed away in strange circumstances. He was the famous physician Peter Hispanus who took the name of John XXI. He was the third Pope in a year and he'd only been in office a few months when he decided to have a new chamber built in his palace at Viterbo. He was working in the new room, probably on his book of remedies for all known ills, when the roof fell in. This brought serious question on his infallibility, since he'd preached that unlike his predecessors, he'd have a long life and a lengthy reign.   *1277*

The giant Partholanus landed in Ireland on the coast of Munster in the late twentieth century – or at least he did according to Keating's incredible *History of Ireland*. Being an industrious giant, he did very well in his new land until his wife made a fool of him with her 'loose behaviour' and this upset him so much that he killed his two favourite greyhounds. A crumb of comfort for other Irishmen though – this was, says Keating, the very first instance of infidelity ever known in Ireland.   *AD 987*

Today's the day...

George III had two lucky escapes in a day. The first was when he was reviewing the Grenadier Guards in Hyde Park, and a man standing close to him was shot in the leg by a bullet that was clearly intended for the King. The second was that very same evening at the theatre in Drury Lane when, as the audience were cheering him, two bullets whizzed past his head and struck the panel behind. The culprit this time was James Hadfield, a soldier with head wounds who thought he was a messenger of Christ, and not surprisingly was found insane. The unflappable monarch was unperturbed and not only did he order the performance to continue, but went to sleep in the interval!   *1800*

A deadly discriminator was patented. It was the world's first working machine-gun, designed by James Puckle – an industrious lawyer who spent most of his time peacefully promoting the English fishing industry. His gun was meant for use at sea and discharged 'soe often and soe many bullets and can be so quickly loaden as renders it next to impossible to carry any ship by boarding'. Mr Puckle thoughtfully incorporated another refinement – it fired round bullets for Christians and square bullets for Turks!   *1718*

May 15

Petulant scientist Ilya Metchnikov was born in the Ukraine. He grew up with a violent temper, but apart from being objectionable, he was also very brilliant. He worked on theories of infection and his particular favourite was 'intestinal intoxication', which he said could be cured by drinking sour milk and eating no raw food. For the last eighteen years of his life, he practised what he preached, believing this to be the answer to longevity and convincing himself that man's natural lifespan was 150 years. It was while he was working on this latter theory that he died – aged seventy-one.   *1845*

Sexual revolutionary Ninon de Lenclos was born in Paris, the daughter of an extremely successful pimp and musician. Her parents died when she was fifteen and she was left with a comfortable income, good looks and a crowd of admirers. Abandoning the artificial coyness of the courtesans of the time, she adopted instead the attitude of an 'honourable man'. She was always totally honest with her numerous and usually aristocratic lovers, though she was surprisingly strict, shunning alcohol and banning lewd conversation. Her wit in the salon was almost as legendary as her artistry in the boudoir, and to communicate both these aspects of her craft she established a 'School of Gallantry'. She lectured her pupils on the psychology of women and techniques of seduction – and if they were found to be lacking she gave them personal tuition. 'Love never dies of starvation,' she said, 'but often of indigestion!'   *1620*

The first air hostess Ellen Church, ex-nurse and trained pilot, took to the skies on board a flight from San Francisco to Cheyenne, Wyoming. Throughout her inaugural trip she was kept busy with a hostess's usual duties – serving the passengers with chicken, fruit salad and rolls. But on the ground it was a different matter. This pioneering young lady had to sweep out the planes, fill them up with fuel and help push them out onto the runway.   *1930*

Today's the day...

Glittering piano player Wladzin Valentino Liberace was born in West Allis, Wisconsin. Mom was a Polish-American concert pianist, Dad a French horn-player and brother George a violinist. He won a music scholarship when he was only seven and was nearly lost to stardom when doctors wanted to amputate an infected finger. Mom saved it with old-fashioned poultices and with all his fingers intact he went on to become 'the heart throb of forty million women'. He still holds the record as the highest paid pianist ever, after a single New York performance in 1954 which earned him nearly £50,000 – significantly more than he would have earned had he followed the career his father had chosen for him. Mr Liberace had always wanted his son to be an undertaker.

1917

The first 'Oscars' were awarded by the Academy of Motion Picture Arts and Sciences in Hollywood. The winning film was *Wings* starring sultry Clara Bow, and the trophy, designed by MGM art director Cedric Gibbons, was known simply as 'The Statuette'. It was given its more familiar name two years later supposedly after Bette Davis' first husband or someone's uncle Oscar. Almost every year since, the awards have contrived to be controversial. Walt Disney has won the most, gratefully accepting some twenty Oscars, but a number of the winners, dubious of its cultural worth, just haven't wanted it. In 1938 George Bernard Shaw refused his when he was nominated for his screenplay of *Pygmalion*. 'It's an insult,' he spluttered, 'to offer me an award as if they'd never heard of me before.'

1929

An unknown traveller in space gave US astronaut Gordon Cooper a shock. He was travelling eastwards over Australia at approximately 17,000mph when he spotted a 'glowing greenish object' fast approaching him. It disappeared – then reappeared ten minutes later when the tracking station on earth saw it too. As Major Cooper prepared to re-enter the earth's atmosphere, the spacecraft's automatic stabilisation system short-circuited and the CO_2 level in the module got dangerously high. But he managed to land safely, and as soon as he'd touched down NASA imposed heavy censorship over the whole affair. They refused to answer any questions about the flight, as did Major Cooper – the only man who really knew what happened 100 miles above Australia.

1963

The Dambusters made their famous raid on the Moehne, Eder and Sorpe dams which held back vast reservoirs vital to the industrial Ruhr. The formation of Lancasters, led by Wing-Commander Guy Gibson, successfully breached the dams dropping Barnes Wallis' bouncing bombs, and sent 350 million tons of water thundering down the Ruhr in a 25ft wall, blotting out roads, railways and airfields; swamping mines, foundries and factories. Of the nineteen planes that left Scampton only ten returned with fifty-six airmen dead or missing. The call-sign for a successful mission was 'Nigger' – the name of Guy Gibson's black labrador. The night before the raid 'Nigger' was run over and killed.

1943

Today's the day...

'The Whitsuntide Working Men's Excursion' to Paris set off from London Bridge – it being the very first 'package tour' and exceedingly well arranged by Mr Thomas Cook. The six-day trip was paid for in advance and forty-six shillings inclusive covered travel and five nights at 'a good second-class hotel', with 'a substantial English dinner'.

1861

The relief of Mafeking ended the 217-day imprisonment of 1,000 British soldiers besieged in this little outpost by 8,000 Boers under their wizened little General Piet Cronje. On both sides, the soldiers had kept their morale up by observing a truce every Sunday. The British took the opportunity to play polo, but the puritanical Cronje was horrified and threatened to shell the field if they didn't stop desecrating the Sabbath. Their commanding officer, the original boy-scout Baden-Powell, put a stop to it, though more out of politeness than anything, since the Boers' aim was so bad there were only thirty-five casualties in the whole of the siege. Among other things, the opposing sides threw stones at each other and the British delighted in sending and receiving messages. One read: 'Four hours bombardment. Killed one hen. Wounded one dog. Smashed one window', and on another occasion a native courier came hurtling back, dodging bullets and shells and proudly announced, 'Mrs Butler is well.' But although everyone cheered resoundingly, no one had a clue who she was!

1900

A thoroughly silly means of propulsion was patented for gullible American balloonists. The idea was a complicated one whereby birds of 'the flying classes – eagles, vultures, condors, etc', would be harnessed by 'corsets' to a frame above the canopy in such a way that they could be steered. It would work because, 'The birds have only to fly, the direction of their flight being changed by the conductor quite independently of their will.' It's obvious really!

1887

Sorry King Alfonso of Spain was born, assumed the throne at sixteen and had his ears pierced in the hope that it would improve his eyesight. It didn't, and neither did it do a lot for his insight – for despite tremendous opposition he tried to amass more power for the crown. He suffered the first of many assassination attempts on his wedding day, and was finally thrown out of Spain by the Republicans in 1931. He was just plain disaster prone. When he went on an official visit to Italy in 1923, and they sent the fleet to meet him, some sailors were washed overboard, a submarine blew up and the officer who met him promptly collapsed and died.   *1886*

A judge caught his death in court. He was Sir Charles Clarke, and he was struck down while judging the duellist Captain Clark for killing Captain Innes in what came to be known as 'The Black Sessions' at the Old Bailey. Three other justices went at the same time and died shortly afterwards, along with several of the counsel, jurymen and members of the public amounting to forty-four persons. The official explanation was a fever brought about by overcrowding, but the more fanciful said that it was 'gaol distemper' brought on a foul wind that blew straight from Newgate into the courtroom.   *1750*

'The injured Queen of England' Caroline of Brunswick was born at the licentious court of her father the Duke. She grew up 'destitute of female delicacy'; appeared topless at a ball in Geneva and once turned up at a hunting party wearing a pumpkin on her head 'for nothing is so cool or so comfortable'. By the time she arrived in England to marry her cousin, the future George IV, she was already suffering from the family malady porphyria and was known as 'the mad princess'. George rejected her totally and her behaviour got worse. She was accused of adultery; is thought to have borne two illegitimate children, and was refused admittance to her own coronation.   *1768*

Today's the day...

The harridan Queen Eleanor of Aquitaine married Henry II of England, five months pregnant with his child. Only six weeks earlier she'd divorced the pious Louis of France who incurred her displeasure by daring to shave off his beard while crusading, and it wasn't long before the two espoused Kings were at war over her dowry – the War of the Whiskers. Eleanor's intrigues dominated Europe for half a century and when she died at the age of eighty-two, she asked that her epitaph be, 'Eleanor, by the wrath of God, Queen of England.' *1152*

The Red Barn Murder was perpetrated at Polstead, Suffolk, when fecund mole-catcher's daughter Maria Marten, mother of three illegitimate children, was slain by one of her lovers William Corder, the son of a prosperous farmer. The girl had become too demanding, so he lured her to the barn – with a promise to wed – then shot, stabbed and possibly strangled her, buried her under the floor and sloped off to London. The following April, Maria's stepmother said she'd dreamed of Maria's fate in the Red Barn, and her father dug till he found the body. Corder was traced and tried at Bury Assizes. He

confessed only to shooting Maria – not stabbing or strangling her –
was hanged in front of a crowd of 7,000 and became the subject of
melodramas and puppet shows. In the time between his crime and his
capture he'd advertised for a wife, married a Miss Moore and set up a
school for young ladies.   *1827*

Socialist, Lord and philosopher Bertrand Russell was born. A
grandson of the Victorian Prime Minister Lord John Russell, he met
both Gladstone and Lenin and said he was ten before he knew anyone
who hadn't written a book. His own principal work *Principia
Mathematica* took a decade to write and the manuscript was so large
it had to be delivered in a horse-drawn cab. When mathematics
became too difficult, he said, he took up philosophy, and when that
became too difficult he took up politics. 'Have you seen him in a
bathing dress ?' said D. H. Lawrence. 'He's all disembodied mind.'
But he married four times and nicknamed one mistress, Lady Ottoline
Morrell, 'Lady Utterly Immoral'. 'I'm as drunk as a Lord,' he once
said, 'but then I am one so what does it matter!'   *1872*

Long-time Prima Ballerina Dame Margot Fonteyn was born in
Reigate, Surrey. She started her stunning professional career at
fifteen, and with Nureyev she took a record eighty-nine curtain calls
after dancing *Swan Lake* at the Vienna Staatsoper in 1964. She changed
her name at the outset, taking her half-Brazilian mother's maiden name
Fontes, but when the family objected to being associated with the
stage, she changed it again to the next name in the telephone
directory.   *1919*

An improvement in privy seats was protected by patent in
America. It consisted of a set of rollers that would fit onto the top of
the seat to secure comfort when sitting, 'yet in an attempt to stand
upon them will revolve and precipitate the user to the floor'.   *1869*

Today's the day...

The Russian disaster plane the *Maxim Gorky* made its first flight.
Designed largely as a vehicle to propagandise Soviet aeronautical
achievement, it had purportedly been built to celebrate the fortieth
anniversary of the start of Maxim Gorky's literary career. It was the
largest plane of its time, having a 260ft wing span – nearly 65ft bigger
than a jumbo-jet. It had eight 900hp engines, accommodation for
eighty passengers, twenty crew, a café, telephone exchange and
printing press, plus a special system of lights to flash political slogans
along its belly at night. A year after its maiden flight, the *Maxim Gorky*
collided with a fighter plane and sixty people were killed. Soviet
aviation's claim to excellence died with them.   *1934*

A dainty device for indenting dimples was patented in America.
Its purpose to 'make the body susceptible' to 'artistic' dimples or to
maintain those already existing. It looked like a brace-and-bit with an
extra arm to which was attached a rolling cylinder. You put the bit
where you wanted the dimple to be, and then you operated the brace
so the cylinder would make the surrounding skin 'malleable'.   *1896*

Henry VIII did Anne Boleyn a favour when he had her head
chopped off on Tower Green. Even as a child she had suffered a
pathological fear of axes and her last wish was to die by the sword.
Henry graciously granted her request even delaying the fatal day while
Rombaud of Calais, the greatest swordsman in the world, was
specially imported for the task. At her trial during which her own
father testified against her, she was unfairly found guilty of multiple
adultery with, among others, her own brother. She spent the night
before her execution in the same room she had spent the night before
her coronation. At midday she stepped up on the scaffold, bravely
refusing a bandage saying she was not afraid of death. She then knelt
erect while Rombaud prepared to strike. He removed his shoes and
stood behind her left shoulder, while his assistant made a noise to

distract Anne's eyes to the right, at which moment Rombaud decapitated her with one giant sweep from the rear. The sad truth is that even if Henry's charges of adultery had failed she would still have lost her head. Henry planned to use her sixth finger and third nipple as proof she was a witch.   *1536*

The hushed-up death of a hero occurred six days after ex-aircraftsman Shaw, better known as Lawrence of Arabia, crashed his Brough Superior motorcycle in a country lane in Dorset. Also involved in the accident were two boys on bicycles, and according to the one eye-witness, Corporal Catchpole, a large, shiny black car. Lawrence split his skull wide open. He was taken to a military hospital and guarded night and day by police. His cottage was ransacked and until the moment of his death, the whole affair was kept a dark secret. Was he merely going too fast, had he swerved to avoid the boys, or was there something altogether more sinister? Shortly before the inquest Corporal Catchpole had been warned not to mention the black car 'in case it confused the issue'.   *1935*

Peachy opera singer Nellie Melba was born in Melbourne, Australia. Really called Helen Mitchell, she was sent off singing to Europe by her brick-maker Daddy and was coached by Madame Marchesi, Sarah Bernhardt, Gounod and Verdi. It wasn't long before she was a raging success – she was made a Dame of the British Empire, nearly married the pretender to the French throne and was said to have had 'as many lovers as she gave encores'. Nellie viewed the entire Edwardian era as 'one long weekend party' and after a lunch at the Savoy, her immortality was guaranteed, regardless of her voice. It was there one day that she gave the great chef Escoffier two tickets for *Lohengrin*. Tickled pink, the chef rushed back to the kitchen and came up with a tasty concoction of peaches, ice cream and raspberry sauce. He called it – 'Peach Melba' – of course!   *1861*

Today's the day...

An automatic 'Poultry Disinfector' was patented in America. The ingenious pneumatic device was placed under the runway of the henhouse. As soon as the foul smelling birds hopped on, both their front and rears were splattered with a healthy spray of sweet smelling disinfectant! *1919*

Make-believe aristocrat Honoré de Balzac was born, the son of the deputy mayor of Tours. Undeterred by being from a bourgeois background, and only 5ft 2in, he adopted a coat of arms, insisted that his small hands showed his noble heritage and wore diamond rings and tightly fitting gloves to show them off. 'Believe everything you hear about the world,' he insisted, 'nothing is too impossibly bad' – and chronicled it all in his mammoth work *La Comédie Humaine* which took twenty years to complete. He wrote from midnight till morning clad in a simple white monk's robe – except it was made of cashmere and tied with a gold belt – and drank so many cups of particularly strong coffee that he's said to have died from caffeine poisoning. Early in life he swore he'd achieve as much by the pen as Napoleon had by the sword and his

later fame really pleased him. It's doubtful, however, if he ever
achieved his ultimate ambition. He wanted to be 'so celebrated, so
famous, that it would permit me to break wind in society'.   *1799*

Gambler and libertine Colonel Francis Charteris was reprimanded
by the House of Commons for allowing debtors to enlist in his regiment.
Charteris wasn't being charitable since although this saved them from
prison, he would then demand a huge fee to grant their discharge. This
was typical of the man whose military record begins with being
drummed out of his first regiment for cheating at cards and being
expelled from the next for stealing. He became enormously wealthy
which helped secure quick pardons on the two occasions he was
condemned for rape. His appetite 'persisted in spite of age and
infirmities' and he even turned his own home into a brothel. But on his
death-bed he had a sudden thought and offered £30,000 to anyone
who could assure him that hell didn't exist.   *1711*

'The Lone Eagle', the blond six-footer 'Lucky' Lindbergh took off
from Garden City, New York in his single engine monoplane *The
Spirit of St Louis* in a bid to win £5,000 by flying non-stop to Paris.
Lindbergh realised that if he was to carry the vast amount of fuel
necessary to sustain him on the 3,800-mile flight, weight would be
critical. He elected to fly solo and with ice-cold logic took no parachute.
He reckoned if he parachuted into mid-Atlantic he wouldn't stand a
chance anyway, and similarly, though he took a small rubber dinghy,
he took no oars as he'd never be able to row to land. He had the
window-panes taken out too and said afterwards it probably saved his
life as the cold sea air constantly pushing in kept him awake. With no
wireless, he was totally isolated and was so thrilled to see a fishing boat
as he neared Europe that he swooped down, cut the engine and yelled
to the occupants, 'Which way is Ireland ?' They were so shocked they
didn't answer.   *1927*

Today's the day...

'The Red Man's Apostle' John Eliot died. He was a zealous Puritan and preached with a vengeance to the Indians of Massachusetts – first in English, then in their own language. His efforts were appreciated and he made a number of genuine converts. With their help he translated the Bible into their particular dialect of Algonquin, and with money extorted from England he printed the first vernacular Bible in North America. He put the Psalms after the New Testament, where they appeared under the title: *'Wame Ketoohomae Uketoohomaongash David'* – which roughly translated means: 'All the Singing Songs of David'.   *1690*

The dashing Scots royalist, the Earl of Montrose was hanged in Edinburgh. He'd returned from exile to raise the country for the refugee King Charles II, but he was betrayed to the Macleod of Assynt and dragged back to the capital in rags on a saddleless horse with his feet tied beneath its belly. His few remaining friends risked life and limb to smuggle fresh clothes to him for his execution and he appeared on the scaffold finely clad in a 'suit of black, a scarlet cloak, a beaver hat and stockings of carnation silk'. As he was brushing his hair in his cell, Wariston, who'd passed sentence on him, came in and remarked that it seemed a rather pointless task. 'It is still my own head,' replied Montrose. 'Tonight it will be yours and then you can do as you will.' He did – and that evening had it skewered on a pike and placed on the Tolbooth.   *1650*

Much manipulated King Henry VI was slain in the Tower of London, allegedly as he knelt at prayer. Thus was removed the devout, scholarly but ineffectual king who stood between the Yorkist Edward IV and the throne. Neither 'a fool nor very wise', Henry spent as much time as possible at the Bible, dressed 'like a townsman', wore the 'shoes of a rustic' and if he had to don his robes, wore a hair shirt underneath. Humble to the point of extinction, he worried a lot about the laxity of his household's morals, and to set a good example rarely swore beyond a muttered 'forsooth and forsooth'. When he was really annoyed, however, he lost all his inhibitions with a shocking 'By Saint John!'   *1471*

'The wasp of Twickenham' little Alexander Pope the poet was born. Deformed by a tubercular disease, he stood only 4ft 6ins high and had to wear a corset to keep his body straight. He was very conscious of the cold and wore a flannel vest, a heavy linen shirt and three pairs of socks to make his legs look fatter. His wit was so savage and often so obscene that one victim said, 'I wonder he is not thrashed.' Then he realised, 'His littleness is his protection; no man shoots a wren.'   *1688*

Bogey married Bacall in a quiet ceremony at the house of his friend Louis Blomfield in Pleasant Valley, Ohio. The ceremony only lasted three minutes and right in the middle the family's boxer dog came in and lay down at the judge's feet. Now listen, blue eyes, you won't believe this – but Bogey cried all the way through!   *1945*

Today's the day...

The worst train crash in British history occurred at 6am at Quintishill, near Gretna Green, when a fast-moving troop train carrying 500 men of the Royal Scots Regiment hit a local train head-on and was telescoped from 213yds to 67yds. Seconds later a London to Glasgow express was derailed by the wreckage and in all, the impacts, fire and exploding ammunition killed 227 and injured 246 people. An absent-minded signalman, James Tinsley, was held accountable for the tragedy. He was late for work and forgot all about the local train – despite the fact that he'd just arrived on it.   *1915*

The first motion picture show in public was given to 147 members of the National Federation of Women's Clubs, visiting Thomas Edison's laboratory at West Orange, New Jersey. The film, viewed through a 1in hole in a pine box, showed a man bowing, smiling, waving his hands, and taking off his hat 'with the most perfect naturalness and grace'. The ladies were delighted and Edison was only too happy to claim the credit for the invention. Actually it was his assistant Dickson who'd done all the work – a claim which though it was proved seventy years later, Mr Edison would never admit.   *1891*

The spoilsport Queen Joanna I of Naples was suffocated by the wicked Charles of Durazzo. He was a little upset because she'd changed her will to make Louis of Anjou her heir instead of him – so he just took the throne by force. Poor old Joanna had survived four tempestuous marriages and, perhaps a little weary, she'd once issued a decree that no man must force his wife to have sexual intercourse more than six times a day.   *1382*

Lord of the stage and peer of the realm Laurence Kerr Olivier was born in Dorking, Surrey into 'an atmosphere of genteel poverty'. At ten, Ellen Terry pronounced him a great actor and at fifteen he made his Shakespearian *début* – as Katherine in *The Taming of the Shrew*!

May 22

With his wavy hair and dandy moustache, he was something of a matinée idol in the forties, but to Hollywood's disappointment the stage always claimed him. Though he's universally acknowledged as 'the greatest actor of our time', even Olivier has problems. After one particularly impressive performance of *Othello*, he retired moodily to his dressing room grumbling, 'I know it was great, dammit, but I don't know how I did it – so how can I do it again ?!'   *1907*

Football's playboy hero George Best was born in Protestant East Belfast. His explosive relationship with Manchester United got off to a bad start when as a fifteen-year-old protégé he got homesick and logically enough – went home. At his best, Best could be magnificent and so nimble was he that he could flick a coin over his shoulder with his heel and straight into his breast pocket. Sadly perhaps, he became more superstar than footballer devoting much of his time to womanising. 'If I'd been born ugly,' he once said, 'you'd never have heard of Pelé.'   *1946*

The ill-gotten composer Richard Wagner was born in Leipzig. His mother was married to a police clerk, but his father was probably an actor who lodged with them. The composer of the great *Ring* cycle which includes the famous 'Ride of the Valkyries', it seems rather appropriate that his early years were mostly spent on the run – his many creditors chased him, his wife and their Newfoundland dog clear out of the country. He cadged ungratefully from a series of patrons until he hit the jackpot with eighteen-year-old mad King 'Lud' of Bavaria, whose insane generosity enabled Wagner to marry his mistress Cosima and build his own opera house at Bayreuth. His mystic-pan-German-aryan-anti-semitism delighted the Nazis, but his heavy-handed technique offended even his gloomy friend Nietzsche. 'Wagner has beautiful moments,' said fellow composer Rossini, 'but awful quarter hours !'   *1813*

Today's the day...

The Thirty Years War got off to a flying start at the Castle of Hradcany in Prague. The militant Catholic, Ferdinand of Bohemia, had been working hard repressing Protestants and sanctioning the closing of their churches. When they protested, they were answered with yet more repression from the Emperor Matthias and so they took some direct action. Led by Count Henry of Thurn they stormed the Castle and captured two Imperial Magistrates, William Slavata and Jaroslav Martinic and their secretary, Fabricius. These unfortunates they ceremonially 'defenestrated' – throwing them out of a window at least 60ft above the ground. Incredibly, they survived relatively unscathed. The Catholics put it down to the intervention of the Virgin Mary, but more objective observers claim they were saved by landing in nothing more holy than a dung heap! *1618*

Misguided medical magician Franz Anton Mesmer was born, the son of a Swabian game-keeper. Inspired by the work of Paracelsus and the grimly named Professor Hell, he believed that 'an invisible magnetic fluid' controlled both mental and physical health, and to treat his patients he often popped them in a bath full of iron filings and hot water and waved a magnet over them. Soon he decided that sheer 'animal magnetism' was enough, and with the help of his staring eyes, elaborate gestures and necromantic clothes, he effected many genuine cures on hysterics, neurotics and hypochondriacs. Inevitably he upset established medical practitioners, but despite his strange behaviour he was by no means a charlatan. He really did believe 'mesmerism' was magical and never for a moment realised that he was the great pioneer of hypnotism. *1734*

The strangest Nazi of them all Heinrich Himmler died by the simple device of biting a cyanide capsule hidden in his mouth, after he'd admitted who he was to his allied captors. He had tried a little late in the day to sue for peace and since Hitler had found out, Herr

Himmler had been wandering around with a patch over one eye, pretending to be a private. This peculiar little man with the pebble glasses, whose consuming interests included necromancy, had fashioned the fanatic SS almost as a personal tool. He thought he was the reincarnation of a Saxon King, and it was he who had institutionalised the mystique of the death's-heads and daggers. He loved magic and ritual, and as a youth he'd been a zealous Roman Catholic. The great irony was that he'd modelled the organisation of the SS on nothing less than the Jesuits – the Society of Jesus.   *1945*

The Texas Rattlesnake and Suicide Sal were killed in an ambush near Gibland, Louisiana. Better known as Bonnie and Clyde, they were just twenty-three and twenty-five years old and had spent the better part of the four years they'd known each other on an indiscriminate spree of robbery and murder. Their accomplices had included Clyde's now dead brother Buck and his wife Blanche, along with one or two lovers for the enthusiastic Bonnie and the homosexual Clyde. A posse of six lay in wait for them. As their car came over a rise, the lawmen opened fire. The car careered off the road and the posse rushed it with their guns blazing. Bonnie sustained fifty gunshot wounds, Clyde – twenty-seven, and soon the souvenir hunters were on the scene searching for grisly relics – one even tried to chop off Clyde's ear.   *1934*

Ben Franklin wrote about bi-focals, which he'd just recently invented, in a letter to one George Whatley. He was at this point Ambassador to France and claimed that with his new bifocals he could go to dinner and, by moving his eyes, see both the food and the person to whom he was talking. Not being 'accustomed to the sounds of the language', he found the movement of the person's features a help in comprehension and so, 'I understand French better by the help of my spectacles.'   *1785*

Today's the day...

'The Ruination of the Rich' gambling magnate William Crockford died, shortly after discovering he'd been outfiddled in fixing the Derby winner and exclaiming, 'I've been done'. Crockford was a millionaire; an enterprising East End fishmonger who'd cashed in handsomely on the contemporary craze for high stakes gambling. Known to have won £100,000 in a single night, he was soon able to open the most sumptuous, and some said most vulgar, club in London – Crockfords. It boasted £94,000 worth of interior decorations, the best food in town and quite the most profitable 'Hazard' table there ever was. Clients included Disraeli, the Duke of Wellington and Talleyrand and 'Crokey' always took the trouble to find out just how much his customers had in money and estates – which he then did his best to acquire. Exactly how many wealthy and noble families he ruined on his way to fame and fortune is not known, but it was said that when he retired in 1840, it was 'much as an Indian chief retires from a hunting country where there is not enough game left for his tribe'.   *1844*

A Minuit bought Manhattan. He was Peter Minuit, third Director-General of the Dutch West India Company, and he bought the entire island from the local Indians for trinkets to the equivalent value of $24. 200 Dutch settlers soon moved in to downtown New Amsterdam – but many thought the whole deal was a foolish waste of time and money, and Mr Minuit was described as 'a slippery fellow, who under the painted mask of honesty was a compound of all iniquity and wickedness'.   *1626*

Empire's Queen Alexandrina Victorina, better known as Victoria, was born the only child of the Duke of Kent and his German wife Victoire of Saxe-Coburg-Saalfeld. When she realised at twelve that she was destined for the throne, she announced 'I will be good' – and just six years later she was called from her bed at 5am and told she was Queen. It took her a while to get used to the idea and when she retired from her first Privy Council meeting with 'slow stateliness' she forgot she could still be seen in the corridor and scampered away 'like a child released from school'. Though in many ways she lived up to her image, she was by no means as dour as she appeared. She enjoyed *risqué* jokes; she and Albert sent each other nude drawings before they were married; she said of her herd of grandchildren that they made the family seem like 'rabbits in Windsor Park' and once at lunch with an ageing and rather deaf Admiral, she came near to hysterics. The old man was maundering on about the sinking of the *Eurydice* and desperate to change the subject, she asked him how his sister was. Undeflected the Admiral continued, 'Well Ma'am I am going to have her turned over, take a good look at her bottom and have it well scraped!'   *1819*

Martin Luther converted John Wesley during a religious meeting in a London backstreet. 'At a quarter before nine o'clock', while listening to Luther's *Preface to the Epistle to the Romans*, Wesley suddenly felt his heart 'strangely warmed'. This experience marked the true birth of Methodism.   *1738*

'King John Bull', Farmer George III was born, the first British-born monarch since Queen Anne and arguably the last real power in politics. Also known as 'Old Nob', he was the son of 'Poor Fred' the Prince of Wales and Charlotte of Mecklenburg – 'a foolish and ignorant woman'. George grew up good-natured but irritable; blunt but eager to please. He always worked too hard and talked too quickly, saying 'What, what?' when anybody told him anything, or he couldn't think of what else to say. More fitted to the life of a country squire than a King, he suffered five attacks of madness from the age of twenty-seven until his death at eighty-two. The first four lasted little more than twelve months all told; the last one a horrifying ten years. Mad the poor soul might have been, but silly he was not. 'I desire what is good,' he said, 'therefore everyone who disagrees with me is a traitor.'   *1738*

Today's the day...

Runaway Reds Burgess and Maclean disappeared on the very day that Foreign Secretary Herbert Morrison had ordered Maclean's interrogation. The two were both in bad books at the Foreign Office for their drunken behaviour – Burgess having been stopped for speeding three times in an hour in Washington, and Maclean having nearly strangled his wife and wrecked a girl's flat in Cairo. In fact the pair of them had been clearly suspect for some time but the Foreign Office had preferred not to believe it. Others did. The historian A.J.P. Taylor said it 'stuck out a mile' that Maclean was a Soviet agent, while Lord Boothby who knew gay Guy Burgess 'wouldn't have trusted him with half-a-crown'.   *1951*

Record-wrecker the black athlete Jesse Owens broke the world records for the 100yds, 220yds, 220yd low hurdles and the long-jump – all in forty-five minutes.   *1935*

The escaped Emperor Napoleon III walked away from the forbidding fortress of Ham, his doctor having told the guards that his Highness had just had a dose of castor oil and could receive no visitors. Off went Napoleon dressed as a workman in carefully muddied clothes, clogs, a wig and a hat, with a plank of wood over his shoulder. Though he eventually fooled sixty sentries and found a way across the reeking marshes, he had one or two nerve-wracking moments. As he walked across the silent courtyard he dropped his clay pipe and it broke on the cobbles with a clatter. Any less a man would have fled leaving the pieces behind him – but not Louis Napoleon. He paused, picked up the broken pipe and in his best workman's voice swore at it profusely.   *1846*

'The Napoleon of Crime' Adam Worth stole 'The Duchess of Devonshire' from Agnews Art Gallery in Bond Street. The Gainsborough painting of the Duchess had been purchased for a record £10,000 and was the talking point of London. Worth slipped into the gallery one night, cut the picture from its frame and was soon sailing home to America with it concealed in a false compartment in his trunk. He repeatedly wrote to Agnews demanding a ransom but they repeatedly refused, saying it would 'compound a felony'. Only after an incredible twenty-five years did they finally agree to pay a measly £1,000 – and then just six months after he got it Worth upped and died.   *1876*

The first hippo arrived in Britain. He was called Obaysch and was a gift from His Highness Abbas Pasha. When he arrived at London Zoo, he was easily tempted into his cage by a sack of his favourite dates and for a while he was quite content to sit next to his Arab keeper uttering the occasional grunt and leering 'with a singular protruding movement of the eyeball'. Now and again, however, he made a run for it and caused great consternation trotting around with 'his huge mouth curled into a ghastly smile, as if he meant mischief'. On one occasion they just couldn't catch him and finally resorted to using not food, but a man as bait. In hot pursuit of a keeper, the hated Obaysch rushed delightedly back to his cage!   *1850*

Today's the day...

The Wild West's most casual killer, John Wesley Hardin was born in Texas. He started his murderous career at fifteen when he slew a negro slave, ambushed and shot the three soldiers sent to arrest him and set a gruesome precedent. Thereafter, with his colts stuffed in his belt, he took at least twenty-four lives – maybe as many as forty – and apart from Sheriffs who were naturally his prey, he showed a marked preference for killing blacks and soldiers. He lived to be forty-two – ten years longer than average for a gunfighter – and managed to fit in a marriage and sixteen years in prison. The bandit son of a preacher, it was ironic that in the caboose he spent his time as a student of law and a Sunday-school teacher. *1853*

The bomber that never flew nose-dived into the Farnborough airstrip killing its crew of three as it was just about to take off for its first and only test flight. The huge wooden Tarrant Tabor triplane – 37ft high and with a 130ft wing span – had six engines, two of them between the top wings. Ironically, engineers had thought it tail-heavy and shortly before taxi-ing they'd put half a ton of lead shot into the nose cone. *1919*

A royal duel took place on Wimbledon Common when George III's son Frederick, Duke of York, fought Colonel Lennox who was said to have insulted the Prince of Wales. He left his hat at Carlton House so he wouldn't be missed, and disguised himself in servant's clothes. At twelve paces Lennox's shot clipped the prince's curls, and having his opponent at his mercy, Frederick then honourably refused to fire. *1789*

Risqué Lancashire troubadour George Formby was born, the son of a music hall comedian, George senior, who was known as 'the Wigan Nightingale'. His father apprenticed him as a jockey, saying, 'One fool in the family is bad enough' – and at the age of ten, he raced in the Earl of Derby's colours, weighing 3st 13lbs. After seeing a poor imitator massacring Dad's material, he couldn't stand it any more and took up the family profession. With his little ukelele in his hand – which he never did learn to tune – the cheeky little chappie recorded 189 'daft little songs', cheered up the thirties and forties with his naughty postcard humour, became the most unlikely of film stars and was awarded the Order of Lenin. *1904*

Winston Churchill's most illustrious ancestor John Churchill, the first Duke of Marlborough, was born. Arguably Britain's greatest general, he never lost a battle, and his string of victories in the War of the Spanish Succession – Blenheim, Ramillies, Malplaquet and Oudenarde – won him Blenheim Palace as a gift from a grateful Queen Anne. In and out of trouble with royalty all his life, he was once caught dallying with Charles II's mistress Barbara Villiers and had to make good his escape by leaping from a window. He was finally disgraced by his opponents after his wife quarrelled with the Queen and went into exile until after Anne's death. In his old age, he was said to be so mean that despite his infirmity, he'd walk home rather than pay a sixpenny fare for a sedan chair. *1650*

Today's the day...

President Truman's sensational confession was made on Ed Murrow's 'Person to Person' television programme. He stated that while asleep in the White House at 3am there came a sharp rapping on his bedroom door. He jumped out of bed but when he opened the door, there was no one there. Reminding the nation that his bedroom was probably the most protected in the world, he said that he believed it was no mortal agency, but the ghost of Abraham Lincoln – and he wasn't kidding!   *1955*

The first millionaire Vanderbilt, Cornelius, was born in Stapleton, New York. At sixteen, he borrowed $100 and magically turned it into 100 million. Called 'the Commodore' as much for his fruity naval language as his tough efficiency, he started the Staten Island ferry, built railways and shipped hopefuls to the California Goldrush. By his old age, he was not only the richest American, he was also one of the oddest. No matter what the weather, he wore fur-lined overcoats, he rarely drank alcohol, but when he did he downed tumblerfuls of gin and he took twelve lumps of sugar in his tea. But strangest of all for a man scared of no one, he always slept in a bed with its legs standing in four dishes of water – to keep the ghosts away.   *1794*

Bard of the Potteries the stammering Arnold Bennett was born in Hanley, Staffordshire. Like his father he became a solicitor, but quickly abandoned law for journalism after winning a competition in *Tit-Bits*. He went on to become the most feared critic of his time and in the words of fellow novelist, Hugh Walpole, 'the only critic who could make a book a bestseller overnight'. As a writer, he was astonishingly prolific; if his annual output fell below 400,000 words he felt he'd been idling. He wrote his 200,000-word masterpiece *The Old Wives' Tale* in a year while casually polishing off two other novels at the same time. His eye for accuracy in these Staffordshire-based sagas even led him to sit by his dying father's bedside making copious notes.

May 27

The down-to-earth epics made him immensely rich. He was called 'the Hitler of the book racket' and, despite his outrageous bow-ties and appalling conceit, he became a social lion. When he moved into a house where every door was panelled with mirrors, he modestly informed society, 'I was born for it.'   *1867*

The revolutionary madonna Isadora Duncan was born in San Francisco where her fatherless upbringing created a lifelong hostility towards formal marriage. She claimed she 'danced in the womb' and this, combined with an unshakable belief that she was the reincarnation of Aphrodite, led her to regard conventional ballet as 'a false and preposterous art' and to develop her own unique, classical style. She copied both her poses and her all too revealing clothes from the figures adorning Greek vases and had many lovers, although this wasn't always easy. While she willingly offered herself, many admirers, over-awed by her talent, refused to defile her. One such frustrated affair with a Russian ended with her suffering a 'wasting disease' which was only cured with immense doses of caviar. Back in America she became the 'Bolshevik hussy' who didn't 'wear enough clothes to pad a crutch', who exposed her breast on a Boston stage declaring, 'This is beauty!' and who had Indianapolis policemen hiding in the wings checking every movement of her knees. Her meteoric life ended with her spending her last days in fraudulent luxury drinking bootleg hootch so powerful it 'would have killed an elephant'.   *1878*

Fire destroyed a complete village leaving 300 inhabitants homeless. Everything was utterly devastated. Lost were all the private houses, the fire station, theatre and even the fort built to protect it all. Fortunately, all the villagers were saved and quickly rehoused. What made this fire so remarkable was that the village, on Coney Island, was called Lilliputia and was the world's first custom-built tiny-town for professional midgets.   *1911*

Today's the day...

Honest George the first Hanoverian King was born. He was fifty-five and happily ensconced in his German electoral princedom when they made him George I of England to ensure the Protestant succession and keep the Popish Stuarts out. He spoke little or no English, was blunt, straightforward, self-indulgent and lazy. His two 'official' mistresses were indelicately referred to as 'the Elephant and the Maypole' and he liked nothing better than an ample woman. This was so much the case that women desirous of his favours would 'strain and swell themselves' with 'all the dignity of an ox' to impress him. 'Some succeeded,' quipped Lord Chesterfield, 'and others burst.'

1660

The first photograph of Christ said to be imprinted on the mysterious Shroud of Turin was taken by Secondo Pia in the city's cathedral. After a journey that is thought to have taken it from the Holy Land via Turkey and Savoy, the Shroud had rested in the cathedral for 320 years, bearing the indistinct front and rear images of a long haired bearded man. When Pia developed his film, he was stunned to find that the images were, in fact, a kind of photographic negative – so that on his negative they appeared the right way round, and for the first time were startlingly well defined. The figure is that of a man 5ft 10in tall, who weighed probably around twelve stone and was between thirty and thirty-five-years old. He appears to have been a victim of crucifixion and bears the wounds of Christ, including what seem to be the marks of a crown of thorns. What caused the images remains unknown but one American physicist has suggested, 'a short burst of radiant energy' – as in an atom bomb blast – or even a resurrection.

1898

The creator of James Bond Ian Lancaster Fleming was born off Park Lane in London. He wrote for 'warm blooded heterosexuals in railway trains, aeroplanes and bed', never really wanted the super-stud secret agent to be a glamorous figure at all, and when Bond had made him a millionaire, was taken aback by the enormity of his success. Slightly dubious of his own work, he was no doubt very pleased when Hugh Gaitskell wrote to him, saying he found 'the combination of sex, violence and alcohol' irresistible. Fleming didn't marry until he was in his middle forties, and in a small way, enjoyed himself *à la* Bond. 'The trouble with Ian,' said a friend, 'is that he gets off with women, because he can't get on with them.'

1908

The youngest ever Prime Minister William Pitt was born, the second son of the Earl of Chatham who was also Prime Minister. The younger could read Latin and Greek at the age of seven, went to Cambridge at fourteen, and entered Parliament at twenty-one. In December 1783, he formed his first government, having already turned the job down ten months before when he was still only twenty-three. William Cobbett called him 'the great snorting bawler' and his likeness to his lordly father was apparently quite staggering. 'He was not a chip off the old block,' commented Edmund Burke, 'but the old block itself.'

1759

Today's the day...

Dead-pan funny man Bob Hope was born in Eltham, London and christened Leslie Townes. When he was four the family emigrated to Cleveland, Ohio and he worked there as a soda-jerk, boxer and newsboy before he went into Vaudeville doing Charlie Chaplin impressions. Immured in Chicago in the twenties, he had a hard time and subsisted mainly on doughnuts and coffee. In fact he says that when a friend bought him a steak for lunch he'd forgotten 'whether you cut it with a knife or drink it with a spoon'. Hope has travelled the world, entertained troops on the battlefront and was given a presidential commendation as 'America's most prized Ambassador of Good Will'. When he went to see the bodies of Lenin and Stalin in their Moscow mausoleum he quipped irreverently, 'A great show but what do they do for an encore ?'   *1903*

A bureaucrat's occupational hazard was reported to have caused a civil servant at the Admiralty to be transferred to another department. It was a mercy really since after spending two years knitting, reading and just sitting in her office, the poor woman had had a nervous breakdown brought about by having just too little to do.   *1945*

May 29

Outpost of Christianity Constantinople fell. Capital of the crumbling Greek Christian Byzantine Empire, it had been besieged for fifty days by the Ottoman Turks, led by sadist, bisexual and sodomite, twenty-three-year-old Sultan Mahomet II. He brought up sixty-eight Hungarian cannon – one of them was a 26ft long monster which weighed twenty tons, was hauled along by 200 men and sixty oxen and fired a 1,200lb cannonball straight through the walls. 10,000 Turks poured through the breach, the defenders of the city were unable to escape since they'd locked all the gates and 2,000 were slain in the first hours. The cautious Papal Legate swiftly disguised himself in beggar's rags, and the Emperor Constantine flung off his insignia and threw himself into the fighting. A decapitated body was later identified as his – by the Imperial Eagle stamped in gold on his sandals.   *1453*

Man stood on top of the world when Edmund Hillary and Sherpa Tenzing struggled up the last treacherous wall of ice to the top of Mount Everest. With heavy oxygen tanks on their backs, the two made their laborious way ever upwards, cutting their steps one at a time in the solid snow and ice. Their oxygen equipment nearly froze up, they were covered in a layer of fine snow and were both beginning to tire when they suddenly looked up and found themselves just a few feet from the summit. On their triumphant return down the mountain, they were met by the support party, breathless for news. With typical antipodean bluntness Hilary announced, 'Well we've knocked the bastard off!'   *1953*

A salivary accident caused consternation in Belfort, France. Unemployed taxi-driver Claude Antoine fractured his skull, legs and wrists in a spitting contest. 'I can spit you all into the ground,' he bragged, and using a long run-up to a second floor balcony, he was unable to stop.   *1977*

Today's the day...

Moosh and Tiggy murdered Pigsticker who'd stolen their bacon and bread. All three were vagrant navvies living in a scrubby woodland near the Barnet by-pass and to them such a theft was no mean felony. William 'Moosh' Shelley and Oliver 'Tiggy' Newman did overreact a little, however, and beat Herbert 'Pigsticker' Ayres to death, smashing his skull in with an axe, wrapping the bloody head in an old sack and burying the entire body in a smouldering refuse tip nearby. One grisly hand beckoned a fellow itinerant and the corpse was uncovered. A guest of Moosh and Tiggy gave them away to the police, and despite their huge bulk, enormous physical strength and three savage dogs, the pair went quietly. At no time did they complain of their fate, but neither did they consider they'd done any wrong. When they were sentenced to hang, Moosh shrugged and said mysteriously, 'They're twenty years too late.'   *1931*

The man who loved statues, President of the Dominican Republic Generalissimo Rafael Leonidas Trujillo y Molina, was assassinated by gunmen who waylaid the presidential car. While in office, this narcissistic and rather nasty gentleman raised over 2,000 images of himself, and generously gave his name to two provinces, the capital city and the country's highest mountain. Not altogether surprisingly, the day of his death is now a public holiday.   *1961*

Joan of Arc was burnt at the stake in Rouen. The daughter not of peasants, but of wealthy farmers in Lorraine, she was not yet twenty and had been talking to the Archangel Michael, St Catherine and St Margaret since she was thirteen. Just a little over two years before her death, they'd told her to save France from the wicked Burgundians and English. Overcoming understandable scepticism, she put on a suit of mail and led an army to re-capture Orleans, had the feeble Charles VII crowned at Reims and went on to try and take Paris. Her 'voices' told her she was going to be captured and true to form she was. Her captors, the Burgundians, sold her to the English for 10,000 golden pounds and the English determined this 'Devil's Whore' should die. In a rigged trial in an ecclesiastical court, she was tried for witchcraft and heresy, harried into a confession and sentenced to imprisonment for life. In recanting her crimes, she'd agreed to give up her habit of wearing men's clothing and it was only when she continued to do so that she was sentenced to the stake. She hadn't really a lot of choice – they'd taken all her women's clothes away. *1431*

Tragedy struck the little big man, the great artist of the music halls and brothels Henri de Toulouse Lautrec, when he was just thirteen-and-a-half years old. Though he'd always enjoyed outdoor sports he was a frail boy, and while trying to get out of a low chair he fell awkwardly and broke his left thigh. The bone never healed properly, and the following year he fell into a ditch and broke his right thigh too. While his body grew to maturity his legs grew no more, and his dwarfishness was emphasised by a kind of hypertrophy – an abnormal enlargement of the extremities. He developed coarse features, a big nose, fat lips, huge hands and a sexual organ so large that the prostitutes he frequented called him 'Teapot'! *1878*

Foul play in a duel was perpetrated by one Andrew Jackson in Logan County, Kentucky. His opponent was Charles Dickinson who'd slandered the 'upright and honourable' Mrs Jackson. They stood 24ft apart and Dickinson fired first. He hit Jackson in the chest but the bullet didn't penetrate and he thought he'd missed. In fact, Jackson was wearing a loose-fitting coat to hide the precise position of his body, and it was this that made the critical difference. Having thus cheated, Jackson shot and killed his adversary in cold blood, and retired from the field with two broken ribs and a bootful of blood. Twenty-three years later, this less than gallant duellist became President of the United States. *1806*

Today's the day...

Beringer's 'lying stones' were found. Dr Johann Bartholomaeus Adam Beringer, professor of natural philosophy at the University of Wurzburg, had been arguing that fossils were 'capricious fabrications of God', designed to test the faith of man. He was consequently delighted by the discovery of stones with impressions of soft-bodied creatures like slugs, and inscriptions in ancient languages – including one apparently signed by God. Even when colleagues confessed that they had made and planted the clay tablets as a hoax, Beringer refused to believe them. He proceeded with the publication of an expensively engraved thesis, *Lithographiae Wirceburgensis*, which made him look so silly he had to buy up all the copies he could find.   *1725*

Posthumously decapitated composer, Austrian maestro Franz Josef Haydn, died aged seventy-seven, and was buried in Hundstrum churchyard. Two days later his body was exhumed and the skull removed for the benefit of Johann Peter, Vienna's prison superintendent and an amateur phrenologist, who pronounced 'the bump of music fully developed'. Haydn's patron Prince Anton Esterhazy later discovered the theft while reburying the composer more grandly at his own chapel at Eisenstadt. He demanded the return of the skull which had passed to his own secretary, Josef Rosenbaum, whose wife displayed it in a glass and ebony case at musical *soirées*. Mrs R wouldn't part with her treasure; her husband palmed off a substitute on the prince, and Haydn's real head was not reunited with its body until 1954!   *1809*

The useless Battle of Jutland – one of the biggest naval encounters ever – was fought in the North Sea. German Admiral Reinhard Scheer's High Seas Fleet of ninety-nine ships aimed to smash British control of the North Sea shipping lanes, and to that end he sent a squadron of battle cruisers out along the Danish Jutland peninsula to lure the British into action. The feint worked and the 148 ships of

Admiral Sir John Jellicoe's British Grand Fleet sailed into battle. By dusk, the better equipped but outnumbered Germans were surrounded – only to break out under cover of darkness. The British blockade was not lifted, however, and the German fleet never ventured forth to fight another battle. Despite the terrible toll, the only result was to demoralise both the navies.

1916

The last Tin Lizzie was produced, virtually unchanged since it was introduced as the Model T Ford in 1908. You could still, according to Ford's famous boast, get any colour you liked 'so long as it was black', and thanks to the introduction of the first moving assembly line in 1913 the price had come down from $850 to under $300. At one point, half of all the cars made in the US were Model Ts – over fifteen million of them – but Ford's son Edsel had finally convinced him to meet increasing competition with a fancy new model. Ford Senior was immeasurably proud of his 'little maid of all work' and appreciated the publicity value of jokes and apocryphal stories made about her. 'What shock absorbers do you use?' he was once said to have been asked. 'The passengers!' he replied.

1927

Today's the day...

The giant who lost his body the 8ft 4in Irish Goliath, Charles Byrne, died aged twenty-two from TB, hastened by 'excessive drinking and vexation at losing a note for £700'. Conceived atop a haystack, Byrne had been on show for 'judicious inspection' and numerous doctors, quacks and anatomists were after his body. Refusing all offers, the dying giant had ordered a lead coffin and hired a team of Irish corpse-watchers to arrange a top security burial at sea. In response, one group of body snatchers prepared a diving bell, while the famous medic John Hunter took the watchers on a drinking spree and convinced them to sell him the lanky cadaver for a record £500. He popped it in his coach and did his rounds as usual, then went home and boiled the flesh from the bones. Meanwhile, with great ceremony, it was not a giant that was laid to rest in Margate harbour, but a giant-size coffin filled with stones.   *1783*

The tragedy of the tragedian, Christopher Marlowe's death was enacted in Widow Bull's tavern in Deptford. The author of the demoniacal *Dr Faustus*, the twenty-nine-year-old Marlowe was no angel himself. An ex-theology student, drunk, forger, atheist, spy and informer, he was due to answer for his seditious and heretical views in the Star Chamber, but never got the chance. Out carousing with three fellow rogues, he found himself enmeshed in an argument over '*le recknynge*' for all their drinking. Aroused and naturally violent, Marlowe started pummelling one man's head with the hub of his dagger. 'It is not surprising to learn that Marlowe was stabbed in a tavern brawl,' said George Bernard Shaw who doubted Marlowe's ability as both writer and fighter. 'What would be utterly unbelievable would be his having succeeded in stabbing anyone else.'   *1593*

Cold-fearing Kirwan, the eccentric Irish scholar and dilettante scientist, died aged seventy-eight. For the whole of his life he was haunted by a morbid terror of catching the common cold. He considered it a mortal sin to leave a door open, offered a bounty for dead flies, studied the weather and kept a roaring fire in his drawing room 365 days of the year. Before venturing out, he always stood in front of it with his coat open to catch all the heat, on the obscure principle that we all need a high calorific value to survive. He walked at a spanking pace, refused to talk out of doors for fear of heat loss, never removed his hat and had tea brought to him in the middle of the night – which his doddering servant, Pope, often poured in his eye! In spite of all his rigorous precautions, it was a cold that killed him.   *1812*

Lord Ted's brolly was struck by lightning. Ex-England captain Ted Dexter was being interviewed for BBC TV, when the blast left him stumped for words. 'I'm sorry if I'm sounding less than electrifying about the cricket,' he said, 'but I've just had a nasty shock.' 'It's never happened to me before,' he added inscrutably, 'I only hope it improves my putting.'   *1978*

The blonde gentlemen preferred – Marilyn Monroe – was born Norma Jean Baker, illegitimate, and actually already in Hollywood. 'Blonde hair and breasts' got her started and nudity played a big part in her life. Asked if she had anything on in a pin-up shot she said, 'Only the radio'; asked if she wore anything in bed she said, 'Chanel No. 5'. Marilyn rarely wore knickers – 'pants gag me' she quipped, and on at least one occasion she got a splinter in the famous backside. Claiming she was only comfortable when she was naked, she once walked down Fifth Avenue on a hot summer's day in a new mink coat, and when asked by a friend what she had on underneath, said 'Nothing' and flashed the coat open to prove it. What Billy Wilder called her 'flesh impact' would have over-awed most men but, after a trial run, Tony Curtis said that kissing her was 'like kissing Hitler', and when she tried her charms on Laurence Olivier she said, 'He looked at me like he had just smelled a pile of dead fish.'   *1926*

Today's the day...

A cut-purse and thief became Lord Chief Justice to Elizabeth I.
He was Sir John Popham a 'huge, heavie, uglie man' who in his youth
consorted with profligates and lifted the occasional fat wallet. Even
when he became Speaker of the House of Commons he was something
of a cheeky gentleman. The Queen once asked him what had passed
in one session. 'If it please your Majesty,' he replied, 'seven weeks!'

1592

The first televised coronation made Princess Elizabeth Queen of
Great Britain and the Commonwealth. Fortunately the blitz had
destroyed the anointing oil – described by Elizabeth I as 'nasty grease
that smelt ill' – and HM was sprinkled with a new batch made to a
recipe of Charles II containing orange blossom, cinnamon,
ambergris and jasmine. It was Norman Hartnell's job to make the
Queen's coronation gown which had to have all the emblems of the
Commonwealth embroidered on it. When he discovered that the
Welsh leek and not the daffodil was to be used, he was horrified at
the thought of covering the Queen in vegetables. It was all right in
the end though – when it was all adorned with diamonds, he admitted,
'It really looked quite edible.'

1953

June 2

The master of charlatans Cagliostro was born in Palermo, Sicily. Pausing only to steal the poor-box and rob his uncle, he took off for Rome, dubbed himself Count and with the help of his beautiful wife, Serafina, he proceeded to fleece the aristocracy. Self-appointed Grand Cophta of an obscure Egyptian masonic cult, he sold love-potions, practised alchemy and foretold the future by summoning the dead. His greatest success was his elixir of life which was pricey, but worth it. Taken after thirty-two days of leeching and starvation, it revitalised elderly patients by making their teeth drop out and their skin peel off. Cagliostro didn't make wild claims for the effects of the brew, however – they only lasted, he said, 5,557 years! *1743*

The *Far from the Madding Crowd* man Thomas Hardy was born in Higher Bockhampton, Dorset, and though he became the great rural novelist, he was forever ashamed of his peasant background. He generally treated real women less sympathetically than his heroines, and in his passion for the sickly schoolmistress, Florence Dugdale, he ignored his first wife's terminal illness. When she finally died, however, he worshipped her memory to the total exclusion of Florence. The trouble was that before he married them he idolised his women, but afterwards he had nothing but contempt for them. 'A good wife is good,' he wrote grudgingly, 'but the best wife is not so good as no wife at all.' *1840*

Brave boy Cornwell died after being wounded in action at the Battle of Jutland. He'd stayed at his post by the forward gun on HMS *Chester* while all his fellows fell dead and dying around him. 'So long as there is one man able to crawl,' said the old naval order, 'a gun must be kept firing.' In Grimsby Hospital, Cornwell was asked how the battle had gone. 'Oh we carried on all right,' he said. After his death, he was awarded the VC and became the youngest ever to receive it. He was just sixteen-and-a-half years old. *1916*

Today's the day...

The longest running comedy in theatre history opened. Written by Antony Marriott and Alistair Foot, *No Sex Please – We're British* has since been seen by over two-and-a-half million people, despite Marriott's original pessimistic prediction that it would only run 'a few weeks'. He and Foot dreamed up the complete plot while having lunch in a Chinese restaurant.   *1971*

The divinely inspired scientist Otto Loewi was born in Germany. Researching into how nerve cells transmit stimuli, he was convinced that a chemical change took place but couldn't work out how to prove it. Incredibly he dreamed of a detailed experiment and rushed to his laboratory at three in the morning to work on it. It proved to be the perfect solution and such an important discovery that he was given the Nobel prize. In fact, he'd been lucky enough to have the same dream twice. But the first time he'd only written the details down – and then couldn't read his own writing!   *1873*

The Guinness Book of Records established a second record-breaking achievement itself according to *The Bookseller*. Apart from being the world's highest selling title with over thirty-five million sales to its credit, it also won the dubious title of the most stolen book from British public libraries!   *1978*

Tricky taxidermist Charles Waterton was born at Walton Hall, Yorkshire. A descendant of Sir Thomas More and six other saints, he disgraced himself in Rome by climbing St Peter's and crowning it with his gloves. The Pope made him take them down again, and thereafter he devoted his considerable wealth and energy to rather bizarre methods of collecting and preserving animals. He once caught a python by tying up its mouth with his braces, and rode a cayman 'for the first and last time' using its forelegs as reins. Back home, he built a three-mile, 9ft high wall around Walton, and created Britain's first bird sanctuary. When he got bored, he made monsters from odd bits of different animals. His masterpiece was a red howler monkey called 'Nondescript', so cunningly embalmed that his visitors were convinced he stuffed humans as well – a belief strenghthened by his strange way of greeting his guests. He liked to hide under the hall table and bite their legs as they passed!   *1782*

The world lost a musical genius when at the early age of thirty-six, the French composer Georges Bizet died, having suffered a heart attack the previous evening, while just a few miles away at the *Opéra Comique* in Paris, the very first all-Bizet concert was being performed. During the concert Mme Galli-Marié, creator of Bizet's immortal *Carmen*, sang the part again. During the scene where Carmen sees death in the cards, she felt a strange chill followed by a shooting pain in her side – 'like the blow of a hammer in her heart'. She struggled through the part, then left the stage saying, 'I saw Bizet's face in front of me, for just a second . . . My God! My God! How pale he was!' By a creepy coincidence, Bizet's fatal heart attack happened at exactly the same moment as Mme Galli-Marié's premonition.   *1875*

The religious gourmet Sydney Smith was born at Woodford, Essex. To please his father, he became a reluctant curate, but never let his frustration diminish his wit, ingenuity or appetite. Convinced that 'digestion is the great secret of life', he calculated that he had personally eaten forty-four horse-waggon loads of food and drink worth £7,000, and used this vast experience to develop a large stomach and several odd ideas. He decided that friendships were destroyed by toasted cheese, lobster with tart produced depression and hard salted meat led to suicides. In his old age he was forced to go on such a strict diet he wished even to be allowed 'the wing of a roasted butterfly'. At the end he comforted himself with his idea of heaven – eating *pâté de fois gras* to the sound of trumpets.   *1771*

Today's the day...

The lawman without a gun Marshal Tom Smith banned firearms in the wild and lawless cow-town of Abilene, Kansas, just as he'd done in his previous job in Bear River, Wyoming. Having once unwittingly killed a man, this ex-prizefighter and New York policeman had no truck with gunfighters, and when faced with pistol-packing trouble-makers he would just punch them in the mouth. So devastating was his right hook that both Bear River and Abilene were at peace for years. *1870*

The last soldier was evacuated from Dunkirk by HMS *Shikari* as German tanks rolled into the town. 338,000 French and English soldiers had been lifted off the beach-head by a vast but motley flotilla of pleasure boats, paddle steamers, yachts and cabin cruisers. Thankfully, the Germans had briefly halted their advance – perhaps believing the British would sue for peace. They were disappointed. 'We shall fight on the beaches,' said Churchill, 'we shall fight on the landing grounds, we shall fight in the fields and in the streets, we shall fight in the hills; we shall never surrender . . .' *1940*

The reluctant acquitted murderess Alma Rattenbury committed
suicide beside a quiet stream in Christchurch, Hampshire. A little
over two months earlier the police had been called to a bizarre scene
at the Rattenbury house. The elderly but wealthy Mr Rattenbury lay
dead, his head beaten in with a mallet. The radiogram was blaring,
Alma was hysterically drunk and started confessing wildly and kissing
the policemen who were arresting her. Along with her pampered,
jealous lover, the eighteen-year-old George Percy Stoner, she was
tried for murder, but only Stoner was sentenced to hang. Distraught,
Alma stabbed herself six times in the chest. 'If only I thought it
would help Stoner,' said her final note, 'I would stay on.' Ironically
Stoner was reprieved just three weeks later.   *1935*

A friendly turtle rescuer saved the life of Mrs Candelaria
Villanueva when the ship she was on caught fire and sank. The giant
sea turtle supported her in the water for over thirty-six hours until she
was rescued. Throughout her ordeal she was kept awake by another
turtle – a tiny one who climbed up her back and gently nipped her on
the ear every time she felt drowsy!   *1974*

A conciliatory Rowland Hill wrote an apologetic note to a
clergyman in Malton who'd complained about a letter being lost in
the post. The irate cleric never got his letter, however – the Post Office
mis-read the address and it ended up in Malta!   *1859*

The Derby's suffragette martyr Emily Wilding Davison was
trampled to death at Tattenham corner. As the King's horse Anmer
approached, she leapt into his path and stood stock-still, arms
outspread as he swept over her. Thundered *The Times*, that bastion
of male Englishness, 'She did not interfere with the race, but she
nearly killed a jockey as well as herself – and she brought down a
valuable horse.'   *1913*

Today's the day...

The master of the insult Gilbert Harding was born. Brought up in a Herefordshire workhouse where his mother was matron, he failed to make the grade as a policeman, teacher and journalist and went on to become the spiky star of early TV panel games. Loved and hated by millions, he was a homosexual, and referred to himself as a 'dreary old phoney'. Women were not his favourite people, and as a celebrated nymphomaniac once disappeared into the distance, he turned to a companion and said, 'Off she goes – in a cloud of lust!'   *1907*

A bunny-pig was born at Knaresborough Zoo – a result of the mating of an amorous rabbit and a guinea-pig. The news was a great comfort to Mary Jackson of Lowestoft, who'd accidentally bred several litters of them some months before and had been told by experts that it was genetically impossible.   *1974*

A poet murdered a priest who had attacked him in an argument over a woman. The versifier concerned was François Villon who wrote poems about everything from drunkenness and prostitution to death and the Virgin Mary. On this occasion, Villon was merely banished from Paris, but later in his career as beggar, brawler, drunkard and thief, he was imprisoned, tortured, and finally exiled for good when he was only thirty-two. Aptly enough, one of his poems was called 'The Legacy' and in it he bequeathed to his barber the clippings of his hair; to usurers some small change, and to the clerk of criminal justice his sword – which at the time of writing was in hock!   *1455*

The Six Day War was launched by Israel after Nasser had ordered the UN peace-keeping force to evacuate Sinai. By the time it was over, the combined forces of Egypt, Syria and Jordan were utterly defeated. The attack had been so stunningly swift that 300 Egyptian planes were destroyed by nightfall – most of them without ever leaving the ground.   *1967*

The original Miss Muffet lost her father when he passed away at Wilton House, Wiltshire. Though the nursery rhyme wasn't collected for another 200 years, this particular Miss Muffet – Patience by name – is thought to be the real one largely because of her father's hobby. Thomas Muffet was an eminent physician, but in his spare time he was also a pioneering entomologist whose 'admiration for spiders', he said, 'has never been surpassed'. *1604*

The second Kennedy was shot. In the Ambassador Hotel, Los Angeles, J.F.K.'s younger brother Robert had just finished a victory speech when he was struck down with three bullets, allegedly from the gun of the twenty-four-year-old Jordanian, Sirhan Bishara Sirhan. Five bystanders suffered gunshot wounds and in all ten bullets were recovered – yet Sirhan's gun was a ·22 that only fired eight shots. Where the other two came from has never been satisfactorily explained. A mysterious woman suspect was questioned and afterwards committed suicide. Sirhan was sentenced to death but the California death sentence was abolished shortly afterwards, and to this day he has never remembered pulling his gun or using it. *1968*

Today's the day...

Viking tennis star the dashing Swede, Bjorn Borg was born. Known to headline writers as 'Iceborg' for his apparent lack of nerves, it was recently revealed that his pulse rate is only thirty-five compared with the usual sixty to eighty. But if he's not highly strung his rackets are – to 80lbs per square inch instead of the normal 56lbs – and he breaks at least one a day. *1956*

The Allies landed. It was D-Day – the start of the biggest sea-borne invasion in history involving 1,213 warships, 4,126 landing craft, 1,087 aircraft, 20,000 vehicles and the components for two artificial 'Mulberry' harbours, each with the capacity of Dover. In all there were 185,000 troops – many of them wretched with seasickness, after they'd had to board landing craft in appalling weather, twelve miles out. With the help of a massively effective naval bombardment, air cover and 'swimming' tanks that could fire while still in the water, the beachheads were quickly secured, though there were 9,000 allied casualties and terrible slaughter on Omaha beach. Just two weeks before, MI5 had been horrified to find that five of the operation's key codewords Overlord, Omaha, Utah, Neptune and Mulberry had all appeared in *Telegraph* crosswords. The poor compiler was given the third degree by the 'word-police' – but it was all just an incredible coincidence. *1944*

England's mistaken hero explorer Robert Falcon Scott was born near Devonport. In 1911 he set off for the South Pole and soon found himself competing with the Norwegian, Amundsen, in what he considered to be a distasteful race. Ignoring the experiences of Arctic explorers, Scott insisted on using just two dog teams, supplemented by three distinctly less effective forms of transport: men – who as draught animals tired easily; ponies – which couldn't stand the cold, and motor tractors that all broke down after the first fifty miles. Since this mistake contributed greatly to his own death and those of his four

companions in the dash for the Pole, it seems ironic that he preferred
not to use dogs, largely because he hated the cruelty involved in
driving them on till they died.   *1868*

The Derby's first hat-trick was won at Epsom by tearaway jockey
Steve Donoghue on the fleet-footed 'Papyrus'. What his enthusiastic
supporters didn't know was that in an earlier race that afternoon he'd
been hit in the face by a stone and was riding with one eye out of
action. Mr Donoghue celebrated his one-eyed win with a riotous party
where he insisted on re-enacting his victory and ended up being towed
round Crafton Galleries mounted on a wooden horse.   *1923*

Dead-keen philosopher Jeremy Bentham died at the age of eighty-
four. He was one of the founders of University College Hospital in
London and left them his entire estate on some rather unusual
conditions. His body was to be dissected, the head preserved and kept
in a glass jar and the skeleton reconstructed, clothed in his usual attire
and topped off with a wax effigy of his face. The whole thing was then
to be seated in a glass and mahogany case and wheeled into the
hospital's board meetings, where he would be registered as 'present –
but not voting'.   *1832*

Today's the day...

Savage south seas painter Paul Gauguin was born in France and brought up in Peru with his mother's wealthy relatives. Driven out by revolution, he returned to Paris and became a successful family man and banker, only to give it all up for art. He became a starving itinerant for his pains and ended up fighting and whoring with Van Gogh in Arles, until Vincent severed his ear and Gauguin severed the relationship. Though his obsession was painting, his preoccupations were money and sex – he had too little of the former and too much of the latter. In 1902 when he was dying of syphilis in Tahiti, his paintings were finally recognised. He wanted to go back to Europe but he was advised not to. 'You are the unknown legendary artist far away,' he was told. 'You have the immunity of the great dead' – and within a year that last remark was quite literally true.   *1848*

The beloved wife of Richard II, Anne of Bohemia died of the plague at Richmond Palace. The King was heartbroken and ordered the palace to be razed to the ground because he never wanted to walk through a doorway alone that they had walked through together.   *1394*

The hard-working killers of Mike Malloy were executed in the electric chair at Sing-Sing. A bunch of New York gangsters, they were led by one Tony Marino and had latched onto life insurance as an easy way of making money. A week after she'd been insured, Tony's mistress was found dead in bed from pneumonia – dead drunk and stark naked – and the gang had collected $800. Malloy, an Irish derelict, was chosen as their next victim. They insured him heavily and started treating him to meals and drinks – wood-alcohol and rat-poison, horse-liniment and nail sandwiches! To the gang's utter disbelief he not only survived, but thrived on it and in desperation they were forced to get him drunk, put a rubber hose in his mouth and fill him up with poisonous gas! In case he liked that too, they kept pumping it in until his face turned purple – just to make sure!   *1934*

The talking mongoose was born according to his own account in Delhi, which would have made him seventy-nine years old when he first turned up in 1931 behind the wooden panelling of the Irving family's lonely farmhouse in the Isle of Man. He said his name was Gef and though the Irvings got only the merest, shadowy glimpses of him, he made his presence felt in all sorts of ways. He was constantly chattering, raiding the larder and leaving droppings, and roamed the island bringing back juicy bits of gossip and the occasional dead rabbit. Though the editor of *The Listener* wrote a book about him and was fired because of it, no amount of investigation could ever prove he was other than what he said he was – 'just an extra extra clever little mongoose'.

1852

The Monarch of the mode Beau Brummell was born, the son of Lord Liverpool's private secretary, descended from a long line of pastrycooks. Through his gambling and extravagance he died destitute in France at the age of sixty-four, but for nearly two decades he had been a figure in his way more important than 'Prinny' the Prince Regent. The two were once great friends but whether it was over the borrowing of a snuff box or the cut of the prince's coat, they fell out most seriously. The *dénouement* came about when the Prince gate-crashed a party thrown by Brummell, Lord Alvanley and friends, and yet again royally snubbed the Beau. 'Alvanley,' said Brummell, loud enough for all the company to hear, 'who is your fat friend?'

1778

A fire-eater got a roasting in court in Manchester when he was fined £75 for driving with excess alcohol in his blood, and disqualified for twelve months. The man, Barry Silva, claimed he'd only drunk two cans of lager and that the problem had come about because he'd swallowed a more than usually large amount of the methylated spirits and lighter fuel he used for his flames.

1978

Today's the day...

Liberace defended himself when he successfully sued William Connor, 'Cassandra' of the *Daily Mirror* for libel. Connor had described the gold lamé pianist as 'a fruit-flavoured, mincing, ice-covered heap of mother love', 'the biggest sentimental vomit of all time' and 'a calculating candyfloss'. The future Lord Gardiner, defending, argued that this crude and cruel calumny was fair comment. Counsel for the plaintiff said it implied that the Candelabra Kid was a homosexual and besides it had made his mother ill!   *1959*

Early Roman capitalist Senator and General Marcus Licinius Crassus was killed in battle with the Syrians at Carrhae in Anatolia. He'd increased his inherited fortune of seven million sesterces to 170 million – almost the entire annual income of Rome – by property speculation, theft, slave dealing, fire and rapine. Having set up his own 500-strong fire brigade, he haggled with property owners about fees while their buildings burned down, and ran an advanced school for slaves – not for their welfare, but to increase their value. Legend has it that the Syrians gave him an apt death. They cut off his head, scooped it out and filled it with molten gold.   *53 BC*

An Irish Quaker tried to convert the Pope and was arrested for his trouble. According to one account, the zealous John Perrot kept his hat on and addressed the pontiff Alexander VII as 'Mr Pope'. In fact, it's unlikely that he ever got as far as an audience, but considering the times and his dangerous impudence, he got off quite lightly. The Inquisition was so astounded that instead of burning him, they put him in the mad house, where he was tortured with 'a dryed Bull's Pizzle'.   *1658*

The first English prelate to be executed – Richard Scrope, Archbishop of York, was despatched on the feast of St William, York's patron saint. After leading a 'priestly rout' of 8,000 men in an insurrection against the administration of Henry IV, he was tricked into dispersing his army, arrested and summarily tried for treason. The crown ineptly allowed his remains to be buried in the Minster and his grave became such a place of pilgrimage and miracle working that it had to be covered with logs and stones. Scrope was a born martyr and he set out to demonstrate his courage and piety on the scaffold. At his own request his beheading took five blows of the axe.   *1405*

The brilliant and arrogant architect Frank Lloyd Wright was born in Wisconsin. Descended from a long line of Welsh preachers, his mother had already decided on his career and hung his bedroom with engravings of cathedrals. He became the pioneer of 'organic architecture'. He designed spectacular homes for wealthy Americans; the Hotel Imperial in Tokyo – one of the few buildings left standing after the 1923 earthquake – and the circular Guggenheim Museum, his 700th job completed in his ninetieth and last year. Wright, who when asked how to improve Pittsburgh said, 'Destroy it and start again', was renowned for his high opinion of himself. When once asked in court to state his profession, he told them he was 'the greatest living architect'. 'I had to,' he said later, 'I was on oath.'   *1869*

Today's the day...

The Gargantuan Tsar Peter the Great was born. A giant of a man he stood 6ft 7in and brooked no argument. He deposed his mentally defective half-brother, packed his sister and his first wife off to a nunnery and when his son opposed his sweeping reforms, he tortured him to death. Not afraid of getting his hands dirty, he was a keen amateur plumber, surgeon and carpenter, once operated on a woman for dropsy and even worked in the shipyards in Deptford. Peter had a great sense of humour. He put a tax on beards and personally clipped them from the chins of reluctant boyars; kept a troupe of dwarfs and cripples to amuse him, and once surprised his guests with a pie containing nothing but a naked lady midget. Not surprisingly it was unwise to upset him, a fact that his favourite mistress, the Scottish Mrs Hamilton, might perhaps have borne in mind. When she was unfaithful to him, he chopped off her head, pickled it and kept it by his bed as a warning. *1672*

The chicken hearted Emperor Nero committed suicide aged thirty-two, after the Senate had declared him a public enemy. He'd already decided to do it three or four times, asked one of his servants if he'd mind going first and was finally pushed into it by the arrival of the cavalry who'd come to drag him off to be beaten to death. Quivering in the arms of his 'wife', the eunuch Sporus, he ordered a grave to be dug for his 'pustular and malodorous body' and stuck a newly sharpened knife in his neck. *AD 68*

Playboy composer Cole Porter was born in Peru, Indiana, the wealthy grandson of an even wealthier millionaire. The master of sophisticated pop-music, he's said to have written 'Always True to You Darling in My Fashion' in the Waldorf Astoria lift between the ground and the forty-first floor. His songs combine sentiment and cynicism in the same way his life did. He was a devoted husband but spent much of his spare time picking up sailors in waterfront bars. He was tough enough to serve in the French Foreign Legion, but dyed his hair, wore gleaming false teeth, lied about his age and added inches to his height on his passport. Mr Porter was a severe and subtle critic – when he disliked a performance by Hermione Gingold he sent her a bouquet of flowers with a live wasp trapped inside. In 1937 his life was marred when he broke both his legs in a riding accident and was permanently crippled. One leg was amputated in 1958 and for the rest of his life he was in constant pain. A simpering woman admirer once asked, 'How are your poor legs ?' The composer replied, 'They're fine. How are yours ?'   *1891*

Dickens died having collapsed the previous evening with a brain haemorrhage. It was exactly five years to the day after he'd helped save other passengers in a tragic train crash at Staplehurst in Kent when ten people were killed. He'd never really recovered from the shock and despite wild seizures, obscured vision and slight paralysis, he'd insisted on continuing with his crushing schedule of lecture-tours and readings. In fact, he'd literally worked himself to death.   *1870*

The sinking of the submarine *Poseidon* led to one of the most heroic nautical escapes in history. The brand new 1,447 ton ship was on manoeuvres in the Far East when it was rammed by the 2,000 ton Chinese steamer *Yuta* and within two minutes had plunged into 100ft of water. Twenty-nine of the crew escaped through the conning tower and the rest drowned, but for six men trapped in the forward torpedo flat. With only the light from one electric torch, they donned their new-fangled Davis escape gear and had to wait for more than three suffocating hours while they flooded the compartment to equalise the pressure, so they could open the hatch. With their oxygen exhausted, they made it to the surface with five of the six still alive. The name of the ship was perhaps a little too apt. Poseidon was a Greek god who had a palace at the bottom of the ocean.   *1931*

Today's the day...

The first of the Salem witches was hanged. She was Bridget Bishop, just one of the 150 respectable citizens accused of witchery by a hysterical band of young girls who for nearly twenty months mesmerised the strict, isolated Puritan community in Massachusetts. Influenced by the black West Indian servant woman Tituba, the 'witch bitches', as they became known, claimed the accused tormented them with the help of the Devil, 'a little yellow bird', and spectres that came in the night. They writhed, swooned and screamed, and pointed the accusing fingers that sent nineteen innocent people to hang and caused one man to be crushed to death with stones. Five years to the day after Bridget Bishop was hanged, seven people were burnt at the stake in Paisley, Scotland, convicted of witchcraft on the testimony of an eleven-year-old girl.   *1692/1697*

Mr Biro patented the ball-point. Laszlo by name, he was a Hungarian proof-reader, sick of filling his fountain-pen. With co-designer brother Georg, he fled to Buenos Aires to escape the Nazis, got backing from the British financier Henry Martin and ended up in an aircraft hangar in Reading producing high altitude, non-leaking 'writing sticks' for the RAF.   *1943*

The outspoken Royal Consort Prince Philip was born on the island of Corfu, the fifth child and only son of Prince Andrew of Greece and Princess Alice of Battenburg. Greece was in revolt, Philip's father was under threat of execution and only with the connivance of George V did the family escape with the boy-prince in an orange box. Father became a Monte Carlo playboy, Mother founded a Holy Order back in Greece and Philip ended up in Kurt Hahn's School for hearties at Gordonstoun. He isn't in fact a Greek, but a member of the Danish Schleswig-Holstein-Sonderburg-Glucksburg royal family, imported into Greece in 1863, descended from both Charlemagne and Queen Victoria, and very blue-blooded indeed. Renowned for his royal turn of phrase, he admits, 'I've never been noticeably reticent about talking on subjects about which I know nothing', and perhaps achieved his greatest notoriety by telling a group of industrialists, 'Gentlemen, I think it is about time we pulled our fingers out!' *1921*

The Star was born. Judy Garland came into the world with vaudeville parents and the unenviable name of Frances Gumm. Pushed by her mother, 'the real life wicked witch of the West', she made her stage *début* at three and at thirteen was bought by MGM who told her, 'You're so fat you look like a grotesque little monster.' They put her on a diet of 'wake-me-up-put-me-to-sleep-now-calm-me-down pills', and by the age of twenty-one she was seeing the psychiatrist daily. Despite the success of her concert career and *A Star is Born*, the remaining twenty-six years of her life were one long chain of ups and downs and public crises. She had five marriages and supposedly attempted suicide twenty times. 'I have a million eyes on me night and day,' she was once reported to have said, 'and I don't know what the hell I'm doing.' *1922*

Today's the day...

Bosky landscape painter John Constable was born in East Bergholt, Suffolk, the son of a prosperous mill-owner. Though known by the village girls as 'the handsome miller', trees interested him more than women and he found art 'under every hedge and in every lane'. The now so familiar naturalism of his paintings was then revolutionary. Never very dynamic, it took him sixteen years to convince his wife to marry him and his friend John Fisher said of him that when he was putting on his breeches he was 'apt to lose time in deciding which leg shall go in first'. He did, however, sire seven children, four of whom also became artists, and as recently as 1978 it was revealed that many of the works thought to be genuine Constables were in fact painted by his talented fourth son, Lionel.   *1776*

The most successful Grand Prix driver ever Jackie Stewart was born in Dumbarton. He followed his brother Jimmy into racing in 1961 and won his first Formula I race just four years later in the Italian Grand Prix. Between then and his retirement at the end of the 1973 season, he clocked up a total of a record twenty-seven wins and got three world championships and an ulcer in the process. They were by no means the first championships the 5ft 4in ace had ever won, however. Years before he had won five British and one European title, not for racing – but for shooting clay pigeons.   *1939*

The brilliant eccentric lady photographer Julia Margaret Cameron was born to the brilliant eccentric family of Jim 'Blazes' Pattle in Calcutta. She married husband Charles there and came home and settled in the arty colony of Freshwater in the Isle of Wight, where her behaviour 'baffled description'. She was the unofficial social secretary of the group headed by Alfred Lord Tennyson, showered everyone with exotic gifts, blew kisses at people in church and was said to have a tendency to shake the house the minute she entered it. She took up photography when she was forty-eight with equal fervour

330

and nobody, with the exception only of Dante Gabriel Rossetti and Garibaldi, ever dared refuse her summons to sit. Poor old Tennyson was forced to pose innumerable times, and it wasn't only in photography that she bullied the Poet Laureate. When he refused to be vaccinated during an outbreak of smallpox, she dragged a doctor to his house and stood outside shouting 'Alfred you're a coward!' *1815*

Le Mans became a nightmare. The twenty-four-hour marathon looked as if it was going to be the fastest and most exciting race ever, until on the thirty-sixth lap disaster struck. As Mike Hawthorn's Jaguar slowed for a pit stop, Pierre Levegh's Mercedes travelling at over 150mph touched Lance Macklin's Austin Healey. The Healey went into a 100yd skid and managed to stop, but Levegh's car flew 15ft into the air, mounted the banking, scythed through the crowd and exploded. In those terrifying few moments, eighty-two people died, and over 100 more were rushed to hospital injured. Incredibly, the race was allowed to continue, though understandably the Mercedes team withdrew. Before the start Levegh was worried. He'd said to his wife, 'Our cars are too fast.' *1955*

Malta's airforce of three leapt into action for the first time, when two formations of Italian bombers made their *début* raid on this strategically vital little Mediterranean island. The three planes were ancient Gloster Gladiators which had missed their aircraft carrier and been stranded in Valetta. For the next seventeen days, manned by a scratched-together group of pilots, the planes were almost constantly in battle, with crew and mechanics working shifts and a fourth plane dismembered for spares. Unbelievably, they kept the ancient and unwieldy planes flying and the Italians on the hop, until they were joined by a group of Hurricanes on 28 June. Aptly enough, the Gladiators that helped to save Malta were christened *Faith*, *Hope* and *Charity*. *1940*

Today's the day...

The crazy Irish duellist George Robert Fitzgerald, dandy, nutcase and improving landlord was executed for the deaths he'd caused while trying to capture Patrick Randall McDonald, the colonel of the Mayo Legion of Volunteers. Fitzgerald had his first duel at the age of sixteen and by the age of twenty-seven had killed twenty-seven men – a mere fraction of his final total. He ran a man through in Paris for stepping on his dog and was once in a coffee-house when a foolhardy knave said, 'I smell an Irishman.' 'You shall never smell another,' replied Fitzgerald and chopped off his nose. He took his father to court for debt and when he wouldn't pay up, manacled him to a pet bear. When they finally caught him hiding in a blanket box, he took it like a man. On the scaffold he drank a bottle of port and jumped. The rope broke. 'You see,' he gleefully announced to the crowd, 'I am once more amongst you unexpected!'
1786

The very first blood transfusion administered to a human was carried out by Jean Baptiste Denys, court doctor to Louis XIV. Denys, whose dangerous experiment was based on work done three years previously on dogs by the Englishman, Lowers, gave the poor boy 9oz of blood mainlined from the carotid artery of a lamb. The patient took on 'a clear and smiling countenance' and recovered. Unfortunately Denys' third such patient died and the transfusions were banned, much to the disappointment of high society Parisian matrons. They'd believed that if they swapped their old blood for new, they'd be miraculously rejuvenated.   *1667*

Frogs fell on England in an amphibious rainstorm over a naval display at Sutton Park, Birmingham. Said an eye-witness, 'There were literally thousands of them. They bounced off our umbrellas and we were afraid to walk for fear of treading on them.' Perhaps more surprisingly than the frog-fall itself is the fact that such hopping showers are not all that uncommon. They were first mentioned in Jerome Caradan's *De Subtilitate* in 1549, and Izaak Walton sensibly commented that if it had to happen, 'it should rain none but water-frogs, for those I think non venomous'.   *1954*

The weather went silly again with what Henry Wicliffe described as 'such an extreme thunder and raine as the like hath seldom beene seene'. The church wall at St Andrew's in Holborn fell down and twelve or fourteen coffins were uncovered. At Bishopsgate, 'People that were dead were taken out of their graves by the violence of the water and swim up and down the streets.' It was said that there 'was a spirit seene upon the waters' – which not surprisingly 'did sore affright the beholders'.   *1626*

The heaviest weight ever lifted by a man was hoisted aloft on the back of the twenty-five stone Olympic and professional weightlifter 'The Dixie Derrick' – Paul Anderson of Toccoa, Georgia. The lift was 6,270lbs or put another way, two large cars or the combined weight of three entire football teams.   *1957*

Today's the day...

The 'infernally impudent' inventor of the steam turbine Charles Algernon Parsons was born. He was only thirty when he came up with his great invention and he was absolutely convinced it would make conventional marine engines obsolete. Unfortunately nobody else was, so in 1894 he built the first ever steam turbine ship, the 100ft *Turbinia*, and three years later took it to the Diamond Jubilee Naval Review at Spithead. There, as assorted royals and admirals looked on helplessly, he hurtled around the assembled battleships of more than a dozen nations. Travelling at an incredible 34½ knots, he left the top-brass spluttering as he quite literally ran rings around the fastest boats sent out to apprehend him. *1854*

The biggest tug-of-war stunt ever pulled took place at a school in Harrisburg, Pennsylvania when 2,274 people tugged on a 1½in-thick nylon rope to disastrous effect. 200 of them were injured, fifty so badly they were taken to hospital – some with severed tendons and at least four children with the tips of their fingers missing. The culprit, apart from whoever came up with the idea in the first place, was the rope. Though it was designed for 3,000 pullers, it snapped. *1978*

The high speed hero of the twenties Sir Henry O'Neal De Hane Segrave was mortally injured when his sleek white powerboat hit a floating bottle, corkscrewed and turned turtle at nearly 100mph on Lake Windermere. Just moments before, he'd broken the world waterspeed record at 98.67mph with an unscheduled but fatal run. He was still alive when he was taken from the water and before he died he was told of his hollow victory. It was Friday the 13th and the tragedy was that he'd broken the record two days before, but thanks to an administrative slip-up, he hadn't been officially timed.

1930

Clean-up campaigner Mary Whitehouse was born, the secondary school teacher who became an international figure when she decided there was too much pornography about. When she first started her campaign in 1963 the strain used to make her physically sick but since then she's given lecture tours in Australia and America, been received by the Pope and withstood attacks with cream pies, bags of flour and torrents of abuse. One official in Australia was rash enough to call her 'that notorious Pom' and his office was promptly mobbed by 200 of her hymn-singing supporters.

1910

Superstitious self-made god Alexander the Great died after a particularly prolonged period of feasting. A brilliant military technician, he never lost a battle and inspired his army to march as many as 400 miles in eleven days. His empire stretched from India to the Persian Gulf and he tried to unite Macedonia and Persia permanently by marrying a Persian wife and bribing 10,000 of his soldiers to do the same. His mother had told him that his father was Zeus, King of the Gods, so he decided he should be a god too. The move didn't make him too popular and when he died at the age of thirty-two, at least one Athenian refused to believe it. 'If Alexander were really dead,' he said, 'the stench of the corpse would fill the world.'

323 BC

Today's the day...

The horrific flight of Alcock and Brown – the first non-stop hop
across the Atlantic – started from Lester's Field, St John,
Newfoundland, by nearly demolishing the earth banks at the end of
the runway. Up by the skin of its teeth, the converted Vickers Vimy
bomber was soon shrouded in fog; an exhaust manifold blew away and
halfway across, the plane nose-dived. For a few terrifying moments,
Alcock and Brown were skipping the white-caps, disorientated and
flying in the wrong direction. The worst wasn't over. Driving snow
blocked the carburettor intakes and Brown, with a crippled leg, had
to clamber out onto the wings not once, but six times to free them.
Finally they sighted land – in the nick of time for the flaps were
freezing up. They touched down near Clifden in Galway, ran smack
into a bog and cartwheeled to a halt. Miraculously, they were
unharmed – perhaps thanks to Twinkletoes and Lucky Jim – two
stuffed black cats who'd flown the Atlantic with them.   *1919*

John Kelly's noisy heart finally gave out on him in New York when
he was only thirty-four years old. Twenty years earlier, he'd been
accidentally shot in the shoulder. Doctors decided it was too dangerous
to operate and left the bullet in him. Five years later his heart
started misbehaving and beat so loud you could hear it 12ft away.
When Dr Galusha B. Balch did a post-mortem the cause was revealed.
John Kelly's bullet had travelled and, without leaving so much as a
scar, had lodged in the wall of his heart.   *1860*

King Priam's treasure of 8,700 priceless pieces was discovered by
the fifty-one-year-old German-American Heinrich Schliemann in the
hill of Hissarlick in Turkey. Since childhood he'd longed to find the
ruins of the supposedly mythical city of Troy, and to finance the
venture he made a fortune as a merchant banker. With his wife
Sophia he set off to find the unknown site which he found
miraculously by instinct and despite a shortage of wheelbarrows he'd

soon got his army of Turkish labourers to slash the hill to pieces, leaving a bewildering mass of ruins and the ramparts of a once walled town. In fact, he'd found nine different layers of settlement. His treasure pre-dated Priam and Helen by 1,000 years and in his enthusiasm to reach it, he'd destroyed what little was left of his beloved Troy.

1873

Barney Barnato casually killed himself leaving his millions behind him. Barney was a charming, resourceful Whitechapel Jew; an amateur conjurer who'd become one of the richest men in South Africa. Having sold his diamond holdings to Cecil Rhodes De Beers Company – reputedly for ten per cent, a seat in parliament and the first Cockney-Jewish membership of the Kimberley Country Club – he was literally bored out of his mind. He decided to return to England to recover his sanity and as the ship passed Madeira, he asked his nephew what time it was. Told it was 3.13pm, he walked up to the rail and jumped overboard.

1897

Dr Death was hanged at Stafford. The notorious William Palmer, genial general practitioner, inveterate gambler and racehorse-owner paid his last debt smiling. Previously, he'd tried to reduce expenses by poisoning six of his natural and legitimate children, his heavily insured wife and brother, his wealthy mother-in-law and uncle, sundry creditors and one John Cook – a fellow punter whom Palmer first relieved of a lucky windfall. When suspicion finally fell on him, he actually attended Cook's autopsy, gave another doctor a shove so the contents of the stomach were spilled and then tried to bribe the coroner. Not surprisingly, he was convicted and the case aroused so much evil publicity for Palmer's home town of Rugeley that the people appealed to the Prime Minister to change its name. 'Why not,' Mr Palmerston is said to have replied, 'they can name it after me.'

1856

Today's the day...

Ben Franklin performed his famous kite experiment at the
corner of Race and Eighth Street in Philadelphia. In the middle of a
fearsome storm, he floated a child's kite, made from a large silk
handkerchief and iron wire, straight into a lowering thundercloud.
With what was either scientific dedication, or plain foolhardiness,
Franklin touched an iron key attached to the string over and over again
with his bare knuckles, and when he did so, the string went rigid and
produced a spark that quite literally electrified the world. Franklin had
demonstrated that lightning was pure electricity, and that it could,
in fact, be controlled (although two scientists who tried to repeat the
experiment killed themselves). The direct practical result was Franklin's
coining of the basic vocabulary of electricity with words like battery,
conductor, condenser, charge and shock; and his invention of the
lightning conductor to protect buildings from the awesome result of
heavenly fire. The church condemned Franklin because he was
'interfering with God expressing his divine wrath'. Fashionable ladies
liked the idea, however. They took to protecting themselves, under
bonnets with lightning conductors on top.   *1752*

June 15

High flying Francis de Rozier was killed trying to cross the English Channel in a balloon filled with hot air and hydrogen. He got off to a good start but, halfway across, the fire caused the hydrogen to explode. Though it could be of little comfort to him, it did at least bring him a double first. He was already the first man to fly in a balloon, and now he'd become the first man to die in a balloon.   *1785*

Harrow School was founded – 'a large and convenient Schoole house, with a chimney in it'. True to what was ever after the public school tradition, the first pupils had a vigorous regime of games to play. They included 'driving a top', 'tossing a handball' and 'running and shooting'. So the boys had to set off to school not with satchels, but with 'bow strings, shafts and bracers.'   *1571*

Liberalising Kaiser Frederick III of Prussia died after a reign of only ninety-nine days. Two years earlier he'd developed a persistent sore throat and doctors discovered what they thought was a cancerous growth. Through the Kaiser's wife, who was Queen Victoria's eldest daughter, they summoned the world's leading laryngologist – Scottish doctor Morel MacKenzie. He was the man who'd founded the world's first throat hospital with beds for in-patients, and he was at the very top of his profession. He assured everybody that it was not cancer, and after a minor operation Frederick was restored to his natural voice again. Victoria invited Morel to lunch at Balmoral, and was so delighted that she knighted him immediately after the cheese and biscuits. All was not well, however. Further investigations established that the pea-sized growth on Frederick's vocal chords was, in fact, cancerous, but by then it was too late to do anything about it. The great MacKenzie had been wrong, and the fact that the Kaiser's death was very possibly caused by a British physician's wrong diagnosis, strained relations between the two countries for years to come.   *1888*

339

Today's the day...

The strange fate of Lord Lovell was decided at the Battle of Stoke. A dyed-in-the-wool Yorkist, he'd made the mistake of fighting with the Earl of Lincoln in the cause of the manipulated teenage impostor Lambert Simnel, who'd been crowned Edward VI in Ireland. Henry VII and his general, the Earl of Oxford, had trounced them roundly. Lincoln was killed on the field; the unfortunate, but lucky Lambert was made a scullion in the King's kitchen and Lord Lovell swam the Trent on horseback to try to make good his escape. He fled to his Oxfordshire house, 'Minster Lovell', where he's said to have hidden in a locked and secret chamber, known only to an old retainer who kept the key. Sadly for Lord Lovell, the old retainer died and this aristocratic rebel was not released until 1708, when a chimney was demolished and they found his bones – which instantly crumbled to dust.   *1487*

The first woman in space Junior Lieutenant Valentina Tereshkova blasted off from Tyuratam in the USSR aboard *Vostok 6*. Flying under the apt call-sign 'Seagull', she was only twenty-six years old and beyond 126 parachute jumps, she had little airborne experience. She orbited the earth forty-eight times in 70hrs 50mins and suffered somewhat from disorientation and space sickness. At a height of 143½ miles she's travelled higher, and at a speed of 17,470mph she's travelled faster than any other woman. Five months after touchdown she married fellow cosmonaut Vladimir Nikolayev and within a year she produced a bouncing baby daughter, and became the world's first space mum.   *1963*

A cricketing record nearly wasn't when dogged Yorkshiremen Percy Holmes and Herbert Sutcliffe made a first wicket stand of an incredible 555 runs. When the Yorkshire captain declared immediately they'd done it, pandemonium broke loose. The scorers claimed they'd made a mistake and put the score-board back to the old record of 554.

Fortunately a clergyman leapt from the crowd and proved the scorers wrong. Poor Percy was suffering from lumbago and was greatly relieved by this divine intervention, but super-cool Herbert was as unruffled as ever. 'My doctor told me if I ever have a heart attack, it'll be a miracle,' he said. 'I've got the lowest blood pressure in Pudsey.'

1932

The too right lawyer Clement Laird Vallandigham was cut off in his prime in Lebanon, Ohio, aged fifty. At the time of his death, he was defending an accused murderer and intended to prove his client's innocence by showing how the so-called victim could easily have killed himself. The defence worked and the defendant was acquitted, but Vallandigham didn't live to see it. Full of enthusiasm, he'd been demonstrating what he meant with a pistol, but he'd forgotten the pistol was loaded!

1871

The first airborne hi-jacking occurred aboard *Miss Macao*, a Catalina flying boat headed for Hong Kong. She'd only just taken off, when a gang of Chinese bandits, led by a notorious outlaw peasant called Wong-Yu Man, took her over – intent on ransoming the passengers on pain of their lives. Bravely if foolishly the pilot resisted. The bandits peppered the plane with bullets and she plunged to her doom. There was only one survivor, and by a cruel stroke of fate he was none other than Wong-Yu Man.

1948

A dropsical death carried off Susanna Wood, wife of James, a mathematical instrument maker of Kent Road. She was fifty-eight years old and had borne her long illness with great fortitude, though it must have been very painful. For, as it says rather indelicately on her tombstone in Bermondsey churchyard: 'She was tapped ninety-seven times and 461 gallons of water taken from her, without ever lamenting her case or fearing the operation.'

1810

Today's the day...

A combined gun and ploughshare was patented for farmers labouring in 'a peaceful avocation in border localities subject to savage feuds and guerilla warfare'. The gun was situated on top of the plough and was 'unrivalled' for firing ball or grape – so long as the farmer didn't forget to unharness his horses first!   *1862*

'The Father of Methodism' John Wesley was born, fifteenth of the nineteen children of a virile clergyman. Fresh from his 'Holy Club' at Oxford, he found his heart 'strangely warmed' after a Moravian meeting and started evangelising. Modestly claiming the world as his parish, he travelled over 224,000 miles, preached over 40,000 sermons and was pelted countless times with stones and rotten eggs. The poor man was a consumptive 5ft 4in, lived on £28 a year and nobly gave the rest of his money away. Rushing through life as if 'his minutes were numbered', he coined the phrase 'cleanliness is next to godliness', advocated a vegetarian diet for fatties and lived solely on potatoes for four years.   *1703*

Giant Roman Emperor Maximinus was killed by his own soldiers as he slept. They weren't taking any chances with this former shepherd from Thrace – he was over 8ft tall and took on heavyweight wrestlers two at a time just for fun. His large features and huge lower jaw suggest he suffered from 'acromegaly' – a glandular disorder which often results in great physical strength and extreme enlargement of the extremities. Even so contemporary writers must have been exaggerating when they said he wore his wife's bracelet – as a ring.   *AD 238*

Giant married giantess when Captain Martin van Buren Bates wed Miss Anna Swan at St Martin's-in-the-Fields, London. He was 7ft 2½in and she was 3ins taller and an ex-Lady Macbeth. The happy couple had come to England from America in a freak show and become great favourites of that connoisseur of oddities, Queen Victoria, who gave the bride a large ring and the groom a big watch as wedding presents. After an enormous reception with the Prince of Wales at Marlborough House and a mammoth tour of Scotland, they returned home to America. After accumulating a fortune, they retired to Ohio to build a tailor-made home. The ceilings were 14ft high; the doors were 8ft 6in high and one of their very first visitors was Lavinia Stratton – the miniature widow of the diminutive Tom Thumb!

1871

The last public guillotining took place at 4.50am on a cold grey morning outside Versailles prison in Paris. Dying to see the German multiple-murderer Eugen Wiedmann foreshortened, a huge crowd had gathered the night before, climbing balconies and trees to get a good view, and drinking heavily. Determined to disappoint them, the police blocked off all the streets so that only a comparatively small mob could see. They whisked Wiedmann out, spreadeagled him, brought the blade down and spirited the pieces away before anyone knew what had happened. When the condemned man had approached the deadly contraption, he'd been ashen and trembling – despite the reassurances of its long-dead inventor Dr Joseph Guillotin. 'The Subject,' he always insisted, 'feels no more than a slight chill on the neck' – though how he knew that he never explained.

1939

Musical America excelled itself with an intimate little *soirée* in Boston, Massachusetts. There assembled an orchestra of 987 and a choir of 20,000 all to be conducted by Johann Strauss II who'd been tempted across the Atlantic by a $10,000 fee and a free passage for him, his wife, his two servants and his Newfoundland dog. Assisted by 100 conductors armed with binoculars, Strauss mounted his lookout tower, tapped his giant illuminated baton and gave the signal to begin. In his own words, 'There then broke out an unholy row such as I shall never forget!' Actually, it was the *Blue Danube*.

1872

Today's the day...

The Battle of Waterloo was fought, ending Napoleon's attempt to rule Europe. Both he and Wellington were at the height of their careers and both were forty-six years old. On the morning of the battle Napoleon told his men, 'Wellington is a bad general, and the English are bad troops. This affair will be a picnic.' But Napoleon who was suffering from such acute haemorrhoids that the pain seriously affected his judgement, underestimated the long-nosed Wellington who led his victorious troops into battle with the cry, 'Damn it! In for a penny in for a pound!' When it was obvious he had the French Imperial Guard at his mercy he asked them to surrender – but received the one-word answer '*Merde!*' The late arrival of General Blücher and his Prussian troops secured the end of Napoleon's brilliant though expensive career that had spanned sixty-two land battles with only two defeats – a military record that cost the lives of three million French soldiers. Strangest of all the Battle of Waterloo wasn't fought at Waterloo, it took place four miles away between the villages of Pancenoit and Mont St Jean.   *1815*

British soldiers first ordered to wear trousers by a proclamation of King George IV stating, 'His Majesty has been pleased to approve of the discontinuance of breeches, leggings and shoes as part of the clothing of the infantry soldiers; and of blue-grey cloth trousers and half boots being substituted.' Until this order British soldiers wore a vast array of leg covering and shoes including multi-coloured full breeches, coloured woollen stockings and thigh-length boots with high heels!   *1823*

America's richest man died a pauper in a cheap Washington hotel. John Sutter owned the land in California where gold was first discovered in 1848. His property was literally invaded by thousands of gold crazy prospectors who illegally exploited the land without paying Sutter a cent. He began the biggest law suit in American history suing the State of California and every 'squatter' for a total of seventy-five million dollars in lieu of personal loss and damages suffered. After five years' legal wrangling he won his case but never saw his compensation. For twenty years he pestered Congress for his dues without success. General William Sherman was sent to inform him that Congress had yet again adjourned his claim without even taking a vote. Sutter, lying ill in bed sank back and said, 'Next year . . . they will surely . . . ' He never finished his sentence but lapsed into a coma from which he never regained consciousness. He died in utter poverty owning the richest land on earth.   *1880*

London's first nude statue was unveiled in Hyde Park. The colossal bronze figure of Achilles commemorated the Duke of Wellington and was sculpted by Sir Richard Westmacott. When the great moment of unveiling arrived an audible gasp was heard from those present – it was completely naked. The embarrassment was even more acute since the statue was commissioned and paid for by 'The Grateful Women of England'. Some time later Achilles miraculously sprouted a bronze fig leaf.   *1822*

Today's the day...

Enthusiastic masochist French boy genius Blaise Pascal was born. Without books or tuition, he worked out Pythagoras' theorem for himself at the age of twelve; solved the thorny problem of conic sections at sixteen and invented the first calculating machine. Far from being conceited, however, he was a keen and humble Christian and was wild about self mortification. He had a special spiked girdle made, which he wore right next to his skin, and whenever he caught himself enjoying anything, he gave it an unscientific thump!   *1623*

The woman who stole a King, Mrs Simpson, was born Bessie Wallis Warfield in Baltimore. Ironically she met the Prince of Wales while chaperoning one of his current married ladyfriends – and went one better than all the others by marrying him. Though it was perhaps ungenerous, the Church of England refused to perform the service and the Royal Family refused her the title HRH. The wedding was at Condé near Tours and though neither of them ever mastered French, it was in France that they held court in a white château thoughtfully provided by the city of Paris for £3 a week. For Wallis, Duchess of Windsor, 'a centimetre in the cut of a dress was of life or death importance'. She was an equally exacting if accomplished hostess, and never had flowers on the table, preferring Meissen china. She'd lapse into Chinese if the conversation was flagging and she scoured the gossip columns to find out which worthwhile socialites were in town. One American dowager complimented her, 'I just love your lunches and your pansies are divine.' 'In the garden?' inquired the Duchess with typical acerbic wit, 'or at the table?'   *1896*

The relief of Aberdeen began when the first victim of the terrible typhoid epidemic that had been sweeping the city was released from Tor-na-Dee Hospital – cured. Though there was only one death, 450 people were struck down and Aberdeen was treated 'like a gigantic leper colony'. Aberdonians were asked to keep out of nearby towns and hotels, tourists stayed away in droves, and lorry drivers threatened to strike rather than go there. When the cause was tracked down to an infected batch of corned beef, shops were ostracised willy-nilly and one shopkeeper actually ran an advertisement saying she definitely didn't have typhoid. Small wonder that when Evelyn Gould, the twenty-three-year-old librarian's assistant, emerged from the hospital cured, she was carried shoulder high by police to the accompaniment of a pipe-band, though the sash they gave her was in questionable taste – it read 'Typhoid Queen 1964'.   *1964*

A riotous military review was forcibly staged at the home of the Wombles on Wimbledon Common. A rumour had swept London that a grand army spectacular would take place and a crowd of 20,000 duly assembled. When a government official announced that the rumour was false, nobody believed him and frustrated at the non-appearance of the military, they set fire to the heath. The local authorities couldn't cope, so a detachment of guards was rushed from the barracks to help, and taking the easy way out they quelled the riot by staging the review.   *1812*

Today's the day...

The noisome Black Hole of Calcutta became living hell for 145 Britons and one Indian woman herded in there on the orders of their conqueror Siraj-ud-Daula, Nawab of Bengal. His aim was to force the British to reveal the whereabouts of a vast treasure and his determination cost 123 lives. Crushed together in the dingy two-windowed cell, a mere 18ft by 15ft, dozens of men died slowly and painfully from asphyxiation and heat exhaustion. When guards offered hatfuls of water through the windows, many more were trampled to death in the rush. In the end those that survived did so by sucking the perspiration from their own clothes. By 6am the following morning after eight-and-a-half hours of suffering, corpses were packed so tightly against the door that it took twenty minutes to push it open. The tragedy was that no one talked – for the very good reason that the treasure didn't exist.   *1756*

Champion old lag John Morgan was jailed for five years for twenty-one charges of theft and falsification of cheques. Mr Morgan, aged sixty, had spent more than half his life in prison: he had twenty-five previous convictions for 445 offences and had first come before 'the beak' in 1936. Said Lord Justice-Clerk Wheatley in court in Edinburgh, trying to decide where to send him: 'I think one place you might go is into the *Guinness Book of Records*!'   *1978*

'The Tasmanian Devil' Errol Flynn was born in Hobart, and was swashbuckling long before he got to Hollywood, as a deck-hand, prospector, plantation-manager, tropical bird hunter and policeman. For a while he was 'dagging the hogget' – castrating lambs with his teeth – on a sheep-station in the outback and somehow he ended up in repertory in Northampton. In his first Hollywood role he played a corpse. 'Nature had given me a unique physique,' he said and he made the most of it. He shared a house with David Niven which they called 'Cirrhosis-by-the-Sea' and after a long string of celebrated affairs, he was hauled before the courts for statutory rape, supposedly committed on two under-age girls of questionable reputation. He was acquitted but the papers had a field day. It was unfortunate for Flynn that one of the girls had testified he made love with his shoes and socks on – at the time he'd just finished playing Custer in *They Died with their Boots On*.

1909

Rommel took Tobruk at his second attempt after the Allies had seized the port seventeen months earlier. Churchill had been pressing for an Allied offensive but while the Allies prepared, Rommel struck. Aided and abetted by the mighty eighty-eight, 'the wonder-gun of the Desert War', he was able to knock out British armour at a range of nearly one mile. His tanks, too, could outmanoeuvre and outshoot the British tanks which incredibly carried auxiliary fuel on their flanks – a habit which made them potential infernos. The inexperienced Lieutenant General Ritchie made matters worse by failing to keep the 1st and 7th tank regiments together. 'If the enemy is foolish enough to allow the scattering of his tank forces,' Rommel had written, 'it will be easy to destroy them piecemeal' – which is exactly what he did. *1942*

Commodore Anson hit the jackpot when after three years of searching the Spanish Main for plunder, he captured 'the Prize of all Oceans' the great treasure galleon *Nuestra Senora de Covadonga*, carrying half a million pounds' worth of booty. Even the Spaniards would have to admit he'd earned it, since he'd lost over 750 men through scurvy, suffered the terrors of the Cape, lost one of his ships in a storm and been forced to scuttle two more. When he captured his silver-laden prize, his crew consisted of ex-slaves, Indians, Dutchmen and Lascars – but even they were better than the complement he'd set out with. Short of men, the Secretary of War had supplied him with 500 Chelsea pensioners – nearly half of whom were nimble enough to jump ship before they'd even reached Portsmouth. *1743*

Today's the day...

The Druids gather at Stonehenge to watch the midsummer sun rise over the Heelstone. In fact, the mysterious monument pre-dates the Druids by a millennium. Built over 500 years, it was started by Neolithic man; the Beaker people hauled sixty four-ton slabs of bluestone 135 miles from the Prescelly mountains in Wales, and it was topped off in the Bronze Age. Recently an astronomer has argued that it may have been a sort of primitive astronomical computer. He discovered that the moon rises over the same stone in midwinter once every 18.6 years and, strangely, Diodorus of Sicily wrote in 50 BC that the moon-god visits Stonehenge – once every nineteen years.

Annual Event

A poisoned partridge made the young artillery officer, Lieutenant Hubert Chevis, ill after he'd only eaten one mouthful in his quarters near the Aldershot barracks. Within twenty-four hours he was dead. The coroner recorded an open verdict but on the day of his funeral, his father received a cryptic telegram from Dublin which said, 'Hooray Hooray Hooray'. Later he received another telegram which read, 'It is a mystery they will never solve' – and they never did.   *1931*

Pneumatic American beauty Jane Russell was born. She was only a dental receptionist (or was it a chiropodist's assistant?) until millionaire Howard Hughes was struck by her attractions. 'I saw the most beautiful pair of knockers I've ever seen in my life,' he is said to have said – and quickly arranged a screen test. Equipped with a specially designed, aerodynamic, cantilevered bra, she made an outstanding première appearance in 1943 in *The Outlaw* – a film that went out with the byline: 'How'd you like to tussle with Russell?' Though she showed her worth as a comedienne in *Paleface*, most of her films seemed solely designed to exploit her ample charms. 'Her breasts,' it was said, 'hung over the screen like stormclouds over a landscape.'   *1921*

Unlucky matador Luis Freg was born. The little Mexican gained the dubious distinction of being gored more often than any other bullfighter. He got the point fifty-seven times, was given the Last Rites five times, but always went back for more. Surprisingly hale and hearty, he finally quit the ring all in one piece – and drowned two years later.   *1890*

Saucy courtesan and schemer Mary Anne Clarke died of old age in Boulogne. In her heyday she was mistress to the 'grand old Duke of York' and lived in great style in Gloucester Place with ten horses, twenty servants and wine glasses costing two guineas a piece. Her overspending led her to be a little naughty and she accepted large sums of money from young officers for using her influence with her lover who was Commander-in-Chief. The poor old Duke was charged with corruption and he and Mary Anne were brought before Parliament to answer for their crimes. Though they found her pertness 'very reprehensible' and the Duke resigned his commission, the pair went unpunished and one member was so charmed by Mary Anne that he sent her a note – '300 guineas and supper with me tonight?'   *1852*

Today's the day...

The Tudor Salome Queen Anne Boleyn was pleased to receive Bishop Fisher's head fresh from the scaffold. Since he'd been opposed to her royal marriage and Henry VIII's supremacy over the church, it gave her great pleasure to taunt his mortal remains. But when she slapped him across the mouth, one of his teeth stuck in her hand and left a painful mark that she carried to the grave. The reviled head was stuck on a pike on London Bridge. Though 'parboyled' it appeared not to deteriorate but 'grew daily fresher and fresher'. Crowds flocked to see the miracle of the 'comely red face' and before the King, disgusted at this posthumous popularity, ordered it thrown in the river, it was said of the Bishop that 'in his lifetime he had never looked so well'.

1535

Admiral Tryon's fatal order was obeyed to the letter and 358 men died as a result. On manoeuvres off Tripoli, he ordered the battleships *Victoria* and *Camperdown* to wheel round and steam directly towards each other. Deaf to the protests of both his second in command and the *Camperdown*'s captain, he stood on the *Victoria*'s bridge watching as if fascinated. Only when it was too late did he give the order to turn; the *Victoria* was rammed deep below the water-line and rapidly started sinking. The crew of 600 jumped for their lives, but many were cut to pieces by the propellers. As the *Victoria* keeled over and went down, Tryon determined to go with her and was heard mumbling, 'It's all my fault.' In that instant nearly 2,000 miles away at a tea-party at Lady Tryon's, the figure of a man walked across the room. He said not a word but to those who knew him, his identity was clear – it was the Admiral himself.

1893

Neurotic big picture painter Benjamin Haydon committed suicide. Though his huge canvases were admired by the likes of Keats and Wordsworth and he taught Landseer and Bewick, his work was not much liked. He struggled on, his wife lost her fortune, he was frequently imprisoned for debt and five of his children died. In desperation he hired part of the Egyptian Hall for an exhibition, but was dismayed to find that his gargantuan paintings had a rival attraction in the form of the midget Tom Thumb. Nobody came to see them, so with a grandiloquent gesture he stood in front of his work, slashed his throat and just to make sure of it, blew his brains out. *1846*

The philosophical lover, English writer Thomas Day, was born. He was exceedingly kind-hearted and decided to find a wife by what he considered to be the proper principles. He adopted two orphan girls Lucretia and Sabrina, to train as possible consorts. Lucretia proved 'invincibly stupid' but Sabrina looked a likely lass, so he put her to the test. He dropped hot wax on her arms and fired pistols up her petticoats. She screamed and he decided she wasn't stoic enough! Only in Esther Milnes did he find a woman who pleased him in every way. She gave up her harpsichord without demur and when he worried about her delicacy, she walked barefoot in the snow to cure it.

1748

Today's the day...

A cocksure con-man appeared at the Old Bailey charged with fraudulently obtaining £2,000 from eight different branches of the London and South Western Bank. Aided and abetted by a bank employee he'd forged a letter to each of the managers indicating that he'd transferred his not inconsiderable account to their particular branch. He then rushed round in a taxi and cashed in excess of £200 at each of them. The long arm of the law finally caught up with him in Madrid and he turned out to be the twenty-three-year-old renegade son of a rich Dutch Jew. In court he insisted on using a rolled-up newspaper as an ear trumpet, and claimed rather smugly that it was all a jolly jape and that anyway he'd given the money away to the poor. The real joke was that he signed all the cheques D.S. Windell – an abbreviation for Damned Swindle!   *1909*

The 327-day King Edward VIII was born to Queen Mary during Ascot week. 'A sweet little boy' and the darling of the nation as Prince of Wales, his attitude to the Kingship was always ambivalent. He was afraid of being a bad king, and when as a young Grenadier Guards officer in the World War I he was itching to see action, he'd written to Kitchener, 'What does it matter if I am shot? I have four brothers.' The staggering thing is that his involvement with the divorcee Mrs Simpson and his renunciation of the crown were predicted by Nostradamus in the sixteenth century and by the father of the Labour Party Keir Hardie only days after he was born. Mrs Simpson had other ideas. 'He was born to be a salesman,' she said as Duchess of Windsor. 'He would be an admirable representative of Rolls Royce. But an ex-King cannot start selling motor cars.'   *1894*

'Our Lady of the Victories' Marie Rose Josephine Tascher de la Pagerie, Empress of France, Napoleon's wife and lucky charm, was born in Martinique. An old Creole woman predicted she'd be Queen and after her first husband Beauharnais had been guillotined, she took

June 23

the first step by marrying Bonaparte in a civic ceremony in 1796. He married her again in the eyes of the Church the very night before they were crowned in 1804 and only divorced her when she failed to give him an heir. He adored her, but was horrified by her extravagance. While he was campaigning in Egypt she consoled herself by spending over a million francs, and her dressmaker's bills were probably the biggest in history. She had one dress covered in tiny toucan feathers and another with fresh pink rose petals – which caused problems when they wilted!

1763

A bibulous bounty was found in the body of a cod-fish when it was opened up by a Cambridge fish-wife. In the Leviathan's tummy was a copy of the treatises of John Frith, a heretic who'd been burnt nearly 100 years before. Ironically, while he was waiting for the stake, Frith had been kept in a fish-cellar and several of his damned companions had died from the overwhelming piscine stink.

1626

Insane hygienist and rejuvenator Dr James Graham was born in Edinburgh and died there exactly forty-nine years later. In between he'd made a substantial fortune out of his vast and exotic Temple of Health – a bizarre institution on the Royal Terrace Adelphi overlooking the Thames. There, assisted by his scantily clad 'rosy goddesses of health' – the most famous of which was Emma Hamilton – he introduced the rich and famous to the restorative powers of electricity and magnetism, Aetherial Balsams and Ambrosial Quintessences. His showpiece was the glass-pillared Celestial Bed guaranteed for £50 a night to cure impotence and sterility, but when he introduced earth-bathing – naked immersion in mud – his popularity waned. He ended his life a religious fanatic, fasting and wearing only cut turfs for fifteen days at a time while he wrote *How to Live for Many Weeks, Months or Years Without Eating Anything Whatever*. He died shortly afterwards.

1745/1794

Today's the day...

A spider became a hero when after two defeats at the hands of Edward II's armies, Scottish King Robert the Bruce smashed the English invader at the Battle of Bannockburn. As every schoolboy knows, the Bruce had been hiding in a cave where he's supposed to have been inspired to fight again by the repeated and eventually successful attempts of the spider to build a web. However apocryphal the story, King Robert's ragged army of 10,000 inflicted 'the most lamentable defeat the English army ever suffered' on twice their number. Yet at the end of the day, the Bruce was quite upset. With the very first stroke of the battle, he'd engaged the English champion Henry de Bohun in personal combat. The Bruce cleft his skull with a single blow, and the stroke broke his favourite battle-axe. *1314*

The first 'Flying Saucers' were spotted by Kenneth Arnold over Mount Rainier in the Cascades region of the Rockies. An experienced pilot and deputy sheriff, he was assisting in an aerial search for a missing plane when he saw nine brilliant, wingless discs flashing across the sky in echelon. He estimated their speed at over 1,000mph – nearly twice the contemporary record for conventional craft. He later described the objects as flying 'like a saucer would if you skipped it across the water'. Newspapers took up the description and the 'flying saucer' was born. More down to earth authorities dubbed them Unidentified Flying Objects while dozens of American astronauts who've seen them call them 'bogeys'. The Soviet statesman Mr Gromyko has offered a simple, if chauvinistic explanation. He boasted they were discuses thrown by Russian athletes training for the Olympics.   *1947*

Good came out of evil when 175,000 Austrians fought 150,000 allied French and Piedmontese in the gruesome Battle of Solferino in northern Italy. In fifteen hours of ghastly slaughter, eighty-eight men died every minute; three surgeons fainted and one grew so tired that two soldiers had to support his arms while he worked. Over 42,000 died in battle, wounds and disease accounted for 37,000 more and in the three weeks it took to clear the corpses, many near death were buried alive. The carnage was witnessed by crowds of holidaymakers, among them a Swiss banker called Jean Henri Dunant, who afterwards wrote a book *Un Souvenir de Solferino*. In it, he promoted the concept of an impartial relief organisation, and it was largely thanks to him that five years later the Geneva Convention founded the International Red Cross.   *1859*

The Argentinian bus driver who went on to become five times world champion racing driver, Juan Manuel Fangio, was born. In his first major race, the aptly named 'Extraordinary Grand Prix', he overturned the car, repaired it himself and went on to finish fifth. His career progressed exceptionally slowly, but at an age when most drivers have retired, he'd battled on to dominate the world's circuits, winning an unequalled twenty-four out of his fifty-one starts. He became champion for the fifth time at the incredible age of forty-six, and since he was easily old enough to be the father of nearly all his rivals, he was lovingly dubbed 'The Grand Old Man of Racing'.   *1911*

Today's the day...

Custer's last stand was fought out at the Battle of the Little Bighorn in Montana, just as Sitting Bull had dreamed it would be three weeks earlier. In the infamous attempt to drive the Indians out of their beloved Black Hills, 'Long Hair', or 'Hard-Arse' as they called him, had stumbled on a vast encampment of Sioux, Cheyenne and Arapaho. He insisted on attacking and foolishly divided his force so he was left isolated with fewer than 300 troops. The Indians led by Gall, Crazy Horse and Two Moon, swept down on them and wiped them out to a man. There were unconfirmed stories of soldiers committing mass suicide; it's even been suggested that Custer took his own life but what is certain is that his body was left unscalped. The sole survivor was an army horse – ironically called Comanche.   *1876*

Popular prophet of doom George Orwell was born Eric Blair in the Raj – in Bengal. After Eton and a spell in the Burmese Imperial Police, he decided to go working-class, became a washer-up and tramp, fought in the Spanish Civil War and ended up a journalist. In *1984* he created his own dismal vision of the future and American academics have suggested that about half its predictions have already come true – including the use of mind altering drugs, data banks, the dominance of three global super-powers, and the corruption of language in 'doublethink' and 'newspeak'. Orwell took life oppressively seriously. 'He wouldn't blow his nose,' said Cyril Connolly, 'without moralising on conditions in the handkerchief industry.'   *1903*

The Korean War began when 240 Communist tanks crossed the 38th parallel by which the peninsula had been partitioned between the Russians and the Americans after the defeat of Japan. Within three weeks a UN security force had cut off the Communist supply lines and effectively won the day. The tragedy was that General MacArthur insisted on trying to 'liberate' the North; the Chinese got involved and the war dragged on for three years. After an estimated four million

casualties, of which the two million dead were predominantly
civilian, the armistice of July 1953 restored the 38th parallel – leaving
both sides exactly where they were when they started. No peace
treaty was ever signed – and technically the North and South are still
at war. *1950*

Pontius Pilate is celebrated as a saint by the Ethiopian Coptic
Church who believe that he and his wife Procula defended Christ,
were converted and became Christian martyrs. More plausible, however,
is the story that he was recalled to Rome for his excesses as Procurator
of Judaea and forced to commit suicide by the mad Emperor Caligula.
Reviled by both Christians and Jews, legend has it that even after death
Pilate had a hard time. His impious body was said to have been
rejected by the waters of the Tiber and to have turned up at Vienne on
the Rhône. It was finally found floating in the lake at Lausanne in
Switzerland. *Feast Day/died circa* AD *39*

Barbed wire was patented by Lucien B. Smith of Kent, Ohio,
though claimants to the honour of its invention also include Alphonso
Dabb, Joseph Glidden, Jacob Glaish and Isaac Ellwood. Within thirty
years, 622 different styles were manufactured and these days American
collectors will pay as much as £75 for a short length of a rare variety.
Styles favoured by the connoisseurs include the Sunderland Kink,
Nadel Two-Twist, Kelly's Diamond and the Corsicana Clip. *1867*

Older women were praised in the wisdom of the US founding
father Benjamin Franklin when he advised a young friend to take a
mature mistress. He pointed out that older women are more discreet,
more improving and less likely to have children. Furthermore 'when
women cease to be handsome, they study to be good'. They are more
practised, 'below the girdle' they are no different, and besides – 'they
are so grateful'. *1745*

Today's the day...

England's fattest King, George IV died aged sixty-seven. For the best part of two years he'd lain a-bed in a steamy room, rising for only five hours every evening and calling for his valets up to forty times a night. Despite his rheumatism, gout and inflamed bladder, he'd breakfast on two pigeons, three beefsteaks, a bottle of Moselle, a glass of champagne, two of port and one of brandy. This morning at 3.30am he said to a page, 'My boy, this is death' – and he was right. In his wardrobe they found all the coats, boots and pantaloons of fifty years, 500 wallets containing £10,000, a pile of love letters, ladies' gloves and dozens of locks of hair. Towards the end poor 'Prinny' had been having delusions. He believed he'd commanded a division at Waterloo and regardless of his vast bulk, he was convinced he'd ridden a winning race at Goodwood.   *1830*

The Pied Piper re-appeared in Hamelin. He'd already piped away all the rats that had fought the dogs and killed the cats, and drowned them in the River Weser. But the townspeople had reneged on their part of the deal and refused to pay him, so he'd come back for revenge. He piped away 130 of their children, leaving only one who was dumb and one who was blind, and sealed them up for ever in a cave on Koppenburg Mountain. They called him the Pied Piper probably because he wore the jester's motley, but the truth is, it's highly unlikely that he ever existed at all. Similar manifestations occur in Greek, Norse and Sanskrit legend and more modern European equivalents have led away various combinations of ants, mice and crickets; and sealed up sundry pigs and sheep. There was said to have been a Pied Fiddler of Brandenburg, a Piping Hermit of Lorch, not to mention the famous Pied Bagpiper of the Hartz Mountains.   *1284*

A party at Prinny's place got a little out of hand in the early hours of the morning, and by the time the Prince Regent had taken his great bulk to bed, strange scenes were occurring outside Carlton House.

About a dozen young women were 'so completely disrobed' they had to send home for clothes before they dare venture out, and one was sufficiently 'unencumbered of all dress' that a serving maid had to wrap her up in an apron to spare her blushes.   *1811*

Lightning struck again in the village of Steeple Ashton, Wiltshire, after a gap of some 203 years. There in the summer of 1670, St Mary the Virgin's steeple had been blasted in a storm and the following autumn two workmen repairing it were killed when it was struck a second time. Today a barn was the victim, and the shaft was so violent that in a nearby house it hurled an eighty-four-year-old pensioner right across the kitchen. The man's name was Mr Bolt.   *1973*

A drinking man's appeal staggered the Judge at Caernarfon Crown Court. Dr Clive Arkle was appealing against the loss of his firearms licence, which police had refused to renew because of his 'intemperate habits and lack of competitive activity'. The doctor claimed there was nothing intemperate about his habits – alcohol, he said, 'tightened up the eyeball' and made him a better shot. To prove his point, he proudly showed the bench a bag of trophies and said that when he won them, he was at the height of his prowess and drinking thirty pints of bitter a day!   *1978*

The absent-minded professor William Thomson, Baron Kelvin, was born in Belfast, the son of an eminent Scottish mathematician. Kelvin was a child prodigy, famous for inventing the tidal gauge and the submarine telegraph cable. It was said that he could think of two things at once, though occasionally this caused problems. His wife was once telling him about the arrangements for an excursion they'd planned to make the following day. Deep in thought, the great scientist suddenly looked up and asked, 'At what time does the dissipation of energy begin?'   *1824*

Today's the day...

Flying saucers visited New Guinea. One big one and two smaller or more distant ones were spotted by the priest Father Gill. They were hanging in the evening sky above the Anglican All Saints Mission on the Isle of Boianai. The big one came nearer until, under a glass dome, four man-like figures could be seen. Father Gill waved at them as did his assistant and amazingly the aliens waved back. The whole mission soon joined in and the UFO danced up and down in response to Father Gill flashing his torch at it. The visitors who disappeared shortly afterwards were well equipped to communicate with the priest. All four had 'curious haloes'. *1959*

The Marquis de Sade had a disastrous orgy. The thirty-two-year-old libertine and his pockmarked valet Latour hired four young harlots in a brothel in Marseilles. He gave them aniseed balls spiked with Spanish Fly, supposedly a ticklish aphrodisiac, and took it in turns with Latour to beat them 859 times, keeping count by cutting notches in the mantelpiece. Unfortunately, the girls got upset about his nail-studded belt and two of them were made ill by the drug. The authorities were less than happy to hear of the Marquis' bizarre practices and as he hotfooted it to Venice, they burnt him in effigy. When he returned they clapped him in the Bastille, where he was kept from the other prisoners for their own protection, and then they sent him off to a lunatic asylum where he organised amateur dramatics! *1772*

The violent death of the Mormon prophet, the thirty-eight-year-old Joseph Smith occurred in Carthage Prison. Along with his brother Hyrum, he'd been jailed for breaking up the printing press of one William Law, a disaffected follower. Law had been churning out pamphlets claiming that the Mormon city of Nauvoo was nothing more than a harem and accusing Smith of using his sacred order of polygamy merely to try and help satisfy his 'insatiable lust'. Other

June 27

religious groups were incensed by the Mormons having all the fun and a mob with blackened faces broke into the prison and shot Hyrum dead. Joseph tried to make a run for it. He jumped out of the window but his body was riddled with bullets before he hit the ground – two storeys down. They propped the corpse up in a chair and just to make sure, they executed it by firing squad.   *1844*

The bonnie boat sped over the sea to Skye, with a disguised Bonnie Prince Charlie and his snoozing saviour Flora MacDonald on board. Flora was staying with her rich relations the Clanranalds on Benbecula, when who should arrive, fresh from his defeat at Culloden, but the fugitive prince, worth £30,000 dead or alive. Flora wangled two passports from her stepfather, a captain of militia, the boat was organised and off they sped. For the trip Prince Charlie took the identity of an Irish maid – 'Betty Burke' – and he sailed fetchingly clad by Lady Clanranald in a quilted petticoat, a white apron, and a flowered gown.   *1746*

Today's the day...

The first charter flight took place, thanks to a short-sighted merchant from Philadelphia, Mr W. A. Burpee. He broke his spectacles just before he set sail from New York aboard the *Olympic*, and ordered the repairers to forward them to him. With a grand gesture, they hired the famous aviator Tom Sopwith who set off with Mr B's specs and, flying low over the *Olympic*, dropped his precious parcel on board!   *1911*

Wise-cracking King of the Lombards Alboyn died, having occupied large chunks of what is now Austria and Hungary. In the process he defeated the Gepidae, killed their King, chopped off his head and made off with his daughter, the fair Rosamund. Tradition has it that she killed him after he'd made one of the worst jokes in history. He'd had her father's skull made into a drinking cup and thrust it across at her saying, 'Here, have a drink with thy father!' She didn't think it was very funny so she gave it back to him, having added a few drops of poison.   *AD 572*

The nineteen-year-old Queen Victoria was crowned at Westminster Abbey. Part-way through the ceremonies, she was horrified to find Lord Melbourne tucking-in to wine and sandwiches from the altar of St Edward's Chapel. Wellington, despite his high boots, made a proper backwards obeisance, but Lord Rolle fell down the steps, prompting one wit to remark that he retained his title by rolling for his sovereign.   *1838*

The shot that shook the world was fired by the teenage Gavrilo Princip. It killed Archduke Ferdinand and precipitated World War I which ultimately cost over twenty million lives. Princip was one of seven assassins planted by the Serbian nationalist Black Hand Gang in the streets of Sarajevo. As the bright-red custom-built touring car passed in front of him, he shot Ferdinand at point-blank range in the

June 28

neck, and a ricochet killed the Duchess Sophie. The ill-fated car
was taken over by the Austrian general, Potiorek, and shortly
afterwards he went insane. An army captain drove it and killed
himself, and the Governor of Yugoslavia lost his arm after crashing
it four times. In all sixteen people were killed in it, and finally
the accursed vehicle was placed in a Vienna museum, where it was
later destroyed by a bomb. Its registration number was A 111-118
which, by a chilling coincidence, makes the date of the Armistice –
11.11.18   *1914*

Freedom's paranoic philosopher Jean-Jacques Rousseau was born
in Geneva. As a boy he enjoyed being whipped by the minister's
sister, and while the Catholic Savoyard spy Madame de Warens gave
him a taste for aristocratic women, he spent much of his life with the
sluttish kitchenmaid Thérèse le Vasseur, whom he eventually married,
but not before she'd already had five children by him. Ironically, for
the author of *Emile*, the bible of idealised education, he sent all five of
them to be taught at the foundling hospital.   *1712*

England's most married monarch, Henry VIII was born. Tall
and golden-haired, cultured and athletic, he was said by the Venetian
Ambassador to be 'the handsomest potentate I ever set eyes on'.
Martin Luther had other ideas. He called Henry 'a pig, an ass, a
dunghill, the spawn of an adder'. Marital problems, gout, corns, a
jousting accident that left him with a permanently ulcerated leg, and
his prodigious appetites soon made Luther's version the more
accurate. Henry is said to have so liked loin of beef that he knighted
it – hence 'Sirloin' – and in one five-year period, his waist expanded
by a massive seventeen inches. The strange thing is that until his
elder brother Arthur died, he was never meant to be King. He spent
his youth studying theology – in training to be an
Archbishop.   *1491*

Today's the day...

The death of the Pink Dream Lady, the pneumatic Jayne
Mansfield, occurred when she was decapitated in a horrific car-crash
on the road to New Orleans. Also killed were the chauffeur and her
man-of-the-moment, the Hollywood lawyer Sam Brody, though
miraculously her three small children survived. Miss Mansfield whose
ample proportions reached a high point of 43-23-37, had been married
three times – most famously to ex-Mr Universe Mickey Hagitay.
They lived in much-publicised passion in The Pink Palace – a house
where everything was pink down to the bed, the pool and the toy
poodles – but it was destined not to last. 'Men are like milestones,'
said the sex-goddess, 'you have to hurry on to the next one on the
road ahead.'

1967

Mass production artist Sir Peter Paul Rubens was born in
Westphalia. Peter became a page, painter and copyist, working mostly
in Italy for the Duke of Mantua and later in his native Netherlands,
where he combined the roles of artist and diplomat. He was always
inundated with commissions and set up a factory of artists to cope
with them. Ever since, it's often been difficult to tell a genuine Rubens
from a partly-genuine or fake one. 'The Last Judgement', he said, was
mostly done by an apprentice but 'could pass for an original', while
'Achilles' was painted by his best pupil, 'but entirely retouched by
me'.

1577

English football was humiliated by the USA in what was supposed
to be a walkover World Cup match in Belo Horizonte, Brazil. The
Americans were unknown outsiders; one player was completely bald
and one wore heavy gloves throughout, despite the blazing heat. The
rocky pitch made accurate passing impossible, which gave the
Americans a distinct advantage. England dominated the match with
running attacks and a hailstorm of shots that never went in. When the
American Bahr finally managed a shot at the English goal, keeper Bert

Williams had it covered – but he hadn't reckoned with the US centre-forward Gaetjens who got in the way. The ball hit him on the ear and ricocheted into the net for the only goal of the match! *1950*

A Choice Collection of Ladies was offered for auction at the Dancing School in Freeman's Yard, Cornhill. They all had independent fortunes, and included 'one tall lusty maiden worth £1,000'; one young widow who buried her husband six months after marriage and a pretty young lady 'unskilled in the tricks of the town'. Not just any Tom, Dick or Harry could buy, however, for bids were only accepted from gentlemen 'who have clear limbs and members entire upon examination'. *1691*

The world's first passenger railway was incorporated by Act of Parliament. Known as the 'Swansea and Mumbles Railway' it ran the $7\frac{1}{2}$ miles between Swansea and Oystermouth. After sail-power had proved to be a terrible flop, each sixteen-seat carriage was drawn by a single horse, rolling over the railway at 5mph, 'with the noise of twenty sledge hammers in full play'! *1804*

Today's the day...

Charles VIII of France was born. The prevailing fashion for long pointed shoes had reached outrageous proportions. It was believed that the longer the shoe, the more illustrious the wearer so a baron's points were 2ft long and those of a prince 2½ft. Charles is believed to have set a new trend for clumpy, square-toed shoes – probably because he had six toes on one foot.

1470

Dapper assassin Charles Guiteau was hanged for the murder of President Garfield. A crowd of four thousand packed into the Washington Jail to catch a glimpse of the condemned man strutting about his cell. Lemonade and cakes were sold to sustain the spectators and 250 of them paid up to $300 to be admitted inside and actually witness the hanging. Guiteau spent the morning shining his shoes and trimming his hair. He'd already made arrangements to donate his body to a certain Reverend William Hicks and had even written his own epitaph. After a huge meal he was taken to the scaffold, but then his nerve broke and he began to whimper. When he actually saw the rope, however, he collected himself and climbed the steps intoning a prayer ending, 'I therefore predict that this nation will go down in blood and that my murderers from the Executive to the hangman will go to hell.'

He then started on a poem he'd written specially for the occasion –
a monologue of a dying child talking to its parents, 'I am going to the
Lordy, I am so glad.' He went on to say it would sound better set to
music, but by then the patient hangman had had enough, and placed
the black hood over Guiteau's head. As the trap dropped, he could
still be heard reciting 'Glory, glory, glory . . .'   *1882*

The first astronauts to die in space perished as *Soyuz II* re-entered
the earth's atmosphere. During the record twenty-three day flight
everything had gone to plan and the only complaint from comrades
Patsayev, Dobrovolsky and Volkov was that they'd got too much work
to do. From the moment the engine braking system fired all contact
was lost, and when the recovery crew opened the hatch they found the
three dead men still strapped in their seats. Their bodies were laid in
state, then cremated and their remains placed in the Kremlin Wall.
During the flight Patsayev had celebrated his thirty-eighth birthday
and his fellow spacemen had presented him with two presents they'd
smuggled aboard – a fresh onion and a lemon.   *1971*

Violent headmaster of Eton, Dr John Keate, excelled himself by
flogging over eighty boys in one day, and surprisingly after this little
marathon, he was cheered by the rest of the school. The 5ft tall
disciplinarian with a face like a bulldog maintained a ferocious regime
and frightened the boys into submission by wielding his cane and
quacking like a duck! He always instructed his pupils to be pure in
heart, advising them 'if not I'll flog you until you are'.   *1832*

Mile-a-Minute Murphy got his nickname by riding his bicycle one
mile in a speedy 57·8 seconds – the first cyclist to do so. He pedalled
along furiously behind a Long Island train equipped with a special
windshield and reached speeds of up to 62mph. The current record is
140mph.   *1899*

Today's the day...

The vast Dominion of Canada was established by the British North American Act, masterminded by John Alexander MacDonald, its first Prime Minister. In those days, it comprised only four million people and four provinces: Quebec, Ontario, Nova Scotia and New Brunswick. The name is said to derive from an Iroquois word meaning 'a group of huts', and the great French writer Voltaire described the country as 'nothing more than a few acres of snow'. In fact, even though today it only has a population of twenty-four million, it's the second largest country in the world – so large that a complete map of it has never yet been made. As for MacDonald, he was so overcome by the British Cabinet's approval of his Act, that he rushed off to the Derby at Epsom where, to celebrate his triumph, he threw bags of flour over racegoers and fired peashooters at them.   *1867*

The third modern Olympic Games opened in St Louis, Missouri. The relative isolation of the southern river city led to a drastic reduction in the number of athletes competing – only 617 as opposed to the 1,300 who had competed in the previous Games in Paris. It lacked some of the usual international flavour too; 525 of the competitors were American, forty-one were Canadian, and the solitary British entrant was in fact, Irish! Even the great Marathon was something of a fiasco. The first man home was Fred Lorz who, unbeknown to the cheering crowd, had got cramp, thumbed a lift back to the stadium and ran in just for the exercise. One of the only two non-Americans competing was Cuban postman Felix Carvajal, who started the race in his everyday clothes, stopped off to pick some apples on his way round and still managed to come in fifth.   *1904*

America's first public library was established by Benjamin Franklin as the Library Company of Philadelphia. Though it still stands today and now houses over a quarter of a million books, it had very small and rather odd beginnings. It was open for only twelve hours a week, and had only fifty subscribers, each contributing forty shillings towards the first parcel of books. As the Minute Book of the time shows, subscriptions were often accepted in kind, and the library's coffers included a collection of fossils, a splendid case of stuffed snakes, an old sword and the ceremonial robes of an Indian chief. After the Revolutionary War, the subscription was reduced to thirty shillings, with an annual subscription of a bushel of wheat. *1731*

High-flier Amy Johnson was born in Hull, the daughter of a herring importer. Always fascinated by anything mechanical, she joined the London Aeroplane Club, and discovered the new delights of aviation. She became the first woman in Great Britain to be granted an Air Ministry ground engineer's licence, swiftly followed by a full navigation certificate. A mere ten months after getting her pilot's licence and having flown no further than from London to Hull, she blithely set off from Croydon on 5 May 1930 – for Australia! She named her tiny Gipsy Moth plane 'Jason' after the trademark of her father's firm, and despite her amazing lack of experience, landed safely at Port Darwin. Unfortunately for 'Jason' she flew on to Brisbane where, as so many of the early fliers did, she missed the aerodrome and crash-landed. A fellow flying enthusiast Jim Mollison piloted her to Sydney and two years later they were married. Shortly afterwards Amy broke the record for a solo flight from London to Cape Town – a record that had previously been held by her husband. *1903*

Henry Fox, first Baron Holland, died. During his last illness, the great English eccentric George Selwyn called to see him and left his card. Aware of his old friend's penchant for attending public executions and viewing corpses Fox, with his last words, instructed his servants, 'If Mister Selwyn calls again show him up; if I am alive I shall be delighted to see him; and if I am dead he would like to see me.' *1774*

Today's the day...

Animal stuffer extraordinaire Walter Potter was born, and his work can still be seen in his memorial museum in Arundel. Inspired by the tale of Cock Robin, he prepared a tableau of the story and stuffed ninety-eight British birds. He went on to stuff thirty-five guinea pigs playing cricket, thirty-seven kittens playing croquet, forty-five rabbits in school, a two-headed lamb, a four-legged hen and a pussycats' wedding with all the guests sporting frilly knickers!   *1835*

Cromwell's first victory overwhelmed the Royalist Cavaliers at Marston Moor and left 3,000 of them lying dead, cut down by the New Model Army as 'stubble to our swords'. He'd attacked suddenly as a clap of thunder rent the air and the Royalist commanders had retired to supper – and the victory was decisive. Returning from the field, Cromwell sent word to Lady Ingleby at Ripley that he and his troops intended to stay there. At first she refused, then stuck a brace of pistols 'in her apron strings' and told him he could come if he behaved himself. He did. 'Had it been otherwise,' said her ladyship, 'he should not have left the house alive.'   *1644*

Paranoiac Papa Hemingway died of gunshot wounds in Ketchum, Idaho. He'd had no novels published for nearly a decade, couldn't write and was convinced 'the Feds' were after him for back taxes. In hospital for depression, he fretted that the electro-convulsive therapy would damage his brain. He'd already tried to shoot himself once; had attempted to walk into an aircraft propeller and jump out of a plane in flight. Above all, his father's death preyed on his mind – he too had died of self-inflicted gunshot wounds.   *1961*

The Orchid Kid went down to the Manassa Mauler in the first boxing match broadcast on the radio and the first to take over a million dollars at the gate. Idolised by the ladies, Frenchman Georges Carpentier slugged it out with Jack Dempsey in a special wooden

July 2

amphitheatre in front of 93,000 people, 400 firemen and a fleet of ambulances. In attendance were John D. Rockefeller, Henry Ford, Teddy Roosevelt, Al Jolson and 'thousands of classy dames'. Dancing like a butterfly, the lighter Carpentier swung into round 2 by punching the Mauler smack on the jaw. Strengthened by gum-chewing, the jaw held out and, ironically, the great punch spelled the beginning of the end for Carpentier. He had hit Dempsey so hard, he'd broken his own thumb in two places.   *1921*

The crackpot Irish quack John Long died after making a fortune 'curing' consumption. A vicious corrosive liniment was his passport to riches and he explained away the violent irritation it caused by saying it was forcing the disease from the body. Even after a patient died and Long was fined for manslaughter, crowds, mostly of women – from 'needy matrons' to 'ladies of the highest rank' – still flocked to his house in Harley Street. His career was cut short at the age of thirty-seven. He caught consumption and refused to take his own 'cure'. *1834*

The murdering Monster of Dusseldorf Peter Kurten was executed, after a ten-month spree in which he had strangled, stabbed, raped and bludgeoned eight women and children to death and attacked fourteen more. In prison, Kurten was a mild man who talked candidly to his psychiatrist, adding that as well as the rapes and murders he'd once killed a swan and drank its blood. He set off for the guillotine looking forward to what he said would be his last and greatest thrill – the sound of his own blood gurgling from his body.   *1931*

Matador Maribel made her name when she killed two bulls in the hallowed Las Ventas bullring in Madrid. The slim eighteen-year-old *senorita* took up bull fighting after trying it at a country party. 'I thought it looked easy,' she said, 'and it was.' Before that, she wanted to be a nun.   *1978*

Today's the day...

The first solo circumnavigation of the globe was completed by the amazing Joshua Slocum. An old sail boat skipper, he'd retired at the age of fifty and been given a dilapidated old sloop by another captain to occupy his time. In just thirteen months Slocum had completely rebuilt the 36ft 9in, nine ton *Spray* – and decided to head around the world. He left Newport, Rhode Island, in April 1895 with precisely $1·50 cents in his pocket. As he travelled east to Gibraltar he was accompanied, he said, by his dead wife's voice. But when he got there he decided to travel west having been warned of Mediterranean pirates. Fighting vast seas and hurricane winds for thirty hours he conquered Cape Horn, spent nine months in Australia, finally crossed the Atlantic for the third time in a single circumnavigation and arrived home 1,166 days after his journey began. He'd travelled 46,000 miles at an average 1.6mph. Astonishingly, the fifty-four-year-old sea dog had never learned to swim. *1898*

A flying accident occurred at a cricket match between Cambridge and the MCC, when a ball bowled by Jehengir Khan to T. N. Pierce struck an unfortunate sparrow crossing its path. 'It is extraordinary,' wrote *The Times*, 'that the rate of mortality of sparrows on cricket grounds is not higher.' With due reverence, the bird was stuffed and mounted by the Museum at Lord's, where you can still see him today – perched on the ball that killed him. *1936*

Sixty unhappy hunchbacks were thrown into London jails as police anxiously searched for the misshapen wretch who had attempted to shoot Queen Victoria as she drove, in her carriage, with her favourite uncle – King Leopold of the Belgians. Horrified witnesses saw the man raise his gun but fortunately it misfired, making only a loud click. Although attacked by the crowd he escaped, but was soon apprehended in the general round-up. John William Bean faced the curious charge that he did: 'Harass, vex and grieve his Sovereign', but received the surprisingly lenient sentence of eighteen months' imprisonment. Clemency was shown when it was proved that his gun was only loaded with harmless pieces of clay pipe.

1842

Ruthless ruler King Louis XI of France was born. The founder of later French dominance in Europe, he was also a music lover constantly seeking new sounds. On one occasion he ordered the Abbot of Baigne, an ingenious inventor of musical instruments, to make him a pigs' choir. The Abbot fulfilled his command by installing a herd of the beasts under a velvet tent, in front of which was a keyboard attached to a row of spikes. When the Abbot pressed the keys, the pigs got poked and squealed 'in such time as highly delighted the King'.

1423

Mathematical wizard Vito Mangiamele, son of a Sicilian shepherd, was examined by the French Academy of Sciences. The learned gentlemen were amazed at his remarkable ability for solving complex mathematical problems at lightning speed, giving them the cube root of 3,796,416, for instance, in just thirty seconds. Vito was eleven at the time.

1839

Today's the day...

Boxing's oddest decision was given in a world lightweight title fight held at Vernon, California. 'Wildcat' Al Wolgast from Michigan defended his title against the wiry Mexican Joe Rivers. After brutally slugging each other for over an hour, Wolgast belted Rivers with a punishing right blow, low to his stomach. At the same time, Rivers landed a crushing left hook to Wolgast's jaw. Both dazed fighters slumped to the canvas simultaneously with Wolgast on top. The confused referee amazed the crowd by simply raising the left arm of the man on top making Wolgast the champ, and counting the poor Mexican out. It was Rivers' unlucky day – and Round 13! *1912*

Original 'Terrible Turk', wrestler Yousouf Ishmaelo died in odd circumstances. Obsessed by the fear of his fortune being stolen, he wore his money belt at all times – in the ring and even in bed! When the ship carrying him home from America collided with another and sank, he still refused to be parted from his beloved belt and despite being a strong swimmer, was weighed down by it. Along with 560 other passengers he drowned. *1898*

The Declaration of Independence was approved by Congress without dissent, on the grounds that the members should all hang together or they'd hang separately. Originally written by the thirty-three-year-old Thomas Jefferson, the first version was thrashed out in a room next door to a stable. In the oppressively hot weather, it soon grew thick with flies which persistently bit the legs of the delegates, and agreement was reached only after thirty-six changes and the elimination of 480 words. Despite such pains taken with its composition, the original was lost and the famous parchment copy, now in the National Archives in Washington, was not signed until 2 August. Seven men actually didn't bother to sign at all and one didn't make good his omission until 1781. Of the fifty-six that did sign, twenty-five were lawyers, and all were committing high treason. *1776*

July 4

Curvaceous Italian film star Gina Lollobrigida was born. Her 36-22-35 hourglass figure has been immortalised in the French language. '*Lollobrigidienne*' is used by artists and surveyors to describe rolling landscapes and hilly terrain. When Humphrey Bogart first met her he said, 'She was the most woman I'd seen for a long time. She made Marilyn Monroe look like Shirley Temple.' *1928*

The 'Fair Play Men' met under the Tiadaghton Elm in Pennsylvania and declared their independence from English rule. They were completely unaware that a few miles away in Philadelphia another group of political dissenters were doing exactly the same! *1774*

Acerbic President Calvin Coolidge was born and it was said by Alice Roosevelt that he was 'weaned on a pickle'. The least industrious of all Presidents he claimed, 'The American public wanted a solemn ass for President and I think I'll go along with them.' He was fond of cat-naps, waking abruptly on one occasion to ask, 'Is the country still here?' Questioned by a reporter about an important meeting he replied, 'I have nothing to say – and don't quote me.' *1872*

377

Today's the day...

The world's first speed limit – 4mph in the country, 2mph in the town – was imposed by the British Government in an attempt to slow down the racier agricultural traction engines. Unfortunately, with the expression 'all road locomotives', the Act put the brake on cars as well. Henceforth all vehicles would not only have to travel at a snail's pace, but be accompanied by three people: one to drive, one to stoke the engine, and another to walk 60yds ahead with a red flag by day and a red light by night. The 'Red Flag Act' as it quickly became known, was operative for a painful thirty-one years, though nicely ridiculed by pioneer car dealer, Henry Hewetson who, noting that no particular size of flag had been decreed, sent his small son on ahead waving an inch of red ribbon, tied to a pencil! *1865*

Founder of Rhodesia Cecil Rhodes was born. Originally he went to Africa to recuperate from a chill caught while rowing – though later he claimed it was because, 'I could no longer stand their eternal cold mutton.' He became one of the richest men in the world – though always dressed like a tramp. In his first will written when he was an impoverished twenty-four-year-old, he bequeathed his non-existent fortune to a secret society dedicated to the 'ultimate recovery of the United States of America' for the British Empire. Ironically his later wealth was used to establish the Rhodes Scholarship for sending American students to study in Britain.   *1853*

The world's greatest showman Phineas T. Barnum was born. Master of the outrageous, crowds flocked to see his 'Cherry Coloured Cat' only to discover an ordinary black alley cat. They were black cherries. Another time people paid twenty-five cents to witness a horse whose head was where its tail should be and vice versa. Barnum had backed it into a stall with its tail attached to the feed trough! Such dubious techniques won and lost him two fortunes, one of which he recouped by giving lectures on 'How to Make Money'. His biblical Christian name, aptly enough, means 'Brazen Mouth'.   *1810*

Outstanding beauty Ann Hamilton married Robert Carnegie, 3rd Earl of Southesk. James Duke of York, heir to the English throne, fell for Ann and despite being chaperoned at all times, managed to pay her 'very particular attention'. Her husband contrived an incredible revenge by deliberately contracting the 'infamous disease', hoping to pass it on to his wife and in turn to the future James II. This historic claptrap only failed because by the time he caught it, the royal romance had ended.   *1664*

A shocking new fashion was revealed at a Paris show by designer Louis Reard. In cotton, printed with an up-to-the-minute newspaper design, it was modelled by exotic dancer Michelle Bernardi. Reard named his 'ultimate' creation after the 'ultimate' new weapon – a huge atomic bomb tested by the Americans four days earlier on a tiny Pacific atoll. The atoll was called Bikini.   *1946*

Today's the day...

A point of odour was raised in the House of Commons when MPs were pelted with horse manure thrown by protesters in the Strangers' Gallery. The Speaker shouted 'Order!' – though some thought he bellowed 'Ordure!' MPs ran out of the chamber since it was an all-party attack showing no ideological preference. Small deposits were scattered throughout the chamber and the house retired for twenty minutes while the mess was cleared away. The question 'Who flung dung?' was later solved when police arrested Yana Mintoff, twenty-six-year-old daughter of the Prime Minister of Malta – she was protesting about the plight of Irish Political Prisoners. Her cause was not publicised though she did at least establish what many have known for a long time – that politics can be a dirty business. *1978*

Strangest rocking chair in history was patented in America. Under the actual seat was fixed a pair of bellows attached to a flexible tube which travelled up the back of the chair and curved over the head of the occupant. When the sitter rocked he pumped fresh air over himself. It was the world's first air cooled rocking chair. *1869*

Czar Nicholas I of Russia was born. A ruthless demi-god yet full of human contradictions. When his Winter Palace caught fire in 1836 and he had only time to rescue his most precious possession, he ordered men to save his portfolio – it contained nothing but love letters from his wife. A chamberlain who incorrectly addressed the daughter of Nicholas was made to pace up and down the palace all night shouting, 'I am a brute! I am a brute!' He once ordered the famous mimic Martineff to impersonate him. Fearlessly the comedian buttoned his coat and strutted around the room in imperial style. When he stopped before the Treasurer he said, 'Sir, pay M. Martineff 1,000 silver roubles!' Nicholas was so amused, he ordered the money to be paid. *1796*

Man for all seasons Sir Thomas More, the ill-fated scholar and ex-chancellor to Henry VIII, was beheaded for high treason on Tower Hill. Just before the axe fell he removed his beard from the block saying, 'It hath never committed treason.' In accordance with the usual custom his head was stuck on London Bridge as a warning. His daughter bribed the bridge keeper to knock it down as she sailed underneath and she caught it. She kept her father's head preserved in sweet smelling spices in a lead box. When she died eleven years later her father's head was placed inside her coffin. 280 years later her body was exhumed and More's head was placed on public display in St Dunstan's Church in Canterbury.   *1535*

Alsatian rescued his owner from drowning after Michael Gibson (twenty-four) got cramp which induced asthma from which Gibson is a chronic sufferer. The twelve-year-old Kim grabbed his master by his T-shirt and dragged him to the bank which proved too steep so he swam a further seventy yards to where the bank was less sloped. Unfortunately when helpers arrived Kim blotted her copy book rescue by guarding him so well nobody could get close to assist. Eventually police calmed Kim into allowing them to take Michael to hospital where he recovered – Kim later won an RSPCA award.   *1977*

'The joker' arrested 140 American thieves in Washington DC. This was the second time ace Detective Lieutenant Robert Arscott and his hand-picked team of tough undercover cops had made a successful mass arrest. The first was after Arscott had opened a phoney warehouse fencing stolen goods operated by policemen using aliases picked from an Italian cookbook. Incredibly 140 thieves fell for the same trick again with Arscott using the cover of the GYA Trucking Company. After the arrest Arscott proved worthy of his nickname, 'The Joker', by revealing that GYA stood for GOT YA AGAIN!   *1976*

Today's the day...

The world licking record was established in London by a team of hand-picked lickers in a tongue tingling twenty-four-hour lick-in. 296,872 Sir Winston Churchill commemorative stamps were licked representing a total of 2,577sq ft of gum – just a little short of the area of a full-size doubles tennis court.   *1965*

Yankee lover Mariano Guadaloup Vallejo, an early Governor-General of California, was born. During the Civil War, he sided with the Union, and loyally spoke out in the Yankees' favour. 'I would rather be swindled by them than by anybody else; they do it so scientifically.'   *1808*

The last Beatle to join the group Ringo Starr was born, weighing in at 10lbs. When he was six, he developed peritonitis, and lapsed into a ten-week coma; recovering from that, he had a birthday party, and in the excitement, fell out of bed and ended up staying in hospital for another year. At thirteen, he was again in hospital for two years with pleurisy, and not surprisingly failed the medical for his first job as a messenger boy! Asked at the height of his fame why he wore so many rings on his fingers, he replied, ' 'Cos I can't get them all through my nose!'   *1940*

The first American saint Frances Xavier Cabrini was canonised for accomplishing 'what seemed beyond the strength of a woman'. Born in Italy, where ironically the first convent she applied to enter rejected her after she failed the medical, she later emigrated to the States where she founded the Missionary Sisters of the Sacred Heart of Jesus. The eccentric Italian writer D'Annunzio refused to talk to her for fear of damaging his genius, though Pope Leo XIII had no such qualms. He was so fond of her he shocked conservative Catholics by enthusiastically hugging her. She travelled extensively and, to protect the young nuns who accompanied her, nearly always first class.   *1946*

Napoleon subdued Europe with the signing of the Peace of Tilsit, after some of the bloodiest battles the continent had ever seen. With the Prussians humiliated, he compromised with Alexander I of Russia, and so that neither should lose face, signed the treaty, exactly halfway between their opposing armies – on a raft moored in the middle of the River Memel.

1807

Knockout fighter Freddie Welsh KO'd American Willie Ritchie in the twentieth round to take the lightweight championship of the world. Victory was particularly sweet, since he had to contribute $500 of borrowed money to make up the $20,000 guarantee that Ritchie demanded, before he'd step into the ring with the wizard Welshman. In his seventeen-year career, Welsh fought 166 bouts and lost only three.

1941

Hunted Queen Mary Tudor sought refuge from the followers of usurper Lady Jane Grey in Sawston Hall, Cambridgeshire. Forced to flee disguised as a milkmaid, her stay was cut short and the house burnt down. As Queen she rewarded the owners, the Huddlestons, by rebuilding it. It's odd that her phantom is said to spend the night there, since she never did.

1553

Today's the day...

Unpredictable Australian composer Percy Grainger was born.
A child prodigy, he was billed by some as one of the twentieth
century's greatest pianists, though in fact he claimed to hate the
piano – except at rehearsals when he would settle down underneath it
for a nap. Sporting one of the earliest Afro haircuts he was, to say the
least, unconventional in appearance. He burnt all his ordinary suits,
insisting they were unhygienic, and had new ones made of towelling
so he could regularly wash them. When he married Ella Strom in 1928,
he wouldn't buy an engagement ring because it represented
subjugation. The ceremony was held in the Hollywood Bowl and the
22,000 guests all paid admission. In typical style, the honeymoon was
spent exploring the uncharted wastes of the Arizona Plateau. In music,
as in life, Grainger had his little idiosyncrasies. He would often stop
in the middle of a concert to tell jokes, though apparently he was
serious when he wrote *The Warriors* for three conductors – one on the
platform, one half on and another hidden from the audience. Refusing
to use Italian terminology, he would give musicians instructions like
'bumping bumpingly', 'hold till blown', 'in walking measure' and 'die
right here'. In one composition he required the organist to fasten down
two keys with a pair of pencils, and in another that he should play
with his nose!   *1882*

The one and only American King was crowned at Lake Michigan.
Leading Mormon James Jesse Strang had lost the battle with Brigham
Young to command the sect after the murder of Joseph Smith in 1844.
He'd attempted to prove his divine appointment by producing two
gold tablets conveniently covered in indecipherable writing – but it
was to no avail. Disgruntled, he left with a band of faithful followers
and moved to the northern shores of Lake Michigan and Beaver
Island, where together they established 'Zion'. There he was crowned
James I, King of Zion, wearing an actor's cloak and a base metal
crown adorned with glass stars. At first his rule was successful,

introducing pensions and welfare schemes, but his majesty ran into trouble when he began pirating 'enemy' boats. Arrested and tried, he defended himself on the grounds of 'being persecuted for religion's sake' and a sympathetic frontier jury acquitted him. Things really came to a head, however, when he ordered all his female followers to wear bloomers. This was too much for the god-fearing band. They conspired to rid themselves of their despotic ruler and with almost indecent haste, they assassinated him.   *1850*

Dapper English politician Joseph Chamberlain was born. At thirty-eight he was able to retire and devote himself almost entirely to politics, but as an orator he was not to everyone's taste. At a particular civic luncheon, the mayor turned to him as coffee was being served and asked, 'Shall we let them enjoy themselves a little longer, or had we better have your speech now?' Much caricatured, he was noted for his monocle and the daily orchid buttonhole he grew himself. Once in Paris, he saw an extremely rare orchid, bought it, and trampled it underfoot. He grew the same species at home and wanted no one else in Europe to have one. As well as his greenhouse, he ran a model dairy farm, and rather obscurely had an extensive collection of black and white furniture.   *1836*

Violent-tempered Don Carlos, son of Philip II of Spain, was born. Severe stammering fits and incapacitating fevers served to increase his rages, and one poor cobbler who made a pair of boots too small for him, was forced to stew and eat them. With his huge head and puny body he presented a grotesque figure as he ran through the streets, grabbing and kissing young girls. He then had the effrontery to insult them for allowing him such favours. His father turned a blind eye to these aberrations, until he discovered that Carlos was hatching a plot to kill him. Philip promptly got his own back – he married his son's fiancée and imprisoned Carlos for life.   *1545*

Today's the day...

Nuns were accused of cruelty to chickens after police broke up a thirty-man sit-in by the Animal Liberation Front at a battery hen unit in Northamptonshire. The unit is run by the sisters of the Order of the Congregation of the Passion of Jesus, and when the demonstrators had dispersed, a delegation was allowed to protest to the Mother Superior about the treatment of her hens. 'Our 10,000 chickens are quite happy,' she said. 'They sit in their cages and sing all day long.'   *1978*

Queen of the romantic novel and health faddist Barbara Cartland was born. Having written over 250 books and sold 100 million copies, she has become the most widely read author of her time. She ascribes much of her astonishing energy to a carefully designed diet supplemented by ninety vitamin pills a day. One major manufacturer announced plans to market one of her own recipes – a virility pill called Zest designed to make both sexes 'warm, generous and loving'. Just like most of her heroines who almost without exception are all virgins and whom she creates at the astonishing rate of 7,000 dictated words at a sitting.   *1901*

Mad English Dr Elliot attempted a double murder in a London street. He fired a brace of pistols at a courting couple at point blank range. Evidently no marksman, he missed and neither was hurt, though the lady's dress was badly singed. In court, Elliot's lawyer defended him on a technicality, saying that since no bullets were found, no one had proved the guns were loaded. Incredibly, Elliot got away with it.   *1787*

Smiling sailor Edward Heath, ex-Prime Minister of England, was born. His keenness for yachting has been responsible for many a jest. An official-looking poster stuck on the side of his craft *Morning Cloud* read, 'Warning by HM Government, Socialism can damage your wealth.' Conversely, when Heath was in Government, Labour Party publicity coined the copy line, 'Come in *Morning Cloud*, your time is up.' His other well known hobby is music, and when offered chop sticks in a Chinese restaurant, he's said to have replied, 'Good Heavens no! I only use those things for conducting.' Apparently when he was at Oxford, he was torn between a career in music or in politics. His tutor advised him that if he was prepared to be as unpleasant as most famous conductors, then that should be his career. With a flourish, the Tory organist explained his decision. 'I didn't want anything to do with unpleasantness, so I went into politics.'   *1916*

The first doughnut cutter was patented by American John F. Blondel. According to which story you believe, he was either a schoolboy bored with the stodgy fillings of Mother's cakes, or a sea captain who designed them to slip over the handles of the ship's wheel, so he could enjoy a snack while steering.   *1872*

Author of strange adventure stories Sir H. Rider Haggard awoke in the night making weird and horrible noises. He'd dreamed that his daughter's black retriever, Bob, was lying dead by some water. His hackles must have risen when three days later Bob was found floating by a weir.   *1904*

US President Zachary Taylor died. Five days earlier he'd been laid low with sunstroke after sitting in the open in the blazing heat of the Independence Day celebrations. The foolhardy man had hastened his own death trying to cool off by guzzling vast quantities of cherries and iced milk. The shock killed him.   *1850*

Philistinic Governor Berkely of Virginia died. Seven years earlier, he'd roughly outlined his philosophy on education: 'I thank God there are no free schools, nor printing, for learning has brought disobedience and heresy into the world, and printing has divulged them.'   *1677*

Today's the day...

Conqueror of the Moor, Rodrigo Diaz de Bivar, El Cid, died according to the legend having devoted his life to driving the tide of Arab invasion from Spain. In the myth, his death wasn't the end of his military career, since his body was supposed to have been embalmed and placed on his horse to spur his troops on in his last victorious battle. In fact, de Bivar was little more than an extra-successful adventurer on the make, who fought as a mercenary not only against the Moors, but with them – taking Valencia in league with the Arab King of Saragossa in a fearful bloodbath. It's curious that to the Spaniards he's known by the Arab name '*Cid*' meaning 'leader', while to the Arabs he's '*Campeador*' – the Spanish word for 'challenger'.

1099

Whistler's Mother gave birth to bouncing baby artist, James McNeill Whistler, whose celebrated portrait of her was actually called *Arrangement in Grey and Black Number One*. Though he told everyone he was born in St Petersburg, he was actually born in Lowell, Massachusetts and it was seven years earlier than he liked to tell.

Pugnacious and dandiacal, he arrived in London fresh from four years in Paris, quickly made friends and just as quickly lost them again. He hated criticism, was incredibly vain and when asked if he believed in hereditary genius, replied, 'I can't tell you; heaven has granted me no offspring.' His home was a riot of colour with the walls yellow, white and blue, and he invited guests round for rather startling breakfasts on Sunday mornings. They were liable to be served something perfectly ordinary such as an egg on toast, but accompanying it would be a bottle of vintage red wine, pink or blue butter and a pastel coloured rice pudding – all to be eaten at the kitchen table with the goldfish bowl in the middle!   *1834*

Asthmatic author Marcel Proust was born. Because of his complaint, he became a reclusive night-owl, sleeping from 8am to 3pm, writing in bed, and often dining alone at the Ritz at four in the morning. In total, he spent six-and-a-half days a week in bed, which was perhaps understandable, since just looking at a flowering chestnut tree through a window could bring on an attack. He had his room lined with cork, and before venturing out would don three overcoats, numerous mufflers, chest padding and collars lined with cottonwool. Attending his brother's wedding thus attired, he was too bulky for the pew and had to spend the entire service standing in the aisle!   *1871*

The royal engagement of Princess Elizabeth and Philip Mountbatten was announced. The £11-a-week naval lieutenant proposed 'beside some well-loved loch, the white clouds sailing overhead and the curlew crying'. The lovers first met in Elizabeth's nursery, where she was playing with a clockwork train!   *1947*

The world's heaviest man died. Robert Earl Hughes from Monticello, Illinois weighed nearly half a ton and his coffin, a converted piano-case, had to be lowered into the grave by crane.   *1958*

Today's the day...

The ghost-ship of doom the *Flying Dutchman* was sighted at 4am, fifty miles off the Cape of Good Hope, by the crew of HMS *Inconstant*. A strange red light appeared and the brig emerged glowing out of the mist in full sail. Since the sixteenth century, this ghostly merchantman had frequently been seen in these dangerous waters, and many a vessel had disappeared or foundered while following her as if impelled by an unknown force. But this particular occasion was unique. For the phantom was seen by thirteen people including a sixteen-year-old naval cadet who became George V, and his brother, the Duke of Clarence. As if giving a command performance, the Dutchman's legend was enacted again. Within hours of the sighting, the man who had spotted the ship fell to his death from the crow's-nest, and when the squadron sailed into port, its commander took ill and died. *1881*

World-famous maestro George Gershwin died. Some months earlier he had lost consciousness while playing with the Los Angeles Philharmonic but had simply skipped a few bars and continued. During another blackout, he'd had the curious sensation of smelling burning rubber. Finally daily headaches and dizzy spells made him agree to a series of tests, but he refused to submit to a spinal tap and so the results were inconclusive. On the morning of 9 July, he could still play the piano but by the evening had fallen into a coma. Neurosurgeons operated to remove a brain tumour but he died without regaining consciousness. *1937*

Early-bird President John Quincy Adams was born in Braintree, Massachusetts. Son of John, the second President, he was a short, fat and eccentric man. He wore the same hat for ten years, was a keen Bible-reader and connoisseur of wine, and constantly had red, rheumy eyes. Every morning at 5am, he'd take a dip in the Potomac River, and one day was surprised to find a young lady journalist sitting on his clothes on the bank. Determined reporter Anne Royall refused to budge until 'Old Man Eloquent' gave her an interview. Modest to a fault, the President agreed.

1767

Enigmatic baldie Yul Brynner was born. The birth is thought to have taken place on an island off the coast of Siberia but he refuses to confirm or deny it, saying 'just call me a nice clean-cut Mongolian boy'. He was raised in Paris, at any rate, and still speaks French when talking about fashions or art, but always uses English for business. His first taste of showbusiness was as a trapeze artist – a sad clown who made awful mistakes but saved himself at the last moment. On one occasion he didn't, fell onto a set of parallel bars and spent seven months in a plaster cast.

1915

A surprising pachydermous mongrel was born at Chester Zoo. Startled keepers were not even aware that the mother, a twenty-one-year-old Indian elephant called Sheba, was pregnant until she was on the point of giving birth. The baby weighed 160lbs and the most staggering thing about it was that its father turned out to be Jumbolina, a seventeen-year-old African elephant. Such a crossbreed had never been known to occur before and experts eagerly looked forward to its maturity to see if this mule-among-elephants might prove a fertile base for breeding stock. Sadly the baby died in his sleep at only ten days old.

1978

Shakespearean censor Thomas Bowdler was born. Though he loved the Bard's works, he considered certain parts of the masterworks to be vulgar and 'unfit to be read by a gentleman in the company of ladies'. His solution was to cut lumps out wholesale – hence the verb 'to bowdlerise'. What's perhaps not so well known is that it was his prudish sister Henrietta who actually did most of the cutting and Dr Bowdler put a lot of it back.

1754

Today's the day...

Great Wagnerian opera singer Kirsten Flagstad born. Although familiar with Wagner's operas from an early age, her second husband had to force her to go and see *Tristan und Isolde* in Vienna. During the opera she almost dozed off – yet Isolde was later to become her most famous role. Before her performances she used to try and relax – by having cigar smoke blown in her face.

1895

Automobile fanatic Charles Rolls was killed. The moneyed co-founder of Rolls-Royce, he was also the first pilot to make a non-stop double crossing from England to France. Taking part in a quick starting and landing competition, his French-built plane broke up in the air earning him another first – the first British aeroplane pilot to lose his life flying.

1910

Wily Roman Emperor Julius Caesar was born. Not by Caesarian operation as is often thought – though his name does, in fact, come from the Latin 'to cut'. Always convinced he'd be powerful, he was captured as a youth by pirates. When he told them that on his release he'd track them down, then torture and crucify them, they laughed.

But once free, he did just that! He liked to see his likeness about the place and as a master of the Roman mint, he got round the law forbidding citizens to stamp their own names on coins. He ordered them to be printed with an elephant, which in the Cunic language signifies 'Caesar'. Having put up his statue inscribed *To The Unconquerable God*, he made a bid for posterity and ordered a month to be named after him – July. As you'd expect he always wanted to look his best – he was fastidiously clean and would shave as close as possible, even plucking out hairs by the roots. Most of all he was grateful for his laurel wreath, since it helped to hide his baldness.

100 BC

A fruity thundercloud hovered over Shreveport, Louisiana. When it broke people ran for cover as they were pelted not by rain, but by green peaches! The weathermen's explanation was that a violent updraft must have transported the fruit across the land. They weren't saying where from.

1961

Sexy Mormon leader Joseph Smith announced that he'd had a divine revelation – to practise polygamy! Followers were stunned as he told them that an angel with a drawn sword had actually threatened to kill him if he didn't. His first wife wasn't impressed, she kicked him out of the house. He didn't worry too much, however, as he already had twenty-five other wives – and eventually made it a grand total of forty-nine.

1843

Sixth-time lucky Henry VIII married again. This time to Catherine Parr, the last of the many. Terrified when he first turned his attention to her she declared, 'It is better to be his mistress than his wife.' After his persistent wooing she finally succumbed and married the lusty King – outliving him and marrying again after his death.

1543

Today's the day...

Man conquered the Matterhorn and the first one up was the Englishman Edward Whymper. Ecstatic because he'd beaten the Italians who'd set out earlier, he wrote in his diary, 'Hurrah! Not a footstep could be seen.' Since then although over ninety have perished in the attempt, at least 100,000 people have followed in his footsteps, including a seventy-six-year-old man and an eleven-year-old girl. In 1948, four foolhardy mountain men froze to death. They'd been trying to get a cow to the top and she, poor beast, froze too.   *1865*

Queen Victoria moved into Buckingham Palace, the first monarch to do so. Of fifty new lavatories installed for her convenience, few worked, and one actually deposited its contents outside her dressing room window. The grand entrance turned out to be too small for the State Coach and had to be moved to Park Lane where it now stands as the Marble Arch. Poor Edward VII had to grow up in Buck House during his mother's forty years' mourning. He called it 'the sepulchre' and it's never been very popular since. George V tried to sell it to a hotel chain; George VI named it 'the ice-box', and Queen Elizabeth described it as 'the house where you need a bicycle'. At banquets, place settings are measured precisely with a ruler, and to make sure the waiters don't get in a jam, there's a set of traffic lights behind the throne.   *1837*

The Third International Spittin', Belchin' and Cussin'
Triathlon in Central City, Colorado, was staggered by an amazing expectoration. Unassisted by wind, competitor Harold Fielding spat a record 34ft ¼in. Dry-mouthed spectators gasped in admiration.   *1973*

Hot-tempered Confederate General Nathan Forrest was born. He enlisted as a private, but was appointed Lieutenant Colonel after raising a battalion of mounted soldiers at his own expense. Sensational cavalry raiding established his reputation, and even as a general he

July 13

always fought alongside his men. Perhaps not surprisingly, he had
twenty-nine horses shot from under him, and when wounded at the
Battle of Tupelo, he insisted on leading a cavalry charge, though he
had to do so in a buggy. An eloquent speaker, he never quite mastered
the art of spelling and in reply to one soldier's third request for leave
he wrote, 'I tole you Twist, godammit know!'   *1821*

Fire destroyed P. T. Barnum's fabulous American Museum in
New York. Though his money survived in a metal safe, he was only
insured for ten per cent of the half a million dollars' worth of damage.
Happily though, all his famous freaks escaped, with heroic fireman
John Denham actually carrying the 400lb Fat Lady to safety on his
own. Perhaps the most spectacular rescue, however, was that of the
Tallest Woman, Anna Swann, said to stand at 7ft 11in. She was
trapped on the third floor unconscious, and fearing the stairs wouldn't
stand her weight her friend, the Human Skeleton, stayed with her.
Eventually the heat drove him from her side, and in the nick of time
she was hauled out by crane and lowered to the ground amidst
enthusiastic applause. As well as the freaks, many wild animals
escaped, causing widespread panic. One exceptionally shrewd
orang-utan climbed a waterpipe and nipped into a nearby newspaper
office, 'doubtless thinking he might fill some vacancy in the editorial
corps of the paper'.   *1865*

Scabious French Revolutionary leader Jean Paul Marat was
murdered. Suffering from a terrible skin disease which caused
unbearable itching, he used to sit in his bath for hours to write
speeches. On this fateful day, he heard a pretty voice at the door, and
instructed the guards to let his visitor in – so he could see the face
behind it. Unfortunately for Marat, it was Charlotte Corday clutching
a sharpened table knife. She stabbed him with a vengeance, and he
died where he sat.   *1793*

395

Today's the day...

Lucky Scottish engraver Sir Robert Strange was born. Fleeing from the blood-soaked moor after the Battle of Culloden, he ran to the home of his sweetheart, Isabella Lumisden, hotly pursued by English troops. When the soldiers arrived they were puzzled to find Miss Lumisden alone in the house, standing quietly humming a rebel tune. When they'd left in some confusion, Sir Robert came out of hiding – from beneath Isabella's hooped skirt. They later married and Robert was appointed official engraver. He was then knighted, ironically by the son of his old enemy, the Hanoverian King of England. *1721*

Accident prone President Gerald Ford was born in Omaha, Nebraska. After an emergency appendix operation, at the age of five, it was discovered he merely had tummy ache and similar disasters have dogged him ever since. His first car ended up in flames after he covered the steaming engine with blankets to keep it warm! During a TV debate with Jimmy Carter, he amazed the American public by reassuring them, 'There is no Soviet domination of Eastern Europe', and climaxed his public blunderings by toasting Anwar Sadat of Egypt with the greeting 'The President of Israel'! *1913*

The Fall of the Bastille in Paris heralded the start of the French Revolution. 8,000 rampaging citizens stormed the notorious prison to free the inmates. To their immense surprise, there were only seven prisoners inside – a motley bunch of four forgers, an Irish Lord and two lunatics. In his diary for the day, King Louis XVI innocently wrote 'Nothing'. *1789*

Folk singer and poet of the people Woody Guthrie was born in Okemah, Oklahoma. He composed nearly 1,000 songs and it was said that 'when you hear them, you hear America singing'. He was haunted by music and plagued by fire. He saw three of his homes burnt to the ground and always suspected his mother or his sister Clara, of starting them. Clara died as a result of burns sustained in the last of the fires, and later his own daughter, Cathy, died in the same way. During World War II, Guthrie joined the Merchant Marine Service and every time his ship had survived yet another torpedo attack, the whole crew would gather around him on deck to sing his songs. He would accompany them, of course, on his trusty guitar. It was inscribed with the words, 'This machine kills Fascists.' *1925*

The 'typical' Englishman actor Terry Thomas was born. Actually his name is back to front. His real surname is Hoare-Stevens and he was christened Thomas Terry. *1911*

Youthful outlaw Billy the Kid was shot by Sherriff Pat Garrett. Only twenty-one at his death, he was said to have killed a man for every year of his life – though in fact he only killed four, and some of those in self-defence. Another great misconception about him concerns his name. Western tradition would have us believe that his real name was William H. Bonney. It wasn't – he changed it to protect his family. Perhaps he should have been called 'Harry the Kid', since his real name was Henry McCarty. *1881*

Today's the day...

Holy weather forecaster St Swithin is remembered in churches and meteorological offices everywhere. On this day, 108 years after he had died incumbent as Archbishop of Winchester, a group of devoted monks decided to move his body from the 'vile and unworthy grave' he'd piously chosen on his death-bed. As the ceremony was about to begin, a sudden cloudburst drenched the funeral party, and it rained for nearly seven weeks thereafter. The monks took this as a heavenly warning not to contradict the Saint's last wish, so they abandoned the idea. He never got his grander tomb, and ever since the weather today is said to presage the weather for the next forty days. If it rains, don't worry – according to the old saying, it's only St Swithin christening the apples.   *971*

The first solo round-the-world flight took off from New York with determined aviator Wiley Post in control. The journey of over 15,000 miles took 7 days, 18 hrs, 49½ mins. It also made him the first man to fly round the world twice. He'd previously done it in the same plane, the Lockheed Vega *Winnie Maw*, but on that occasion he was accompanied by a co-pilot. Perhaps it was just as well, since the intrepid Wiley only had one eye.   *1933*

The first close-up photographs of another planet were received from *US Mariner IV*. The planet in question was Mars and it took over eight hours for the signals to be compiled in Johannesburg, South Africa. They had to get them right – after all, they'd travelled 135 million miles.   *1965*

The world's longest living man was born. A French Canadian boot-maker, he was called Pierre Joubert, and was to live for 113 years, 124 days – a proven record which, despite less well-attested claims, still remains unchallenged.   *1701*

July 15

The world's tallest man died aged only twenty-two. Robert Pershing Wadlow of Manistree, Michigan, contracted cellulitis of the feet which was aggravated by his poorly fitting brace. His last recorded height was a gigantic 8ft 11·1in.   *1940*

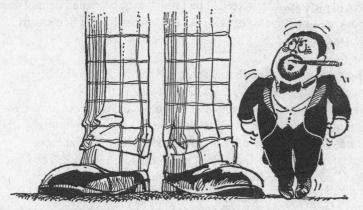

The world's shortest man died. He was the famous General Tom Thumb, a tiny American showman whose real name was Charles Sherwood Stratton. He stood only 30½in high at the age of eighteen, and kept growing all his life. When apoplexy finally carried him off, he was forty-five and stood a towering 40in small.   *1883*

Butch Cassidy surrendered after a strange and short parole. The son of a strict Mormon family, Robert Leroy Parker as he was really called, had been tried for cattle-rustling and sentenced to two years' imprisonment. The night before he was due to start his sentence, he appealed to a friendly warder to let him free for one night, promising faithfully to return in the morning. The trusting soul let him go, and off he went. True to his word, he came back this morning, but where he spent the night and who he'd seen is still a mystery to this day.   *1894*

Today's the day...

A one-legged pauper in a tantrum threw his wooden leg at the Poor Committee who'd provided him with it in the first place when his own false limb had broken. Peg-leg Taylor insisted the leg was too short, but the Committee had said if he wanted another new one, he'd have to pay a shilling a week. The Lord Mayor overruled them. For a poor man like Peg-Leg he said, 'A new wooden leg might incite to greater industry.'   *1828*

The first atomic bomb was detonated at Alamogordo in the arid desert of New Mexico. In the midst of a violent thunderstorm, the device was hoisted to the top of a steel tower and the tense forty-five-minute countdown began. When it came, the explosion lit up the whole countryside sending a 'huge multi-coloured surging cloud' over 40,000ft into the sky, destroying the real clouds in its path. The blast which followed knocked some of the observers flat and caused the launching tower to vaporise completely. 235 miles away the sun appeared to rise and fall with a roar of thunder. Inhabitants were alarmed, but the US army tried to pass it off. They said an ammunition store had exploded.   *1945*

Chairman Mao took the plunge in the Yangtse River to prove he was perfectly healthy. In fact, if the Chinese communiqué was correct, the seventy-two-year-old supremo was Superman. He was said to have swum nine miles in sixty-five minutes – which breaks every known amateur record.   *1966*

Record damages for breach of contract were awarded to the Bank of Portugal against Waterlow's, the London printers who printed their bank notes. Much to his chagrin, Sir William Waterlow had been taken in by the brilliant master-forger Artur Alves Reis, who'd sent an official-looking batch of documents to London, authorising Waterlow's to print 580,000 five-hundred escudo notes for Portuguese Angola.

Waterlow's went ahead and printed, and back in Portugal, Reis built up a vast business empire based on his counterfeit fortune. When he was finally caught and sentenced to sixteen years in jail, the suit was brought against the hapless printers. Counsel for the firm claimed that damages should only be awarded for the costs involved in printing the notes. After all, no one else had suffered; Reis' money had been accepted at its face value and in fact, technically, the notes weren't even counterfeit as they'd been printed and produced in exactly the same way as legal tender. Despite this convincing legal and financial conundrum, Waterlow's lost – and it cost them £610,932. *1930*

The last Tsar Nicholas II was murdered along with his entire family in a filthy cellar in a bleak house in Ekaterinburg, at the foot of the Urals. The fabulously wealthy Imperial family had been held prisoner for months, condemned to a diet of black bread and broth, allowed not a moment's privacy and unable even to look out of the window, which had been painted over. Shortly after midnight, the Tsar and Tsarina, their four daughters and sickly young son were herded down to the dank vault, shot, bayoneted and finally clubbed to death. The bodies were partially burnt, dumped down a mine shaft, then doused with acid. Though this is the generally accepted version, rumours have always been rife that all or some of them survived. Perhaps after all, Nicholas II finally achieved his ambition. 'Thank God,' he said when he signed his abdication, 'I can now do what I have always wanted to do. I can go to my home in the Crimea and raise flowers.' *1918*

Relaxed Red Indian athlete James Thorpe was presented with two well-deserved gold medals. It was said that this great all-rounder had once appeared as his high school's entire athletics team, and now he'd taken the Stockholm Olympics by storm, becoming the only man to win both the Pentathlon and the Decathlon. When King Gustav made the presentation, Thorpe greeted him with a laconic 'Hi, King'. *1912*

Today's the day...

Russia and America shook hands in space after the historic *Apollo-Soyuz* docking. Short of sleep and struggling with language problems, the crews of the spacecraft had to cope with a TV transmission as well as the manoeuvre itself. In the end the *Soyuz* camera broke down and there were no pictures of *Apollo* docking at all. Once locked together, smells of burning emanated from the *Apollo* Module, and the Russians couldn't find a replacement TV cable. Exasperated, Commander Leonov cut calls from Moscow short and at the end of a three hour struggle finally managed to wriggle through the hatch to dine with his US counterparts. As they gulped down their borsch and turkey, exchanging flags, plaques and medals, the convivial picture was flashed back to earth. There was one final problem – the camera was upside-down!   *1975*

'*L'ange de l'assassination*' Charlotte Corday was executed just four days after she'd murdered Marat. At her trial, her ice-cool courage had alarmed her accusers. Arriving at the scaffold, executioner Sanson tried to shield her view of the guillotine but she peered round him saying, 'I have the right to be curious, I've never seen one before.' Mounting the steps with great composure, she threw herself on the plank and Sanson so admired her courage he didn't pause to strap her down but immediately let fly the blade. His assistant, Le Gros was not so noble: he grabbed the severed head, brandished it in front of the mob and slapped its cheeks. Even the bloodthirsty Parisians were outraged. Sanson dismissed Le Gros on the spot and it was said that the face of the dead Charlotte blushed with anger at the insult.   *1793*

'Yankee Doodle Dandy' James Cagney was born. Too poor for a lengthy education, he worked in a store, a pool-room and a restaurant, before deciding he'd make more money in vaudeville. Just a year after signing his contract with Warner Brothers, he was cast as second lead in *Public Enemy* – but took over the starring role after three days' shooting. His hoarse-voiced, wheedling gangster is probably the most mimicked of all Hollywood roles, but in fact he didn't say many of the things that are attributed to him and the actual words of the all-time Cagney quote are, 'You dirty double-crossing rat!' The really surprising thing, however, is that this greatest of hoodlums got his first job in the show *Every Sailor* – as a chorus girl.   *1899*

The Royal Family announced their change of name. With World War I at its height, King George V was urged to relinquish the Germanic royal nomenclature 'Saxe-Coburg-Gotha', brought to Britain by Queen Victoria's husband Albert. He adopted instead the resoundingly English 'Windsor'.   *1917*

A mass breakout at a maximum security prison near Lisbon left guards feeling piqued. They had, they protested, noticed certain irregularities and they fully intended to investigate the disappearance of 200 knives and quantities of electric cable; the lack of prisoners at roll-call and the fall-off in attendance at film shows – they'd just 'never got around to it'. In the meantime 124 prisoners escaped and the guards only found out when one of the prisoners told them.   *1978*

Today's the day...

A new golf ball was patented by an English addict called Pedrick. The proposed ball was to be fitted with hinged flaps designed to fly out when the ball started to spin – so steadying its flight. 'If this can be achieved,' argued Mr Pedrick, 'considerable benefit will have been added to the general happiness of mankind.' *1967*

Spain's noblest fighting bull was mercilessly butchered by hungry fascist soldiers on the night of the outbreak of Civil War. He was 'Civilon', who by his amazing gentleness had become a national celebrity, allowing children to feed and pet him. Shortly before his death, he'd been brought to Barcelona to fight his first 'corrida', and a massive crowd had flocked to the stadium to see if this gentlemanly taurean would actually do battle. He did – and frightened the life out of two picadors in the process. Spectators were so impressed with his courage that they called for the *indulto* – the pardon – for him, and it was immediately granted. Then his 'handler', Alvarez, was dared to enter the ring and when he did so, nervously clutching a handful of hay, Civilon charged at him and, before an astonished crowd, nuzzled him and docilely followed him out of the arena. *1936*

404

Jane Austen contributed to medical knowledge by her death at the age of forty-one. She'd written that her skin had gone 'black and white and every wrong colour', and her doctors were unable to diagnose her illness. Her descriptions of it were so painstaking, however, that medical authorities now positively assert that she died of Addison's Disease – a fact which makes her not only the first person known to have died from it, but the first ever to have accurately recorded a case history. Asked in her last moments if she wanted anything, she replied, 'Nothing but death,' and her wish was mercifully granted.   *1817*

'The Grand Old Man of Cricket' W. G. Grace was born in Gloucestershire and started playing the first-class game at the age of fifteen, combining his sport with his studies for a medical degree. In his thirty-seven-year playing career, this bearded and intimidating giant of a man hit 54,896 runs, 126 centuries and on ten separate occasions scored over 200 runs. He was not only a batsman, however, but a great bowler and all-round fielder, taking a grand total of 2,876 wickets. In 1879, he decided to devote more time to surgery and made a speech of partial farewell. 'I have bowled many a maiden over in my time,' he said, 'but now to make up for that, I hope to set many a one on her legs again!'   *1848*

The satirical giant William Makepeace Thackeray was born in Calcutta. He squandered away a substantial fortune and survived hand-to-mouth writing for numerous publications under pseudonyms like 'Yellowplush' and 'Michael Angelo Titmarsh'. *Vanity Fair* brought him fame and fortune and he became something of a literary patriarch. 6ft 3in and weighing between fifteen and eighteen stone, he was said to look like 'a colossol infant'. He had 'a little dab of a nose', which was broken once in a fight at school and once more when he fell off a donkey. His loving aunt was always worried about his huge head, but the doctor told her not to trouble herself because 'the big head has a lot in it'.   *1811*

Today's the day...

The most unfortunate coronation in British history occurred when the tubby Prince Regent became George IV in a sorry ceremony in Westminster Abbey. Prinney so despised his Queen, Caroline of Brunswick, that he not only didn't invite her, but had the doors barred when she tried to get in. The King's fabulous and costly robes proved too much for him on what was an intolerably hot day, so he had to be supported by eight sons of peers, and was only stopped from fainting at the altar by a swift application of smelling salts. At the banquet afterwards, the Earl Marshal biffed Lord Gwydor with his staff of office; the King had so over-indulged he had to be bled, and the one and only coronation medal was raffled for a dinner. *1821*

The world's first lonely hearts ad appeared in an English publication. It said: 'A gentleman about thirty years of age that has a very good estate would willingly match himself to some young gentlewoman that has a fortune of £3,000 or thereabouts.' The ad appeared in the aptly titled *Collection for the Improvement of Husbandry and Trade*. It wasn't followed by any similar ad from a woman for over thirty years, and in 1727 when a Miss Morrison of Manchester was bold enough to enter the fray, the Lord Mayor had her placed firmly in the local lunatic asylum. *1695*

The much-married singer Ethel Merman was born. Her fourth attempt at wedlock was particularly unsuccessful and in her autobiography there is a chapter covering the event, which is entitled 'Marriage to Ernest Borgnine'. Below the title is a blank page – and when asked to explain, Miss Merman said, 'I only speak of events which are important to me!' *1909*

Frank Sinatra married Mia Farrow, the then twenty-one-year-old star of *Peyton Place*. She was thirty years Sinatra's junior and one year younger than his son. Among the many barbed comments that followed, Sinatra Wife No. 2 Ava Gardner, said, 'I always knew Frank would end up sleeping with a boy', and the bride's mother added, 'At his age, he should marry me.'   *1966*

Washington was invaded by UFOs at around 10 pm. For some hours, five strange blue and white lights danced in the sky around the White House and surrounding countryside. They came back exactly a week later in great strength, and between six and twelve of them ran rings around an F.94 jet intercepter sent up to investigate them.   *1952*

The first Wimbledon final was played. The total of twenty-two players had to pay a one guinea entrance fee, provide their own racquets and wear 'suitable shoes without heels'. Fifteen dozen of the new flannel-covered balls had been purchased and a neighbour of the All England Croquet and Tennis Club had provided the seating in return for four guineas and the loan of a lawn mower! A racquets player and rank outsider Spencer Gore took the title, though he considered the rules 'terribly confusing' and didn't really think his original close-to-the-net volleying style had any future in the game. The final had been scheduled to take place a week earlier but the players and the 200-odd spectators agreed it would have to wait while they all went off to watch the obviously more important Harrow *v* Eton cricket match.   *1877*

Nasty but lovable tennis player Ilie Nastase was born in Bucharest. He's won every major title but Wimbledon and can lay claim to being the most controversial star who ever stalked a court. He's a unique stylist – unpredictable, fast and cunning, and it's been said by many authorities that were it not for his mercurial temperament, he would have been the greatest player in the world. The terror of linesmen everywhere, he's been known to appear at the nets wearing everything from a false moustache to a pyjama top.   *1946*

Today's the day...

'Operation Valkyrie' nearly killed Hitler, in what was the third
try of the ninth attempt on his life. With the backing of numerous
non-Nazi generals, the one-armed, one-eyed assassin Colonel Von
Stauffenberg, Chief of Staff of the Reserve Army, arrived at the
'Wolf's Lair' – the Fuhrer's heavily fortified forest retreat in
Rastenburg, East Prussia. In his brief-case was a hunk of plastic
explosive captured from the British and fitted with a ten-minute fuse.
In the conference room, Von Stauffenberg placed the brief-case a little
over 6ft away from Hitler and excused himself to take a phone call.
The 'bomb' exploded, but thanks to an unlucky accident, the meeting
had been moved from a concrete bunker to a wooden building, and the
blast thus uncontained was not lethal enough. It killed one person,
injured several and left the Fuhrer relatively unharmed. It had singed
his hair, hurt his eardrums and bruised his back, but instead of killing
him, it had only blown off his trousers.   *1944*

The original Vamp Theda Bara was born. She stunned audiences in
her 1915 *début* movie *A Fool There Was*, which was inspired by
Kipling's poem 'The Vampire' – hence the expression. She was not
only the first film *femme fatale* and sex-symbol, but the first female
product of the publicity machine. Famed for her expression 'Kiss me
my fool', she was called 'the reddest rose in hell', 'the Devil's
handmaiden' and her heart was 'a charnel house of men's dead hopes
and withered ambitions'. She 'caused fifty children and 150 wives to
beg her to give back their daddies and their husbands', and was 'the
vengeance of her sex upon its exploiters'. Her name was an anagram
of death and she played just about every man-killing heroine from
Cleopatra to Mata Hari. The incredible myth, however, was no more
than that. She was a quiet girl, whose wickedest act was to falsify her
age by 5yrs on the young side, and who lived with her parents before a
lifelong happy marriage. 'The Vamp' was only Theodosia Burr
Goodman, 'a nice little Jewish kid from the Mid-West'.   *1885*

The Declaration of Independence was slandered by the American public. *Miami Herald* reporter, Collin Dangaard, had a copy typed and asked people's opinion of it in a series of street interviews. 'Commie Junk' they said. 'Be careful who you show that anti-government stuff to.' The intrepid reporter then asked a crowd of young Christians who they thought had written it. 'A communist', 'a redneck revolutionist', came the pious replies, and one saintly devotee chimed in, 'Someone ought to tell the FBI about this kind of rubbish!'

1970

The Sultan who was insulted by an Englishman, Mahmud II, was born. Very prickly about the casual attitude of Western diplomats, he had the door of his throne-room lowered, so they would have to crawl through it in proper submissive pose. The aristocratic British envoy Lord Ponsonby thought that it was beneath his dignity, and made his point as tastefully as possible by crawling through backwards – thus facing the perplexed Potentate with his rotund English rump.

1785

Today's the day...

Wronged patriot Lord William Russell was executed at Lincoln's Inn for plotting to assassinate Charles II. He was convicted on perjured evidence and his trial was a travesty. Russell stoically accepted the verdict, but his wife and friends wouldn't. They bribed the King's mistress to help them obtain a pardon, and Lady Russell threw herself bodily at the King's feet, begging for her husband's life. 'If I do not kill him,' Charles said, 'he will soon kill me.' On the morning of his execution Russell rose early and wound his watch saying, 'Now I am done with time and am ready for eternity.' He thought a violent death 'desirable' and 'the pain of one minute . . . not equal to the pain of drawing a tooth.' Unfortunately, the executioner bungled. The first stroke of the axe went astray and only on the second blow was his head actually severed. *1683*

Scotland's bard Robbie Burns died, killed by his doctor's cure. He was suffering from rheumatic fever, aggravated by heavy drinking. The doctor sent him to the spa town of Brow Well on the Solway Firth, and there he had not only to drink the evil iron waters, but wade up to his armpits in the mud of the estuary. Burns endured it for a month then, pestered by creditors, he rushed home, collapsed and expired. A son was born to him posthumously and, ironically, he was christened Maxwell – in honour of the doctor. *1796*

Man walked on the moon when Commander Neil Armstrong left the lunar module *Eagle* and stepped out into the 'Sea of Tranquillity'. The landing had been a tricky one. The site was strewn with boulders 'as big as small motor cars', and dust whirled up from the moon's surface like 'a fast moving ground fog'. Once they'd touched down, fellow lunarnaut Buzz Aldrin celebrated his relief by taking communion with a tiny chalice he'd brought with him. During their sortie on the moon, the two men collected nearly 48lbs of rock and soil, and left behind an assortment of commemorative plaques and scientific equipment, including an ultra-sensitive seismometer. So sensitive was it that the first signal it sent back was the impact of the astronauts' boots, thrown out of the module before take-off.   *1969*

Famous fattie Daniel Lambert died, weighing out at an incredible 52st 11lb. A happy, healthy chap, his death was quite unexpected and caused enormous problems. He needed a coffin 6ft 4in long and 4ft 4in wide, and it took twenty pall bearers to push it into the grave. The biggest problem, however, was getting him into it in the first place. He passed away in a ground floor room at the Waggon and Horses Inn at Stamford, Lincolnshire, and a wall and a window had to be demolished to get him out.   *1809*

Bonaparte won the Battle of the Pyramids when his troops vanquished over 78,000 fierce Mamelukes. Known ever after in the East as 'the Sultan of Fire', he'd said to his men, 'From yonder Pyramids, twenty centuries behold your actions.' It's thought, however, that the French were less inspired by his words than by the thought that Mamelukes always carried their personal hordes of gold into battle.   *1798*

Action man writer Ernest 'Papa' Hemingway was born in Oak Park, Illinois, the son of a country doctor and an 'all time, all-American bitch'. Mother wanted him to be a cellist, but he became a journalist instead and started 'collecting experiences'. Adventuring, hunting, drinking and womanising, he worked hard to cultivate a he-man image, and come the Spanish Civil War, 'Papa' had a field day writing and unofficially fighting. He was a war correspondent on the D-Day landings and became a GI hero. Acting like one of his own characters, he amassed a following that amounted to a private army and was accused of single-handedly 'impeding the orderly advance of the official forces'!   *1899*

Today's the day...

Movie-loving gangster John Dillinger was shot dead by federal
agents outside the Biograph Cinema in Chicago. The great 'Public
Enemy Number One' had just been to see his favourite actress Myrna
Loy in *Manhattan Melodrama* – though in the real drama that followed
he never even had time to fire his gun. Chief of the FBI, Edgar Hoover,
had never liked him. 'Dillinger,' he said, 'is cheap, boastful, selfish,
tight-fisted and pug ugly.' *1934*

The Paris Olympics ended. They'd been held in the Bois de
Boulogne, and had featured the first woman gold medallist, Charlotte
Cooper, who won the women's singles tennis. It was an unfortunate
venue for discus and hammer throwers, however, since many of their
best throws landed in the trees. *1900*

Crazy, mixed-up Chi Chi the giant panda died in her sleep, aged
fifteen. Now preserved in London's Natural History Museum, she
was found as a six-month-old cub in the Szechuan Province of China,
where pandas are so rare that only nine westerners have positively
seen them in the wild. She was taken to Peking Zoo and then sent on a
European tour. London Zoo acquired her in 1958, and she soon vied
with Guy the Gorilla as the most popular attraction. She was very
much a slimline panda, weighing in at only 235lbs, as compared to the
cuddly 400lbs of Moscow's Ping Ping. Though supposedly vegetarian,
it was soon discovered that her favourite food was roast chicken,
followed closely by blackcurrant jam and spaghetti. Her sexual
appetite also proved to be a little out-of-the-ordinary. She rebuffed
two attempts to mate her with her Russian cousin An An, and
demonstrated her preference by making passes at her keeper! *1972*

Spanish Prime Minister Count Gasper de Olivares died. A child
prodigy, he was made head of the University of Salamanca – at
the ripe old age of twelve. *1645*

Philip the Handsome of Spain was born. On his death his distraught wife Joanna kept his corpse in her bed for three years. Funnily enough she became known as Joanna the Mad. *1478*

Fast moving Finn Lasse Viren was born. At the 1972 Olympics he revived the great Finnish running tradition by winning both the 5,000 and 10,000 metres. It was a remarkable feat, particularly since in the longer race he tripped over the fallen Tunisian, Gammoudi, at almost exactly the halfway stage. He not only kept going, but covered the last 800 metres in an astonishing 1min 56.2secs, to complete the course in a world record-breaking time. He'd had plenty of practice though, since he was the village policeman. *1949*

Verbal clown William Archibald Spooner was born in London. Though generally robust he was an albino and suffered defective eyesight as a result. It is thought that this caused some of his verbal confusions which were legion and later, of course, dubbed 'spoonerisms'. His most famous include: 'It is kisstomary to cuss the bride' and 'You hissed my mystery lecture'. Perhaps best of all, however, is his description of Queen Victoria. He called her 'our queer old dean' – and she wasn't amused! *1844*

Today's the day...

Edmund Kean hot-footed it from America, clutching the toe-bone of fellow actor Frederick Cooke, who'd drunk himself to death in New York, ten years earlier. Kean had had him reburied and stole the bone in the process. On his return to England, he was greeted by the Drury Lane Company, whom he obliged to kiss the blackened relic – 'the toe-bone of the greatest creature who ever walked the earth'. Kean took it home with him and preserved it with the greatest reverence. When it went missing he was absolutely distraught and his wife was forced to keep her guilty secret from him – she'd thrown it down the well.

1821

Unfortunate cabin boy Richard Parker was murdered by the three other survivors of the wreck of the yacht *Mignonette*. Twenty days earlier, they'd abandoned ship in the South Atlantic with just two tins of vegetables and not a drop of water. In their holed lifeboat they struggled to keep alive, and after several days they caught a turtle which they'd consumed in eight days. Drenched by spray and roasted by the sun, they were on the verge of madness. Richard Parker, tormented by thirst, had drunk sea water and collapsed. The men saw him as their only means of survival. The captain killed him, and they ate him a piece at a time until they were rescued. Forty-six years earlier Edgar Allan Poe had written a story entitled *The Narrative of Arthur Gordon Pym of Nantucket*. In it, four survivors of a shipwreck were marooned in an open boat, and to survive they'd killed and eaten one of their number. His name was Richard Parker.   *1884*

Author of *The Big Sleep* Raymond Chandler was born of Irish-American parents in Chicago 'so damned long ago that I wish I'd never told anybody when'. Educated at Dulwich College, young Raymond gave up a job with the Civil Service and failed as a journalist. He borrowed some money and returned to America with such a pronounced English accent that he was nicknamed 'Lord Stoopentakit'. He became an oil executive and fell in love with Cissy Pascal, the wife of a friend and eighteen years his senior. Mother violently disapproved and it wasn't until two weeks after her death that they were married. Cissy was then fifty-three, a captivating strawberry blonde who preferred to do housework in the nude! Nine years later, with Cissy in her sixties, Chandler was sacked for constantly being drunk and having affairs with his secretaries. Asked if he was anything like his characters Chandler replied, 'Yes . . . I am very tough and have been known to break a Vienna roll with my bare hands. I am very handsome, having a powerful physique and I change my shirt regularly every Monday morning.'   *1888*

Sprightly Christobella, Viscountess Say and Sele, died aged ninety-five. Passionately fond of dancing, even in her eighties she still gave balls and parties at Doddershall House, tripping 'on the light fantastic toe' and wearing out her partners, often forty years younger. At ninety she declared she'd chosen 'her first husband for love, her second for riches and her third for rank', and had every intention of starting all over again – in the same order.   *1789*

Today's the day...

First ejection seat escape landed plucky aircraft fitter, Bernard Lynch, over Chalgrove Aerodrome, Oxfordshire. Travelling at 320 mph, he exploded out of his Gloster Meteor at 8,000ft, and parachuted to the ground – straight into the backyard of a pub! He'd been chosen for the test, he said, because 'everyone in the factory elected me as the person it was hardest to kill!' *1946*

Truman told Stalin of the bomb at the Potsdam Peace Talks. The casual mention of an American weapon 'of special destructive force' elicited no particular response, however, save that Stalin said he hoped they'd make good use of it against the Japanese. So secret was this news of the great man's approval that when Secretary of State Stimson telegraphed the coded message, 'Doctor most enthusiastic that the little boy is as husky as his big brother', the cipher clerk thought Stimson had just become a father – though in fact, he was seventy-eight at the time. *1945*

The one that got away came back. Amateur angler O.T.Wertz hooked a perch in Chappell, Nebraska, but it broke his line and swam away. Disgruntled at his bad luck, Mr Wertz moved a mile up river and started again. On reeling in his next catch, he was amazed to find it was the same fish, with the same piece of line still in its mouth. *1926*

The liberator of South America Símón Bolívar was born in Venezuela. Raised by a slave after the death of his parents, he led numerous armies to free no less than five nations from Spanish rule – including Upper Peru, which was re-named Bolivia in his honour. Though effective, his military tactics were extremely unorthodox. On one occasion, he tied cow hides to the tails of fifty of his horses, stampeded them into the Spanish herd which panicked and overran the sleeping Spanish troops. In the confusion, Bolívar's men swooped down and promptly routed the enemy. 'Old Iron Tail' as his soldiers called him, inherited a fortune but blew it all in the cause of liberty. When he finally retired in 1830, his departure was delayed because he didn't have enough money to pay his passage.   *1783*

World's first private detective, ex-actor and thief, François Eugene Vidocq born in Arras, France. Originally recruited to the police as a snitch, he put his unique knowledge of the underworld to good use when in 1892, along with four other villains, he formed the famous French *Sureté*, and went on to pioneer such modern methods of investigation as fingerprinting, graphology and ballistics. In 1832 he formed his own detective agency, but so successful was he that his own creation, the *Sureté*, grew jealous and closed him down. They were convinced he planned crimes just to embarrass them.   *1775*

Author of over 1,200 works, Alexander Dumas was born to one of Napoleon's generals and a Haitian slave. Plagiarising many of his swashbuckling plots, he wrote books like *The Count of Monte Cristo* and *The Three Musketeers*, aided and abetted by a team of collaborators he called 'the factory'. Bragging he would never marry, he nevertheless claimed to have fathered over 500 children, finally getting his come-uppance when the guardian of his latest love bought all his debts and gave him the choice – get wed or go to prison! An incurable insomniac, he was ordered by his doctor to stand under the Arc de Triomphe at 7am each morning and eat an apple. Neither the apple nor the site were important – it was a ruse to get him into regular sleeping habits. He also kept a pet vulture named Jurgutha.   *1802*

The world's first parachute death occurred in Greenwich, England. Intrepid inventor Robert Cocking designed a brand new parachute. It was 17ft in diameter, shaped like an inverted umbrella and was no good. Halfway down from the balloon it collapsed, and poor Cocking plunged to his death.   *1837*

Today's the day...

Louis Blériot conquered the Channel. At 4.40am, he stood beside his famous 'flying bicycle' in a field near Calais, and to make sure he got his bearings right, asked, 'Tell me, where is Dover?' Minutes later the intrepid aviator was airborne at the joystick of the 25hp monoplane. He made the journey in just 36½mins and underlined his reputation as a notoriously bad pilot by crash-landing near Dover Castle. He was not, surprisingly, the first man to fly across the Channel, for many had gone before him. But he was the first man to do it in an aeroplane – the others had all been in balloons.   *1909*

The Channel was conquered again – this time in the first ever crossing by hovercraft. The *SRN 1*, as it was called, took eight months to build, and happily wobbled its way across, despite swells several times its own hover-height. Its trip from Calais to Dover took 2hrs 3mins. It had taken exactly fifty years and all the resources of modern technology to get across those few miles of water 86½mins slower than Blériot.   *1959*

An officer but no gentleman James Barry died, aged seventy. On his death it was discovered that 'the most skilful of physicians and the most wayward of men' was in fact a woman. Jilted by a lover, Barry had joined the British Army and stayed with it for fifty-two years.

Red-headed, with a temper to match, she became a noted duellist and was frequently sent home for breaches of discipline. One observer did detect 'a certain effeminacy in his manner' but thought no more of it, praising instead her conversation which 'was greatly superior to that which one usually heard at the mess-table'. Even her servant of thirty years never guessed the truth, and it was left to the coroner to reveal the dark secret of the world's only female Inspector General.   *1865*

Hanging in chains was abolished. For centuries, it had been the common form of execution for pirates and murderers. Felons were either hung by their wrists, or chained in an iron cage and left to waste away from starvation, thirst and exposure. Executioners and other assorted cut-throats did well out of it, though, for since it was such a slow and painful death, friends and relatives of the victim would often cough up bribes to have them despatched by quicker, if not altogether painless means.   *1834*

Conquering wooer Emperor Constantius I of Rome died in York. In his early days in Britain, he'd captured Colchester, and was captivated by the resident King's daughter, Helena. A marriage was arranged, and since peace and love were clearly the order of the day, the King held a massive banquet to celebrate. There, like any good host should, 'he called for his pipe, and he called for his bowl and he called for his fiddlers three'. You see, the merry old soul was the original 'Old King Cole'.   *AD 306*

The gruesomely mis-named Pope Innocent VIII died in Rome at the age of sixty. In the vain hope of restoring his lost vigour, in his last months he took to sucking the breasts of pregnant women, and drinking the warm blood of young boys. From his vampirish attentions three of the poor little urchins died – and then fortunately, so did the Pope.   *1492*

Today's the day...

Lusty Moll Cutpurse died of dropsy, aged seventy-five, after a life of amazing dissolution. Born Mary Frith, she became a prostitute, forger and fortune-teller, but achieved her greatest fame as the seventeenth-century equivalent of a pick-pocket. Caught four times and burnt on the hand, she nevertheless went on to ambush and rob the Commander-in-Chief of the Parliamentary Army, Lord Fairfax – shooting him in the arm and killing his servant's horse. For all her escapades she dressed as a man, and took her little dog with her everywhere. She was one of the first women smokers, and though incredibly ugly, she was very successful with men – she beat them into submission. She didn't actually pick pockets though, since they weren't worn for another century. Instead, as her nickname suggests, she cut her victims purse-strings.   *1659*

New York State was admitted to the Union. Although America's leading producer of manufactured goods, the home of its financial capital, the largest city and the largest port, it ranks only thirtieth in overall size. Among its odder achievements is the fact that in 1938 it became the first state to insist that prospective marriage partners applying for a licence should take a test for syphilis.   *1788*

Teetotal Swiss psychologist Carl Gustav Jung was born. Originally a disciple of Sigmund Freud, he later developed his own ideas on the libido and the unconscious and claimed that Freud's theories viewed the brain 'as an appendage to the genitals'. The rift deepened when Jung discovered Freud's secret passion for his sister-in-law and offered to analyse him. Freud huffily refused, saying, 'I cannot risk my authority', and their relationship was never the same again. The quarrel was a particularly poignant one, since though it's not widely known, in 1909 Freud had formally adopted the then thirty-four-year-old Jung as his son.   *1875*

July 26

Portly King Farouk was forced to abdicate. He took off from Egypt in such a tearing hurry that he had to leave behind many of his personal possessions. These have been said to include a massive collection of American comics, fifty walking sticks, 1,000 ties, seventy-five pairs of binoculars, a famous $20 American eagle (which had previously disappeared from the US Coin Museum), and an unrivalled collection of pornographic books and photographs.   *1952*

Lexicologist Sir James Murray died. As chief editor of the *Oxford English Dictionary*, he was in touch with many eminent men in the world of letters, but few more valuable to him than W. C. Minors. The incredible thing was that Minors, a United States doctor, was a convicted murderer and insane to boot. The two men only met once – in Broadmoor Lunatic Asylum, and it was from here that many of the definitions and references in the august *OED* were supplied by this erudite American madman.   *1915*

Luscious-lipped rock star Mick Jagger was born in Dartford, Kent. Intending to pursue a business career, he went to the London School of Economics, but was soon singing in a blues group with Alexis Korner. In 1962 the Rolling Stones were formed, and Jagger soon became famous as the man every middle-class parent would hate his daughter to marry. He's said that he doesn't like rock and roll, that he'd rather be dead than singing 'Satisfaction' when he's forty-five, and that he likes to play Vivaldi first thing in the morning. These days of course, he's verging on the respectable, still making music and busy being a beautiful person. His mother, however, who calls him Michael, has said that he could always make a living as an impersonator. Perhaps he could do Gerald Ford, who must be very nearly unique in not knowing until recently who he was. 'Mick Jagger?' he said, 'Isn't he that motorcycle rider?'   *1944*

Today's the day...

The second Alexander Dumas was born. During one of his many famous quarrels with his illustrious parent, his first play opened. Father Dumas attended the opening night, and sent a polite note to his son saying, 'Dear Sir, I went to see your play and liked it very much.' Dumas *fils*, ever ungrateful, replied: 'Believe me, sir, I am honoured to have the esteem of a man of whom I have always heard my father speak most highly.'

1824

The Gentleman Highwayman Captain McClean was arrested at his St James' Street lodging. The arresting officers found there 'a wardrobe of clothes, three and twenty purses, the celebrated blunderbuss and a famous kept mistress.' 3,000 people visited him in jail on one day, and at his trial, six highly respectable young women testified to his good character. If his lady victims were pretty enough, the lovable rogue always stole a kiss after robbing them

1750

Frogmen amazed the Queen of England by putting on a unique display at the Royal Naval College. Wearing special, non-bubbling breathing equipment, they played underwater draughts.

1962

July 27

Cynical English poet and historian Hilaire Belloc was born in a thunderstorm, in France. Something of a free-wheeler, one of his first writing jobs was as a cycling correspondent for the *Pall Mall Gazette*. While at Oxford, he was a devoted walker, amazing his fellow students by legging it to London in a record 11hrs 30mins. Always the realist, he thought that writing should be offered for sale 'just like butter', and that 'nothing should impede the truth . . . save a substantial amount of money'. He had no illusions about his lecturing techniques, either: 'First I tell them what I'm going to tell them, then I tell them, and then I tell them what I've told them.'   *1870*

The double execution of a single murderer horrified witnesses at Auburn Prison, the home of the new electric chair. The unfortunate felon, William Taylor, was given too strong a charge, and on receiving the 2,000 volt shock, lunged violently and broke the contacts. Doctors worked frantically to keep the semi-conscious and badly burned Taylor alive, giving him morphine to dull the pain, until the chair was repaired. 1hr 9mins later he was executed a second time – despite cries for mercy in the face of an Act of God – and the same doctors then performed his autopsy.   *1893*

St Pantaleon was executed on the seventh attempt, surrounded by a halo, and succumbing finally to decapitation. Previous tries, by burning, drowning, liquid lead, wild beasts, putting him to the sword, and breaking him on the wheel had all failed. Despite such determination on the part of his executioners, his only crime was that as a doctor, he'd refused to charge his patients.   *Feast Day*

Septuagenerian author and critic Gertrude Stein died. Paradoxical to the end, she turned to a friend and asked, 'What is the answer?' The friend understandably remained silent. Miss Stein looked at her and said, 'In that case what is the question?'   *1946*

Today's the day...

Blind composer Johann Sebastian Bach died of an apoplectic stroke. Years of close copying had destroyed his vision though inexplicably his sight was miraculously restored during his last ten days. Many of his manuscripts were lost, though the immortal *St Matthew Passion* was rescued from a cheesemonger about to use it as wrapping paper. His last composition was a hymn entitled 'When in the Hour of Utmost Need', and just before he died he re-named it 'Before Thy Throne O Lord I Come'. *1750*

The last public execution in Scotland took place, when wife and mother-in-law murderer and corrupt medical man, Dr Edward Pritchard, was hanged before an estimated crowd of 100,000 in Glasgow. A totally amoral, but very plausible character, he forged testimonials to secure practices and gave lectures on his 'travels'. 'I have hunted the Nubian lion,' he once said, 'on the prairies of North America.' When his wife was dying from slow poisoning with antimony, he had her examined by another doctor, who prescribed small quantities of iced champagne. When she was later seized with agonising cramps, it was concluded she'd overdone the treatment and was drunk. Both mother and daughter died in the same bed, with Pritchard crying with well rehearsed grief, 'Come back my dear Mary Jane! Don't leave your dear husband!' He then went and wrote to his bank manager about his overdraft. *1865*

The most complicated and dangerous *Skylab* mission was launched. *Skylab 3* quickly developed a serious gas leak and the broken parasol sunshield caused the cabin temperature to rocket. A rescue mission was planned but the astronauts succeeded in making emergency repairs. After fifty-nine days they returned landing upside down in 8ft waves – the roughest sea for any splashdown. Prior to the launch, programme director William Schneider predicted a 'dull and boring flight'. *1973*

July 28

The royal odd couple married. Short-sighted, fat and frowning
Princess Anne, future Queen of England, married tall, fat and
asthmatic Prince George of Denmark. While she was desperately
boring, George was no social comet either. According to Anne's uncle
Charles II, 'I've tried George drunk and I've tried him sober and
there's nothing in him!'   *1683*

The world's most famous widow Jackie Kennedy Onassis was born
in Southampton, NY, the daughter of Black Jack Bouvier, a wealthy
banker. At the age of six she had read her first Chekhov story and
already decided to become a circus queen on the flying trapeze, and in
her high school year-book she listed her ambition as 'Not to become a
housewife'. This she failed to do when she became the First Housewife
of America. At her husband's inauguration she said, 'I feel as though I
have just become a piece of public property.' Indeed she probably
became the world's most photographed citizen and one set of famous
full frontal photos took a team of ten determined snapshooters fifteen
months to get. Her lack of sympathy with photographers is a little
surprising, since she once worked for a Washington paper as their
'Inquiring Camera Girl'. From being the widow of one of the most
powerful men in the world, she became the wife of one of the richest.
This proved extremely useful since her ability to spend is legend. Other
inside information says she is such a tightwad that after parties she
has all unfinished drinks poured back into decanters.   *1929*

Time Lord and 1964 Nobel Prize winning American physicist Charles
Hard Townes was born. His invention of Maser – microwave
amplification by stimulated emission of radiation – made it possible for
atomic clocks to measure time with utter accuracy. True to the
tradition of the best scientific discoveries, Townes wrote the principle
on the back of an envelope, while sitting on a Washington Park bench
waiting for a restaurant to open, so he could have breakfast!   *1915*

425

Today's the day...

Tormented genius Vincent van Gogh died of a self-inflicted bullet wound in his chest. Suffering from acute depression and the noise of the city which was 'bad on his head', he had shot himself then stumbled to an inn where doctors pronounced his condition inoperable. He survived nearly two days, suffering little pain and calmly awaiting his end smoking his pipe. He had always asserted dying held no fear for him and was convinced his would be a 'smiling death'. When it came he was in the arms of his beloved brother Theo saying, 'Do not cry I did it for the good of everybody.' *1890*

Sex-mad Italian fascist Benito Mussolini was born, the son of a blacksmith, and inherited his famous square jaw from his mother. Named after Benito Juarez, the Mexican revolutionary, he was a strange paradox of tyrant and sentimentalist. He treated his wife and family with great tenderness, but his many mistresses with extreme cruelty – stabbing his first paramour in the thigh. When in power, he made outward show of propriety by closing down fifty-three Roman brothels, while luring strings of young girls to his lair. 'He has these women seven at a time,' said his most famous mistress Claretta Petacci, and he liked to ravish them, often without even taking his trousers off. Despite passing virulent anti-semitic laws, *Il Duce* also managed to fit in two Jewish mistresses, and was at pains to demonstrate his romantic attitude to life, saying, 'I am not a statesman really, I am more like a mad poet.' *1883*

One of the most expensive afternoons in history resulted in the birth of Charles Lennox, Duke of Richmond. Illegitimate son of the Merrie Monarch Charles II and his French mistress Louise de Keroualle, he was conceived during a quick break from the Newmarket races, with the French ambassador acting as pimp and introducing the King to the ambitious and beautiful courtesan. Though totally undistinguished, Lennox was granted Richmond Castle, a large chunk

426

of Scotland and a levy of one shilling on every cauldron of coal shipped to London from Newcastle. With a curious hint of heredity, his one great passion was horse-racing – the prompt for his conception.   *1672*

Prophet and streaker William Simpson walked through the English Parliament with a chafing-dish of burning brimstone, shouting 'Repent, repent!' Simpson liked to smear his face with smut to symbolise the moral darkness that pervaded society, but today he really outstripped himself – because apart from the chafing-dish he was stark naked. He claimed as his justification that the prophet Isaiah had walked naked too, and that anyway he had an express command from God to do so.   *1667*

The wettest Olympics ever held opened in London, featuring the first bantamweight-weight-lifting contest. The winner, stocky 4ft 8in American Joseph de Pietro, caused quite a stir, having such short arms that he was only just able to raise the bar above his head. Czech Emil Zatopek won the 10,000 metres after training in heavy army boots, while the hero of the games, seventeen-year-old American Bob Matthias, struck gold in the Decathlon, despite a tremendous downpour throughout the gruelling twelve-hour day. Asked what he would do next, the new champion is said to have replied, 'start Shaving.'   *1948*

Strapping six-footer Mary Queen of Scots, twenty-two-year-old widow of four-and-a-half years, married her dissolute nineteen-year-old cousin Henry Stewart, Lord Darnley, at 5.30am. Their courtship had been spent in Darnley's sickroom where the royal widow fell madly in love with the measle-ridden 6ft 2in teenager. For her wedding in Holyrood Palace to the 'properest and best proportioned long man' she had ever seen, she wore a black mourning gown which, with hindsight, seems very apt indeed since she was later to connive in her syphilitic husband's death. He was blown up and stabbed.   *1565*

Today's the day...

An attempt to introduce bull fighting into England failed dismally.
Hundreds of eager spectators turned up in Artillery Yard in London
expecting to witness a bloody and exciting combat. A mounted
Spanish cavalier 'in a careless posture' faced a fearsome English bull.
But despite being prodded several times with a spear, the reluctant
bovine refused to fight. Realising that the audience was getting
agitated, another member of the troupe jumped on the bull's back and
the crowd was briefly amused by a bucking-bull display. They
nevertheless felt cheated, wrecked the scaffolding and marched off in
triumph – taking the bull with them!   *1683*

The Beatles gave it all away when they closed their trend-setting
Apple Boutique in Baker Street, London. The shop staff were told to
give everything away and the first customer to get a nice surprise was
snub-nosed actor Michael J. Pollard, of *Bonnie and Clyde* fame, who
bought some shirts and jackets and was told to keep his money. The
only sad person in the £10,000 give-away bonanza was poor Ringo
Starr, who went along to take advantage of his own offer and came away
with nothing saying, 'I couldn't find anything that fitted me.'   *1968*

The proudest moment in English football came when England
won the World Cup at Wembley – exactly as team manager Alf
Ramsey had predicted three years earlier. The West Germans opened
the account after thirteen minutes. Six minutes later, Geoff Hurst
headed an equaliser and the score remained at one-all until half-time.
In the seventy-seventh minute Martin Peters scored a 6yd sitter and
Ramsey's prophecy seemed well on the way to fulfilment. Then, in the
last moments of full time, the Germans scored a sensational equaliser.
After the whistle Ramsey calmly told his weary team, 'You won it
once. Now go out and win it again.' In the tenth minute of extra time,
Hurst scored a controversial goal which the Germans claimed did not
go over the line. With literally the last kick of the match, Hurst scored
again and became the first player to get a hat trick in a World Cup
Final. There was no more argument. England were quite simply the
best team in the world!   *1966*

Father of the assembly line, Henry Ford, was born. He built his
first car in his spare time in a brick shed at the back of his house in
Detroit. It had no brakes, but it got him financial backing and he began
full-scale production. His revolutionary methods achieved a production
rate of 1.6 cars every minute. In his factory he was a total autocrat –
the labour force was carefully screened and any worker who didn't
spend his wages in the approved manner was fired. Yet at home he
called his dominating wife 'Mother'; was so superstitious that if he put
a sock on inside out he wouldn't change it; collected violins; loved
bird-watching and enjoyed folk dancing. He hated smoking and was a
food faddist who adored weird concoctions like soya bean ice cream,
and often ate nothing but carrots for days. His billion dollar fortune
was based on the success of 'Tin Lizzie', the car that every American
could afford – and he fought hard for many years to retain the original
design. When finally he changed it and accepted a new look Fancy-Ford
it inspired the hit song 'Henry Made a Lady out of Lizzie'.   *1863*

Today's the day...

Spain's greatest treasure trove was lost off the coast of Florida. Under the command of General Juan Esteban Ubilla, the fleet of eleven galleons laden with gold and silver, pearls and emeralds, had lumbered out of Havana six days earlier. They knew full well that they ran the risk of meeting a hurricane, but they preferred to encounter that rather than the wrath of King Philip. In the Straits of Florida a strange mist closed in around the ships and General Ubilla fatalistically remarked, 'It's coming.' At 2am the hurricane struck, and caught in its very eye the ships were hurled about and dashed to pieces. Such was the force of the winds that within five minutes the fleet had been decimated and over 1,000 men killed. There were some miraculous survivals; one ship was thrown intact onto a coral reef and the crew of another were washed ashore clinging to the dismembered deck as a life-raft. It was a brief respite however – on the orders of the Governor any crewman caught ashore with treasure was promptly strangled. *1715*

Morte d'Arthur **was published** by Caxton. The courtly tale of the Arthurian legend proved to be extremely popular, not only in England but abroad, and many enjoyed the 'noble and joyous book'. What wasn't so well known was that Sir Thomas Malory wrote his definitive tale of knightly love and chivalry while he was in prison – for armed assault and rape. *1485*

Lightning struck the rustic sweethearts John Hewitt and Sarah Drew. That very morning they'd obtained parental consent to their marriage, but while toiling in the fields, a fierce thunderstorm blew up and they rushed to take shelter under a pile of barley. When the storm had cleared, the two lovers were found in a 'tender posture' lying dead underneath. The poet Alexander Pope was so struck by the tragedy that he penned their epitaph: 'Hearts so sincere th'Almighty saw well pleased / sent his own lightning, and the victims seized.' *1718*

The Scot who paid America's National Debt died. He was James
Swan of Fifeshire who emigrated to Boston when he was only eleven.
He took part in the Boston Tea Party, got wounded twice at Bunker
Hill and made a fortune using his wife's inheritance to speculate on
confiscated lands. He lived extravagantly but his luck changed and
heavily in debt, he sailed to France. With the help of his friend
Lafayette he built up his fortune again through contracts with the
French navy. Having gained financial control of the debt owed by
America to France, he managed to liquidate it in 1795 and triumphantly
reported, 'The entire American debt does not exist any more'. Eight
years afterwards he was sued by a German firm for non-payment of his
own debts, and was flung into a debtor's prison in Paris. He died there
twenty years later. *1830*

Astronauts Scott and Irwin bounced across the moon in the
first moon-buggy – their Lunar Roving Vehicle. The tough little
machine could negotiate obstacles, carry twice its own weight and had
an effective range of ten kilometres. It bumped about a bit though – the
astronauts described it as 'a real bucking bronco'. *1971*

The first criminal captured by wireless. Wife-poisoner Dr
Crippen was arrested aboard the SS *Montrose* just before she docked in
Quebec. His cleverly planned escape hadn't accounted for Mr Marconi's
device, though. Just prior to his arrest he was seen to look up at the
ship's wireless aerial and say, 'What a wonderful invention it is!' *1910*

A blow against freedom was struck when the world's first film
censorship law was passed in the United States. The penalty for
ignoring the new federal ruling was a fine of up to $1,000, one year's
hard labour or, for serious offenders, both. This seemed particularly
harsh since the law dealt not with outrageous obscenity or vice, but
simply the interstate transportation of films showing prize fights! *1912*

Today's the day...

'The slowest suicide bid in nautical history' ended after two Norwegian fishermen completed the first two-man rowing of the Atlantic. Frank Samuelson and George Harbo had been drunkenly bragging around New York bars that one day they would conquer the ocean using nothing but oars. A wily reporter took them up on their boasts with headlines they couldn't ignore. Three months later, the two intrepid rowers entered their 18ft long dory, loaded with 600 cans of food, seventy gallons of water and five pairs of spare oars. At first their only enemy was monotony. They rowed in shifts, subsisted on a diet of cheese, salt beef, fish, chocolate and tea and swore at each other to keep their spirits up. Then, after thirty-three days, disaster struck. A violent storm overturned the boat and left the two men clinging to the upturned keel. Miraculously they managed to right it and finally, after fifty-five days, they landed on the coast of St Mary's in the Scilly Isles. Their first words to a startled stranger were, 'Pardon me, sir, but would you kindly tell us where it is we're at?' *1897*

New York dog owners were told to clean up. In a city which averages sixty tons of 'canine waste' a day, a law came into effect making dog owners liable for a $50 fine if they didn't clear up after their pets. The only problem was that police officers actually had to witness the event, and one poor official crouched for hours behind some bushes before he finally got his dog. *1978*

Nelson trounced the French fleet at the Battle of Aboukir Bay. Anchored close to shore with their guns pointing seawards, the French were convinced their position was impregnable. However Nelson had brilliantly outmanoeuvred them, by taking them on both sides at once. Shortly before 10pm the French flagship *L'Orient* caught fire and Nelson ordered boats to be launched to rescue the Frenchmen he'd just been attacking. On board the blazing ship the sailors found ten-year-old Giacomo Casabianca crouching by the side of his dead

August I

father, refusing to leave until his father gave the order. Shortly
afterwards the ship blew up with an explosion that was heard fifteen
miles away. The young boy perished but was immortalised in the
poem: 'The boy stood on the burning deck / Whence all but he had
fled.' Ironically, at the height of the battle, one of the women on board
the English ships had given birth – to a son.   *1798*

Henry III of France was stabbed to death in the royal toilet, by a
fanatical monk Jacques Clement. Immediately after the assassination,
Clement was grabbed and stabbed to death himself. But the French
public were not cheated of an execution. Clement's corpse was
dragged to court where after a full judicial hearing it was solemnly
sentenced to death. In the public square, it was attached to four horses,
ripped apart and finally cremated with the ashes being thrown into
the river.   *1589*

Reluctant Roman Emperor Claudius was born. When the Imperial
Guards came to inform him that he was Caesar they found him
trembling behind door curtains. Though tall and quite handsome with
unusually white hair, he had weak knees which made him stumble as
he walked and when excited he would slobber, his nose would run, and
his head would roll uncontrollably from side to side. He also stammered,
and suffered such violent stomach aches he often contemplated suicide
as a cure. He passed a law making it a public holiday every time there
was an earthquake; planned a decree allowing men to pass wind at his
table; and slept through one court case then woke and delivered the
verdict: 'I decide in favour of the party which has told the truth.' But
he wasn't so silly and was in fact a memorable historian – which is
strange because the charge of absent-mindedness made against him is
quite justified. After ordering his wife's execution for adultery he
calmly sat down to dinner and demanded, 'Why is her ladyship not
here?'   *10 BC*

Today's the day...

The 'Red King' of England William Rufus was killed, allegedly mistaken for a deer, while out hunting in the New Forest – exactly the same way his nephew had been killed just three months earlier. Curiously enough, just before the hunt started, he's supposed to have given two specially-made arrows to Walter Tirel, traditionally the man who 'inadvertently' shot him, saying he knew that he was a man who could inflict 'death dealing strokes'. Even more strange is the tale that just before his death Rufus shouted to Tirel, 'Shoot in the Devil's name or it will be the worse for you.'   *1100*

Wild Bill Hickok was shot in a saloon in Deadwood. The ex-marshal had ridden in with a friend intending to do some prospecting, but in fact he'd spent most of his time gambling. The original of the Western gunfighter, Hickok had said he never wanted to kill another man – and for once in his life, he was careless and sat with his back to the door. In came Jack McCall, unnoticed. He pointed his Navy Colt at Wild Bill's head, and at a range of 18ins, he fired. The bullet smashed through the skull, flew out through the cheek and struck another man

August 2

in the arm. McCall fled, narrowly avoided a lynching and then, strangely, was acquitted at a Vigilante trial. Six months later he was tried again and this time with a full muster of evidence, he was hanged. No motive was ever established and all he would say was that he shot from behind because, 'I didn't want to commit suicide.' In Wild Bill's hand were two black aces, two black eights, and the jack of diamonds – still known to this day as 'The Dead Man's Hand'. *1876*

The greatest ham of them all, overworked actor John Palmer, died in Liverpool after 'a convulsive sigh' in the fourth act of a play called *Stranger*. On first seeing him perform, Garrick had recommended him to join the army and even got an appointment for him. But somehow he became one of the most popular players of his time. Dubbed 'Plausible Jack', he ingratiated himself with audiences in a 'pharisaical way' acompanied by the 'nice conduct' of his pocket-handkerchief. In private life he was exactly the same and when he approached Sheridan after a quarrel he whined, hand on heart, 'Oh if you could see my heart, Mr Sheridan.' To which the sharp Irish wit replied, 'Why Jack, you forget – I wrote it.' *1798*

The most mysterious death of any US president occurred after Warren Gamaliel Harding fell ill while travelling on a train down the Pacific Coast from Alaska. He was installed in the Palace Hotel, San Francisco, where he died from causes that are not reliably known. One doctor suggested apoplexy, another pneumonia, and the official cause of death was ptomaine poisoning from eating bad crab meat. Harding was in danger of public disgrace and impeachment for the corruption of his administration, and both suicide and murder are strong contenders. His wife may have personally cooked the crab, and no one else at the meal was affected. More pointed still is the fact that Mrs Harding, jealous of the President's mistress, had shown little emotion at the funeral, having refused to allow an autopsy. *1923*

Today's the day...

'Fiery face' King James II of Scotland was killed while trying to storm the besieged town of Roxburgh. He was inordinately proud of his specially prepared cannons and his French bombardier whose aim was so accurate he could hit 'within a fathom' of any target. But as he was gloating over a barrage of artillery, one of the guns blew up and poor James was killed by his own pride and joy.   *1460*

The soldier poet Rupert Brooke was born in Rugby, Warwickshire. He was handsome and charming and his romantic poetry captured the imagination of war-torn Britain. His sonnet 'The Soldier' – 'If I should die, think only this of me . . .', and his tragic early death made him an almost legendary figure. Yet strangely he never saw a shot fired in anger and he died from the combined results of a mosquito bite and sunstroke. One of his little known poems can be seen in a Grantchester pub – it reads : 'If I had a wife who could Scrub,/My cottage at Melbury Bubb,/I would breakfast at ten/And sit with some Men,/ Drinking Beer all the day in the Pub.'   *1887*

America's proudest father Mr Coolidge swore in his own son Calvin as US President in a unique ceremony in Vermont. Calvin had been holidaying at his birthplace and was fast asleep when the news of Warren Harding's death arrived. After waking the household Mr Coolidge who, apart from being a storekeeper, was also a notary public, gave the oath of office to his son. Calvin was his usual cool self and his first act as President was to say goodnight and go back to bed.   *1923*

Denmark's bungling robber made his *début* in a street in Copenhagen. He burst into a goldsmith's shop and demanded money from the girl behind the counter. She told him to go away. He insisted, but so did she, and so empty-handed off he went next door to the chemist's. He told the chemist he had a gun in his pocket, and the chemist gave him more than £50 to keep it there. Success. The robber made good his escape and hailed a taxi – or at least a car with a light on the roof. It turned out to be a police car. No problem for a cool-headed crook, except as he popped his head in the window to give the uniformed 'taxi-driver' his destination, his description was broadcast over the radio. He was not only caught red-handed, but very red in the face!   *1978*

The last notorious English highwayman Jerry Abershaw was hanged before an admiring crowd on Kennington Common in London. With traditional aplomb, he had displayed his contempt for the court by donning his own hat as the judge assumed the black cap to pronounce sentence of death. He returned to the death cell where he drew sketches of his exploits on the walls, using the juice from blackcherries, and with apparent unconcern he travelled to the gallows cheerfully waving to the crowds with a flower in his mouth. Just before he swung he shocked everyone by suddenly kicking off his boots. He did this just to prove his mother wrong – she'd always said he would die with them on.   *1795*

Today's the day...

Two English women witnessed the Dieppe Raid – the premature attempt to invade Hitler's Europe – which ended in appalling defeat, with nearly 4,000 casualties and hundreds of prisoners. Unwittingly the women, Agnes Newton and her sister-in-law Dorothy, had taken a room in a boarding house directly opposite one of the six military beach-heads. It was pitch dark, they were terrified and saw nothing, but between 4am and 7am – an hour before surrender – they heard the shells and machine guns, the dive-bombing and the cries of the wounded. Their account is extraordinary, because the raid took place precisely nine years and fifty weeks earlier. Their experience couldn't be explained by the weather or atmospherics, and they couldn't have read about it in such detail – because the official account wasn't published until five months after they had duplicated the dreadful tale it told. *1952*

America's meanest millionaire Russell Sage was born in a covered waggon in Oneida County, New York. Through shrewd investment and large scale money-lending, he amassed a seventy million dollar fortune. Yet he wore $4 second-hand suits, and hosted business lunches where only apples were served. In 1891 a crazed robber entered his office and threatened to blow the place up unless he was paid $1,200,000. Sage shoved an unfortunate clerk between himself and danger, and in the resultant explosion the hijacker was killed. Sage recovered but refused to pay the poor clerk a single cent compensation. Perhaps he wanted to live up to his mother's name – Prudence. *1816*

Queen Elizabeth the Queen Mother was born Elizabeth Bowes-Lyon in Glamis, the most haunted castle in Scotland. She's noted for her hats, her pearls, and her racehorses, and despite being a great-grandmother, she's still a keen fisherman, reads *The Sporting Life*, keeps over 150 engagements a year and makes at least one foreign tour. Queen after the marriage of her brother-in-law

Edward VIII and Mrs Wallace Simpson, she did sterling work in wartime London, particularly in the hard-hit poorer areas. When Buckingham Palace came in for a pasting in an air-raid, she said, 'I'm glad we've been bombed. It makes me feel I can look the East End in the face.'

1900

'Fanatic poet' Percy Bysshe Shelley was born at Warnham, Sussex, and chased through life in what seemed to be a perpetual frenzy. 'Cursing his father and the King', he was thrown out of Eton for stabbing another pupil, and was sent down from Oxford for his aggressive atheism. He was constantly reading, fell asleep anywhere, ate dried bread and flicked pieces of it at passers-by with stunning accuracy. He wrote with 'quivering intensity' and his verse, said critic Lionel Trilling, 'should not be read, but inhaled through a gas pipe'. A keen, but incompetent sailor, he once tried to leap overboard to rescue a hat. He liked to sail paper boats made from bank notes and sailed them on a pond just a few yards away from the Serpentine, where his wife drowned herself in despair. He too drowned, of course, and it's not really surprising since he used to steer with a book in one hand, the tiller in the other – and he couldn't even swim!

1792

Today's the day...

Marilyn Monroe died alone in her bedroom from 'acute barbiturate poisoning'. She'd been taking tranquillisers all the previous day and when Peter Lawford had phoned her in the evening, her voice was slurred and unsteady. He'd been alarmed when she suddenly ended the conversation by asking him to 'Say goodbye to Pat, say goodbye to the President, and say goodbye to yourself, because you're a nice guy.' He'd wanted to go to her right away, but his manager insisted that as brother-in-law to the President he could be seriously compromised. Later that evening he contacted the live-in psychiatric nurse who reported that the light was on in Marilyn's room and everything was all right. At 3.30am when they broke into the room, Marilyn was dead – stretched across the bed with the phone in her hand. Her body lay unclaimed in the County Morgue until ex-husband Joe DiMaggio took charge. He arranged the funeral and barred all her Hollywood friends saying bitterly, 'If it hadn't been for some of her close friends she wouldn't be where she is.' All these years later, he's never re-married and still sends flowers to her grave three times a week. 'I pay the florist to send them,' he says calmly, 'to never stop sending them.'   *1962*

Richard the Lionheart won the Battle of Jaffa against overwhelming odds. Vastly outnumbered, the English had been taken completely unawares by a Turkish attack at sunrise. They'd had to arm so quickly that some of the soldiers rushed into battle 'even without their breeches'. In the midst of battle, Richard's own horse fell under him. The Turkish commander Saladin grudgingly admired the bravery of his enemy and sent Richard two fresh horses. Richard gratefully accepted the gift and by sunset he was victorious. It wasn't Saladin's only gift to Richard, however, in the course of their fierce encounters. Once when the chivalrous Saracen had heard the King was ill, he'd sent him pears and peaches, and snow from Mount Ascalon to soothe his fevered brow.   *1192*

Houdini was sunk in a bronze coffin in a hotel swimming pool. He stayed there for 1hr 30 mins, and when they hauled him up he was running with perspiration and his pulse was racing. His doctors told him to rest, but he insisted that the best cure for exhaustion was physical exercise and he rushed off to the gym to play handball for over an hour.   *1926*

The transatlantic cable was given a rousing send-off. At Valentia on the west coast of Ireland, two specially constructed steam frigates, the *Agamemnon* and the *Niagara*, were all set to take their leave and start laying the cable across the sea to Newfoundland. To celebrate the Anglo-American venture, a special coat-of-arms appeared with the Union Jack and Stars and Stripes together for the first time. Crowds flocked to see the departure, tents had been set up and the sightseers enjoyed themselves dancing jigs and eating potatoes out of huge, steaming cauldrons. The official banquet was presided over by Lord Carlisle, Lord-Lieutenant of Ireland, and he sent the ships off with a grand farewell speech which ended, 'It is a rule and condition of final success to fail the first time.' It proved to be rather an unfortunate choice of words. Ten miles out from the shore the cable broke. It was hurriedly repaired, but after another 300 miles it broke again – and disappeared into 10,000ft of water.   *1857*

The classic leading man Robert Taylor was born Spangler Arlington Brough in Filley, Nebraska. He signed up with MGM straight out of drama school and stayed with them for a record twenty-six years. He never argued about his films as he 'figured they knew what they were doing'. In return they promoted him as the romantic hero and he became one of the biggest box office draws of the thirties. One of Hollywood's most modest stars he summed up his career by saying, 'I was a punk kid from Nebraska who's had an awful lot of the world's good things dumped in his lap.'   *1911*

Today's the day...

Hollywood's amiable tough guy Robert Mitchum was born in Bridgeport, Connecticut. His career started in a Hopalong Cassidy film and in all, he's made more than 100 movies, mostly playing himself and occasionally acting. He has no illusions about his talents and wrote an autobiography called *It Sure Beats Working*. He's far from being the typical 'star'; he's aggressively unpretentious, served six days on a chain gang for vagrancy and went to prison on a drugs charge and made no secret of it, and has been married to the same woman since 1941. He claims his success was fortuitous: 'I came back from the war and ugly heroes were in', and awards himself little distinction: 'The only difference between me and my fellow actors,' he once said, 'is that I've spent more time in jail!'

1917

A strange new snack was born. It was 5am and a peer of the realm had been gambling all night. Loath to leave the table, he ordered a servant to bring him a hunk of beef wrapped up in two slices of bread. The peer was of course the Earl of Sandwich, but sadly the legend is untrue. The ubiquitous sandwich was undoubtedly named for him, but the Romans had eaten sandwiches too. They called them by the less appetising name of *offula*.

1762

August 6

The most inquisitive Archbishop of Canterbury, Matthew Parker was born. He had an extremely long nose, which he insisted on poking into everyone else's business. Hence the expression 'Nosey Parker'.   *1504*

The Savoy Hotel opened in London. The builder had been instructed to install private baths in seventy rooms. He took a deep breath and asked, 'Are the guests amphibious?'   *1889*

The death of Pope Paul VI coincided with some strange events. He collapsed while assisting at a private mass and having suffered a massive heart attack, he died at 9.40pm. At that precise moment his alarm clock, which was always set for 6am, started ringing. Minutes later a colossal cloudburst drenched a valley in north-eastern Italy, which eventually resulted in the worst flooding in twenty-five years. The older inhabitants needed no meteorological explanation. They said, 'The Angels are weeping.'   *1978*

The first Poet Laureate Ben Jonson died, a poverty-stricken old man. 'A great lover and praiser of himself', he'd written some of the finest plays in the English language and been an intermittent friend of Shakespeare, the poet Donne and the philosopher Bacon. He'd also earned himself a thoroughly bad reputation. He was a heavy drinker, killed a fellow actor in a brawl and was accused by a contemporary of having murdered the playwright Marlowe. Before he died, legend has it that he begged 18ins of ground from Charles I. It was granted him in Westminster Abbey, and he was buried in it, standing upright. The second part of the legend, at least, was proven when 212 years later the grave was disturbed. His leg bones were found upright in the sand, and his skull still retaining some of its red hair, fell with a thud between them.   *1637*

Today's the day...

Exotic and voluptuous spy Mata Hari was born. Though legend often has it that she was a Polynesian princess, she was born Margaret Gertrude Zeller – in Holland. After an unsuccessful marriage to a Dutch officer stationed in Java, she ended up in Paris where she earned her living as a prostitute and dancer. She never stripped completely since she had extremely small breasts, which she invariably covered with sea shells. She had literally hundreds of lovers, and with one of them worked out a spectacular stage routine for which she adopted her famous pseudonym, meaning 'eye of the morning'. The Germans soon spotted her potential as a source of securing information from British and French officers, but when things got too hot for her she fled to London and offered to become a double agent. The British spy master told her to stick to dancing and sent her packing. She returned to Paris, where she was trapped by the French, and subsequently shot. It's ironic that her daughter also became a spy – for the British in Korea. She, poor girl, met the same fate as her mother.   *1876*

A poignant suicide note was written by washerwoman Catherine Allsop. She'd written it in pencil on a scrap of paper before hanging herself in her best Sunday dress. The note was used as her epitaph, and these touching lines are taken from it: 'Dear Friends, I am going/ Where washing ain't done, nor sweeping, nor sewing;/But everything there is exact to my wishes,/For where they don't eat, there's no washing of dishes./Don't mourn for me now, don't mourn for me never,/I'm going to do nothing for ever and ever.'   *1905*

The first rugby game was played to Australian rules between Melbourne Grammar and Scotch College. The first team to get two goals would be declared the winner. The trouble was there were forty men a side, and the goal posts were nearly half a mile apart. Play started at lunchtime, and after three hours, Scotch College scored.

Bad light stopped play and the game was resumed a fortnight later, though nothing was added to the score. A week after that they started again, but still no-one could get a goal and the game was abandoned. The joke was, that its inventor T. W. Wills was educated in England, and the school he went to was Rugby.   *1858*

The uncrowned Queen of England Caroline of Brunswick died so suddenly that there were rumours of poisoning. There was certainly no love lost between her and her chubby husband, King George IV. He actually locked her out of Westminster Hall at his coronation in July, and it's said that this caused her rapid decline. In fact, she was struck down with a mysterious illness in the Drury Lane Theatre. Her last words were typically curt. To the priest who was muttering prayers over her, she snapped, 'Pray louder that I may hear!'   *1821*

Major British anthropologist Dr Louis Leakey was born. In 1960, he and his wife found the remains of what was then thought to be the oldest specimen of pre-*Homo sapiens* 'Humanity', dating back between 1,750,000 and 2,300,000 years. This venerable being was originally called pre-*Zinjanthropus* to distinguish it from *Zinjanthropusboisei*, the younger 'Nutcracker Man'. Along with the brain case and lower jaw however, they discovered chipped stone tools, probably used for making weapons. Armed with this extra evidence, they renamed the 4ft tall creature *Homo habilis* – handy man.   *1903*

A crazy tightrope stunt surprised New Yorkers. It began when twenty-seven-year-old Frenchman, Philippe Petit, dodged security guards, and used a crossbow to fire his rope from one of the mighty twin towers of the World Trade Center to the other. He leapt into action, and 1,350ft above the teeming traffic, he made a successful crossing. He was arrested immediately and sentenced to perform his act in Central Park, for under-privileged children.   *1974*

Today's the day...

The great Anglo-German painter Sir Godfrey Kneller was born. He suffered from agonising headaches and the only thing that cured them was a sniff of gunpowder. He claimed that God was the most ingenious of all beings, and he was the most ingenious of all painters. His prodigious output of portraits was maintained by an army of assistants, who painted the bodies of the sitters, while he saved himself for the heads. If there's a certain sameness about them, it's because he used his 'most buxom mistress' Mrs Voss as the model for practically every lady he painted.   *1646*

French scholar Jacques Basnage was born. He wrote the first definitive history of the Jews, which became the basis for the science of Jewish history. It's odd that a race so renowned for their scholarship and traditions should have left this task to such a man. He was a gentile Protestant pastor.   *1653*

The twenty-first British Prime Minister George Canning died, four months after taking office. It has been suggested that his death was hastened by the criticisms of his opponents which gravely affected his 'sensitive constitution'. A statue was erected to him on Palace Yard in 1832, and in 1867, while it was being moved to Parliament Square, the dead Prime Minister fell over and killed an unlucky Mr Riley.   *1827*

Freaky American artist Andy Warhol was born. When he started his Campbell's soup tin paintings in 1962, the soup cost about twenty cents and one painting at least, went for around $1,300. In 1978, the same can of soup cost nearer thirty-three cents, and the same painting cost $95,000. Despite this super-success, Warhol has said, 'Machines have less problems, I'd like to be a machine.' *1931*

Graduate actor Dustin Hoffman was born. In 1964 he retired from acting because he said it wasn't possible to make enough to live on. His resolve lasted for a few months, while he earned a living as a teacher, and then he took a small part in a small play. In that production he appeared with another unknown actor called Jon Voigt. Five years later, they appeared together in *Midnight Cowboy*, when hungry Hoffman was paid a quarter of a million dollars. *1937*

The Great Train Robbery took place between Sears Crossing and Bridego Bridge in the depth of Buckinghamshire. The first police call reported, 'You won't believe this but they've stolen a train.' The slick operation had lasted a mere forty-two minutes, long enough for the gang of fifteen to shift two tons of mailbags containing a total of two-and-a-half million pounds. They each got paid £140,000 for their trouble. In the van afterwards one of the gang sat quietly on the huge sacks of money quoting the *Rubaiyat of Omar Khayyam*. There was so much money about they even lit their cigarettes with it. All had been meticulously planned down to the last detail, but the police got their big break when the man paid to burn down the hideaway, Leatherslade Farm, didn't bother and they found numerous fingerprints. Despite all this, only a seventh of the money has ever been recovered and that's been found in some very strange places: £147,000 was found in a car after one of the gang had rented a garage from a policeman's widow; £100,900 was found in a plastic bag at the roadside by a passing motorcyclist, and £47,254 in two potato sacks in a public call box. *1963*

Today's the day...

'The Father of Angling' Isaak Walton was born. He wrote the world's first definitive work on the sport under the catchy title, *The Compleat Angler, or the Contemplative Man's Recreation. Being a Discourse of Fish and Fishing, not unworthy of the perusal of most Anglers*. This remarkable book full of fine prose contains many quaint suggestions. For example he advises that a live frog is excellent bait, but it should be impaled on the hook 'as though you loved him, in order that he may live the longer'.
1593

Cack-handed antipodean tennis player Rod Laver was born. On leaving school his first job was as a clerk for the Dunlop Rubber Company who later paid him a small fortune to endorse their products. He became the first man to win the coveted Grand Slam twice – Wimbledon, Australia, US and French titles. He carries a lasting memorial to his fabulous career – his left playing arm is one third as big again as his right arm.
1937

Female matador Conchita Cintron was born in Chile. At the age of twenty-two, she travelled to Spain where although her unique talents were widely acclaimed, the authorities refused to allow her to fight on foot, because they considered it too dangerous for a woman. This characteristic arrogance ignored the fact that back in South America she had already killed over 400 bulls – all on foot.
1922

Poor Eddy was finally crowned King Edward VII of England. His original coronation, set for 26 June, had been cancelled because he needed an emergency appendicitis operation. This not only upset the china industry which had spent a fortune marketing commemorative cups, but also his tailors who had to alter all his official robes and costumes because he lost 6in around his waist. As it was the first coronation for sixty years, court officials busied themselves researching correct procedure since everyone who officiated at his mother's

August 9

coronation was long dead. Parliament were especially thrilled at the event since, 'For the first time in English history, the heir apparent comes to the throne unencumbered by a single penny of debt.' During the actual ceremony Edward kindly raised the aged Archbishop of Canterbury from his knees – he had got stuck in an attitude of prayer. *1902*

A bizarre offer was made to seven prisoners in London's notorious Newgate jail. They were offered their freedom if they agreed to become human guinea pigs in a medical experiment to test the rights, or maybe wrongs, of Dr Charles Maitland's ideas on inoculation. The prickly choice between a slow lingering death in the rat infested hell holes of Newgate and a chance of a pardon was no choice at all. The seven unnamed jailbirds became the first men in England to be inoculated. All seven survived to make medical history and enjoy this well-earned freedom. *1721*

Exhausted statesman Viscount Castlereagh had an extraordinary audience with dilettante King George IV. After months of overwork he finally cracked; in the middle of the meeting he suddenly broke down and began to confess that he had committed high treason and several murders. The stunned King gently recommended him to a good physician. *1822*

Disgraced US President Richard Nixon made his emotional farewell to the White House staff after admitting that, because of the Watergate matter, he *might* not have the support of Congress. The tremendous strain clearly showed as he rambled on about riches, his saintly mother and America's need to produce more plumbers. His final words were reminiscent of his previous political farewells – he said *au revoir*. One of President Ford's first acts was to grant Nixon a full, and absolute pardon for any crimes he may have committed. *1974*

Today's the day...

Tragedy struck Franklin Delano Roosevelt when, after fighting a forest fire, he took a dip in the icy water of Fundy Bay. He came out without the glow he expected, and was soon complaining of aches in his legs. The first doctor to attend him advised vigorous massage, which as it turned out was the worst possible treatment, for the thirty-nine-year-old future President had poliomyelitis and within two days was paralysed from the waist down. Cold comfort for Roosevelt that eighty per cent of sufferers feel nothing worse than a feverish cold, and often never realise they've had polio at all.   *1921*

The unfortunate Bishop of Peterborough, White Kennet, was born. At twenty-eight, out hunting, his gun exploded and fractured his skull. He underwent the dangerous operation of trepanning, where bone is removed to relieve pressure on the brain. While undergoing this treatment – without anaesthetic – he dictated a Latin poem to a friend, though afterwards he could never remember composing it!   *1660*

The first dukedom was created by Queen Victoria when stylish James Haworth was appointed Duke of Abercorn. A pernickety peer, his servants had strict orders to wash their hands in rosewater before serving food and the maids had to wear kid gloves while making the beds.   *1868*

The ship that never sailed the *Vasa* was launched in Stockholm harbour, having consumed forty acres of timber in its building. With a 164ft mast, sixty-four gleaming bronze cannons and a crew of 133, it was the mightiest craft of its day. At its launching a sudden storm turned it turtle, and within minutes it plunged 110ft down to the sea-bed. There it lay for 332 years until it was salvaged, and without so much as a shot being fired, the great warship was turned into a dry dock museum.   *1626*

August 10

American chewing faddist and dietician Horace Fletcher was born.
At the age of forty-six he was refused insurance because of his
constant indigestion and 50lb excess weight. The diet he devised was
so successful he wrote two bestsellers on the philosophy of good
eating. Basically, food should be chewed thirty-two times – once for
each tooth – until it 'swallowed itself'. Soup had to be swilled for
twenty seconds. Fletcherism swept America and disciple, author Henry
James, claimed it saved his life and improved his disposition. But
gradually it fell into disfavour because meals took so long to eat and
people preferred hot food!   *1849*

Lightning struck an unfortunate umpire during a cricket match
at Berwick-on-Tweed. Although he recovered, he found great
difficulty in walking – the flash had welded solid an iron joint in his
leg! By a striking coincidence the event took place on the eighty-ninth
anniversary of the day Elihu Thompson of Lynn, Massachusetts,
patented the first electric welder.   *1975/1886*

Today's the day...

English poet and *bon viveur* Richard Monkton Milnes died. He led an extremely active social life and ate on the grand scale. 'My exit,' he declared, 'is the result of too many entrées.' *1885*

Ugly English miser Joseph Nollekens was born. A fine sculptor he was often rude to his sitters, reminding one mature lady that no bosom was worth looking at beyond the age of eighteen, and keeping another waiting while he washed his feet. A pair of candles would last him a year and his wife fed their dogs by taking them for a stroll round the butchers' stalls. Not surprisingly he left £200,000. *1727*

1, 500 ships of the British Armada set sail from Portsmouth under Henry V. Amongst the 2,500 men at arms and 8,000 archers was a party of fifteen minstrels for the King's personal use. As the fleet moved out three ships caught fire, but Henry, ever the optimist, capitalised on the mishap declaring it to be a divine blessing. Since he went on to conquer Northern France, marry the French King's daughter and get appointed heir to the French throne, he may well have been right. *1415*

Sentimental song-writer Carrie Jacobs-Bond was born. A child prodigy, she was dogged by poverty for most of her life, at one point working as a saleswoman, though she continued her song-writing – on wrapping paper. It was only after a chance meeting with Victor P. Sincere that her first songs were published, titled *Seven Songs as Unpretentious as the Wild Rose*. Despite writing some of the most popular songs of the day including 'Just a-Wearyin' for You' and 'The End of a Perfect Day', she always felt she ought to have done better things but a shortage of cash had forced her to write 'little songs that would sell'. *1862*

Disappointed American astronomer Asaph Hall identified two tiny dwarf satellites orbiting around Mars. Hall was over the moon about his discovery only to find that the Laputan astronomers in Swift's *Gulliver's Travels* had discovered exactly the same thing – 115 years earlier.   *1877*

Ruthless Rodrigo Borgia was created Pope. A good job too, since in the seventeen days it took to elect him, he ordered the assassination of 220 men who had opposed him.   *1492*

Ailing American statesman Thaddeus Stevens died. Already ill, his failure to get President Johnson impeached caused an acute relapse. Friends visiting his death-bed remarked on his healthy appearance. 'Gentlemen,' he replied, 'it is not my appearance that I am concerned about just now – it's my disappearance.'   *1868*

Philanthropic American industrialist Andrew Carnegie died. Insisting he wanted to leave this world poor, he gave away over 308 million dollars in his eighty-three years. But he still didn't achieve his ambition – he had twenty-two million left.   *1919*

Today's the day...

Chubby dandy King of England George IV was born. Despite being fat all his life (at thirty-three he weighed seventeen stone), he was a slavish follower of fashion – even to his own discomfort. He bled himself to look pale and elegant and pretended to take snuff though he hated the stuff and never actually sniffed it. To hide his bloated neck he took to wearing high collars which became all the rage, and appointed himself a field marshal so he could dress up in the uniform. On a visit to Scotland he even donned a kilt. With his portly figure he felt rather foolish but was cheered by a diplomatic comment from Lady Jane Hamilton Dalrymple: 'As your majesty stays so short a time in Scotland, the more we see of you the better.'   *1762*

'When Irish Eyes are Smiling' was published. Just one of the many songs about Ireland written by Ernest R. Ball, on this occasion with Chauncey Alcott. A popular singer, Ball also wrote 'Rose of Killarney' and 'Ireland is Ireland to me'. He even died after singing a medley of Irish songs – though in fact he was American.   *1912*

The grouse shooting season opens in Britain on the 'Glorious Twelfth'. Always an aristocratic pursuit, it even had a hand in the loss of the colonies. When a group of American colonialists arrived with peace proposals, George III was engrossed in his grouse shooting and left discussions to his ministers. The mission failed of course, making George's outing a very expensive one for Britain.   *Annual Event*

Extravagant gourmet and gambler Diamond Jim Brady was born. From lowly beginnings he quickly made a personal fortune and with 200 suits, fifty top hats and two million dollars' worth of jewellery, he always lived up to his maxim: 'If you're going to make money, you've got to look like money.' He had twelve gold-plated bicycles all with ruby studded handlebars and his most exotic one had mother of pearl handgrips with emeralds and sapphires mounted on the spokes of the wheels. His monstrous appetite was legend too. One restaurateur called him 'the best twenty-five customers I have'. He would eat his way through six lobsters, two whole ducks, sirloin steak, pastries and twenty-one boxes of chocolates at a sitting, claiming his secret was always to leave 4ins between his stomach and the table. When the two met he knew he'd had enough!   *1856*

The first shot of World War I was fired by a British soldier, when Allied troops invaded Togoland forcing the unconditional surrender of the German Governor. The name of this intrepid Briton was Alhaji Grunshi – he was a Regimental Sergeant Major in the Gold Coast Regiment.   *1914*

Guinness Book of Records **twins,** Ross and Norris McWhirter were born, within twenty minutes of each other. Always keen on memorising facts, they were recommended to Guinness MD Sir Hugh Beaver by aspiring young executive Chris Chataway. When Beaver met the twins he mentioned that he loved to holiday in Turkey. Norris immediately replied, 'Turkish is the language with the fewest irregular verbs – just one.' They got the job and now have their names in their own book as authors of the world's biggest-selling title.   *1925*

Wasp-waisted French actress Anna Held died, officially of a diseased spinal cord. The newspapers suggested, with good foundation, that to preserve her figure she had her lower ribs removed and death was caused by wearing her corsets too tight.   *1918*

Star of BBC 'Brains Trust' Professor Joad was born. A great logician, he once confounded British Rail by jumping aboard a train when it made an unscheduled stop. Told by a porter he couldn't get on as the train didn't stop there, he replied with irrefutable logic, 'In that case don't worry – I'm not on it.'   *1891*

Today's the day...

A breakthrough in chamber-pots was patented in England. Its object was 'to obviate the necessity for putting the thumb inside the vessel when holding the same, as is now generally the custom'. 1889

An historic drive reached its halfway stage when Charles Creighton and James Hargis of Missouri arrived in Los Angeles after chugging 3,340 miles from New York. Twenty-three days later, they made it back again. The incredible thing was not the distance, but that they did it each way without stopping the engine – and entirely in reverse. 1930

Chilling film-maker Alfred Hitchcock was born, the son of a London greengrocer. The maker of over fifty of the world's most terrifying films, whose motto is 'make the audience suffer', 'Hitch' is a lover of practical jokes. He once paid a £3 debt with 2,880 farthings, and on leaving a crowded lift exclaimed loudly, 'I didn't think the old man would bleed so much.' After the dreaded *Psycho* with its horrible bathroom murder, he was asked what to do about a woman who'd seen it and was now too terrified to take a shower. He replied, 'Have you considered having her dry cleaned?' 1899

August 13

'**The Girl of Western Plains**' Phoebe Anne Oakley was born in Patterson, Ohio. Dubbed 'Watanya Ciciha' – 'Little Sure Shot' – by Sitting Bull, she was probably the greatest shot who ever lived. She could knock a dime out of the air, slice a playing card sideways-on at thirty paces, and in a single day shot 4,772 out of a possible 5,000 flying glass balls. At Victoria's Jubilee celebrations she appeared before the Queen, who called her 'a very clever little girl', and at a command performance in Germany she shot a lighted cigarette out of Kaiser Bill's mouth. Perhaps the most surprising thing about her, however, is that until she went there with the show, this most famous of Western heroines had never once seen the Wild West.   *1860*

Charles V officiated at his own funeral, having been told by his confessor, the monk Regla, that it would be good for his soul – a matter of some importance to this very devout Holy Roman Emperor. A special catafalque was erected and the morbid monarch turned up in procession with his entire court clothed in 'sable weeds' and carrying candles. Symbolically giving up his life to his maker by giving his candle to a priest, he watched his coffin interred in its tomb and then adjourned for lunch. He spent the afternoon sitting outside in the blazing heat and was struck down with sunstroke. The funeral was performed again in little more than a month, and this time when the coffin was interred, Charles was in it – for good.   *1558*

A rifle got shot in one of the most amazing incidents of World War I. Private W. J. Smith of the Sixth Battalion, Queen's Own Royal West Kent Regiment, was in action near Armentieres, when he aimed his Lee-Enfield .303 at the hideaway of a German sniper. The sniper spotted him and fired first, and the bullet went straight down the barrel of Private Smith's rifle and smashed the bolt. Smith himself was unharmed. This particular August 13th was a Friday.   *1915*

Today's the day...

The father of modern journalism, press baron Lord Alfred Harmsworth died. After launching the *Daily Mirror* and the *Daily Mail,* he acquired that most august of papers *The Times.* The enormous strain affected him mentally and he began to suffer from megalomania. His delusions made him impossible to be with, but an attempt to improve his health with a world tour only convinced him that enemies were plotting to poison him. Shortly before his death he hinted at his own obituary saying, 'I should like a page reviewing my lifework by someone who really knows, and a leading article by the best man on the night.' *The Times* obliged. *1922*

Modern motoring headaches began with the introduction on the streets of Paris of various legal regulations. Plates bearing registration numbers and the owner's name and address were authorised; double parking was outlawed and unless absolutely necessary so was parking on pavements. As a final insult driving tests were made compulsory. All drivers had to be over twenty-one and not only be aware of the laws, but also have a working knowledge of the engine and be able to perform instant repairs. Strangely, because his department controlled all steam engines, the tests were under the personal supervision of the Chief Engineer of Mines. *1893*

The last execution in the Tower of London took place on the miniature rifle range. German spy Josef Jakobs had been captured within minutes of parachuting into England. Because he broke his ankle on landing, he was executed seated on a Windsor chair. Among his possessions was found a solitary cold sausage. *1941*

Big spending William IV came under fire during a heated debate in the House of Commons. A row had erupted over his excessive expenditure on the renovation of Buckingham Palace. Radical reformer William Cobbett argued that while there was not a man in

Britain who would begrudge the royal family anything necessary 'to their splendour, pleasure or magnificence ... these feelings should not be shocked by flagrant expenditure and unfeeling waste ... even the poorest labourer would gladly work a day extra rather than see St James' Palace or Windsor Castle pulled down. I cannot say so of Buckingham Palace. No one would complain of its being pulled down.' They did – so it wasn't!

1833

Eighteenth century ham and rake Richard Barry, Seventh Earl of Barrymore, was born. His mad Irish father and eccentric English mother weaned a spectacularly assorted brood. The three brothers and one sister were all known after famous London sites. His sister swore so profanely she was called 'Billingsgate' after the fishmarket where the porters' language is legendary. His club-footed brother was cruelly known as 'Cripplegate'; the youngest brother was nicknamed 'Newgate' after the only jail in which he was never held a prisoner, and for more obvious reasons Richard was dubbed 'Hellgate'. He was expelled from school after wrecking the furniture and chasing the headmaster all over the grounds. His practical jokes began with simple pranks like removing inn signs and road notices to confuse travellers, but they developed into elaborate plots like unsuspecting house guests finding corpses waiting for them under the bed-sheets. Later in life, he concentrated on his hobby of founding clubs. Naturally enough the first was 'The Humbugging Club' dedicated to playing practical jokes. Later additions included 'The Warble Club' for drunken singing, 'The Two O'Clock Club' which never met until two in the morning, and best of all, 'The Bothering Club' for making people's lives as uncomfortable as possible. He collected a vast army of creditors and to avoid them bought himself a rotten borough, since as an MP he could not be arrested for debt. At the age of twenty-four he died in a shooting accident, after squandering a fortune of £300,000

1769

Today's the day...

The world pea pushing record was smashed by twenty-three-year-old swimming pool attendant Helga Jansens of Peterborough. Overcoming the obvious difficulties of hill runs and squashed peas, she established a new record of two miles. This is not to be sniffed at – she pushed the pea with her nose!   *1978*

The busiest canal in the world was blessed with her first customer. The passenger cargo vessel SS *Ancon* made the fifty mile journey along the Panama Canal cutting the 13,000 mile journey from New York to San Francisco to a mere 5,200 miles. Unfortunately, the success was short-lived because just as the journey was being hailed as a landmark in naval history, a series of landslides made further transits impossible. Five years later, the canal was officially opened and today over 15,000 vessels make the trip each year. It is the only canal to connect two oceans and strangely, because of the curve of the Panamanian Isthmus, any ship sailing westwards actually emerges twenty-seven miles *east* of the Atlantic entrance.   *1914*

Lawrence of Arabia was born in Wales, the illegitimate son of an Irish nobleman and his English governess. He fell in love with the

Middle East while researching a thesis on crusader castles, and quickly learned Arabic – though he always spoke it with a pronounced English accent. While spearheading the Arab revolt he became an almost mythical figure, and the Turks put a £20,000 price on his head as *El Aurens*, the train wrecker. Leading his men from the back of a camel or the front seat of a Rolls Royce, he eventually took Damascus ahead of the mainstream of the British army, but he returned home a bitter man, disillusioned with the political disenfranchisement of the Arabs. To show his disgust, he resigned his commission and joined the RAF as Aircraftsman 'Ross' and later 'Shaw'. He took to being flagellated and wanted 'to eat dirt until its taste is normal to me'. Though he became a legend in his own lifetime his best friend, Mrs Bernard Shaw, called him 'an infernal liar', while he described himself in true masochistic style as 'an Irish nobody'. *1888*

Napoleon was born on a carpet in the hallway of his parents' house in Corsica. As a boy he hated the French and wanted to join the English navy to help destroy them. He attended a girls school where 'being a pretty boy and the only one there I was caressed by every one of my fair companions.' Although he spoke fluent Italian and good English he didn't master French until his early twenties. His amazing military career was hallmarked by his survival – in sixty major engagements he had nineteen horses shot from under him, but never suffered a scratch. After proving his invulnerability by deliberately exposing himself to enemy fire he said, 'I am condemned to live.' His many odd personal habits included perfuming his horse, pinching the ears of those who pleased him, looking at corpses and relaxing by reading logarithms. Strangest of all his personal quirks was his massive conceit. Although one painter described his face as a 'bloated suet mask' he was convinced of his own perfection. Boasting about his curiously full breasts he said, 'Any beauty would be proud of a bosom like mine.' *1769*

Today's the day...

Popeye the Sailorman died. Or rather his voice did – the voice of seventy-four-year-old Harry Foster Welch, who'd also provided the vocals for Bluto and Olive Oil. Amongst Welch's greatest fans was a certain Mel Blanc – otherwise known as Bugs Bunny.   *1973*

Liechtenstein celebrates its national day. This tiny Roman Catholic principality of only 61·8 square miles sits snugly between Austria and Switzerland. In the true spirit of compromise the inhabitants speak German but spend Swiss francs. With only eleven miles of railway, fifty policemen, three cinemas, a five-man government and one newspaper, it's the only country in Europe where women don't get the vote. In its defence, however, it should be said that it does have the world's second largest false teeth factory.   *An annual event*

Seventy-year-old William Harrison disappeared from the beautiful Cotswold village of Chipping Camden. He'd set out to collect rents and then vanished completely in what was described as

August 16

'one of the most remarkable occurrences which hath happened in the memory of man.' All that was left of him was his hat, comb and scarf, lying in the road spattered with blood. His servant John Perry was accused of the murder and confessed, naming his mother and brother as accomplices. Despite the absence of a corpse, the trio were summarily hanged. Perry's mother, widely believed to be a witch, was hanged first and buried beneath the gallows while John's body still dangled overhead. An inquisitive female onlooker approached on horseback to catch a glimpse of the supposed witch; the horse reared, she knocked her head on the hanging man and fell headlong into the open grave. Though justice had been seen to be done, the mystery of the missing body lingered on. Two years later it was solved when the 'murdered' man cheerfully walked back into the village with a fantastic tale of being kidnapped and sold into slavery. The shock was so great that his wife promptly hanged herself and the population of Chipping Camden was left to puzzle over why Perry confessed to a murder he didn't commit and sentenced himself and his family to death.   *1660*

Itinerant English oculist John Taylor was born. An undoubtedly skilful eye surgeon who numbered King George II among his clients, he nevertheless acted like a complete charlatan. Audiences paid to watch his operations and he would harangue them in showman-like fashion promising his cures to be 'the true Ciceronian, prodigiously difficult and never attempted in our language before'. At a dinner with the Earl of Dumfries in Edinburgh he recieved his come-uppance when, in his usual braggart style, he informed the table he could tell their thoughts just by looking into their eyes. 'Pray sir,' asked Lady Dumfries, 'do you know what I am thinking?' Taylor replied that he did, and m'lady went on, 'Then it's very safe, for I am sure you will not repeat it.' Taylor later disappeared to the continent and eventually passed away in a convent in Prague. Before he died, however, he went blind.   *1703*

Today's the day...

'The King of the Wild Frontier' Congressman Davy Crockett was born in Hawkins County, Tennessee. He prided himself on his lack of education, maintained that correct spelling was 'contrary to nature', and only went to school for six months to improve his chances of marrying. More at home shooting bears than dining at the White House, he astounded an usher who'd announced 'Make room for Colonel Crockett', by striding into the room exclaiming, 'Colonel Crockett makes room for himself.' When visiting Louisville Zoo with Governor McArthur of Ohio, he remarked that there was a distinct similarity between the baboon and their friend Judge W. He turned round and saw the judge standing right behind him. With great solemnity Crockett removed his hat and looking first at the judge, then at the baboon, remarked, 'Gentlemen I owe one of you an apology, but I do not know which!'   *1786*

The ultimate blonde Mae West was born in Brooklyn, daughter of a heavyweight boxer and a corset model. At six she was playing Little Lord Fauntleroy, before studying dancing and becoming 'The Baby Vamp'. In vaudeville she wrote all her own material and her show *Sex*

in 1926 caused such a row she was jailed for ten days for obscenity. In her first film, with George Raft, she 'stole everything but the cameras', and 'sashayed' into the limelight with her reply to the hat-check girl. 'Goodness,' said the girl, 'what beautiful diamonds.' 'Goodness,' replied Miss West, 'had nothing to do with it, dearie.' William Randolph Hearst was so incensed by her predatory sexuality he mounted a press campaign to pressure Congress into censoring her – but to no avail. Her drawling one-liners are legendary. 'I used to be Snow White, but I drifted.' 'It's not the men in my life, but the life in my men that counts.' When she was told that the RAF had christened their inflatable lifejacket a 'Mae West' she remarked, 'I've been in *Who's Who* and I know what's what, but it's the first time I've been in a dictionary.' *1892*

A sculptor was killed by his muse. The son of a Liverpool tax collector and jeweller, John Deare was apprenticed in London at sixteen and worked with 'great application' to create magnificent mantelpieces and monuments. At twenty he won the coveted gold medal from the Royal Academy and was sent to Rome to study. His works were eagerly sought after but it was his very devotion to work that caused his sudden death. He caught a cold after he'd been sleeping on a strangely shaped block of marble – 'expecting to get inspiration in his dreams for carving it'. *1798*

The first transatlantic balloon crossing was successfully completed when the huge black and silver balloon *Eagle II* sank gracefully to the ground in a wheat field in Normandy. With its crew of three Albuquerque businessmen, it had floated along for five days on its 3,200 mile trip across the waves. Within minutes of landing it had been torn to shreds by eager souvenir hunters who'd been following its progress from the coast. The only person who wasn't too thrilled with it all was the owner of the field – Madame Coquerel – whose $3\frac{1}{2}$ acres of ripe wheat had just been ruined. *1978*

Today's the day...

Emperor Menelek II of Ethiopia was born. He was a very peculiar ruler, with some very curious ideas. He believed in the power of the Bible so completely that whenever he was ill, he would eat a few pages. When he heard about the awesome chair the Americans used that delivered instant death to wrongdoers, he was beside himself with joy and ordered three. Unfortunately, he failed to realise that since Ethiopia had no electricity, they wouldn't be of much use. He employed his initiative, however, and used one of them as a throne. *1844*

Elvis Presley was buried in Memphis, Tennessee, amid a herd of fans and celebrities. It was estimated that 130,000 mourners had paid their respects before the burial, including Jacqueline Onassis. Sixteen cream coloured Cadillacs inched their way to the mausoleum, decked with over 3,000 floral arrangements. Sobbing women rushed to their cars to follow, and a second service had to be arranged for nearly 1,000 fans locked out of the first one. *1977*

Pepys saw *The Loyal Subject* at the Cockpit Theatre and beheld 'the loveliest lady that I ever saw in my life'. Afterwards they went for a drink together, but this was one occasion when Pepys' wife had no need to be jealous because his drinking companion was none other than Edward Kyanston – an actor who made his living playing the female. He once caused Charles II a good deal of confusion, when the King impatiently demanded why he was being kept waiting for the play to start. He was astounded when the master of the company replied that the leading lady was still shaving! *1660*

History repeated itself for Captain Antonio Misa of the Philippine Airlines, when a bomb ripped a hole in his BAC 1-11 jet. The bomber had been sucked out of the hole by the sudden drop in air pressure, but the rest of the passengers were all unharmed. Thinking quickly, the

captain instructed them to put on their oxygen masks, while he eased
the plane down from 24,000 to 10,000ft, and then landed at Manila
Air Force Base. The amazing thing was that not only had the Captain
had a similar experience before, but it had occurred in the very
same plane. 'We are very proud of Captain Misa,' said an airline
official, 'he reacted beautifully . . . just as he did in 1975.'   *1978*

The ill-fated film director Roman Polanski was born to Polish
parents in Paris. He calls himself 'a student of fear' and since his life
has been at least as bizarre and terrifying as his movies, he ought to
know. His mother died in Auschwitz, and at fifteen he narrowly
avoided death at the hands of a triple murderer. In 1969, his beautiful
wife was ritually slaughtered by the Manson 'Family' and many of
his colleagues have died. The man who wrote most of his film music
had a brain haemorrhage; the man who gave him his first break in films
was killed in a car crash; David Stone who translated the script of
Repulsion succumbed to appendicitis and one of his best friends was
killed jumping on a train. His appetite for the macabre is unrelenting.
Shortly after his wife's death, he filmed the cheerful tale of Macbeth.
Asked if he was going to give Shakespeare equal billing he replied,
'Why should I? For one thing, it's already fairly well known that he
was the author. For another thing he hasn't got an agent.'   *1933*

A strange marriage by proxy was contracted in England between
Louis XII of France and Princess Mary Tudor, the sister of
Henry VIII. Since it was a political alliance, it was important that it
be fully solemnised. So the French King sent the Duc de Longueville
to represent him, and after the 'wedding' Mary undressed and went to
bed. Longueville bared one leg and otherwise fully clothed leapt
in to join her. He touched her with his naked limb and then to the
satisfaction of all but the bride, the marriage was said to be
consummated.   *1514*

Today's the day...

Sweet-smelling Roman Emperor Augustus died a fragrant death. Right to the end, he'd anoint various parts of his body with different perfumes – a human pot-pourri, it included mint for the arms, palm oil on the chest, and essence of ivy for the knees. *AD 14*

England's first Astronomer Royal John Flamsteed was born to a family of brewers. Attacked by rheumatic fever of the joints when only fifteen, he was unable to attend school, and instead spent his time studying the heavens – producing some very impressive calculations at an early age. His illness, however, slowed him down and so he went to Ireland to be stroked by the famous faith healer Valentine Greatrakes. Unfortunately the treatment 'found not his disease to stir'. He sought a fixed viewing point from which to study the stars and came up with the novel idea of lying on his mattress at the bottom of a deep well. *1646*

Crazy comic Groucho Marx died. Years earlier Irving Berlin had written the perfect epitaph for him. 'The world would not be in such a snarl /If Marx had been Groucho instead of Karl.' *1977*

August 19

Pioneer aviator Orville Wright was born. Younger than his brother Wilbur, he became the first man to achieve powered sustained flight in the plane they'd built together. As a child, he'd been something of a prodigy – he repaired sewing machines at the age of five, made and sold kites to his friends and built a printing machine at the age of thirteen. Neither he, nor his brother went to high school, and their juvenile money-making ventures included collecting the bones of dead cows and selling them for fertiliser. A sorry twist to the tale is that Orville also earned the dubious distinction of being the world's first pilot to kill his passenger – a certain Lieutenant Selfridge, badly injuring himself at the same time. *1871*

Wild West baddie Wes Hardin died aged forty-one, shot in the back of the head, just a year after his release from a twenty-year prison sentence. Believed to have killed over fifty men (twelve before he could shave), this son of a Methodist minister was inappropriately christened John Wesley, after the famous English preacher. *1895*

The most successful jockey in history Willie Shoemaker was born, weighing in at only 2½lbs. This handicap, however, didn't stop 'the Shoe', as he was known, from breaking the world record in his first full year of racing, with no less than 388 winners. Since 1949, in fact, the pint size (4ft 11in) ninety-eight pounder, has ridden 30,000 races, winning 7,000 and a grand total of over sixty-three million dollars. Spectacular even in defeat, he lost the 1956 Kentucky Derby, though well in the lead, when to the amazement of the crowd, he misjudged the finishing line. *1931*

Scottish steam-engine pioneer James Watt died. He spent his retirement playing with a new invention – a machine which copied sculpture. The copies were presented to his friends as the work 'of a young artist just entering his eighty-third year'. *1891*

Today's the day...

Churchill made his famous tribute to the RAF. Since 13 August the 'Battle of Britain' had raged in the sky above south-east England while the RAF and the Luftwaffe desperately fought for supremacy. Though constantly outnumbered and stretched to the limit, Fighter Command had battled on and in five days destroyed 236 German aircraft, compared to their own loss of ninety-five. In the House of Commons, Churchill echoed the sentiments of the nation when he uttered those immortal words, 'Never in the field of human conflict was so much owed by so many to so few.' *1940*

Tchaikovsky's *1812 Overture* had its première in Moscow. Allegedly written for the consecration of the Temple of Christ, it was composed to be performed outdoors with the accompaniment of actual artillery in the battle scene. At a recent concert in Atlanta, Georgia, the conductor decided to emulate the composer and use real explosives. The blast shook the audience, set off the fire alarms and as the fire brigade hurtled to the scene, filled the concert hall with smoke. *1882*

Ronald Ross celebrated 'Mosquito Day' when he finally located a malarial parasite in the stomach of a spotted-winged mosquito. The discovery meant that the attack against the disease could be taken to the swamps and rivers where the insects bred, and in the second attempt to build the Panama Canal it had its first dramatic success. So drastic was the reduction in malarial deaths that Colonel Gorgas, the engineer in charge, claimed it was the discovery of the little parasite 'that enabled us to build the canal'. *1897*

Leon Trotsky was assassinated on a lazy summer afternoon in the fortress he'd built around himself at Coyoacàn, Mexico. He'd been feeding his rabbits when, for the fourth time in a fortnight, Frank Jacson arrived to ask his advice on an article he'd been writing. The two men disappeared into the study, where Jacson took out an ice-pick, shut his eyes and plunged it into Trotsky's head. Guards rushed in and attacked the assassin, beating him so hard that one of them broke his hand. Trotsky told them to leave him alone, and insisted he be 'made to talk'. Twenty-six hours later the great revolutionary was dead, and Jacson, alias Ramon Mercader never 'talked', not then or throughout his twenty years' imprisonment. It's ironic that on that fateful day he wasn't searched, even though he was wearing a bulky overcoat in the blazing heat. The guards were too busy fitting a new security system.   *1940*

The Russian invasion of Czechoslovakia began one hour before midnight, taking the country completely by surprise. Alarmed by Secretary Dubcek's 'socialism with a human face', Brezhnev sent in the tanks and more than 200,000 troops. As Russian armour rumbled through the streets, there was a spirited but vain resistance. Dubcek had no choice but to sign an agreement providing for the stationing of Soviet troops in Czechoslovakia; it was meant to be a 'temporary' measure, but 90,000 of them are still there today. When last heard of, the ousted Dubcek was working for the Forestry Commission in Bratislava – unable to see his friends and under constant surveillance by the Secret Police, whose powers he'd sought to limit.   *1968*

'Living Encyclopaedia' Samuel Latham Mitchill was born in Long Island. His irrepressible interest in the world led him to poke his nose into everything: agriculture chemistry natural history and geography not to mention politics and philosophy. Dubbed a 'chaos of knowledge' he was a prolific writer and inveterate speech giver; wanted America to be called 'Fredonia' and insisted that the Garden of Eden lay in Onondaga Hollow, New York State. He took himself very seriously and once published a pamphlet of 'Some of the Memorable Events in the Life of Samuel L. Mitchill' – there were 192.   *1764*

Today's the day...

The most bloody woman in history Hungarian Countess
Elizabeth Bathory died. After striking one of her maids, she noticed
that where the blood she had drawn fell on her skin, the flesh felt
exquisitely silky. Convinced that bathing her complete body in blood
would preserve her beauty, she began her ghastly ten year reign of
terror. She kidnapped 610 girls who were dragged to the dark dungeons
of her castle and hung in chains. They were extremely well fed since
she believed the fatter they were, the richer their blood. When ready,
their veins were sliced open and drained through pipes, which led to a
bath where the naked countess joyously wallowed in the tepid
plasma. It was claimed that when her vampirish craving reached its
peak she would bite victims to death. This bloody human dairy
continued until 1610, when she was arrested, tried and condemned to
a living death walled up in her own room. For the remaining three-and-
a-half years of her life, the evil Countess saw no light and never
uttered a sound.   *1614*

Silly Billy King William IV of England was born. He was the
third son of George III who named him after his own father's third
son. His unfortunate talent for tripping over, getting in people's way
and telling dirty jokes very badly, earned him the nickname Silly Billy.
The genial, bumbling Billy had a great love of the sea and at the age
of thirteen joined the navy as an ordinary midshipman. Years later
when he was Lord High Admiral, the government threatened to
resign unless he stopped secretly taking squadrons out to sea, just
to play war games.   *1765*

English boxer and politician John Gully was born. After retiring
from the ring he became a financial wizard and later MP for
Pontefract. He always admitted, however, that he owed his success to
boxing, which strangely he learned while he was in prison for
debt.   *1783*

August 21

The world's most famous smile, Leonardo da Vinci's 'Mona Lisa', was stolen from the Louvre in Paris. The thief was an Italian waiter who, posing as an official photographer, quite literally walked off with it under his arm. It took police two years to track him down, and after being arrested he said that as a true patriot, all he wanted to do was return it to its rightful home in Italy. For two years the world's most valuable painting was kept hidden under his bed. *1911*

'Beautiful exceedingly' English traveller and writer Lady Mary Wortley Montague died. Her physical beauty is questionable, because an early attack of smallpox left her without eyelashes and she covered her pockmarked face with cheap white paint so coarse 'you would not use it to wash a chimney'. Her interest in smallpox deepened when her only brother died of the disease. While in Turkey, she experimented with inoculation achieving such success that on her return she tried to introduce 'ingrafting' into England. She was publicly ridiculed and denounced from the pulpit for trying to take the decision of life and death away from God. She summed up her own life with her last words, 'It has all been very interesting.' *1762*

Today's the day...

The father of contemporary electronic music Karlheinz
Stockhausen was born. On the sleeve notes of his CBS recording
Complete Piano Music, he listed everything that had been eaten and
drunk by the pianist during the recording, including 'an omelette
with salami and a portion of Ceylon tea, high grown'. His instructions
to musicians are equally elucidating – 'Think nothing. Wait until
there is complete silence in you. Start to play (a sound). As soon as
you begin to think, stop.' He's confused audiences the world over,
not to mention critics. His professor slated one performance, only
to be told by the composer that he was trying to see a chicken in an
abstract painting. His choristers fare little better. He calls them cows
and rhinos, while some of them show their appreciation for his music
by actually wearing ear plugs.   *1928*

Fifteen terrorists attacked De Gaulle in the twenty-second and
worst of the world-record thirty-one attempts on his life. He, his wife,
son-in-law and driver were motoring through the Paris suburb of
Petit Clamart, when they were sprayed with a searing volley of 150
shots. Security guards chased off the gunmen, who were led by Lt Col.
Jean Marie Bastien Thiry – a man who ironically had just been
decorated by De Gaulle with the cross of the *Légion d'Honneur*.
Oddly enough, the General sustained only one injury. While wiping
glass splinters from his coat he scratched his finger, wiped his face
and left a small speck of blood on his cheek. With amazing sang-froid
he stepped out to inspect the airforce guard of honour and
immediately after he turned to his steward and said, 'Whisky, and
some beer for my wife.'   *1962*

Handel scored a hit with the first performance of his *Water Music*.
The diplomatically inept composer had been Kapellmeister to George
Elector of Hanover, but frustrated by the confines of this provincial
European Court, he came to England and was granted permission to

474

stay for 'only a reasonable time'. He stayed rather longer, thanks to the patronage of Queen Anne, who gave him a life pension. Unfortunately when Anne died, she was succeeded by none other than George Elector of Hanover, who became King George I of England. Poor Handel dared not show his face at court until Baron Kilmannsegge made a shrewd suggestion. The King was making a triumphant procession down the Thames from Whitehall to Limehouse. The Baron was in charge of the arrangements and asked Handel to write some music. He did and it was played in the barge directly behind the King's. George was so delighted that even when he learnt who the composer was, he could do nothing but forgive his errant Kapellmeister. *1715*

Vitriolic American writer and wit Dorothy Parker was born. She was not crazy about other women writers, especially novelists. 'As artists they're rot,' she said, 'but as providers they're oil wells, they gush.' When she failed to meet a *New Yorker* deadline she said she was sorry but 'somebody was using the pencil'. *1893*

The much maligned Richard III was butchered at Bosworth Field, as he vainly struggled to reach the usurper Henry Tudor. Despite Shakespeare, it is unlikely that he was a hunchback and certainly did not waste his last words offering his kingdom for a horse. He'd been betrayed by Lord Stanley who'd deserted him in the thick of the battle and he ended his life screaming with some accuracy, 'I will die King of England! I will not budge a foot ... Treason! Treason!' Before the battle, Richard was seen to be grinding and gnashing his teeth, and when he found a sentry snoozing he stabbed him, saying, 'I found him asleep and have left him as I found him.' By a weird mischance, this last English King to die in battle was the third King Richard to die by violent means, and cautious monarchs have avoided the name ever since. *1485*

Today's the day...

Ill-fated King Louis XVI of France was born. Etiquette demanded that people should back away from him if he walked towards them and he loved backing them into walls. Guests at Fontainebleau had to bring their own furniture and food, while the Queen had to put up with his rather odd hobby of locksmithing. To escape her dislike of the activity, he used to hide away in a secret workshop, where he was said to have created a master key that would open any lock in France. He and Marie Antoinette were respectively twenty and nineteen when grandfather Louis XV died and they came to the throne. The new King fell on his knees, and said, 'Guide us, protect us, oh God. We are too young to reign.' The crown used at his coronation in Rheims Cathedral in June 1775 cost nearly a million pounds. His kingship cost him his head. *1754*

The great lover Rudolf Valentino died of peritonitis, ten minutes after noon in the Polyclinic Hospital, New York. During his traumatic career, he had been much attacked by the press for using pink powder. It clearly played on his mind, for on his death-

476

bed, he asked his doctors, 'Do I act like a pink powder puff?' Several women were driven to commit suicide, two in front of the hospital. A London girl poisoned herself, and in Paris an elevator boy became the only male casualty. 100,000 telegrams were sent, a memorial was built in Hollywood, and still today there's a special ceremony of remembrance every year. The most spectacular mourner was his ex-wife Jean Acker, whose theatrical display of grief waned a little when she discovered he'd only left her $1. Numerous paternity suits were filed against his estate, despite the fact that neither of his marriages was ever consummated.

1926

The world's worst poet, William McGonagall of Dundee, died of a cerebral haemorrhage. He had been a weaver until the age of fifty-two, when he suddenly discovered his genius for creating appalling rhymes and horrifying metre. He was convinced his verses were inspired, and claimed the Emperor of Brazil had left his country just to come and see his famous poem 'The Railway Bridge of the Silvery Tay'. Without honour in his own country, however, he was pelted with fruit at recitals, and turned away when he went to present his poem 'Balmoral Castle' to Queen Victoria. Although his name is now immortal, it was spelt wrong on his death certificate. His wife, fortunate woman, couldn't read.

1902

Saint Ebba the younger – a king's daughter – was born in Northumberland. When her father was taken by the Danes she became a nun, and eventually Prioress of Colringham. To protect her chastity and that of her holy sisters, she cut off her nose and persuaded them to do the same, so that 'their beauty might be of no bait' to the wicked Vikings. When a fresh lot of Danish raiders arrived, however, and found a convent full of noseless nuns, they expiated their ugly lust by burning the convent and the nuns with it.

Feast Day

Today's the day...

The bloodthirsty Mongol leader Genghis Khan died, probably taking posthumous pleasure from the fact that his funeral escort murdered everyone who even looked at his coffin. His butchery began early. After his first success he had seventy enemy chiefs boiled alive – just as a warning. He never took prisoners and all corpses had their stomachs ripped open, because people hid precious jewels by swallowing them. The dead were then decapitated and the heads stacked in vast gory pyramids. Genghis Khan slaughtered more people than any other man in history – twenty million souls, at that time one tenth of the world's population. *1227*

Mount Vesuvius erupted in the most famous volcanic disaster in history. The town of Pompeii was slowly covered under noxious fumes and white ashes. The nearby town of Herculaneum was smothered under a river of mud 60ft deep. Some inhabitants chose to sit it out in cellars while others were more ingenious, running through the streets protecting themselves with pillows tied over their heads! The most famous victim of the volcano was Pliny the Elder who was killed by his own curiosity. He insisted on studying the eruption at first hand and at the end of the day showed his unconcern by taking a long hot bath and going to bed. He suffocated. Paradoxically the eruption not only destroyed Pompeii, but also preserved it for all time. *AD 79*

A silly expression was born with the gruesome murder of eight-year-old Fanny Adams at Alton, Hampshire. While picking black-berries she was approached by a young man who offered her a halfpenny to follow him. She refused but quickly accepted when he upped the figure to 2½d. Later that day her dismembered body was discovered literally piece by piece – her eyes were actually found floating in the nearby River Wey. The murderer was quickly apprehended and executed. Around this time British sailors were

478

being issued with a new diet of low grade tasteless tinned meat, and the grizzly joke went around the ports that they were eating 'sweet Fanny Adams'. The term fell into popular use to describe anything that was tasteless or worthless.   *1867*

The first man to swim the English Channel Captain Matthew Webb dived off the Admiralty Pier, Dover. After twelve miles the sea was so calm he could distinctly recognise a tune being played by the Dover Band. Fighting clogging seaweed, stinging star fish and advancing tides he made the twenty-one mile journey in 21hrs 45mins. A considerate hotelier at Cap Griz Nez hired a band to 'hush him to slumbers' but it only kept him awake! Webb's style was so perfect the water had rubbed a straight raw line across his neck.   *1875*

The world's oldest man was found in a Hungarian limestone quarry. He didn't have much to say since he had been dead for about 450,000 years besides which he had no mouth! All that was discovered was his occipital bone – the lower part of the head where it merges with the neck. His name has been withheld until next of kin have been informed.   *1965*

Today's the day...

German philosopher Friedrich Nietzsche died insane. A brilliant professor at the age of twenty-four, he was the man who developed the concepts of 'nihilism', 'the superman' and 'the will to power', but his life was plagued with suffering. Intense headaches, vomiting, temporary paralysis and loss of speech dogged him and in 1888 he finally snapped. He was committed to an asylum, and though he partially recovered, he was to serve another twelve years of life, before dying of an apoplectic fit. The son of a Lutheran minister, he had coined the phrase 'God is dead'. Perhaps the Almighty was getting his own back.   *1900*

Balding heart-throb Sean Connery was born. An ex-coffin polisher and muscleman, he made his stage *début* in *South Pacific* and changed his name from Thomas to Sean in 1953 – coincidentally the same year Ian Fleming wrote his first Bond novel *Casino Royale*. Early contenders for the part of 007 included Trevor Howard, Peter Finch, James Mason and Richard Burton. Connery got it, despite refusing to make a screen test.   *1930*

The story of one of the great non-executions began when the house of Mary Breeze of Sydney, Australia, was robbed by person or persons unknown. Breeze reported it to convict-turned-constable Luker, who was found the following day, with his head beaten in. Governor King took personal charge of the investigation; all roads were blocked and five men arrested. Joseph Samuels and James Hardwicke were found guilty of murder; Hardwicke was reprieved, but Samuels was taken by cart to the gallows at Brickfield Hills. When the cart was driven from beneath him, 'the suspending cord was separated' and the condemned man fell to the ground. They tried again and 'the line unrove until the legs of the sufferer trailed on the ground'. They tried a third time and again the rope snapped. There was an outcry from the crowd, and soon after, a reprieve from the Governor. Samuels recovered but within a year, a convict of the same name escaped from Newcastle prison in an open boat and was never seen again, and so it's believed was ended the story of the man they couldn't hang – he drowned. *1803*

A real-life Jonah was swallowed by a whale off the Falkland Isles. Leaving the whaler in a rowing boat, thirty-five-year-old English steersman James Bartley headed for a large school of sperm whales. In a *mêlée* of harpooning, one of the wounded animals upskittled the boat and swallowed Bartley as he tried to jump clear. Later that day, the crew collected the bodies of the dead whales that had floated to the surface, and began stripping them. Curled up in the intestines of one, the amazed seamen discovered their lost shipmate, alive but unconscious. Brought round by massage and brandy, he could remember only being in the company of live fish, surrounded by hot slime which gave way 'like soft india rubber'. The event had left an indelible impression however – the whale's enzymes had bleached Bartley's body white. *1891*

The seventeenth modern Olympics opened in Rome. Heroine of the track events was Wilma Rudolph, the first American girl to win three gold medals. Challenged to an unofficial race by eighteen-year-old light-heavyweight boxing gold medallist Cassius Clay, she left him behind 'so fast it was pitiful'. Wilma, one of nineteen children, was asked how she could run so fast. She replied, 'Man, in my family, you had to run fast if you wanted to eat!' *1960*

The world's first parachute wedding was solemnised at the New York World's Fair when Arno Rudolphi was married to Anne Hayward by the Reverend Homer Tomlinson. These three, plus the best man, maid-of-honour and four musicians were all suspended from the ceiling in harness. *1940*

Today's the day...

The first artillery barrage in a major battle took place at Crécy, where Edward III, his son, the Black Prince and their 9,000 men faced the 30,000 strong French army of Philip VI. The first cannon, however, which were little more than iron pots filled with gunpowder, rocks and bits of iron, were as dangerous to their owners as they were to the enemy – what really won the day was the withering fire of the English long-bow men. Disdained by the French mounted knights as a faint-hearted rabble, they nevertheless outshot and outdistanced the enemy's crossbows. In all, eleven princes, 1,200 knights and 10,000 soldiers were destroyed. The victory was won at a cost however – the English force was to be known as the barebottom army because it was riddled with dysentery.   *1346*

The fastest century was scored by English cricketer Percy Fender, playing for Surrey against Northampton. It took this bionic batsman just thirty-five minutes.   *1920*

The amazing Chevalier D'Eon fought his last duel in Southampton, dressed as a woman, as usual. Though he'd commanded a company of dragoons in the Seven Years' War, it was in drag, as a secret agent and duellist, that he made his greatest claim to fame. This fight was against a Frenchman named De Launey. Unhappily, De Launey's foil broke, and the remaining five inches of blade pierced the Chevalier through the shoulder. The wound was not properly cared for, and though he lived for another fourteen years, it almost certainly caused his death. The irony was that Europe's greatest swordsman was only beaten because he fell on his opponent's steel after tripping on his own skirt.   *1796*

The father of modern chemistry Antoine Lavoisier was born. He financed his research by investing a million francs of his family's money in *Ferme Generale* – the notoriously corrupt French company of profiteering tax farmers. He even married a tax farmer's daughter, who at fourteen was half his age. In his defence, however, it should be said that he coined the words 'oxygen' and 'hydrogen', and discovered that the average weight of matter expelled by human sweat in a twenty-four-hour period is 52·89oz! Unfortunately, come the Revolution, this carried very little weight. He was arrested by an officer who told him that the Republic had no need for scientists, prosecuted by the infamous Marat, and guillotined for a list of crimes which not only included tax farming, but the fiendish and inscrutable offence of 'watering the people's tobacco'. *1743*

The most famous ghost story of World War I was witnessed by both friend and foe, during the British retreat from the bloody field of Mons, in Belgium. Outnumbered by more than two to one, the British decided to stand and fight it out. At 3.30pm, the Second Corps stood waiting for the *coup de grâce*, when a phantom army of angels appeared, striking terror into the Germans and holding them at bay. The British grasped the opportunity and fled, saving eighty per cent of their force. A month later a version of the story appeared in the British *Evening News*, only this time the spectral regiment was led by Saint George. Arthur Machen, who wrote the article, claimed it was pure fiction – but how else do you explain how 50,000 weary Tommies so miraculously escaped from a German army nearly three times as strong in both men and guns? *1914*

Keen Christian novelist John Buchan was born. At the age of five, he was kept in bed for a year, after his head had been run over by the wheel of his pram. Years later, illness confined him to his bed again, and there he wrote *The Thirty-Nine Steps* at the age of thirty-nine. In 1935 he became Governor General of Canada, and was made a Red Indian Chief. Summing up his religious views, he said, 'An atheist is a man who has no invisible means of support.' *1875*

Today's the day...

The island of Krakatoa blew up with the loudest recorded explosion in history. Its giant volcano Rakata had lain dormant for 200 years but recently deep rumblings had been heard and nearby islanders had watched fearfully as mile-high fountains of dust came belching out of its crater. The air was thick with vapour, a black pall of smoke hung over the island and lumps of pumice rained down from the sky. At 10am Rakata erupted and blew the island to smithereens. The blast was heard nearly 3,000 miles away, rocks were hurled for thirty-four miles and a Dutch scientist described how 'the bottom of the sea seemed to have cracked open so that subterranean fires belched out'. In the tidal wave which followed over 36,000 people were killed, and the waves made their mark over 7,500 miles away at Cape Horn.   *1883*

Movie mogul Samuel Goldwyn was born. A glove salesman from Minsk, he was given the name 'Goldfish' when he entered the United States but changed it when he realised the immigration officer's little joke. Regarded as one of the founders of Hollywood, he became famous for his sayings like 'Include me out', and 'In two words: im-possible'. He summed up his whole movie-making philosophy when he said, 'What we want is a story that starts with an earthquake and works its way up to a climax.'   *1882*

The Duke of Bourbon was discovered, hanged in his bedroom. Suspicion immediately alighted on his English mistress, Sophie Dawes, who'd spirited the elderly Duke away to the remote Château de St Leu some weeks earlier, accompanied only by her nephew and a shady priest. Since he'd spotted her in a London brothel nearly twenty years earlier, Sophie had profited greatly from her association with the Duke. Provided with a scapegoat husband, the Baron de Feuchères, she'd been accepted at the French court and was much sought after – especially by those wishing to have their children named as heirs to the childless Bourbon fortune. In the end she persuaded the old Duke to leave

August 27

everything to the second son of the Duc d'Orléans, and it was when
Orléans became King that Bourbon had suddenly died. The frail old
man had apparently managed to strap two cravats round his neck and
hoist himself up on the window catch. A long court enquiry ensued and
it seemed certain Sophie would be arrested. Then suddenly the King
intervened, the case was dismissed and the suspect murderess was
awarded part of the Bourbon Palace, the Château de St Leu and a
legacy of eight million francs.

1830

The shortest war in history was fought when the English fleet
popped into Zanzibar harbour for a quick game of cricket. Spotlessly
clad in their 'whites', the officers were just about to leave their ships
when the Sultan of Zanzibar declared war on them. Rear Admiral
Rawson demanded the Sultan's surrender but he refused, so the fleet
turned their guns on the town. In less than thirty-eight minutes they
reduced the palace to rubble, killed and injured 500 soldiers, sank the
Sultan's one and only battleship and accepted his capitulation – and
not a ball was bowled.

1884

Today's the day...

Captive host Renwick Williams celebrated his imprisonment
with a party in London's notorious Newgate jail. Known as 'the
Monster' for his attacks on young girls with a knife concealed in a
bunch of flowers, he was caught after stabbing Anne Porter, and tried
on two counts. One was for wounding her, and the other for 'wilfully
and maliciously spoiling, tearing, cutting and defacing her clothes'.
Strangely enough, the latter was a capital offence, and Williams was
sentenced to death. On appeal, however, it was decided that he had
damaged her clothes only accidentally, in pursuance of the attack. So
with stunning illogicality his sentence was reduced from hanging, to
two years inside. Helping him celebrate were forty guests, including
defence witnesses and fellow prisoners. Tea was served to the
accompaniment of flutes and violins, and guests later enjoyed a cold
buffet with wine, before leaving at 9pm in strict accordance with
prison rules. Appropriately, the event became known as the 'Monster's
Ball'. *1790*

The world's first oil rig struck it rich, at Titusville, Pennsylvania.
The owner, ex-railway guard and drifter, Edwin Drake, had
originally been sent to inspect the site by the Rock Oil Company,
simply because he was available, and cheap – he still had his railroad
pass. Drake sank all his life savings into the project but missed the
great moment of the strike, was apparently unmoved by it and never
really made a great deal of money out of it. He became a Justice of the
Peace, but lost what small fortune he had on Wall Street, and was
found years later wandering the streets in a ragged coat, incapacitated
by neuralgia. The inscription on his monument tells of his sad ending –
'Oppressed by ills, to want no stranger, he died in comparative
obscurity.' After his death a young man was sent to make an investment
report on Drake's Well, and though through oil he was to become one
of the richest men in the world, he said there was little opportunity for
profit. His name was John D. Rockefeller. *1859*

August 28

Wagner's opera Lohengrin was first performed. It contains the 'Bridal Chorus' better known as 'Here Comes the Bride'. What isn't quite so well known is that it's sung as Lohengrin and his new bride Elsa are getting undressed ready to go to bed. The first tenor to sing the title role, Joseph Tichatschek, is supposed to be responsible for one of the most famous funnies in opera. In the first act, Wagner's hero is supposed to arrive on stage in a boat drawn by a swan. Unfortunately during one performance, someone pushed the boat out before the passenger had boarded. Completely unabashed, Tichatschek calmly turned around and asked, 'What time does the next swan leave?'   *1850*

The world's first radio commercial was transmitted, by Station WEAF in New York City. The ten-minute spot featured a new property development at Jackson Heights described in glowing terms by a certain Mr Blackwell of the Queensborough Corporation. It was broadcast at 5.15pm every day for five days, after which the company proudly announced they had sold two of their apartments. The cost of their historic campaign was a mere $100.   *1922*

Today's the day...

Faraday began work on the production of electricity from
magnetism. Having built an iron ring with a couple of coils of insulated
wire, he connected one to a battery, and the other to a magnetic needle.
He'd made, in fact, the first electric transformer. He wrote, 'I think
I may have got hold of a good thing but I can't say; it may be a
weed instead of a fish I shall pull up after all my labours!' It was a very
big 'fish' indeed, for Faraday's 'good thing' was to become the dynamo
and his experiment the very beginning of the age of electricity. *1831*

The English monopoly on cricket was broken in an historic Test
Match, when the Australians beat the mother country, for the first
time, by only seven runs. The next day an obituary appeared in the
Sporting Times – 'In affectionate remembrance of English Cricket,
which died at the Oval. Deeply lamented by a large circle of sorrowing
friends and aquaintances. The body will be cremated and the ashes
taken to Australia.' Thus the legendary 'Ashes' were born, and two
years later the English cricket captain was actually presented with an
urn said to contain them, though authorities disagree as to whether they
were in fact the ashes of the bails or the stumps used in the earlier
match. Either way, they were borne home that year and the urn, which
was made in Melbourne, hasn't been back to Australia since. This is
because the 'Ashes' that are annually played for, in the words of the
Oxford English Dictionary, are 'an imaginary trophy'. *1882*

The amazing Blondin sky-walked across Sydney Harbour, 50ft
up on a 3in tightrope. Watched by 16,000 Australians, under
what his manager described as 'the biggest top in the world', he
went backwards and forwards dressed first as a knight in silver armour,
and then in athletics clothes. He did headstands and back rolls;
crossed while blindfolded and inside a sack, and finally carried a coal
stove out into the middle, lit a fire, cooked an omelette and washed it
down with champagne. Thereafter his tour was a sell-out, with

audiences particularly impressed by his nocturnal exploits, where with fireworks fixed to a wheelbarrow, and with his balancing pole and helmet, the blazing funambulist leapt across his rope, lighting up the antipodean twilight.   *1874*

The fast and furious Earl of March, later the Fourth Duke of Queensbury, won a bet with Irish horseman and gambler Count Theobald O'Taffe, that he could travel nineteen miles in an hour in a four-wheel carriage. 'Old Q' as he was known, had a super-light spider carriage constructed of wood and whalebone, with an all-silk harness, the whole thing weighing only 2½cwt. To this he hitched four of the finest blood horses he could find, set off at 7am, and made the distance in just 53mins 27secs. Though it's not known how much 'Old Q' made in side-bets, it's doubtful that he recouped the cost of the carriage. He needn't have worried – he was the richest man in England.   *1750*

The Star of David became the official emblem of the Jewish people at the 'First Zionist Congress' in Basle, Switzerland. It wasn't the first congress, however, since there had been one twelve years earlier in Kattowitz. Neither was the famous six-pointed star a uniquely Jewish symbol. In fact, none of the twelve tribes had ever had a symbol of their own, and the irony is that this very distinctive one which dates back some 4,000 years, has often been found in Moslem mosques.   *1897*

The most famous Chinese dish was created by the chef of the Chinese Ambassador to America. Seeking to please the palates of both American and Chinese diplomats at a banquet, the ingenious Oriental literally threw together lots of different bits and pieces. When asked what it was he replied '*Tsa Sui*' meaning 'various things'. The nearest American pronunciation was that great Chinese favourite 'Chop Suey' – created in New York.   *1896*

Today's the day...

Ruthless but careful King Louis XI of France died. An epileptic,
who took liquid gold for his troubles, he was served by numerous
dubious medics. One such quack predicted that the King's mistress
would die in eight days, and sure enough, she did. Louis had the man
brought before him, told his servants to throw him out of the window
when he gave the word, and said, 'You pretend to know exactly the fate
of others. Tell me, this moment, what will be yours?' Quick as a flash,
the quack replied, 'Sire, I shall die just three days before Your Majesty.'
Cautious to a fault, Louis spared him. *1483*

The strange case of the 'Shark Papers' first came to light when
Lieutenant Whylie came aboard HMS *Ferret* to breakfast with his
friend Lieutenant Michael 'Fighting' Fitton. Britain was at war with
America, and the previous day, Whylie in his cutter HMS *Sparrow* had
caught the US blockade runner *Nancy* and taken her to Port Royal,
Jamaica. She couldn't be taken as a prize, nor her crew condemned,
because her skipper, Captain Briggs, had thrown her papers overboard,
and replaced them with forgeries. By an amazing coincidence, however,
'Fighting' Fitton had been doing a spot of fishing before breakfast, and

had caught a huge shark. When they opened it up, they were staggered to find the missing papers in pristine condition, inside. The two officers rushed back to port and the jaws of justice closed around the unfortunate Captain Briggs.   *1799*

Short fat miser John Camden Neild died in his sparsely furnished house in Chelsea, after a lifetime of incredible meanness. Despite doubling his inherited fortune of £250,000 he never bought a bed, wouldn't have his socks mended or his patched old clothes brushed, for fear they'd wear. He lunched on a boiled egg and dry bread; wouldn't wear his overcoat saying it was beyond his means; and travelled with the local coal merchant, whom he paid a penny, rather than cough up for a cab. In his will this 'frigid, spiritless specimen of humanity' bequeathed nothing to his faithful housekeeper who had cared for him for twenty-six years – on one occasion stopping him from committing suicide. Instead he left almost his entire £500,000 fortune to Queen Victoria.   *1852*

Lenin survived a remarkable assassination attempt, as he left the Michelson factory in Moscow. He had just delivered a 'Victory or Death' speech to the workers. The nearly blind Fanya Kaplan and her sister Dora, who had recently returned from Siberian exile, tried first to harangue him about food shortages. Accounts vary as to which of them pulled the gun, which shot him three times in the neck, shoulder and chest. There is some doubt too, as to whether Dora was shot dead on the spot or executed later, though it's known that Fanya died in prison. It was four years before Lenin was strong enough for an operation, when astounded surgeons discovered that one of the bullets was a dum-dum that had failed to fragment on entry. Even more curious was the discovery that the bullet had been smeared with deadly curare. Neither bullets, nor deadly poison it seemed, could destroy the hero of the Soviet Union.   *1918*

Today's the day...

Screwball Roman Emperor Caligula was born. Originally called Gaius, he was given his famous nickname, which means little boot or 'bootikin', when as a child he wore a miniature version of the 'caliga' – the soldier's boot. On coming to power at the age of twenty-five he appointed himself god and replaced the heads of all the statues of the other gods with his own. He made his horse, Incitatus, a senator, and committed incest with all three of his sisters. When his favourite, Drusilla died, he forbade the entire population to laugh or take a bath. It became a capital offence to mention goats in his presence and anyone who criticised his games was sawn in half. His hobbies included watching executions and tortures, and scalping people who had more hair than he did. He complained that times were bad because there hadn't been any massacres, earthquakes or fires and to console himself kept two little books full of the names of people he intended to murder. In less than a year, he blew his fortune of twenty-seven million gold pieces, and to recoup the loss, took a share of the earnings of all Rome's prostitutes, and held public auctions of other people's property. After three years, ten months and eight days of this nonsense, a handful of the disaffected had the good sense to murder him. *AD 12*

The birth of tough-guy Emperor Commodus was celebrated in Rome. Strong, good-looking and ruthless, he took personal pleasure in murdering his own victims, under the guise of a gladiatorial contest. Since no-one dared beat him, he won all of his 1,031 fights, mostly by strangulation. He commanded that he be worshipped as Hercules, but that little availed him when his lover slipped him a Mickey Finn, and with a nice touch of irony had him strangled. *AD 161*

Jack the Ripper struck in real style for the first time, when he mutilated Whitechapel prostitute Mary Anne Nichols, popularly known as Polly. A notorious drunk, she had been thrown out of the local doss-house, shouting, 'Don't worry – I'll soon get the money!'

August 31

She was found with her head very nearly severed from her body, and disembowelled by two gashes from lower abdomen to breast. The style of the killing has led some criminologists to believe that Polly was the first of all the Ripper victims (and not Martha Turner who three weeks earlier had been stabbed thirty-nine times, but suffered none of the more typical 'skilfully performed' mutilations). As in almost all Jack's fiendish works, Polly was dispatched in absolute silence. He always cut their vocal chords first. *1888*

The world's only financial composer was born. His name was Joseph Schillinger and all his compositions were inspired by the money pages of the *New York Times*. He would draw a graph of the fluctuating prices of commodities like gold and wheat, and use the resulting curves to add to his stock of melodies. *1895*

Demon batsman Sir Gary Sobers became the first cricketer to score six sixes in a single over, batting for Nottingham against Glamorgan. The unhappy bowler Malcolm Nash watched helplessly as the final ball, which is now in Nottingham Musem, soared over the stands and fell into the road, where it was picked up by an ecstatic little boy. *1968*

Today's the day...

The phantom anaesthetist made his first attack in Mattoon, Illinois. His victim said he had prised her window open and sprayed her with a sweet-smelling gas which paralysed her legs and made her vomit. Over the next twelve days, twenty-four more women made official complaints, many giving intimate descriptions. Though a police drag-net was mounted, the Phantom was never caught, and is now thought by psychologists to have been no more than a figment of mass hysteria.

1944

The longest papal conclave ended when Theoboldi Visconti, Archdeacon of Liège, became Pope Gregory X. His predecessor Clement IV had died three years earlier, but the College of Cardinals spent an amazing thirty-one months in the Vatican without coming to a decision. Finally they were put on bread and water, and quite literally had the roof taken from over their heads. A divine revelation quickly followed.

1271

The most amazing directive ever given by an English judge was delivered at the trial of Quakers William Meade and William Penn, the founder of Pennsylvania. Charged with conspiracy and causing a riot, their real crime had been to hold religious meetings forbidden by the Anglican Church. The jury found them 'guilty of speaking in Gracechurch Street', which of course was not a crime. Furious, the judge refused to dismiss them saying 'We will have a verdict, with the help of God, or you shall starve for it.' After two nights in prison, 'without meat, drink, fire or tobacco', they changed their verdict – to not guilty. The apoplectic judge fined Penn and Meade for not wearing their hats in court; fined the jury a steep forty marks and imprisoned them for two months, from where they claimed their release every six hours. In the furore that followed, the illegality of punishing juries was established and Penn's point proved – that unjust laws are powerless against upright people.

1670

September 1

Ape-man writer Edgar Rice Burroughs was born. Under the *nom de plume* of Norman Bean, he sold his first Tarzan story in 1912 and got just £700 for what he thought was a lousy yarn. His hero nevertheless became the subject of forty films and twenty-six books, translated into fifty-six languages. Yet in 1969, the books were banned from Los Angeles libraries because, reprehensively, Tarzan and Jane weren't married. *1875*

The youngest King of England Henry VI toddled to the throne aged nine months, on the death of his father, the hero of Agincourt. He signed his first royal decree with a thumb print appointing Dame Alice Butler his nurse and giving her licence 'to chastise him reasonably from time to time'. At the age of four he opened parliament for the first time, sitting on his mother's knee. *1422*

Sun King Louis XIV of France died four days before his seventy-seventh birthday, after a reign of seventy-two years 110 days – the longest in European history. Throughout his life, he'd been plagued by minor ailments. Gross over-eating gave him constant stomach pains, for which he took powders of crab, viper, lead and pearl. He used 'oil of gold' as an enema, and on one memorable occasion his doctors' efforts were rewarded when they reported that 'at last, after six hours, his bowels moved'. With all his teeth and a large piece of jaw missing, he took to gobbling his food whole and often it entered his nose or left through it. Though he made the disreputable business of surgery respectable, by allowing Monsieur Felix to remove an anal fistula, it availed him nothing in his last days of pain. His legs became gangrenous and turned black, and he was simply too old for amputation. Turning to a weeping servant he said, 'Why are you crying? Did you think I was immortal?' His heart was preserved and later came into the hands of the bizarre English epicure, Dr Buckland – who ate it. *1715*

Today's the day...

Ex-Prime Minister Edward Heath's yacht *Morning Cloud III* was sunk in a Force 9 gale in the English Channel. Skippered by the unfortunately named Ronald Blewitt, it was struck by a huge wave and two of the six crew members were swept overboard. One was hauled back again, but the other sadly was lost. As the yacht turned about to look for him, it was struck by a second wave and Christopher Chadd, Mr Heath's godson, was also taken by the sea. The rest of the crew took to the life-raft and were rescued eight hours later. All the *Morning Cloud*s were unlucky. At the 1973 launch of this one, a crew member's wife fell into the slipway and was knocked unconscious. The second was sold and embarrassingly and inauspiciously re-named *Opposition*. While the first was smashed to pieces, on this very same day, Mr Heath was engaged in promoting a new thriller by John Dyson. It was called *The Prime Minister's Boat is Missing*.   *1974*

The last of the famous Blaydon Races was run, as usual amid much controversy. When 'Anxious Moments' came in at 5–1, sceptics demanded that jockey and saddle should be weighed again. It was found that the horse had run at 14lbs underweight and a riot ensued. The weighing-in room and the stewards' room were set alight, bookies were chased around the grounds and several jockeys were thrown in the River Tyne. Thus an English institution ended with a splash.   *1916*

The Great Fire of London started, and was spotted as early as 3am by the diarist Samuel Pepys, who thought it 'far enough off' and went back to bed. It spread with a fury, however, and with such an intensity that buildings some distance away burst into flames, causing Londoners to believe it was arson. Astrologer William Lilly claimed he'd predicted it, and was hauled before an extraordinary session of Parliament to explain himself. Frenchman Richard Hubert, 'a poor distracted wretch, weary of life' actually confessed, and was tried and executed, though he wasn't even in London when it began. According to an inscription,

September 2

now erased, it was all a 'horrid plot for extirpating Protestant and Old English liberty and introducing Popery and Slavery'. An even less likely theory is celebrated on a lesser known monument, high on a wall near the old Smithfield market. It's a little naked fat boy, said to represent the sin of gluttony, which was thought to have caused the fire, because it started at Pudding Lane and ended at Pie Corner. The fire lasted four days, destroyed 13,200 houses and left 80,000 people homeless – though amazingly only six were killed.   *1666*

A golfer's dream was realised by Norman L. Manley at the Del Valle Country Club, Saugus, California. On the 330 yard par 4 seventh hole he hit a hole in one, and then on the 290 yard par 4 eighth, he did it again. This double albatross, as it's called, is considered the greatest feat in golfing history.   *1964*

Toothsome Duchess Isabella of Rutland died. Wife of the fourth Duke of this one time smallest and now defunct English county, she was an incredibly vain woman. When she lost a front tooth, she insisted that her poor maid have one pulled also, and had it transplanted into her own aristocratic mouth.   *1831*

Today's the day...

The bloodiest coronation ever seen in Britain was the crowning of Richard the Lionheart. A Jewish money-lender tried to enter Westminster Abbey bearing a gift for the new king, who was his best customer. For daring to defile a Christian sanctuary, he was immediately 'smitten with a man's fist'. The incident sparked off a wave of anti-semitism and while the ceremony continued inside the Abbey, hundreds of Jews were being slaughtered out in the streets. Ironically this very day, remembered for its injustice, is also regarded as the limit of legal memory and is therefore the birthday of British Justice.   *1189*

Handsome blond-haired hero Alan Ladd was born in Hot Springs, Arkansas. Before entering films, the 5ft 6in teenager became West Coast diving champion and a hot dog salesman on a stall appropriately called Tiny's. His small stature, however, was not to hamper his career since leading ladies obligingly stood in trenches or he gallantly stood on boxes. He described his own appearance as being 'like an ageing choirboy'. Raymond Chandler was more accurate, he said Ladd was 'a small boy's idea of a tough guy'.   *1913*

'A bastard tertian ague' killed Oliver Cromwell. His body was embalmed, given a lavish funeral and interred in Westminster Abbey. Two years later, when the monarchy was restored, the well-preserved corpse was exhumed amid great rejoicing and dragged to Tyburn where it was publicly hanged in the gallows and beheaded – the executioner taking eight strokes and bending Cromwell's nose in the process. Spiked on a pole, the head was paraded through the streets and stuck on the roof of the English Parliament. For twenty-four years the hideous face stared down on passers-by, until a violent storm blew it to the ground. A sentry picked it up and later bequeathed it to his daughter who sold it. For the next 250 years the 'Monster's Head' brought misfortune to all who owned it. By 1960, it was kept in an oak box, one-eared, battered and wartless, but still clearly the head of England's only dictator. In a final touching ceremony, it was laid to rest in the grounds of his old college, Sidney Sussex, Cambridge. The site remains a closely guarded secret – so its safekeeping will never be a headache again. *1658*

A garlic and brandy cocktail was patented by Nathan Hart. This British recipe instructed people to mix a couple of garlic bulbs with a bottle of Three Star brandy and then slowly warm the mixture for seven days. Hart stated that this odd brew was a sure cure for consumption. *1904*

Great Britain stood alone and declared war against the might of Nazi Germany. Just before Prime Minister Chamberlain made his historic broadcast, the BBC transmitted a selection of light music. Half an hour later, the first air raid warning was sounded. It was a false alarm and hundreds emerged from dug-outs just as the pubs opened for the lunchtime session. The Duke of Windsor asked for his kilt to be laid out and marched up and down defiantly playing the bagpipes. The Duke of Devonshire asked his chauffeur what he thought of Hitler and with classic understatement he replied, 'Well your Grace, it seems to me that he should know by now that he is none too popular in this district.' *1939*

The first world champion racing driver, Giuseppe Farina, won his title by winning the Italian Grand Prix at Monza. He was famous for his temperamental moods and on several occasions gave up in the middle of races because he'd decided he couldn't win. His career was starred by so many horrific stunts, he couldn't remember the number himself. He nevertheless survived to retire in 1957 but three years later he died while on his way to watch the French Grand Prix – he was killed in a car crash. *1950*

Today's the day...

Famous English executioner William Marwood died. While still a cobbler, he wrote to the authorities protesting of the inhumanity of choking people to death by hanging. He worked out that by adjusting the length of rope to the weight of the body, the victim's neck would be dislocated and death instantaneous . 'Give them as long a drop as possible,' he said, 'but not too long or decapitation would result.' The authorities were so impressed that they appointed him hangman in 1874. He replaced the traditional villains and ruffians to become the first gentleman hangman and the first to be called 'executioner'. Always dressed very soberly, and considering himself an important civil servant, he held the post for only four years, but became the father of the science of execution. He was taken very seriously and the nearest anyone made to a joke about him was the little rhyme, 'If pa killed ma, who'd kill pa ? Marwood.'   *1883*

The army Jeep went into production as a civilian vehicle – the Willys Model CJ–2A. Designed by Carl K. Pabst and originally built by the American makers of the Austin 7, its first army trials had been supervised by Colonel Dwight D. Eisenhower. A competitive Ford prototype carried the initials GP for general purpose and it's been claimed that's where the name came from. Others insist however, that it was borrowed from E. C. Segar's dog-like cartoon character, 'the Jeep' who lived on orchids, could make himself invisible and run up and down walls. During World War II, 649,000 Jeeps were manufactured – with one factory completing one every eighty seconds.   *1945*

The first hand-held roll film camera was patented by original happy snapper George Eastman. It was a fixed focus box, which weighed 22oz, carried a hundred exposures and took round photographs 2½ins in diameter. When it came to a name, Eastman thought it should be 'short, vigorous and incapable of being misspelt'. He started with the letter 'K' believing it to be a 'strong, incisive sort of letter' and came up with the word Kodak, which satisfied the trademark laws, since it was completely meaningless.   *1888*

America's first test cricket team beat one of the best teams in the world, the West Indies, at Giants' Stadium, in the first match ever played on astroturf. 6,674 people paid $50,000 to see Gary Sobers and his Caribbean All Stars lose in an afternoon of gentle English cricket. Except it wasn't. Instead of discreet applause, boundaries, catches and wickets, the crowd were greeted by an electronic scoreboard flashing up messages like 'Give that man a hand!', 'Did you see that?' and 'Boing!'   *1977*

Mighty Turkish Sultan Suleiman the Magnificent died. Though he always kept a full harem of wives, he was enraptured by reports of the beauty of the Italian Duchess of Fondi – 'the fairest flower of the West'. Knowing she'd never consent to marry him, he decided to kidnap her, and incredibly he mobilised the entire Turkish fleet of 1,000 ships to bring her to him. She was warned and fled, and the most powerful monarch in the world wept for three days.   *1566*

Today's the day...

The ugliest man in England died. His name was John Heidegger. He was in charge of the King's entertainment and confirmed his ugly title in a contest with the most hideous old hag Lord Chesterfield could find in Soho. Hogarth actually made a face-mask of him, tapped him on the shoulder and surprised him with it. The poor man was so frightened, he fainted.

1749

Outlaw Jesse James was born, the son of a Baptist Minister. Far from being the Robin Hood of Western myth, he was a cold-blooded, vicious crook. As one of Quantrill's raiders he took part in the massacre of 150 citizens of Lawrence, Kansas, while in fifteen years of hold-ups with his own gang, he personally killed at least ten people and stole some $200,000. At 5ft 11in and heavily bearded, he was at least tall, dark and handsome – though his eyelids were granulated, and looked like the skin of a plucked chicken. He had a strange nickname too, which came about in rather an odd way. Having accidentally shot off the tip of the middle finger of his left hand, he yelled – 'If that ain't the dingus-dangest thing!' Thereafter he was called Dingus – a name rightly feared.

1847

French hero King Louis XIV was born to Anne of Austria after twenty-three years of childless marriage. Called 'Dieudonne' (the God-given), he had two teeth and wet nurses 'suffered greatly from his voracity'. The engineer of French ascendancy in Europe, he hated Paris because of childhood memories of the rebellions of the Frondes, and for half a century never spent a night there, preferring his fabulous Palace of Versailles. Among his many eccentricities, he would often conduct official business sitting on a commode, and his many amours became legend. It was said that if he wasn't the father of all his subjects, he was of many. He had 413 beds – one with a special erotic bedspread – and even at seventy he made demands twice daily on his last and long-time favourite, the seventy-four-year-old Madame de Maintenon.

September 5

Troubled by his conscience, he paid a woman to talk to him twice a week for eighteen years, since 'she made an honest man of him', and his sister-in-law said, 'The King thinks himself a saint, because he no longer beds with young women!'

1638

American *avant-garde* composer John Cage was born. His works astound critics, confuse the public and generally defy explanation. During one piano concerto, for instance, he asks for turkeys to be released from a coffin, while in *The Wonderful Widow of Eighteen Springs*, the pianist has to keep the keyboard closed and strike only the outside of the instrument. His *Water Music*, more logically, calls for a musician to pour water from one container to another at intervals regulated by a stop-watch, and accompanied by the shuffling of playing cards and static from a radio. Perhaps some sort of answer lies in another work – *Four Minutes and Thirty-Three Seconds* – described as 'a piece in three movements, during which no sounds are intentionally produced'. The musicians just sit there silently holding their instruments, because for Cage, there's music everywhere if only we listen.

1912

America's most obdurate criminal was hanged at Fort Leavenworth. Carl Panzram freely admitted to thousands of burglaries and twenty-one murders and was totally unrepentant – 'I hate the whole darn human race,' he said, 'including myself.' Finally he killed the civilian foreman of the prison laundry and was sentenced to hang. 'I look forward to that as a real pleasure and a big relief,' he said, and wrote to President Hoover demanding his constitutional right to be executed. He told the Society for the Abolition of Capital Punishment not to interfere and added, 'I wish you all had one neck and I had my hands on it.' He even hustled the guards up to the gallows and said to the hangman, 'While you're fooling around, I could hang a dozen men.' He didn't get the chance.

1930

Today's the day...

Twenty-fifth US President William McKinley was shot at a public reception in the Temple of Music, Buffalo. Twenty-eight-year-old labourer and fanatical anarchist, Leon Czolgosz had approached the President with his hands wrapped in a white handkerchief, concealing a ·32 calibre revolver. At seven minutes past four, he fired two bullets at such close range that the powder stained McKinley's vest. The first bullet struck his breastbone, the second ripped through the walls of his stomach. Czolgosz screamed, 'I have done my duty' and was immediately knocked down by soldiers and security men. Despite McKinley's plea to be easy with him, they punched, kicked and even tried to bayonet the fallen assassin. A black waiter who joined in and started to cut his throat said, 'He never even flinched. Gamest man I ever saw.' McKinley died eight days later from gangrene of the pancreas. When asked his name, Czolgosz answered 'Fred Niemen' – Fred Nobody. So nobody killed the President.   *1901*

Playboy King Carol of Rumania was deposed by his pro-Nazi Prime Minister. Fearing for his life, he fled in the dead of night with his mistress, Magda Lupescu, and the pair were forced to lie together on the floor of their train, as agitators pelted it first with stones and then with bullets. Strangely enough, it had been his antics with Miss Lupescu which had first lost him his throne fifteen years before. He made his comeback in 1930 when, taking advantage of a weak government, he usurped his own son, crowned himself again, and brazenly installed his paramour in a magnificent mansion near his palace. This time there was no coming back.   *1940*

The *Mayflower* set sail from Plymouth with 103 pilgrims seeking religious freedom in the New World. The seas were so rough that the wickedly overcrowded ninety foot ex-whaling vessel sprang leaks, cracked a main beam and had to drift with its sails down for days. Most of the passengers were perpetually sick; one went overboard, but was saved; two died and two more were born. Before the epic voyage to freedom began, the *Mayflower* had never carried passengers and ironically, on her very next voyage, landed a cargo of slaves in America. What's left of this great puritan ferry can now be seen in England's Chalfont St Giles. Some of the ship's timbers are now part of a barn.

1620

The first great American sculptor Horatio Greenough was born. In 1833, the Government commissioned him to sculpt a massive statue of George Washington for the Capitol. After eight years, he produced the first major American marble statue, only to find that it was too big to go through the door. The door was enlarged, but then the floor couldn't take the strain. So the huge figure, scantily clad in a classical robe, was put out in the cold where the public condemned it as immoral. In his defence Greenough could only say that had he known the figure was to go outside, he would've made sure it was properly dressed.

1805

English eccentric Joseph Capper died. A wealthy grocer, he'd retired early and devoted much of the rest of his life to a bizarre sport that astounded his contemporaries. With stunning accuracy, he would swat flies with his walking stick, claiming that if he had the chance, this is what he would do to the entire French nation.

1804

An assassin cut down Dr Hendrik Vorwoerd, Prime Minister of South Africa, stabbing him again and again in the neck and chest. The Dutch born defender of the apartheid system had survived a shooting six years earlier, but this time was taken unawares as Dimitric Tsafondas, a government messenger, approached, wearing his official uniform. The only message, however, was death. Tsafondas was declared insane and at his trial the judge said he could as little try this man 'as I could try a dog'.

1966

Today's the day...

The James Gang were decimated in the famous raid on the First National Bank in Northfield, Minnesota. Practically the entire town turned out against them, cutting off their escape. Jesse and brother Frank made it through the cordon, but their confederates, the infamous Younger brothers, were all badly wounded and captured. Cole, the eldest, was riddled with eleven bullets, but as he was taken to the caboose, he still managed to stand up and bow to the ladies. Their near fatal mistake had been to shoot the bank clerk for not opening the safe and the shot alerted the town. Ironically the safe wasn't even locked! By a strange twist of fate, it was five years later to the day that Jesse James made his last hold up, robbing a train at Blue Cut, Missouri. Eight months after that, he was shot dead himself. *1876*

The first gloved boxing match under the Queensberry Rules ended in defeat for the great John L. Sullivan who relinquished his heavyweight crown to Gentleman Jim Corbett in this marathon bout at the Olympic Club in New Orleans. Sullivan, the much loved 'Boston Strong Boy', held out to the twenty-first round when heavily bleeding, he was knocked down twice and finally KO'd by the San Franciscan Corbett. After the fight Sullivan admitted that like so many champions, he'd 'fought once too often'. *1892*

The 'Virgin Queen' Elizabeth I was born to the ill-fated Anne Boleyn. At thirty-one, however, she was bald and her face pitted from smallpox. She grew emaciated, and had to pad her cheeks with cottonwool; her eyebrows fell out; she got leg ulcers, and her teeth were reduced to a few blackened stumps through her excessive liking for sugar. In an age when people rarely washed, her abnormally acute sense of smell must have increased her suffering. Perhaps it also explains her own enthusiasm for cleanliness – she would bathe once every three months, 'whether she needed it or not'. *1533*

September 7

A ghoulish experiment was performed in the name of humanity two hours after the execution of French murderer Menesclou. The bold Dr Amirault wanted to prove whether or not the guillotine was a painless form of death. In front of witnesses, he pumped blood from a living dog into the decapitated head. The face lost its ghastly pallor and became flushed with life. The eyelids twitched, the lips began to move and the Doctor reported that had the vocal chords not been cut, speech would almost certainly have followed. The event lasted only a couple of seconds, but Amirault was sure the victim must have heard the crowd roar and seen the blade as his head rolled into the basket.   *1880*

The world's oddest shower fell on Leicester, Massachusetts, when instead of cats and dogs, it actually rained frogs and toads. Though witnesses rushed into the streets to scoop up the animals in buckets, the official explanation claimed that they'd merely overflowed from a nearby pond. What they never did explain was how the unfortunate amphibians landed up in gutters and on rooftops.   *1954*

Today's the day...

New York was renamed in honour of James Duke of York, the future James II of England, after the old Dutch town of New Amsterdam surrendered to the British. The first English Mayor of New York was a traitor named Captain Thomas Willet who had betrayed the Dutch despite receiving tremendous kindness while living among them. The swift surrender is not surprising since the total defence force of the town consisted of the farcical 'Rattle Watch'. This absurd platoon of only eight volunteers was expected to alert the town by shaking children's rattles.

1664

Royal strangers King George III of England and Princess Charlotte Mecklenburg-Strelitz were married in St James' Palace, London. It was a political marriage and the young couple had never even met right up until the moment Charlotte reached the altar. After the ceremony he gave her the following advice: 'Never be alone with my mother. She is an artful woman and will try to govern you.' She followed his warning and their happy fifty-seven-year marriage produced fifteen children.

1761

St Augustine the oldest surviving city in the United States was founded by Pedro Menendez de Aviles. He first sighted the Florida coast eleven days earlier – St Augustine's Day – and an advance party established base. After scouts ensured the coast was clear of hostile Indians, Aviles triumphantly arrived amid a fanfare of trumpet calls and the booming of cannons. He celebrated the joyous event by immediately attacking a nearby French camp, slaughtering 132 innocent souls.

1565

Daredevil stunt driver Evel Knievel attempted to leap across the mile-wide Snake River Canyon in Idaho. The designer of his custom built £400,000 Sky Cycle 2 was offered a bonus of £40,000 if Knievel survived. Evel claimed the bike only had five safety features, and the fifth was the Lord's Prayer! A few seconds after taking off mechanical trouble struck, the automatic parachute opened and Evel floated gently down. For this 'failure' Knievel reportedly received $250,000 in cash – it cost him a banged nose.

1974

The world's first mid-air collision occurred between two aeroplanes flying over Wiener-Neustadt in Austria. One pilot broke a leg but the other escaped unhurt. They had been unable to avoid each other since childhood – they were brothers.

1910

England's most absent monarch King Richard I was born. Far from being the chivalrous 'Lionheart' he was in fact a mean, power crazy, homosexual cannibal. Although he reigned for nearly ten years he was only in England twice – a grand total of 160 days. His wife Berengaria was even less enthusiastic – she never set foot in England in her life. This didn't worry Richard who was horrified when it was suggested that as a penance for his waywardness he should sleep with her. Richard was always away on his absurd crusade to retrieve the Holy Lands from the pagan infidels. On these journeys he always kept a supply of live prisoners so when food supplies ran low there was always a tasty dish to set before the King.

1157

Today's the day...

Kidnap victim Jeffrey Jackson, British Ambassador to Uruguay, was released by left-wing guerrillas who had held him captive for eight months. On his return to England he made a touching tribute to Marks and Spencer. He presented the company with their vest which he had worn throughout his ordeal.   *1971*

A letter in *The Times* gave birth to one of the world's great landmarks. In the centre of London stood an empty plot of land and the writer suggested England should take advantage of 'this favourable opportunity . . . by erecting in the centre of the square some worthy monument . . . to the immortal Nelson'. Thirty-two years after his death someone at last got around to thinking of England's greatest naval hero – the result was Nelson's Column in Trafalgar Square.   *1837*

A little-known mutiny in the British Army took place at a training camp near Boulogne in France. To toughen young soldiers up for war, a sadistic régime kept them marching at the double over sand-dunes all day without food or drink. The men finally snapped when a corporal shot a recruit for talking to a woman. All hell broke loose. Military policemen were thrown over bridges, one officer had his throat slashed, while others were paraded through the town in wooden boxes. Peace was restored only after the Brigadier cancelled training and made a peace token of ten days' wages. The affair was hushed up but interestingly enough most of the mutineers were ordered to the front line of the bloody Battle of Passchendaele – few survived.   *1917*

William the Conqueror was killed by a joke! He was extraordinarily obese – 'the protuberance of his belly deformed his royal person', and his old enemy Philip I of France cruelly quipped, 'When will this fat man be delivered of a child?' In a fury William set off to avenge this insult. On the way to Paris he pillaged the town of

September 9

Mantes but while riding through the ruins his horse stumbled jumping a ditch. William was thrown forward and impaled on the pommel of his saddle which fatally burst open his bowels. Deciding this was divine punishment for his evil past he spent his last days vigorously repenting. He confessed he had subjugated England by slaughter and by persecuting it beyond endurance. He ordered the release of all prisoners and finally bequeathed £5,000 in silver to the town of Mantes to repay them for the damage he had caused. After he died his faithful servants performed one last service – they robbed his body.   *1087*

The stunted, bespectacled French painter Toulouse-Lautrec died as the result of two strokes. During his last illness, the ravages of drink and syphilis affected his mind so badly, he imagined microbes were crawling all over his body and he flooded his bedroom floor with kerosene to destroy the phantom swarm. A heavy smoker, the final paralytic stroke probably saved him from burning himself alive.   *1901*

The Golden State, California, became the thirty-first to be admitted to the Union. It has the biggest population – twenty million; the oldest living thing in the world – the 4,500-year-old Bristle Cone Pine in the Inyo National Forest; the tallest living object – the 366.2ft Howard Libbey Coast Redwood, and the most massive living object – the gigantic Californian Big Tree, in Sequoia National Park. It also has America's largest population of chickens!   *1850*

Last of the legendary Hollywood moguls Jo Levine was born. His career is modestly condensed in a handout for his film *A Bridge Too Far*: 'God didn't create Hercules or Mike Nichols or Sophia Loren or Mel Brooks or Dustin Hoffman or Julie Christie or Marcello Mastroianni or countless others of the biggest and brightest stars in the entire entertainment industry. No, it wasn't God, it was some guy from Boston – a guy named Levine, Jo Levine.'   *1905*

Today's the day...

The song that rocked Victorian England was copyrighted in New York. Written by Canadian ex-bandsman Henry J. Sayers, it was called 'Ta-Ra-Ra-Boom-Der-E' and for a year it was overlooked. It took Imperial Britain by storm. The capital went 'stark mad' over it, and within days, everyone was singing it in the theatres and in the streets. The odd thing was that it was far from original. Over eighty years before, a tune had been published in Austria called 'Ta-Rada Boom Di-E', and the phrase had appeared in Germany as 'Tarara Bumtara'. Unabashed, Henry admitted he'd borrowed it and even gave the source. He'd first heard it in a brothel in Missouri!   *1891*

The man 'everybody complained about' author and critic Cyril Connolly was born in Coventry, the son of an army officer. He went to school with George Orwell, and was at Balliol with Graham Greene. About to come home after a spell in America, he wrote to a friend that he was coming back with a wife, £500, a set of diamond studs, and a decent box for the ferret. 'That's what everybody comes to America to do,' he added, 'and I don't think I've managed badly for a beginner.'   *1903*

Golf's all time 'best putter' Arnold Daniel Palmer was born in Latrobe, Pennsylvania, the son of a club professional. He started playing at the age of five and became US Amateur Champion in the early fifties. In 1954 he bet $100 for every stroke over eighty against $100 for every stroke under seventy-two. He shot four-under, bought an engagement ring and eloped with his sweetheart Winnie Walzer. He became the first golfer to earn over $100,000 in a year and by 1968 had become golf's first millionaire. His contribution to the game has been enormous, not least in helping to make it the hugely popular spectator sport it is today. Bob Hope once asked him for his opinion of the Hope swing, and Arnie replied, 'I've seen better in a condemned playground.'   *1929*

September 10

Troubles started for an American inventor, Elias Howe of Spencer, Massachusetts, when he patented the first ever lock-stitch sewing machine. Despite the fact that he'd shown it could do more work than five girls, manufacturers thought it would be unreliable and workers thought it would mean unemployment. His machine was also attacked on moral grounds. *The New Orleans Medical Society Journal* even went so far as to suggest that seamstresses operating it should be given bromide. It would stop them, it said, getting excited by the rhythmic motion of the pedal!   *1846*

The resurrected robber Patrick Redmond was hanged at Gallows Green in Cork. When it was all over and the crowd had dispersed, an actor called Glover attended the body and 'by means of friction and fumigation' brought it back to life again. Overjoyed at being snatched from the jaws of death, Redmond got roaringly drunk and in the evening decided to go and thank Glover for his vital assistance. The only trouble was that Glover was performing at the time, and the audience on perceiving a man they'd seen hanged in the morning, fainted in droves.   *1766*

Today's the day...

Oddball Governor of New York Edward Hyde third Earl of Clarendon was censured for his bizarre behaviour. Once arrested as a drunken vagrant by one of his own officers, he taxed men who wore wigs and charged admission to state dinners. The real reason for his eventual dismissal, however, was more outrageous still. He spent most of his administration dressed up as a woman – claiming that if he was to represent Queen Anne, he should do it as faithfully as possible. In his wife's clothes he would sit in the window of the Governor's mansion and disport himself on the ramparts of the fort. He even appointed an official staymaker.   *1708*

Self-styled prophet and seer Roger Crab died. A famous eccentric he lived up to his name by becoming a hermit. He gave up eating meat and as his ethics got the better of his appetite he ended up subsisting on water, dock leaves and grass. He wore sackcloth, dispensed physic to the locals and when he was imprisoned for breaking the Sabbath, a friendly dog brought him bread. Perhaps all is explained by the fact that while fighting for the Parliamentary army in the English Civil War, he received a severe blow on the head.   *1680*

September 11

Bungling murderer Henry Wainwright, a popular Victorian
entertainer, shot his mistress, cut her throat and buried her corpse in a
warehouse. Bankruptcy forced him to get rid of the building, and
exactly a year to the day after the murder he dug up her body and, to
his horror, found it in perfect condition. He sliced it up, made parcels
of the pieces, then hailed a cab and got a young man named Stokes to
help him load them. The curious lad opened one and a severed hand
fell out. As Wainwright was driven away smoking a cigar to disguise
the awful smell, Stokes called the police and had him arrested. He
went to the scaffold probably reflecting on his fatal mistake. Instead of
burying the body in quicklime which would have destroyed it, he
buried it in chloride of lime which preserved it.   *1874*

Gory Scots hero William Wallace enjoyed strange fruits of victory
after he and his men had massacred 50,000 English troops at the
Battle of Stirling Bridge. Having had the 'fat and fair' body of
despised English treasurer Hugh de Cressingham flayed, he had the
skin cut into little pieces and flung in the air. Not satisfied with this, he
had another body stripped from 'head to heel' and made into a
swordbelt, which he proudly wore thereafter.   *1297*

The world's first television play was transmitted by Station WGY
in Schenectady, New York. Though J. Hartley Manners' *The Queen's
Messenger* had only two characters, there were four actors. This was
necessary since the old-fashioned cameras were immobile, the play
went out live and close-up shots of the actors' hands were needed to
break the monotony. The actors couldn't be in two places at once, so
'their' hands were in fact the hands of doubles.   *1928*

The first British Women's Institute was founded in Wales, in the
little Welsh town of Llanfairpwllgwyngyllgogerychwyrndrobw-
llantysiliogogogoch.   *1915*

Today's the day...

John F. Kennedy married Jackie Bouvier, in a match that was blessed by the Pope, and celebrated by Archbishop – later Cardinal – Cushing. 800 people came to church and a further 3,000 rushed a police cordon trying to see the happy couple. Jack had met Jackie at a dinner party where he 'reached across the asparagus and asked her for a date'. Her mother had always told her to judge a man by his letters – but all the young socialite ever got from her intended was a postcard, saying, 'Wish you were here. Cheers Jack.'   *1953*

Odd moraliser Mason Locke Weems became one of the first two priests ordained in the American Episcopal Church in a ceremony reluctantly performed by the Archbishop of Canterbury, who had at first refused to give the benefits of Anglicanism to colonial rebels. Weems, who wrote the *Life of Washington* which contained the famous cherry tree incident, was given to stumbling about bars imitating drunks in order to redeem them. For a holy man he was also inordinately interested in sexual matters. He wrote *Hymen's Recruiting Sergeant*, a pamphlet designed to 'extinguish the pestilence of celibacy', and once preached from the text, 'I am fearfully and wonderfully made', concluding, 'There I must stop, for should I go on, some of the young ladies present would not sleep a wink tonight!' *1784*

Bawdy King Francis I of France was born. An odd mixture of gallant patron of the arts and cheat, by far his favourite pastime was to make love indiscriminately and 'go a-whoring anywhere!' On one occasion he visited one of his royal doxies, who was otherwise engaged with another. Hearing the King approach, she hid her lover behind a pile of branches in the fireplace. The King enjoyed his stay and before leaving decided to relieve himself by 'watering the green branches', thus drenching his unknown and unfortunate rival. Not altogether surprisingly, Francis contracted and probably died of syphilis. *1494*

September 12

Tetchy Lord Cardigan shot Harvey Tuckett in a duel on
Wimbledon Common over an article the ex-officer had written
criticising milord's treatment of a captain in his regiment. Duelling
was a crime punishable by transportation, so both participants were
arrested by a plucky constable, and for the first time in seventy years,
an English peer was tried for a felony – intent to murder and grievous
bodily harm. Cardigan, later leader of the Charge of the Light Brigade
and the most disliked man in the British army, chose as was his right
for his case to be heard by the House of Lords. Incredibly, they found
him not guilty. The 'old boy network' had exploited a legal loophole.
The victim was named in full on the indictment as Harvey Garnet
Phipps Tuckett, and since no-one had previously known his middle
names, they couldn't technically identify him.   *1840*

Cleopatra's Needle was erected on the Thames embankment.
Despite its name, the famous obelisk was standing in Egypt when
Moses was found in the bulrushes, and was there a good 500 years
before the great Queen was born. Inside the pedestal were put some
'important reminders of the British Empire', including *Bradshaw's
Railway Guide*, *Whitaker's Almanack*, a 2ft rule and a dozen pin-ups of
Victorian ladies.   *1878*

Licentious Emperor Andronicus I was murdered by an angry mob,
having rashly annoyed his most powerful subjects, the Byzantine
aristocracy. He was publicly humiliated and tortured for three days,
and finally hung by the feet between two pillars and run through with a
sword. It was from among the wives of these same nobles that he had
always chosen his mistresses, compensating their husbands by giving
them hunting parks and the right to nail antlers over the gates. The
expression 'to wear the horns' is thought to be derived from this
practice. It means to be cuckolded.   *1185*

Today's the day...

The strangest lynching in history took place in Erwin, Tennessee. After a vicious attack, a man had been brutally killed, and angry townspeople determined to bring the culprit to justice. She was quickly identified as a heavyweight female called Mary, who was noted for her exceptionally large ears. She was soon captured and taken to a railway siding where she was unceremoniously strung up. Incredibly, the powerful steel cable they used for a rope snapped in two. It was replaced with another and poor, sad Mary was cruelly hoisted aloft. What made the lynching so bizarre was that Mary was not a woman, but a rogue circus elephant.   *1916*

Freak weather made citizens swelter at Al'azizyah in Libya. The temperature soared to 136.4°F making today the hottest day ever recorded.   *1922*

The British won the Battle of Quebec after scaling the rocky Heights of Abraham in the dead of night. With a massive, but sustained volley of musket and grape-shot, they utterly decimated their enemy and within fifteen minutes, it was all over. French losses were ten times those of the British and the commanders on both sides,

September 13

Montcalm and Wolfe, were mortally wounded almost simultaneously. At his death, Wolfe became a national hero, and one dubious poet wrote: 'He marched without dread or fears /At the head of his bold Grenadiers /And what was more remarkable – nay, very particular/ He climbed up rocks that were perpendicular!'   *1759*

Phineas P. Gage got a hole in the head when he was working on the Rutland and Burlington Railroad. The twenty-five-year-old American navvy was caught unawares by a premature explosion, and such was the force of the blast that it drove a $3\frac{1}{2}$ft long crow-bar straight through his left cheek and out through the top of his head. While he was understandably dazed, Gage was fully conscious as he was taken to a nearby hotel. There he was treated for his wounds and chatted quite cheerfully with his doctor. Though he later lost the sight of his left eye, he made an astonishing recovery and his mental capacity was totally unimpaired – despite a $3\frac{1}{2}$in hole in his skull.   *1847*

A head-case was tried in a court at Maidenhead, when retired architect Andrea Gigli was charged with riding his moped without protective headgear. He was found guilty and though conditionally discharged, tore up his licence in disgust. He claimed his machine was so slow that boys could overtake him on push-bikes, and that at that kind of speed his own headgear was perfectly adequate. He'd been apprehended wearing not a helmet, but a plastic mixing bowl.   *1978*

A ticklish industrial problem was resolved when two seventeen-year-old pillow-stuffers were given their jobs back in a Merseyside bedding factory. Feathers had flown when fellow workers walked out on hearing of the girls' dismissal. They'd been fired because they'd refused to continue to operate their pillow-stuffing machines. Apparently, every time they brought the contraptions into action, their skirts flew up, and the feathers tickled their thighs!   *1978*

Today's the day...

The Duke of Wellington died, carried off by a fit at the age of
eighty-four. Despite his immense fortune, he had lived out the last
years of his life in almost monastic style. At his residence in Walmer
Castle, he observed a strict routine. He slept on a narrow military bed,
rose before 7am, took a turn round the ramparts and breakfasted on
'plain tea and bread and butter'. In complete contrast, his funeral was a
lavish and magnificent event. Witnessed by a million and a half people,
the cortège wound its way to St Paul's with the Iron Duke's coffin
mounted on an eighteen ton carriage, made from the metal of captured
guns. Unfortunately, the carriage broke down in St James' Park and
the procession was held up for two hours while they repaired it. A
stickler for punctuality in life, the Duke was actually late for his own
funeral.   *1852*

Britain lost eleven days overnight, when it finally got around to
adopting the Gregorian Calendar – 170 years after the rest of Europe.
Pope Gregory XIII had devised the system to annul the ten extra days
accumulated by the Imperial Roman calendar. There were riots all
over Britain. People believed their lives had been foreshortened and
politicians were attacked with cries of 'give us back our eleven days'.
The population was understandably confused – after all yesterday was
2 September and today is 14 September.   *1752*

Isadora Duncan was garrotted by her shawl, which caught in the
wheel of her prospective lover's sports car. It was an appropriately
bizarre end to a hectic life in which she'd scandalised Europe and
America with her sensual dancing, married an alcoholic Russian poet
and been denounced as 'a Bolshevik hussy'. In Paris in 1912 a gipsy
flowerseller had cursed her with three numbers – 13, 25 and 27. In
1913, both her children drowned, in 1925 her husband hanged himself,
and the year of her death completed the curse.   *1927*

September 14

Itinerant aquatinter William Daniell completed his round Britain trip. Determined to produce a comprehensive collection of pictures of the British coast, he had taken ten years to get back to his starting point at Land's End in Cornwall. During that time he'd walked, ridden and occasionally sailed the whole of the 4,650 mile coastline. He published the 308 aquatints himself and sold them as part works for 10s 6d an issue. His work was highly praised and the Royal Academy were so impressed they made him a member in preference to Constable. Aquatinting was soon overtaken by lithography, however, and Daniell's work became unfashionable. Just over 100 years later, all but three of his original copper plates were valued as a job lot – at £15.   *1823*

A weary Handel finished the *Messiah* just twenty-four days after he'd started it. Supplied with the libretto, he'd immured himself in his room at Brook Street, London, hardly eaten anything and lived almost entirely on coffee. Indeed he was so involved with the work that when he finished the 'Hallelujah Chorus', his servant found him in tears declaring, 'I did think I did see all heaven before me, and the great God himself.'   *1741*

Today's the day...

Jumbo the elephant was killed by a train. Owned by Phineas T. Barnum, he was believed to be the largest African bush elephant ever held in captivity – though in fact, Barnum never allowed him to be measured. After a show in Ontario, Jumbo, along with his tiny stablemate, a baby elephant called Tom Thumb, was being led back to his private carriage along a supposedly unused railway track. Suddenly an unscheduled freight train came hurtling round the corner, mesmerised Jumbo with its blazing headlights and smashed into them. Tom Thumb was thrown aside with a broken leg but Jumbo took the full force on his head and was killed. The impact was so great that the train was derailed and the driver was killed as well. At the autopsy, veterinary surgeons discovered that Jumbo was still growing and must have stood a full 11ft at the shoulder when he died. They also discovered something odd in his stomach, presumably sucked up from admiring fans during his many performances. It was a small fortune in coins. *1885*

The first hydrogen balloon voyage in Great Britain was made by youthful Italian attaché Vincent Lunardi. Watched by huge crowds, with the City Artillery carrying arms in case of riot, he ascended into the wide blue yonder from Moorfields, London. Pausing only to lighten his load by dropping his cat off at North Mimms, Hertfordshire, he sailed breezily on to Standon near Ware. There, his descent was assisted by a courageous young lady who grabbed a rope and steadied the floating apparition as it sank back to earth. Local labourers had refused to help – they were too frightened! *1784*

The first tanks to be used in battle lumbered into the mist through the mud of the Somme. According to one German eye-witness, as the flame-spurting monsters crawled towards them a soldier yelled, 'The Devil is coming', and the troops took to their heels. So terrifying were they, that one single tank captured an entire village and another a

September 15

trench of 300 soldiers. What the enemy didn't know was that the tanks were hopelessly inefficient, the crews were untrained, and on the way to the front seventeen out of the shipment of forty-nine had broken down.

1916

Prolific thriller writer Agatha Christie was born. Though in all her books sold over 300 million copies, her greatest mystery occurred in real life when in 1926 she disappeared. Several weeks later she was discovered living under an assumed name in a hotel in Harrogate – a supposed victim of amnesia. Stranger still is that the 'plot' of her missing time was never revealed.

1890

The railway claimed its first passenger victim when MP William Huskisson was struck down by Stephenson's *Rocket*. It was the great day of the opening of the Liverpool–Manchester Railway, and at Newton-le-Willows the procession of trains had pulled off the main line to take on fresh water. Huskisson stepped across the track to greet his old rival, the Duke of Wellington. As they were warmly shaking hands, the *Rocket* appeared steaming swiftly towards them. The rest of the party nimbly escaped, but Huskisson was confused and landed right in its path. Seriously injured he was rushed to nearby Eccles at a record 36mph, but died the same evening. Ironically it was Huskisson who'd championed the cause of the railways and introduced the very bill which brought about the Liverpool–Manchester line.

1830

'The Greatest' Muhammad Ali proved it again when he seized his world title back from Leon Spinks at the Superdome, New Orleans. Leon had been living it up in the nightclubs and as he failed miserably to beat off Ali, fourteen years his senior, his seconds yelled to him to 'boogie'. He didn't, and his coach left the ringside in disgust after only six rounds. Spinks had held the title for a brief 214 days, the shortest reign in heavyweight history.

1978

Today's the day...

Peter 'Columbo' Falk was born in New York. With his characterisation of the scruffy, shambling, but shrewd police lieutenant, he's become one of the highest paid TV actors in the world. In his early days, however, he had two other claims to fame. One was his glass eye – the result of a tumour he'd had when he was three – and the other was his skill at baseball. During one particularly important match, the umpire gave a very doubtful decision against him, so he took out his eye and said, 'Sir, you need this more than I do.'   *1927*

Controversial Dr John Colet died. He became Dean of St Paul's and used much of his vast fortune in founding St Paul's school. It started with 153 pupils – the number of fish caught by St Peter. There were to be no holidays no use of tallow candles and no cock fighting. The Dean was buried in his Cathedral, and after the Great Fire his monument and coffin were damaged. Inside, Messrs Wyld and Greatorex saw the corpse preserved in a strange liquid. They tasted it, but found it 'insipid'; then they prodded the body with a stick and reported that 'it felt like boyled Brawne'.   *1519*

September 16

Hitler's successor the Grand Admiral Karl Doenitz was born.
Despite his rabid anti-semitism, he said he only discovered 'the
demonic side' of Hitler's nature too late. It must have been very late,
since he was loyal to the day of Hitler's death, when he became
Führer himself. He ruled Germany for nine days, and was imprisoned
for ten years. Compared to Hitler, he said, 'we are all worms'.   *1891*

A bizarre custom got under way for the last time when Louis XVIII
of France died. It had long been a tradition that dead French Kings
were embalmed, but not buried for forty days. While their bodies were
kept discreetly hidden, a wax effigy would be put on display, *couchant*
on an ermine robe. The weird thing was that the effigy was treated as
if it were the King alive. Almost all the usual ceremonies took place,
protocol and etiquette were strictly observed, meals were served and
the King's wine tasted. The problem with Louis was that in life he'd
been a great glutton, so for this last lying-in, ministers ordered that
the food and drink part of the ceremony be discontinued. They were
worried that people would laugh so much, it would break the palace
windows!   *1824*

The hero King Henry V was born in Monmouth Castle. Legend has
it that in his youth he 'yntended gretly to riot and drew to wylde
company', but as soon as he assumed the Crown, he's supposed to have
become a paragon of virtue. What is certain, however, is that
Shakespeare's bluff Prince Hal was an extremely ruthless man who
fought two bloody campaigns that climaxed at Agincourt. Shortly
afterwards, in 1422, Henry died unheroically of dysentery. He was
interred in a marble tomb in Westminster Abbey, under an effigy with
a head of silver. Unfortunately vandals stole the head during the
dissolution and Henry was headless for more than 400 years. He now
has a replacement at last, but instead of silver, Hal's new head is made
of plastic.   *1387*

Today's the day...

Tippling eccentric 'Sir' Jeffrey Dunstan died. A foundling raised in the workhouse of St Dunstan's Church, he became a wig collector and though crippled and dirty, married a 'fair nymph'. He first came to fame as the 'Mayor' of Garrett – a fake borough in Wandsworth for which mock elections were held after every General Election. Its original purpose was to prevent encroachment on the common; voters qualified by having had an 'amour' there and candidates just had to be able to drink a lot! Dunstan was Mayor for twelve years, adopted the title 'Sir' and managed to survive the excesses of three elections. He finally succumbed after one particularly 'jovial meeting' when he consumed 'rather more than his usual quantity of juniper'. His friends pushed him safely home in a wheelbarrow but he died just a few hours later – 'smothered in liquor'. *1797*

The killer whale 'Old Tom' was found dead on the beach at Twofold Bay, New South Wales. For the best part of a century, he and his pack of fellow killers had actually helped the fishermen of the bay catch fin and humpback whales, by driving them towards the boats, biting their tails and bumping their blow-holes. The killers ate only the lips and the tongues, leaving the rest for the whalers. They'd even beat their flukes in warning if the whales turned up and the men didn't. 'Old Tom', who came alone this year, clearly enjoyed himself. He liked to grab the harpoon lines and get towed through the water. *1930*

The Emperor of the United States announced his existence to a startled public with a proclamation in the *San Francisco Evening Bulletin*. In it, Joshua Abraham Norton, a bankrupt 'forty-niner', declared himself Norton I and ordered representatives of the States to come and meet him. A month later he issued an edict abolishing Congress and when he heard it was still sitting, ordered the army to 'clear the halls' immediately. He was ignored by most as a 'harmless madman' but the people of San Francisco fêted him, fed him, paid his

September 17

rent and generally kept him in comfort for the next thirty years. In his garish outfit smothered with gold braid, the Imperial sabre at his side, he paraded the streets followed by his faithful hounds – Lazarus and Bummer. He ate in all the best restaurants; rode free on trains and claimed a place of honour for himself at public functions. The ironical thing was that the one and only Emperor of the United States wasn't even American. He was born in the East End of London.   *1859*

Edward the dancing Duke of York died at the tender age of twenty-five. George III's favourite brother, he'd been living it up in Monte Carlo when he was 'so stimulated by the ladies' one evening and so exhausted by his 'prodigies of dancing' that he caught a fatal chill. While his body was lying in state in London, a fourth son was born to George III, and named after the dead Duke. This Edward became Queen Victoria's father. He was a happy little soul and always said, 'The circumstances of my birth were ominous of the gloom and struggle which awaited me.'   *1767*

The lonely voyage of *The Resolute* came to an end when she was spotted by Captain Buddington in the Dewis Strait. He was amazed, for *The Resolute* was one of the five British ships abandoned over a year earlier by Sir Edward Belcher, off Melville Island – nearly 1,000 miles away. Incredibly the ship had negotiated the tricky passage through the Barrow Straits and the Lancaster Sound on her own – and though bleached by Arctic storms, she'd survived intact. She was towed back to America where, to celebrate her amazing voyage, she was magnificently re-fitted with a $40,000 grant from Congress, and sailed back across the Atlantic as a gift for Queen Victoria. With great ceremony the ship was handed over – but the Admiralty couldn't decide what to do with her. Finally they made up their minds and after all she'd been through *The Resolute* was stripped of her splendid American fittings – and left to rot.   *1855*

Today's the day...

800 million Chinese paid a last tribute to their leader Mao Tse-Tung at the beginning of a memorial service. For just three minutes, one fifth of the population of the world stood in silence.   *1976*

A ram did a grand slam when he saw his reflection staring back at him from the window of a high street bank in Mold, North Wales. Indignant at the stranger making eyes at his ewes, the ram charged the window and smashed straight through into the bank. The rest of the flock followed – just like a crowd of sheep!   *1978*

'The Hercules of Literature' Samuel Johnson was born in Lichfield, Staffordshire. Poverty forced him to leave his Oxford college with 'a bitterness which they mistook for frolic' – and he was hard-up ever after. He always gave money to beggars, however, and when a friend reproached him for it, saying they'd only spend it on gin and tobacco, the generous Sam retorted, 'And why should they be denied such sweeteners of their existence?' He was obsessed by food and the very sight of it affected him 'as it affects wild beasts and birds of prey'. He gulped sixteen cups of tea at a sitting and once covered his plum pudding with lobster sauce and wolfed the lot down without noticing. Conscious of his almost grotesque ugliness and racked by a nervous tic, he totally disarmed an admiring group of women by announcing, 'Ladies, I am tame; you may stroke me.'   *1709*

The enigmatic Greta Garbo was born in Stockholm. Her first job was working up a lather on men's faces in a barber's shop, then she sold hats in a department store and starred in a film about the Co-op Bakery. Brought to Hollywood by Louis Mayer in 1925, she couldn't speak a word of English and was billed as 'The Norma Shearer of Sweden'. In fact, she got her first part because Miss Shearer didn't want it and was acclaimed as the Spanish peasant girl in *The Torrent*. With the talkies growing more and more popular, the studio was worried the public wouldn't like her husky Scandinavian drawl. They needn't have bothered – her first screen words were 'Gimme a visky' and audiences loved it. Shy to the point of being a recluse, she avoided publicity as much as the other stars courted it, but denies ever saying 'I want to be alone.' In her own words, 'I only said I want to be *let* alone!'

1905

The unsociable socialite Gerald Tyrwhitt-Wilson Lord Berners was born at Apley Park in Shropshire. Although he listed his recreations as 'none' in *Who's Who*, he was an accomplished artist, author and musician: he wrote six novels, an opera and five ballets and built a 140ft high tower on his estate at Faringdon. He was delighted with it because it was 'entirely useless' and pinned a notice to the door: 'Members of the public committing suicide from this tower do so at their own risk.' When travelling he hated company and would keep his railway carriage to himself by donning black spectacles and beckoning in passers-by with a sinister grin. If someone did join him he'd soon scare them off – he'd sit and read a newspaper upside-down and take his temperature every five minutes.

1883

Today's the day...

A shopkeeper with a headache Melville Bissell patented the first carpet sweeper. Proprietor of a china-shop, Mr Bissell suffered terribly from the effects of the dusty straw he used to pack his goods. To clean up the shop and clear his head, he designed the sweeper with a box to catch the dust, and demonstrated it at church socials. *1876*

The first beauty contest was won at Spa in Belgium by eighteen-year-old Bertha Soucaret from Guadeloupe. Instead of flashing smiles and thighs, the finalists wore crinolines, and were kept secluded before being driven to the judging hall in a closed carriage. *1888*

Canine-crazy King of France Henry III was born. Henpecked by his mother Catherine de Medici who more or less ran the country, he'd little else to do but give himself up to voluptuousness. 'Covered with scent and crimping his hair', he spent most of his time with ladies, sporting a perfumed necklet and wearing two pairs of earrings at once. But his real passion was for little dogs. He drove around Paris collecting them and even raided convents to steal them from the nuns. With over 2,000 spread around his palaces, there were seldom less than 100 in evidence, sprawling on velvet cushions, being alternately fondled and incited to 'a deafening clamour'. Deciding which ones to take on his daily walk 'cost the King emotion', so with sycophantic inventiveness, one of his chamberlains designed a satin-lined carry cot. With this hung around the royal neck, Henry could then transport twenty of the little darlings at a time! *1551*

Dirty dog Lord Chancellor Henry Brougham was born near Cowgate in Edinburgh. So slovenly and ill-kempt was he, that one disgusted lady exclaimed, 'You never saw such an object, or anything half so dirty', while the Prince Regent publicly ordered him to wash his filthy hands before dining at their club. He roared his speeches in Parliament with 'such lungs and such a flow of jaw that surpassed the imagination', and fortified himself in debates with mulled wine and a hatful of oranges which he'd sit and suck – noisily. Though he founded the University of London, and fought hard for the abolition of slavery, he's best remembered for the 'odd little sort of garden chair on wheels' he designed – the carriage called the brougham. When the Duke of Wellington commented on the inevitable fame his design would bring, the cantankerous old man said it was certainly better than being remembered for a pair of boots!

1778

The first aerial passengers soared into the sky in a gaily painted hot air balloon, launched from the Palace of Versailles. Masterminded by the Montgolfier brothers, the balloon rose to a height of 1,700ft, travelled two miles and landed safely eight minutes later. The motley crew consisted not of people, but a sheep, a duck and a cockerel, all of whom appeared unharmed by their experience – except that the cock had been kicked in the wing by the sheep! Louis XVI and his Queen were very impressed, but when they eagerly approached the machine to examine it, they were driven back by the 'noxious smell'. To get the 'right balance of gas', the brothers had insisted on burning damp straw, together with hundreds of old shoes and the odd bit of decomposing meat.

1783

The silent witness of Salem – eighty-year-old Giles Corey – was crushed to death, having been charged, but not condemned, for witchcraft. Amid the hysteria of the infamous witch-trials, he saw it would make no difference which way he pleaded, so he refused to plead at all. Affronted by mute rebuff, the justices deemed that he should suffer the medieval process of '*peine forte et dure*'. As heavier and heavier weights were placed on his chest he gasped, 'More weight' to hasten his death, but said no more. The savagery of the torture was made worse by the fact that the process was illegal – it had been outlawed in Massachusetts over fifty years before.

1692

Today's the day...

The first safety lift was demonstrated by Elisha Graves Otis at New York's Crystal Palace. He was hoisted aloft on his platform and to the horror of the assembled crowds, he then ordered a workman to cut the rope. Happily his safety brake worked and he ceremoniously bowed to the assembled audience and doffed his hat. His invention gave free rein to skywards building in New York. Businessmen who'd been contemplating moving out of the city because of lack of space just built taller buildings and the famous Manhattan skyline began to emerge. Lifts were far from being a new idea, however. Archimedes built a weight-lifting device in 236 BC; animals were lifted to the arena of the Roman Colosseum; and Louis XV had a 'flying chair' at Versailles. He used it to go up one storey – to visit his mistress's bedroom. *1853*

The stigmata of Padre Pio first appeared. As the thirty-one-year-old Franciscan monk knelt at prayer he suddenly felt faint and lost consciousness. When he came round he was bleeding from wounds in his hands, feet and side – the marks of the crucifixion. Suddenly a phenomenon, he was virtually besieged by crowds in the monastery of

September 20

San Giovanni Rotondo and many claimed he appeared to them in visions and effected miraculous cures. Gifts poured in from all over the world and he was allowed to accept the money if he passed it on to the church. A one million pound hospital was built nearby at Foggia and the people of his birthplace, the tiny village of Pietrelcina, prospered when pilgrims flocked there by the thousand. Doctors made many attempts to stop the bleeding, including cauterisation, but it was all to no avail. Padre Pio continued to bleed from his wounds until he died – forty years later.   *1918*

Shapely Italian actress Sophia Loren was born Sofia Scicolone in the back streets of Naples. In the allied advance on Italy she was scarred by shrapnel and forced to sleep in railway tunnels with her mother and sister. At school she was so skinny she was nicknamed 'Toothpick' but blossomed out and won a beauty contest at the age of fifteen. Her mother won one too as the best double for Garbo, and the pair of them moved to Rome and got parts as extras in *Quo Vadis?* After twenty-seven bit parts, some naughty photographs and some tutoring from Carlo Ponti, she became an international star. She adores spaghetti, finds diets 'too boring' and insists that 'glamour is humbug'. Though she's now a French citizen, her last home in Italy was a fifty roomed mansion outside Rome with mosaic floors, fountains, frescoes, a 135ft swimming pool and Louis XVI bedsteads.   *1934*

The most crowded tennis match ever took place when 30,472 people packed into the Astrodome at Houston, Texas. On court were Billie Jean King and Bobby Riggs, a man twenty-six years her senior. Billed as the 'Battle of the Sexes', the protagonists presented each other with gifts before the match began. Billie Jean got a giant candy bar and gave her opponent – a true male chauvinist pig – a little piglet called Larimore – Rigg's middle name. Billie trounced Bobby.   *1973*

Today's the day...

Canada was given away. James I gave Nova Scotia and effectively the whole of the country to Sir Alexander Stirling. Charles I confirmed the grant and added what amounted to supreme power over Canada's inhabitants and natural resources. The two had given Sir Alexander – who later became Earl Stirling – a land that was vastly larger than all their dominions. 'From sea to sea, all continent lands, with rivers, bays and torrents.' The problems it brought him, however, were as vast as the gift. After trying to develop his estates, 'this poet who aimed to be King', the ex-Secretary for Scotland died a bankrupt.   *1621*

'The man who invented tomorrow', futuristic writer Herbert, George Wells was born in Bromley, Kent. Wells had first developed a taste for literature when he was bedridden as a child after breaking his leg. Later he worked in a shop, hated it, threatened to commit suicide and so impressed his old headmaster with his histrionics, that he gave him a job as a teacher. Once again illness helped him. He was badly injured in a football match, and while recovering, took up writing. He was married twice, and had many affairs, and as he grew older and deafer, his behaviour grew more than usually eccentric. When his neighbours asked him to turn down his radio, he said he would if they'd de-bark their dog. His garden, he believed, was blighted by an overhanging tree, and he made a point of shaking his fist and shouting at it every day. 'That bloody sycamore' he said, '. . . is a complete repudiation of any belief in an intelligent God!'   *1866*

Victor the giraffe died at Marwell Zoo Park in Hampshire. Six days earlier, the slim eighteen footer had mysteriously done the splits and despite the efforts of the zoo staff and the fire brigade, he'd been unable to get up again. He became a national celebrity overnight and millions of people tensely awaited the outcome. This afternoon, he was wrapped in a canvas jacket and winched up – but the strain proved too great for the nervous animal and his heart failed. Victor was fifteen and could have expected to live another five years. The rumour was that he collapsed while trying to mount one of his wives, and though a zoo spokesman said, 'There is no reason to believe that,' Victor nevertheless had sired a posthumous heir. *1977*

The oddest reason for stealing a truck was given to police in Memphis, Tennessee, when they charged the culprit, Henry Jackson. He said he needed the vehicle to get him to Jackson, where he hoped to get a job as a policeman. He asked the arresting officer rather plaintively, 'Will it affect my chances of getting the job?' *1978*

King Edward II was brutally murdered above 'a charnel house' in Berkeley Castle. He'd been deposed by his Queen Isabella and her confederate Mortimer for indulging his counsellor's 'covetous rapine, spoil and immoderate ambition'. De Gournay and Maltravers were sent to do the deed. They held him down with either a mattress or a table and 'put into his fundament an horn and through the same, they thrust up into his body a hot spit'. The effect was disembowelment, without leaving a mark on his body. It was said that he died 'a natural death', but his screams could be heard 'without the castle walls'. *1327*

The angel Moroni appeared to Joseph Smith in Manchester, near Palmyra, New York. He told the eighteen-year-old youth of the location of a series of golden plates buried in the hill of Cumorah. The plates told the tale of the descendants of Lehi the Israelite, who after a great journey had arrived in the Americas in the seventh century BC. In 1827 Smith was allowed to get possession of them and was given two stones – the Urim and the Thummim – which enabled him to 'see' and with three helpers, to translate. What he produced was nothing less than the Book of Mormon. The volume was published in 1830, and with little regard for disbelievers, the angel took the plates back to heaven. *1823*

Today's the day...

Captain William Lynch immortalised his name with a proclamation. In it, he stated that the citizens of Pittsylvania County, Virginia, had sustained 'great and intolerable losses' at the hands of 'lawless men and abandoned wretches'. Along with some fellow Pittsylvanians, he believed that the justiciary of the time wasn't meting out enough 'justice' and so they took it upon themselves to provide 'such corporal punishment as shall seem adequate'. They held only the most cursory trials, which generally consisted of beating the victims into confession, and horse-whipping was the general punishment. Hangings inevitably occurred, however, and hence the word 'lynch' passed into the language.   *1780*

'The Battle of the Long Count' was fought between Jack Dempsey and Gene Tunney at Soldier's Field, Chicago. It was Dempsey's chance to win back the world title he'd lost to Tunney a year earlier; excitement was at fever pitch and the audience was studded with stars. Though badly beaten in the early rounds, he floored Tunney in the seventh. Unfortunately, he didn't retire immediately to a neutral corner and the count didn't start until he did. Estimates of the total length of the count vary between fourteen and seventeen seconds – long enough for Tunney to regain his senses and slog on to a points victory that robbed Dempsey of his title for good and all. Sickened, the ex-champ wrote, 'I couldn't get out of Chicago quick enough.'   *1927*

'The Three Legged Wonder' Sicilian Francesco Lentini died aged seventy-seven. His third limb is thought to have been part of an undeveloped twin and it was very nearly as long as his other two. He cheerfully claimed he was the only man who carried his own stool around with him, and said that when he bought shoes, he bought two pairs and did a good deed by giving the odd one to a one-legged friend.   *1966*

September 22

Royal spouse Captain Mark Phillips was born. A common interest in horses spurred his romance with Princess Anne, though only five weeks before their engagement they denied the existence of a romance at all. After their marriage in 1973, struggling genealogists traced the Phillips family back to Edward I – and there have certainly been some interesting ancestors in between. His father is a sausage manufacturer, his great-great-grandfather was a coal miner, and he's a direct descendant of Sir John Harrington who built the first flush-toilet and was banished from court for telling dirty jokes. His nickname in the royal family – supposedly coined by Prince Charles – is 'Fog'.   *1948*

The beating headmaster Dr Richard Busby was born. For fifty-five terrifying years he was the headmaster of Westminster School. He declared that his rod was his sieve and that 'whoever could not pass through that sieve was no boy for him'. He caned his pupils as a matter of course, whether they deserved it or not, and it was common practice for boys to be sent home with a leather patch on their pants as a substitute for the part that had been worn away by the flogging. It was all, he claimed, 'for my young friends' intellectual welfare'.   *1606*

Today's the day...

Julius Caesar's heir, the noble Augustus was born. Though he was a tiny man, he wrested control of the Empire from his partner Mark Antony and ruled it with a rod of iron, from a pair of built-up shoes. The cold affected his bladder, so in the winter he wore four tunics, a heavy woollen gown, a chest protector, underpants and woollen garters. For an emperor, he had very few vices, being mainly interested in power, gambling and women, especially other men's wives and 'young maidens of ripe years'.   *63 BC*

The decisive Battle of Salamis probably altered the whole course of European history when the Greeks stemmed the advance of the Persians. By pretending to disperse his ships, the Greek Commander Themistocles lured the Persian fleet into the straits below Mount Aegaleos. There the narrowness of the passage robbed them of the advantage of their superior numbers. While the Greeks lost only forty ships, the Persians lost 200 – and it was said that the sea turned red with the blood of the slain.   *480 BC*

The star who married more times than Henry VIII, Mickey Rooney was born. He first married Ava Gardner and has gradually worked his way through another seven wives, including poor Miss Muscle Beach who was murdered by her lover. Rooney is quite philosophical about it all. He claims that when he said to the Justice of the Peace 'I do' – the Justice replied, 'I know, I know!'   *1922*

Tricky Dicky made his Checkers speech in a TV and radio broadcast that cost $75,000. As Eisenhower's vice-presidential candidate, he was hoping to explain away an $18,000 secret fund set up for him by a group of Californian businessmen. Having demonstrated his basic honesty by one or two obscure devices, like the fact that his wife didn't have a mink coat, he came to the real highlight of the show. He admitted that he had received a gift. A man in Texas had sent him a dog. It was a cocker spaniel, 'And our little girl, Tricia, the six-year-old, named it Checkers. And you know, the kids love the dog, and I just want to say this right now, that regardless of what they say, we're going to keep it!'

1952

The first conviction for swearing by the act of 1745 took place in a London court when a 'ticket porter' was fined three shillings. The new act worked on a sliding scale so, for instance, a soldier or sailor would have been fined less; a 'gentleman or person of superior rank' considerably more. This was by no means the first naughty language act however. For in 1623 James I – who was known for a colourful turn of phrase himself – had signed a similar one, which provided a twelve-penny fine for each swear-word or curse. It's thought to be this earlier law that gave rise to the strange forms of 'polite' cussing that afterwards occurred, with expressions like 'Zounds', 'Odds Bobs', 'Egad', 'Lackadaisy' and best of all 'Gadzooks'.

1746

Today's the day...

The jockey baron Thomas Ward was born in the village of Howley, near York. He rose to fame and fortune on the back of a horse, riding first for the Prince of Liechtenstein and then for Charles Louis of Bourbon, the Duke of Lucca. As confidential servant to Charles, he solved the Dukedom's money troubles by selling political subservience to Austria and cutting down on the stable expenses. He was made Master of the Horse and then Minister of the Household and brought himself instant popularity by lowering the price of corn. He spoke German, French and Italian fluently with a very distinguished accent, but his uneducated native tongue always gave him away – so he was careful to avoid speaking English.   *1809*

The hungriest Roman Emperor Vitellius was born, and his natal horoscope was so bad his parents despaired. Brought up in Capri amid the sexual excesses of the Court of Tiberius, it's hardly surprising he grew up to be infamous for every sort of vice. His favourite was gluttony, with cruelty running a close second. He gorged himself three or four times a day, invited himself to everybody else's banquets and cost them a fortune – at least 4,000 gold pieces a visit. With exotic tastes, he concocted a dish dedicated to the goddess Minerva full of flamingo tongues, peacock brains and pike livers, all specially shipped from the furthest corners of the Empire. His ravenous appetite knew no bounds. He'd eat other people's leftovers if he was peckish, and in the temple the priests had to be careful or he'd snatch pieces of burnt offering from the altar!   *AD 14*

Chronicler of the Jazz Age Francis Scott Fitzgerald was born in St Paul, Minnesota, to an eccentric mother descended from 'straight 1850 potato-famine Irish'. At the tender age of twenty-four, his first novel *This Side of Paradise* was an instant success, and he was catapulted into the limelight as the personification of the Roaring Twenties and the spokesman of New York Society. 'I who knew less of New York than

September 24

---

any reporter of six months' standing and less of its society than any hall-room boy in a Ritz Stag line.' He married the dashing Zelda Sayre and tried hard to live up to being 'rich, famous, young and beautiful', saying, 'Sometimes I don't know whether Zelda and I *are* – or whether we're characters in one of my novels.'   *1896*

Dainty man of letters Horace Walpole was born, the fourth son of Robert Walpole, Earl of Orford. 'Slender, compact and neatly formed', he wore lavender suits in the summer, and was an MP for over twenty years. In his spare time, he indulged his passion for the odd. He altered his cottage at Strawberry Hill until he'd transformed it into 'a little Gothic castle'. He filled it with antiques and curiosities and then opened it to the public and charged admission. He was so unlike the rest of his family that wagging tongues had it that he wasn't sired by Sir Robert at all – but by Lord Carr of Hervey.   *1717*

Gun-happy sea-farer Matthew Barton was made an admiral after sailing the seas for fifty-seven years. The belated promotion didn't do him much good, however, for his health was so bad he never went to sea again. To console himself, he converted the roof of his house at Hampstead to look like a ship's quarter-deck. It was mounted with cannons, and on great occasions he'd fire them across the heath.   *1787*

The revolutionary physician Paracelsus died penniless and alone. He believed 'not even a dog-killer can learn his trade from books' and on his arrival at Basle University shocked everyone by burning the venerated medical works of Galen, Avicenna and Averroes. Worse still, he lectured in German, not Latin, and in such an extravagant style that the word 'bombastic' was coined from one of his many Christian names. A sloven spendthrift and drunkard, he had 'neither scholarship nor piety' and dabbled more and more in sorcery, declaring, 'If God will not help me, then the Devil will.'   *1541*

Today's the day...

The bravest British footballers created a legend in the World War I Battle of Loos. As the London Regiment's 18th Battalion went over the top, they pelted hell-for-leather into No Man's Land kicking a football before them.

1915

The guillotining of the prophet Jacques Cazotte took place in Paris. Cazotte was a writer and a staunch royalist, and four years before he'd made a remarkable prediction. At a dinner party, he'd foretold the fate of most of his fellow guests in the Revolution that was to come. In particular he told the playwright Chamfort 'you will cut your veins ... but will not die for months', while the Marquis de Cóndorcet could look forward to 'taking poison to cheat the executioner'. Both these prophecies were fulfilled – and as Cazotte had said, most of the other guests ended up on the scaffold. The question is, did he know that he'd be there with them?

1792

A fungus killed the Pope. Poor Clement VII had eaten it believing it to be a mushroom. In fact, as he found to his cost, it was a death-cap toadstool.

1534

September 25

Jack the Ripper's first letter arrived at the Central News Agency. It said, 'Dear Boss, I keep on hearing the police have caught me, but they won't fix me just yet ... I am down on whores and I shan't quit ripping them till I do get buckled. Grand work ... The next job I do I shall clip the lady's ears off ... My knife's nice and sharp, I want to get to work right away ... Yours truly Jack the Ripper. P.S. Don't mind me giving the trade name.' It was, in fact, the first time the name had ever been used and the chances are it was this that guaranteed the Ripper's immortality. Five days later the body of Catherine Eddowes was found. The right ear, as predicted, was snipped.   *1888*

Samuel Pepys drank his first cup of tea. He'd probably been impressed by broadsheets that had started appearing two years earlier, praising its virtues. 'It maketh the body active and lusty' said one. 'It helpeth headache, giddiness and heaviness thereof ... it easeth the brain and strengthens the memory ... is good for colds, dropsies and scurvies and expelleth infection.' Jonas Hanway, tea's 'most violent foe' disagreed. He said later that tea 'had lessened the vigour of men and deprived English women of their beauty'.   *1660*

A cormorant's stomach revealed a strange secret. The bird had been flying low over the river near Ripon in Yorkshire. A fish leapt out of the water and the cormorant gobbled it up and retired to the bank to eat it. The hunter who watched this display shot the bird and when its 'maw' was later opened, there was found inside a gold brooch valued at £10. It had probably been lost in the water and first swallowed by a fish.   *1825*

Dwight Eisenhower got annoyed with so-called agricultural experts he described as 'synthetic farmers'. 'Farming looks mighty easy,' he said, 'when your plough is a pencil and you're a thousand miles from the cornfield.'   *1956*

Today's the day...

The *Queen Mary* was launched by her royal namesake with a bottle of Australian wine. The largest liner of her time, she was originally going to be called 'Queen Victoria', and the Chairman of Cunard had called on King George V to seek his approval. He told the King that they were going to name the great ship after 'one of England's noblest Queens', but before he actually said which one, George had concluded that his own wife Mary was meant. 'Oh!' he said, 'Her Majesty will be so pleased' – and after that, there wasn't a choice!   *1934*

The last album the Beatles recorded together was released. Surprisingly it was not 'Let It Be', which was issued later, but the much more impressive 'Abbey Road'. Beatle-buffs claimed that the cover confirmed their fears that Paul had died and been replaced by a double. The picture showed the four walking across a zebra crossing in Indian file – Paul was the only one barefoot, and the only one out of step. The album gave the local council problems too. The Abbey Road sign was stolen so many times, they had to leave it off – and the road was nameless for months.   *1969*

September 26

The inventor of the bouncing bomb Sir Barnes Wallis was
born. Though his invention made him the boffin-hero behind Guy
Gibson's famous World War II dambusting raids, it was not the only
thing he's ever come up with. He also made important contributions to
the development of both the swing-wing plane and Concorde. More
significant, however, is the weapon he designed to repel the Norman
invaders at a Bank Holiday reconstruction of the Battle of Hastings –
it was the world's first aerodynamic custard pie.   *1887*

Nelson's successor at Trafalgar Admiral Lord Collingwood was
born. He became one of the best loved commanders in the fleet;
flogged only once a month and rarely gave more than a dozen lashes –
which at the time was remarkably mild. His humanity, it was said, was
only exceeded by his patriotism, and when walking on his estate he
always took a pocketful of acorns to plant. That way, he reckoned,
there'd be plenty of oak trees for England's ships in the future.   *1750*

'The Empress of the Blues' Bessie Smith died in a car crash in
Mississippi, amid rumours that she'd bled to death while a white had
been given preferential treatment. She'd recorded her first track,
'Downhearted Blues' in 1923, but her music was too real for
Depression America and her career was already on the wane. She was
buried in an unmarked grave and it wasn't until 1970 that a group of
admirers gave her a headstone. One of them was rock singer Janis
Joplin, who was to die shortly afterwards herself. Joplin said of Smith,
'She showed me the air and taught me how to fill it.'   *1937*

An ex-con broke into prison. The man was Terence O'Neill and
the chosen clink was Lewes. He scaled a 20ft wall to stay the night
because, he said, 'I've been in the prison so many times, it was like a
sanctuary'.   *1978*

Today's the day...

The Railway Age was born with the opening of the George Stephenson-built Stockton and Darlington. The total length of rail was somewhat over twenty miles and the rolling stock included six goods waggons, six passenger coaches, a director's coach, fourteen waggons for workmen and the train – called *Locomotion*. A local reporter was staggered by the display. 'The engine', he wrote, 'started off with this immense train of carriages and such was its velocity that in some parts the speed was frequently twelve miles per hour!' The Americans, however, weren't so impressed. One writer claimed that the railways would make stay-at-homes gadabouts, honest men liars, and encourage widespread intellectual decline.   *1825*

Much maligned monarch Louis XIII of France was born in Fontainebleau. He was once playing the game 'battledore' with his mistress Madame d'Hautefort, when the shuttlecock fell into the low neck of her dress and lodged in her cleavage. The courtesan told him to come and get it, but 'to avoid a trap set by the evil one', he went and got the firetongs and removed it thus. He tried the same trick to try and get hold of a secret letter which was kept in his wife's ample bosom. Unfortunately this time, the Queen and her maids mocked him so much he fled in embarrassment and they burnt the naughty note.   *1601*

The campaigning caricaturist and illustrator George Cruikshank was born. Seeing two women hanging at Newgate one day for forgery, he was horrified both by the ease with which the £1 note could be copied and by the severity of the sentence. He produced a superb counterfeit but added the hangman's tree and the words 'not to be imitated'. His friend William Hone published it, and caused a sensation – and soon after forgers were no longer hanged. His next target was drink, though he'd long been a hell-raising drinker himself and his father was an alcoholic. The man who'd been once left by his

546

September 27

fellows perched on top of a lamp-post totally inebriated, now became a teetotaller with equal zest. He accused his poor mother of 'first lifting the poison chalice to my lips' – though in fact she'd tried to wean him off it – and at a huge celebration for his silver wedding anniversary, he served just tea and toast.   *1792*

'Baggy Pants' Banks, the splendid Miss Sarah Sophia as she was known to her intimates, passed away in the family house in Soho Square. She was a collector of curiosities, coins and engravings, but it was her dress that impressed people and wherever she went they stood agog. She often wore an old 'Barcelona quilted petticoat' which had a hole in either side so she could rummage in two huge pockets stuffed with books. Over the top of this she wore a gown and progressed through the streets followed by a 6ft servant with 'a cane almost as tall as himself'.   *1878*

A real-life gunfight took place in true Hollywood style in Hays City, Kansas. Sam Strawhim's gang had threatened to kill Wild Bill Hickok for stopping them shooting up the saloon. In the street outside, Bill took the glasses they'd stolen and walked back into the bar. Strawhim followed him and threatened to break every glass in the place. Bill stood with his back to Sam and said, 'Do, and they'll carry you out.' Sam drew. Bill saw his reflection in the mirror, whirled round and shot him dead.   *1869*

The *Queen Elizabeth* was launched on Clydebank by Queen Elizabeth – later styled the Queen Mother. At the time, it was the largest passenger vessel ever built; it was 1,031ft long, 118ft wide; originally weighed 83,673 gross tons and with 168,000hp turbines, could travel at 28½ knots (32.8mph). Unfortunately the big ship started travelling too quickly and began to slide down the ramp before Her Majesty had started her speech.   *1938*

Today's the day...

The original Marathon was won by a breathless messenger who hotfooted it twenty-four miles from the scene of the Battle of Marathon to the City of Athens. 'Rejoice we conquer,' he gasped – then dropped dead.   *490 BC*

The Pope died a solitary death. Sixty-five-year-old Albino Luciani had been in good health when he was elected John Paul I only thirty-three days before. Cheerful and gregarious, he seemed overwhelmed by the loneliness of his office and told one foreign cardinal, 'I am in a place where everyone comes to complain about something. I don't know who I can have a friendly conversation with.' His secretary Father Magee found him dead in bed in the morning, his reading light still on and a copy of Thomas à Kempis' *Imitation of Christ* open before him. A bell was within reach, but his nearest aide was out of earshot and doctors estimated he'd died about six-and-a-half hours earlier – alone in his room without receiving the last rites.   *1978*

Gentlemanly boxer John Jackson was born in London. Polite to a fault, he offered to finish one fight sitting on a chair after he'd slipped and dislocated his ankle. He opened his 'Gymnastic Academy' at Old Bond Street and aristocrats flocked to take lessons from him. Among them were Lord Byron who sparred regularly with him in an attempt to 'renew my acquaintance with my muffles'. Asked by George IV to provide a bodyguard for his coronation, Jackson chose some of his best fighters and they all lined up outside Westminster Abbey – bruisers dressed up as pageboys!   *1768*

Tom Cribb saved the honour of English boxing when he beat the American ex-slave Tom Molineaux in just twenty minutes. The crowd of 20,000 was disappointed the fight was so short, as in a previous match Cribb and Molineaux had battled on for thirty-three rounds. On the very morning of the fight the American consumed 'a boiled fowl, an apple pie and a tankard of ale', and by the fourth round was 'heaving fearfully'. Short of wind he lunged about the ring, was finally floored and carried off with a broken jaw and two broken ribs. Seven years later he died in poverty – aged only thirty-three.   *1811*

Legendary sex-kitten Brigitte Bardot was born in Paris to wealthy middle-class parents. She studied ballet, worked as a model and became a household name when Vadim promoted her as the sexually liberated woman – 'the impossible dream of married men'. More renowned for her lifestyle than her acting ability, after three marriages and innumerable lovers, she commented, 'Nobody has any security in loving me . . . sometimes eight days is too long to be faithful.'   *1934*

Kindly author Thomas Day was killed, a victim of his own theories. A 'most virtuous human being' he believed kindness could control any animal, and set off to visit his mother on an unbroken horse. Unfortunately the animal threw him off, Day landed on his head and died an hour later.   *1789*

Today's the day...

Horatio Lord Nelson was born in Burnham Thorpe, Norfolk, one of the eleven children of a poor country parson. A midshipman at twelve and a captain at twenty-four, he lost the sight of his right eye at Calvi and his right arm at Santa Cruz – and both times he was on land. He became an Italian Duke and an English Baron – though he'd have preferred to be a Knight of the Bath because he liked the colour of the sash. For a hero, he cut a 'poor figure'. He stood only 5ft 4in, Lady Hamilton led him about 'like a keeper with a bear', and he was always 'bedecked with stars, ribbons and medals'. For the Duke of Wellington, he was two people – personally 'a vain and silly fellow'; militarily 'a very superior man'. As his relationship with Lady Hamilton developed, she got fatter and he got thinner – until he was nothing more than 'a miserable collection of bones'. He once said, only half in jest, 'I have all the diseases there are,' and strange as it may seem, all his life he was 'always tossed about and always seasick'. *1758*

The man who lived a dream William Beckford was born. Left a millionaire at ten, he became a great traveller, black magician and collector of exotica; kept a pet dwarf and a dog called Viscount Fartleberry. Having written the bizarre fantasy *Varthek*, he spent the rest of his life intermittently living the book. Returning from exile after a homosexual scandal, he surrounded his estate with a 12ft high, seven mile long wall and built England's most elaborate folly Fonthill Abbey. In the whole vast edifice, there was not a single mirror, and such was his aversion to women that he had alcoves built in the corridors, so the maids could hide when he passed. *1759*

The first metropolitan police force appeared on the streets of London. They were called 'Peelers' after their creator Sir Robert Peel. They wore reinforced top hats to protect them from assault and to use as platforms for peering over walls. Of the first 2,800 bobbies recruited, 1,790 were quickly dismissed – for being drunk on duty. *1829*

September 29

Original rock'n'roller Jerry Lee Lewis was born in Ferriday, Louisiana. He created a storm with 'Great Balls of Fire', 'A Whole Lotta Shakin' Goin' On' and his marriage in 1958 to his thirteen-year-old cousin. After two decades, however, he's still selling records and playing piano with his foot. 'They call me the killer,' he says, 'I mow people down with rock'n'roll.'   *1935*

The scientist who fooled Stalin Trofim Lysenko was born of semi-literate peasant stock. Though poorly educated himself, he developed a half-baked theory that suggested that genetic improvement could be wrought in plants and animals merely by controlling the environment. Anyone who opposed his views, he said, was 'an enemy of the proletariat', and both Stalin and Khrushchev agreed. He produced trees that grew in barren soil and a prize herd of super-milk-yielding cows. Scientists who questioned his views were removed from their posts and occasionally sent to Siberia, and he controlled the Soviet scientific hierarchy for nearly thirty years. The trouble was nobody else could reproduce his amazing achievements – though that really wasn't surprising – they were fakes!   *1898*

'The tuneful cowboy' Gene Autry was born in Tioga Springs, Texas, the son of 'the singing baptist minister'. He took up Morse Code in a telegraph office in Oklahoma and after an accidental meeting with Will Rogers took his advice and became a singer. In the mid-thirties with a string of hits behind him, he became film's first singing cowboy, acquired 'Champion the Wonder Horse' and fired off a bizarre mixture of ballads and bullets that made him a star from then until well into the fifties. These days he controls a business empire that turns over more than forty million dollars a year, but way back then he was just a lonesome cowboy who couldn't act, but could play guitar and ride – well almost. He once fell off Champion in a rodeo in Madison Square Gardens.   *1907*

Today's the day...

A foreign war broke out in London. The French and Spanish ambassadors were on their way to Whitehall when their coaches clashed. In the narrow lane that led to the City there was only room for one, and of course neither would give way. Within minutes their retainers launched into a pitched battle, and the streets were soon strewn with wounded. Despite the ferocity of the fight, no clear decision was reached and both parties left the field in disarray. Though the Spaniards had held their own against superior numbers, they had to give way in the end. If they hadn't, Louis XIV said he'd make this fake war a real one. *1661*

Reckless spendthrift Squire John Mytton was born. His father died before he was two and unchecked, the boy ran wild. He was expelled from Eton and Harrow, took up drinking at an early age and was soon downing eight bottles of port a day – topped up with *eau-de-Cologne*. With total disregard for the cold, he'd wear only the thinnest clothes and was once spotted stalking duck in winter – stark naked. His wardrobe, however, consisted of 152 pairs of trousers, 152 overcoats, 700 pairs of boots, 1,000 hats and 3,000 shirts. He threw bundles of money to the winds, quite literally, and in the last fifteen years of his life, he got through nearly half a million pounds. Like the gentleman he was, he took great care of his horses. He let them warm themselves by the fire, and once actually killed one when he gave it a bottle of mulled port. He terrified his guests by riding a bear into his own dining room, and terrified himself as a cure for hiccups – he set fire to his nightshirt. His servants rescued him and despite severe burns he happily announced, 'The hiccups is gone by God!' *1796*

Devious skinflint Daniel Dancer died. With his long-suffering sister, he'd lived in a decrepit mansion in Harrow, with a tree sprouting out of the roof. They lived on scraps of meat and hard dumplings which they boiled up once a week – while Dancer scoured the fields looking for

September 30

bones. He was once delighted to find the body of a sheep and carried it home on his shoulder, so his sister could make pies. He collected pocketfuls of dung, bits of wool and old iron; swathed his body in haybands and rarely washed. When he did, he'd never use soap or a towel, and on sunny days, he'd take a dip in his neighbour's pond and scrub himself down with sand. His one and only friend was Lady Tempest, who on one memorable occasion sent him a trout stewed in claret. In the cold weather it had frozen, but since Dancer was too mean to make a fire, he sat on it in bed till it thawed.   *1794*

The bill was paid for the Boston Tea party on behalf of the citizens of Jackson County, Oregon. Though nobody else had paid, they still felt they owed something to the merchants, Davison and Newman of London, who 188 years before had lost their tea. Mayor Snider of Medford carefully worked out that Jackson County represented four ten-thousandths of 1 per cent of the population of America. Taking everything into account, he conscientiously sent the company a cheque for the exact amount due – $1.96 cents.   *1961*

Jack the Ripper committed double murder. The jeweller Diemschutz found the first body huddled by the wall in Berner Street at 1am. Though it was surrounded by 'quite two quarts of blood', the body was still warm, and since it wasn't mutilated, it looked as if Jack had been disturbed. An hour later, a constable on patrol in nearby Mitre Square found the second victim. This time, the Ripper had done his worst – the woman had been disembowelled; and her left kidney, a piece of her ear and some of her entrails were missing. The women were identified as Elizabeth Stride and Catherine Eddowes – both well-known prostitutes. Ironically Catherine had been arrested earlier in the evening for being drunk and disorderly – but a brief forty-five minutes before her death the police had released her.   *1888*

Today's the day...

The world's only white gorilla was found in Spanish Equatorial Guinea, clinging to the body of his dead mother. Estimated to be about two years old, he was taken to Barcelona Zoo where he was christened 'Capito de Nieve' – not a very apt name for what would eventually be an enormous strapping male gorilla – it means 'Little Snowflake'.   *1966*

The mad Tsar Paul I was born. Alternately ignored and threatened by his mother Catherine the Great, he grew up to be just a little strange. He'd have people arrested for wearing pantaloons or 'vests without sleeves', and if they dared to mention baldness or snub noses – particularly his – he'd have them flogged. When people knelt to him, he liked to hear the crack of their knees on the floor, and insisted they made loud smacking noises when they kissed his hand. Because one man had a dirty button on his uniform, he made his entire bodyguard march 2,000 miles to Siberia, and when the English Ambassador's coach went where it shouldn't have, he not only had the horses and the postilions whipped, but the coach as well! In 1807 after he'd reigned for just five years, the army staged a coup, and just as his mother had arranged the death of his father, so Paul was strangled in a plot that was organised by his son.   *1754*

'Everybody's tomboy' film star Julie Andrews was born at 6am in Walton-on-Thames. Her parents had a music hall act and were amazed to discover that as well as goofy teeth, bandy legs and a squint, their little daughter had a four-octave voice and an 'adult larynx'. Starting off in revues and pantos, she first came to international fame in *My Fair Lady* in 1956. After *Mary Poppins* and *The Sound of Music*, Kenneth Tynan praised her 'thrice-scrubbed innocence', and Miss Andrews tried to dispel it by wearing a badge which said 'Mary Poppins is a junkie'. Paul Newman called her 'the last of the really great dames', while someone less flattering said she was like a nun with a switch-blade.   *1935*

October 1

A countess was killed by cosmetics. She was Marie Countess of Coventry and her death was said to have been hastened by an excess use of white-lead make-up. Marie was one of the two empty-headed Gunning sisters, who were considered to be the greatest beauties of their age. A cobbler once made 2½ guineas just by exhibiting a shoe he made for her, and such were the crowds that followed her about that the royal household gave her a fourteen-man military escort. She was the original dumb blonde and her *faux pas* were legion. Towards the end of his reign, she told her ageing but adoring fan, George II, 'of all the sights of London, there is only one I am really anxious to see – and that's a coronation.'   *1760*

Bloody Mary, England's hated Catholic queen, was crowned. She was taken from the Tower in 'a chariot of tissue, drawn with six grey horses all betrapped in red velvet', and she wore a blue velvet gown trimmed with ermine. Trumpets blew and the streets were thronged; 'Peter the Dutchman' stood on one leg on the weathercock of St Paul's waving a flag, and perhaps not surprisingly, the Queen ended the day with a headache.   *1553*

555

Today's the day...

The last Plantagenet King Richard III was born, the twelfth of thirteen children. He almost certainly didn't have a hunchback and by turning him into some kind of monster, Sir Thomas More, the Tudors and Shakespeare probably perpetrated one of the most successful character assassinations of all time. Not that Richard was entirely without blemish. He married the wealthy widow of the Prince of Wales, and had his mother-in-law imprisoned for life. He stood by while his brother George mysteriously drowned in a cask of wine; packed his nephews off to the Tower, probably killed them, seized the crown and prepared to marry their sister after his own wife had conveniently died.

1452

Moustachioed madcap Groucho Marx was born in New York. He wanted to be a doctor but the family couldn't afford it and his mother, the daughter of a magician, was determined her sons would go into showbiz. Along with Gummo and an out-of-tune female singer, he was launched on the vaudeville circuit as one of 'The Three Nightingales'. Later they were joined by Harpo, became 'The Four Nightingales' and, according to Groucho, 'played in towns I wouldn't let them bury me in . . . even if the funeral was free'. Apart from the famous films with his brothers, he wrote two plays, and several books; compered a TV chat show and 'insulted nearly everyone worth insulting'. He married three times, was always chasing the ladies in his films and insisted he still did so in his later years except that, 'I only chase them now if they are running downhill!'   *1895*

The world's most beastly army helped the revolutionary Bernardo O'Higgins lead Chile to independence. Trapped with fellow patriots outside Santiago, wounded and low on ammunition, O'Higgins had a brilliant idea. As the Spanish troops were closing in, he rounded up reinforcements from the village and sent them charging through the enemy, clearing a path for his escape. His terrifying storm-troopers consisted of a herd of horses, cows, pigs and mules, backed up by ducks and chickens!   *1814*

'The Father of India' Mohandas Karamchand Gandhi was born in Junagadh. Contrary to his strict Hindu upbringing, at eighteen he was eating meat, dabbling in atheism and smoking. In London studying law, he bought himself a silk hat and spats, took dancing lessons, and learnt English from an Irish priest so he spoke it with a brogue ever more. Twenty years as a 'second-class citizen' in South Africa changed him completely. He developed the concept of 'soul force' – '*satyagraha*', took a vow of celibacy and dressed simply in a loin-cloth and sandals. Back in India, he organised 'passive resistance' to English rule and became 'Mahatma' – 'great soul' – though Churchill insisted he was just 'a seditious Middle Temple lawyer now posing as a fakir'. Gandhi was certainly odd. He slept with young girls to test his chastity, worked at a spinning wheel for two hours a day and carried his false teeth in his loin-cloth. His diet and drinking habits were a little eccentric too. On a visit to England, he insisted on keeping a goat in his hotel room – and milked it every day.   *1869*

Today's the day...

A courageous confidence trickster was hanged at Shrewsbury. He was one Richard Johnson and he conned the Under-Sheriff into promising that he'd be laid in his coffin without being stripped. Half an hour after he'd swung, the reason became clear when someone noticed he still showed signs of life. What he'd done in fact, was to make a special harness that would prevent the rope from killing him – and by wearing a 'double shirt and a flowing periwig' he'd been able to hide it and dupe officialdom. It did him no good, unfortunately, for he was immediately hanged again 'in an effectual manner'. *1696*

The happiest of marriages was contracted between labourer's daughter Sarah Hoggins and a divorcee called Henry Cecil – whom nobody in the village of Hodnet in Shropshire knew much about. Some thought he was a highwayman, since he popped off from time to time and came back with money. Two years after the wedding, however, Mr Cecil's uncle died, and he had to reveal his true identity. On the decease of his elderly relative he'd become none other than Lord of Burleigh and Earl of Exeter – and the doughty peasant Sarah, 'a plain, but honest girl', was staggered to find herself a Countess. *1791*

October 3

The greatest shoplifter of all time thirty-three-year-old
Australian part-time teacher Richard Jeakins was jailed for three years
at a court in Knightsbridge. In his flat, which he called 'the Palace',
police had found £90,000 worth of stolen property, including a
painting by William Blake worth £17,000; a £7,000 Picasso print;
two valuable ikons, two colour TVs, two hi-fi sets and forty cashmere
sweaters. Mr Jeakins, who was described by psychiatrists as suffering
from 'erotic kleptomania', was finally caught in possession of
stolen washing-up liquid when the tyres on his getaway bicycle had
been deflated by forty-year-old store detective, Sylvia 'Pussy'
Keeble.   *1978*

A fallen woman Sarah Lloyd admitted that she'd let 'her abandoned
seducer into the dwelling house of her mistress'. Together they'd
robbed and set fire to the premises, and for her part in the felony poor
wicked Sarah was hanged at Bury St Edmunds in Suffolk. With her
last words she spoke the immortal line: 'May my example be a warning
to thousands.'   *1799*

The trans-American golfer drove a ball into the Atlantic Ocean. He
was Floyd S. Reed and he started swinging on the Pacific shoreline
nearly thirteen months before. His trip across the national fairway
spanned nearly 3,500 miles. It took him well over 100,000 strokes and
in the various roughs, bunkers and other hazards along the way, he
lost more than 3,500 balls – at least one for every mile.   *1964*

The first sex symbol of the circus New-Orleans-born Adah Isaacs
Menken made her English *début* at Astley's. For this first London
appearance she came on strapped to the back of a 'wild horse',
performing the sensational 'Ride of Mazeppa'. The linen outfit she
was wearing crept 'only slightly towards her knee', and according to
one shocked critic 'did not much trouble the sewing machine.'   *1864*

Today's the day...

Donald Hume got away with murder when he killed Stanley Setty, his partner in a business that dealt in stolen cars and forged petrol coupons. Hume was an illegitimate psychopath, who was jealous of Setty's opulent life-style and finally snapped when his partner kicked his dog. He stabbed him with an SS dagger, dismembered the body, wrapped up the pieces and dropped them from a hired plane over the Channel. One of the parcels floated ashore and was discovered by a shocked wildfowler on the Essex mudflats. Hume was arrested but incredibly, was found not guilty of murder and sentenced to only twelve years in prison as an accessory. Five months after his release in 1958, he sold his confession to the Sunday papers, flew to Switzerland and took to robbing banks. In 1959 he was charged with the slaying of a Swiss taxi-driver and while he was awaiting trial, wrote a 60,000-word novel on a subject close to his heart. It was entitled *The Dead Stay Dumb*. *1949*

Soviet master spy Richard Sorge was born in southern Russia. He became one of the leaders of the German Communist Party, was promoted to Comintern headquarters in Moscow and established spy rings in Germany, China and Japan, where he was taken for a harmless drunken journalist. Although he was captured in Japan, it's never been clear whether he was executed or exchanged. However, to mark his 82nd birthday, a statue was unveiled to him in Dresden. It was inscribed to 'a tireless Socialist scout'. *1895/1977*

Penniless composer Henry Carey died. Although he's often credited with writing 'God Save the King' and composed the evergreen 'Sally in our Alley', he was nevertheless always short of money. His widow and six children were left 'entirely destitute', and a benefit was held at Covent Garden to support them. Happily they managed to survive and continue the line, and Carey's great grandson was none other than the famous actor Edmund Kean. *1743*

October 4

Britain's first public escalators were introduced at Earl's Court tube station. The public was understandably nervous of the new moving staircases, so sensitive railway officials took direct action. They employed a man with a wooden leg to ride up and down all day. *1911*

Deadpan hero of the silent screen Buster Keaton was born on tour in Kansas. His parents were acrobats in vaudeville and by the time he was three, Buster was in on the act. When Father took to drinking, they all abandoned acrobatics for their own safety and Buster, already a celebrity, was offered a part in a 'Fatty' Arbuckle film. Together they made seventeen short movies, in one of which Buster gives his only on-screen laugh! In his own films, he was famed as the little man with the flat hat and the 'great stone face' who reacted little in the midst of crazy disasters. In the thirties, contractual difficulties and a broken marriage drove him to drink, and until a revival of interest in the sixties, his career was at a low ebb. Shortly before the war he was reduced to acting as a comedy consultant for Red Skelton. The sad joke was that the films he was working on were all re-makes of his own movies. *1895*

Today's the day...

The world's biggest airship burst into flames shortly after
2.05am near Beauvais in France. She was 777ft long; her gas bags
made of bullocks' intestines bulged with $5\frac{1}{2}$ million cu.ft of
hydrogen, and as she had shown in her maiden voyage, she was
immensely difficult to control. Having narrowly avoided demolishing
a house, she'd plunged and plummeted her way across the Channel
pelted by rain and buffeted by 35 knot winds, crossing the French
coast at a height of only 250ft. Nearing Beauvais, she went into a
shallow, almost gentle dive and as she collided gracefully with a hill,
she was torn apart by the exploding hydrogen and 'fired up in an
instant from stem to stem'. Only six of the fifty-four observers and
crew survived, and among the dead was the Air Minister Lord
Thompson. When pressed about the R101s poor performance he'd
said, 'Except for the millionth chance, she's as safe as a house!'   *1930*

The first 'Monty Python's Flying Circus' bewildered British
audiences, who nevertheless took to it much quicker than the
Americans. Horrified US censors actually dared to cut the last two
words out of a sketch in 1975, when two men were shown in a bath
and the voice-over said: 'They washed their arms, their legs, and then
they washed their naughty bits!'   *1969*

The Daltons' last hold-up ended in disaster when they tried to rob
two banks simultaneously in Coffeyville, Kansas. The three brothers,
all ex-peace officers, arrived in town with two accomplices, armed to
the teeth with Colt 45s and Winchesters and wearing false whiskers.
Bob and Emmett held up the First National while Grat, along with
Bill Powers and Dick Broadwell, tried to take the Condon bank. Their
hairy disguises were easily seen through by locals who knew them, and
as the gang tried to make their escape, they were confronted by angry
townspeople. In the ensuing battle, four citizens including the Marshal
were killed and the gang were 'all cut down'. Bob, Grat, Powers and

Broadwell all died, while Emmett was shot in the arm and hip. After ten years in jail he was pardoned. He became a real estate agent and Hollywood scriptwriter, and played bit parts which showed that crime doesn't pay. 'It never paid and it never will,' he said, 'and that was the one big lesson of the Coffeyville raid.' *1892*

Marlene Dietrich showed what she was made of when she appeared at the Sahara Hotel, Las Vegas, in what appeared to be a see-through dress. Marlene claimed it wasn't her glittering rhinestone outfit that was at fault, however, but the pressmen's flashbulbs, which could 'shoot through a black sweater!' *1955*

The spy in drag Chevalier D'Eon was born in Burgundy. He grew up with a 'girlish bust', a beardless face and a dandy's taste in clothes, and though he was a brave soldier and one of the best fencers in the army, Louis XV got him to dress up as a woman to spy at the Russian court – as a lady-in-waiting to the Tsarina. By the time he was posted to England as Secretary to the French Ambassador, his fame had gone before him. People started gambling on the question of his true sex, and such enormous stakes were involved that odds were actually quoted on the Stock Exchange. Outraged, D'Eon tried to seek redress, but an English court declared him to be a woman, and the French King concurred. To make matters worse, his pension and the right to return to France were made dependent on his dressing permanently in skirts, and when he once demurred, he was clapped in a convent. It took his death in 1810 to resolve the problem when the surgeon Copeland performed an autopsy and declared, rather late in the day, that 'the male organs were perfectly formed'. *1728*

Women were forbidden the veil by Shah Riza Khan of Persia. Defending his action in removing the traditional female covering he said, 'It is not as if the faces of our women were sad to look upon.' *1928*

Today's the day...

The Reno Brothers committed the first train robbery in America. Inspired by their cavalry raiding in the Civil War, they decided to rob a moving train on the Ohio and Mississippi Railroad. As it slowed down for a bend near Seymour, Indiana, they jumped on board and seized more than $10,000 in gold and cash. However a stout safe remained, which they knew contained more valuables. For over an hour William Reno tried to open it but finally – cursing, kicking and firing at it with his gun – he had to ride off and leave it behind.   *1866*

The fourth Arab/Israeli War broke out, once again plunging the Middle East into turmoil. It was a peculiarly sad day for hostilities to begin, for it's both the Jewish Day of Atonement and the beginning of the Moslem Feast of Ramadan – two of the most important festivals in the opposing forces' religious calendars.   *1973*

'The Swedish Nightingale' Jenny Lind was born in Stockholm. As she was illegitimate, she was boarded out during her childhood and sent first to live with the local parish clerk and then at the Widows' Home. Admitted to the Royal Theatre School when she was only nine, she sang in her first opera when she was eighteen and by the time she was

October 6

twenty had raised the money to travel to Paris and study with Manuel
Garcia. 'A thin, pale, plain-featured girl', she was transfigured when
she sang and 'Lindomania' swept through Europe. Admirers in
Vienna tried to draw her carriage themselves; in Stuttgart they ripped
apart her bedclothes for souvenirs and when she arrived in London,
Queen Victoria tossed her bouquet at her feet and 'the old Duke of
Wellington' hung about her 'like an enamoured grandfather'.   *1820*

The silent film era ended when the first full length 'talking picture'
opened in New York. It was *The Jazz Singer*, a twenties 'weepie', and
starred Al Jolson singing such numbers as 'My Mammy', 'Toot Toot
Tootsie Goodbye' and 'Blue Skies'. The soundtrack was almost
entirely music and apart from one scene there wasn't supposed to be
any other dialogue. However they'd reckoned without Jolson who
after one song ad-libbed and quipped prophetically, 'You ain't heard
nothin' yet!'   *1927*

Gruff broadcaster Gilbert Harding insulted his fellow diners when
he began his after-dinner speech, 'I have been dragged along to this
third-rate place for a third-rate dinner for third-rate people . . .' He
got no further as he was firmly asked to leave. He should have been
more careful – he was addressing the annual dinner of the Hounslow
Magistrates.   *1953*

Self-styled King of Haiti Henri Christophe was born in Grenada.
He modelled himself on Napoleon, rose through the ranks of the army
from cook to general, and had himself crowned Henry I of Haiti in a
hastily-built cathedral. He dressed his officers in gold lace, silk
stockings and 'white smallclothes', rode around in an elegant
London-built carriage drawn by four grey horses, and created an
aristocracy which included the unfortunate titles of Duc de Marmelade
and Comte de Limonade.   *1767*

Today's the day...

The Battle of Lepanto halted the advance of the Ottoman Empire when the allied Christian forces roundly defeated the Turkish fleet. One of the heroes of the battle was a young Spaniard who rose from his sick-bed to take part in the fray. In the fighting he lost his left hand but it was afterwards said that the loss 'added to the glory of his right'. The young man's name was Miguel de Cervantes and he was to create one of the greatest characters in literature – Don Quixote.   *1571*

Music-hall star Marie Lloyd died, aged only fifty-two. Worried about her troublesome husband, her rheumatism and the increasing popularity of the cinema, she'd been working harder than ever. Off-stage she was frightened and lonely, threw endless parties and lavished money on people she'd hardly met. At the Alhambra, her doctor warned her not to go on, but she ignored him. Singing one of her most famous tragi-comic songs 'One of the ruins that Cromwell knocked abaht a bit', she was staggering about the stage in keeping with the character, when she fell heavily. The audience applauded and cheered loudly at this new bit of play-acting, but in fact she'd collapsed – and she died shortly afterwards.   *1922*

The Wigwam Murder was discovered when the mummified body of a woman dressed in a 'tatty green and white frock' was found on Hankley Common in Surrey. Identified as Joan Pearl Wolfe, she'd been engaged to a Canadian-Indian soldier, August Sangret, who was stationed nearby. When he was interviewed by the police, Sangret remained impassive but gave them a detailed 17,000 word statement in which he told of a wigwam he'd built in the woods where he and Pearl used to meet. When the girl's shattered skull was pieced together by forensic experts, they found unusually shaped stab wounds in the front of the head which could only have been made by an instrument with 'a beak-shaped point'. A private in Sangret's unit recalled seeing an unusual knife during the summer. It had been stuck in a tree in the woods above a curious little shack – Sangret's wigwam. With the evidence of the knife Sangret was hanged – without it he would probably have been set free.

1942

Raddled writer Edgar Allan Poe died in Baltimore. Although a lifelong alcoholic, he had just taken the pledge and joined the Temperance Society giving several public lectures on the evil of drink and the pleasures of abstinence. The city was in the throes of an election when Poe mysteriously disappeared. He turned up five days later semi-conscious in the gutter and it's believed he may have been used as a 'repeater' – a multiple voter using false names. Suffering from *delirium tremens*, he lived in agony for four days and finally expired screaming 'Lord help my poor soul.' He was buried in the grim cemetery of Westminster Presbyterian Church, with no headstone and his grave forlornly marked 'Number 80'. Twenty-six years later, he was exhumed and reburied in a magnificent monument and when his body was examined, his features were still 'easily discerned' and his teeth as 'perfect and white as pearl'.

1849

Today's the day...

The first horse-race won by a woman jockey was a triumph for millionaire's daughter Eileen Joel. She and five other girls had entered the race through a loophole. The Newmarket Town Plate, originally sponsored by Charles II, was open to any amateur rider and since no gender was specified, the girls took the organisers at their word and ran away with the race. Miss Joel sailed past the post elegantly attired not in a riding cap, but a cloche hat. *1925*

Sergeant Alvin York bamboozled the Germans in the Argonne in World War I. The young Tennessee soldier and six other men found themselves surrounded by the Hun on Hill 223. So packing his pistol and a Springfield rifle, the Sergeant started blazing away in true comic book style. He killed twenty Germans single-handed and the rest were so confused by his fusillade, they thought they were surrounded and gave up the ghost. The seven Americans returned to a hero's welcome – with 132 prisoners. *1918*

10,000 British women were blackmailed by a letter that arrived in this morning's post. It had been sent by the aptly named Chrimes brothers, who had made a speciality of tablets that were supposed to promote abortion. Not satisfied with their ill-gotten gains from this procedure, they sent the threatening letter to all their 'patients', demanding money or exposure for the 'fearful crime' the poor women had tried to commit. The Chrimes' crime was exposed and they were sentenced to thirty years' hard labour. *1898*

Ernesto Che Guevara was captured. Disillusioned with the new Cuba he'd helped Castro to create, he was betrayed by one of the very peasants he was fighting for. At first, he was said to have succumbed to injuries sustained in an ambush, but it seems altogether more likely that the fatal neck and chest wounds were administered after capture. His corpse was hurriedly disposed of, however, and the Bolivians countered suspicion with a gory trophy – they cut his hands off and triumphantly identified him by his bloody fingerprints. *1967*

Man fought dog in a trial by combat near Notre Dame in Paris. The dog's master, a Monsieur Aubry de Montdidier, had been murdered and secretly buried in an unmarked grave. With admirable initiative, the faithful hound had led a human friend to the site and the body was discovered. Some time later, the normally docile animal came across the Chevalier Macaire and flew at his throat. Suspicions were aroused, and on hearing of them, the King ordered the trial. Though the man had the advantage of a cudgel, the dog won, and no doubt spurred on to righteousness by the fangs about to despatch him, the cowardly knight confessed. *1361*

The first, permanent waving machine swept into action in Karl Nessler's London Salon, replacing the dreaded Sevegas method which involved sea-water, clay and chicken bones. There were, however, a few drawbacks. Potential curlies had to pay ten guineas, wear over 20lbs of hardware and sit there for a hair-raising six or seven hours. *1906*

Today's the day...

Magistrates tried to impose a drinking ban on forty-year-old
Arthur Mason, but they couldn't – he was too drunk to understand
what they were saying. Shortly before, Arthur had been convicted for
being drunk and disorderly for the fifty-ninth time and the JPs now
wanted to make it an offence for anyone to serve him. The court was
adjourned until the next day when Arthur, who'd managed to stay
sober, was fined and the ban imposed. The day after that, publicans in
his native Basingstoke were all ready to refuse to serve him – but he
didn't turn up. When asked where he was, a neighbour said he'd gone
elsewhere – to try and get a drink!   *1978*

Charles II's long-time mistress Barbara Villiers died. She was
Duchess of Cleveland, Countess of Castlemaine and Southampton
and Baroness Nonsuch, and as well as being exceedingly beautiful, she
was said to be both vicious and foolish. For more than a decade, she
was the King's favourite and bore his children. She was not asked to be
and never was faithful, and apparently 'lavished her fondness on a
crowd of paramours from Dukes to rope-dancers'. When he finally
discarded her, Charles saw she was well cared for; she survived
numerous other lovers, and passed away aged sixty-eight, suffering
from dropsy and 'swelled to a monstrous bulk'. It's said that her ghost
still haunts the site of Walpole House where she died – looking for her
long lost beauty.   *1709*

'The Divine Sarah' had an accident. The beautiful Miss Bernhardt
was playing Floria in *Tosca* – a part which called for her to commit
suicide by jumping from the parapet of the Castel San Angelo –
which she duly did. Unfortunately, the stage hands had forgotten to
put down mattresses and she landed heavily on her right knee. The
next day she embarked for New York, and the ship's doctor's hands
were so dirty that she refused to let him treat the now hugely swollen
joint. The delay in treatment proved disastrous, and over the next eight

years the leg deteriorated until she could barely walk at all. Finally the leg threatened her life and it was removed. She was never able to walk unaided again, and when she met Harry Houdini she said to him, 'You do such wonderful things. Could you bring back my leg?'   *1905*

John Winston Lennon was born in a Liverpool Maternity Hospital in the middle of an air raid. His father, a ship's steward, had already left his mother and the boy was brought up by his Aunt Mimi and his Uncle George. As the career of the Beatles – the band he'd once said were 'bigger than Jesus' – ground to a close, he married Yoko Ono; staged their famous lie-in for peace; appeared naked with her on an album cover and for a while wouldn't go into a recording studio without consulting *I Ching* – the Chinese 'Oracle of Change'. Lennon has adopted many causes – from the anti-apartheid movement to children's charities. He had his hair cut off and sold it, auctioned the piano on which he composed 'Imagine' and paid for a full page advertisement in *The Times* arguing that marijuana should be legalised.   *1940*

Elvis and Priscilla were divorced. They ended their six-year marriage in the Santa Monica Superior Court and in exchange for his freedom, Mr Presley gave up substantial properties, shares in two music publishing companies, $750,000 and $4,000 a year for their daughter Lisa. The couple left the court arm in arm, and kissed – before they parted for good.   *1973*

A man was caught at the altar as his marriage vows were about to be pronounced in a parish church near Leeds. A woman rushed in with several children in tow and claimed the groom was her husband. The man didn't argue; he left his bride-to-be and went quietly with Wife No. 1. 'Ee lass,' he said with remarkable aplomb, 'I've 'ad no breakfast. Shall us go 'ome and get some?'   *1861*

Today's the day...

England's greatest mad scientist Henry Cavendish was born. He devoted his entire life to his studies; couldn't bear to talk to people; was terrified of women and sacked his maids if they so much as crossed his path. He ate mostly mutton; did most of his thinking up a tree and held up the advance of science for years by not publishing his very brilliant results. He was a pioneer of electricity and often shocked himself to measure the strength of currents. He was the first person to investigate thoroughly the properties of hydrogen; the first to analyse water and nitric acid; and the first to notice the existence of inert gas. Most remarkable of all, he determined 'G' – the gravitational constant – and was then able to work out that the earth weighs 6,600,000,000,000,000,000,000 tons – or thereabouts! *1731*

The fit and fecund Donald McCleod arrived in London. He was a soldier who'd served under three sovereigns and was determined to do something about it when the Chelsea authorities decided to dock his pension. In company with his eldest and youngest sons, he marched south from Inverness, settled the dispute and marched back home again. A feat that was the more amazing because McCleod was 101, his eldest son was eighty and his youngest eight years old. *1789*

The improvident Dr Thomas Sheridan died. He was the playwright Sheridan's grandfather, a brilliant scholar and churchman who always had a suitable pun or epithet for every occasion – and always put his foot in it. On George I's birthday, he preached a sermon from the text 'sufficient unto the day is the evil thereof' – and justly said of himself, 'I am famous for giving the best advice and following the worst.' On his dying day, he was sitting with friends after dinner and the conversation turned to the weather. 'Let the wind blow east, west, north or south,' the learned Doctor pronounced, 'the immortal soul will take its flight to the destined point' – and having said that, he leaned back in his chair and expired. *1738*

October 10

Buxom Dolly Parton 'busted out the front' of her dress seconds before she was named country entertainer of the year at Nashville's Grand Ole Opry. Hastily wrapped in a fur stole to hide her star attractions when accepting the award, she said afterwards, 'It was just the strain on real thin material . . . it's like my Daddy said – you shouldn't try and put 50lbs of mud in a 5lb sack!'   *1978*

Farmer and composer Giuseppe Verdi was born in the village of Le Roncole, near Parma. His first opera was performed when he was twenty-six and his first major success *Nabucco* came just three years later in 1842. After *Rigoletto* he was assured of lasting success when critics said that women couldn't watch it 'without sacrificing both taste and modesty'. Verdi wasn't cut out for stardom, however, and so hated barrel organs grinding out his most popular arias, that he bought every organ in town – all ninety-five of them – so he wouldn't have to listen. He liked best of all to spend time on his farm, where he kept seventeen cows, four oxen and a herd of sheep – and he often included animals in his operas. During a London performance of *Aida*, a horse suddenly forgot its manners; Sir Thomas Beecham, conducting, quipped: 'Disgusting spectacle – but Gad – what a critic!'   *1813*

Erik Satie's *Vexations* was given its first solo performance at the Arts Laboratory, Drury Lane. The composition consists of a short piece of music repeated very slowly with as little variation as possible 840 times. It had previously only been played by pianists in relays, but today Richard Toop decided to go it alone. The performance took over eighteen hours and Toop stayed fresh by munching black bread, cucumber sandwiches and chocolate. The following year, he did it again and made it last twenty-four hours, and the year after that an Australian tried an encore. He played for seventeen hours and peacefully slipped into a coma.   *1967*

Today's the day...

The Bohemian Hussite General John Zizka died of plague. Known as the 'Old Blind Dog', he'd lost the sight of both eyes in battle by late middle-age – but it didn't stop him fighting. On his death-bed, Zizka ordered that his corpse be flayed and his skin made into a military drum, so that he could lead his army into battle even after he was dead. Unfortunately the talisman didn't work. His forces were overthrown and the macabre instrument was used by his enemies to strike fear into his own men.   *1424*

Beans man H. J. Heinz was born of German parents in Pittsburgh, Pennsylvania. He started peddling home-grown vegetables at the age of eight, but his first grown-up business selling grated horseradish went bust after six years. Within twelve months he was back in action, and formed his famous company to manufacture 'pickles, condiments and pre-cooked food'. A crude but clever marketing man, he plagiarised the idea of many varieties from a shoe manufacturer, and though he actually made sixty at the time, he chose the number fifty-seven because the mystical last digit had 'alluring significance to people of all ages'. While the famous ketchup was one of his first products, the even more famous 'baked beans' came much later. Today 850 million cans of baked beans are produced each year.   *1844*

Famous first lady Eleanor Roosevelt was born. She grew up both 'ugly and old-fashioned' and her mother rather cruelly called her 'Grannie'. When she married her cousin Franklin Delano Roosevelt, their uncle Teddy said, 'There's nothing like keeping the name in the family.' She was probably the most influential and energetic of president's wives, though the position offended her sense of the sartorial. 'You are no longer clothing yourself,' she said, 'you are dressing a public monument.' As for her effect on government, one columnist came up with a now immortal quote 'F.D.R. is twenty per cent mush and eighty per cent Eleanor.'   *1884*

October II

The world's first adding machine that was both reliable and accurate, was patented by the ingenious American inventor Dorr Eugene Felt, of Chicago, Illinois. He had figured out the basic principle three years earlier, though his prototype machine looked more like a surrealist xylophone. He constructed the odd looking contraption with a jack knife, using an old macaroni box, staples, elastic bands and meat skewers for punch keys. He named his clever little machine the Comptometer. *1887*

The world's weirdest kidnapping occurred in Pascagoula, Mississippi, when two dock workers Charles Hickson and Calvin Parker were whisked off by a UFO. Under oath they testified that they had been taken aboard and examined by three silvery-skinned eyeless creatures that had slits for mouths and three odd appendages where a human's nose and ears would have been. They were examined for twenty minutes, photographed and returned unharmed to a local pier. The most amazing thing about their story is that despite public ridicule they maintained it – even under deep hypnosis. *1973*

Today's the day...

Christopher Columbus discovered the New World – in the nick
of time. His crew were scared they'd sail off the edge of the earth, so
he'd promised them not to go more than 700 leagues west. He'd been
showing a false log for over two months and they'd guessed the truth
and threatened to mutiny. He persuaded them to wait just two more
days, and luckily they spotted a flock of birds which showed that
landfall was near. The King and Queen of Spain had promised a
reward of 10,000 marivedos for the first man to glimpse terra-firma,
and after two false alarms it was spotted during the night by Rodrigo
de Triana. As the new day dawned, Columbus, clad in his red and
ermine cloak, landed on the beach, planted the Spanish flag and fell on
his knees in prayer – a sight which totally baffled the natives. To the
end of his days, Columbus was convinced that this island he'd named
San Salvador lay off the coast of Asia and that in fact he'd discovered
a part of Japan. Poor Rodrigo didn't get his reward incidentally –
Columbus pocketed it himself.   *1492*

King John lost his crown while touring the country looting and
pillaging. The King and his entourage were crossing a tributary of the
Wash when the mist came down, the tide came in and his baggage
waggons disappeared in the quicksand. Enraged, John marched off to
the nearest monastery and gorged himself on peaches and newly
brewed ale. He was so ill the next morning he was convinced the
monks had poisoned him but, whether they did or not, he died a
week later.   *1216*

Yorkshire's incredible animal man Jemmy Hirst was born at
Rawcliffe, Humberside. He went hunting on a bull; tried to train
piglets as gun dogs and when invited to visit George III, replied that
he was too busy teaching an otter to fish for him. Eventually he did
arrive at court – in a 9ft round lambskin hat, and a waistcoat made from
the skins of drakes' necks! The Duke of Devonshire collapsed into

paroxysms of laughter when he saw him. Jemmy stood it for a moment
then threw a glass of water in the Duke's face and pulled his nose
saying 'the poor mon was in hysterics'. Then he shook King George
firmly by the hand and declared, 'Eh, I'm glad to see thee such a plain
owd chap. If thou comes to Rawcliffe, step in and give me a visit.'
Suppressing his laughter the King politely enquired what he thought
of London to which Jemmy replied, 'I like it weel enow, but I hadn't
any idea that there were sae mony fools in it!'   *1829*

Nurse Edith Cavell was shot by a German firing squad. A vicar's
daughter from Norfolk, she chose to stay at her post as matron of a
Brussels hospital during the German occupation, despite being
offered safe conduct to Holland. Instead she helped over 200 French
and British soldiers flee the country and was finally arrested when the
Germans discovered a letter of thanks from one of the escapees. To
everyone's surprise she made a full and complete confession which
totally ruled out any possible defence at her trial. Throughout her
life Nurse Cavell always had 'a veritable horror of lying', and now her
honesty had led to her death.   *1915*

'The Beast' Aleister Crowley was born in Leamington, the son of a
prosperous brewer. Father was a member of the strict Plymouth
Brethren, but it didn't take his son long to find his own way in life.
Apart from his sex orgies, drug taking and black magic rituals, he
found time to study with the Yogis in India and the Buddhists in
Tibet; climbed 20,000ft up in the Himalayas; walked across the
Sahara and scaled Mount Popocatepetl in Mexico. He painted dwarfs
and 'freaks of all sorts' in New York, wrote over sixty 'vile books' and
sold his own 'Elixir of Life' and sex-appeal ointment. He claimed the
ointment made him irresistible to women and it certainly had some
strange effect. Both his wives went mad and five of his mistresses
committed suicide.   *1875*

Today's the day...

Stubborn Emperor Claudius was murdered a bit at a time by his
wife Agrippina. First of all she fed him a dish of poisoned mushrooms
at dinner. He collapsed but his servants just thought he was drunk
again and carted him off to his room. There Agrippina got impatient;
Claudius was still alive – so she got the physician to come and tickle
the back of his throat with a feather dipped in poison. They gave him
a poisoned enema too, but Claudius kept on breathing and in the end
they had to smother him with a cushion.

AD 54

'The Jersey Lily' Lillie Langtry was born, the daughter of the
conservative clergyman Dean le Breton. At the age of twenty-one she
met yacht owner Edward Langtry and 'to become mistress of the
yacht, I married the owner'. In London, her beauty was acclaimed;
she posed for Millais, Whistler, Burne-Jones and Rosetti, and along
with Queen Victoria and Sarah Bernhardt, she became one of Oscar
Wilde's three favourite ladies. After her famous four-year affair with
the Prince of Wales, she took to the stage and became the subject of
many a scandal. Touring America for the first time, she was found
with a man in a St Louis hotel room and when the local newspaper
urged citizens to boycott her performances, the theatre took a record

October 13

$31,000 in a fortnight. Back in Europe, she had trouble with George Baird, Baron Auchmeddon – one of the richest men in England. Jealous of her chatting to Robert Peel in Paris, he went berserk; smashed up the furniture, beat Lillie about the face and almost choked her to death. He tried to apologise by giving her gowns, jewels, racehorses, a cheque for £50,000 and a magnificent 220ft yacht. It was called *The White Lady* – but the press promptly dubbed it *The Black Eye*.   *1853*

Intrepid Victorian explorer Mary Kingsley was born. Both her parents died within weeks of each other when she was thirty, so she took herself off to 'skylark and enjoy myself in Africa'. An agnostic, she travelled as a trader carrying mainly cloth and tobacco, and once saved her life by bribing a ferocious native with a dozen ladies' blouses – noting with interest that he wore them 'with nothing else but red paint and a bunch of leopard tails!' She awoke one night to a strange smell in her tent and found a shrivelled hand, toes, eyes and ears hanging in a bag above her bed. Unperturbed, she carefully placed them into her pillbox hat – 'for fear of losing anything of value'. Back in London she lectured to the School of Medicine for Women on a subject that the ladies no doubt found fascinating – 'African Therapeutics from a Witch Doctor's Point of View'.   *1862*

The Devil of Woodstock first appeared when Cromwell's Parliamentary Commissioners moved into Woodstock Manor. Strange noises were heard, bedclothes whisked off, candles blew out and buckets of water came down the chimney. The Roundheads stood it for nearly three weeks, but one evening it was so bad they spent the entire night together in prayer and left at first light next morning. Twelve years later the mystery was solved. A faithful Royalist servant confessed that there weren't any spooks – he'd been the 'ghost' all the time.   *1649*

Today's the day...

Man broke the sound barrier 42,000ft above the Edwards air-base in Muroc, California. The supersonic craft, a Bell XS-1 experimental rocket plane, had been carried aloft under the belly of a Boeing B-29 Superfortress. At 5,000ft its pilot, wartime air-ace Chuck Yeager, had climbed through the bomb doors and into the little plane – called *Glamorous Glennis* after his wife. The order was given to 'drop'; the rockets fired and he accelerated to a stunning speed of 670 mph – Mach 1.015. He hadn't actually told the real Glennis what he was going to do that day, and it was only when it was all over that another officer told her – she was married to the first supersonic man.   *1947*

America's hero president Dwight D. Eisenhower was born in Denison, Texas. His rise was astonishing. In 1940 he was just a lieutenant-colonel and by 1943 he was Supreme Allied Commander in Europe. He claimed he'd refuse a presidential nomination if he was offered one – and in 1952 he was duly elected. He described himself as 'a dynamic conservative'; was the only US President to have held a British knighthood; had numerous heart attacks and played golf. But despite the 'I like Ike' slogans, he was not without his critics and for one, the most powerful man in the world was just 'a cardiac case whose chief interest is getting away from his job as often as possible'.   *1890*

'The Legless Acrobat' Eli Bowen was born in Ohio, one of ten children – the rest of whom were perfectly normal. Eli, though strong, well-built and handsome, had his feet joined straight onto his hips. Inevitably, he graduated to the freak show and the circus, and visited England with the 'Greatest Show on Earth'. Not only was he able to get about quite happily, but he also did tumbling tricks and performed feats of amazing agility on a pole. But quite his most popular turn was when he helped a friend ride a tandem. The friend concerned was Charlie Tripp – the amazing 'Armless Wonder'.   *1844*

The Battle of Hastings was fought not at Hastings but seven miles away on Senlac Hill, near Pevensey. King Harold's Saxons were depleted and exhausted by the long march south after their victory over Hardrada at Stamford Bridge. They were said to have celebrated their arrival the night before and gone into battle hungover. William had two horses killed under him, and it was a close-run thing until Harold and most of his house-earls were slain. As well as the arrow-in-the-eye, it's likely that Harold's body was hacked to pieces. Before the fight, the Conqueror had put his coat-of-mail on inside out. He claimed it was a good omen, since he was about to turn his dukedom into a kingdom – and of course, that's exactly what he did.

1066

The Star of the Silents Lillian Gish was born in Springfield, Ohio. She made her stage *début* at the age of five and worked alongside the infant Mary Pickford who later introduced her to the movies. In 1978 she appeared in her first movie for ten years – Robert Altman's *A Wedding*. When asked why she did it, she said Altman had told her she'd die in it and it would be amusing. 'Now I've died lots of times in movies . . . but never has it been amusing – so I signed.'

1896

Today's the day...

Victoria proposed to Albert when the two royal twenty-year-olds were sitting in her chambers. He'd arrived a few days earlier, having lost his luggage and turned up for the evening's entertainment in a morning suit. Victoria, who'd not been too keen at first, soon thought him 'beautiful'. She loved his 'delicate moustachios', 'slight whiskers', 'broad shoulders' and 'exquisite nose', and had summoned him for the express purpose of popping the question. 'It was a nervous thing to do,' she wrote, 'but Albert could not propose to the Queen of England. He would never have presumed to take such a liberty!' *1839*

The clumsiest US President married a Bloomer – Betty Bloomer, a fashion buyer, ex-model and dancer, who'd just divorced her first husband. Gerry Ford had been dating her for a year; he'd proposed seven or eight months earlier, but put off the wedding till now in case her past jeopardised his chances in the primaries of his first Congressional elections. At the wedding, Ford wore one brown shoe and one black shoe. Afterwards, he took his bride to a football game, before a one-night honeymoon in a Detroit hotel. *1948*

The crazy Roman poet Virgil was born during an earthquake in Cisalpine Gaul. He studied medicine and astronomy, became a wealthy courtier and among other things wrote the *Aeneid*. He was something of a lecher and once tried to seduce the daughter of a local senator by getting her and her servants to hoist him up to her room in a basket. Halfway up, she had second thoughts, fastened the rope and left him hanging there all night. Virgil was certainly odd and many strange stories grew up about him. He was supposed to have founded Naples on a pile of eggs, which shook and caused tremors. He was said to own a brass bridge that would take him anywhere, and a bath that could cure anything. Perhaps the strangest story about him, however, is true. The triumvirate that ruled Rome were confiscating the property of the rich. One exception was made for burial plots. So Virgil built a great

October 15

mausoleum on his land for 800,000 Sesterces – about £50,000 – and gave what he claimed was a favourite family pet, the most lavish animal-funeral in history. The pet was a fly. *70 BC*

Hitler's favourite philosopher Friedrich Nietzsche was born. He was the son of a Lutheran pastor and became an aggressive atheist. He thought that women were 'ruled by the womb', only became scholars if there was 'something wrong with their sexual organs', and ought to be dominated, preferably with a whip. It was this weak and sickly academic who created the word 'superman' and helped give the Nazis the philosophical base for their Aryan ideal of the 'Master-race'. 'I am not a man,' he said, 'I am dynamite . . . There will be associated with my name, the recollection of something terrifying.' *1844*

A UFO appeared in the West End of London. Cars smashed into each other, a motor-cycle hit a taxi and a cyclist collided with some railings. Doughty policemen hurtled down Park Lane to apprehend the aliens and when they got to the Marble Arch end, they found a tin foil kite equipped with a red light stuck in a tree. A shame-faced American inventor named Sam Da Vinci claimed the contraption and said, 'I just went to the bathroom for a few minutes and when I came back it was gone!' *1978*

The first manned ascent in a balloon took place when Pilatre de Rozier and his unwieldy Montgolfier hot-air craft rose 84ft before being restrained by a tether. Spurred on by his success, he convinced the Marquis d'Arlandres to join him a little over a month later for the first unfettered five-mile voyage over Paris. They travelled at an average of 12mph which must have worried Louis XVI who'd originally banned the attempt because it was too dangerous. He'd suggested that instead of the two aristocrats, they should send some criminals aloft. *1783*

Today's the day...

The Houses of Parliament burnt down as Turner made water colour sketches of the blaze. The 500-year-old buildings burned for days and the destruction was enormous. In the previous session an MP named Hume had vainly proposed that a larger and more prestigious House of Commons be built. As the fire tore through the fabric, a wit in the crowd remarked, 'There goes Hume's motion – being carried without a division.'   *1834*

Oscar Fingal O'Flahertie Wills Wilde was born in Dublin. He was a brilliant scholar and took a first at Oxford along with a bout of syphilis that ruined his teeth and was never properly cured. Though he claimed that 'in love one always begins by deceiving one's self and ends by deceiving others', he nevertheless married Constance Lloyd and fathered two children. After the huge success of his plays came the fall from grace, the scandal of his 'indiscreet homosexuality', his persecution by the maniacal Marquess of Queensberry and two years' hard labour. Even that didn't dull his wit, however, and once when standing on a railway station with some other convicts in the pouring rain, he quipped, 'If this is the way Queen Victoria treats her convicts, she doesn't deserve to have any.'   *1854*

The mystery of 'the Captain of Kopenick' began when an unknown officer ordered a detachment of guards to arrest the Burgomaster and Treasurer of this little town near Berlin. The captain enlisted the help of the local police, lined the residents up in the square and explained that irregularities had been found in the town's financial affairs. It was his duty he said to take both the culprits and the missing money back to headquarters. After some argument 4,000 marks were produced, the captain gave a receipt, sent his men off to Berlin with the captives and then disappeared with the money. It was over a week before the mystery was solved, when it was discovered it was all a hoax. The captain was in fact, an aged cobbler called Wilhelm Voigt, who was captured and sentenced to four years' hard labour. The Kaiser was so amused by his audacity, however, that he pardoned him after twenty months, and Voigt was able to retire with a pension. *1906*

The Cardiff Giant was discovered by two well-diggers on William Newell's farm in New York State. It was the perfectly fossilised remains of a man 10ft 4½in tall and weighing nearly 3,000lbs. Scientists and churchmen inspected the fossil and pronounced it to be genuine, but Dr Andrew White, President of Cornell University, did the sensible thing and had a piece of the fossil analysed. It turned out to be plain old gypsum and Newell's cousin George Hull finally admitted it was a fake. Unabashed, he and Newell turned the giant into a tourist attraction, at fifty cents a look. Showman P. T. Barnum tried to buy it from them and when they wouldn't sell, he put a 'Cardiff Giant' of his own on display. They asked for an injunction against him, but the judge refused. He couldn't see what was wrong in exhibiting a fake of a fake. *1869*

'The Michigan Assassin', heavyweight bruiser Stanley Ketchell fought big Jack Johnson for his world title. In the twelfth round, Ketchell surprised the Champ and put him on his back, but the giant black man recovered quickly and with the very next punch he knocked Ketchell out cold. The punch was so hard that Jack later found the challenger's two front teeth – they were embedded in his glove. *1909*

The Ripper sent a parcel to Mr George Lusk, Chairman of the Whitechapel Vigilance Committee. Inside there was a piece of murdered Kate Eddowe's kidney and a note. It read: 'From Hell, Mr Lusk Sir, I send you half the kidney I took from one woman – prasarved it for you. T'other piece I fried and ate; twas very nice. I may send you the bloody knife that took it out if only you wait a bit longer. Catch me when you can, Mr Lusk.' *1888*

Today's the day...

Libertine and hell-raiser John Wilkes was born. He lived a life 'strained with every vice' and was a member of the notorious Hellfire Club which indulged in orgies and fake black magic. An 'incomparable comedian', he once nearly frightened his fellow members to death when he took along a black baboon in a chest and released it just as they were calling up the devil! With hardly any teeth, 'his eyes sunken and horribly squinting', he was nearly as ugly as his enemy Hogarth painted him. Nevertheless, 'private society' found him 'pre-eminently agreeable', and his looks never caused him any problems with the ladies, either. When he was Lord Mayor of London, his mistress was a lady who'd once given Casanova the brush-off! *1727*

'The Love Goddess of the forties' Rita Hayworth was born in New York. Originally called Margarita Cansino, she was the daughter of a Latin-American dancer and was spotted performing at the Agua Caliente Club in Los Angeles. After two years of electrolysis they got rid of her low hairline and she was ready to go. Unfortunately, although she was a talented dancer, she couldn't sing – so the famous musicals with Kelly and Astaire were each and every one of them dubbed. *1918*

The Princess Etheldreda died and was canonised St Audrey. She was the daughter of an Anglian King, married twice, but remained a virgin and founded the monastery of Ely. Her death was caused by a throat tumour, which she saw as a punishment for her childhood love of necklaces. *Feast Day*

The wolf-children of Midnapore were dug out of a termite mound by the Reverend Joseph Singh. Their 'wolf-mother' was killed and the 'two little ghosts' were found curled up with two cubs. Covered in mud, with long matted hair and calluses on their elbows and knees, the children – both girls – were otherwise quite fit and appeared to be about three and five years old. Singh bundled them into bamboo cages and took them back to his orphanage where he bathed them, shaved their heads and named them Amala and Kamala. They prowled around on all fours, curled back their lips and growled, slept little, and when they did, lay on top of one another like puppies, grunting and grinding their teeth. Within a year Amala was dead, and while Kamala was trained to stand upright and speak a few words, four years later she died too. Faced with the spectre of the wolf-children morosely crouched on their haunches, the Reverend Singh often wondered if it would have been better had he never found them. *1920*

Bionic stuntman Evel Knievel was born in Butte, Montana. He was christened Robert, became a safe-cracker and changed his name when he shared a cell with Awful Knaufle. He's broken 100 bones in his numerous crashes but his most spectacular disaster to date was in Las Vegas, when he tried to leap 150ft over a fountain, broke his pelvis and had to be pinned back together again. He's so used to operations, however, that he now doesn't bother with anaesthetic. 'We just split a bottle of Wild Turkey and I get a spinal – that way I get to watch.' *1939*

Today's the day...

Wordy English novelist and poet Thomas Peacock was born. He coined the expression, 'If "ifs" and "ands" were pots and pans, there'd be no work for tinkers' – and he also invented one of the most improbable words in the English language. It's used to describe the human physique and it's fifty-one letters long: osseocarnisanguineoviscericartilagininervomedullary.   *1785*

The great gunboat diplomatist Viscount Palmerston died and proved himself right. Shortly before, he'd been discussing his mortality with his physician. 'Die my dear doctor,' he said. 'Why that's the last thing I'll do.'   *1865*

Russia published her first Top Ten with Abba's disc 'Money' at No. 1 and an Elton John track at No. 6. Whether due to censorship or some inscrutable point of party philosophy, this premier Top Ten had only seven entries.   *1977*

A dog's lonely vigil came to an end when his body was found at his home – a patch of grass on the roadside near Bradford-on-Avon, Wiltshire. For seven years, Winston, the golden labrador, had steadfastly stayed there waiting for his master. He was fed, kennelled and cared for by the staff of a local hospital, who believe his vigil started after he'd escaped from a car crash in which his owner was killed.   *1978*

The missing balloonist Solomon Andrée was born in Gressna in Sweden. He became interested in balloons in his early twenties and when years later he became a professor of science, he dreamed of sailing one to the North Pole. He managed to get the backing of Alfred Nobel and the King of Sweden and after a false start, he, along with an engineer called Fraenkel and a physicist named Strindberg, sailed off for the north in the balloon *Eagle* in 1897. They released a homing pigeon shortly after take-off and were never heard of again. The mystery looked like it would never be solved until incredibly, thirty-three years later, Norwegian sealers found the remains of the men and Andrée's diary. It told how the ice had brought the *Eagle* down 500 miles from the Pole; how they'd trekked south for two months and lived off polar bear meat. What it didn't explain is how they died. They were well-clothed and far from starving, but the last entry in the diary was incomprehensible.

1854

'The Beau of Bath' Richard Nash was born. In the early 1700s when the spa town of Bath was made a fashionable resort, 'Beau', as he was then known, had the good luck to be appointed Master of Ceremonies. He became virtual dictator of the town, set up the Assembly Rooms, laid down codes of conduct, travelled about on a post-chariot drawn by six greys and pursued countless affairs. 'Women are as plentiful as mushrooms,' the modest Mr Nash once said, 'they're always to be had for the asking.'

1674

Habitual portrait painter Sir Joshua Reynolds began his career when he started an apprenticeship with Thomas Hudson 'a man of little skill and less talent'. The 'boss' was a man who liked to pose his sitters in the same position over and over again, and something of that rubbed off on Reynolds. He usually painted men with their hats under their arms, but one man insisted he wanted to wear his. Old habits die hard and when the picture was delivered the man had one hat on his head – and another under his arm.

1741

A topsy-turvy picture went on show in the Museum of Modern Art in New York. It was the French painter Henri Matisse's brilliant '*Le Bateau*' and it attracted big crowds. But it wasn't until 116,000 people had seen it, forty-six days later, that anyone noticed – it was hanging upside down!

1961

Today's the day...

America won her independence when Lord Cornwallis surrendered at Yorktown. He'd held out there for over three weeks waiting for the navy to arrive but finally his ammunition ran out and he'd had to give in. He sent his second-in-command, General O'Hara, to hand over his sword to George Washington, and as the soldiers marched towards surrender they played 'The World Turned Upside Down'. The news of the great American victory was quickly relayed to Washington DC and the first person to inform the public there was a German nightwatchman. He marched the streets shouting 'Cornvallis isht taken!' *1781*

Australia's national poet Adam Lindsay Gordon was born in the Azores. Expelled from Cheltenham and the Royal Military Academy, he earned a living boxing at country fairs, won his first steeplechase when he was nineteen and was mysteriously bundled off to the Antipodes a year later. He became an Australian Mountie, scribbled his poems sitting on horseback and bluntly proposed to his wife when she nursed him after a bad fall. 'I like your ways. If you like we shall get married next week.' He lost all his money, couldn't sell his poems and finally committed suicide at the age of thirty-seven. With poems such as 'The Sick Stock-Rider' he was hailed as 'most Australian' -- in fact he only lived there for seventeen years and often talked of returning 'home' to England. *1833*

Self-imposed castaway Alain Bombard set off across the Atlantic in a rubber dinghy. A French doctor, he was determined to prove that it was possible to survive at sea by eating fish and plankton and drinking limited amounts of seawater. It wasn't a very good start: he didn't catch any fish for five days; a giant wave covered the dinghy and encrusted everything with salt; his mainsail tore and his spare one blew away. He lost track of time, watched in horror as a swordfish attacked his vulnerable boat and nearly lost it completely when he dived overboard to save a cushion. He cheered up when he saw pieces of driftwood, a butterfly and a fly, since he'd read in a handbook they were signs of approaching land. When it didn't appear he was so depressed that he wrote his will and in it urged his wife to take legal action against people who give false information in handbooks. He finally landed at Barbados on Christmas Eve in a terrible state – he was seriously anaemic, 56lbs underweight and had developed vision defects – but the point was he was alive, so his painful experiment had been a great success. *1953*

Notoriously brutal judge Sir Francis Page died aged eighty. A practising judge until his death, he tottered out of court one day and was stopped by a friend who asked how he was. With unintentional humour the judge replied, 'My dear sir, you see I keep hanging on, hanging on!' *1741*

An unfortunate pallbearer met his end at a funeral at Kensal Green cemetery. The day was damp, the grass was slippery and as they turned towards the grave he slipped, and the heavy lead coffin fell on top of him and crushed him to death. *1872*

Today's the day...

The tiny architectural giant Sir Christopher Wren was born. He came to fame as Surveyor General to Charles II and, odd as it may seem, his renown as the creator of St Paul's has overshadowed the great depth of his genius. After the Great Fire, he not only designed the great cathedral and sixty other London buildings, but planned a whole new London – funds for which were not forthcoming. He was an Oxford professor, mathematician, astronomer, geographer and anatomist, contributing much to medical knowledge and inventing a deaf and dumb language that he claimed could be learned in half an hour. His diminutive stature, however, was the cause of much amusement. When the King came to see his new Wren-built hunting lodge at Newmarket, he complained the ceilings were too low. Wren insisted they weren't. So Charles, a small man himself, crouched down to Wren's height and minced around the room saying, 'Aye Sir Christopher, I think they're high enough.' *1632*

A cobra bit a keeper at London Zoo and the man – one Edward Horatio Girling – swiftly died. It seems harsh to blame the snake, however, for although it was well before lunch, Girling was drunk and had been 'wilfully and rashly' manhandling the beast. The Secretary of the Zoological Society 'ascertained that the deceased had obtained his last supply of gin at the Albert Public House' – at eight o'clock in the morning. *1852*

The famous film of the Bigfoot was shot by Roger Patterson and Bob Gimlin in the wilderness of northern California. They'd been riding along the banks of a creek when their horses reared and threw them and they got their first glimpse of the American Yeti. Halfway between an ape and a human, it stood 7ft tall, weighed an estimated 350lbs and was covered in shiny black hair. With surprising presence of mind, the fallen Patterson grabbed his camera and ran after the creature, filming it as it made off into the dense undergrowth. Not surprisingly, his film caused a storm of controversy. The consensus of expert opinion seems to be that though the beast looked convincing, its gait was suspect; it had large breasts, but otherwise appeared to be male. All agree that if the film was a fake it was an incredibly good one. If it really was the Bigfoot, however, it was discovered in a very apt site. The creek was just north-east of a place called Eureka!   *1967*

The First Lady married the Pirate. Jacqueline Kennedy had met Aristotle Onassis five years before and their romance had blossomed despite much opposition from both families. Daughter Christina Onassis referred to her new stepmother as 'my father's unfortunate compulsion', while Ari's jilted lover Maria Callas bitched, 'Jackie was smart enough to give a grandfather to her children.' According to an ex-Onassis aide, a 173-clause marriage agreement was drawn up. It provided for separate bedrooms, no children and the couple only had to spend Catholic and summer holidays together. Jackie was guaranteed £21,000 a month – £6,000 of it for clothes. If she left him in the first five years, she'd get twelve million pounds, while if he left her he'd pay six million pounds for each year the marriage survived. When Ari came to sign it, Teddy quipped, 'Now remember – no invisible ink.'   *1968*

Numerical religious nutcase Thomas Horne was born. He spent seventeen years of his life counting every word and letter in the Bible. He concluded that there were 773,693 words and 3,566,480 letters – and if you don't believe him, count them yourself!   *1780*

The *Sunday Times* was first published. Its principal object was 'to instil an invigorating spirit suitable to the character and exigencies of the time'. True to this formula, it warned of an international conspiracy to promote the tyranny of kings and emperors, and several issues later proclaimed that George IV was mad.   *1822*

Today's the day...

The first effective electric light bulb worked for 14hrs 30mins, before it 'busted'. Invented by Thomas Alva Edison of New Jersey, it came after a series of experiments designed to perfect the glass bulb and find a suitable material for the filament. In the end, he used carbonised sewing thread, but had previously tried a fine red hair which he plucked from the beard of a friend. *1879*

Britain's most talkative poet Samuel Taylor Coleridge was born in Devon. Crossed in love at Cambridge, he joined the Dragoons and soon established himself as the regimental buffoon by constantly falling off his horse. He once caught Charles Lamb in conversation by grabbing hold of a button on his coat. Lamb sliced the button off with a knife and escaped. When he returned five hours later, Coleridge was still rooted to the spot, talking to the button. Only his addiction to opium seemed to calm him down, and it was when he was under the influence that he composed 'Kubla Khan'. He awoke and started transcribing it, but was interrupted by a visitor to whom he talked so long and hard that the dream faded and the poem was never finished. *1772*

October 21

'England expects that every man will do his duty' was signalled
to 'amuse' the fleet by Lord Nelson and at 11.30am the Battle of
Trafalgar started. The combined French and Spanish line was cut to
pieces but at the height of the battle, a sniper's musket-ball took
Nelson in the shoulder. He died at 4.30pm, the precise moment of the
enemy surrender. He'd asked Hardy not to throw his body overboard,
and so it was preserved in a cask of brandy – thought to be a better
preservative than rum. The spirit was drawn off and refreshed several
times, which led to the apocryphal belief that the sailors were drinking
it. Ever since, splicing the main brace has also been referred to as
'tapping the Admiral'.   *1805*

The worst tornado in British history killed four and injured
fifty-six in the town of Widecombe, Devon. Unlike the human
inhabitants, the local cattle seemed to know what to expect. They all
ran away – and were saved.   *1638*

The embalmed wife of Martin Van Butchell appeared in an
advertisement in the *St James's Chronicle*, which pointed out that only
those introduced by friends could visit the corpse ensconced in his
living room. Van Butchell charged admission and had kept his wife
unburied, since he was only entitled to her property 'so long as she
remained above ground'. The mummy was far from being his only
eccentricity however. He earned his living as a false-teeth and truss
maker and seller of quack remedies. Inveterately publicity seeking, he
would paint his white pony with black and purple spots and ride around
London carrying the jawbone of an ass for protection.   *1775*

The Can-Can was first performed in Offenbach's *Orpheus in the
Underworld* in Paris. 'The idea,' wrote Mark Twain, '. . . is to expose
yourself as much as possible!'   *1858*

Today's the day...

'Pretty Boy' Floyd was gunned down by the FBI in a field in Ohio. He was a big, strong farm boy from Oklahoma who'd been driven to crime during the terrible rural poverty of the twenties. Christened Charles Arthur, he'd been dubbed 'Pretty Boy' by the madam of a Kansas City whorehouse and the name stuck throughout his short career as a professional machine-gunner and bank robber. After a brief partnership with Killer Miller, which ended in a gun battle with police in Bowling Green, he took to the hills where, protected by his friends and kinfolk, he lived a life of strangely casual criminality. On one occasion, he was wandering down the street with his machine gun under his arm when he met someone he knew. The man asked how he was and what he was doing in town. Pretty Boy said he was fine and was going to rob the bank. Another man overheard, but instead of trying to tell the police, he just smiled at Floyd and said, 'You give 'em hell!' *1934*

Admiral Shovel made his biggest mistake when he was commanding HMS *Association* just off the Scilly Isles. A common sailor dared to remind him that there were dangerous rocks nearby and Shovel ordered him hanged for his impudence. As they roped him up, the man cursed the Admiral with some well-chosen words from Psalm 109. Minutes later the ship was wrecked on the rocks; the dazed Shovel was murdered by an old woman for his ring, and ever since it's been thought unlucky to quote the Bible on ships at funerals. *1707*

The histrionic Hungarian composer Franz Liszt was born in the village of Raiding, which is now part of Austria. He was a child prodigy and before he was out of his teens, had given piano recitals in every European country except Norway and Sweden. He was exceptionally tall, extremely good looking, an extravagant dresser, long-haired and immensely vain. 'Lisztomania' was actually a contemporary expression, used to describe the adoration he was accorded and the mad fashions he inspired. Liszt was a staggering snob and of all his many love affairs, the two greatest were with a countess who bore him three children, and a princess – the cigar-smoking Carolyne Von Sayn Wittgenstein – who after fifteen years' cohabitation wanted to marry him. He took holy orders instead, but was neither notably pious nor even polite. When the Tsar dared to talk during one of his concerts, Liszt was infuriated and stopped playing with a flourish. When asked what was wrong, he replied with ostentatious humility, 'When the Emperor speaks, all should be silent.'

1811

A giant tortoise was given to Captain James Cook by the King of Tonga. The beast was called Tu'malilia and it's believed that it was the very same animal that passed away peacefully in 1966 – 193 years later.

1773

'The eighth wonder of the world', the 'divine' actress Sarah Bernhardt was born in Paris, the illegitimate daughter of a successful Dutch Jewish prostitute. Educated in a Catholic convent and at the Conservatoire, legend has it that she was expelled three times – once for imitating a bishop, once for throwing stones at soldiers, and finally for sleeping with one! From her early twenties onwards, she became more famous than any other actress before or since, but she was also an accomplished sculptor, painter and writer. She was loved by the Princes Napoleon and de Ligne, adored by the Prince of Wales, and went hunting with the Tsar. In all, it's been estimated she had more than 1,000 lovers, and kept a menagerie that included not only cats and dogs, but monkeys, pumas and a lion. Though she lived to be nearly seventy-eight, she had the romantic premonition that she would die young, so she got into the habit of travelling with her own coffin, which was a gift from her mother. She's said to have slept in it, made love in it and used it as a table to serve tea to critics.

1844

Today's the day...

God created the world, according to a seventeenth-century Vice-Chancellor of the University of Cambridge, Archbishop James Ussher. The good Lord apparently did it at 9am on a Sunday, and though there are over 140 different versions of the date of creation, Ussher has God on his side – today's date is the only one that tallies with the chronology of the Authorised Version of the Bible. *4004 BC*

The Royalists beat the Roundheads – but only just – in the first major battle of the Civil War at Edgehill in the Cotswolds. Both armies were badly organised and both commanders – King Charles I and the Earl of Essex – were hugely inexperienced. Prince Rupert's cavalry practically won the battle for Charles with a dashing charge – but they nearly lost it again by failing to re-group and thundering off into the distance. They returned just in time to save the day, only to see the King throw away their hard-won advantage by falling back to Oxford instead of marching on London. Before the battle, Sir Jacob Astley royalist infantry commander, had prayed: 'O Lord, thou knowest how busy I must be this day: if I forget thee, do not thou forget me.' *1642*

The Battle of El Alamein began with a barrage of 1,000 guns that rained fire and destruction on nearly 100,000 Italian and German troops. Montgomery's forces outnumbered them nearly 2 – 1 in both men and tanks, and had gained control of the air. The battle, vitally important to both sides, turned into a hard-fought slogging match that lasted almost a fortnight. At last, Rommel was forced to allow his commanders to ignore Hitler's 'victory or death' command, and the seemingly invincible Afrika Korps was all but routed. They left behind 20,000 prisoners; Allied losses amounted to 13,500 killed or injured. 'It may almost be said,' said Churchill, 'that before Alamein we never had a victory. After Alamein we never had a defeat.' *1942*

October 23

Dillinger scooped his biggest haul from the Central National Bank in Greencastle, Indiana. While a driver waited outside in a hot Studebaker tourer, the outlaw and three accomplices crammed a sack with $75,346 in the five minutes they'd allotted themselves. As they were about to make off, Dillinger spotted a customer standing at the counter with a stack of dollar bills. 'Is that your money or the bank's?' he asked. 'Mine,' the man replied. 'Then keep it,' said the self-styled Robin Hood, 'we only want the bank's.'

1933

Murdering Winnie, twenty-three-year-old doctor's wife Winnie Ruth Judd, was arrested in Los Angeles after a railroad attendant had found the axed-up pieces of her two friends Agnes Le Roi and Helwig Samuelson in a bloody trunk. After a convincing courtroom performance in which she tried to tear her clothes off and asked permission to jump out of the window, she was declared insane. During the next thirty-seven years, she made seven successful escapes from her Arizona asylum, was then found to be sane, sent to prison and finally paroled in 1971. She said to the parole board, 'I'm terribly sorry.'

1932

Today's the day...

The Queen of the Gipsies Margaret Finch was buried at Beckenham, Kent at the advanced age of 109 years. A famous travelling lady, she eventually settled in Norwood, where she constantly sat on the ground with her chin resting on her knees and her pipe in her mouth. This 'so contracted' her sinews that in the end she couldn't get up and had to be buried in 'a deep square box'. *1740*

The fun-loving ghoul Emperor Domitian was born. He loved to murder people and delighted in lulling them into a false sense of security before sentencing them – so if he started with 'a preamble full of clemency' it was a sure sign of a fatal ending. He liked to see his victims squirm and changed his mind occasionally just to keep them on their toes. At one particular banquet he sat his chief senators down to dinner in an entirely black room, on black couches, with a little monogrammed tombstone in front of them. The meal was served by naked black-painted slaves 'as terrible to behold as ghosts', while Domitian made polite conversation about murder and massacres. Then just when their fear and indigestion had convinced them they were not long for this world, he sent them home and showered them with gifts. It will come as no surprise to discover that Domitian's favourite hobby was sticking pins into flies. *AD 51*

'A street-brawl' championship fight gave the heavyweight crown of Britain and the Commonwealth to John L. Gardner when beaten Billy Aird threw in the towel after five action-packed rounds. Afterwards, the new champ complained that Aird had bitten him, just before the final bell. 'I didn't bite him,' said the affronted loser, 'I kissed him.' *1978*

The daredevil widow Annie Taylor rode over Niagara in a barrel. A forty-three-year-old schoolteacher from Michigan, she made her claim to fame strapped in a stout, $4\frac{1}{2}$ft high wooden barrel, bound with seven hoops of iron and padded inside for protection. Resplendent in a long black dress and broad-brimmed hat, she coyly changed into a short skirt before easing her ample form into the barrel. She yelled '*Au revoir*' to the cheering crowds, was set loose and bobbed off towards the 160ft drop over the Horseshoe Falls. At the bottom, the barrel bounced miraculously clear of the rocks and she was promptly fished out by her aides. It was lucky they were there on cue – because as they found out later, the intrepid Annie couldn't swim.   *1901*

Al Capone's career ended when he was sentenced to eleven years for tax evasion and was carted off to the cage wearing a heather-coloured suit. For a while at least, he was able to continue running his 'organisation' from jail. He was put in a one-man cell with a private shower, allowed to make phone calls and was visited by his 'associates'. Two of his most important guests were the warring New York gangsters Lucky Luciano and Dutch Schulz. Capone had summoned them for a peace conference and it was held in the death chamber with Al presiding in the electric chair.   *1931*

Today's the day...

The unbelievable Battle of Balaclava took place and the Light
Brigade spent most of the morning watching the Heavy Brigade and
others doing the fighting. Their turn came at 11am when an order
that got confused somewhere between the Commander in Chief Lord
Raglan and the brigade commander Lord Cardigan, sent all 675 men
hurtling towards the wrong set of guns with heavy artillery and rifle
fire on both flanks. They were faced not only with dozens of blazing
cannons pointing their way, but upwards of 20,000 Russians who
could hardly believe their eyes. In all 475 horses died and 247 men
were killed and injured. The battle itself was an English victory
which is quite remarkable really, since Cardigan was more
interested in his yacht and Raglan, who'd lost an arm at Waterloo,
sometimes thought he was still fighting the French.   *1854*

The Battle of Agincourt was fought by around 5,000 Englishmen
and well in excess of 20,000 Frenchmen. Henry V set up his tiny
dysentery-stricken army in a narrow neck of land with its flanks
protected by woods – and at dawn it started. While between 100 and
400 Englishmen were lost, French fatalities amounted to between
7,000 and 8,000, and their bodies blocked the battlefield in piles, head
high. For luck, Henry had worn the famous 'Bastille Ruby', which now
rests in the Imperial British Crown. Only recently it was discovered
that the lucky 'ruby' is in fact a fake.   *1415*

The artist with the longest name Pablo Diego José Francisco de
Paulo Juan Nepomuceno Crispin Crispiano de la Santisima Trinidad
Ruiz was born. He's better known as Picasso – his mother's maiden
name which he chose to use, not only because it's shorter, but because
it's 'more musical'. In his long life he had two wives, five significant
mistresses, three daughters and two sons. He produced over 20,000
works in total and twenty-three major oils in one month during 1936.
In 1966 an exhibition of his pictures was insured for twenty-one

October 25

million pounds – more paintings by Picasso have been stolen than those of any other major artist – and on one canvas he pre-empted Muhammad Ali by writing 'I am the King.'   *1881*

The last British King to lead his troops in battle, George II, died at 7.15am. He was also the last King of England to be buried in Westminster Abbey and his coffin was placed alongside his wife's with the sides removed, so their remains could be together eternally. Unfortunately the late Queen Caroline was a terrible nagger and certainly wouldn't have approved of the way George died. The poor old Hanoverian had a stroke while sitting on the toilet!   *1760*

The biggest bowl of punch in the world was brewed up on the orders of Sir Edward Kennel for the English Navy. It was made in a huge marble dish and used eighty casks of brandy, one of Malaga and nine of water, 25,000 limes, 1,300lb of sugar, 80 pints of lemon juice and 5lb of nutmeg. This was enough for 6,000 officers and crewmen, but the aroma was so strong that the serving boys were soon overcome and had to be replaced once every fifteen minutes.   *1599*

Today's the day...

The exiled Emperor His Imperial Highness Muhammed Riza Shah Pahlavi, King of Kings and Sun of the Aryans was born. The child of a donkey driver, he became the Shah of Persia, by taking over the throne in 1941, when Britain and Russia forced his father to abdicate. For the next thirty-seven years he ruled the ancient kingdom with a mixture of quasi-mystical divine right, US aid, oil revenue, western arms and a secret police force. He's been married three times, once lost nearly three-quarters of a million pounds in one game of poker, and before leaving his riot-torn capital managed to get out enough money to make him one of the richest men in the world. 'Since my childhood,' he once told a journalist, 'nay since my birth, I have been living under the protective wing of Almighty God!'   *1919*

History's most horrifying sadist was 'mercifully' strangled before he was burned. He was the forty-four year old Gilles de Rais, sometime lieutenant of Joan of Arc and a Marshal of France. If the evidence extracted from his 'associates' under torture is to be believed, this once brave and pious knight had retired to his estates and turned into a monster. He'd become an alchemist and black magician; committed bestial sexual assaults on children and often worked up his passion by torturing or decapitating them first. He was said to have kidnapped and killed more than 120 boys and girls, and after each revolting spectacle, he'd plunge into a coma. The question is, was the evidence true – or was it merely an elaborate plot hatched between the Church and the local duke to rob a very rich man of his lands?   *1440*

The spy they wouldn't believe Elyesa Bazna turned up at the residence of the German First Secretary in Ankara and offered his services. He was the valet of the British Ambassador Sir Hughe Knatchbull-Hugesson, and working under his code name 'Cicero', he supplied his Nazi masters with a stunning amount of spectacularly top-secret information for more than six months. He gave detailed

October 26

information about bombing raids; the conferences of allied heads of
state; the key to the major British cipher and incredibly the plans for
'Operation Overlord' – the D-Day invasion of Europe. The Germans
were staggered and fortunately they convinced themselves the
information must be false – it was simply too good to be true. In the
end, they got very little out of it, and 'Cicero' got very little out of
them. They paid him nearly £300,000 mostly in English banknotes –
and nearly all of them were forged.   *1943*

'The greatest boy actor in the world' Jackie Coogan was born in
Los Angeles to parents who had a vaudeville act. He made his first
film when he was three and shot to fame at the ripe old age of six,
acting alongside Charlie Chaplin in *The Kid*. He became the youngest
ever dollar millionaire and before his career began to wane, his savings
should have amounted to $4 million. His mother and stepfather had
appropriated the lot and when, after his marriage to Betty Grable he
sued them, he was awarded only $126,000 which barely covered his
debts. This outrage helped prepare the way for the child actors' Bill
to protect the financial interests of little stars – and it was called 'the
Coogan Act'. The strange thing is that he didn't see the film that
started it all for years. Chaplin showed the preview of *The Kid* after
his bedtime and when he should have been watching it, he was fast
asleep.   *1914*

The Football Association was born in a pub at a meeting that took
place in the Freemason's Tavern in Lincoln's Inn Fields. The historic
meeting was not very productive, however, and only served to widen
the schism between the footballers and the rugby footballers – 'the
dribblers' and 'the hackers'. What was agreed was that the rules drawn
up in 1857 in Sheffield were too brutal. So from now on: 'No player
shall be allowed to wear projecting nails . . . on his boots' and better
still, 'No player shall be held and hacked at the same time.'   *1863*

Today's the day...

'That damned cowboy' the incredibly energetic, twice Republican President Theodore Roosevelt was born in New York. From being a sickly, short-sighted, bookish child whose favourite reading was *Wind in the Willows*, he took to being a tough guy by sleeping in damp grass. For his third attempt at the presidency, he stood as the independent 'Bull Moose Candidate', and though he got the biggest vote of any third party ever, a lot of people – including George Bernard Shaw – were glad to see him lose. Roosevelt's idea of 'getting hold of the right end of the stick', said G.B.S., 'is to snatch it from someone who's using it effectively and hit them over the head with it'. *1858*

The beleaguered explorer Ernest Shackleton ordered his crew of twenty-six and a stowaway to abandon ship after they'd been stuck in the ice for nine months, 1,200 miles from nowhere, in the middle of the frozen Weddell Sea. The ship's timbers snapped 'with a noise like heavy gunfire', and for another five months the men had to camp on the ice until the break-up, when they were able to launch their boats and row to Elephant Island. There were still 800 miles to go.

Shackleton took five men and set off through the terrifying waves for South Georgia – arriving on the wrong side from its lonely whaling station, with a mountain range between them. Just thirty miles short of it, they got stuck on a rocky ridge as night began to fall. With nothing to lose, they linked arms and slid down it at nearly a mile a minute. 'My hair fairly stood on end,' said one of them – but they made it and eventually rescued the others. Shackleton's ship had been called *Endurance* and his motto more appropriately still was: 'By endurance, we conquer.'

1915

Renegade Confederate 'Bloody Bill' Anderson was killed when he ran into a troop of Union Soldiers in Missouri. One of the most vicious of Quantrill's raiders, Bill took a delight in gunning down unarmed men and always carried at least eight revolvers, four rifles, a hatchet and a sabre. The only man ever known to escape him was an Englishman called James Thorp. 'If you kill me,' the man cried, 'you'll have to answer to the Queen!' Anderson was mystified. 'What in hell does he mean?' he asked and rode off in a hurry – not so much merciful as confused!

1864

Jane Austen wrote a bitchy letter to her sister. In it she said: 'Mrs Hall of Sherborne was brought to bed yesterday of a dead child . . . owing to a fright. I suppose she happened unawares to look at her husband.'

1798

Puckish Welsh poet Dylan Thomas was born. A natural actor, he'd play all kinds of different roles according to the company he was keeping at the time: a country gentleman in his hairy tweeds, a BBC verse reader in his grey suit or a drunken poet 'with a fag in the corner of his mouth and a dirty raincoat'. Chattering on one morning, sipping some illicit 'champagne wine tonic', he suddenly stopped in full flow. 'Somebody's boring me,' he said quietly, 'I think it's me!'

1914

Today's the day...

Everybody's Mummy and Daddy Adam and Eve were created at tea-time – or so said Archbishop Ussher, the man who decided when the world started. Adam appeared at precisely 4pm and his name means 'earthy'; Eve popped out of his rib, of course, and her name means 'living' or 'life'. It's thought highly unlikely that she tempted him with an apple. An apricot, say the experts, was probably what caused all the trouble, though the Moslems insist it was an ear of wheat or a grape, and others believe it must have been a fig – or where did they get the fig leaves ?

4004 BC

The pioneer of polio vaccine Jonas Salk was born in New York. He became a research microbiologist working in various US medical schools, and by 1952 had produced his first viable vaccine. After three years of testing, it received such a tremendous blast of publicity that some hastily-made samples were used too soon and eleven people died. The Salk vaccine clearly worked, however, and within ten years it had reduced the incidence of polio by a staggering ninety-five per cent. Salk was rightly lauded, and at one of many testimonial dinners he was heard to whisper ruefully, 'I wish I'd discovered a preventative for Chicken *à la* King.'

1914

The original South Seas explorer Captain James Cook was born in the village of Marston, Yorkshire. He grew up to become map-maker on Wolfe's expedition to Quebec, and in his subsequent voyages travelled further South than any man had done before. He charted the coasts of New Zealand and Australia; discovered Hawaii and sailed the Pacific from top to bottom. But though he had good reason to suspect its existence, he never 'discovered' Antarctica. He was 'a modest man', 'most friendly, benevolent and humane'. For restless natives he prescribed a mild peppering with birdshot, while those who stole merely had their heads shaved. He looked after his crew too, and they never got scurvy, though they undoubtedly got sick of his cure.

He forced molasses and apple vinegar down them, and gave them his murderous 'portable broth'. Its secret ingredient was sauerkraut – and on one voyage they got through nearly four tons of the stuff. *1728*

The high-speed surgeon Robert Liston was born in Ecclesmachan, Linlithgow. Before the arrival of anaesthetic, surgeons needed to operate fast and Liston was one of the fastest – in fact the gleam of his knife and the sound of his sawing were said to be 'almost simultaneous'. With great physical strength as well as skill, he would amputate a leg at the thigh, compressing the artery with his left hand and sawing away with his right – and if he happened to need both hands for the job he'd clench the saw between his teeth. *1794*

The most expensive wine in the world was drunk when thirty guests paid £750 a ticket to enjoy a sip of an 1864 *Château Lafite* claret. The shindig was organised by John A. Grisanti, a Memphis restaurant-owner, who'd bought the wine for over £9,000 and was donating the proceeds of the party to the local children's hospital. The wine director of Christie's was flown to Memphis especially to open the bottle, and guests sipped the 114-year-old wine with great ceremony. All except one that is, who with little of the 'reverence' shown by his colleagues took his share home in an empty vodka bottle. *1978*

The Statue of Liberty was dedicated or, to give it its full name, 'The Statue of Liberty Enlightening the World'. It was erected by the citizens of France and the US as a monument to democracy. The French paid for the statue; the Americans for the pedestal. The frame was made by Charles Eiffel of the tower fame and 'Liberty' was created by Frederick Bartholdi. She was shipped across the Atlantic in bits in 214 packing cases; President Grover Cleveland did the honours and it wasn't long before the entire copper-covered Amazon oxidised and turned green! *1886*

Today's the day...

'Old Drum' got a bellyful of buckshot. He was Missourian Charlie Burden's best hound dog and it looked like he had been killed by Charlie's miserable neighbour and brother-in-law Leonidas Hornsby. Charlie decided to sue and the case went to four trials. Finally he was able to hire the eminent lawyer George Graham Vest and he pleaded for Old Drum so eloquently that the jury awarded three times the maximum legal damages. Vest's summing-up – or at least part of it – has since become immortal, for in it he coined the expression that 'a dog is a man's best friend'. *1870*

Elizabeth I's favourite pirate Sir Walter Raleigh was executed on a trumped up charge of conspiracy, arranged by James I after he'd kept the old adventurer in the Tower for thirteen years. Despite the wealth and honours showered on him, Raleigh had been something of a failure. He'd failed to establish a successful colony in Virginia, and failed to find his last goal – the golden city of El Dorado. He was pipped at the post in introducing tobacco to Europe by the Frenchman Jean Nicot and even the story that he laid his cloak in the mud for the Queen to walk on is now known to be an invention. He was quite a character, however, and at the end he scandalised everyone by smoking a pipe immediately before he was beheaded. He felt the edge of the axe and said, 'This is a sharp medicine, but it will cure all diseases' – and two strokes later his head was severed. It was put in a red leather bag and given to his wife. She kept it by her all her days, and so after her did their son. *1618*

A pampered puppy flew first class from Heathrow to New York accompanied by a gentleman companion called of all things, Mr Fox. After landing, 'Claret' as she was called, was taken to the Waldorf Astoria where she was collected by her new owner the following day. Her little jaunt had cost £800, but that was nothing to her new owner. He was called Frank Sinatra. *1978*

October 29

The last minute masterpiece *Don Giovanni* was first performed and to everyone's relief it was a great success. The libretto had been written by a rake called Da Ponte, who was a 'Don Juan' himself – and when Mozart got bored he was inspired afresh by a visit from Casanova. The biggest problem, however, was the overture, which the horrified manager realised he hadn't heard the night before the opening. Mozart said, 'It's all in my head' – but in fact he hadn't written it. He stayed up all night and the orchestra got it complete only half an hour before the curtain rose. *1787*

The Yorkshire joker Jemmy Hirst died aged ninety-one. He'd already had two coffins made ten years before. One he'd used as a cupboard and the other for making money. He would ask visitors to step inside, slam it shut and not let them out till they paid – a penny from the men and a garter from the ladies. Jemmy always said you could tell a woman's character from her garters – and he had a collection ranging from fancy silk to whipcord! He instructed that a Scots piper should lead his coffin to his grave, and better still that it should be carried by twelve old maids. *1829*

Today's the day...

The end of the world was nigh when the 500,000 ton asteroid
Hermes went whizzing past the earth – closer than one had ever done
before. Luckily it missed us by 485,000 miles, but in astronomical
terms that's a very close shave!   *1937*

Martians landed near Princeton, or at least that's what most
Americans who tuned into CBS radio believed, convinced by Orson
Welles' version of the H. G. Wells' classic *The War of the Worlds*.
Thousands heard terrifying reports of gleaming bear-sized monsters
killing police with heat rays. Panic engulfed America: in Newark, New
Jersey, twenty families rushed into the streets using wet towels as gas
masks; in Pittsburgh one woman was found clutching poison shouting,
'I'd rather die this way than that', and in Minneapolis another ran into
a church screaming hysterically, 'This is the end of the world! You
might as well go home to die. I just heard it on the radio.' After the
play Welles publicly apologised while secretly rejoicing that Campbell's
Soups were now offering lavish sums to sponsor him. A year later a
production of the play in Equador caused the same panic, but this time
the studios were attacked and six of the cast murdered.   *1938*

The world's first television star was a fifteen-year-old office boy
named William Taynton. He had been cheerfully working at his job
in Frith Street in London's Soho when he was suddenly seized by the
mad Scottish boffin who had a secret laboratory in the office above.
Bundled up the narrow stairs he was plonked down on a chair in front
of a weird looking contraption lit up by intense white light. Frightened
by the machinery and third degree lighting, Taynton backed off out
of range. He was given half a crown, repositioned and then magically
his well paid features appeared on the screen. As the boffin – John
Logie Baird – later recalled, 'It is curious that the first person in the
world to be seen by television should have required a bribe to accept
that distinction.'   *1925*

October 30

'The Highwayman's Case', probably the oddest ever in an English court, was heard in London. Two 'gentlemen of the road', John Everet and Joseph Williams, entered an oral agreement to share equally all loot and expenses. Inevitably, after a successful run during which time they 'dealt with' over £2,000, they argued about the payout. Unbelievably, Everet sued Williams for his share. The thought of two obvious thieves using the courts to allot their swag was too much for the judge, who dismissed the case as both scandalous and impertinent. Though neither man could be touched, Everet's solicitors were 'attacked for contempt and fined £50'. Within five years, however, both scoundrels were hanged – and soon after one of the solicitors was convicted of robbery and transported. *1725*

The joke that named a religious sect was quipped by a local magistrate named Gervasse Bennet. The itinerant English preacher George Fox had formed his own breakaway sect which he originally called 'Children of Light'. This was later changed to 'Truth's Friends', or more formally the 'Religious Society of Friends'. On this occasion at Derby he stood up and told Justice Bennett to 'quake and tremble at the word of the Lord'. Unruffled, Bennett instantly mocked Fox saying that he made all his followers 'Quakers'. It is probably the best remembered bad joke in history. *1650*

The reluctant dramatist and keen politician Richard Brinsley Sheridan was born in Dublin, the son of a famous actor and orator. He inherited his father's eloquence and in a voice that was 'singularly mellifluous', he would hold Parliament spellbound by his speeches. Constantly harried by creditors, he was obliged to keep writing – but kept putting it off. Two days before the première of *The Critic*, he still hadn't written the last scene. Desperate, the proprietors lured him to the theatre, laid on a supply of pens, paper, anchovy sandwiches and claret in the green room – and locked him in. *1751*

Today's the day...

'That most illustrious of magicians' the escapologist Harry Houdini died from a ruptured appendix. He'd always boasted he could take a punch from anyone, but some days earlier a college-boy-boxer had hit him in the stomach and he'd collapsed, coughing blood. He'd still insisted on going ahead with his famous 'water trick' whereby he was manacled and suspended upside down in a huge fish tank. But he'd had to be hauled out after giving the distress signal which was ironically the 'thumbs up'. He was rushed to hospital and lingered in a coma until today. When he finally succumbed, friends said he'd waited for Halloween so it would make a good headline.   *1926*

The annual holiday for ghosts and ghouls is celebrated. Officially it's the 'holy even' before All Saints Day – 'Halloween'. But unofficially it's been marked in a distinctly unholy way since time immemorial. It's the end of the Celtic year, dedicated to the Cult of the Dead and enjoyed by witches and warlocks everywhere. People used to dress up like spirits so they wouldn't be harmed – or light fires to frighten the real ones away. The Celts burned people and animals, and the Romans worshipped 'Pomona' the Goddess of Orchards – and hence one source for the custom of 'bobbing' for apples. The traditional turnip lanterns, on the other hand, came from Ireland and were created for the unfortunate 'Jack O'Lantern'. The poor lad was welcome neither in heaven nor in hell, but wandered the land with his turnip lamp in his hand – lit by a coal from the devil.   *Annual Event*

The mystery of the lone sailor began when Donald Crowhurst, the last entrant in the *Sunday Times* single handed round-the-world yacht race set off from Teignmouth five hours before the deadline. He was determined that the publicity from the voyage would save his electrical company from bankruptcy and he'd sold the film rights to the BBC. In December, he cabled a record one-day sail of 243 miles;

in May he sent word he'd rounded Cape Horn – but in July a cargo ship found his yacht abandoned. The log book revealed that for the last eight months he'd just been circling the south Atlantic, waiting for an opportune moment to sail home. There was plenty of food on board, and the only thing missing was the ship's chronometer – apart, that is, from Crowhurst – and the reason why.   *1968*

Prince Charles was dubbed 'Hooligan of the Year' by Mr John Bryant of the National Council of the RSPCA. 'Not content with fox-hunting,' HRH 'killed five wild pigs, pheasants and hare' while on a trip to Vienna. Mr Bryant further suggested that the Prince should get a prize – 'a vandal's flick-knife or a can of aerosol paint'.   *1978*

A self-confessed werewolf was put to an excruciating death. The lycanthrope in question was Peter Stubb and he'd told a court in Bedburg, Germany, how a magic belt had made him commit many murders by turning him into 'a greedy and devouring wolf, with eyes that sparkled like unto brands of fire'. The judges could find no belt, and pronounced their awful sentence. Stubb was laid on a wheel; his flesh was 'pulled off from the bones' with red hot pincers; his arms and legs were broken and he was finally beheaded – all in the presence of 'many peers and princes of Germany' who had come to see justice done.   *1589*

The Reformation began almost by accident when Martin Luther nailed his '95 Theses' to the church door at Wittenberg. Things got out of hand, however, and inadvertantly Luther had sparked off a movement that split the Church in two. He ended up getting married, having six children and claiming that the Pope was no better than 'any other stinking sinner'. At first, despite the insults, Pope Leo X wasn't bothered. 'Luther is a drunken German,' he said. 'He'll feel different when he sobers up.'   *1517*

Today's the day...

The world's most famous ceiling was unveiled in the Sistine Chapel. Michelangelo had not wanted to do it, because he felt himself to be a sculptor and not a painter. Though everyone was convinced it would be a failure, he persevered, dismissing his assistants and completing the 5,808sq ft of vault alone. It took him four-and-a-half years, with most of his working time spent lying down on the job, with his head thrown back and paint dripping on his face. Thereafter, the poor man could only read by holding the paper high above his head. Pope Julius, who'd commissioned the work, originally only wanted a fresco of the twelve apostles. What he got was the complete Bible story from the creation to the flood, which like some vast time machine, visitors to the chapel see in reverse chronological order. *1512*

Eighteenth-century stud Giovanni Jacopo Casanova made a classic escape. He'd been imprisoned not for cheating at cards, womanising or immoral behaviour – which he certainly was guilty of – but for reciting one of his own poems, which apart from being obscene, mocked the Holy Mother Church. He was taken to the dreaded 'Leads' in the Venetian Ducal Palace from which no-one ever escaped. He fashioned a spike from an iron bar and made a lamp fired by the oil from his salad. Working six hours a day he bored an escape hatch, but by a cruel stroke of fate, the day before his break-out he was moved to a new cell. This time he co-operated with his neighbour, a debauched monk named Balbi. He smuggled the spike into the monk's cell in a Bible, which he claimed he was going to use as a tray for a dish of macaroni. A hole was made in the adjoining wall and in Balbi's ceiling. They lifted one of the lead plates off the roof, from which the prison got its name, and made good their escape in a gondola. With unbelievable cheek Casanova spent his first night of freedom in the house of the Chief of Police, who was out hunting him. The officer's wife was home.   *1756*

A Douglas DC6B airliner exploded near Longmont, Colorado, and all forty-four occupants were killed. FBI investigators discovered that the mother of a known criminal, John Gilbert Graham, had been on board. The unfilial fellow had taken out a huge travel insurance on her life shortly before the flight. It was proven that with unbelievable sang-froid, he'd planted an alarm clock and dynamite bomb. Instead of profiting from this indiscriminate murder, however, he was sent to the gas chamber.   *1955*

Voyeur of war, American writer Stephen Crane, was born in Newark, New Jersey, the fourteenth son of an itinerant Methodist Minister. A frail child who didn't attend school until he was eight, he loved to play strategy games with armies of buttons, and once nearly killed a friend playing 'burying dead soldiers'. He grew up 'giftedly profane' and married Cora Howorth, ten years his senior and the proprietress of the Florida brothel, the Hotel de Dream. His first significant work was called *Maggie: A Girl of the Streets*. It was so 'impossibly grim' that he had to publish it himself, and fearing for his newspaper job, used the *nom de plume* Johnston Smith. The book only sold about 100 copies and the remainder were used as fuel to keep his apartment warm.   *1871*

Today's the day...

Empty-headed Queen Marie Antoinette was born in Austria. Despite her fame as a beauty, she had weak inflamed eyes and a gross bust. She did have an exceptionally fine complexion, however, and an 'elevated manner, which announced a Queen'. Modest in the extreme, she wore a long flannel gown buttoned right up to the neck in the bath, yet still made an attendant hold a sheet in front of her when she emerged. Frivolous and extravagant, she arrived in Paris at the head of a cavalcade of fifty carriages, refused to eat anything but chicken, and would only ever drink water. Her own mother was among the many who recognised her daughter's faults. She declared, 'I know my daughter's frivolousness and her aversion to concentrating – and she doesn't know a thing!'   *1755*

***Lady Chatterley's Lover* was found not guilty.** It was Lawrence's last novel and had been prosecuted under the Obscene Publications Act of 1959. Lawrence regarded it as 'an honest, healthy book, necessary for us today', and claimed he was trying to make 'the sex relation valid and precious, instead of shameful'. Happily the jury agreed with him and for the first time the book was legally available in the UK. The trial and its verdict were much talked about, even in the House of Lords. Viscount Gage related how one peer had been asked if he'd allow his daughter to read it. 'Certainly,' he'd replied, 'but I wouldn't allow my gamekeeper to.'   *1960*

The first crossword to be published in Britain appeared in the *Sunday Express*. It was compiled by Liverpool-born Arthur Wynne who, at the time, was living in America. The thirty-four clues were Horizontal and Vertical as opposed to Across and Down, and the day before publication it was discovered that the crossword contained the American spelling 'honor'. Panicky wordsmiths worked frantically to alter it. By the time they'd finished, it was totally different – and the troublesome word didn't even appear.   *1924*

November 2

Grand old Irish writer George Bernard Shaw died, aged
ninety-four. A keen vegetarian, he'd already had a vision of his funeral
with his hearse followed by herds of animals, flocks of poultry and a
small travelling aquarium of live fish, 'all wearing white scarves in
honour of the man who perished, rather than eat his fellow creatures'.
He'd always kept fit and active in his old age and maintained 'a fine
slender figure' despite his incorrigible sweet-tooth which led him to eat
sugar by the handful. He did make one concession to his advancing
years, however, by giving up swimming, but still continued with his
favourite hobby of pruning trees. In fact, that's what he was doing
when he fell and fractured his thigh and was rushed to hospital. He
wanted to die at home in Ayot St Lawrence where he'd spent so many
happy years with his beloved wife Charlotte. He was eventually
allowed back there, but despite the ministrations of his nurse and
cook, who on doctor's orders even tried putting a little whisky in the
teetotaller's soup, his mind was made up. On his death-bed he
declared, 'Sister you're trying to keep me alive as an old curiosity, but
I'm done, I'm finished, I'm going to die.' And that's exactly what he
did.   1950

Today's the day...

Queen Matilda wife of William the Conqueror died. She'd been married for some thirty years and at only 4ft 2in, she was the shortest ever Queen of England. She'd been reluctant to have anything to do with William at first, saying she would never marry a bastard. Not being a man to take 'No' for an answer, however, he ambushed her as she left church one day, swung her round by the hair and threw her into the mud, where he beat and kicked her. She seemed to like it though, and took to her bed vowing that she would marry no-one but him. They married and had four sons and five daughters. Mindful of his own experience William was chary of the taunt of illegitimacy for his children, and the marriage was a conspicuous model of fidelity and happiness, in an age of loose living. After her death he built Matilda a richly adorned tomb and it's said that the conquering King mourned her for the rest of his life. *1083*

Mona Lisa got toothache four years after she started sitting for the great Leonardo. Her elderly husband, Signor Giaconda, had commissioned the painting to hang in his dining room, and throughout the sessions had paid for twelve violinists to serenade his beautiful young wife. Da Vinci preferred to paint on dark, thundery evenings to capture the strange effects of the light. On this particular evening, Signora Giaconda had rushed to the studio in the rain, and then sat in a draught. The result was a horrendous toothache, which was so painful that she was prepared to go through the torture of having three teeth pulled out. Leonardo went to great lengths to put matters right. He got replacement teeth, torn out of corpses, fitted to a copper band, and persuaded the lady to wear the gruesome contraption. Her gums were too sensitive however, and she had to give up wearing it. The smile was ruined, and the painting was never completely finished.   *1507*

Roy Plomley had the idea for 'Desert Island Discs' while he was standing in his pyjamas about to go to bed. He immediately sat down and wrote to the BBC and the first programme was broadcast on 21 January 1942. The many famous people who've been marooned over the years have taken some very odd things with them. Dame Edith Evans chose the theme music from *Rawhide*, while Elizabeth Schwarzkopf went for seven of her own records out of the eight allowed. Hermione Gingold chose as her luxury the Albert Memorial; Oliver Reed plumped for an inflatable rubber woman, and Harvey Smith refused to take a book on the grounds that he'd never read one in his life.   *1941*

Panama was declared independent. Formerly a part of Colombia, it's the 107th largest country in the world and the 115th in population. The workers there start young – official lists of the workforce include anyone aged ten or over. Everyone's paid in coins too, since the Panamanian Bank doesn't issue any bank notes. Its most famous export, the Panama Hat, is something of a misnomer. It was originally made in Ecuador – Panama was just the distribution centre.   *1903*

Today's the day...

The National Security Agency was founded by President Truman. Mainly concerned with making and breaking codes and the analysis of foreign countries, it's the biggest, most secret intelligence agency in the free world. With 100,000 personnel, it's five times bigger than the CIA and its electronic sophistication is so great that it's claimed to have picked up the conversations of Kremlin leaders on their car telephones. Not surprisingly, their own security is extremely tight and at their base in Fort Meade, Maryland, visitors are given a marine escort even when they go to the men's room.   *1952*

Gangling Abraham Lincoln married plump, pretty Mary Todd at the home of the bride's sister in Springfield, Illinois. Some months earlier he'd left her with the preacher and had become so profoundly depressed that friends kept knives and razors out of his reach. The new ceremony was arranged for a Friday and, though traditionally it's a bad day for weddings, they wouldn't change it for fear of changing their minds. It was all so sudden that the icing on the wedding cake was still warm! Lincoln did at least have time to have Mary's wedding ring engraved with 'Love is Eternal'. A strange message for someone who when asked where he was going, a few hours before the wedding, replied 'To the Devil'. During his stormy marriage he must often have reflected on that reply – especially when his wife chased him out of the house with a carving knife.   *1842*

Dr James Simpson had a chloroform party. Anxious to experiment with the new 'curious liquid' he invited his two assistants Dr Duncan and Dr Keith to supper. His wife, his niece Miss Petrie and a naval officer were also present. Each was given a tumbler of chloroform and the sickly sweet stuff soon got the party going. Shy reticent Miss Petrie blossomed forth announcing, 'I'm beginning to fly! I'm an angel, oh I'm an angel!' – then she fell into a deep sleep. Dr Keith had a good laugh, which got louder and louder with everyone

November 4

joining in and the navy man crowing like a cock! Dr Simpson forsook his chair to stand on his head and his wife, who made a valiant effort to rescue him, collapsed in a snoring heap on the floor. When Dr Simpson came to, he realised that this new substance was far stronger than ether and announced to the now-awake party that chloroform was obviously the perfect answer to painless childbirth. Dr Simpson's slapstick party was, in fact, a great milestone in medical history.   *1847*

Gatling patented his machine-gun – arguably the most important invention of the US Civil War. The prototype could fire 350 shots a minute – nearly six a second – but fortunately for the Confederacy, it didn't impress the US Chief of Ordnance. Only when the war was over, did the authorities realise its full potential, and it was developed to shoot at an amazing 1,200 bullets a minute – or twenty a second. The paradox is that the inventor of this lethal machine served in the Union Army as a physician-dedicated to preserving life.   *1862*

The Beatles played at the Royal Command Performance, an event which seemed to mark their acceptance by the Establishment. Twenty-six million people watched the charity show on television; tickets at the Prince of Wales theatre were four times their normal price and the Queen Mother, Princess Margaret and Lord Snowdon all attended. Introducing one song, John said, 'The ones in the cheap seats clap your hands,' – then he looked towards the Royal box and added – 'the rest of you just rattle your jewellery!'   *1963*

A unique hair transplant operation was patented by Dr Aurel Popovic. The jolly doctor claimed his technique was so wonderful that it rendered 'the artificial nature of the hair covering thus produced completely unnoticeable'. The only drawback was that the operation was rather painful, as it involved individually sewing new hairs to the scalp – and fixing them there with rust-proof gold hooks.   *1909*

Today's the day...

The Gunpowder Plot was exploded only hours before Parliament was to open. In the early hours, notary's son Guy Fawkes was arrested and thirty-six half-barrels of poor quality gunpowder were discovered in a cellar under the House of Lords. The Plot was betrayed by Baron Monteagle, and Fawkes and company suffered the full force of the law. For the original Guy, James I ordered that, 'the gentler tortures be first used unto him, *et sic per gradus ad ima tenditur*', which loosely translated means 'and by degrees into hell'. On the rack, Fawkes confessed and implicated his colleagues. The first recorded celebration of the anniversary took place in Bristol in 1607; fireworks were first used to mark the event seventy years later, and until 1859, it was actually illegal *not* to celebrate it. The cellars are still searched before the opening of each new Parliament, and in 1978 a receipt for the illicit gunpowder was found in the Office of Public Records. It had cost 15s 6d to remove it from the House of Lords to the arsenal at the Tower of London.   *1605*

The hole-in-the-pole man Captain John Cleves Symmes was born in New Jersey. Like Plato and Halley before him, he decided the earth was hollow, and contained a number of other worlds in concentric spheres. Unlike his predecessors, however, he decided that these worlds could be entered through holes 4,000 and 6,000 miles wide at the North and South Poles respectively. He drummed up hundreds of devotees to his theory, and prevailed upon a Kentucky Representative to put his case for Government backing to the Congress. He wanted to follow the birds' winter migration by ship and reindeer sled, hoping to disappear through the northern hole to find: 'a warm and rich land, stocked with thrifty vegetables and animals, if not men'. Congress, needless to say, refused.   *1780*

Radiant German Konrad Roentgen discovered the X-Ray. He'd been working on cathode rays and was fascinated by the way they made certain chemicals luminous. Today, he put the cathode tube in a cardboard case in a darkened room, and was amazed to find a chemically coated sheet of paper glowing some feet away. He took the paper into the next room and still it glowed, showing the powerful penetration of – he knew not what. He called these strange invisible manifestations X-Rays because he still didn't know exactly what they were. Within two months an eighty-year-old man had had his hand publicly X-rayed, and shortly after, the New Jersey legislature heard a bill designed to prevent their use in opera glasses. It was feared they might enable people to look through women's clothing! *1895*

Guy the gorilla arrived at London Zoo, direct from his home in the French Cameroons. He was only eighteen months old, weighed less than 25lb, and sat in a wooden box clutching a tin hot-water bottle. Though he occasionally had wild tantrums, he was generally good-natured. He was given to catching sparrows but, unlike other primates at the Zoo, he wouldn't eat them. Instead, he'd just hold them in his huge hands, peer at them through his fingers and then let them fly away. *1947*

Today's the day...

A weird underwater craft was spotted in the Pascagoula River, Mississippi, by two amazed fishermen, the Ryan brothers. They could hardly believe their eyes and immediately contacted the local coastguard station who sent Charles Crew and Alan Nations to take a look. They confirmed that there was a shiny metal craft about 3 ft long and 4 in wide, with a bright amber light, silently gliding along just below the surface. Despite frenzied attempts, they failed to catch the world's first Unidentified Submarine Object – and perhaps that was a lucky escape. Twenty-six days earlier, two men had claimed they'd been kidnapped in the same area – by a UFO.   *1973*

Depressive composer Peter Tchaikovsky died. Haunted by 'an indefinable terror – though from what, the devil only knows', he'd already tried to commit suicide the hard way by standing all night in an ice-cold river. He only succeeded in catching pneumonia and, to his disgust, survived. After his break with Madame von Meck, the patron whom he'd never met, his depressions increased. Suffering from gastric trouble, he went to lunch with his brothers and favourite nephew in St Petersburg. He ate nothing but drank a glass of water. Either deliberately or thoughtlessly, he drank it unboiled and straight from the tap, when he knew full well the city was gripped by an epidemic of cholera. Almost inevitably, he caught the disease and since the only cure attempted was to throw him into a bath of scalding water to kill the germs, he died. His last and favourite work was the *Symphonie Pathétique*, an appropriate requiem for his miserable life.   *1893*

Louis Philippe, Duc d'Orléans was guillotined. The richest man in France, he'd renounced all his titles at the outbreak of revolution and joined the insurgents as Philippe Egalité. Despite his exemplary conduct, he couldn't win – the royal family considered him a cowardly disgrace, while his new political bedfellows were embarrassed at such an ally and would never really trust him. He ended up in the tumbrils just like the rest of the aristocracy, but he presented himself bravely like 'a soldier marching to battle'. Immaculately dressed, he wore a blue dress coat, a white stiff ribbed cotton vest, leather breeches, and his hair coiffed as though going to a ball. The executioner wanted to remove his brightly-polished, narrow-fitting boots, but Louis stopped him saying with a smile, 'They will be much easier to remove afterwards. Come, let us have done!'

1793

Prince Henry, Prince of Wales, died aged eighteen. He was the son of James I and the elder brother of the future Charles I. Much loved and admired, his popularity irritated his unlovely and dribbling father, who in a fit of peevishness once asked, 'Will he bury me alive?' The Prince was a keen sportsman, and during his last autumn insisted on playing tennis, despite tiredness and severe headaches. Wearing only a cotton shirt, he played a full match in the freezing weather, and the following day he couldn't get out of bed. He was clearly seriously ill, and doctors argued over how to treat him. Some were reluctant to bleed the heir apparent, but others felt they should proceed 'as though he were some meane person'. They settled on cutting a cock in half, laying the pieces on each of his feet. It didn't work, and though many thought his father had poisoned him out of jealousy, the cause of death remained a mystery. Years later, physicians realised that Henry was the unfortunate victim of the world's first closely attested case of typhoid.

1612

An historic letter to President Roosevelt was unearthed from the State Department's files. It was prompted by his re-election and came from a twelve-year-old Cuban schoolboy, who offered to tell the President where to find 'the biggest of iron of the land' for building ships. He admitted, 'I don't know very English', but knew enough to add, 'If you like, give me ten dollars bill, green American.' The letter came from the Roman Catholic *Colegio de Dolores*. It was signed Fidel Castro.

1940

Today's the day...

The first performance of *Rhapsody on a Theme of Paganini* was given by the composer, Sergei Rachmaninov. A few days earlier he had met Benno Moiseiwitsch, who though twenty years his junior, was already a noted pianist and one of the foremost exponents of Rachmaninov's work. The maestro confessed he was worried about a series of difficult chord jumps in the Rhapsody's twenty-fourth variation. Moiseiwitsch assured him that the best thing in the world for difficult chord jumps was a glass of *crème de menthe*. Though he didn't usually drink, Rachmaninov agreed to try it. The performance was a great success, and the composer swore by the remedy thereafter. He sent Moiseiwitsch an autographed score, and entitled it the *Crème de Menthe Variation*.   *1934*

Scientific genius Marie Curie was born in Warsaw. She could read at four, and had a phenomenal memory. When she arrived in France, she lived on three francs a day, and ate so little, she once fainted in class. Eventually, she won the Alexandrovitch Scholarship for 600 roubles, and when she'd saved enough she paid it all back, saying it had helped her, now it must help someone else. In 1895, she married Pierre Curie, who though a noted physicist himself, gave up his own work to help Marie. Their early experiments were done in a damp shed with no floor, and for over three years they struggled financially and physically with the awesome task of purifying tons of pitchblende, to isolate the new elements of radium and polonium. When they shared the Nobel Prize for Physics in 1903, the Curies were too exhausted to go to Stockholm to collect it, but were overjoyed that they could now afford a bathroom.   *1867*

Handsome, tub-thumping evangelist Billy Graham was born. He worked on his father's dairy farm, where he became 'the fastest milker in Mecklenburg county'. His handy, expressive style earned him the name of the 'Preaching Windmill', and in his early days he was such a determined fundamentalist that he claimed that heaven was exactly 1,600 miles above the earth. Taking a relatively modest salary, he runs a super-efficient team of crusaders, who answer his average of 50,000 letters a week from a stock of forty specimen replies. He has only once, as far as is known, watched TV on the Sabbath, and that was to see the Beatles. His favourite benediction is a good down-home one – he usually signs off, 'May the Lord bless you real good.'

1918

Forger John Austin became the last to die at Tyburn. He followed an estimated 50,000 other souls who had perished there in its 587-year history. Arguably the most bizarre execution of all occurred in 1447, when two felons were to be hanged, drawn and quartered. They were duly strung up, cut down still alive, and marked for quartering, before the ritual disembowelment. Suddenly a reprieve arrived and since the hangman wouldn't part with their clothes, which were part of his fee, they had to wait until they'd recovered, and walk back to the City naked.

1783

Futuristic surgeon Gaspare Tagliacozzi died. Centuries ahead of his time, this remarkable Italian from the city of Bologna pioneered plastic surgery. He was the inventor of 'rhinoplasty' – the restoration of lost noses – and he specialised in those organs mutilated by 'syphilis and a nose-destroying pope'! His method was based on the even earlier work of a Sicilian named Branca, and involved transplanting a flap of skin from the forearm. Stitched into place and held there by leather straps, arm and nose were only separated when the graft had taken. Crudely, this is the same basic technique used today and it all occurred, of course, 300 years before the birth of anaesthesia and medical hygiene. The Anatomical School of his home town remembered him by commissioning a statue of him, holding a nose.

1599

Today's the day...

Horrifying writer Bram Stoker was born. Immortalised by his creation of the frightful vampire Count Dracula, he based his unsavoury character on the historical figure of the bloodthirsty Vlad the Impaler – a warlike nobleman who plunged his prisoners onto sharpened stakes. He was also known as Draculaea, from the Rumanian for 'Son of the Devil', and in all executed a total of 40,000 people between 1452 and 1462, while he ruled a terrified Wallachia. Stoker, who was made of milder stuff, did all his research in the civilised surroundings of the British Museum, and never once paid a visit to the dreaded Transylvania, where our toothy hero had his castle. It's said that the author got his idea from a nightmare he had after eating a plate of crabs. *1847*

The courageous Madame Rolande achieved immortality with her famous last words, uttered as she waited on a Paris scaffold and gazed at the Statue of Liberty. In fact, it was the translators who created 'Oh Liberty, Liberty, what crimes are committed in thy name,' because what she actually said was, 'Oh Liberty, Liberty, how they have played with you.' As she rode the tumbril to the gallows, she

November 8

noticed that another condemned prisoner, Lamarde, was ashen with fear. With exquisite charity, she renounced her privilege of dying first, saying, 'At least I can spare you the suffering of seeing my blood.' The executioner, one Sanson, had orders to take her before the other, but when he asked her to ascend the fatal stairs, this doughty lady gently rebuked him: 'Surely,' she said, 'you will not be so impolite as to refuse a woman her last request.'   *1793*

The world's strangest footprints were photographed by mountaineer explorer Eric Shipton. They were found in the Himalayas and measured 12½ by 6in. He'd rediscovered that most famous of unknown animals the Yeti – the Abominable Snowman, said to be a cave-dwelling nocturnal six-footer, rank smelling, incredibly strong and capable of uttering high pitched whistles. Most remarkable of all, however, is the fact that the busty females have such large breasts that when running or bending down they throw them over their shoulders.   *1951*

Kennedy could have won the Presidency by fraud. In his memoirs Nixon suggests voting irregularities, as does Lyndon B. Johnson. Alistair Cooke wrote shortly after it was all over that Kennedy had been worried that Nixon would appeal to the Supreme Court; while a noted American columnist claimed that J.F.K. said he'd have done exactly that, had he been in Tricky Dicky's position. The election was certainly a close-run thing and the question remains – was Kennedy so popular in some districts that more people voted for him than there were registered voters ?   *1960*

James Christie the auctioneer died. He founded his famous company in 1766, knowing nothing about it – he just liked the idea. He threw extravagant dinner parties for connoisseurs of antiques and picked their brains till he was the foremost authority in the land.   *1803*

Today's the day...

Self-indulgent spendthrift Edward VII was born into the bleak world of Victorian morality which he was destined to scandalise time and time again. Victoria and Albert were baffled by their eldest son's intractability and sent him to get his 'bumps' read. The sycophantic phrenologist reported that the bumps representing morality and the intellect were growing apace, so poor Edward was sentenced to an even stricter regime. Under the beady eye of Baron Stockmar he was given up to seven hours of self-improving study a day. Not surprisingly, the Prince reacted against his stifling upbringing, and as soon as he was old enough, became a fast-living glutton and rake. When he seduced a young Irish actress in a military barracks outside Dublin, Albert was horrified. Despite illness and bitterly cold weather, he went to see his recalcitrant son; returned home, and died shortly afterwards. Victoria blamed Edward, and never forgave him. She excluded him from all matters of state, and secluded herself at Windsor. It's been said that his most lasting impression on history was the vogue for leaving the bottom waistcoat button undone – he was so fat, he had to. For Lord Northcliffe, however, he was, 'the greatest monarch we've ever had – on a racecourse!'   *1841*

The Great Fire of Boston began in the early evening and devastated sixty-five acres in the heart of the business section of the city. With its tightly-packed narrow streets and wooden buildings, the site was ideal for a raging inferno. A handful of startled spectators watched the fire erupt in a tower of flame four floors high but no-one reported it. When it was finally brought to the attention of the authorities, there was some delay getting the horse-drawn fire engines to the scene, as most of the horses were ill. Crowds of trippers poured into the city and there was a holiday atmosphere as they strolled around buying souvenirs of the fire from street urchins – twisted bits of metal, scorched pieces of leather and even blackened hard-boiled eggs.   *1872*

November 9

Welsh poet and playwright Dylan Thomas died in St Vincent's Hospital, New York, at the tragically early age of thirty-nine. Though the official cause of death was given as 'an acute alcoholic insult to the brain', recent opinion suggests it was a doctor's misguided injection of morphine which actually killed him. Tormented by his inability to write, he'd taken to consuming vast amounts of whisky, and though advised by doctors to give up alcohol completely, he'd set out on a 'final' binge, commenting before he collapsed, 'I've had eighteen straight whiskeys, I think it's a record.' He once wrote, 'I'd fallen in love with words, words were to me as the notes of bells, the sounds of musical instruments, the noises of wind, sea and rain.' Before he slipped into his final coma, he said, 'I wish the words would lie down and go to sleep.'

1953

Razor-sharp actress Katharine Hepburn was born to a wealthy family in Hartford, Connecticut. Her famous partnership with Spencer Tracy got off to rather a shaky start when they starred together in *Woman of the Year*. 'I'm afraid I'm too tall for you Mr Tracy,' she said. 'Don't worry Miss Hepburn', he replied, 'I'll soon cut you down to my size!'

1909

Today's the day...

Stanley found Livingstone in Ujiji on the shores of Lake Tanganyka. Financed by James Gordon Bennett of the *New York Herald*, he'd set off some two years before, taking in a tour of Asia, before starting his epic 900-mile, 236-day journey from Zanzibar to the heart of the 'Dark Continent'. In his own words, he was 'totally ignorant of the interior'; took a mass of supplies, an army of porters, and two white companions – Farquhar and Shaw – neither of whom survived the trip. Overcoming wild animals, dysentery, malaria and mutiny, he lost over four stone in weight and drove his men on with threats and beatings. With short interludes in civilization, Livingstone had been in the bush for twenty-two years; no white man had seen him for six years, and rumour was rife that he'd 'gone native', and married an 'African princess'. In fact, the 'disagreeable and brusque' old man Stanley had been warned about, turned out to be more than a little charming, and terribly ill. Stanley's arrival gave him a new lease of life, and an odd father and son relationship grew up between these two men of wildly different background and outlook. Henry Morton Stanley of Missouri was in fact John Rowland – a Welshman – child of the workhouse and veteran of the American Civil War. He believed he was twenty-eight when he arrived in Ujiji, though he was actually thirty. Livingstone thought the date was 24 October; Stanley at first thought it was 3 November. He greeted the great missionary with the immortal words, 'Dr Livingstone, I presume', because he couldn't think of anything else to say, and whenever he wrote about it afterwards, he could never decide whether or not to add a full stop, or a question mark!

1871

The incredible 'Vibratory Generator' was first demonstrated by its inventor John Worrell Keely. Employing among other odd bits of equipment, a goose quill and a bath tub, the generator was one of his earliest attempts to harness the 'etheric force' he'd found in ordinary water. The generator's successor, which took fourteen years to build, was the 'Harmonie Vibration Liberator'. Compounding 'quadruple negative harmonics' with 'ethereal disintegration', this amazing machine built up tens of thousands of pounds of pressure per square inch. With a little more time and a lot more money, Keely argued, he could produce a motor that, with less than a gallon of water, would power a steamship from New York to Liverpool, and with only a quart, would drive a train from Philadelphia to San Francisco. Alas, he died in 1898, before his achievement came to fruition, and when a team of investigators examined his workshop, they found that the 'etheric force' was produced by a huge pump hidden under the floorboards. It was compressed air.   *1874*

Richard 'the Voice' Burton was born in Pontrhydfen, Wales, with the surname Jenkins. By general agreement a considerable actor, he has attracted more attention for his vast consumption of alcohol and his two marriages to Elizabeth Taylor. He gave up the hard stuff when he was on three bottles a day, and was given two weeks to live. He also gave up Miss Taylor. He once claimed, 'Monogamy is one of man's greatest inventions', and is now trying it out with Suzy, ex-wife of ex-World Champion racing driver, James Hunt. She thought she was marrying 'a drunk and a roaring madman' he said, but ended up with 'a little goody-two-shoes!' Burton the actor has starred in over thirty films. He's recorded a definitive version of Dylan Thomas' *Under Milk Wood*, and played Becket, Faustus, Henry V and Othello, to name but a few. After his portrayal of the Bard's Prince of Denmark at the Old Vic, Winston Churchill paid him a visit in his dressing room. 'My Lord Hamlet,' the old boy growled, 'may I use your lavatory?'   *1925*

Prince Charles was asked for a kiss by a girl working in a biscuit factory in North London. The Prince refused to give her so much as a peck. He said, 'My mother wouldn't like it!'   *1978*

Today's the day...

Expatriate animal lover Francis Henry Egerton, 8th Earl of Bridgewater, was born. He lived in Paris and was in the enviable position of having sufficient fortune to gratify 'the most extravagant caprices that ever passed through the head of a rich Englishman.' He filled his house with dogs and cats, dressed them all in the latest fashions, had miniature shoes made for them and sat them in armchairs at his dinner table every day, where they were waited on by servants while they ate. He never wore a pair of shoes more than once and in his later years filled his garden with partridge and pigeon – all with their wings carefully clipped so that even with his failing eyesight he could still shoot them.

1756

Loud-mouthed General George S. Patton was born on an 1,800 acre ranch at San Gabriel, California. His father believed that children could learn best by having the classics read aloud to them; and consequently when Patton was twelve he still couldn't read for himself and only managed to get through Westpoint Military Academy by dint of his phenomenal ability to memorise everything and repeat it verbatim. He described himself as 'the best damn butt-kicker in the whole United States Army', and was nicknamed 'Blood and Guts'. The name arose because he delighted in telling new recruits, 'You've got to spill their blood or they'll spill yours. Rip 'em up the belly or shoot 'em in the guts.' Paradoxically he was also something of a mystic. When asked if he read the Bible he replied, 'every goddam day'; he also wrote poetry and firmly believed in reincarnation, claiming to have 'subconscious memories' of six past lives. He certainly surprised General Alexander who remarked, 'You would have made a great marshal for Napoleon if you'd lived in the eighteenth century.' Patton quietly replied, 'I did.' *1885*

World War I ended. The Armistice was signed at 5am and it was decreed that there should be 'a cessation of hostilities six hours after the signing'. At the eleventh hour of the eleventh day of the eleventh month a curious hush descended on war-torn Europe, and the peace has been commemorated by two minutes' silence ever since. *1918*

The last great Australian bushranger Ned Kelly was hanged in front of a crowd of 5,000 people outside the jail at Melbourne. Mindful of his mother's instruction to 'die like a Kelly', he walked steadily to the gallows, and accepted the rope around his neck with a laconic, 'Such is life.' His trial had been a travesty with the defence not being allowed to call any witnesses or even re-examine any of the evidence. With Justice Redmond Barry as judge, the 'guilty' verdict was a foregone conclusion. Two years earlier he'd sentenced Kelly's mother to three years in prison and said at the time that if he could get his hands on Ned, he'd like to sentence him to fifteen. He now pronounced the death sentence on the bearded twenty-six-year-old ending with the customary words, 'May the Lord have mercy on your soul.' 'I will add something to that,' retorted Kelly, 'I will meet you there.' Two days after Kelly was hanged, Judge Barry was suddenly and mysteriously taken ill – he died twelve days later. *1880*

Today's the day...

The original 'Daring Young Man on the Flying Trapeze' made his *début* at the *Cirque Napoléon* in Paris. Twenty-one-year-old Jules Leotard had been practising for several wet years jumping from one moving trapeze to another above the swimming pool in his father's gymnasium in Toulouse. There were already trapeze artists on the static bar, sometimes suspended from a hot air balloon, but Leotard was the first to discover that if he released the trapeze at the right time his own momentum would carry him through the air to catch another. His first appearance caused a sensation; he was likened to 'a tropical bird jumping from branch to branch', and overnight he became the darling of Paris. Leotard ties, walking sticks, medallions and even pastries went on sale and his fellow artists were so impressed they presented him with a medal. Apart from the song, he's best remembered today for the tight-fitting elastic garment he designed – it was of course the leotard.   *1859*

The headless hen refused to die, which rather surprised Mr Herbert Hughes of the Belvidere Hotel, Sault Ste Marie, Michigan, who'd just chopped its head off with an axe. The maid ran screaming from the room when the chicken she was about to pluck sprang into life. For the next two weeks crowds thronged to the hotel to see it and Mr Hughes fed it by squirting food down its foodpipe with a syringe. The happy hen lived on for seventeen days, and only died when her windpipe healed over and she choked.   *1904*

Chemist and composer Alexander Borodin was born, the illegitimate child of a lusty ageing Prince and a nubile young dairymaid. As was the custom, the baby was registered under the name of one of his father's serfs – a certain Mr Porphyri Borodin who hadn't had anything to do with it. Papa paid well for his indiscretion, however, and young Alexander was taught by private tutors who fostered his great interests in life – chemistry and music. He qualified as a doctor and worked in an army hospital before spending three years abroad, mostly at the University of Heidelberg. On his return he married Ekaterina Protopopova, a talented pianist who introduced him to the works of Chopin, Schumann and Liszt. Appointed professor of Organic Chemistry at the Academy, he was awarded a rent-free flat. It was to be his home for life and also a refuge for stray cats, penniless students and absent-minded friends – a bohemian collection which increasingly drove his wife to stay with her parents. He joined a group of amateur musicians – a select five which included Mussorgsky, a clerk in the Civil Service, and Rimsky-Korsakov, a naval officer. With their encouragement, he took to being a 'week-end' composer but not surprisingly it took him rather a long time to complete anything. His first symphony took five years; his second, seven and his opera *Prince Igor*, begun in 1869, was still unfinished when he died – eighteen years later.

1834

Her Serene Highness Grace Kelly was born in Philadelphia, daughter of a millionaire Olympic sculls champion. While making Hitchcock's *To Catch a Thief* on the French Riviera, she met Prince Rainier of Monaco and amidst storms of protest, announced her intention of giving up her career to marry him. Her co-star Cary Grant remained unruffled. 'After all,' he said, 'what could she have become? Only an older actress, not a better one.'

1929

Nessie had her first photo taken. As Mr Hugh Gray was walking along the shore of Loch Ness, the calm water erupted and a large body appeared in a cloud of spray. Mr Gray hastily snapped five photographs before the thing disappeared but when the film was developed, four were blank. However, the remaining one contained an image of 'an object of considerable dimensions'. Technicians confirmed the photo hadn't been tampered with but zoologists dismissed it as a bottle-nosed whale or even a rotting tree trunk!

1933

Today's the day...

Daredevil diver Sam Patch died, having first come to fame when the Chasm Bridge was built. The then unknown twenty-year-old cotton spinner from Rhode Island suddenly announced he was going to jump from the mighty structure as soon as it was finished, and dive 90ft into the Passaic River below. Police tried to stop him but he fooled them by jumping from a nearby precipice first, and went back later to dive from the bridge. Exhilarated by his success, he began to make a habit of jumping off various cliffs, bridges and high points, occasionally accompanied by a bear he'd found on his travels. After diving from Goat Island, half the height of Niagara, he set his sights on the dangerous Genesee Falls. The date was fixed for the unpropitious Friday the 13th, and crowds of sightseers lined the banks of the river to watch Sam take his dive. After his usual little speech, he jumped and fell 125ft to the river below, but he hit the water awkwardly and disappeared without trace. Four months later his mangled body was found at the mouth of the river – frozen inside an icefloe.   *1829*

Consumptive Scottish writer Robert Louis Stevenson was born in Edinburgh, the son of a lighthouse builder. His father was horrified

November 13

at the thought of him becoming a writer so he became a law student and took to frequenting low haunts, and consorting with prostitutes. Since childhood he'd been obsessed with the character of Deacon Brodie, an eminently respectable citizen who nightly took to the streets to cheat and steal, and in 1886 he used him as the basis for his study of 'man's double being' – *The Strange Case of Dr Jekyll and Mr Hyde*. He wrote the whole book, and rewrote it totally, in only six days. Despite his interest in the dark side of life, he was extremely fond of children, wrote *Treasure Island* to amuse his stepson and once gave his birthday away with all its 'rights and privileges' to little Annie H. Ide – saying that should she violate the conditions, the birthday would revert to the President. When Annie died, aged sixty-eight, President Truman wistfully enquired whether he might have it, but the family politely declined.   *1850*

Churchill was struck by an enemy missile. The man who emerged unscathed from wars in India, France, Cuba, South Africa, the Sudan and the Netherlands, finally met his match in the House of Commons. During a heated debate on the Home Rule Bill, Ulster MP Ronald McNeill flung a copy of the *Orders of the House* at him and gashed his forehead. The Speaker later presented the book to Winston who kept it as a reminder of the only time he'd been 'wounded in action'.   *1912*

The bra was patented in America by heiress Mary Phelps Jacob, who'd made her prototype from two handkerchiefs, and registered the uplifting concept under the apt name of Caresse Crosby. Earlier claims for its invention date back to primitive 'bust improvers' in the England of the 1900s, and of course to the legendary Otto Titzling, a claim that's almost certainly a hoax. Mary took the idea to her bosom, insisted it was fit for 'vigorous exercise' and said of her ancestor the pioneering steamboat man Robert Fulton, 'I believe my ardour for invention springs from his loins.'   *1914*

T.D.—33   641

Today's the day...

Prince Charles was born on a gloomy Sunday evening at
Buckingham Palace. He splits his income from the Duchy of
Cornwall with the Government; owns the site of Dartmoor Prison,
and a 550 acre farm. A trim eleven stone, he dresses conservatively,
has five grey suits exactly alike and presents a slight problem to his
tailor, as his right shoulder is out of alignment from playing too much
polo. Dubbed 'the Clown Prince' by the international press corps, his
jolly exploits get maximum publicity. He amused President Nixon
for over an hour in the Oval Office at the White House – an interview
that's now presumably on tape – and when he danced with topless
beauties in a fertility rite in Fiji, he quipped, 'It certainly beats the
Changing of the Guard.' He's inevitably plagued by photographers,
and when he was in the Navy, his ship was boarded by a small army of
them in search of some royal snap-shots. They were taken to see the
duty officer, a young lieutenant, who said he wasn't going to incur the
Prince's wrath by disturbing him, and anyway he was 'pompous, not
very bright and probably wouldn't agree to meet them'. Disgruntled,
the pressmen disembarked not realising they'd been had. The young
lieutenant was none other than HRH himself!   *1948*

Princess Anne married Captain Mark Phillips amid great
celebrations on her big brother's birthday. The same afternoon the
'Wedding Handicap Chase' at Wolverhampton was won by a horse
called 'Royal Mark'.   *1973*

Witch-hunting Senator Joe McCarthy was born in Wisconsin. As
an officer in the wartime marines he had an undistinguished career,
but invented a stunning record for himself as 'Tail Gunner Joe'
complete with thirty flying missions and a war wound. Once a Senator
he started 'the fight against Communism' to distract attention from
his tax evasions and dubious legal practices. For openers, he announced

to a startled women's club in West Virginia that there were 205 communists in the State Department. They were astonished and so was the State Department who wired McCarthy for the names. He promptly changed the number to fifty-seven, then increased it to eighty-one. His lying, erratic behaviour has often been attributed to his consumption of alcohol but it's recently been alleged he was a morphine addict too, and obtained regular supplies with the blessing of the Narcotics Department who feared a scandal. *1908*

Miserly scholar Jacky Barrett, Vice-Provost of Trinity, died leaving £80,000. Obsessively mean, his rooms in the college were never cleaned and never heated, and students once had to revive him with brandy when they found him nearly frozen to death. A glutton, he dined in the Common Room where the food was free, and only ever bought bread and milk for breakfast. When his maid Catty was fetching the milk one day, she fell and broke her leg. Uncharacteristically, Barrett went to visit her in hospital – his first question was, 'Where's the jug?', his second, 'Where's my change?' *1821*

Crafty Old Thomas Parr died aged 152, after being brought to London to see King Charles I. Thomas first got married when he was eighty, committed penance for adultery when he was 105 and married again at 120 after his first wife died. After three leases of land had expired, Parr persuaded his landlord to grant him another lease for the duration of his life. He reluctantly agreed but on hearing that Old Parr had gone blind, sent his son to reclaim the property. As soon as he was told who was approaching the house, Parr told his wife to put a pin by his right foot. As soon as the lad started arguing about the lease, Parr pretended to spot the pin, bent down and picked it up. The boy went scurrying back to his father and told him that Old Parr's sight had been miraculously restored. *1635*

Today's the day...

The 'English Samson' William Joyce appeared before King William III. As his performance he lifted a solid piece of lead, weighing over a ton; and roped to an 'extraordinary strong horse' kept it at a standstill even when it was whipped. His Majesty was 'mightily well pleased' but the day before, Joyce had surpassed all these feats by uprooting a tree at Hampstead. Its trunk was 1½ yds round. *1699*

The last of the Manchu Emperors Pu Yi came to power, at the grand old age of 2 yrs 9 mnths. Everywhere he went he was followed by a band of servants carrying clothes, food, medicines and umbrellas – and in his early days, a collection of chamber pots. He was the only person entitled to wear the Imperial Yellow; his clothes and hats were lined with it and his apartments decorated in it. Not surprisingly, he remembered his childhood in 'a yellow mist'. After the Republican government took over, he stayed on at the Imperial Palace until 1924, got married when he was sixteen and became known as 'Henry Pu Yi'. It's believed he worked as a clerk in one of Mao Tse Tung's ministries and the 'Lord of Ten Thousand Years' ended up as an odd-job man at the Botanical Gardens in Peking. *1908*

November 15

'Motherly and auspicious' Tzu Hsi died after ruling China in all
but name for over fifty years. The beautiful daughter of a noble
Manchu family, she was disgusted at being selected as only a third-
class concubine for the debauched Emperor Hsien Feng. She got her
own back by studying the 'arts of love' with the Chief Eunuch An
Te-Hai and soon became the power behind the throne. On her first
trip to the Imperial boudoir she stayed for three nights and two days.
The Emperor had to be treated for exhaustion and Tzu Hsi quickly
consolidated her position by becoming pregnant and presenting him
with his longed-for male heir. When the Emperor died, she
confounded her enemies by seizing the omnipotent Imperial Seal and
thereafter she ruthlessly plotted and murdered anyone who got in her
way. She hastened her son along the debauched road to his death, and
devised some particularly nasty ends for her enemies, ordering one
unfortunate to be sliced 'into a thousand strips' while he was still alive.
Intolerant of foreigners, she called the British 'the long nosed hairy
ones', and the Japanese 'the dwarfs from the eastern islands'! On her
death-bed an official implored, 'Let Old Buddha please quiet herself
and recover from her illness.' Candidly she replied, 'No I have sinned
enough. I will die.'   *1908*

Pitman's shorthand manual was published under the off-putting
title *Stenographic Sound-hand*. It wasn't the first shorthand system,
however, since as early as 63BC a Roman – Marcus Tullius Tiro –
had devised a set of 'notqe' to record the speeches in the Senate, and
Dr Timothy Bright had dedicated a shorthand manual to Queen
Elizabeth I in 1588. But Isaac Pitman's was the first to use sound
symbols and 'grammalogues' for words in common use. He set up a
correspondence course to teach it by post and although it eventually
became standard in the UK, it took some time. As late as 1882
newspaper, court and Parliamentary reporters were still using as many
as thirteen different systems.   *1837*

Today's the day...

The Emperor 'made from mud and blood' – Tiberius – was born. He grew up to be hugely strong, and could poke his finger through an apple. He drank heavily and indulged in bizarre sexual practices. He often killed his 'lovers' when he'd done with them, and once broke the legs of two priests who complained when he sexually assaulted them. The long life of the 'Old he-goat' became one long chain of cruelties, typified by a singular story. He was visiting a prison when a terribly tortured captive begged to be put out of his misery. Tiberius smiled and said 'No. We are not friends again, yet.'   *42 BC*

A woman fought at the Battle of Washington Heights, near New York. She was called Margaret Corbin and had joined her husband John when he went to the Revolutionary War with the Pennsylvania Artillery. At the height of the battle, John was killed and Margaret took his place at the cannon, and fought on until she was badly wounded. She was captured but, because of her sex, allowed to go free. She was given a grant, a soldier's half-pay for life, a new suit of clothes, and a place in history as the first woman to fight for the US in a battle, the first to be wounded and the first to be pensioned off.   *1776*

November 16

Pizarro captured the Inca Atahualpa in the one-sided battle of Caxamarco. The Spanish adventurer had advanced deep into the Inca's golden kingdom, as native troops, who had never seen a horse, fell back before their invaders, believing them to be at least centaurs, and probably Gods. Pizarro sent his brother and one Hernando de Soto to request an interview with Atahualpa, a civilised and intelligent man, who dearly expected civilised behaviour from his European visitors. They met this evening in the great square of Caxamarco and called upon the Inca to become a Christian and do homage to the Emperor Charles V. Not unreasonably, Atahualpa refused, and the trap – for it was hardly a battle – was sprung. Though the Inca had between 3,000 and 4,000 men, they were not armed for a fight, and Pizarro's 177 Spaniards, bristling musket and sword, massacred them in their hundreds. The 'battle' which brought centuries of Inca rule crashing in ruins had lasted just thirty minutes.   *1532*

East Anglian fisherfolk were horrified when Alan Castleton was refused permission to appeal to the House of Lords over the ancient and venerated right to dredge mussels off the coast of Norfolk. It was hardly surprising, since the presiding Justice was Lord Salmon, and the opposing counsel none other than Mr Michael Fysh!   *1978*

Napoleon applied for a US patent in New York. He was Napoleon S. Guerin and he'd designed the first cork-filled life-jacket. Though widely used, it didn't gain Federal approval for a frustrating thirty-six years, when after the sinking of the SS *San Francisco*, this ignored invention proved its worth by saving 287 lives.   *1841*

Clean-living German composer Paul Hindemith was born. He was once sued by a gas company for loss of business, because the heroine of his opera *Neus Vom Tage* sang the praises of taking a bath in water heated by electricity!   *1895*

Today's the day...

Field Marshal Viscount Montgomery was born the son of an
Anglo-Irish vicar in the poor parish of Kennington, South London.
Christened Bernard Law, he was only two years old when his father
was made Bishop of Tasmania and the family with all five children
moved to Hobart. In World War I, he was badly wounded, narrowly
avoided being left for dead and was awarded the DSO for gallantry.
When he was nearing forty, he decided to get married and planned his
wooing like a military operation. He went to Switzerland where he
thought he'd find plenty of eligible English women, and came back
with Elizabeth Carver, a young and artistic widow with two children.
They were idyllically happy for a brief ten years, when Elizabeth died
tragically, of blood poisoning. Montgomery threw himself into his
army life and at the outbreak of World War II, he was made a Major
General. As an officer, he was a stickler for discipline and a fanatic
about physical fitness. He didn't eat meat, fish or eggs; sent overweight
officers on cross-country runs, and told Eisenhower to put his cigarette
out. He once boasted to Churchill, 'I do not smoke or drink, and I am
one hundred per cent fit.' But for once he was outdone when the obese,
cigar-puffing Minister replied, 'I smoke and drink, and I am two
hundred per cent fit!'   *1887*

The Suez Canal was finally opened, thanks mainly to the efforts of
one man, Ferdinand de Lesseps, who'd weathered a storm of criticism
to get the job done. The very idea threw Europe into turmoil – some
said it interfered with the laws of nature, and the British, worried
about strategic links with the Empire in India, brought great pressure
to bear to stop the project altogether. In exasperation, de Lesseps
appealed to Napoleon III to arbitrate, and work resumed in earnest in
1864. Five years later the opening ceremony was performed, and a
great flotilla of ships carrying the Empress Eugénie and representatives
of most of the royal houses of Europe set off down the canal.
Unfortunately, the night before, an Egyptian frigate had run aground

November 17

and blocked the canal completely. An army of men worked frantically to move the wreckage, and the great waterway was finally cleared, just minutes before the ceremonial fleet hove into sight.   *1869*

Hard-drinking womaniser Ernst Udet committed suicide. Between the wars Udet became a stunt pilot, skimming over glaciers and through narrow Alpine valleys. He performed the impossible by landing on the Mont Blanc glacier and made an amazing flight between moving icebergs for the film *SOS Iceberg*. He used his experience in stunt-flying to design his brainchild, the deadly accurate Stuka dive-bomber, even adding a terrifying siren which he named the 'Trumpet of Jericho'. Although a General in the Luftwaffe, his flamboyant ways didn't please the Nazi hierarchy and he frequently clashed with the equally flamboyant Goering. When the Luftwaffe was shattered in the Battle of Britain, Udet was made a scapegoat and personally reprimanded by Hitler after Rudolf Hess flew to Scotland on his abortive peace mission. Seeing his future crumbling, the general took himself off to his exotic apartment and shot himself with a Mexican revolver. The propaganda machine promptly went into action. Hitler arranged a magnificent State funeral, Goering gave a moving oration and an official statement declared that Udet met his death 'while testing a new weapon in the fulfilment of his duty'.   *1941*

The remains of Alexander T. Stewart were stolen from St Mark's-in-the-Bouwerie, New York. The family received a ransom demand for a staggering $200,000 from a certain Harry G. Romaine, but after many secret meetings it was reduced to $20,000, whereupon a sack of bones was handed over, and the family paid up. They reburied the pricey remains in the basement of the Garden City Cathedral on Long Island, surrounded by a complex system of alarms. But the mysterious bone-snatcher, Harry G. Romaine was never caught.   *1876*

Today's the day...

The talking Mickey Mouse was officially born. Conceived in the previous year, legend has it that Disney got the idea for his first and greatest superstar from the mice playing in his studio wastebasket. He was going to call the critter Mortimer, but his wife suggested Mickey and Mickey it became. Disney himself did the original voice-track, and since then the mighty Mouse has appeared in over a hundred films. He's won an Oscar, been awarded a medal by the League of Nations, and received more fan mail than any other star, man or mouse. On his fiftieth anniversary in 1978, a surprisingly youthful Mickey did a whistle-stop tour on the railroad from California to 'the Big Apple'. He gave a performance at the White House for the Carters; was given a party at the Museum of Modern Art in New York, and was churlishly refused permission to board a bus in Nottinghamshire, England. A spokesman for the bus company, naturally horrified, told shocked press men, 'We are looking into the matter!'   *1928*

Louis XIV had a delicate operation for the painful condition of an anal fistula. The lucky surgeon was Monsieur Felix, who'd spent months practising on less exalted sufferers of the same complaint. Assisted by two physicians, two assistant surgeons, the King's confessor and four apothecaries, Felix wielded the knife. Fortunately for him the operation was a success. He was given a title, an estate and 300,000 *livres*. Surgery was put firmly on the road to respectability, and noble men all over France rushed to their local surgeons complaining of anal fistulae they didn't have, and begging to undergo 'the King's operation'.   *1686*

Pollster and academic Doctor George Gallup was born. The pioneer of public opinion gathering by random sample, he's often been associated with the advertising business, recently much to his chagrin. Stuck one night at Chicago Airport without any money, he was forced to spend the night on a bench, as his American Express

November 18

card had expired and he possessed no other credit cards, nor any means of identification. Shortly before, he'd appeared in an advertising campaign for American Express, featuring people whose names are well-known, but whose faces aren't. The copy line read, 'They may not recognise my face, but they recognise the American Express card.'

1901

Bad-tempered librettist William Schwenk Gilbert was born in the Strand, to a Hampshire family of 'yeomen grocers'. A lazy pupil at school, he was a lazy clerk in the Privy Council Office, writing songs all the while. He became a barrister, then a cartoonist – under his childhood nickname of 'Babs' – and finally achieved recognition as a playwright. He met Sullivan in 1870 – *Trial by Jury* followed, then *HMS Pinafore*, and their fame was ensured. Gilbert was an extremely vitriolic and touchy man, and as he got older, plagued by gout and arthritis, he gradually became intolerable. When one famous lady fell heavily on the stage, he didn't enquire after her health, but said, 'Very good. Very good. I always knew you'd make an impression on the stage one day.'

1836

Today's the day...

A healthy hat-frame was patented, which was designed to prevent headaches caused by weighty head-gear. It rested on the shoulders and allowed the wearer's head to move independently of the hat. The ultimate idea was to wear a hat big enough 'to avoid the use of a parasol or umbrella'.

1912

German composer Franz Schubert died at the age of thirty-one probably from abdominal typhoid. He'd become ill at the end of October after eating fish in a local tavern and although he claimed he'd been poisoned, typhoid was common in the unhygienic Vienna of the 1820s. Since the death of Beethoven nineteen months earlier, he'd seemed obsessed with death. After Beethoven's funeral he'd drunk a toast 'To him who will be next', and his last songs, the *Winterreise* disturbed his friends by their morbid beauty. Schubert did nothing to allay their fears by telling them, 'You hear the rustling of the wings of an angel calling me home.' After his death, great stacks of manuscripts were cleared from his room and one bundle of possible masterpieces was sold as wastepaper for eight shillings.

1828

Queen Mary's night out was censored. On a rare trip to the cinema the Queen was to view *The Wicked Lady*, a Restoration drama, but two of her ladies-in-waiting went along first and found some of the language decidedly unsuitable. They complained, but it was too late to delete anything. Propriety, however, was maintained for while Queen Mary was watching, the soundtrack was turned down so low during the offending passages, it was virtually inaudible!

1945

President Lincoln made his most famous speech on the battlefield of Gettysburg, where 7,000 Union and Confederate soldiers had been killed some four months earlier. Senator Edward Everett was the principal speaker at this ceremony and his speech lasted a full two hours. The President followed with a brief address of only three minutes. Despite the legend Lincoln didn't write his speech on an envelope on the train but had worked on it for nearly two weeks and re-written it five times. In it, he said, 'The world will little note, nor long remember what we say here.' Little did he know that his speech would become part of the American heritage, and his closing words the watchwords for democracy everywhere – 'that government of the people, by the people, for the people, shall not perish from the earth'.

1863

The last of the backwood's presidents James Abram Garfield was born in a log cabin in Ohio. Distinguished for bravery in the Battle of Chuckamanga during the Civil War, he entered Congress and after an unbroken seventeen years was nominated for the Presidency. Dubious of the 'evil effects of presidential fever', he nevertheless won the 1880 election by a narrow margin. In his first weeks as President he received a number of threatening letters but dismissed them noting, 'Assassination can no more be guarded against than death by lightning, and it is best not to worry about either.' Six months later he was dead – from an assassin's bullet.

1831

'The Battle Hymn of the Republic' wrote itself, according to Julia Ward Howe who committed it to paper. Some Union soldiers had adopted 'John Brown's Body' as their marching song using the tune of an old southern hymn 'On Canaan's Happy Shore', and Mrs Howe had heard them singing this on the road to Washington. Although she'd always had difficulty writing poetry, she quickly wrote down the five verses, changed only a few words when she re-read it and always insisted, 'I was just an instrument, it really wrote itself'. It was published in *Atlantic Monthly* in February 1862, but some months later a released prisoner, Chaplain Charles McCabe, sang it before President Lincoln and it became the most famous anthem not only of the Civil War, but of America. She was paid $4 for it.

1861

Today's the day...

Princess Elizabeth married Prince Philip in Westminster Abbey, despite her father's earlier objections on the grounds of her youth. She was twenty-one; he was twenty-six – an exile of the Greek Royal House. They were third cousins and both directly descended from Queen Victoria. Five kings were in attendance, and the whole congregation rose spontaneously to honour the arrival of the grand old man, Winston Churchill. Among the princely presents was a fabulous ninety-six ruby necklace from Burma; a filly from the Aga Khan; a refrigerator from the WVS; a wastepaper basket from her dresser; a piece of crocheted lace made by Gandhi himself and an amazing 32,000 food parcels sent from America, and eventually distributed to needy widows. Her bouquet was laid on the Tomb of the Unknown Warrior, and she and Philip left by open landau for Waterloo Station. In the landau with the royal couple was a special guest. It was Crackers, her pet corgi, sitting snugly in a nest of hot-water bottles.   *1947*

The great English lights mystery was solved. For six months, the flashing road lights outside the Longton Road School in Stone, Staffordshire, had refused to work. Now after careful analysis and shrewd detective work, intrepid officials discovered why. They'd never been switched on!   *1977*

Beethoven's only opera *Fidelio* was first performed in Vienna. He was distinctly unhappy about it. The name had been changed from *Leonore* against his wishes; he'd rewritten one duet eighteen times; composed four different overtures and practised the songs on his friends in his 'detestable voice'. The night was a disaster. Napoleon had captured the city a few days before and the cream of society had fled. It was below zero, and only a few French officers turned up. According to one critic: 'It has no melodic ideas and not a trace of originality – just endless repetitions and a perpetual hubbub in the orchestra.'   *1805*

November 20

A demonstrator was killed in Trafalgar Square. The young radical solicitor, Alfred Linnel, was ridden down by a mounted policeman. He was given a public funeral with his coffin draped in socialist flags. Said MP Cunningham Graham, 'It was bad taste of the people of London to parade their insolent starvation in the rich and trading portions of the town. They should have starved in their garretts, as no doubt members of Her Majesty's Government and most of the upper classes would have wished them to.' *1887*

A marathon lie on a bed of nails began in Sydney, Australia. Clad in the requisite turban and loin-cloth, Zjane Azzar settled down on a mattress of 6in spikes, only 2in apart. Though at one point his pulse dropped to a dangerous level, he lasted 25hrs 9mins, keeping himself fresh with cigarettes, ice cream and hamburgers. When he got up he said, 'My body has been dead for fourteen hours,' and fainted. The record now stands at over sixty-five hours, and though there seems little point in it, one famous fakir claims to have lasted 111 days. *1969*

Today's the day...

One of Cole Porter's biggest hit musicals opened at the Alvin Theatre on Broadway. It was conceived by Vinton Freedley, who was out fishing in the Pacific to escape his creditors after a previous Broadway disaster. All the stars, librettists, and Mr Porter himself had been signed up before a word was written. The story was put together by four writers including P. G. Wodehouse, and everything was so rushed that when rehearsals began, only part of the first act had been finished. The source of no less than five hit songs – a personal record for Porter – it included 'You're the Tops' and 'I Get a Kick Out of You', which was later banned for daring to mention drugs. Originally called *Hard to Get*, the name of the musical was changed to *Bon Voyage*. Nobody could really decide what to call it, and finally because of all the last minute changes, it was dubbed *Anything Goes*. *1934*

An amorous art lover appeared in court. She was Ruth Olive Van Herpen and she was accused of damaging a painting by American Jo Bear, which was on loan to the Oxford Museum of Modern Art from a New York Gallery. The damage, which cost hundreds of pounds to restore, was caused by a kiss which implanted nasty lipstick stains on the canvas. After psychiatric and social reports, Mrs Van Herpen was conditionally discharged. 'I only kissed it to cheer it up,' she said, 'It looked so cold.' *1977*

The witch of Wall Street Hetty Green was born to a wealthy Quaker family. The inheritor of millions, she was a true artist among misers. She lived only in cheap boarding houses, and a broken-down flat; chewed one onion a day for sustenance, and when relations came to dinner she ate nothing but boiled eggs and sandwiches from a paper bag. She had only the bottoms of her petticoats washed to save on laundry bills, and though she controlled whole railroads, she refused to issue free passes to the workmen. When her son got in debt she wired him 'Not a cent', and when he got an infection in his knee, she refused to pay the doctor's bills and through lack of treatment, he later lost a leg. She would travel about in a carriage, which had previously been used as a chicken coop, and liked to sit alone, cross-legged on the floor of the Chemical National Bank to transact her business. She was terrified of being murdered for her money, thought everyone was trying to poison her, and grew so paranoic that she would hide in doorways to make sure no one was following her. In case anyone should want to follow in her footsteps, she gave this advice on making money: 'Never speculate on Wall Street; never maintain an office; eat slowly; don't stay up at night; don't drink iced water and keep out of draughts.'   *1834*

The English public hangman Edward Dennis died. He had reigned fifteen years and been immortalised in Dickens' *Barnaby Rudge* as one of the ringleaders of the attack on Newgate Prison, who ended up on his own gallows. The truth, however, is stranger than the fiction. He was walking home when he saw the mob looting a Catholic chandler's. He claimed that he was forced to join them – 'My will was innocent,' he told the judge, 'but my body compelled.' He was nevertheless sentenced to hang and incredibly his last wish was that the authorities should appoint his son as hangman. He was kept in a separate cell lest his fellow rioters should tear him to pieces – but he was reprieved at the last minute and had the dubious honour of hanging them all himself.   *1786*

North Carolina was admitted to the Union. Among its quainter attractions is an event held annually at Spivey's Corner – 'The National Hollerin' Contest'. It originated in the odd custom that farmers had of yodelling their hellos to each other early in the morning, and is now considered something of an art. It's sponsored by the local fire department, and has made its home town the hollerin' capital of the world.   *1789*

Today's the day...

Blackbeard, the scourge of the Spanish Main was killed. His real name was Edward Teach and he was born in Bristol. He was a burly 6ft 4in, had 'flashing eyes' and a 'fearsome gaze'. He had a harem of fourteen wives, and his long black beard was twisted into rat's tails, which when courting he decorated with silk ribbon. At dinner with his officers, he would blow out the candles and fire a brace of pistols under the table, saying, 'If I don't shoot some of my crew occasionally, they'll forget who I am.' When fighting, this 'fury from hell' would stick slow-burning tapers under his three-cornered hat so his eyes glowed, and smoke seemed to pour from his ears. £100 was offered for him dead or alive, and when Lieutenant Maynard cornered his boat in shallow waters, a bloody fight was inevitable. They fired pistols at each other and fought with sword and cutlass. Then one of Maynard's men slashed Blackbeard's neck from behind. He fell, but fought off a dozen men. Maynard shot him repeatedly and when he'd sustained twenty-five savage wounds, he died. They flew his famous black beard from the bowsprit. *1718*

November 22

John F. Kennedy was shot in Dallas, Texas at 12.30 pm in an open-
top Lincoln Continental travelling at 11 mph. According to the
Warren Report, which is much contested, the first bullet passing
through Kennedy somehow altered course and wounded Texas
Governor John Connally. A second bullet was fired and missed. The
third blew a hole in the President's head. Mrs Kennedy held onto her
husband all through the 'silent terrible ride' four miles to the Parkland
Memorial Hospital, and before they took him away she slipped her
wedding ring onto his finger. He died officially at 1 pm. Secret
Service men found three pieces of the President's skull in Elm Street
where he'd been shot and, according to some reports, the hole gouged
by the bullet was 5in across. His brain was removed in the autopsy
and preserved. He was buried without it and, incredibly, it was lost.
Though it's not widely known, J.F.K. was living on borrowed time.
He had a sort of slow-motion leukaemia, took cortisone and had
a drug pellet embedded in his thigh. It's also claimed he had
Addison's Disease which, though eventually crippling, has the
odd side-effect of keeping the sufferer young looking. He once told
reporters, 'I'll probably last until I'm forty-five' – he was forty-six
when he died. Whether or not Lee Harvey Oswald was the sole
assassin is still in serious doubt. His mother Marguerite Oswald
certainly believes he's innocent and, for reasons best known to herself,
claims he's an unsung hero. On the morning of the assassination
Kennedy had said, 'If anybody really wanted to kill the
President . . . all one had to do was to get into a high building some
day, with a telescopic rifle, and there'd be nothing anybody could
do.'
1963

English physician John Lettsom was born. He was a brilliant
doctor, despite his favourite self-denigrating epigram: 'When people's
ill, they come to I,/I physics, bleeds and sweats 'em;/Sometimes they
live, sometimes they die./What's that to I? I lets 'em.'
1744

Today's the day...

Miming Harpo Marx was born. The world's most famous mute, he could of course speak, but swore never to do so again on the stage, when critics complained they couldn't hear his tiny voice. He made his amateur *début* as a schoolboy, when he visited his neighbour's house in the guise of a prostitute touting for business, and was so convincing that the man was delighted and his womenfolk fled. He claimed among other things, that he'd 'played piano in a whore-house', 'sat on the floor with Garbo' and 'horsed around with the Prince of Wales'. He liked to shock guests by greeting them in the nude, and could sleep anywhere including the dentist's chair. *1893*

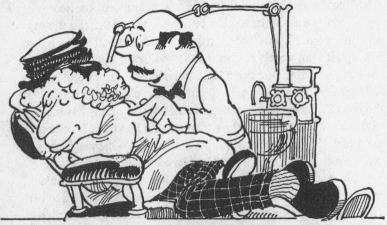

American doctor Hawley H. Crippen was hanged in London for the murder of his wife Cora, an aspiring music-hall artiste who preferred to be known as Belle Elmore and whose real name was, in fact, Kunigunde Mackamotzi. In February 1910, friends became suspicious when she disappeared. Crippen was seen with a young woman sporting his wife's jewellery, and when he placed a notice in *The Era* announcing Cora's death in California, the police were called in. Crippen was questioned and his house at Hilltop Crescent was searched, but nothing was found. Chief Inspector Drew was just about to abandon the case, when he heard that Crippen had disappeared with his mistress, the dowdy little typist Ethel le Neve. The house was searched again and what remained of Cora was found. An international police hunt drew a blank until the eagle-eyed Captain Kendall, master of the SS *Montrose* bound for Quebec, noticed a rather strange 'father and son' on board. The 'son' wore boy's clothes all right, but there was nothing 'filial' about the way 'he' gazed into his father's eyes! The Captain radioed Drew, who caught a faster ship to Quebec and was waiting when the culprits arrived. A four-day trial at the Old Bailey found Crippen guilty, but much to his relief, cleared le Neve of involvement. In his farewell letter from Pentonville Prison he wrote, 'My last prayer will be that God may protect her and keep her safe from harm, and allow her to join me in eternity.' He was buried with her photograph and letters. Fifty-seven years later, when Ethel died as plain Mrs Smith in Dulwich Hospital, her last request was to be buried with a locket – containing a picture of Hawley Harvey Crippen.   *1910*

The peace of the bar-room was shattered when the first jukebox was installed in the Palais Royal Saloon, in San Francisco. It was powered by an Edison phonograph, had four 'listening tubes' and cost a-nickel-a-go. It was called a 'juke-organ' from a slang word with a very apt meaning. A 'juke' was in fact a brothel, or more accurately 'a disorderly house'.   *1889*

An amazing feat of endurance began when the SS *Ben Lomond* was torpedoed and sunk in the South Atlantic. The sole survivor was the diminutive steward Poon Lim who, after two hours in the water, managed to find a life raft in which he survived for a record 133 days. With only sixty days of rations, he had to fish for food with a hook fashioned from a spring in the raft's flashlight, and claimed his amazing resilience stemmed from eating goat's meat as a child.   *1942*

Today's the day...

The storm over evolution broke when Charles Darwin published his *Origin of Species*. Though he didn't see why it should 'shock the religious feelings of anyone', people nevertheless raced to abuse him, led by Bishop 'Soapy Sam' Wilberforce and the Church in full cry. The irony was that while Darwin's theory was the most far-reaching to date, it was by no means the first of its kind. Lamarck, Lyell, Wallace and Malthus had all in their different ways broached the subject, and escaped relatively unscathed.   *1859*

'The French Tiger' Clemenceau died more than a decade after he'd led his country to victory in World War I. He'd often slept fully clothed, after first changing into an unstarched shirt and replacing his shoes with slippers. During his fatal illness the doctors insisted he undressed, but despite this indignity, he kept his fighting spirit to the last. His final wish was with characteristic belligerence, that he be buried standing, facing towards Germany.   *1929*

Noël Coward's biggest flop was booed off the stage on its opening night in London. It was called *Sirocco* and Ivor Novello and Frances Dobie acted the star parts so badly that the audience fell about laughing. Somebody shouted, 'Give the old cow a chance' and Miss Dobie paused in mid-speech to thank him for his gentlemanly interjection. The audience split into two camps, one cheering and one booing. When the curtain came down Coward lived up to his name by fleeing across the stage instead of making a speech, and the leading lady inexplicably cooed, 'Ladies and Gentlemen this is the happiest night of my life.'   *1928*

The first public flush-toilets for dogs were installed at specially selected sites in the streets of Paris. As if this were not luxury enough, the concrete bowls were fitted with tall posts for dogs who preferred more traditional methods.   *1978*

Boy King Louis XIII married Anne of Austria. They were only fourteen at the time, and the youthful French ruler was so nervous, his mother had to take him to his wife's bedroom. He arrived wearing his furry slippers, and his mother was so anxious to finalise the match that she left him to consummate his marriage in front of two loyal nurses who later claimed positive results. Not surprisingly, the little monarch didn't sleep with his wife again for four years and was just three years short of his silver wedding before he sired a child.   *1615*

The resurrection of a rapist occurred when seventeen-year-old William Duell was hanged on 'The Tyburn Tree'. The boy's youth and the fact that he was a simpleton, didn't sway his judges, but gained him the sympathy of the crowd. His body swung for 20 mins and was then removed for dissection. A lackey was 'washing him to be cut up' when, miraculously, he came back to life and after 2 hrs was completely restored. The surgeons notified the sheriffs who by law had to hang him again the same day. By this time, however, a huge mob had gathered, which kept the officers at bay. At the stroke of midnight, they silently dispersed and William Duell was saved.   *1749*

Today's the day...

Whistler's famous court case was heard. The critic and scholar
John Ruskin had written some rather nasty and somewhat fatuous
remarks about the artist's work, and Whistler had over-reacted a
little by bringing a libel action. What Ruskin had actually accused
Whistler of were things like 'Cockney impudence', selling 'unfinished'
pictures and asking 'two hundred guineas for flinging a pot of paint
in the public's face'. He clearly didn't like impressionistic painting,
and so the question that ended up being discussed was the old
chestnut of 'What is art?' No clear decision was reached, though
Ruskin said he'd never write a critique again if he lost. He did. He
resigned his chair at Oxford and retired from public life. Whistler was
awarded one farthing damages, and had to move out of his house and
hock his most treasured possessions to cover the costs.   *1878*

The much-loved Pope John XXIII was born in Sotto il Monte in
Northern Italy, the fourth son of a family of fourteen. Dogged by
illness through much of his childhood, the then Angelo Giuseppe
Roncalli was not a very conscientious pupil, and only got into the
local seminary by the skin of his teeth. Once ordained, however, he
had a brilliant career. He was made a Bishop, became Apostolic Vicar
to Bulgaria and Papal Nuncio in France. His travels meant he was into
his seventies before he was given a diocese and made Patriarch of
Venice. He became Pope in 1958 and in his own unique way was quite
a revolutionary. He was eminently approachable, forbade people to
kneel when they came to see him and brought a touch of humour to
the Holy See. Somewhat overweight, he claimed he was always asking
God to have patience with fat men, and when an Anglican Bishop was
granted an audience, the following ensued. 'Are you a theologian?'
the Pope asked. 'No,' replied the nervous prelate. 'I'm so glad,' said
the Pope, 'neither am I.' When asked how many people worked
in the Vatican, his Holiness reflected a moment and said,
'About half!'   *1881*

November 25

The 'Bane of the Bar-room' Carrie Nation was born in Kentucky and grew to be a strapping six-footer. Spurred on by the death of an alcoholic husband, she became the kind of temperance campaigner who could drive a man to drink. Pausing only to pick up a preacher for a second husband, she became Chairman of the Women's Christian Temperance Union in Medicine Lodge, Kansas, and started talking to God. He apparently told her to smash up saloons, which is exactly what she did. In her first year, she took in twenty, and wreaked havoc wherever she went. Screaming 'Glory to God. Peace on earth and goodwill to men!', she broached casks, smashed bottles, tore down pin-ups and struck terror into hardened drinkers. The mayhem continued until her death in 1910, and little signs were posted by nervous bartenders all over the USA. They read, 'All Nations welcome – except Carrie.'   *1846*

The longest-running show in the world opened in London at the Ambassador's and celebrated its Silver Jubilee with the 10,391st performance at the St Martin's Theatre. It was – and is – of course, *The Mousetrap* by Agatha Christie – first written as a radio play for Queen Mary's eightieth birthday. Its producer Peter Saunders thought it would last 'a year – or longer' but by its twenty-fifth anniversary it had been seen by over four million people; 142 actors had played in it and it had outlived its creator by more than three years. Spare a thought however, for Romulus Films. They bought the film rights in 1956, with the condition that no film should be released until six months after the show had closed in London. They're still waiting.   *1952/1977*

Gilbert and Sullivan's Opera *Iolanthe* was premièred – three days after Sullivan had finished the overture. It was the first time electric lights had been used in the theatre as props – the fairies wore them on their heads, with the batteries concealed in their hair.   *1882*

665

Today's the day...

The World's Biggest Liar won his title at a public house in Cumbria. To gain his prize he told the tale of how he shot a tiger in Africa and brought it home on a bicycle.   *1978*

A geologist popped a toad in the hole. He was Dr William Buckland, an eminent scientist, and he was determined to test the hoary old stories of toads being found alive in the middle of rocks. He built an elaborate honeycomb of sandstone and limestone, slipped in various sizes of toad, and covered the edifice with soil. After a year all the toads in the sandstone were dead, along with some of the tinier ones in the limestone. This porous rock, however, let in enough air and water for the bigger ones to survive a while longer, but at the end of another year they were all dead too. Expertise with frogs and toads appears to have run in the Buckland family and William's son, the famous fish collector, Frank Buckland, was once called upon for advice by Queen Victoria. She had a plague of frogs at one of her houses which, believe it or not, was called 'Frogmore', and wondered what she should do. Buckland, nothing if not a practical man, said, 'Let out the ducks', and the ducks ate the amphibians for tea.   *1825*

November 26

The inventor of the motor car Karl Benz was born. He started making gas engines in 1880, fell in love with the idea of a belt-driven 'horseless carriage' and finally came up with the first petrol car – a three-wheeler capable of between 8½ and 10mph. The first model appeared in Mannheim in 1885, and the first saleable version was ready two years later. One day his wife 'stole' it from him and set out on a joy-ride. When a wire short-circuited, she had the presence of mind to insulate it with her garter! Mr Benz, however, had trouble with the speed limit, and so he invited a government minister to take a ride, having carefully arranged for the milkman to overtake him in a horse and cart. When the minister told him to go faster Benz said it was illegal. The minister insisted and the problem was solved.   *1844*

The San José lynchings took place in a park near the town's Santa Clara Jail. Two young men, Thomas Thurmond a garage worker and John Holmes a high-school student, had kidnapped Brooke Hart, the twenty-two-year-old son of a well-to-do store and hotel owner. The bumbling kidnappers hit their victim with a brick, weighted him down and threw him into the sea. He came to and started screaming, so they shot him and then demanded $40,000 ransom from his father. After a succession of threats, notes and phone calls, they were easily apprehended and ensconced in the jail. When the body was found, pandemonium broke loose. A mob of 15,000 stormed the jail and Governor Rolfe refused to send the embattled sheriff a detachment of state troopers. The two men were dragged from their cells and beaten. Thurmond, found hiding in the pipes above the cell's toilet, was hanged first, and Holmes, one of whose eyes had been put out, quickly followed. He pleaded with the mob to let him go. They just laughed and in the aftermath Governor Rolfe publicly expressed his approval. 'I'd like to parole all the kidnappers in San Quentin and Folsom,' he said, 'and give them to the fine, patriotic citizens of San José.'   *1933*

Today's the day...

A bride married a ghastly bridegroom in the parish of South Pool, England. She was Miss Dorothy Ford and she'd been engaged to William Street, the rector of the local church. Shortly before the big day, William had been killed in a riding accident and a broken-hearted Dorothy found herself at a funeral, instead of a wedding. Soon after, friends of the couple began to have terrible recurring nightmares. William would appear as a ghostly apparition, complaining that he could not rest in peace until he'd redeemed his pledge to Dorothy. Finally it was decided to exhume the poor soul and go through with it. The coffin was disinterred and placed in front of the altar, and Dorothy stood beside it and took her marriage vows. Neither she, nor anybody else, ever saw her husband again.   *1667*

A miniature robber was broken on the wheel in *La Place de Grève* in Paris. Poor Louis Dominique Cartouche had been born of lowly parents some fifty-nine years before. He grew up to be a tiny 4ft 6in, lived for a time with gypsies and stayed determinedly illiterate, putting his intelligence to use in other ways. In between love affairs with numerous ladies, all of whom were a good head taller than him, he put together the most notorious band of pick-pockets and cut-throats France has ever known. They held up coaches, stole ships' cargoes, burgled palaces and even pillaged the Louvre. Such a charming little devil was Louis that people went to great lengths to help him avoid capture, but he was eventually betrayed and ended up in the *Conciergerie* – chained, and beaten before being taken to the wheel. The execution was witnessed by a huge crowd, many of whom had reserved their places weeks before. When the deed was done his broken little body was appropriated by one of his executioner's assistants. The man took it home and exhibited it to ghouls for one sou a look.   *1721*

The English weather did its worst when the greatest storm on record raged around the British Isles. It had started in a small way the day before, but between the hours of midnight and 7am, it reached a hurricane crescendo. Over 8,000 people died in twenty-four hours; more than 800 churches, 100 houses and 2,000 chimneys were destroyed; 300 vessels were lost at sea or smashed at their moorings and 400 windmills fell down. In Kent, 17,000 trees were uprooted, in Gloucestershire 15,000 sheep were killed, and the Bishop of Bath and Wells was crushed in his bed by falling masonry. Perhaps the oddest casualty of all, however, was Henry Winstanley, the designer of the first Eddystone lighthouse. He was unfortunate enough to be visiting the building when the storm struck. When it subsided both he and the lighthouse had disappeared off the face of the earth.   *1703*

A famous Polish strong-man made an exhibition of himself in Washington, DC. Anxious to attract attention to his stage act in 'Keith's Theatre', the 225lb Siegmund Breitbart drove through the streets, chained to the drivers' seat of a waggon with a load of fifty people. The waggon had no shafts, and the team of horses was connected to it solely by a harness, which ended in a mouthpiece clenched between Breitbart's teeth.   *1923*

Today's the day...

The longest surviving heart transplant patient received his new lease of life today. The lucky man, Emmanuel Vitria of Marseilles, was given the heart of a twenty-year-old car crash victim, and recovered to enjoy a full life keeping fit by jogging, swimming and cycling. Sadly, the chief surgeon at his operation, Professor Jacques Henry, subsequently died. The cause of death was a heart attack. *1968*

Visionary and poet William Blake was born, the son of a London hosier. He first had religious visions as a child and his parents, although sceptical at first, realised he was exceptionally gifted and educated him at home. At the age of ten he went to Par's Drawing School in the Strand, acknowledged as the finest in the country. In his spare time he wrote poems and bought old prints with his pocket money, becoming known as the 'little connoisseur' at one sale room, where he was a regular customer. At the age of fourteen he was apprenticed to James Basire, engraver to the Society of Antiquaries, and learnt the craft he was later to use in publishing his beautifully illuminated poems. Jilted by the vivacious Polly Wood he retreated, hurt, to his friend William Boucher's house in Battersea. There he met Boucher's daughter Katharine and poured out the sad story to her. 'Do you pity me?' he asked when he'd finished. She said she did. 'Then I love you,' Blake declared and a year later they were married. She became his helpmate for life and when Blake was 'under his very fierce inspirations' the long-suffering Katharine would sit up night after night at his side 'motionless and silent . . . without moving hand or foot'. *1757*

Hangman Albert Pierrepoint got a nasty shock for he'd met the murderer he was about to hang before. In fact he'd even sung duets with him, because James Henry Corbitt was a Saturday night regular at Pierrepoint's pub in Hollinwood, which was aptly called 'Help the Poor Struggler'. Corbitt was usually accompanied by a woman whom everyone took to be his wife, but when her body was

670

found strangled in a hotel room with 'whore' written on her forehead in indelible pencil, she was discovered to be his mistress. Although he'd read about the murder, Pierrepoint never connected the two until he came face to face with his victim at Strangeways Prison. Corbitt had always greeted him, 'Hallo Tosh', to which he'd always replied, 'Hallo Tish, how are you?' One last time they greeted each other in the death cell, in the usual way, and then set off for the scaffold.

1950

Commander Richard Byrd flew over the South Pole in a Ford Trimotor monoplane. When he was twelve he'd written in his diary that he'd decided to be the first man at the North Pole and to toughen himself up insisted on only wearing light underwear and no overcoat. When he broke a bone in his foot, smashed his ankle and went lame, it looked as though his ambition was doomed. He was retired from his chosen career in the Navy but, undeterred, decided to take up flying. His lessons were fraught to say the least; he crashed-landed twice and once hit another plane head-on. Not easily discouraged he went ahead and became a qualified pilot. Then he hit problems; he wanted to make test flights but was refused because of his foot; he wanted to pilot one of Amundsen's planes and was refused because he was married. Determined as ever he went out and got private finance for his venture. In 1926 he flew over the North Pole, and tackled the South Pole three years later. He returned to America to a hero's welcome and the man who'd been retired from the Navy was made an Admiral. Suitably enough for someone who'd flown over the top and the bottom of the world, he was known as Dicky Byrd.

1929

'Puss' the geriatric tabby cat was said to have enjoyed her thirty-sixth birthday, to become the oldest cat who ever lived. Sadly, the excitement must have proved too much for her, for the following day she died.

1936

Today's the day...

The devout and deadly King Philippe IV of France died after a busy reign of twenty-nine years. Said to have contributed much to the greatness of France, he fasted often, wore a hair shirt and let his confessor beat him. His death from a lengthy illness came as a shock to his doctors, since 'neither his pulse, nor his urine' indicated his condition was 'mortal'. On his death-bed he gave his eldest son, the King of Navarre, some sound advice – and added that if it wasn't followed, he would personally arrange divine retribution.   *1314*

Geographically incompetent composer Gaetano Donizetti was born. He created a grand total of sixty operas all written at breakneck speed. When he was told that Rossini had written *The Barber of Seville* in three weeks, he shook his head and said, 'Yes, yes, Rossini always was a lazy fellow.' At least Rossini made sure of his settings, unlike Donizetti who set his works as far afield as Siberia and the Caribbean, and with a master-stroke placed one very firmly 'in the mountains near Liverpool'.   *1797*

***Madame Butterfly*'s creator** Puccini died. He'd been busy with *Turandot* when he noticed he had a sore throat – a symptom that had often troubled him since he'd swallowed a goose-bone at a dinner. This time it was more than a tickle, however, for his doctors discovered he had cancer. He was successfully treated with radium, only to be struck down with a heart attack. With his dying breath he cried, 'My poor Elvira! My poor wife.' It was the first concern he'd shown her for years, and it was strange, since they hated each other.   *1924*

The author of *Little Women*, Louisa May Alcott, was born. Brought up in Concord, Massachusetts, her life was far from being the idyllic picture painted in the book. As a writer she was financial head of the family of four girls, and had to keep her selfish father, a transcendental nut-case, who tried vainly to set up 'advanced' schools and a utopian community called *Fruit-lands*. A tomboy as a child, she was physically unattractive, developed an abiding and unrequited passion for her near neighbour Henry Thoreau, and died an 'unwilling virgin'. During the Civil War, she worked in Washington as a nurse, fell ill from the strain, was accidentally overdosed with calomel and suffered from mercury poisoning for the rest of her life. Out of her rather sordid background, she managed to write the ultimate 'girls' story', which was an immediate bestseller. She thought the book that immortalised her was a failure, and though it was adored by generations of young ladies, she found it very boring. *1832*

Blank looks greeted a prize-winning picture when it went on display at Liverpool's Walker Art Gallery. The £3,000 masterpiece consisted of a large canvas painted entirely in white, with artistic strokes from the blade of a palette knife. Entitled 'Untitled No.9', it had 'Top' written on two sides at the back of the canvas. This understandably confused the hangers, but all was explained when painter William Turnbull pointed out that it was 'a gravitationally orientated picture'. *1978*

Today's the day...

The ultimate British Bulldog Winston Leonard Spencer-Churchill was born two months prematurely at Blenheim Palace, to the American socialite Jenny Jerome and the English statesman Lord Randolph Churchill. Through this unlikely match his ancestors and relatives included an admiral, two generals, a royal mistress, eight Dukes of Marlborough, Franklin Delano Roosevelt and the Iroquois tribe. Educated at Harrow and Sandhurst, he became a soldier and war correspondent; saw action in six wars; served six sovereigns and spent a total of sixty-two years as Member of Parliament. The ups and downs of his political career took him from the Tory to the Liberal party and back again; to Downing Street as Chancellor of the Exchequer, and out into the political wilderness as a lone prophet of the coming catastrophe. Prime Minister at last in 1940, he survived the war years on 'cigars, brandy and crisis'. His vituperative wit was as famous as his oratory, and when Lady Astor said, 'Sir, if you were my husband, I'd poison your coffee.' He replied, 'Madam, if you were my wife, I'd drink it.' The overweight Labour MP Bessie Braddock once accused him of being drunk. He said, 'And you madam are ugly, but tomorrow, I shall be sober.' For all his acknowledged ego mania, it has to be said that he took a modest view of his war-time achievement: 'It was the nation . . . that had the lion's heart, I had the good luck to be called upon to give the roar.' *1874*

The father of *Tom Sawyer* and *Huckleberry Finn* was born Samuel Langhorne Clemens, in Florida, Missouri. His father kept a store and became a Justice; his mother kept thirty-eight cats and became a very old lady; and Sam kept playing hookey and became a printer's apprentice, Mississippi steamboat pilot, soldier, miner and journalist, taking the immortal *nom de plume* of 'Mark Twain'. He was the first author to use a typewriter, and his obsession for 'money-making' schemes cost him several fortunes. 'When I was young,' he once claimed, 'I was so handsome, women became spellbound when I came into view. In San Francisco, in rainy seasons, I was often mistaken for a cloudless sky.' As age crept up on him, he said, 'I have achieved my seventy years in the usual way: by sticking to a scheme of life that would kill anyone else.' As for moderation: 'I have made it a rule never to smoke more than one cigar at a time . . . never to smoke when I am asleep and never to refrain when I am awake . . .'   *1835*

Oscar Wilde died penniless and in debt in a French hotel where he'd registered illegally under an assumed name. The tragic Irish playwright, poet and wit, persecuted for his homosexuality, succumbed to an illness believed to be either meningitis or a mastoid infection. Whatever it was he knew the end was near, remarking characteristically that he was 'dying beyond his means'. During his last few days he woke from a nightmare and confided to his friend Reggie Turner, 'Reggie, I dreamt I was dining with the dead.' 'My dear Oscar,' Reggie responded in the very style of the master, 'I'm sure you were the life and soul of the party!'   *1900*

The Crystal Palace died in a vast and eerily quiet conflagration, its acres of glass running to the ground in molten rivers. Between three and five million voyeurs came to watch it burn as the breeze whipped up the flames and firemen struggled to get through the crowds. It had stood on its present site at Sydenham, South London, since 1854 – a vastly enlarged version of the original Great Exhibition building that had opened in Hyde Park three years before. Though it took no human life, the fire claimed the lives of twelve birds in the aviary, injured four firemen, marked the end of an era for the tottering British Empire, and caused the General Manager, Sir Henry Buckland, to burst into tears. With a sad irony the great Victorian writer, William Makepeace Thackeray, had once described it with a metaphor that now proved to be literally true. He called it 'this great blazing arch of lucid glass'.   *1936*

Today's the day...

Cromwell's Parliament decided to sell Hyde Park. First enclosed by the Convent of Westminster, it passed to the crown in Henry VIII's reign and was made a public park and racecourse in 1637. The Commonwealth Government sold it in three lots for £17,000 and one of the purchasers, Antony Deane, a 'sordid fellow', decided to recoup some of his money by charging admission: a shilling for a coach and sixpence for a horse. The park got its revenge however. One day Cromwell was driving through in his coach; the horses bolted, he fell out and a pistol went off in his pocket.   *1652*

Downtrodden hero Woody Allen was born. He doesn't like taking baths as, 'It washes off the natural juices that keep you young.' Eager to improve his mind, he relates, 'I once took a course in speed-reading and was able to go through *War and Peace* in twenty minutes – it's about Russia!'   *1935*

Jolly Irene fell out of bed on Coney Island. It took five hefty policemen to get her back in – she was the Ringling Brothers' famous fat lady and weighed 650lbs.   *1937*

Kirov was assassinated in what is thought to have been a convoluted plot to help Stalin to absolute power. Leonid Nikolayev had been chosen for the job, an ex-prison guard of 'weak intellect and hideous appearance'. At approximately 4.30 pm Kirov was on his way back to his office after taking a call from the Kremlin, Nikolayev appeared and shot him through the back of the head from about 6ft away. Kirov fell dead and his assassin fainted, then made a belated attempt at suicide by cutting his throat with a razor. Kirov's bodyguard, Borisov, was bundled into a van and taken off to the headquarters of the secret police. En route the van crashed and curiously enough, although all the other passengers emerged unscathed, Borisov – the only witness – was dead.   *1934*

December 1

King Henry I died from 'a surfeit of lampreys', a fish he'd been told not to eat as it always disagreed with him. A brawny, black-haired man he was 'heavy to sleep' and prone to snoring; had as many as twenty illegitimate children and succumbed to 'female blandishments . . . not for gratification of incontinency but for the sake of issue.' Usually temperate, he was 'plain in his diet', 'never drank but to allay thirst' and ate – except in the case of lampreys – 'rather satisfying the calls of hunger, than surfeiting himself'. An unfortunate physician was offered a great reward to come and remove the dead King's brain. As soon as he did, he was struck, 'with the stink thereof' and promptly died.   *1135*

The poet Dryden reluctantly married Lady Elizabeth Howard, the sister of his friend Sir Robert. Twenty-five-year-old Elizabeth had something of a reputation through her 'questionable intimacy with a dissolute nobleman', and her brothers bullied Dryden into marrying her. On one occasion she complained she might have more of his time if she were a book and the poet retorted, 'Let it be an almanack, for then I shall change you every year!'   *1663*

Spenser copyrighted *The Faerie Queene* at Stationers' Hall. The poem, designed to 'fashion a gentleman or noble person in virtuous and gentle discipline', was written in the ideal setting on his country estate in Cork. When Sir Walter Raleigh read part of it he was enchanted and introduced Spenser to Queen Elizabeth. She declared it was of 'wondrous worth' and permitted the poet to read it to her at 'timely hours'. The Earl of Southampton was similarly affected when Spenser took the poem to him. Having read a few pages, the Earl told his servant to give Spenser £20; reading on he ordered another £20, then £20 more and finally turned the poet out of the house, 'for if I read on I shall be ruined'.   *1589*

Today's the day...

First mention of Jack Ketch the executioner was made in a
pamphlet entitled *The Plotter's Ballad*, confirming in print that he'd
been appointed official hangman. Notorious for his ham-fisted
butchery, he was accused of bungling Lord Russell's execution after
accepting money from him to make a clean job of it. In another
pamphlet *The Apologie of John Ketch Esquire*, he replied to his accusers,
saying that it was all Lord Russell's fault, since he 'did not dispose
himself for receiving the fatal stroke in such a position as was most
suitable' – although he did admit that his attention strayed as he was
taking aim. In 1682, he went on strike for higher wages, but three
years later he was making a mess of things again. After three
ineffectual attempts to behead the rebellious Duke of Monmouth, he
flung down his axe shouting, 'I can't do it!' Under threats from the
sheriffs, he took it up again, dealt the Duke another two blows and
finally had to resort to the gruesome device of a knife to make an end
of him. About this time, the 'Punchinello' puppet show was brought
into England from Italy. The executioner in the show was instantly
dubbed Jack Ketch, and children have been laughing at his exploits
ever since.   *1678*

December 2

Original sadist the Marquis de Sade died in a lunatic asylum. Nine years earlier he'd made a will and left strict instructions that his body was to be buried on his estate at Malmaison in 'the first thicket on the right', and sown over with acorns so that it would subsequently disappear. His wishes were totally ignored and this fervent atheist was given a Christian burial complete with a stone cross for his tombstone. However, shortly afterwards, his grave was robbed and his skull ended up in the possession of Gall the phrenologist. On examining it, he announced that it was 'small and well-shaped', and especially prominent were 'the bumps of tenderness and love of children'. *1814*

Atomic energy was produced for the first time when the geiger counters started clicking in a disused squash court at Chicago University. Under the leadership of Enrico Fermi, scientists from Columbia and Princeton Universities had banded together to construct a 'pile' – a lattice arrangement of uranium and graphite calculated to produce the controlled chain reaction of nuclear fission. Although the first yield was only half a watt, within ten days it was 200 and was later measured in kilowatts. The scientists rejoiced; they'd actually managed to produce pure energy and usher in the Atomic Age. What they'd also done, of course, was to pave the way for the atomic bomb and given the world the means of destroying itself. *1942*

The second Eddystone Lighthouse burned down, fifty-two years after the original had been destroyed in a storm. The lighthouse had been rebuilt in wood by a Mr Rudyerd, who at ninety-four was now its keeper. Along with his fellow lighthousemen, he valiantly fought the blaze – but in vain. After the fire, he kept insisting that he'd swallowed some molten lead as it fell from the roof. Everyone discounted his story as impossible, but twelve days later he went into spasms and died. On opening up his stomach, the surgeon found a flat, oval piece of lead weighing over $7\frac{1}{2}$ oz. *1755*

Today's the day...

The bloody Irish joker John Toler was born. Chief Justice of Ireland for twenty-six years, his rise to prominence was extraordinary, since his knowledge of the law was minimal. He managed to combine buffoonery and sadism, and would sleep throughout a hearing, waking in time to pass his own brand of death sentence. Any poor wretch brought before him could expect little mercy, for in one day's hearings, he sentenced ninety-six men to death and didn't trouble much about justice. He once astonished a court by dismissing a case where the accused was indisputably guilty. He said, 'I hanged six men last Tipperary Assizes who were innocent, so I'll let this poor devil off now to square matters.' *1745*

A human heart was transplanted successfully for the first time ever by Dr Christiaan Barnard and a team of thirty assistants at the Groote Schuur Hospital in South Africa. The patient was Louis Washkansy, a fifty-four-year-old wholesale grocer who suffered from diabetes and had had a number of heart attacks. The transplant was his last hope. The operation was completed, having taken a total of 192 minutes and Washkansky's response was remarkable. All signs of heart failure vanished; his swollen legs resumed normal shape and his diabetes became easier to control. Dr Barnard's main fear was infection, and in the end it proved to be justified, for the patient died after eighteen days from an infection of the lungs. The irony was that as the autopsy showed, his heart had maintained good circulation to the death. *1967*

Cheated inventor Samuel Crompton was born. Living with his widowed mother in Lancashire, he earned a meagre living playing the violin in the Bolton Theatre, and helped with the spinning. Realising the limitations of his mother's primitive equipment, he set out to build a super-efficient spinning machine. The result of his labours was a cross between the existing machines of Arkwright and Hargreaves, and since it was a hybrid he called it the 'Mule'. Unable to afford a patent and harassed to the point of exhaustion, he sold the 'Mule' for a measly £67 6s 6d, and he didn't get all of that. Thirty years later, he was awarded a miserable £5,000 compensation. It was invested badly and he lost that too – ironically in the failure of a company that spun cotton.

1753

Chimney crazy priest Robert Stephen Hawker was born in Devon. After a brilliant career at Oxford, he took the cloth and was soon installed as vicar of Morwenstow in Cornwall. A great lover of architecture, he wanted to be reminded of his favourite churches, and so he had five chimneys of his house built as exact replicas of their towers, and with the sixth he commemorated his mother by copying her tomb. Perhaps his greatest love, however, was for his cats, nine or ten of which were usually to be seen gambolling around the church during services. Hawker didn't mind this a bit, but when one of the beasts caught and ate a mouse on a Sunday, he could no longer turn the other cheek. With due reverence for formality, he took the sacrilegious feline and promptly excommunicated it.

1803

Today's the day...

The Napoleon of Africa crowned himself Emperor in a sports
stadium in Bangui, capital of one of the continent's poorest countries,
the Central African Empire. The fifty-six-year-old former paratroop
sergeant Jean-Bedel Bokassa sat regally on his ample throne, carved in
the belly of a huge gilded eagle, and swapped his simple twenty-four
carat gold crown for the Crown Imperial, worth nearly three million
pounds. Wrapped in a cosy ermine robe and wearing a toga
embroidered with Bonaparte's bee symbol, the Emperor withstood
temperatures of 100°F, clutched his 6ft diamond-encrusted sceptre
and watched topless girls swaying to the rhythm of tribal dances and
Beethoven's Ninth. As the young Empress Catherine looked on,
wearing a dress studded with three quarters of a million pearls, loyal
troops fired a 101-gun salute, and the celebrations started in earnest.
24,000 bottles of champagne, hundreds of pounds of caviar and a 7ft
high cake were consumed and the bill came to a staggering
£16,660,000 – a quarter of the Empire's annual income.   *1977*

An anxious émigré left South Africa by a very peculiar route. No
doubt keen for company, he asked three total strangers if they'd like a
free trip overseas. The men eagerly piled into his car, but when
they saw where he was heading, they quickly changed their minds.
Politely, the man stopped and let them out – and then to their horror
drove straight into Durban Bay. As the car slipped slowly beneath the
waves the man smiled, waved – and drowned.   *1978*

Diminutive satirist Samuel Butler was born, four years to the day
before his reverend father, the Bishop of Lichfield died. Probably his
two most famous works are *Erewhon*, which is a deliberate anagram of
the word 'nowhere', and *The Way of All Flesh*. But as well as being an
author he was a painter, philosopher, theoretical biologist, and
composer. He loved poking fun at people but always did it gently, and
his epigrams are legion. He coined 'Invention is the mother of

necessity', claimed that 'Cleanliness is almost as bad as godliness', and that 'Life is one long process of getting tired.' He was not all that keen on the Protestant Work Ethic and said, 'All animals except man know that the principal business of life is to enjoy it.'

1835

Mildly paranoic Prime Minister Lord Liverpool died. He was the eighteenth Prime Minister of England and had a morbid fear of opening letters in case they brought bad news. One day his secretary found him prostrate on the library floor. He'd been smitten with apoplexy and didn't survive the year. In his hand, there was an opened letter.

1828

The great Scottish historian Thomas Carlyle was born in Ecclefechan. He was troubled by dyspepsia all his life and would often tell people, 'I have a rat gnawing in the pit of my stomach.' To make matters worse, he couldn't stand noise, and his special soundproof room was so ineffective that he claimed it was 'the noisiest room in the house'. For thirteen years, he struggled with his life of Frederick the Great, saying that, 'A well written life is almost as rare as a well spent one.' His irascibility made him many enemies, as did the fact that he was a conversational bully – though at least he was honest about it. 'Let me have my own way in everything,' he said, 'and a pleasanter creature does not exist.' Yet with his intimates he was all sweetness and light, and if anything, too quiet. When his great friend the Poet Laureate Alfred Lord Tennyson came to visit, they would say hello and goodbye to each other, and sit for two hours in between – smoking their pipes in absolute silence.

1795

The author of *Leviathan* philosopher Thomas Hobbes died. With his parting words, Hobbes demonstrated that his grasp of philosophy was greater than his understanding of syntax. He said, 'I shall be glad to find a hole to creep out the world at.'

1679

Today's the day...

Hollywood's most honoured son Walt Disney was born. He first
began drawing cartoons professionally when he was ten, for free
weekly haircuts, but when he went for his first job interview, he was
told he didn't have any real talent. On the way home in a train, he
remembered a little mouse that used to play around in his studio. The
mouse became Mickey, and appeared in the world's first 'talkie'
cartoon *Steamboat Willie*, which was a bootleg production.
Paradoxically Mickey eventually financed Walt, and has made more
money out of his off-screen activities than in his numerous starring
roles. It isn't surprising then to hear that Walt once said, 'I love Mickey
more than any woman I've ever known.'   *1901*

Mozart's presentiment was fulfilled when he died aged thirty-five.
Three months earlier he had been approached by a man dressed
entirely in grey, who had commissioned him to write a Requiem – and
ask no questions. Mozart became convinced the mysterious stranger
was the Messenger of Death and began to work feverishly. His
anxiety, compounded by malnutrition and strain, caused his health
to deteriorate rapidly. Amid paranoic delusions of being poisoned by
rivals, he continued to compose the fateful work. After singing the part

of the *Lacrymosa* he lapsed into silence, athough continued to mouth the rhythm silently. He died within hours and was given a pauper's burial and to this day the true site of his grave remains unknown. Strangely, the man in grey was the servant of an eccentric nobleman, who genuinely wanted a Requiem for his deceased wife.   *1791*

Home-grown President Martin Van Buren was born. He was an incredibly vain man and his enemies claimed he wore his study carpet threadbare in front of the mirror, and whether that's true or not, it is known that to preserve his trim figure, he wore ladies' corsets. His term was marked by such persistent financial crises that he earned the nickname 'Martin Van Ruin'. In 1848, four years after losing power, he attempted to become President again, and his popularity was such that he didn't get a single electoral vote.   *1782*

Handel was saved by a button. He'd lost a very lucrative pupil to his friend and fellow composer Mattheson and he found this blow to his pride a little hard to take. A duel was arranged on the spot, and the chubby Handel who made an excellent target, was saved by his dandy outfit. As Mattheson lashed out with his sword, the blade struck one of Handel's shiny brass buttons and snapped. Always quick to spot a way out, Handel nobly forgave his adversary, and not only did the two make up, they became better friends than ever.   *1704*

Military prankster George Armstrong Custer was born. His lighthearted approach and childish love of high jinks marked the whole of his career. At his father's house he used to throw live cartridges into the fire, and when the old man came to visit him in Texas, he would tie firecrackers to his chair and roar with delight to see him leaping around the room, looking for the 'Injuns'. But Custer was always forgiven his pranks, because he was the very image of a dashing soldier.   *1839*

Today's the day...

The infant crowned King Henry VI was born, inheriting a weak body, an impaired mind and at the age of nine months, the throne of England. Though affairs of state were handled by a council, the tiny monarch approved all decrees with a thumb-print, while sitting on his mother's knee. Excessively pious in later life, he was said at the age of two to have bewailed defiling the Sabbath when he was taken to the House of Lords on a Sunday. Six years later, he was crowned and prophetically, since he was deposed and murdered, he found the crown too heavy for his little head, and had to be helped staggering from the platform.

1421

The first artificial echo was made by the amazing phonograph designed by the mechanical genius Thomas Edison. Earlier in the year he had rapidly sketched a model he wanted made. He gave the drawing to John Kruesi who innocently asked what the odd-looking gadget was supposed to be. 'A talking machine' said Edison. Kruesi simply laughed. When it was finished Edison shouted into the horn 'Mary had a little lamb!' After a few adjustments, for the first time in history, man really spoke to himself. Kruesi leapt back in astonishment.

December 6

Even Edison was surprised, 'I was always afraid of things that worked first time . . . but here was something there was no doubt of.' To help promote his pet invention, he asked many famous celebrities to record messages for posterity. Sir Arthur Sullivan said, 'I am terrified by the thought of all the hideous and bad music which might be put on records.' Edison was not personally worried since, of all things, the inventor of the talking machine was deaf.   *1877*

The worst non-military explosion in history destroyed half of Halifax, Nova Scotia. In the harbour two boats were on a collision course. The Belgian relief ship *Imo* accidentally rammed the French munitions ship *Mont Blanc*. The impact turned the explosives-laden *Mont Blanc* into a floating volcano which erupted leaving the thriving capital a city of the dead. The suburb of Richmond was totally flattened. Freight cars were thrown over two miles. At an orphanage all 200 children died and a telegraph operator four miles away was killed by flying metal. What little luck was available that day went to the unwilling human cannonball, who was blown nearly a mile but survived after landing in a tree. The full statistics of the tragedy will never be known but at least 1,600 people died, 8,000 were injured and 2,000 were listed as missing. Materially, damages were estimated at over thirty million dollars. The cause of this horrifying disaster was said to be 'a confusion of whistles'.   *1917*

The precocious saint St Nicholas is celebrated. He's the original Father Christmas, of course, but he's also the patron of schoolboys, sailors, thieves, virgins, Turkey, Greece and pagan communist Russia. Among his miracles, he's said to have resurrected two little boys who were sliced up by an innkeeper and pickled in brine, and even as an infant he was working towards canonisation. Soon after his birth, he's supposed to have stood up in the bath and thanked God, and while still on the breast, refused to sup on Fast days.   *Feast Day*

Today's the day...

Operation 'Z' crippled the US Pacific Fleet as it lay at anchor unwarned and unprepared in Pearl Harbour. At 7.44am, over 350 Japanese fighters, bombers and torpedo planes poured in from six carriers out at sea, and wreaked havoc on their unsuspecting victims, who didn't even know they were at war. As the band aboard the *Nevada* played 'The Star Spangled Banner', the bombs and torpedoes flew thick and fast. Four battleships were sunk outright; four were badly damaged, and the quays were in chaos with a dozen other ships floundering or sinking. Nearly 200 aircraft were destroyed on the ground, and the death toll amounted to almost 2,500, with over 1,000 more wounded. Masterminded by Admiral Isoroku Yamamoto, the raid went ahead a day earlier than scheduled. It missed its main targets – four US aircraft carriers that were no longer in port – but otherwise it went exactly to plan. Amazingly, the US Navy had considered the possibility of a raid on Pearl Harbour earlier. In 1932 Admiral Frank A. Schofield had actually predicted it could happen, and to show just how vulnerable the base was, he mounted a mock attack. It proved that in theory the harbour was a sitting duck, but little was done about it and nine years later the Japanese proved it in fact.   *1941*

'The half-Queen of France' Madame du Barry was executed. Mistress of the late Louis XV, she'd fled to England in the Terror, but foolishly returned home and was arrested. Once a beautiful courtesan, she'd become coarse and bloated and no one was more struck by the change than Sanson, her executioner, who'd been her friend twenty years before. When he went to the *Conciergerie* for her, she broke down shrieking and screaming that she was innocent, and it took three men to hold her down while they cut her hair and bound her hands. In the tumbril on the way to the scaffold, her screams and impassioned pleas for mercy silenced the crowd, and she had to be carried to the gallows and lashed, struggling convulsively, to the plank. Sanson was so overcome by it all, that he couldn't execute her himself and signalled for his son to do it. The crowd watched silently and were so moved by her exhibition that Madame Vigée-Lebrun remarked that if all the other victims had not been so brave, the Terror might have ended earlier, since the populace is more easily stirred by pity, than by admiration'. Madame du Barry's head was taken to the Cemetery of the Madeleine, where it was handed over to a man who made a wax model of it. He was Curtius, director of the Wax Museum in Paris and uncle of Marie Grosholtz – better known as Madame Tussaud.   *1793*

The Roman orator Cicero was assassinated after his speeches had offended Mark Antony once too often. He was beheaded and the hands that had written the offending orations were cut off. Both head and hands were sent to Rome and hung on the rostra where the orators spoke. There Antony's wife Fulvia, who had often been the butt of Cicero's barbed wit, also got her revenge. Unable to match the orator's tongue in life, she got her own back in death. She tore the tongue from the head and stabbed it with a hairpin over and over again.   *AD 43*

American novelist of the Plains Willa Cather was born in Back Creek Valley, Virginia. When she was ten, the family moved out West to the desolate flatlands of Nebraska which were to be her inspiration. She had a very odd upbringing. Her mother was exceedingly vain, always wore the latest fashions, and apart from beating the children when they disobeyed her, she left them entirely to their own devices. As a reaction to her fashionable mother, Willa cropped her hair, wore boys' clothes and signed herself 'William'. She rode through the wild country on horseback, made calls with doctors she knew and was so obviously advanced at school that they let her come and go as she pleased. Her favourite amusement was vivisection and she said that her idea of seventh heaven was to be able 'to amputate limbs'.   *1873*

Today's the day...

The vagabond Queen Christina of Sweden was born, the only child of the country's hero monarch, Gustavus Adolphus, who was killed when she was six. Brought up as a boy, she could outride and outshoot most men; wore men's clothing and swore like a trooper. She loved to shock people, and got her chambermaids to sing bawdy songs to the French ambassador. Then in 1654, she stunned everyone by abdicating, leaving her cousin Charles X nothing but a crown, two carpets and an old bedstead. She left Sweden 'shouting with joy'; horrified her countrymen by becoming a Catholic; and ended up in Rome where she was to plague three successive Popes. When Cardinal Medici upset her, she fired a cannon at his door, and while trying to enlist French support in her bid for the throne of Naples, she upset the court by asking if Louis XIV's *valet de chambre* could come and undress her. Often described as a 'libertine' and 'hoyden', she was accused of having love affairs with numerous men and women including a high-ranking churchman and a nun. But in fact, the chances are that this notorious Queen died a virgin.   *1626*

Corpulent poet and lawyer John Davies died, rid at last of his embarrassing wife Eleanor. This rather odd woman had discovered an

December 8

inaccurate anagram of her name 'Reveal O Daniel' and it had convinced
her she was imbued with the spirit of the prophet and could therefore
see the future. In 1623, she found that John's name very nearly spelled
'Jove's Hand' and spurred on by the discovery, predicted his death
within three years and went straight into mourning. A few days before
death finally came, she told him it was about to and he replied: 'Weep
not while I am alive and I will give you leave to laugh when I am dead.'
It was a biographer of the period, however, who had the last laugh,
when he too found an anagram in her name. 'Dame Eleanor Davies',
he wrote, spells 'never so mad a ladie!'   *1626*

Multi-faceted singer and movie star Sammy Davis Jr was born.
He made his stage *début* at the age of four, worked with his father and
uncle in the 'Will Martin Trio', lost an eye in a car crash at the age of
twenty-nine, and adopted the Jewish faith. This self-acclaimed
'one-eyed Jewish negro' has given over a million dollars to the Civil
Rights movement, and when he married Swedish actress Mai Britt, he
was quoted as saying, 'I don't care if we have polka-dot children' – a
remark he avidly denies. Apart from singing and acting, Mr Davies
drives nineteen cars, plays piano, vibes, drums, trumpet and bass, and
is renowned for his impressions. When he did the late Nat King Cole
on a radio show, the singer turned to his wife and said, 'I don't
remember recording that.'   *1925*

Ancient Briton Henry Jenkins died in Yorkshire at the reputed age
of 169 years. Though he could neither read nor write, he would give
convincing details of the Battle of Flodden 157 years earlier and had
no trouble giving an authentic picture of life in the reign of Henry VIII.
Often dismissed as a fraud, his case is nevertheless convincing. There
were five other centenarians in his village who could never remember
him as anything else, but 'a very old man.'   *1670*

Today's the day...

Superstar Issur Demsky was born in New York – better known as Kirk Douglas. On his way to the top, he earned a living as a parking lot attendant, a bell-hop and a soda-jerk, working out his aggressions in amateur wrestling. At various times, he's played a one-eyed viking, a trapeze artist, Van Gogh and a Jewish refugee. When he was offered a part in the Warner Brothers film called *Young Man with a Horn*, a co-star quipped, 'It should be a cinch . . . he never stops blowing it.'

1916

England's blind visionary and poet John Milton was born. Called 'the Lady' for his pale skin and beautiful auburn hair, his major interests in life were God, the Classics and himself. Many of his famous political and social pamphlets were written not out of a sense of cause, but out of personal bitterness. When the first of his three marriages was an immediate failure, for instance, he wrote a great diatribe on the iniquitousness of the divorce laws. According to Dr Johnson he thought 'woman was made only for obedience; man made only for rebellion.' In 1652, he was struck blind and thereafter wrote his finest verse, including the epic *Paradise Lost*. He often composed lying in bed, where he could dictate as many as forty-two new lines without pausing, and frequently crammed 300 words into a single sentence.

1608

The 'Thug in Robes' Chancellor Edward Thurlow was born in Norfolk. Thrown out of school, he eventually made it to Cambridge where 'he distinguished himself by his idleness'. He wheeled and dealed his way into a Baronetcy and when he was finally made Lord Chancellor, his first act was to adjourn the Parliament. He had a vast house built, but insisted the architect cheated him and lived out his life in the cottage next door. He was lucky in his friendship with King George III, but didn't get on so well with his fellow Lords and Bishops. One prelate, with whom he was staying at the time, asked if he'd like to come and hear him preach in the local church. 'No,' replied the Lord Chancellor, 'I am obliged to listen to enough of your damned nonsense in the House of Lords, but there I can answer you. I'm damned if I'm going to hear you when I can't reply.'   *1731*

Oh-so English comedienne Hermione Gingold was born. Though always popular in Britain, she achieved her greatest success in America, and had to make frequent transatlantic trips. Returning home once, she was stopped by a English immigration officer and asked the purpose of her visit. 'To see my two sons,' she replied, 'both of whom are older than I am!'   *1897*

The world's longest running TV soap opera was born in Manchester, having had its name changed from *Florizel Street* to *Coronation Street*. An everyday story of working-class Salford folk, it was created by Tony Warren, and more than one critic thought it would never last. To date it has topped the British TV ratings 200 times and is rarely out of the top ten shows. It's employed 2,000 actors and actresses and sixty-nine hard-pressed script writers. It's currently with its fifteenth producer, and is the Poet Laureate John Betjeman's favourite programme. The first words spoken were 'That sign needs changing', and since then the street sign has appeared in nineteen different countries including Canada, Greece and most surprising of all – Thailand.   *1960*

A self-propelled bicycle was patented by early conservationist, Elijah Burgoyne. Noticing how bumpy the roads were at the time, he decided you could 'store-up' the bumps as fuel. He converted the saddle into a plunger to work a compressed air-pump, that fed a turbine, which powered the wheels. The trouble was, the roads just weren't bumpy enough, and for the rider, bouncing was more tiring than pedalling.   *1919*

Today's the day...

The legendary first American bathtub was revealed by Mr Thompson of Cincinatti, who'd been inspired by its use in England. It was celebrated at a party, where all the guests tried it out. They liked it – but nobody else did. Doctors said it was dangerous. In Boston it was banned. In Virginia a penal tax was imposed on it, and while in Philadelphia they put one in a prison, it wasn't to be used in the winter. Only in 1851 did it finally become respectable when President Fillmore installed one in the White House. All this is faithfully recorded by H. L. Mencken in the New York *Evening Mail* of 28 December 1918. Amazingly, it was the first time the story had been told, and soon it was used as a telling example of the ingrained conservatism of the medical profession. Mencken was extremely embarrassed, because the whole thing was a hoax. He confessed, but it did no good – nobody would believe him.   *1842*

A spy was hanged by the nose. He was Karl Richter, an SS officer who was parachuted into Britain and given the alias 'Otto Schmidt'. Captured and sentenced to die, he was to be executed by the famous hangman Albert Pierrepoint. When Pierrepoint arrived in his cell, however, the massively built Richter was exceptionally unwilling to go. As the priest made a run for it, a fierce battle ensued, and four prison officers just managed to hold Richter long enough for Pierrepoint to put the straps on. As Pierrepoint threw the lever, his victim leapt into the air. The rope slipped and caught between his lip and his nostrils, in which position it snapped his neck in two. The amazing thing is that the mighty Richter had been arrested by a single, unarmed country copper.

1941

The Nobel Prize was born when its creator died. Alfred Nobel was a wealthy Swedish chemist and inventor; a strange, self-effacing man who never married and had a long, platonic affair with his secretary, Bertha. Though his riches were considerable, he cared little for money and scribbled down his will two weeks before he died, leaving nothing to his relations. Instead, he directed that his property be sold and the money invested to provide annual prizes for those whose work had benefited mankind in the previous year. The prizes were to be awarded internationally in five categories: physics, chemistry, medicine, literature and his pet love – promoting the cause of peace. It's particularly ironic, since his fortune was based on his invention of 'Nobel's Safety Powder' – a substance that's better known as dynamite.

1896

The Countess who joined the Labour Party was born Frances 'Daisy' Maynard. She was vastly rich and married Lord Brooke, the heir to the Earldom of Warwick. Indulged by her long-suffering husband, she spent a fortune promoting working-class education. The Labour movement never really accepted her, however, and eventually, like her aristocratic friends, it spurned her. Unable to adopt the working class, she adopted exotic animals instead. When she died in her seventies the first thing her son had to do was cancel an order for a herd of Highland cows.

1861

Today's the day...

The dreaded Reno brothers were lynched at New Albany County Jail. They'd terrorised entire counties in Southern Indiana, and local people wanted not a trial, but bloody revenge. They formed themselves into a Vigilantes' Committee; cut the telegraph lines; dressed up in red masks and surrounded the two-storey caboose. The Sheriff was wounded trying to protect his prisoners, and the three brothers and their accomplice Charlie Anderson were dragged up the stairs and hanged from a second floor balcony. Frank went first and his neck was immediately broken. William went next cursing and shouting that his father's ghost would return for vengeance. Then came Simeon who put up a terrific struggle, and finally the taciturn Anderson swung without a word. For over half an hour this 'branch of the tree of evil' struggled and fought and slowly choked to death. *1868*

America's strangest monument was dedicated to an agricultural pest at Enterprise, Coffee County, Alabama. The beastie had ruined hundreds of farmers by chewing up their cotton, and the survivors had to diversify their crops. Their profits rose threefold and in gratitude they immortalised the boll weevil. *1919*

Bald but lovable film producer Carlo Ponti was born. He is twenty-one years older and 6in shorter than his celebrated wife, Sophia Loren. He says of her loving terminology that, 'For dear, she calls me *polpettone* (meat loaf). For very dear, *pepperone* (pepper). But when she loves me most of all, she calls me *sappli* (fried rice ball with mozzarella cheese)!' *1913*

Dentistry took a great leap forward when Connecticut practitioner Horace Wells decided teeth could be drawn painlessly with the help of nitrous oxide. He had a toothache at the time and asked his friend J. M. Riggs to test his theory. It worked and he felt no more 'than the prick of a pin'. Here was a discovery that would make him famous.

December 11

Soon off he went to demonstrate it to other doctors. In his inexperience he administered too little gas and the patient howled with pain. Then he administered too much and the patient nearly died. Defeated, he resigned his practice and became a bird fancier, travelling round Connecticut with a flock of singing canaries. The correct dosage was not discovered for another twenty-four years, and on 21 January 1848 this disappointed man took his own life by severing a femoral artery – having first dampened the pain by inhaling chloroform.   *1842*

Edward VIII broadcast to a hushed nation. Shows stopped in theatres and cinemas, no telephone calls were put through and not a soul moved in the streets. At 10 pm Edward began in a trembling voice to explain that he 'found it impossible to carry the heavy burden of responsibility and to discharge my duties as King as I would wish to do, without the help of the woman I love'. The speech lasted seven minutes and brought to an end a reign of only 325 days. Mussolini heard it in Rome; the Pope listened alone in his room, and Mrs Simpson herself lay on the sofa in her villa in Cannes with a handkerchief over her eyes. When it was over, the audience at the London Palladium stood and applauded. One hour later Edward motored towards Portsmouth and lifelong exile, and thus ended the rule of the King who was never crowned.   *1936*

The Duke of Portland bought Tirpitz the Pig for £440 in a bizarre auction at the Portland Hotel, Chester. Tirpitz had been shipwrecked in naval action in the Pacific, and English sailors had been moved to save his bacon. He was sold in aid of the British Red Cross, and was auctioned again the following year, when his Lordship went the whole hog and bought him a final time for £505. In all the noble porker raised £1,785 for the piggy banks of three different charities and after his death in 1919 he was stuffed and presented to the Imperial War Museum – the first British prisoner-of-war pig.   *1917*

Today's the day...

A farcical football match was finally abandoned. Drenched by sleet and snow in the freezing cold, the players of Burnley and Blackburn Rovers were having an extremely rough game. In the second half when two players from opposing sides started to fight, they were ordered off and were followed by the whole of the Blackburn team, except for plucky goalkeeper Herbie Arthur who bravely stood his ground. The referee re-started the game but it wasn't long before Burnley scored a goal against their lonely opponent. As Arthur quite rightly appealed, it was offside – but he delayed so long taking his free kick that the referee gave up the game in despair. *1891*

A hopeful Wagner demanded a huge loan in a letter to his great admirer Baron Robert Von Honstein. *Tristan und Isolde* had been abandoned as hopeless after fifty-seven rehearsals – yet even with his career in virtual ruin, Wagner's amazing ego was left intact. Believing that genius had a natural right to other people's money, he blithely wrote to Honstein, 'I hear that you have become rich . . . I require an immediate loan of 10,000 francs . . . now let me see whether you are the right sort of man.' Convinced that he was 'conferring an honour'

December 12

on his admirer, Wagner was astounded when his request was actually refused. He promptly wrote another letter scolding Honstein for his impropriety, adding, 'Your answer could only pass muster on the assumption that you are totally ignorant of my works.' Fortunately the ebullient composer did eventually find a sympathetic patron – mad King Ludwig of Bavaria. *1861*

Australian schoolgirl Shane Gould made swimming history, when she smashed the world record in a 1,500 metre free-style race by a full eighteen seconds, and became the first woman ever to hold every single free-style record. At the 1972 Olympics she presented such a daunting prospect that American girl swimmers tried to boost their flagging morale with T-shirts emblazoned 'All that glitters is not Gould!' *1971*

The Hovercraft was patented. Its inventor Sir Christopher Cockerell originally called it the 'Ripplecraft' and got the idea for this new mode of transport from watching the steel runners of skates and sleighs. He noticed they melted a thin layer of ice which formed a film of water and acted as a lubricating agent over the snow. With this in mind, he constructed the first prototype hovercraft using a vacuum cleaner, a tin of coffee and a tin of cat food! *1955*

Brilliant French novelist Gustave Flaubert was born. Surprisingly he was not a naturally gifted writer and would work for hours on a single phrase. He rewrote his masterpiece *Madame Bovary* five times, never looking at the previous manuscript, and was so involved with the famous scene where Madame Bovary gives her husband poison that he was sick three times. *1821*

Strange things happened in Central Park. Young Dorothy Arnold went in by the 79th Street entrance – and was never seen again. No trace of her was found but on the same day, at exactly the same place, a swan suddenly appeared – from nowhere. *1910*

Today's the day...

Roasted bedbugs were the order of the day. A nit of an inventor had designed an extraordinary bedbug exterminator. It consisted of electrifying the bedstead with a number of tightly packed circuits. When an unwary bug crossed from one to another it would close the circuit receiving such a shock that it would 'more than likely change its mind and return in the direction it came'. Not everyone was bitten by the scheme which was eventually scratched!   *1898*

Walking medical disaster Dr Samuel Johnson died. As a child he contracted scrofula which left him pock-marked, partially deaf and so short-sighted that when he read his eyelashes almost touched the page. He suffered such severe depressions he was frequently tied to a chair to prevent him from committing suicide. He finally had a stroke and succumbed to pneumonia. Though in great pain he deliberately stopped taking opium so his mind would be clear. He also stopped drinking wine so as not to be drunk when he met his maker. He unwittingly hastened his death by plunging a pair of scissors deep into his calves to bleed his legs. The last words of this compiler of the first great English dictionary were, 'I am about to die,' but he said them in Latin.   *1784*

December 13

Phlegmatic English surgeon Joseph Henry Green died. On his death-bed, he demonstrated the same cool professional judgement that he'd shown throughout his life. After diagnosing congestion he felt his own pulse, calmly said 'stopped' – and then died.   *1863*

Butch American actor Van Heflin was born. In the 1955 Broadway production of Arthur Miller's *A View from the Bridge* he became the first major actor to kiss another man on the lips. Although it always drew gasps from the audience he admitted he never received any passionate letters from 'the boys'.   *1910*

America's first abdominal operation was performed by Dr Ephraim McDowell of Danville, Kentucky. He had been called to help deliver the child of Mrs Jane Todd Crawford, but after examination he realised that she was not pregnant but actually suffering from an enormous ovarian tumour. He advised her that although an operation was extremely dangerous, without it she would die anyway. With typical frontier courage she travelled the sixty miles back to McDowell's surgery on horseback resting her massive tumour on the horn of the saddle. Using no anaesthetic or any trained assistance, McDowell cut her open. During the grisly twenty-five-minute operation her intestines lay on the operating table while he removed 15lb of gelatinous material and the sac which weighed 7½lb. Incredibly Mrs Crawford survived, and lived to be seventy-eight – outliving the man she made famous as 'The Father of Ovariotomy'.   *1809*

South African statesman Balthazar Johannes Vorster was born. His life has been dominated by the number 13. Born on 13 December, he was the 13th child of his family. He was appointed to the Cabinet after 13 years in Parliament and was named Premier on 13 September 1966 – at a time when his golf handicap was 13! He resigned the Presidency in September 1978 after being in power 13 years.   *1915*

Today's the day...

George Washington killed himself through his own stubbornness. Two days earlier he had returned soaking wet from a lengthy afternoon ride in the rain and snow, and disregarding the advice of his secretary Lear, refused to change his sopping clothes. He developed a throat infection and complications set in. His disregard for self-preservation was typical. In the Revolutionary War, he'd blithely had two horses shot from under him, and four bullets pierce his coat, yet leave him unharmed. He suffered a great deal too, having had smallpox, consumption, amoebic dysentery, rotten teeth, pleurisy, malaria and Kleinfelter's Syndrome, which may have left him sterile. This morning he awoke unable to breathe. His doctors made matters worse by bleeding him twice at the neck and the end was clearly in sight. With his last words he said, 'I die hard, but I am not afraid of dying.' In his will, he bequeathed to his brother his prize possession – Ben Franklin's 'fine crabtree walking stick'.   *1799*

Half-hanged Anna Green swung for half an hour at Oxford, with her friends pulling on her feet to hasten her death. She'd been cut down and flung in her coffin, when it was noticed she was still breathing. Despite a hefty kick in the stomach administered by an onlooker, she wouldn't stop. Doctors were called in and revived her. She was allowed to go free and lived to have several children. Superstitious midwives were surprised that none of them were affected by their mother's nightmare experience, though at very least, they must have been highly strung!   *1650*

A modern colossus was topped out in New York. It was the amazing 110-storey World Trade Center, whose soaring twin towers reach a staggering altitude of 1,377ft – more than a quarter of a mile in the sky. During excavations for the monster building, 1.2 million cubic yards of earth were removed and dumped in a vast area on the shores of the Hudson River. So as well as providing accommodation

December 14

for some 50,000 workers, this gargantuan edifice has created another 23.5 acres of New York.

1970

Victorious viking Roald Amundsen conquered the South Pole – the first man to do so. Favoured by fair weather, it had taken him – and his accompaniment of four men, four sledges and fifty-two dogs – fifty-three days. Marking the spot with the Norwegian flag and a flimsy tent, he left a letter to King Haakon and a note asking his rival Scott to deliver it, in case he didn't get back. It's odd to consider that his lifelong ambition had been to reach not the South, but the North Pole. As he said at the time, 'I have never known any man to be placed in such a diametrically opposite position to the goal of his desires . . . can anything more topsy-turvy be imagined.'

1911

Beloved Albert the Prince Consort died and ironically, considering his keen interest in sanitary reforms, it was typhoid that carried him off. Victoria plunged herself into the longest, most excessive public mourning in modern history. Even thirty-nine years after his death she could still record in her journal: 'I could go mad from the desire and longing! Oh, how bitter, how hot are the tears that I often pour forth in the evening in his room, kneeling beside his chair.' The public manifestation of this 'inexpressible grief' was the building of the massive, much mocked and rather bizarre Albert Memorial in Hyde Park. It has a frieze containing sixty-one human figures, forty-two men, nineteen women, and nine animals. Albert died in 1861 aged forty-two; he was born in 1819 and had nine children. Even this great edifice, however, wasn't enough for the 'little black widow'. Until her last day on earth, she maintained Albert's sick-room exactly as it had been at the fateful hour. The medicine bottle remained untouched and the wash-stand was refilled every day. Most moribund of all – at night she went to bed clutching his nightgown and a plaster cast of his hand.

1861

Today's the day...

The world's first Society for the Prevention of Cruelty to Children was founded in New York, based upon the work of Elbridge Thomas Gerry. In the spring of the year a young child named Mary Ellen was discovered after being taken from a charitable institution by a couple whose only purpose seemed to be to torture her. Social workers were helpless, as there was no legal machinery for them to work with. Then they had a brainwave. There was an American Society for the Prevention of Cruelty to Animals and since the child could be considered as an animal, she came under their jurisdiction – and they did in fact save her. Within weeks they were inundated with child abuse cases, and Gerry was enabled to set up his society to deal with them. Though this was the first time in history children were protected by their own special laws, he was reviled by some as 'an interfering zealot' and a 'meddlesome bureaucrat'.   *1874*

Nasty Emperor Nero was born to his almost equally nasty mother Agrippina. With his father dead and his mother in exile, he was raised by two men – a barber and a dancer. When Agrippina came home again, she was supposed to have committed incest with Nero and, with basest ingratitude, he then tried to kill her three times. He poisoned her – she took the antidote. He made her a crushingly heavy collapsible bed – she avoided it. He made her a collapsible boat – and she swam to safety. When he wasn't trying to dispose of his mother, Nero was exceedingly vain. He tried to keep slim by laying a slab of lead on his chest, and wouldn't eat apples in case they affected his voice. His love life was equally insistent. He raped the vestal virgin Rubria. He masqueraded as a bride, married a man, and on his wedding night imitated the cries of a virgin being deflowered. Quite his best variation though was to marry his favourite, the transvestite Sporus, whom he'd tried to turn into a woman by castration. As the contemporary Roman joke ran – the world would have been a happier place if Nero's father had married such a wife.   *AD 37*

December 15

Money magnet Jean Paul Getty was born in Minneapolis, Minnesota. He joined his father's oil company in 1914 and vowed to make a million dollars in two years. He did, and later invested in some barren land on the borders of Saudi Arabia in a little known place called Kuwait. Within four years it was pumping out sixteen million barrels of oil a year. He lived to become the richest known private citizen in the world. Much of his money went to feed his incurable addiction to collecting works of art, and so painfully conscious of this was he, that he tried shock treatment to cure it. He added up what he'd spent on art in a particular feverish period of collecting and was horrified to find that it ran into seven figures.

1892

Long-time escaper Leonard T. Fristoe was recaptured after forty-six years of illicit freedom. In 1920, he'd been sentenced to life for killing two deputy sheriffs, but three years later, broke out and lived happily with his wife and children under an assumed name. Today, at the age of seventy-seven, he was turned in at Compton, California – by his own son.

1969

Today's the day...

History's most famous tea party took place in Boston Harbour.
The 'party' was a symbolic protest stirred up against the unjust tax of
threepence a pound on tea, imposed by the distant British Government.
Under a bright newish moon, approximately 110 Bostonians stealthily
approached three British ships each containing 114 tea-chests. The
rebels were disguised as Mohawk Indians in costumes made from
blankets, shawls, cast-off dresses and red woollen caps. Their skins
were smothered in red ochre blended with axle grease and soot.
Unfortunately the act almost ended in a potty farce. As it was low tide
the chests thrown into the harbour began to build into huge stacks so
high one chest actually fell back onto the ship. Many of the Indians
ruined their costumes jumping into the water to smash open the canvas-
covered chests. Meanwhile the 'secret' raid was being admired from the
quayside by a large audience which actually hampered the fifty-five-
minute operation. The point was made at the cost of one broken
padlock and one concussed Indian who had been knocked out by a
falling chest. Strangely the world's most celebrated tea party ended
with the uninvited guests sinking the tea in the drink.   *1773*

Scruffy, deaf German composer Ludwig van Beethoven was born.
His tutor was most discouraging declaring, 'He has learnt nothing, and
will never do anything in decent style.' However Mozart was more
enthusiastic. After the eighteen-year-old Ludwig auditioned before
him he said, 'Some day he will make a big noise in the world.' He
certainly did – once hitting the keys of his piano so hard six strings
snapped. He had enormous black hairy hands which were particularly
thick at the finger-tips. Before composing he always bathed them in
cold water claiming it helped him concentrate – but if this failed he
resorted to pouring the freezing water over his head. Beethoven's
concentration was so great he went around blithely muttering to
himself, abandoning most of the social niceties and was once so badly
dressed he was arrested for vagrancy. As his deafness increased, he

became even more of a social outcast, refusing to go to dances because he couldn't keep in step to the music. His composing was not affected since he taught himself to hear through his teeth! Biting on a long piece of wood touching the piano he could hear the vibrations. Despite this dreadful handicap he wrote immortal musical masterpieces, but modestly summed up his own talent saying, 'Beethoven can write music, thank God, but he can do nothing else on earth.'   *1770*

'The Master' Noël Coward was born in Teddington. His mother was nearly deaf so to help her hear he developed the famous clipped style of talking. Noël built an early reputation as a superb actor, though his writing career started more slowly. His first, and forever unpublished, novel was called *Cherry Pan* telling the unlikely tale of Peter Pan's daughter. However the royalties from his later writings were so large he bought a magnificent mansion in Switzerland 'overlooking an absolutely ravishing tax advantage'. The multi-talented Thespian was asked: 'Why the nickname "The Master"?' In a rare flash of modesty he said, 'Oh you know – Jack of all trades, Master of none!'   *1899*

Gangly Abraham Lincoln met dumpy Mary Todd at a party in Springfield, Illinois. After a tedious series of emotional ups and downs, the long and the short of it was they married. Their future disharmony seemed obvious from the start. She informed him that her name was spelled with two 'd's. He said, 'Why? One was enough for God!'   *1839*

English writer Somerset Maughan died in France. He chose to be buried in the grounds of his old school which is odd since as a child he'd detested it. Shortly before he died he remarked to his nephew, 'You know dying is a very dull, dreary affair and my advice to you is to have nothing whatever to do with it.'   *1965*

Today's the day...

Mr Coke collected his new hat – a 'low crowned hard felt' he'd designed to protect his head from overhanging branches while he was out hunting. To the utter amazement of his hatters, Lock's of St James's, he put the new hat on the floor and stamped on it twice. Finding it undamaged, he walked off into history with it firmly on his head. Although Lock's still call it the 'Coke' and in America it's known as the 'Derby', it's more popularly known by the name of its maker – Mr Bowler.

1849

The Wright Brothers made history when they flew their plane for the first time on the beach at Kitty Hawk, North Carolina. They'd spent a lot of time there studying the seabirds and the locals regarded them as 'just a pair of poor nuts'. However, with this ornithological information in mind, they'd built the muslin covered *Flyer I* with its 12hp engine and 40ft wing span. Gingerly they dragged it on its truck to the top of a 100ft high sand dune, ominously named Kill Devil Hill. With a 27mph wind whistling around them they solemnly shook hands

December 17

and Orville climbed into the plane, refusing to wear a coat because
of the extra weight. The engine roared and with Wilbur steadying
a wing tip, the *Flyer* rolled forward faster and faster, then took
to the air – the first self-powered, controlled flying machine. The
flight only lasted twelve seconds but it proved the brothers' theories
right – and their father wrong. He'd said, 'It's given only to God and
angels to fly!'   *1903*

Barbara Mackle was kidnapped for 'kicks'. Her abductors Gary
Krist and Ruth Eiseman-Schier whisked her away to a hillside near
Atlanta, Georgia and buried her in a box in a 9ft deep pit. In total
darkness with only a tube to breathe through, she was immured for
eighty-three hours until the half a million dollar ransom was paid.
Pursued by FBI men, Krist tried to make his getaway by sailing a boat
across the Gulf of Mexico – but it sank. At his trial, Krist was silent
until he was sentenced, when he sarcastically remarked 'Kidnapping?
The only kidnapping I know anything about is Robert Louis
Stevenson's.'   *1968*

Spiritualist statesman William Lyon Mackenzie King was born in
Ontario. Canada's Prime Minister for a total of eighteen years, he was
re-elected six times, the last when he was seventy. He always 'kept his
own counsel', never married and after the death of his dear friend
Henry Harper, never had any close friends either. He didn't smoke or
drink, and was so restrained that once when he raised his hat in public
the newspapers hailed it as 'The Prime Minister Lets Go!' His
constant companion was a little Irish terrier Pat II and in his diaries
he recorded what it ate, how it breathed and what its bowel movements
were like. He saw 'visions' in his shaving mug and on the clock-face;
communicated with his dead mother through a medium and when he
was awarded the Order of Merit, felt that Pat II deserved it 'a thousand
times more than I do.'   *1874*

Today's the day...

The original Joey the Clown, Grimaldi, was born into a theatrical family. His first performance was at fifteen months as a dancer and he soon appeared disguised as a variety of small animals. He rapidly became famous and was once booked to appear nightly in two theatres several miles apart. Not pausing to change he jumped into a coach in his fantastic costume and hurtled through the streets. This came to be a ritual and attracted crowds of people who would make sure the road was clear so Grimaldi didn't miss his cue. An odd looking character with a fat face, stunted body and extraordinary nose, he was the first major clown to paint his face white and in his honour all white faced clowns now share the name of Joey. Off-stage the great funny man suffered from melancholia. Seeking help he went to a doctor who advised him to go and see Grimaldi and have a good laugh. Sadly the little clown replied, 'But, Doctor, I am Grimaldi.' *1779*

Willowy blonde Empress Elizabeth of Russia was born.
Daughter of Peter the Great, she was taller than the rest of the dumpy women at court and liked to show it off by wearing men's clothes. Dressed in a soldier's uniform, she deposed her cousin Regent Anna

December 18

and once in power, insisted that men should attend balls in whalebone petticoats, women's gowns and head-dresses while the women wore the trousers. Despite her penchant for masculine apparel, she still had 15,000 dresses and made it tricky for the ladies by making it an offence to wear a dress of the same pattern as her own. Her capricious and nervy disposition once delayed the signing of an important peace treaty renewal with Austria. When she got as far as 'Eli . . .', a wasp landed on the end of her pen – she flung the pen down and the royal signature wasn't completed for another six months.   *1709*

The renowned 'Dirty Dick' died in Edinburgh, an aimless wanderer, ruined by a 'loose woman'. His real name was Nathaniel Bentley, a Londoner, whose life presents an amazing paradox. As a young man, he'd lived sumptuously – cared for by servants, elegantly dressed and extravagantly coiffed; the darling of society ladies, and a regular visitor to the French Court. On his father's death, however, he was left two hardware shops which he couldn't sell. He knocked them into one, appointed a manager and took himself off to Paris. On his return, it soon became apparent that he'd undergone a total change of character. He turned up at the shop shabbily dressed in patched clothes and second-hand boots. He let the shop windows get as 'dirty as the back of a chimney' and let the inside dissolve into squalor. What prompted the change was never known, and when a concerned customer suggested he do something about it, Dick replied, 'It is of no use, sir; if I wash my hands today, they will be dirty again tomorrow!'   *1809*

'Million Dollar Legs' Betty Grable was born. As the most famous pin-up of World War II, it's often said she helped the allies win. Enamoured GIs boosted their sagging morale by requesting copies at a rate of 20,000 a week. She got her nickname when she took out a hefty insurance policy on her famous legs. At one million dollars that made them twenty per cent more valuable than Fred Astaire's.   *1916*

Today's the day...

Poor Richard's Almanack **was published** and soon gobbled up by the almanac-hungry American colonists. Full of quips and homilies, it piously advocated thrift on one page and talked about ogling young girls on another. Its author, Richard Saunders, was clearly a bumbling but very wise old man, nagged by his wife and not very well off. In his Introduction, he said he'd like to say that he'd written it for the public good, but 'the plain truth of the matter is, I am excessive poor and . . . the printer has offered me a considerable share of the profits.' As it turned out, the book was an enormous hit, and popularised such adages as: 'Make haste slowly', for instance, and 'God helps them that help themselves'. The wise old man whom everybody wanted to meet was, of course, none other than Benjamin Franklin – who at the time was a hoary twenty-six years old.   *1732*

Britain's first painless tooth extraction was pulled off by an American dentist. He was Dr Francis Boott, and he'd convinced his hapless niece Miss Londsdale, that with the help of a wonderful new substance called ether he could cure her toothache without tears. She agreed; he applied the vapour, and his friend Dr James Robinson plucked out the offending molar. Though afterwards she said all she could remember was a 'heavenly dream', the patient had in fact howled throughout the operation.   *1846*

The great English painter Turner died. Christened Joseph Mallord William, he grew up to be small, 'of ruddy complexion', with clear blue eyes, a prominent nose and crooked legs. He was an extremely clumsy man and such a bad gig driver that he was nicknamed 'Over Turner'. Dedicated to his own brand of realism, he got himself into some perilous situations. As the Houses of Parliament blazed, he calmly made water colour sketches of the inferno, and at the age of sixty-seven, he had himself lashed to the mast of a ship for four hours, just so that he could capture a storm. 'I didn't expect to escape,' he said, 'but I felt bound to record it if I did.' The result was 'The Snowstorm', which one critic cruelly dubbed 'Soapsuds'. Turner was much attacked for his wild and visionary work. He developed a pathological fear of publicity, and when he moved to Cheyne Walk, he wouldn't even tell his landlady his name. His last days were spent sitting admiring the sunsets and he's commemorated by a plaque on the very tree under which he sat. He died in bed, with the winter sun streaming in on his face, and his last words were 'The sun is God'.

1851

Lord Henry Brougham got a nasty shock in Norway. This 'man of letters, man of science, advocate, orator, statesman and Lord High Chancellor' had agreed with 'G' while they were at college years before, that the first one to die would, if possible, come back to demonstrate the validity of life after death. Lord Henry was in his bath after a hard day's travelling, when 'G' appeared and sat on a chair. The doughty peer thought he'd been dreaming but on his return to Britain, he got a letter from India saying that 'G' had died on the very day he turned up at the foot of the bathtub.

1799

Veteran faker Walter W. Williams died in Houston, Texas, supposedly aged 117. Celebrated as the last survivor of the Civil War, this self-acclaimed Confederate trooper and 'honorary General', claimed to have been born in Mississippi in 1842. Famous for his fighting yarns, he was given $3,000 a month as a pension for 'services to the Confederacy' and was serenaded on his birthday by a band playing 'Dixie'. He was buried with full military honours, and a day of mourning was decreed to mark his passing. Walter's little 'joke', however, was not discovered until some years later when it was found that he was actually born in 1855 – which meant that when the Civil War was all over, this precocious old soldier was, at most, ten years old.

1959

Today's the day...

Harry Ramsden's fish and chip shop opened in a 10ft by 6ft
hut in Guiseley, Yorkshire, laughingly referred to as 'the gateway
to Bradford'. In 1931 he built a huge and 'extremely handsome
apartment' to replace the hut, and created the biggest fish and chip
shop in Yorkshire – and the world. Though Harry himself sold out
after twenty-one years, his chippie is still frying and has long since
become an English institution. It has thick carpets, chandeliers and
stained-glass windows, and at the last count, fries nearly 180 tons of
fish and 400 tons of chips in 44 tons of beef dripping every year.   *1928*

Australian wit and statesman Sir Robert Menzies was born, in
his own words 'a reasonably bigoted descendant of the Scottish race'.
At the age of four, a phrenologist felt his bumps and said he'd be a
successful public speaker. At school, his headmaster said he'd be
'Prime Minister of Australia one of these days'. They were both right:
he became the longest serving PM ever, and developed a nice line in
heckler-bashing. One man shouted to him, 'Tell us all you know, Bob –
it won't take long.' He replied, 'I'll tell you all we both know, it won't
take any longer.' When a woman declared, 'I wouldn't vote for you
if you were Archangel Gabriel', he answered her, 'If I were the
Archangel Gabriel, madam, I'm afraid you wouldn't be in my
constituency!'   *1894*

Paranormal Israeli Uri Geller was born in Tel Aviv. At the age of
three, he experienced a 'high-pitched ringing in his ears', saw 'the sun
blotted out by a silvery mass' and was knocked over backwards by a
pain in his head. He found that he could read his mother's mind, and
move the hands of watches without touching them. In his first
television appearances, he bent viewers' spoons and mended watches
by the thousand. He's repaired space scientist Wernher von Braun's
calculator; stopped a cable car in mid-air, and perfectly reproduced a
telepathically transmitted drawing while in a room shielded from

electrical transmissions. In one remarkable experiment, he moved a magnometer, creating a magnetic force half the strength of the earth's, and not surprisingly, he's impressed scientists, psychologists and paranormal researchers all over the world. One Swedish housewife, however, wasn't at all impressed. She claimed that while she was watching him on TV, he'd bent her contraceptive coil, and caused her to get pregnant! When asked about the future of Israel, Golda Meir said 'Don't ask me. Ask Uri Geller.'

1946

English satirist and rake Paul Whitehead died. A leading member of the notorious Hellfire Club, he collapsed shortly after the death of his imbecile wife. An avowed atheist, he wouldn't be buried in consecrated ground, and asked instead to be interred in a mausoleum above the caves at High Wycombe, where the Club celebrated its famous orgies. He willed his heart to fellow profligate Sir Francis Dashwood, with instructions that it be kept in a marble urn. It became a great tourist attraction and was shown to visitors for a small fee. It rapidly decayed however, and shrivelled into an ugly black ball – 'as black in death as it had been in life'. It was later stolen by a heartless thief.

1774

Today's the day...

The first major operation in Europe using anaesthetic was performed at University College Hospital, London. Previous attempts to dull the pain of surgery had involved alcohol, hypnotism and the presence of a priest – none of which were entirely successful. The patient was Frederick Churchill, a butler of thirty-six, with a suppurating wounded knee. Surgeon Robert Liston had decided to amputate. He'd heard from the American Dr Boott of the wonders of ether, and got a well-known chemist Peter Squire of Oxford Street to fashion an inhalant device to administer it. The 6ft tall, muscular Liston was famous for the speed of his operations – indeed once he was a little too hasty and in amputating a man's leg at the thigh cut off one of his patient's testicles and two of his assistant's fingers! Everything went smoothly this time, however, and with Squire acting as anaesthetist the patient quickly became insensible and the leg was off in twenty-five seconds. The gently sleeping Churchill never felt a thing and was whisked back to the ward five minutes after he'd left it. Liston was jubilant at his success declaring, 'The Yankee dodge, gentlemen, beats mesmerism hollow.'   *1846*

Forefathers Day is celebrated in America in memory of the landing of the Pilgrim Fathers. The original band of Pilgrims probably landed on 26 December but the first celebration wasn't held until a century and a half later, and then on 22 December. In 1895 the Commonwealth of Massachusetts decided they really must fix a definite date for the landing – so they did, and made it 21 December. The famous Pilgrim's Rock has moved around a bit too. It was originally identified by the Plymouth Colonial Club in 1774, who'd had it pointed out to them by Deacon Ephraim Spooner, who'd been shown it nearly forty years earlier by the ninety-five-year-old Thomas Fraunce, who'd been told it was the Pilgrim's Rock when he was a little boy! When the Club decided to move it from its place on the beach, it split into two pieces. Undeterred, they dragged the top half to the town square and then in

December 21

1834 took it on a flower-decked cart to the Pilgrim Hall. Halfway there a wheel broke and so did the rock. In 1880 it went back to the shoreline again, but in 1920 for the 300th anniversary it was on the move again. This time it shattered completely and the pieces were piled into the pit of an ornate Grecian-styled temple kindly donated by the Dames of America. In confused conclusion, Forefathers Day is probably being celebrated on the wrong day, around the wrong rock, in the wrong place.   *1620*

Bel esprit and beau Benjamin Disraeli was born. Quite a dandy, he wore brightly coloured velvet trousers, canary-yellow waistcoats, glittering chains and large rings on the outside of his gloves. When he was first Prime Minister, straight-laced Queen Victoria said, 'I do not approve of Mr Disraeli.' But the old charmer soon won her round. He would flatter her outrageously; wear primroses to remind her she'd given him some at Windsor; and call this most dumpy little woman 'Faery' and 'Gloriana'. He admitted his methods were less than subtle, but said, 'Everyone likes flattery, and when it comes to royalty, you should lay it on with a trowel.' He never flattered Mr Gladstone, however, and his dislike of him was legend. His most famous comment on the relationship came when he was asked to distinguish between a misfortune and a calamity. He said, 'If Mr Gladstone fell into the Thames it would be a misfortune, but if someone pulled him out again, it would be a calamity!'   *1804*

Pantomime hero Dick Whittington's will was published. The real Dick wasn't a footsore scullion with a friendly pussy, but a prosperous merchant whose trading ship was called *The Cat*. He built up a business dealing in wool, leather, cloth and pearls, and became one of the wealthiest men in the land. It's no wonder he was so famous: he'd lent £10,000 to the King, been temporary Mayor of London and knighted – all by the time he was twenty.   *1423*

Today's the day...

The gold-toothed boy was born in Silesia, and during his childhood became the cause of much academic concern. Learned men argued as to whether the cause was physical, astrological or religious. The great scholar Jacob Horstius of Helmstadt University wrote a book about it, and the title alone ran to twenty-one words. It was postulated that the magical event presaged a crusade against the Turk, but amid all the feverish speculation, hardly anyone thought to examine the boy. Finally a local man, Dr Rhumbaum, did. He noticed a tiny gap at the top of the tooth and the mystery was explained. The parents had moulded a gold button over it, and some of the best minds in Europe had been had.

1585

A living fossil came out of the sea, dredged up in the nets of a trawler from a depth of forty fathoms, near the mouth of the Chalumna River in Cape Province, South Africa. It was the Coelacanth – a primitive deep-water fish thought to have been extinct for seventy million years, and belonging to a group with fleshy limb-like fins, from which all land vertebrates are said to be descended. The captain of the ship described it as being brilliant steel blue, with dark blue eyes. It was 5ft long, weighed 127lbs, survived for four hours, and was acquired by Miss Courtenay-Latimer, Curator of the East London Museum. Rapid decay caused only the skin and skull to be kept, and from this, the famous ichthyologist, J. L. B. Smith identified the beast, giving it the generic name *Latimeria* in the lady's honour. Despite the offer of a £100 reward, fourteen frustrating years were to pass before another specimen was found off Anjouan Island – and still only twenty have been discovered to date. It was arguably the most important zoological find of the century; the scientific world was amazed, but the Anjouan Islanders were unimpressed. They were already familiar with the fish, and when repairing punctures, they used its thick scales to roughen up the inner tubes.

1938

The original Groucho made his *début* in a cartoon strip by Gus Mager, about a ham-fisted master sleuth called Sherlocko the Monk. The strip became something of a cult and vaudeville characters appeared with names like Henpecko, Tightwado and Nervo. A monologuist named Art Fisher, suggested the Marx Brothers should adopt similar names. Harpo because he played the harmonica; Chico because he liked the ladies; Gummo because he wore gumshoes, and Groucho because he was moody. Only he ever appeared in the strip, and the original was an aggressive 5ft 10in dental patient with a toothache who smashed windows with a stick.

1910

The great French surgeon Ambroise Paré died aged eighty and is now acknowledged to be among the fathers of modern surgery. He invented a new and less painful way of labour for difficult pregnancies; and an amazing series of artificial limbs, including a hand with a quill holder, and another where the fingers moved separately by cogs. Though unusually innovative, humane and modest, he was nevertheless a child of his times. He refused to treat witches since they were issue of the devil, and after successfully treating wounded soldiers, he would often say, 'I dressed him – but God healed him.'

1590

Today's the day...

Van Gogh's famous mutilation occurred, when he sliced a good half of his right ear off with a rusty razor. He'd been having a series of disastrous affairs and the last, with a prostitute named Rachel, drove the depressive masochistic artist to prune himself. He took the ear piece to the local brothel, handed it to Rachel and said, 'Keep this object carefully.' *1888*

Benjamin 'Beast' Butler, the Union General, was outlawed by Confederate President Jefferson Davis in a unique proclamation that declared him to be a 'common enemy of mankind', who if captured should be 'immediately executed by hanging'. The Beast's real crime was not so much his repressive rule of New Orleans, which he had taken eight months earlier, but his treatment of Southern ladies who 'by word, gesture or movement' showed contempt for Yankee soldiers. In his infamous *General Order No 28*, he decreed that each of these haughty belles should be treated as 'a woman of the town'. When they turned their backs on him in disgust, the General added, 'These women know which end of them looks best.' *1862*

December 23

The French Critic Sainte-Beuve was born. He fought a duel with an umbrella in one hand and a pistol in the other. It was pouring with rain, and he said, 'I don't mind being killed, but I'll be damned if I'm going to catch cold!'   *1804*

'Old Q' the Rake of Piccadilly died aged eighty-five. Toothless, practically totally deaf, and squinting, he passed away in a bed strewn with seventy love letters from women ranging from whores to Duchesses. He was the fourth Duke of Queensberry, and his great loves, apart from women, were gambling and his health. The richest man in England, he insisted that he 'had to buy love' and spent a fortune on potions, cures and quacks. Every morning, he bathed in milk scented with almond powder, which servants afterwards sold. He paid dairymaids to breathe on him for fresh air, and was cared for constantly by two doctors, one of whom he paid the then massive sum of £600 a year. During the last seven-and-a-half years of his life, he was visited by an apothecary named John Fuller, an amazing 10,555 times – 9,340 during the day; 1,215 at night, and an average of 3·8 calls in every twenty-four hours. Fuller was paid just £73 10s for his trouble, and only after suing Old Q's executors did he finally get a further payment of £7,500. The old hypochondriac eventually died after a bout of over-eating, when he consumed vast quantities of peaches and nectarines. He was no doubt very annoyed with himself, since he'd laid a £500 bet that he'd die in late November.   *1810*

Hansom registered the idea for his cab and promptly sold the patent for £10,000. It was designed for safety, rather than looks – and it looked very peculiar. It had huge wheels, nearly as high as the roof; it was very low slung; had no windows, and its driver sat at the front. He never got his money, and to add insult to injury, the Hansom Cab which eventually immortalised his name was nothing like the real one and was actually designed by a man named Chapman.   *1834*

Today's the day...

The cruel and clandestine Ku Klux Klan was founded in the cellar of a ruined mansion in Giles County, Tennessee. The six founder members were all high ranking Confederates, demoralised, defeated and disenfranchised by what they saw as a conspiracy of 'yankees, blacks and carpetbaggers'. The Klan claimed to be a social club, designed 'to cheer up our mothers and girls', but in fact it was dedicated to the persecution of 'uppity niggers' and radical Unionists. Its first 'Grand Wizard' was the hell-fire slave-trader, General Nathan B. Forrest, and it's odd to consider that this now virulently anti-Semitic organisation survived its early days only with the help of former Attorney General, Judah P. Benjamin – who was a Jew. The idea for the bizarre costume is said to have come from one of the very earliest meetings when a man stood guard on a tree stump, wrapped in his old Confederate cloak; a recently freed slave saw the eerie apparition and fled in terror. *1865*

Multi-millionaire maniac recluse Howard Hughes was born. At eighteen, he had himself legally declared an adult; took over his recently dead Texan Daddy's drill-making company; bought out the other shareholders for $325,000 and eventually made conservatively estimated profits of $746 million. His three great loves were women, speed and movies, which he did his best to combine in producing mediocre and massively expensive epics. He dallied with dozens of starlets; discovered Jane Russell; designed her famous cantilevered bra, and wouldn't let his chauffeurs exceed 2mph when driving movie beauties in case the bumps spoilt the firmness of their breasts. He became an aviator, and broke records flying around the world in a plane packed with ping-pong balls, so it would float if it crashed in the sea. In his film, *Hell's Angels*, the flying stunts were so dangerous that the first four pilots were killed and Hughes badly injured himself trying to show others how it should be done. As he grew older, he grew weirder and weirder. He became a total recluse, surrounding himself

December 24

with teetotal Mormons and getting obsessed about his health. Windows
were blacked out; no one was allowed to touch him; everything was
sterilised or wrapped in tissues and men were sent to catch flies by
hand. He wore the same shirt for months on end and stank like a skunk;
his hair grew to chest length, was dry cleaned and only rarely cut, and
then with specifically German scissors and a new comb for every three
strokes. His diet decreased to biscuits, sweets and cakes, all cut square,
and the occasional blood transfusion to top him up. Near death, his
6ft 4in frame lost so much weight that rolls of skin hung loose around
his buttocks, and to the end of his days he was known out of earshot
as 'Saddlebags'.   *1905*

A solitary soul survived a plane crash in the Peruvian jungle,
when a total of ninety-one passengers and crew died, either on impact
or within hours of the disaster occurring. She was seventeen-year-old
Juliane Koepcke, and she owes her life to a meteorological freak. The
updraughts caused by the turbulent air of a storm, cushioned the
descent of the plane after it had exploded at 9,000ft. For ten days,
with her arm inflamed and fed on by fly larvae, she struggled through
tangled and snake-infested vegetation along the banks of the Rio
Shebonya, before she was found by woodcutters. Her mother had died
in the crash, and the tragedy was heightened in that it could have been
avoided. They had only caught the plane because somebody had
mistakenly told them their scheduled flight was cancelled. Afterwards,
the courageous Juliane said it was her dearest wish to fly in a helicopter
or a seaplane – because 'airliners are so boring'.   *1971*

Naughty King John of England was born. He was small and hairy,
short, fat and bald, and when he lost his temper – which was often –
he would gnash his teeth, roll his eyes and throw straw and sticks in
the air. But when he was really angry, he would roll on the floor, bite
the legs of chairs and 'gnaw them like a maniac'.   *1167*

723

Today's the day...

Father Christmas comes a-calling all around the world. In Switzerland his lovely wife Lucy helps him out. In Holland, *Sinte Klaas* is followed by dastardly Black Peter who snatches naughty children, pops them into bags and whisks them off to Spain! In France, *Bonhomme Noël* is accompanied by *Père Fouettard* who makes sure mischievous *enfants* don't get good presents. But to tell the truth, Old Man Christmas, Joulupukki, actually lives on the arctic circle in a Lapland town called Rovaniemi where his ten assistants help him answer over 6,000 letters every year from eager children everywhere. Best of all, Santa Claus still visits England even though since Henry VIII's Reformation, the Catholic Church has said he shouldn't. But he does, doesn't he?   *Annual Event*

The industrious genius of gravity Isaac Newton was born, so small 'he might have been put in a quart jug'. At Cambridge he worked long and hard in his room and would often wander out, forget where he was going and wander straight back again. He never took any exercise and was always very secretive about his studies. With good reason, it turned out, as a lot of his work was concerned not with mathematics or astronomy but with the occult and alchemy. In fact, the great scientist of the 'Age of Reason' was busily searching for the philosopher's stone and the elixir of life.   *1642*

There was a conflagration at the coronation when the new King William the Conqueror was crowned in Westminster by Eldred Archbishop of York, who had also crowned the vanquished Saxon King Harold. At the climax of the ceremony the congregation cheered, and the Norman guards thought the outcry meant treachery and before anybody could enlighten them, they set fire to many of the surrounding buildings. William, incidentally, had refused to use the old crown and had a new one made from Byzantine gold encrusted with jewels – just so it would be better than Harold's.   *1066*

December 25

The King of the Jews, Jesus Christ was supposedly born in Bethlehem, though many scholars disagree about both the year and the place. There are no contemporary accounts of his life and he himself left no known written word. However, in an ancient manuscript sent to Rome, a Governor of Judaea, Publius Lentulus, describes him as being 'tall and elegantly shaped; his hair falling in graceful curls, agreeably couching on his shoulders; his cheeks without blemish and of roseate hue, and his beard thick, reaching a little below his chin and parting in the middle'. As an insight into Christ's character, the man added that though he was known to weep frequently, 'no man has seen him laugh'.

Circa 7 BC

Columbus was sunk when the good ship *Santa Maria* ran aground off Hispaniola and was claimed by the sea. Anchoring his other ships, Columbus landed and with salvaged timbers he built a fort called Navidad – from the Spanish for nativity. He spent Christmas with the pagan natives, in what because of a shipwreck was the first recorded European structure in the New World.

1492

The first personal Christmas cards ever printed decorated the mantelpieces of America. They were sent from Glasgow, bore a picture of the sender on the cover and inside had little drawings of 'Christmas in America'. In fact the lady who'd gone to all the trouble of getting them made faraway on Clydeside was none other than the little sharpshooter herself – Annie Oakley.

1891

It doesn't often snow. Though traditional, white Christmases have not often been recorded in recent years – there have only been around half a dozen in fact since 1900. It's not only the change in the climate that's brought this about, it's because for more than two centuries Christmas has been early. When they changed the calendar in 1752, they brought it forward by eleven days.

Annual Event

Today's the day...

Boxing Day is traditionally celebrated in the British Isles.
Nothing to do with pugilism, the name comes from an old custom
where apprentices would visit their master's customers hopefully
proffering a box for donations. The boxes were marked TIP – 'To
Insure Punctuality' – often thought to be the origin of the word 'tip'.

An annual event

The première of Gilbert and Sullivan's first opera, *Thespis,*
took place at the Gaiety Theatre, London. Written in less than three
weeks, it was put on after only a week's rehearsal – and it showed.
Although it was supposed to end at 11 pm, on the opening night Act
Two was still 'yawning' on at midnight. The appalling production was
said to have 'marred the pleasant effect of Mr Sullivan's music and
destroyed the pungency of Mr Gilbert's humour'. After the last night,
Gilbert and Sullivan shook hands and parted. Happily they got back
together again and produced another thirteen operas, before their final
break – after a row about the price of new carpet.   *1871*

Tongue-tied comedian Alan King was born. Nervous about
meeting Queen Elizabeth after a Command Performance, he spent
days practising his greeting – 'How do you do your Majesty.' The
dreaded moment finally arrived. 'How do you do Mr King' she said.
'How do you do Mrs Queen' he replied.   *1927*

Chain-smoking Communist Mao Tse-tung was born, in the remote
Hunan Province of China. Shovelling manure in his father's paddy
fields left him little time to study, but he caught up with his more
literate colleagues later, thanks to his alleged ability to read four times
faster than them. He survived the longest march in military history in
1934, when he led the First Red Army in a gruelling 6,000 mile
rearguard action against the Japanese and Chiang Kai-Shek
Kuomintang forces. Despite offers of up to £62,000 on his head he

December 26

still managed to keep the loyalty of his followers. Once in power he became renowned for his maxims like, 'Political power grows out of the barrel of a gun' and he identified sins against the Party with convenient labels such as 'closed-doorism' and 'mountaintopism'. *1893*

Delicate elegant poet Thomas Gray was born. After his childhood home burnt down he had a morbid fear of fire; always kept a rope ladder by him and prudently insured himself with the London Assurance. While studying at Peterhouse, Cambridge, a group of hearty undergrads decided to take advantage of his well-known phobia and placed a large water butt under his window. They sounded the alarm and right on cue Gray flung open the window and shinned down the ladder in his nightgown – straight into the middle of the tub. Disgusted at these juvenile pranks, he moved to Pembroke College. Luckily he took his rope ladder with him, for it was there that he really did have a narrow escape when part of the building was destroyed – by fire. *1716*

Prematurely enlightened Emperor Frederick II was born. Formally crowned King of Sicily at three-and-a-half, he was married at fourteen, a father soon after and invited to be Holy Roman Emperor at eighteen. Known as the 'Wonder of the World' he spoke six languages, had learned discourses with Muslim scholars, defied the Pope, decided all religions were 'impostures', and was described by Dante as the father of Italian poetry. He also won battles, built castles with bathrooms and running water, and had an extravagant menagerie including the first giraffe in Europe. *1194*

Eccentric physician Messenger Monsey died, leaving strict instructions for his body to be dissected and the remnants thrown away. He'd adopted a surefire way of extracting teeth by tying a piece of strong catgut around the tooth, attaching the other end to a bullet and firing it from a fully charged pistol. *1788*

Today's the day...

The voyage which revolutionised man's thinking began, as the
Beagle set sail with the untried naturalist Charles Darwin on board.
She was a ten gun brig of 242 tons; 90ft long and 24ft 8in in the beam.
She was commanded by the fascinating figure of Captain Robert
Fitzroy. A direct descendant of Charles II through his famous
mistress Barbara Villiers, he was a strange and severe man. Darwin,
who was then still under sentence of becoming a reluctant clergyman,
had volunteered as the ship's unpaid naturalist, and the two made an
odd pair. The voyage, and Darwin's observations of the different
adaptations of the Galapagos Island finches, led of course to the *Origin
of Species* and the theory of evolution. It changed him from a man who
'did not doubt the strict and literal truth of every word in the Bible',
into the champion of free thinkers – and its outcome in his work
horrified Fitzroy, himself a deeply religious man. Fitzroy was bitterly
ashamed of his involvement with the 'sacrilegious theory' and though
he went on to become a Vice Admiral and Governor of New Zealand,
he committed suicide at a relatively early age. How much he must have
regretted not following his first inclination to reject Darwin's
application for the job. He was going to do so, because he didn't like
the shape of his nose.   *1831*

Marlene Dietrich was born in Berlin – Maria Magdalene von
Losch Dietrich. She was not born on any of the other days or in any of
the other years she's enjoyed confusing people with. She became
Hollywood's highest paid actress; made her first major film *The Blue
Angel* in 1930; her most recent *Just a Gigolo* in 1978; she still has a
36–24–36 figure and still has to suffer being called 'the world's most
glamorous grandmother'. In 1934 she became an American citizen.
Hitler wanted her to be his mistress but she refused and then worried
that if she'd agreed she could have helped the Jews. Her lovers have
included Douglas Fairbanks Junior, Maurice Chevalier, Yul Brynner
and sundry other artists and actors. Noël Coward called her 'a realist

December 27

and a clown'. Hemingway said, 'If she had nothing but her voice, she could break your heart with it.' Cocteau thought she was 'like a frigate with all sails flying', and Richard Burton summed up the paradox of her age and beauty. He said, 'She's like a skeleton risen from the grave. Beautiful and extraordinary.'

1901

***Peter Pan* was first performed** at the Duke of York's Theatre. It was written by James Barrie for the Llewellyn Davis children, and everybody but Barrie thought this then revolutionary tale of a little boy who never grew up, would be an absolute disaster. The great H. Beerbohm Tree even thought Barrie had gone mad. After a fairly dismal first two weeks, however, it was a roaring success, and has been practically every Christmas since. Children of the time were terrified of the wicked Captain Hook, who was played by Sir Gerald du Maurier, the novelist Daphne du Maurier's father – and were carried fainting from their seats. One of the most memorable lines comes from Peter himself, 'To die will be an awfully big adventure.'

1904

Today's the day...

Hairy Highlander Rob Roy died, to the tune of his piper playing the old lament 'I shall never return'. Immortalised by Sir Walter Scott as a Robin Hood character who stole from the rich and gave to the poor, in reality he operated a flourishing protection racket and extorted a handy five per cent from farmers for the safety of their cattle. Any who didn't pay up were stripped of all their possessions while those who did had the guarantee that if their cattle were stolen, Red Robert would get them back. Uncommonly strong, his legs were said to resemble those of a Highland bull, 'hirsute, with red hair and evincing muscular strength similar to that animal'. *1734*

Fiery composer Maurice Ravel died. He suffered from aphasia which made it impossible for him to compose and sometimes even to speak, so he decided to risk a brain operation. The operation was unsuccessful but afterwards at least he could talk and pathetically asked his friend Roland Manuel, 'Tell me not everything I wrote was bad.' Often quoted as his last words they're not in fact. These came later when, admiring his bandaged head in a mirror, he declared, 'I look like a Moor.' *1937*

The Tay Bridge collapsed into the swirling flooded waters of the river, taking with it a train and claiming over 300 lives. The two-year-old bridge had been one of the great wonders of modern engineering stretching over a mile and a half, with eighty-five huge spans constructed of metal girders. The 4.15 pm train from Edinburgh was right on time and reached the bridge about 7.30 at the height of a terrible storm. With its seven carriages packed full of people, it was signalled onto the bridge, but barely two minutes later thirteen of the central girders suddenly collapsed. 'A comet-like burst of fiery sparks sprang out as if forcibly ejected into the darkness from the engine. In a long visible trail the streak of fire was seen till quenched in the stormy waters below.' There were no survivors, for apart from the terrible

December 28

conditions, the doors of every carriage were locked. With uncanny precognition, the sonorous poet McGonagall, a native of Dundee, had written when the bridge was opened, 'I hope that God will protect all passengers/By night and by day/And that no accident will befall them while crossing/The Bridge of the Silvery Tay.'   *1879*

Chewing-gum was patented by William Finley Semple, a genial dentist from Mount Vernon, Ohio. He saw it as an excellent way to exercise the jaws, stimulate gums and scour the teeth. One doctor published a dire warning that its use would 'exhaust the salivary glands and cause the intestines to stick together'. That didn't stop people chewing, however, and it's come in handy in some sticky situations. The RAF dirigible R-34 wouldn't have made it across the Atlantic without it. Halfway over a leak was discovered in the water jacket of one of the engines. All the glues and putty on board failed to mend it so the captain handed out packets of gum to his crew. After some rapid chewing, they were able to block up the offending hole with the well-masticated mass. According to one crew member, they then offered up a vote of thanks to gum manufacturers everywhere.   *1869*

Today's the day...

The massacre of Wounded Knee, South Dakota, left between 150 and 300 Indian men, women and children dead, with the loss of some twenty-five soldiers killed and thirty-nine wounded, mostly by their own stray bullets and shrapnel. The US Government had ordered that Indian 'fomentors of disturbances' be rounded up – in particular Big Foot, Chief of the Minneconjou. The previous day Big Foot, who was dying of pneumonia, surrendered to General Whiteside of the 7th Cavalry. A camp was made at Wounded Knee Creek, where the Indians, who were to be disarmed, were surrounded by soldiers and watched over by two men on Hotchkiss machine-guns. During the night, the soldiers celebrated the 'capture' of Big Foot with a liberal helping of whisky. In the morning the Indians were ordered to disarm, and though they did so quietly, the soldiers insisted there weren't enough guns – they wanted them all. In fact, only two more were found but one of them belonged to a young brave who said the gun had cost him a lot of money and it was his. He brandished it above his head. He was grabbed, the gun went off, pandemonium broke loose and the Indians were fired upon 'like we were buffaloes'. It was later reported that the brave who brandished the gun could not have heard the instructions – he was deaf. *1890*

St Thomas à Becket was martyred and Henry II was finally rid of his 'turbulent priest'. The four barons, Fitzurse, de Tracy, de Morville and le Breton galloped to Canterbury to put an end once and for all to the struggle between Church and State. They found the Archbishop in a chapel near the North transept of the cathedral and Fitzurse struck the first blow. De Tracy struck next, and nearly severed the arm of Becket's friend Grim, who tried to parry the blow. He struck again and knocked the martyr to his knees. Le Breton sliced scalp from skull and his sword snapped in two as it struck the pavement. One of the barons' men strode forward, trod on the dead man's neck, thrust his sword into the open wound and scattered the brains on the floor.

December 29

The killers fled and within hours pilgrims were clamouring to dip their hands in Becket's blood. Under the Archbishop's robes, they were staggered to find the humble black habit of a Benedictine and the hair shirt of a penitent. *1170*

Loquacious prig William Ewart Gladstone was born of Scottish parents in Liverpool. The greatest Liberal of all, he started out as a Tory; made a maiden speech in defence of slave labour; became a Tory Chancellor of the Exchequer; saw the light; crossed the floor of the house; became Liberal Prime Minister four times and spent a total of sixty-one years in Parliament. An interminable speaker, with 'a gleaming vulture's eye', he would point his bony finger and pound his despatch box so hard that he would often drown what he was saying. He must be one of the few people who've ever used the word 'antidisestablishmentarianism' in normal speech, and liked to ease his vocal chords with a lubricant of sherry and egg. Disraeli described him as 'a sophisticated rhetorician, inebriated with the exuberance of his own verbosity.' Queen Victoria wasn't keen on him either – she said 'He speaks to me as if I were a public meeting.' Thick of neck, flat of foot, with his massive ears on a line with his mouth, the old boy had some very strange habits. When he wasn't walking at precisely 4mph, he was probably trying to reclaim a fallen woman, or chopping down a tree with one of his thirty axes. What convinced most people of his dottiness, however, was the sight of Mrs Gladstone scurrying round the hatters early in the morning, cancelling the twenty top hats her husband regularly ordered. *1809*

The Haymarket Theatre opened in London. Haunted by Old Buxton, the ghost of a former actor-manager, it's also the theatre where Prime Minister Robert Walpole was so rudely portrayed that he jumped up and boxed the leading actor's ears, and created the Lord Chamberlain's Office to censor all future productions. *1720*

Today's the day...

A nice Roman Emperor was born – at last. He was called Titus; was an excellent scholar, a brave soldier and exceedingly generous. To keep in touch with the common people, he used the public baths, and once when he realised he hadn't done anyone a favour, he turned and said, 'My friends, I have wasted a day.' Probably the only really nasty thing he ever did was to burn down the Temple in Jerusalem and God made him pay for that, said the Jews, by only allowing him to reign for two years. The irony is, that this classical Mr Nice Guy is best remembered for his great love affair with Berenice, who was not only a Jewess, but twelve years older than him, twice married and lived in public incest with her brother.   *AD 41*

Lecherous quack Simon Forman was born. Famous for bedding his female patients and receiving stolen goods, he was nevertheless rarely short of patients. His 'chirugery' had three rooms – one for 'normal' medical practice like wart reading and breast massage; another reserved for the magical arts and a third devoted to marriage guidance, where couples could ask for advice or pick up their aphrodisiacs. Perhaps his most astounding cure was that of the knight, Sir Barrington Molyns, who was suffering from a nasty attack of 'stinking sweet and venomous worms' up his nose. Forman diagnosed demons – obviously – and gave the man some demonifuge and a quick rub down with some heavy stones. This produced a loud ringing in his ears, and convinced him the demons were leaving. Stage two of the treatment was to immerse the patient head first in a stagnant pond full of frogs at midnight, and the most amazing thing of all is – it worked.   *1552*

Lascivious Gregorian Rasputin was murdered by Prince Felix Yussopov and three accomplices, who lured him to what promised to be a wild party in a cellar. There, while the phonograph played 'Yankee Doodle Dandy', they convivially stuffed him with fancy cakes and a bottle of Madeira, all liberally laced with cyanide. What they didn't know was that the debauched holy man suffered from alcoholic gastritis, which prevents the stomach secreting hydrochloric acid – the catalyst needed to make cyanide a poison. At 2.30 am he was happily studying an ivory crucifix when Yussopov could stand no more and shot him. Rasputin fell, but as the Prince examined the body, the monk transfixed his assassin with one hypnotic eye. They fought and Yussopov fled. Rasputin burst into the courtyard and was shot over and over again. Some reports state that he was stabbed as well and in all, it's agreed, that Yussopov tried to finish him off with a truncheon. The four men trussed the body up, and pushed it through a hole in the ice on the River Neva. When the remains were recovered a few days later, an examination revealed that one arm was free of its cords and the victim's lungs were full of water – Rasputin had survived assassination and died from drowning.   *1916*

The 'absolutely fireproof' Iroquois Theatre in Chicago burned in the worst theatre fire in US history. It was a new building; had only been open for thirty-eight days, and shouldn't in fact have been opened at all, since it wasn't finished. It was however, extremely 'safe'. It had eleven fire exits and a lot of money had been spent on a new asbestos safety curtain. It had seats for 1,602 people, though on this night 1,830 attended. The fire started as a 'double octet' began singing 'In the Pale Moonlight'. To create a moonlit effect, a lighting man had changed a white light for a blue one, and the electrics sparked and set fire to a chunk of scenery. The fire spread and soon was so fierce that it was decided to lower the asbestos curtain, but it stuck two thirds of the way down and the stage became a funnel for the fire. The next quarter of an hour was one of unmitigated horror as people rushed for the exits, many of which were bolted or hidden with curtains. In all the carnage, however, only one performer was killed. She was acrobat Nellie Reed, leader of the Flying Ballet, whose wires had stopped the safety curtain from dropping.   *1903*

Today's the day...

A gentle giant died when he was caught by a gang of poachers in the mountain forests of Rwanda and speared five times in the chest. They took his head for a trophy and cut off his hands to be made into ashtrays for tourists. The giant in question was 'Digit', a twenty-stone member of the vanishing tribe of rare mountain gorillas. Despite his colossal strength, Digit's gentleness was beyond question. Millions of people had witnessed it on the BBC's 'World About Us' programme, when this huge primate approached the American zoologist Dr Dian Fossey, took her notebook and pen for a brief examination, returned them to her, and lay at her side to sleep.   *1977*

The Ratcliffe Highway murderer, seaman and labourer John Williams hanged himself in his cell at Coldbath Fields Prison. In a short spree before Christmas, he'd massacred two families, an apprentice and a maid. His body was placed in a cart, and escorted past the houses of the victims by '300 constables with swords drawn'. This done, it was thrown into a ditch at the crossroads of Cannon Street and New Road, covered in quicklime, a stake driven through its chest and the grave left unmarked. The idea was to restrain the wandering soul of the sinner, and if the stake didn't hold him down and the ghost arose, he'd be so confused by the crossroads that he wouldn't know which way to go and might lie down again. Perhaps not surprisingly, this exotic execution was dealt with by De Quincey in his book *Murder, Considered as One of the Fine Arts.*   *1911*

It's Hogmanay and though nobody really knows what it means, the Scots lexicographer Jamieson says it's 'the name appropriated by the vulgar' for New Year's Eve. Various suggested origins include 'Hogmoney' – oatmeal cakes traditionally given to children, 'Hagman heigh!' – the cry of the woodman asking for his annual gratuity, and '*Hagia-mana*' which signifies 'Holy Month' in Ancient Greek. The most likely solution, however, lies in the word '*Aguillanneuf*', which is what the Normans used to shout instead of Hogmanay. So, sadly for Scotland, not only are bagpipes originally Turkish, Haggis English and St Andrew a Galilean – but Hogmanay is probably French!

Annual Event

The Dutch Hippocrates Herman Boerhaave was born in Voorhout, near Leyden. He became the arbiter of medical Europe and his bed-side manner of teaching was so popular that the university 'had to pull down its walls' to accommodate his students. So great was his fame that when a Chinaman sent him a letter addressed to 'Boerhaave Europe', it got there! He wrote a book called *The Onliest and Deepest Secrets of the Art of Medicine* and willed that it should be auctioned after his death. It brought £2,000 in gold, but when the eager buyer opened it, he found just ninety-nine blank pages. The only words were on the fly leaf. They said: 'Keep your head cool, your feet warm and you'll make the best doctor poor.'

1668

The year ends – traditionally. So we'd like to wish a happy New Year to all our readers.

Annual Event

Index

Aberdeen 347
Abernethy, Dr John 193
Abershaw, Jerry 437
Abominable Snowman 631
Aboukir Bay, Battle of 432
Abu Simbel 23
Abyssinia 212
Aconcagua, Mountain 33
Adam and Eve 608
Adams, Fanny 478
Adams, President John Quincy 390
adding machine 575
Addinsell, Richard 31
Agincourt, Battle of 602
Agrippina (mother of Nero) 704
air hostess 277
airship 562
Alamein, Battle of 598
Alaska 178, 184
Albert, Prince Consort 48, 87, 582, 632, 703
Alcatraz, Bird Man of 176
Alcock, John William 336
alcohol 546
Alcott, Louisa May 672
Alexander I 383
Alexander the Great 335
Alexandra of Denmark 144
Alexei, Tsar 69
Alfonso, King (Portugal) 19, 281
Alfonso, King (Spain) 281
Ali, Muhammad 523
Alkemade, Sergeant Nicholas 174
Allen, Margaret 'Bill' 29
Almanack, Poor Richard's 712
Amin Dada, Idi 7
Amirault, Dr 507
Ampère, André Marie 48
Amundsen, Roald 41, 320, 703
anaesthetic 184, 716
anaesthetist, phantom 494
Andersen, Hans Christian 191

Anderson, 'Bloody Bill' 607
Andrée, Solomon 588
Andrews, Julie 554
Andronicus I, Emperor 517
Anjouan Island 719
Anne of Austria 663
Anne of Cleves 6
Anne of Russia, Empress 54
Anne, Princess 642
Anne, Queen 425
antiques 631
Anything Goes 656
appetite 455
April Fool's Day 188
Arabs 564
archaeology 262, 336
Archer, Fred 27
architecture 325
Armstrong, Archie 146
Armstrong, Neil 410
Arnold, Walter 60
Arscott, Robert 381
art 322, 330
'Ashes' 488
assassination 64, 65, 96, 106, 109, 154, 194, 214, 253, 306, 364, 433, 470, 504, 505, 535, 676, 732, 735
Astaire, Fred 366
asthma 389
astronauts 100, 106, 369, 431
Astronomer Royal 132, 468
astronomy 102, 104, 150
Aswan Dam 23
Atahualpa (Inca) 647
Atchison, David Rice 133
athletics 141, 158, 258, 296, 401, 413, 427
Atlantic Ocean 432
atom bomb 400, 679
Attems, Count Von 224
Attlee, Clement 11
Augustus, Emperor 468, 538
Augustus the Strong 271

Aurungzebe, Emperor 108
Austen, Jane 405, 606
Austin, John 629
Australia 224, 371
Autry, Gene 551
aviation 15, 16, 74, 109, 250, 253, 257,
  260, 284, 287, 298, 336, 339, 371, 392,
  398, 416, 418, 469, 509, 580, 617, 671,
  708, 723
Aviles, Pedro Menendez de 508

'Babe' Ruth 78
Bacall, Lauren 289
Bach, Johann Sebastian 166, 424
Bacon, Francis 205
Bader, Douglas 109
Baird, John Logie 58, 612
Balaclava, Battle of 602
Ball, Captain Albert 260
Ball, Ernest, R. 454
ballet 149, 159
balloon flight 18, 465, 522, 531, 583, 588
ballpoint pen 328
Balzac, Honoré de 286
Bankhead, Tallulah 66
bank notes 400
Banks, 'Baggy Pants' 547
Bannister, Roger 258
Bannockburn, Battle of 356
Bara, Theda 408
barbed wire 359
Barber of Seville 124
Bardot, Brigitte 549
Barnard, Dr Christiaan 680
Barnato, Barney 337
Barnum, Philo 12
Barnum, Phineas T. 12, 379, 395
Barrett, Jackie 643
Barrie, James M. 77, 196, 264, 729
Barry, James 418
Barry, Madame du 688
Barry, Richard 459
Barrymore, John 97, 222
Bartlett, Adelaide 220
Bartley, James 481
Barton, Matthew 541

baseball 78
basketball 45
Basnage, Jacques 446
Bastille, Fall of 397
Bathory, Countess Elizabeth 472
bathtub 694
Battle of Britain 470, 649
BBC 37
Beagle, HMS 728
Bean, John William 374
Beatles 80, 382, 428, 544, 571, 623
Beauharnais, Alexandre 354
beauty contest, first 530
Beck, Martha 139
Becket, St Thomas à 14, 732
Beckford, William 550
bedbugs 700
Beecham, Sir Thomas 244, 245
Beethoven, Ludwig van 176, 654, 706
'Beetle' car 43
Bell, Alexander Graham 32, 131, 145
Bell, Dr Joseph 260
Belloc, Hilaire 423
Bell Rock lighthouse 68
Bennett, Arnold 178, 300
Bennett, James Gordon 7
Bentham, Jeremy 321
Benz, Karl 667
Beringer, Dr Johann Bartholomaeus
  Adam 308
Berkeley, George 148
Berlin, Irving 258, 268
Bernhardt, Sarah 570, 597
Berry, James 83, 113
Best, George 291
Best, Samuel 138
Bevin, Ernest 254
bicycle 693
Bigfoot 592
Bikini 379
Billy the Kid 397
Birdseye, Clarence 137
Biro, Laszlo 328
Bishop, Bridget 328
Bishop, Washington Irving 270
Bizet, Georges 130, 315

Bjorkland, Penny 68
Blackbeard 658
Blackburn Rovers F.C. 698
Black Hole of Calcutta 348
Black Prince 482
Blake, William 670
Blanchard, Pierre 18
Blaydon Races 496
Blériot, Louis 418
Bligh, Captain 242
Blondin, Charles 488
Blood, Colonel 264
blood transfusion 332
Boabdil, King 9
boat-race 172
body-line bowling 41
Boerhaave, Herman 737
Boer War 280
Bogarde, Dirk 180
Bogart, Humphrey De Forest 50, 289
Bokassa, Emperor Jean-Bedel 682
Boleyn, Anne 55, 284, 352
Bolivar, Simon 416
Bolivia 416
boll weevil 696
Bolshevism 231
Bombard, Alain 590
Bond, James 303
Boniface VIII, Pope 50
Bonnie and Clyde 293
Booth, Hubert Cecil 116
Booth, John Wilkes 238
Booth, Richard 188
Boothby, Lord 90
Boott, Dr Francis 712
Borg, Bjorn 320
Borgia, Rodrigo 453
Borgnine, Ernest 53
Borley Rectory 120
Borodin, Alexander 638
Boston, Great Fire of 632
Boston Tea Party 431, 553, 706
Boucher, Katharine 670
Boult, Sir Adrian 9
Bourbon, Duke of 484
Bouvier, Jackie 516

Bowdler, Thomas 391
Bowen, Eli 580
Bowes-Lyon, Elizabeth 239
bowler hat 708
Bow Street Runners 105
boxing 128, 221, 273, 372, 376, 472, 506, 523, 536, 548, 585, 600
Boxing Day 726
bra 641
Brady, Diamond Jim 454
'Brains Trust' 455
Brando, Marlon 193
Brasher, Christopher 258
Braun, Eva 226, 247
Breitbart, Sigmund 669
Brooke, Rupert 436
Brougham, Lord Henry 530, 713
Brown, Arthur Whitten 336
Brummell, Beau 323
Brutus 154
Brynner, Yul 391
Buchan, John 483
Buckingham Palace 48, 394, 458
Buckland, Dr William 666
Buffalo Bill 118
bull-fighting 254, 351, 373, 404, 428, 448
bunny-pig 318
Bunyan, John 102
Burgess, Guy 296
burial, premature 126
Burke and Hare 88
Burnley F.C. 698
Burns, Robbie 410
Burraway, Alice 90
Burroughs, Edgar Rice 495
Burton, Richard 154, 635
Burton, Sir Richard 163
Busby, Dr Richard 537
Butler, Benjamin 'Beast' 720
Butler, Samuel 682
Byrd, Richard 671
Byrne, Charles 310
Byron, Lord 49

Cabrini, Frances Xavier 382
Caesar, Julius 154, 392, 538

Cage, John 503
Cagliostro, Alessandro di 313
Cagney, James 403
Caillaux, Henriette 156
calendar 124, 520, 725; Gregorian 520; Julian 175
California 344, 382, 511
Californian Big Tree 511
Caligula 52, 492
Callaghan, Stephen 107
Calmette, Gaston 156
camera 501
Cameron, Julia Margaret 56, 330
Cameron, Lord 212
Canada 370, 534
Can-Can 595
Canning, George 208, 446
Cape Canaveral 106
Capone, Al 28, 54, 95, 601
Capper, Joseph 505
Cardiff Giant 585
Cardigan, Lord 517, 602
Carey, Henry 560
Carlyle, Thomas 683
Carmen 130, 315
Carnegie, Andrew 453
Caroline of Brunswick 196, 246, 281, 446
Carpentier, Georges 372
carpet sweeper 530
Carroll, Lewis 59
Cartland, Barbara 386
Cartouche, Louis Dominique 668
Caruso, Enrico 117, 222
Casanova, Giovanni Jacopo 190, 616
Cassidy, Butch 399
Castlereagh, Viscount 449
Castro, Fidel 627
Castro, Ines Pires de 19
Cather, Willa 689
Catherine de Valois 11
Catherine the Great 191, 250
Cato the Younger 76
cats 671
Cavell, Edith 577
Cavendish, Henry 572

Cazotte, Jacques 542
censorship 431
Cervantes, Miguel de 566
Chamberlain, Joseph 385
Chamberlain, Neville 499
chamber-pots 456
Chandler, Raymond 415
Chaplin, Charlie 219
Charge of the Light Brigade 602
Charles I 64
Charles II 70, 78, 108, 240, 570
Charles V, Emperor 115, 457
Charles VIII (France) 368
Charles, Prince 614, 635, 642
Charlie, Bonnie Prince 363
Charlotte, Princess 508
charter flight, first 364
Charteris, Colonel Francis 287
Chartists 206
Chataway, Christopher 258
Chatelard, Monsieur de 101
Chequers 21
Chesebrough, Robert Augustus 274
Chevis, Lieutenant Hubert 350
chewing gum 731
Chiang Kai-Shek 726
Chi Chi 412
children, cruelty to 704
Chile 557
China 644, 645, 726
Chinese cuisine 489
chloroform 60, 622
Chrimes brothers 568
Christie, Agatha 523, 665
Christie, James 631
Christina of Sweden, Queen 690
Christmas 725
Christmas cards 725
Christobella, Viscountess 415
Christophe, Henri 565
Chung Ling Soo 171
Churchill, John 299
Churchill, Lord Randolph 53
Churchill, Winston S. 11, 29, 53, 266, 316, 470, 635, 641, 654, 674
CIA 622

Cicero 604, 689
Cid, El 388
Cintron, Conchita 448
Civil War (English) 246
Civil War (American) 43, 210
Clarence, Duke of 21, 44
Clark, Jim 133
Clarke, Mary Anne 351
Claudius, Emperor 433, 578
Clemenceau, Georges 662
Cleopatra's Needle 517
Coates, 'Cockadoodle' 84
Cobbett, William 458
'Coca-Cola' 182
Cockerell, Sir Christopher 699
Cocking, Robert 417
Cody, William F. 118
Coelacanth 718
Coleridge, Samuel Taylor 51, 594
Colet, Dr John 524
collecting 7
Collingwood, Admiral Lord 545
Columbus, Christopher 576, 725
Comédie Humaine, La 286
comedy, longest running 314
Commodus, Emperor 492
Compleat Angler 448
Comstock, Antony 139
Concorde 129
Connally, Governor John 659
Connecticut 22
Connery, Sean 480
Connolly, Cyril 512
Connor, William 324
Constable, John 330
Constantinople 305
Constantius I of Rome 419
Coogan, Jackie 605
Cook, Captain James 242, 608
Cook, Dr 229
Cook, Thomas 280
Cooke, Alistair 631
Coolidge, President Calvin 377, 436
Cooper, Alice 75
Cooper, Gary 261
Copenhagen, Battle of 191

Copernicus, Nicolaus 104
Corbett, 'Gentleman' Jim 506
Corbin, Margaret 646
Corbitt, James Henry 670
Corday, Charlotte 395, 402
Cordobes, El 254
Cornwallis, Archbishop of Canterbury
    179
Cornwallis, Lord 590
coronation 208, 312, 448
Coronation Street 693
Count of Monte Cristo, The 417
Coward, Noël 35, 662, 707
Crab, Roger 514
Crabb, Commander Lionel 'Buster' 224
Crane, Stephen 617
Crapper, Thomas 30
Crassus, Marcus Licinius 324
Crawford, Joan 171
Crawford, Mrs Jane Todd 701
creation, date of 598
Crécy, Battle of 482
cremation 31
Crème de Menthe Variation 628
Cribb, Tom 548
cricket 41, 340, 374, 405, 482, 488, 501
crime 381, 417
Crimean War 270
Crippen, Dr 431
Crippen, Hawley H. 660
Crockett, Davy 464
Crockford, William 294
crocodile 105
Crompton, Samuel 680
Cromwell, Oliver 65, 227, 236, 372, 498,
    676
Cronje, General Piet 280
Crosby, Bing 251
crossword puzzles 618
Crowhurst, Donald 614
Crowley, Aleister 577
Crown jewels 264
Cruft, Charles 144
Cruikshank, George 546
Crystal Palace 249, 675
'Cucaracha, La' 241

742

cuckoo 129
Cullinan, the 56
Culloden, Battle of 396
Cup Final, FA 243
Curie, Marie 628
Curie, Pierre 628
Custer, George 85, 358, 685
Cutpurse, Moll 420
cycling 369
Czechoslovakia 471
Czolgosz, Leon 504

Daily Mail 458
Daily Mirror 458
Daimler, Gottlieb 150
Dali, Salvador 269
Dallas, Texas 659
Dalton Bros. 562
Dambusters 279
Dancer, Daniel 552
Daniell, William 521
Darnley, Lord 427
Darwin, Charles 219, 662, 728
Davenant, Sir William 200
Davies, Peter Llewellyn 196
Davis, Bette 196
Davis, Joe 217
Davis, Jr, Sammy 691
Davy, William 132
Day, Thomas 353
D-Day 320
Deare, John 465
decapitation 65, 82, 92, 204, 236, 284,
    308, 325, 352, 364, 381, 402, 410, 478,
    498, 507, 610, 678, 688
Declaration of Independence 376, 409
De Gaulle, Charles 128, 474
De la Cloche, James Stuart 208
Dempsey, Jack 372, 536
Dennis, Edward 657
dentistry 696
Denys, Jean Baptiste 332
D'Eon, Chevalier 482, 563
Derby (race) 255, 321
'Desert Island Discs' 621

Devil 83
Dexter, Ted 311
diamonds 56
Dickens, Charles 34, 80, 327
dictionary 216
Dietrich, Marlene 563, 728
Digby, Sir Everard 65
Dillinger, John 412, 599
Dillinger gang 136
DiMaggio, Joe 440
'Dirty Dick' 711
Disney, Walt 77, 81, 132, 650, 684
Disraeli, Benjamin 224, 717
diving 111, 223
diving record 168
Doenitz, Admiral Karl 525
dogs 140, 144, 381, 432, 530, 569, 621,
    662
Dolly Sisters 27
Domitian, Emperor 600
Don Carlos 385
Don Giovanni 611
Donizetti, Gaetano 672
Donoghue, Steve 321
doughnut 387
Douglas, Katherine 106
Douglas, Kirk 692
Doyle, Sir Arthur Conan 260
Dracula, Count 630
Drake, Francis 195
drinking fountain 229
driving 123, 570
driving tests 151, 458
dropsy 341
Druids 350
Drury Lane Theatre 104, 115
Dryden, John 273, 677
Dubcek, Alexander 471
Duck, Stephen 166
Ducornet, César 25
Duell, William 663
duelling 82, 166, 253, 298, 307, 332
Dumas, Alexandre 417, 422
Duncan, Isadora 301, 520
Dunkirk 316
Dunlop, John 123

Dunstan, 'Sir' Jethrey 526
Duryea, Charles and Frank 224
Dustin, Hannah 245

eagle 121
Earp, Wyatt 162
earthquakes 178, 199, 222
Eastman, George 501
Ebba, Saint 477
Eddystone lighthouse 669, 679
Edgar I 269
Edgehill, Battle of 598
Edison, Thomas Alva 88, 290, 594, 686
Edward the Confessor 14
Edward I 234
Edward II 535
Edward III 482
Edward IV 183
Edward VI 107
Edward VII 394, 448, 632
Edward VIII 354, 697
Edward, Prince of Wales 144
Edward, Duke of York 182
Egerton, Francis Henry 636
Egypt 421
Einstein, Albert 153, 222
Eisenhower, President Dwight D. 500,
    543, 580
Eleanor of Aquitaine, Queen 282
electric chair 37, 139, 322, 423
electricity 338, 488
electric light bulb 594
elephant 127, 391, 518, 522
Elephant Man 209
Elizabeth of Russia, Empress 710
Elizabeth I 172, 195, 506, 677
Elizabeth II 228, 312
Elizabeth, Princess (later Queen
    Elizabeth II) 78, 133, 312, 389, 654
Elizabeth, Queen Mother 238, 438
Ellerton, Simeon 10
Ellington, 'Duke' 245
Elliott, Dr 386
Empire State Building 248
end of the world 612
English Channel 18, 418, 479

escalators 561
Etheldreda, Princess 586
Etna, Mount 146
Eton School 369
Everest, Mount 305
Everet, John 613
evolution 662, 728
exploration 98, 158, 182, 320, 606, 608
explosion 687

Faerie Queen, The 677
Fairbanks, Douglas 180
Fairfax, Lord 420
fakirs 655
Falk, Peter 'Columbo' 524
Fangio, Juan Manuel 357
Faraday, Michael 488
Farina, Giuseppe 499
Farinelli, Carlo 53
Farouk, King 421
Farrow, Mia 406
Father Christmas 724
Fawkes, Guy 624
Felt, Dorr Eugene 575
Fender, Percy 482
Ferdinand, Archduke 364
Ferdinand V (Spain) 9
Fernandez, Raymond 139
Fidelio 654
Fielding, Henry 123, 230
Fields, W. C. 63
Figaro, Le 156
Fischer, Bobby 143
fish 37, 718
fish and chips 714
Fisher, Bishop 352
Fitzgerald, Edward 33
Fitzgerald, Francis Scott 540
Fitzgerald, George Robert 332
Fitzroy, Captain Robert 728
Flagstad, Kirsten 392
Flamsteed, John 132, 468
Flaubert, Gustave 699
Fleming, Ian Lancaster 303, 480
Fletcher, Horace 451
Flores, Ralph 74

Floyd, 'Pretty Boy' 596
flushing toilets 30, 70, 662
Flying Dutchman 390
flying saucers 356, 362
Flynn, Errol 348
Fondi, Duchess of 501
Fonteyn, Dame Margot 283
football 32, 243, 291, 366, 429, 698
Football Association 605
Ford, Bob 192
Ford, Miss Dorothy 668
Ford, Henry 429
Ford, Model T 309
Ford, President Gerald 396, 449, 582
Forefathers' Day 716
Foreign Legion 142, 327
forgery 190, 546
Forman, Simon 734
Formby, George 298
Forrest, General Nathan 394, 722
Fox, George 613
Fox, Henry 371
France, Anatole 219
Francis I (France) 516
Franklin, Benjamin 38, 220, 293, 338, 359, 712
fraud 354
Frederick II, Emperor 727
Frederick III, Kaiser 339
Frederick Louis, Prince of Wales 165
Freedley, Vinton 656
French Revolution 93, 235, 395, 397, 630
Freud, Sigmund 258, 420
Fristoe, Leonard T. 705
frogs 333
frozen foods 137
Fry, Charles 236
'Furnace, Sam' 22

Gable, Clark 68
Gagarin, Yuri 143
Gage, Phineas P. 519
Gainsborough, Thomas 274
Galli-Marié, Mme 315
Gallup, Dr George 650

Galton, Francis 98
gambling 120, 152, 294
Gandhi 65, 557
Garbo, Greta 152, 528
Gardelle, Theodore 104
Garfield, President James Abram 652
Garland, Judy 329
Garrick, David 104
gas lighting 61
Gatling, R. J. 623
Gauguin, Paul 13, 322
Geller, Uri 714
General Strike 254
Genghis Khan 100
George, St 232
George I, 302, 475
George II 248, 603
George III 62, 276, 295, 454, 508, 527, 576
George IV 76, 196, 246, 281, 344, 360, 406, 446, 449, 454
George V 44, 403
George VI 78
George of Denmark, Prince 425
Gerry, Elbridge Thomas 704
Gershwin, George 91, 390
Getty, Jean Paul 45, 705
Gettysburg 651
ghosts 120, 483, 668
ghost ship 92
giants 310, 342, 585
Gibbon, Edward 262
Gibson, Wing Commander Guy 279
Gibson, Michael 381
Gilbert, Sir W. S. 15, 651, 726
Gilbert and Sullivan 15, 651, 665, 726
Gingold, Hermione 327, 693
Giotto 20
giraffe 534
Gish, Lillian 581
Gladstone, W. E. 717, 733
Glenn, Lt-Col John 106
Goddard, Professor Robert Hutchings 31
Godfrey, Sir Edmund Berry 108
Goering, Hermann 67
Gogh, Vincent van 322, 426

gold 52, 344
Goldie the Eagle 121
gold rush 53
Goldsmith, Oliver 178
gold-toothed boy 718
Goldwyn, Samuel 484
golf 47, 186, 404, 497, 512, 559
Gordon, Adam Lindsay 590
Gordon, General George Charles 57
gorilla 534, 625, 736
Gorky, Maxim 284
Gould, Shane 699
Goya, Francisco José 13, 218
Grable, Betty 711
Grace, W. G. 405
Graham, Billy 628
Graham, Dr James 355
Graham, John Gilbert 617
Grahame, Kenneth 141
Grainger, Percy 384
Granada (Spain) 9
Grand National (race) 173, 174
Grant, Cary 40
Grant, President Ulysses Simpson 209
Gray, Thomas 727
Great Exhibition (1851) 249
Great Fire of London 246, 496
Great Train Robbery 447
Greeley, Horace 72
Green, Anna 702
Green, Hetty 656
Green, Joseph Henry 701
Greenough, Horatio 505
Gregory X, Pope 494
Grey, Lady Jane 383
greyhound 183
Grimaldi, Giuseppe 170
Grimaldi, Joseph 710
grouse 454
Guevara, Ernesto Che 569
guillotine 46, 128, 236, 343, 373, 402,
    507, 542, 626, 688
Guinness Book of Records 314, 455
Guiteau, Charles 368
Gulliver's Travels 453
Gully, John 472

Gunning sisters 555
Gunpowder Plot 65, 624
gurning 136
guru 188
Guthrie, Woody 397
Guy the gorilla 625
Gwynn, Nell 70, 78

Hagemore, Reverend Mr 7
Haggard, Sir H. Rider 387
hair transplant 623
Haiti 565
Haley, Bill 211
Halifax, Nova Scotia 687
Hall, Asaph 453
Halley's Comet 234
'Halloween' 614
hamburger 217
Hamilton, Ann 379
Hamilton, Duke of 95
Hamilton, Lady Emma 238, 550
Handel, George F. 474, 521, 685
Hanger, George 186
hanging 29, 65, 83, 112, 117, 155, 174,
    201, 368, 419, 424, 437, 463, 480, 484,
    501, 503, 513, 558, 657, 663, 667, 670,
    696, 702
Hansom, J. A. 721
Hansom cab 721
Hardin, John Wesley 298, 469
Harding, Gilbert 318, 565
Harding, Warren Gamaliel 435
Hardy, Thomas 26, 313
Harlow, Jean 130
Harmsworth, Lord Alfred 458
Harrison, Colonel
Harrison, William 462
Harrow School 339
Hartnell, Norman 312
Hastings, Battle of 581
Hathaway, Anne 232
Hawker, Robert Stephen 681
Hawthorn, Mike 331
Haydn, Franz Josef 308
Haydon, Benjamin 353
Haymarket Theatre 733

Hayworth, Rita 586
Hearst, Randolph 96, 222, 244, 465
heart transplant 51, 670, 680
Heath, Edward 386, 496
heaviest man 389
Hebrides 148
Hedley, Captain J. 16
Heenan, John 221
Heidegger, John 502
Heinz, H. J. 574
Held, Anna 455
Heliogabalus, Emperor 146
Hellfire Club 715
Hemingway, Ernest 'Papa' 372, 411
Henry I 677
Henry II 134, 282, 732
Henry III (France) 115, 433, 530
Henry IV 165, 686
Henry V 452, 525, 602
Henry VI 288, 495
Henry VII 11, 61
Henry VIII 6, 14, 55, 60, 284, 365, 393
Henry, Prince of Wales 627
Henry, Joseph 241
Hepburn, Katharine 633
Herculaneum 478
Herschel, William 150
Hess, Rudolf 266, 649
Heyerdahl, Thor 240
Hickok, Wild Bill 434, 547
high jump 158
highwaymen 155, 176, 200, 437, 613
hi-jacking 341
Hill, Rowland 25, 317
Hillary, Edmund 305
Himalayas 631
Himmler, Heinrich 292
Hindemith, Paul 647
hippopotamus 297
Hirohito, Emperor 244
Hirst, Jemmy 576, 611
Hitchcock, Alfred 456
Hitler, Adolf 67, 120, 226, 247, 249, 262, 266, 408, 525, 649, 728
Hobbes, Thomas 683
Hobbit, the 10

Hoffman, Dustin 447
Hogmanay 736
Hollywood 40, 68, 126, 196, 251, 348, 440, 442
Holmes, Percy 340
Holmes, Sherlock 260
Homo Sapiens 447
Honstein, Baron Robert von 698
Hood, Thomas 252
Hoover, President Herbert
Hope, Bob 304
horse-racing 27, 255, 321, 469, 568
Horton, ACW/2 194
Houdini, Harry 199, 441, 614
House of Commons 8, 380
hovercraft 418, 699
Howard, Catherine 92
Howard, Charles 135
Howard, Lady Elizabeth 677
Howe, Julia Ward 652
Hughes, Howard 197, 722
Hugo, Victor 119
'Humanity Martin' 17
Hume, Donald 560
Huskisson, William 523
Hyde, Edward 514
Hyde Park 676
hypnotism 292

Ibsen, Henrik 164
Importance of Being Earnest, The 94
Incas 647
incest 90
Incredible Conjurer 36
Indian Mutiny 267
Innocent VIII, Pope 419
'Innocents, The' 12
inoculation 449, 473
Inquisition 98, 325
insurance 272
inventions 84, 89, 97, 99, 116, 123, 126, 131, 144, 187, 209, 213, 241, 283, 284, 286, 293, 425, 513, 530, 532, 545, 594, 634, 651, 667, 680, 686
IQ, highest 139
Ireland 158, 454

Ireland, William Henry 190
Iroquois Theatre, Chicago 735
Isabella, Queen (Spain) 9
Isabella of Rutland, Duchess 497
Ishmaelo, Yousouf 376
Israel 252, 318, 564
Ivan the Terrible 160

Jack the Ripper 21, 492, 543, 553, 585
Jackson, President Andrew 20, 64, 155, 307
Jackson, Jeffery 510
Jackson, John 548
Jacobs-Bond, Carrie 452
Jaffa, Battle of 440
Jagger, Mick 421
Jakobs, Josef 458
James I (Scotland) 95, 106
James II (Scotland) 436
James IV 158
James, Frank 25, 506
James, Jesse 25, 192, 502, 506
Japan 244
jazz 136
Jeakins, Richard 559
Jeep 500
Jefferson, President Thomas 213, 247, 376
Jeffries, Dr John 18
Jellicoe, Admiral Sir John 309
Jenkins, Captain 205
Jenner, Edward 275
Jesus Christ 30, 725
Jews 157, 214, 446, 489, 734
Joad, Professor 455
Joan of Arc 306
Joanna I of Naples, Queen 290
Joey the Clown 710
John XII, Pope 274
John XXI, Pope 275
John XXIII, Pope 664
John, King 576, 723
'John Brown's Body' 652
John of Gaunt 73
John Paul I, Pope 548
John Paul II, Pope 89

Johnson, Amy 15, 257, 371
Johnson, Jack 585
Johnson, President Lyndon B. 631
Johnson, Dr Samuel 216, 528, 700
Jolson, Al 565
Jonah 481
Jonson, Ben 443
Josephine (wife of Napoleon) 142, 354
Joubert, Pierre 399
journalism 458
Joyce, William 644
Judd, Winnie Ruth 599
jukebox 661
Julius, Pope 616
Jullien, Louis 232
Jumbo the Elephant 142, 522
Jung, Carl Gustave 420
Justinian, Emperor 195
Jutland, Battle of 308

Kaplan, Fanya 491
Kean, Edmund 415
Keate, Dr John 369
Keaton, Buster 561
Keely, John Worrell 634
Kelly, Grace 639
Kelly, Ned 637
Kelvin, Baron 361
Kennedy, President J. F. 516, 631, 659
Kennedy, Mrs Jacqueline 425, 516, 593, 659
Kennedy, Robert 319
Ketch, Jack 678
Ketchell, Stanley 585
Khan, Genghis 478
Khartoum 56
Khrushchev, Nikita 86, 203, 220, 224
kidnapping 126, 709
Kim the Korean genius 139
King, Alan 726
King, Billie Jean 533
King, Martin Luther 194
King, William Lyon MacKenzie 709
King's Evil 240
Kingsley, Mary 579
Kirov, Sergei 676

748

Kirwan 310
Kneller, Sir Godfrey 446
Knievel, Evel 508, 587
Koepcke, Juliane 723
Kon-Tiki 240
Korean War 358
Krakatoa 484
Kraken 267
Kreisler, Fritz 71
Kruesi, John 686
Ku Klux Klan 722
Kurten, Peter 373
Kuwait 705

Labouchere, Henry 34
Ladd, Alan 498
Lady Chatterley's Lover 618
Laënnec, René Théophile Hyacinthe 101
Lambaréné 32
Lambert, Daniel 411
Langtry, Lillie 578
Larwood, Harold 41
Latimer, Irving 177
Laud, Archbishop 146
Lauda, Niki 110
Lavoisier, Antoine 482
Lawrence, D. H. 618
Lawrence of Arabia 285, 460
Lazaros, Peter 243
lead shot 42
Leakey, Dr Louis 447
Lear, Edward 271
Leatherslade Farm 447
Lee, Mother Ann 125
Lee, John 112
Lee, General Robert E. 43
Lee of Fareham, Lord 21
Le Mans 331
Lenclos, Ninon de 277
Lenglen, Suzanne 99
Lenin, V. I. 46, 231, 491
Lennon, John Winston 571
Lennox, Charles 426
Leo X, Pope 615
Leo XIII, Pope 382
Leonardo da Vinci 621

Leonov, Aleksey 160
Leotard, Jules 638
Lepanto, Battle of 566
Lesseps, Ferdinand de 648
Lettsom, John 659
Levine, Jo 511
Lewis, Jerry Lee 157, 551
Liberace, Wladzin Valentino 278, 324
libraries 370
licking 382
Liechtenstein 462
life-jacket 647
lift, first safety 532
lightning 338, 361, 430, 451
Lilly, William 246, 496
Lincoln, Abraham 91, 214, 238, 622, 651, 707
Lind, Jenny 564
Lindbergh, Charles 74, 126, 287
Linnel, Alfred 655
Lisle, Claude Rouget de 235
Liston, John 169
Liston, Robert 609, 716
Liszt, Franz 596
Little Women 672
Liverpool, Lord 683
'Living Skeleton,' The 207
Livingstone, David 162, 634
Llanfair P. G. 515
Lloyd, Marie 566
Loch Ness Monster 639
Loewi, Otto 314
Lohengrin 487
Lollobrigida, Gina 377
Lonely Hearts ad, first 406
Long, Dr Crawford Williamson 184
Long, John 373
longest living man 399, 691
longest name 125
Loren, Sophia 533, 696
Louis, Joe 273
Louis Philippe, Duc d'Orléans 626
Louis XI (France) 375, 490
Louis XII (France) 467
Louis XIII (France) 546, 663
Louis XIV (France) 495, 650

Louis XVI (France) 46, 128, 476, 502, 531
Louis XVIII (France) 525
Louisiana 247
Lourdes 89
Lovell, Lord 340
Lowell, Percival 102, 150
Ludke, Bruno 202
Luetgert, Adolph 249
Luftwaffe 649
Lumisden, Isabella 396
Lupescu, Magda 504
Lusitania 260
Luther, Martin 295, 615
Luvibond, Lady 92
Lynch, Bernard 416
Lynch, Captain William 536
Lysenko, Trofim 551

MacArthur, General Douglas 358
McCall, Jack 23, 434
McCarthy, Joe 642
Maclean, Donald 296
McClean, Captain 422
McCleod, Donald 572
McCoy, Kidd 128
MacDonald, 'Fighting Mac' 175
MacDonald, Flora 363
MacDonald, John Alexander 370
McDowell, Dr Ephraim 701
McGonagall, William 477, 731
MacGrath, Cornelius 144
machine-gun 276, 623
McIndoe, Sir Archie 254
MacKenzie, Morel 339
McKinley, President William 96, 504
Macmillan, Maurice Harold 86, 147
McWhirter, Norris 455
McWhirter, Ross 455
Madame Bovary 699
Madame Butterfly 672
Mafeking, relief of 280
Mahdi 56
Mahmud II, Sultan 409
Mahomet II, Sultan 305
Mahon, Charles James Patrick 159

Maigret, Georges Simenon 92
Maine (battleship) 96
Maintenon, Madame de 502
Maitland, Dr Charles 449
malaria 470
Malcolm, Sarah 138
Malloy, Mike 322
Malta 331
Mamelukes 411
Mangiamele, Vito 375
Manhattan 294
Manners, J. Hartley 515
Mansfield, Jayne 366
Mantell, Captain Thomas 19
Mao Tse-tung 400, 528, 726
Marat, Jean Paul 395
Marathon 370, 548
March, Earl of 489
Maria Theresa, Empress 272
Marie-Antoinette, Queen 46, 58, 476, 618
Marlborough, Duke of 299
Marlow, Christopher 310
marriage 8, 85, 218
Mars 398, 453
Marseillaise, La 235
Marten, Maria 282
Martians 612
Marwood, William 500
Marx Brothers 556, 719
Marx, Chico 169
Marx, Groucho 468, 557
Marx, Harpo 660
Marx, Karl 256
Mary, Queen 651
Mary, Queen of Scots 82, 101, 383, 427, 555
Masada 214
Mata Hari 444
matches 200
mathematical wizard 375
Matilda, Queen 620
Matisse, Henri 589
Matterhorn, 394
Matthias, Bob 427
Matthias Corvinus, King (Hungary) 115
Maugham, Somerset 54, 707

Maximinus, Emperor 342
Mayflower 504
Maynard, Frances 'Daisy' 695
Maynard, Lieutenant 658
Meade, William 494
medical items 8, 51, 275, 332, 336, 341, 346, 405, 418, 495, 608, 627, 650, 680, 700, 701, 702, 716, 719, 721, 727, 734
Medici, Catherine de 212
Meir, Golda 252
Melba, Nellie 285
Mencken, H. L. 694
Menelek II, Emperor 466
Menken, Adah Isaacs 559
Menzies, Sir Robert 714
Merman, Ethel 406
Mesmer, Franz Anton 292
Messiah 521
Metchnikov, Ilya 277
meteor 190
Methodism 342
Metropolitan Police 76
Michelangelo 137, 198, 616
Mickey Mouse 650, 684
Midnight Cowboy 447
Miller, Arthur 701
millionaires 44, 197, 254, 294, 300, 438, 722
Milnes, Richard Monkton 452
Milton, John 692
Minors, W. C. 421
Mintoff, Yana 380
Misa, Captain Antonio 466
'missing link' 219
Miss Muffet 319
Mitchill, Samuel Latham 471
Mitchum, Robert 442
Mohocks 149
Moiseiwitsch, Benno 628
Molière, Jean Baptiste 100
Monaco Grand Prix 215
Mona Lisa 473, 620
money 44, 438, 491, 552, 657, 705
mongoose, talking 323
Monroe, Marilyn 311, 440
Mons 483

Monsey, Messenger 727
Montague, Edward Wortley 218
Montague, Lady Mary Wortley 473
Monte Carlo 152
Montgolfier brothers 531
Montgomery, Field Marshal Viscount 598, 648
Montrose, Earl of 288
Monty Python's Flying Circus 562
moon 213, 410, 431
Moors 9, 388
More, Sir Thomas 81, 380
Mormons 362, 384, 393, 399, 535
Morning Cloud III 386, 496
Morrisey, P.C. John 28
Morse, Samuel 241
Morte d'Arthur 430
Mortison, C. Louis 84
Mother's Day 266
motor car 60, 151, 458, 667
motorcycle 150
motor racing 133, 215, 226, 330, 331, 357, 499
mountaineering 33
Mousetrap, The 665
Mozart, W. A. 58, 611, 684, 706
'Mule', the 681
Munchhausen, Baron 268
murder 69, 138, 139, 162, 223, 249, 282, 306, 317, 322, 435, 515, 560, 566, 661
Murray, Sir James A. H. 69, 80, 421
Murrow, Ed 237
music 67, 166, 503
music-hall 566
Mussolini, Benito 243, 426
Musters, Pauline 119
mutiny 510
Mutiny on the Bounty 242
Mytton, Squire John 552

Naismith, James 45
Napier, General Sir Robert 212
Napoleon 142, 211, 230, 247, 256, 344, 354, 383, 411, 461, 654
Napoleon III 33, 227, 296
'Napoleon of Crime' 296

Nash, Richard 589
Nastase, Ilie 407
Nation, Carrie 664
National Security Agency 622
Neild, John Camden 491
Nelson, Lord 191, 238, 432, 550, 595
Nelson's Column 510
Nero 326, 704
Ness, Loch 639
Nevison, John 155
Newgate Prison 449, 486, 657
Newman, Paul 57
Newton, Isaac 724
New Year's Day 175
New York 395, 420, 508, 702
New York Tribune 72
Niagara 600
Nicholas, St 687
Nicholas I, Tsar 380
Nicholas II, Tsar 401
Nicklaus, Jack William 47
Nietzsche, Friedrich 480, 583
Nightingale, Florence 270
Niven, David 126
Nixon, President Richard M. 23, 449, 538, 631
Nobel, Alfred 695
Nobel Prize 695
Nobel Prize for Physics 314, 628
Nollekens, Joseph 452
Norris, Francis 99
North, Lord Frederick 212
North Carolina 657
Northington, Lord 33
North Pole 199, 229, 248, 671
Norton, Joshua Abraham 526
No Sex Please - We're British 314
Nostradamus 354
Novello, Ivor 35
nuclear protesters 527
numbers 701
Nureyev, Rudolph 159

Oakley, Annie 457, 725
Oates, Captain L. E. G. 158, 182
Obscene Publications Act, 1959 618

O'Higgins, Bernardo 557
oil 486
oldest living thing 511
'Old Q' 721
Oliver of Malmesbury 234
Olivier, Laurence Kerr 290
Olympic Games 87, 199, 370, 401, 412, 427, 481, 699
Onassis, Aristotle Socrates 44, 593
opera 124, 285, 392, 564, 573, 672
orchid 168
Origin of Species 662, 728
Orsini, Count Felice 33
Orwell, George 358
'Oscars' 278
Oswald, Lee Harvey 659
O'Taffe, Count Theobald 489
Otway, Thomas 214
Outlaw, The 351
Owens, Jesse 296
Oxford English Dictionary 69, 80, 421

Padre Pio 532
Page, Sir Francis 591
painting 322, 446
Pakenham, General Sir Edward 20
Pall Mall 61
Palmer, Arnold Daniel 512
Palmer, John 435
Palmer, William 337
Palmerston, Viscount 588
Panama 621
Panama Canal 460
panda 412
Pantaleon, St 423
Panzram, Carl 503
Paracelsus 541
parachute 417, 481
Paré, Ambroise 719
Parker, Dorothy 475
Parker, Matthew 443
Parker, Richard 414
Parliament 37, 584
Parliament Square 446
Parr, Catherine 393

Parr, Thomas 643
Parsons, Charles Algernon 334
Parton, Dolly 573
Pascal, Blaise 346
Pascal, Cissy 415
Patch, Sam 640
Patrick, St 158
Patton, General George S. 636
Paul I 534
Paul VI, Pope 443
Paulus, Field Marshal Friedrich 67
pea pushing record 460
Peace, Charles 116
'Peach Melba' 285
Peacock, Thomas 588
Pearl Harbour 688
Peary, Robert 199, 229
Pedrick, Arthur 99
Pedro I (Portugal) 19
Peel, Sir Robert 76
Pelée, Mount 262
Penn, William 494
Pennsylvania 494
Penny Post 25
Pentagon, the 35
Pepys, Samuel 11, 112, 466, 543
Perceval, Spencer 253
permanent waving 569
Persia 237
Persia, Shah of 237, 604
Pertinax, Emperor 180
Petacci, Claretta 243, 426
Peter Pan 77, 196, 264, 729
Peter the Great 326
Petit, Philippe 445
Philip II (Spain) 385
Philip IV (Spain) 203
Philip V (Spain) 53
Philip VI (France) 482
Philip, Prince (Duke of Edinburgh) 328, 389, 654
Philippe IV (France) 672
Philip the Handsome 413
Phillips, Captain Mark 537, 642
Phipps, William 111
phonograph 686

photography 56
Picasso, Pablo 602
Pickford, Mary 180, 202
pick-pockets 420
Pied Piper 360
Pierrepoint, Albert 670, 694
pigeon 202
pigs' choir 375
Pilgrim Fathers 156, 716
Pilgrim's Progress 102
Pinocchio 81
Pitman, Isaac 645
Pitt, William 303
Pitt the Younger, William 50
Pizarro, Francisco 647
Pliny the Elder 478
Plomley, Roy 621
Pluto (planet) 102, 150
Podelicote, Richard 234
Poe, Edgar Allan 42, 415, 567
Poet's Corner (Westminster Abbey) 26
poisoning 177
'Poker Alice' 120
Polanski, Roman 466
police force 550
Pompeii 478
Ponti, Carlo 676
Pontius Pilate 359
Pope, Alexander 289
Popeye the Sailorman 462
Popham, Sir John 312
Popovic, Doctor Aurel 623
Porter, Cole 326, 656
Portland, Duke of 697
Poseidon 327
Post, Wiley 398
postage stamps 173
post-box 235
Postle, Arthur 141
Post Office 25, 235, 317
Potsdam Peace Talks 416
Potter, Walter 372
Powell, Baden 280
Presley, Elvis Aaron 20, 173, 466, 571
Priam, King 336
Price, Dr William 30

753

Primrose Hill 109
Prince Regent 360, 323
Private Jackie 118
Prohibition (USA) 36
Promenade Concerts 245
Proust, Marcel 389
Psalmanazar 252
psychoanalysis 258
public loo 70
Puccini, Giacomo 672
punch, biggest bowl of 603
Pushkin, Alexander 82
Pu Yi 644

'Quakers' 613
Quebec, Battle of 518
Queen Elizabeth (liner) 547
Queen Mary (liner) 544

R101 562
'Rabbit Woman' of Godalming 233
Rachel (French actress) 122
Rachmaninov, Sergei 628
Radcliffe, James 114
radio 487
radium 628
RAF 470
Raglan, Lord 602
railways 367, 546
Rainier, Prince 639
Rais, Gilles de 604
Raleigh, Sir Walter 610, 677
Ramsden, Harry 714
Ramsey, Alf 429
Raphael 198
Rasputin 734
Ratsey, Gamaliel 176
Rattenbury, Alma 317
Ravel, Maurice 730
Red Barn Murder 282
Red Baron 228, 250, 260
Red Cross 357
'Red Flag Act' 378
Red Indians 245, 358
Redmond, Patrick 513
Reed, Floyd S. 559

Reformation 615
Reger, Max 163
Reichstag 120
Reis, Artur Alves 400
Relativity, theory of 223
Reno brothers 564, 696
Resolute, The 527
revenge 245
Reynolds, Sir Joshua 274, 589
rhinoplasty 629
Rhodes, Cecil 378
Rhodesia 378
Richard I ('Lionheart') 157, 440, 498, 509
Richard II 17, 73, 94, 322
Richard III 475, 556
Richter, Karl 694
Richthofen, 'Red Baron' von 228, 250, 260
Ritchie, Willie 383
Rivals, The 39
Rivers, Joe 376
Robert the Bruce 356
Robeson, Paul 204
Rob Roy 730
Rockefeller, John D. 486
Rocket 523
rocking chair 380
Rock 'n' Roll 211
Rockwell, Norman 73
Roentgen, Konrad 624
Rogers, Ginger 267
Roget, Peter Mark 40
Rolande, Madame 630
Rolling Stones 421
Rolls, Charles (see also Rolls-Royce) 179, 392
Rolls-Royce 79, 231, 392
Romanov dynasty 401
Rombaud of Calais 284
Rommel 349, 598
Rooney, Mickey 538
Roosevelt, Eleanor 574
Roosevelt, President F. D. 64, 96, 210, 450, 574, 627
Roosevelt, President Theodore 606
Ross, Ronald 470
Rossetti, Dante Gabriel 270

Rossini, Gioacchino 124, 672
Rousseau, Jean-Jacques 365
rowing 432
Rowland, Walter Graham 121
Royal Family 403
Royal Festival Hall 9
Rozier, Francis de 339
Royce, Henry (*see also* Rolls-Royce) 179, 231
RSPCA 17
Rubens, Peter Paul 366
Rudolf, Crown Prince 62
Rudolph, Wilma 481
Rufus, William 434
rugby 444
Rugby School 444
Rumania, King Carol of 504
'Rump', the 227
Ruskin, John 665
Russell, Bertrand 283
Russell, Jane 351
Russell, Lord William 410, 678
Russia 250, 326, 401, 402
Ryan, Tommy 128

Sade, Marquis de 362, 679
safety-pin 207
Sage, Russell 438
Sai Baba 140
St Paul's Cathedral 116
St Valentine's Day Massacre 94
Sainte-Beuve 721
Saladin 440
Salamis, Battle of 538
Salem 531
Salem Witches 328
Salk, Jonas 608
Salomon, Haym 16
Salt Lake City 13
Samuels, Joseph 480
Sandringham 44
sandwich 442
San Francisco 222
Sangret, August 566
Sanson 128, 236, 402, 688
Santa Claus 724

Sargent, Sir Malcolm 245
Satie, Erik 573
Savoy Hotel 443
Sayers, Henry J. 512
Sayers, Tom 221
scalping 117
Schillinger, Joseph 493
Schliemann, Heinrich 336
Schmeling, Max 273
Scholl, Aurelian 219
Schopenhauer, Arthur 110
Schubert, Franz 67, 166, 651
Schweitzer, Albert 32
Scott, Captain Robert Falcon 182, 320
Scott, Sir Walter 41, 730
Scrope, Richard 325
Seddon, Frank 223
Segrave, Sir Henry O'Neal de Hane 335
Selfridge, H. G. 26, 154
Selwyn, George 371
Semple, William Finley 731
'serendipity' 60
Severus, Emperor 75, 181
Seward, William H. 184
sewing machine 513
Shackleton, Ernest 606
Shakers 125
Shakespeare, William 200, 232
Sharp, William 130
Shaw, G. B. 278, 619
Shearer, Norma 528
Shelley, Percy Bysshe 439
Sheridan, Richard Brinsley 39, 115, 613
Sheridan, Dr Thomas 572
Shipton, Eric 631
Shoemaker, Willie 469
shoplifting 559
shorthand 645
Shovel, Admiral 596
Shreveport, Louisiana 393
Siamese twins 13, 39, 268
Siddal, Elizabeth 270
Siddons, Sarah 274
Siegel, Bugsy 122
Silly Billy 472
Simnel, Lambert 340

Simpson, Dr James 622
Simpson, Mrs W. 346, 354
Simpson, William 427
Sinatra, Frank 406, 610
Sirhan, Sirhan Bishara 319
Sistine Chapel 616
Six Day war 318
Skeffington, Sir Lumley 'Skiffey' 170
Skye, Isle of 28
Skylab 424
Slade, Jack 145
Slocum, Joshua 374
smallest person 119
smallpox 275
Smith, Bessie 545
Smith, Joseph 362, 384, 393, 535
Smith, Sydney 315
snakes 91
snooker 217
Sobers, Sir Gary 493
Solferino, Battle of 357
Sopwith, Tom 364
Sorge, Richard 560
Soubirous, Bernadette 89
sound barrier 580
South Pole 41, 671, 703
space flight 31, 100, 106, 128, 143,
    160, 213, 340, 369, 398, 402, 410,
    424, 621
Spain 9, 388
Spanish Civil War 358
speed limit 378
Spencer, Herbert 241
Spenser, Edmund 677
Spinks, Leon 523
spiritualism 186
Spitz, Mark 87
Spooner, William Archibald 413
Sporting Times 488
'Spring Heeled Jack' 103
spying 444, 560, 604
squid, giant 28, 267
Staël, Madame de 230
Stalin 134, 416
Stalingrad 67
Stanhope, Lady Hester 148

Stanley, Dean 11
Stanley, Henry Morton 634
Star, Belle 72
starling 136
Star of David 489
Starr, Ringo 382, 428
Statue of Liberty 609
Stauffenberg, Von 408
steam turbine 334
Stein, Gertrude 423
Sterne, Laurence 161
Stevens, Thaddeus 453
Stevenson, Robert Louis 640
Stewart, Jackie 330
stigmata 532
Stimson, Henry Lewis 416
Stinsford, Dorset 26
Stirling, Sir Alexander 534
Stirling Bridge, Battle of 515
Stoker, Bram 630
Stockhausen, Karlheinz 474
Stonehenge 350
Stowe, Harriet Beecher 164
Strang, James Jesse 384
Strange, Sir Robert 396
Stratton, Charles S. ('Tom Thumb') 12
Stratton, Sherwood 399
Street, Rev William 668
striptease 151
Stroud, Robert Franklin 177
Stubb, Peter 615
Suez Canal 648
Suffolk, Duke of 250
suffragettes 127, 317
suicide 22, 63, 76, 99, 212, 247, 317, 326,
    329, 353, 426, 435, 444, 626
Suleiman the Magnificent 501
Sullivan, Sir A. S. 15, 651, 665
Sullivan, John L. 506
Sunday Express 618
Sunday Times, The 593
Sureté (French) 417
surgery 60, 171, 184, 254, 650, 670, 716,
    719
surgery, plastic 609, 629
surname, longest 106

survival 74, 174, 240, 248, 327, 374, 414, 432, 589, 590, 606, 661
Sutcliffe, Herbert 340
Sutter, John 52, 344
Sutton Hoo 262
Swan, James 431
swearing 539
Swinburne, Algernon Charles 197
Swinton, Sir Ernest 29
Swithin, St 398
Sydney Harbour 488
Symmes, Captain John Cleves 624

Tagliacozzi, Gaspare 629
tallest building 248
tallest living object 511
Talleyrand-Périgord, Charles Maurice de 93
Tamerlane the Great 100
tank 29, 522
Tarzan 495
Tate, General William 90
taxidermy 372
Tay Bridge 730
Taylor, Annie 600
Taylor, Elizabeth 154, 168, 635
Taylor, John 463
Taylor, Robert 441
Taylor, William 423
Taylor, President Zachary 387
Taynton, William 612
Tchaikovsky, Peter Ilyich 470, 626
tea 543
telephone 32, 131, 145
television 59, 515, 612, 693
Temperance Movement 206
temperance societies 36
tennis 99, 113, 320, 407, 533
Tennyson, Alfred Lord 330
Tensing, Sherpa 305
Tereshkova, Valentina 100, 340
Thackeray, William Makepeace 405
Theodora, Empress 195
Thirlby, Bishop 179
Thirty-nine Steps, The 483
Thirty Years War 292

Thomas, Dylan 607, 633
Thomas, Terry 397
Thompson, Farmer 201
Thornhill, Sir James 272
Thorpe, James 401
Three Musketeers, The 417
Thurlow, Chancellor Edward 692
Tiberius, Emperor 646
Tichatschek, Joseph 487
tightrope walking 107, 445
Tilsit, Peace of 383
Times, The 71, 458
Tin Lizzie 309
Tippett, Sir Michael 9
Titanic 216
Titus, Emperor 734
toads 666
Todd, Mary 622, 707
Todd, Mike 168
Toler, John 680
Tolkien, John Ronald Reuel 10
Tolpuddle Martyrs 160
Tombaugh, Clyde 102
Tom Jones 123, 231
Tom Thumb 12, 399
tooth extraction 712
top hat 35
tornado 180
tortoise 597
Toscanini, Arturo 174
Toulouse Lautrec, Henri de 307, 511
Tower Hill 204
Tower of London 458
Townes, Charles Hard 425
Towton, Battle of 183
toys 114
trade unionists 161
Trafalgar, Battle of 545, 595
Trafalgar Square 655
traffic lights 8
train crash 290
Transatlantic cable 441
transvestism 29, 115, 134, 419, 420, 482, 514, 563, 690, 710
Transylvania 630
trapeze artists 638

757

treasure 111, 349, 430
Treasure, Royal 234
Tristan und Isolde 392, 698
Trollope, Anthony 235
Trotsky, Leon 470
trousers 344
Troy 336
Trujillo y Molina, Rafael Leonidas 306
Truman, President 300, 416, 622
Tryon, Admiral 352
Tsafondas, Dimitric 505
Tuckett, Harvey 517
tug-of-war 334
Tunney, Gene 536
Tupelo, Battle of 394
Turin, Shroud of 302
Turner, J. M. W. 712
Turpin, Dick 200
turtle 317
Tussaud, Madame 689
tutu 149
Twain, Mark 674
Tyburn 629
typhoid 347, 627, 703
tyre 123
Tyrwhitt, Gerald 529
Tzu Hsi 645

Udet, Ernst 649
UFOs 19, 278, 356, 362, 407, 575, 583, 626
Uganda 7
ugliest man 502
Uncle Tom's Cabin 164
underground railways 24
underwater record 155
Uranus 150
Ussher, Archbishop James 598, 608
Utah 13

vaccination 275
vacuum cleaner 116
Valentino, Rudolf 258, 476
Vallejo, Mariano Guadaloup 382
'Vamp', the 408
vampirism 472

Vanbrugh, Sir John 177
Van Buren, President 685
Van Butchell, Martin 595
Vanderbilt, Cornelius 300
Van Gogh, Vincent 185, 720
Van Heflin 701
Van Herpen, Ruth Olive 656
Van Meter, Homer 136
Vasa (ship) 450
'Vaseline' 274
Vatican 494, 664
Vaucanson, Jacques de 114
Verdi, Giuseppe 573
Vere, Robert de 17
Versailles, Palace of 502
Verwoerd, Dr Hendrik 505
Vesuvius 478
Vetsera, Maria 62
Vicar of Wakefield, The 178
Victoria Cross 313
Victoria, Queen 12, 48, 87, 121, 144, 249, 294, 339, 364, 394, 582, 632, 654, 666, 703, 717, 733
Vidocq, François Eugene 417
View from the Bridge, A 701
Villiers, Barbara 299, 570
Villiers, Lady Elizabeth 204
Villon, François 318
Viren, Lasse 413
Virgil 582
Virgin Mary 89
Vitellius 540
Voigt, Jon 447
Voigt, Wilhelm 584
volcano 146, 262, 484
Vorster, Balthazar Johannes 701

Wadlow, Robert Pershing 398
Wagner, Richard 291, 487, 698
Wainwright, Henry 515
Wales 515
Wales, Prince of 346
Walewska, Marie 6
Walker, John 200
Wall Street 656
Wallace, Edgar 189

758

Wallace, William 515
Wallis, Sir Neville Barnes 545
Walpole, Horace 60, 541
Walton, Isaak 448
Wandering Jew 230
Ward, Seth (Bishop of Sarum) 16
Ward, Thomas 540
Warhol, Andy 447
War of Jenkins' Ear 205
War of the Worlds, The 612
Warren Report 659
Warsaw Concerto 31
war, shortest 485
Washington, George 111, 702
Watergate 449
Waterloo, Battle of 344
Waterlow's 400
waterspeed record 335
Waterton, Charles 314
Watt, James 42, 469
weather 180, 211, 333, 361, 398, 507, 518, 669
Webb, Captain Matthew 479
Weems, Mason Locke 516
weight-lifting 333
Wellington, Duke of 12, 166, 344, 520
Wells, H. G. 534, 612
Wells, Horace 696
Welsh, Freddie 383
Wembley Stadium 243
werewolf 615
Wertz, O. T. 416
Wesley, John 295, 342
West, Mae 40, 464
Westmacott, Sir Richard 345
Westminster Abbey 11, 26, 107, 406, 498, 525, 654
Westminster Hall 446
whales 481, 526
whisky 149
Whistler, James 66, 388, 665
Whistler (mother of James) 66
'White Christmas' 258
Whitehead, Paul 715
Whitehouse, Mary 335
Whittington, Dick 717

Whylie, Lieutenant 490
Whymper, Edward 394
Wiedmann, Eugen 343
Wigwam Murder 566
Wild Bill Hickok 547
Wilde, Oscar 94, 584, 675
Wilhelm II, Kaiser 48, 59
Wilkes, John 586
Wilkinson, Dr John 8
William the Conqueror 510, 620, 724
William III 140, 208
William IV 458, 472
Williams, Rev John 124
Williams, John (murderer) 736
Williams, John (dreamer) 253
Williams, Joseph 613
Williams, Renwick 486
Williams, Walter W. 713
Wills, Helen 99
Wills, T. W. 445
Wilmot, John 206
Wilson, Edward 'Beau' 204
Wilson, Harold 146
Wimbledon 407
Wimbledon Common 347
Wind in the Willows, The 141
Windsor, Duchess of 347, 354
wine 609
Wingate, Orde Charles 172
wireless 431
witches 463, 531
Wodehouse, P.G. 656
wolf-children 586
Wolfe, James 519
Wolgast, 'Wildcat' Al 376
Women's Institute 515
Wood, Sir Henry 245
Woolf, Virginia 257
Woolworth, Frank Winfield 110
World Cup football 429
World Trade Centre, New York 445, 702
World War I 364, 455, 457, 483, 510, 522, 568, 637
World War II 223, 320, 349, 499
Worth, Adam 296
Wounded Knee 732

Wren, Sir Christopher 116, 592
Wright Brothers 708
Wright, Frank Lloyd 325
Wright, Orville 469
Wroe, John 221
Wynne, Arthur 618

X-Rays 624

Yeti 631
York, Sergeant Alvin 568
Yorkshire 107

Young, Brigham 384
Younger, Cole 34, 506
Yussopov, Prince Felix 734

Zangara, Joseph 96
Zanzibar 485
Zatopek, Emil 427
Ziegfeld, Florenz 167
Ziegfeld Follies 167
zip, first 187
Zizka, General John 574
Zurbriggen, Matthias 33